Revised Printing

Literary Culture

Reading *and* Writing *Literary* Arguments

General Editor
L. Bensel–Meyers

Editors
Susan Giesemann North
Jeremy W. Webster

UNIVERSITY OF TENNESSEE
KNOXVILLE

Contributing Editors

Tanya Bennett
Joan Burton
Allison E. Carey
Jo Angela Edwins
Kevin Eubanks
David A. Haines, Jr.
Steven Harthorn
Kristi Larkin Havens
Leslie LaChance
William B. Larsen
Mary Moss
Nathaniel Preston
Laura Rutland
Daniel Schierenbeck
Melissa Putman Sprenkle
David Sprenkle
Walter Squire
James C. Thompson
Stephanie Lewis Thompson
Patricia Waters
Robin Wright

Pearson
Custom
Publishing

Please visit our website at www.pearsoncustom.com

ISBN 0–536–02824–9

BA 990428

PEARSON CUSTOM PUBLISHING
160 Gould Street/Needham Heights, MA 02494
A Pearson Education Company

Copyright Acknowledgments

Contents

Preface

*L*iterary Culture is a custom-published textbook for English 102: "English Composition II" at The University of Tennessee, Knoxville. Specifically tailored to address the needs of both students and instructors of this second term of first-year composition, this book focuses on teaching students how to read and write about literature while developing their research skills. The literary anthologies we have used in the past, because they were attempting to reach both the first-year writing course and the sophomore "Introduction to Literature" course, were often bulky and expensive. Also, because they tended to focus on literature as an aesthetic form, they made it difficult for students to learn how to respond to literary works as cultural arguments, as a kind of writing authors use to respond to the very human concerns embedded in their time and culture. We hope this new book—our choice of selections, how we have chosen to organize them, and the specific, rhetorical questions that follow each work (including a casebook to demonstrate the many different rhetorical situations within which arguments about literature take place)—can make it easier for students and teachers to engage rhetorically with the cultural issues at the heart of literary works.

Each of the units has been developed by teachers in the composition program at UTK, and any proceeds from the sale of the book will go back into the composition program to further the training of new teachers. The Contributing Editors, drawing upon their experience of what most inspires students of English 102, were responsible for each unit, choosing the readings and formulating the questions that follow. The result clearly reveals how much these teachers care about helping students to enjoy reading and writing about literature. The units focus on developing students' communication skills by helping them become more sensitive to the variety of perspectives literary rhetoric exposes us to, using reading and writing about literature to help students experience and decide for themselves how they want to value the many worlds and peoples that surround their lives.

The book is the product of many hands, with the primary vision coming from the Editors, Susan North and Jeremy Webster, both experienced Assistant Directors of Composition at UTK. These two scholar-teachers shaped the overall structure and soul of the text. They tirelessly edited the individual units, gathered permissions for the readings, and developed the introductory chapters that prepare students with the skills and terminology they need to experience and respond to literature as written argument. Without the Editors' tireless dedication and wisdom, we would not be able to provide you with this less expensive alternative to the several texts we used in the past to teach the highly-stylized, rhetorical discourse that both responds to and reshapes our cultural attitudes toward human behavior.

—L. Bensel-Meyers,
General Editor & Director of Composition, UTK

UNIT
ONE

*Reading and Writing
Literary Arguments*

Introduction

Every day we are confronted with many different kinds of texts. During the course of a single 24-hour period, we might read a textbook, an article in a news magazine, a newspaper editorial, a short story, or part of a novel. We do not, however, encounter only written texts. News broadcasts, soap operas, advertisements, movies, and sitcoms are also texts. What all these texts have in common is that they involve the use of language, either written or spoken, or visual elements to communicate something. What they communicate may be an informational message or an emotional one or, what is more likely, a combination of the two. Texts, however, do not give up their messages easily. Language is a code. Sometimes this code is difficult to understand. At other times it can be readily deciphered, but our senses can still misperceive its message. As a result, we must interpret the messages we receive through texts carefully, and that is not always as easy as it sounds.

How do we learn to interpret all these messages? Most of us have learned to interpret texts by doing it, much like we learned to talk or walk. There is certainly nothing wrong with that kind of life knowledge. Most of us depend on it to get through our daily lives. But if we want to develop our skills, we need to work harder and concentrate our attention. Professional basketball players, for example, do not rely on the skills they learned playing hoops at the neighborhood park. Instead, they sharpen their abilities by practicing hard and studying the fundamentals of the game. Gourmet cooks, too, progress beyond basic cooking by learning about ingredients, terminology, and techniques of the culinary arts. Interpreting texts, too, is a skill that can be improved by studying the techniques and fundamentals of literary theory and rhetorical analysis.

Why do we need to develop our skills at interpreting texts? In part, we need those skills because we are constantly confronted with texts in our daily lives. When we are faced with a high-pressure salesperson trying to sell us a car, we need to be able to distinguish truth from exaggeration. We need to interpret the loan documents that we sign when we buy that car or a house. We need to know how to listen to politicians, to religious leaders, to our bosses, our families, and our friends. Furthermore, we live in a world where more information is available than at any time before in human history. The traditional texts—books, magazines, and newspapers—are augmented by audio-visual media—television, radio, and movies. The growth of the internet and the worldwide web mean that we receive more and more messages every day.

Without sharpening our interpretive skills, we simply cannot deal with this vast amount of information. Unless we can distinguish between reliable and unreliable information, we run the risk, like Chicken Little, of appearing foolish when we mistake a falling acorn for the falling sky. In short, we need to improve our interpretive skills so that we can understand our world, so that we can communicate effectively with one another, and so that we can control our own lives.

As members of an academic community, we encounter many different kinds of texts. We read historical accounts, psychology textbooks, biology reference guides, to name just a few. In English classes, we read argumentative essays, poems, short stories, plays, and novels. Many of the kinds of texts we encounter in college are different from those we've encountered before. Not only do we have to read unfamiliar kinds of texts, we have to produce them as well. For instance, we must interpret the results of a chemistry experiment and write up those results in a form that is accepted by other chemists. Engineers must study and interpret problems and design appropriate solutions to fit those situations, and, at every step of this process, must produce written reports detailing their work and giving reasons to support their recommendations. These reports, too, must conform to the expectations of their discipline.

Why Study Literature?

In this book, you will learn an argumentative approach to reading and writing about literature. You might wonder why you should study literature if you intend to be an engineer or a chemist, a social worker or a doctor. One reason is simply that the interpretation of literature is a very complex task that sharpens your ability to decipher other kinds of texts as well. Remember that we said earlier that language is a code. We might say that literature is a code within a code. The messages in literary texts are not straight-forward; they are wrapped up in figurative language and things like setting, characterization, and plot. It takes a lot of work and skill to unravel their meaning. Another good reason for studying literature as a way to develop interpretive skills is that literary scholars have a vocabulary for talking about the way language is used to make meaning. We can, for instance, talk about figurative use of language and how the use of certain kinds of figures alter our perception of a situation. What we learn from our study of literature—the interpretive skills, the understanding of how language can alter our understanding of the world—can be transferred to other contexts. We might, for instance, be better able to make up our own minds about the effect of violent television and films on our culture. The close reading that we must do in order to interpret a poem may help us to pay closer attention to the results of a physics experiment. Determining the best critical approach to use in analyzing a novel is much the same as deciding what tests to use to determine the contents of an unknown sample in chemistry. Just as the information you learn in other classes—history, chemistry, art—will help you understand literature better, what you learn by studying literature can transfer to those other contexts.

Of course, the study of literature is not only a means to success in other disciplines; it is worthwhile for its own sake. Sciences help us understand how the physical world works, but they cannot always explain the subtle nuances of human social interaction. The arts and the humanities focus on human beings and their relationships with other human beings and with the natural world. The study of literature combines the analytical methods of the humanities with the emotional expressiveness of the fine arts. Literature speaks to us on an emotional as well as an intellectual level. As we struggle to account for our emotional responses to a given literary text, we are also learning something about the nature of our humanity. Sometimes, the complex lessons which a literary text has to teach cannot be communicated in any other way. A poem like Robert Frost's "Stopping by the Woods on a Snowy Evening," for example, has become an American cultural icon precisely because it evokes a whole range of complicated emotions related to the conflict between obligations and the need for solitude. Thousands of words have been written to "explain" the ambiguous emotions that poem communicates.

It is also important to study literature because it is part of a cultural heritage of a people. Culture is a term which generally refers to the complex set of ideas, art, history, laws, values (i.e., things we think are worthwhile), and beliefs that are common to a group of people. While some of the elements of culture such as laws are codified, most of them are not. We learn our culture in the same way that we learn language, by being immersed in it as we grow from infancy. As a result, we often accept cultural beliefs and values without question. Unquestioned beliefs and values can be dangerous, however, when we are confronted with new and unfamiliar situations. An example of the consequences of unexamined values is the crisis oil-dependent countries faced in the 1970s when OPEC, the consortium of oil-producing countries, decreased the amount of oil available for export to other countries. The result of this action was a sharp increase in the price of gasoline and other products made from petroleum. In America, the crisis came about in part because we valued large automobiles which used lots of gasoline. Americans had never before questioned the consequences of our love for big cars. As a response to that crisis, American automobile companies began making smaller, more fuel efficient cars, and cultural values shifted. We might analyze this change in the kind of automobiles Americans value in terms of other belief and value systems.

Cultural values are so deeply-ingrained that, often, they are not visible except when they are challenged (as in the oil crisis). How, then, is it possible to question something that is so deeply buried within the consciousness of a cultural group? The study of literature allows us to glimpse the values that we are not always able to see. By questioning the beliefs and values of the characters in a novel, for example, and by comparing them with our own beliefs and values, we can begin a process of self-discovery. Literature can help us understand not only our own cultural values, but also those of people from other cultures, enabling us to decide for ourselves how we want to live our own lives.

Why Study Argument?

Finally, it is important to consider that word "argumentative" in our description of what this book is about. As a college student, you are being trained to investigate the unknown. No matter what your major is, you will learn skills that enable you to push back the frontiers of ignorance. Once you make a discovery or come to a conclusion about what you've studied, your task is to inform others about what you have found and to enter into a kind of conversation with others in your field about your findings. This conversation helps you enlarge your own understanding of what you have discovered at the same time that it leads others to accept your findings as valuable new knowledge. This is what we mean by argument: the way an individual uses language in order to come to an agreement with others (or one's self!) about what we should believe, value, or do. This book will help you develop your argumentative skills in two ways. First, it helps you identify the argumentative strategies of other writers as you study the various selections in this book. In some selections, the arguments will be easy to identify. In others, in poems and short stories, the arguments are much more subtle and will take work on your part to dig out. Second, you will improve your argumentative skills by developing arguments of your own. Because the arguments in literature are so subtle, there are often many ways to interpret them. You will have your own ideas about the arguments in a text; your classmates will likely have different ideas. Your task will be to identify what is at issue in a text and develop your own arguments to secure the agreement of your classmates. As they attempt to do the same thing, you will, together, be engaged in the sort of conversation that leads to discovery and agreement about what the literature has to teach us.

How This Book Is Designed

In order to facilitate these discoveries, this book is divided into several units. The first unit is designed to introduce you to ways in which literary texts make arguments and to help you begin the process of writing your own arguments about literary culture. Chapter One introduces you to the technical vocabulary of literary criticism, while Chapter Two discusses rhetoric, the art of argument and persuasion. In Chapter Three, you will gain some experience examining the arguments that literary texts present.

Units Two through Six present small collections of literary texts, all of which address a consistent theme. These texts include essays, poems, short stories, and plays so that you can see how different kinds of texts can address a topic in different ways. Unit Two, "Everyday Use," looks at the human relationships between families and friends and how those relationships affect and are affected by the larger culture of which they are a part. Unit Three, "Lives of Fantasy and Reality," looks at the connections between life as it is and life as we dream about how it should be. The selections in Unit Four, "And Justice for All?" examine questions of social justice in our own and other cultures. In Unit Five, the "big" questions of "Living, Dying, and the Quest for Meaning" are addressed. Unit Six, "Nature, Technology, and Romancing the Self" looks at the relationship between human beings, technology, and the natural world. In Unit Seven, we introduce William Shakespeare's play, *A Midsummer Night's Dream,* not simply as a masterpiece, but also an argument about the nature of love and the degree to which romantic relationships are constrained by cultural values. Finally, Unit Eight is a casebook which includes a variety of texts by a single author, along with critical commentary on her work. Judith Ortiz Cofer is a contemporary Latina writer who has written essays, poems, and short stories. The texts in this unit offer you a glimpse of the literature of a culture that is different from mainstream American culture, but not so alien that it is difficult to understand. The critical commentary will help you begin to understand the arguments which the literary texts are making and will situate them within the contexts of both Puerto Rican and American culture. Finally, these critical commentaries offer an example of how literary research, like the research in any academic discipline, is constituted as an argument.

Chapter One
Talking About Literature

What is literature? What is an argument? If the purpose of this textbook is to help you think about literature as argument, it is important to settle those two questions at the beginning. Unfortunately, these are very difficult questions to answer and, by the time you finish this book, you will probably still be wondering about them. However, by that time, you should have gained some knowledge of terms and strategies that will allow you to deal with the questions more effectively. You will also have put your knowledge to work, interpreting various texts, developing experience that can help you interpret other areas of your life.

What Is Literature?

Suppose you were given a novel by Jane Austen and an article from the most recent issue of *The New England Journal of Medicine* and were asked to choose which one was literature. You probably would not hesitate to choose the Austen novel. And most people would agree with that choice. But consider for a moment that it is a very common practice to call professional texts "literature." For instance, doctors often say that they have consulted "the literature" on a particular ailment, meaning that they have read medical encyclopedias, textbooks, and journal articles to learn more about the disease and its treatment. So, you could choose the article from *The New England Journal* and be perfectly correct in your choice. But if, as most of us would have done, you chose the novel by Jane Austen, your choice was probably determined by a very different understanding of the meaning of the term "literature." That understanding probably tells you that literature consists of texts like novels, poems, Shakespearean plays, and other similar kinds of texts. But knowing that these sorts of texts are literature doesn't explain *why* they are literature.

Generally speaking, when we talk about the kind of "literature" that a Jane Austen novel represents, we are talking about texts that are "belletristic." That word comes from a French phrase, *belles lettres* (pronounced "bell letr") which literally means, "beautiful letters." In other words, "literature" consists of beautiful texts, those written or produced to be works of art or those we have come to value as works of art. The idea of valuing literary works for their artistic merit goes back to Greek civilization; although the official designation originated during the

18th century, it has remained popular for a long time. One great value of the belletristic approach to literature is that it leads us to reflect on the importance of beauty to human society. This approach is, in many ways, a very useful way of talking about literature because it leads people to ask what kind of thing makes a literary text beautiful. As a result of the belletristic approach to literature, we have developed a professional vocabulary for talking about texts, many of which we will use in this textbook. But along with the usefulness of the belletristic approach to literature, there are some pretty significant problems.

Perhaps the most serious problem with seeing literature as "belles lettres" is the problem of a standard of beauty. We've probably all heard the old saying, "Beauty is in the eye of the beholder." That old saying means simply that each of us has a different standard for deciding what is beautiful. Or, that the perception of beauty can be affected by many other factors. Think, for instance, of the fairy tale, *Beauty and the Beast,* and how the Beauty's perception of the Beast is altered as she comes to know him and to care for him. So, whose standard of beauty do we use in determining what is literature? Is it possible for a Beatles song to be a piece of art in the same way that a Shakespearean sonnet is a piece of art? It depends on who you ask.

The other problem with this definition of literature is the notion that a text is only created to be artistic. That is a very limited definition. Most people who are considered "beautiful" or "handsome" will tell you how stifling such a perception can be. People want to be treated as complete persons, to be appreciated for their intellect and their personality, not just for "a pretty face" or a great body. While a text cannot care whether you love it only for its looks, its author might. Texts are not the products of random events in a chaotic universe. Rather, they come into being as a result of an author's deliberate and careful work. They represent the author's attempt to tell us something about ourselves and the world in which we live. Texts may be intended to entertain us, to educate us, to influence our opinion, to move us to action. Sometimes, they accomplish any or all of these goals even without the author's conscious intention. If we simply think about texts as "beautiful letters," we may fail to understand why the text affects us as it does, or even miss the message altogether.

If defining literature in terms of "belles lettres" is problematic, we might look at other characteristics of literary texts in order to find a criterion that will lead to a more comprehensive definition. The Austen novel we chose as literature, for instance, might be considered "literature" because it is about something that isn't "real." In other words, the novel is about an imaginary sequence of events as opposed to, for example, a newspaper story about something that actually happened. If we apply the "reality" criterion to other literary works, we find that many of them are written from the author's imagination instead of from "real" life. Of course, we can find problems with this criterion, too. Many so-called "fictional" texts are about events that actually happened. A number of Shakespeare's plays, particularly those designated as "history" plays, dramatize actual events. And certainly, we wouldn't say that a Shakespearean play isn't literature.

Another issue to consider is to what degree the "realism" of a text is determined by whether the events it describes actually occurred. Think about the Austen novel for a minute. Jane Austen's novels are, in many ways, very realistic. They describe in great detail the life of many different types of people who lived in the 18th century, including discussions of how they made their living, what their homes were like, what they wore, how they traveled, and even how they spoke. The fact that the events of the novels didn't actually take place doesn't affect how accurately they portray life of that era. We might say that even though the stories aren't real, they are "true." In fact, an Austen novel might give us a truer sense of the life of the English middle-class during the late 18th century than a newspaper account from that time.

Another problem with applying the term *literature* only to fictional works is that it keeps us from considering as literary a whole range of "beautiful" texts that are "real." Abraham Lincoln's "Gettysburg Address" or Martin Luther King, Jr.'s "Letter from Birmingham Jail" would not be considered literature under this criterion, but are nevertheless beautiful and important texts. Books by authors such as Joan Didion and Truman Capote, who write in a literary style about actual events, would also be excluded.

Finally, we need to consider the "reality" of literary texts themselves. While literature may be about events that aren't real, a literary work often takes on a powerful cultural life of its own. Consider Shakespeare's play *Romeo and Juliet*. This play, written in 1595 and based on a poem written in the 1560s, continues to symbolize the tragedy of forbidden love. Movie versions were made in the 1960s and 1990s. Even people who have never read a Shakespeare play know about Romeo and Juliet. The play has become a part of our cultural heritage and its characters are as real to us as Charlemagne or Joan of Arc.

One thing that is important to understand about both these ways of viewing literature is that they sometimes cause us to forget what a powerful effect literary texts can have over our lives. Because the literary work is not "real," we sometimes treat it as unimportant. Because it is beautiful, we appreciate it without questioning it. Thus, we have a tendency to push "art" into a separate category in our culture. James Agee once said that to designate a text as art was to strip it of all its power. By characterizing art in this way, we risk treating it as a mystery that we cannot understand. We've all heard people say, "I don't know what art is, but I know what I like." If we stick our heads in the sand and refuse to consider how art functions in a society and why it is such a powerful cultural force, not only do we lessen its impact, but we give others a degree of control over us. Several years ago, a certain film about gang warfare in the inner city was said to have set off violent incidents in several places. That, of course, was an extreme case, but we have all had the experience of reading a book that made us cry, seeing a film that made us angry, or, perhaps, hearing a poem that moved us deeply. If we simply accept this response at face value, we may fail to realize that the work of art affects us much as an argument does. When someone engages us in an argument, we know that we are being persuaded, and we have some control over the outcome of the argument. If we ignore the persuasive power of art, we give up any control over how the argument it makes affects us.

It should be clear that it is a difficult, if not impossible, task to agree on a strict definition of literature. But perhaps a strict definition of literature is not that important. Rather than asking whether a given text is literature or not, we might rephrase the question. We should ask, "How has the author of this text used literary techniques to make an argument?" and, "Why does this piece of literature affect me in the way it does?"

For Practice

1. Consider a text (poem, play, novel, or film) that you believe to be a work of art. Why do you think so? Because someone told you? Because you personally think it is art? What makes it art?

2. Consider a text that you like but that is not considered art by most people. You might choose a rock-and-roll song, a comic book, or a situation comedy. Why do you like this text? Do you personally consider it art? Why or why not?

3. Think about a text that has made you cry, or made you angry, or has moved you deeply in some way. Do you think your response was what the author intended? Why or why not? Identify specific things in the text that elicited your response.

What Is Argument?

Many of us tend to think about argument as something to avoid. We think of an argument as an angry disputation between two or more people. Generally, we believe that somebody has to win an argument, and that means that somebody else has to lose. In this book, we want to look at argument differently, as a way of reaching agreement with other people. Much of what you will do in the academic world and in your life outside college will involve using argument to resolve disputes. Arguments become necessary when people do not agree about a state of affairs or what should be done about that state of affairs. Most reasonable people would not, for example, argue about whether two and two make four; that is a mathematical fact that is beyond dispute. Unfortunately, there are few parts of our life where there is such universal agreement. In the many instances where the answer is less certain, we can use argument both as a means of discovering what we believe about a given controversy, and for coming to agreement with others who might believe differently.

An argument is nothing more than the reasons we put forward for resolving a disagreement. Suppose, for instance, a group of us decide to go to a movie but we each want to see a different film. We could resolve our differences in several ways. One of us could make a decision and impose it on the others. Or we could draw straws. Or we could each offer our reasons for wanting to see a certain film, negotiating some agreement in time to see one of the movies. The set of reasons that each of us offers is an argument.

Some arguments are very clearly arguments: a debate between presidential candidates; a court case where defense and prosecuting attorneys present arguments to a jury. Other arguments, however, are delivered in more subtle ways, not so clearly marked as arguments, but nevertheless intended to persuade an audience. Think of the speeches that politicians give on national holidays, or the eulogies that you have heard at funerals. These speeches are not intended to move us to action but to reinforce commonly held values. On Memorial Day, for example, the president might extol the virtues of giving up one's life for one's country. At a funeral, the minister might praise the dear departed for being a good parent, an active participant in civic life, or a good church member. Such arguments are not only limited to praise. The president might reinforce cultural values just as effectively by criticizing someone who had desecrated the flag. These kinds of arguments, which the ancient Greeks called *epideictic* or the rhetoric of praise and blame, are intended to strengthen cultural values. They are sometimes all the more persuasive because they are not obviously arguments.

Most literary texts are examples of very subtle arguments. Remember that we said earlier in this chapter that authors create texts to tell us something about ourselves or about the world we live in. The author of a poem, or a play, or a short story, or a novel, tries to persuade us to agree to a certain vision of the world. And quite often, we simply take for granted the arguments in a literary text without ever questioning them as we would more traditional arguments. Sometimes the arguments in a literary text are obvious. In the *Iliad*, for example, the Greek forces, after ten years of war, argue whether to continue fighting or give up and go home. Various Greek leaders offer arguments about what course of action they should take. At other times, however, the arguments in literary texts are like epideictic rhetoric. They reinforce or change cultural values simply by presenting them in a positive or negative light. These arguments are sometimes more powerful because we don't recognize their persuasive force and fail to question them as we might a more traditional argument.

We might examine, as an example of a literary text that makes an epideictic argument, the old situation comedy, *I Love Lucy*. In that television program, which was incredibly popular for many years and continues to be watched in re-runs, Lucy, an American woman, was married to Ricky Ricardo, a Cuban immigrant and bandleader. In the 1950s, when *I Love Lucy* first appeared on television, marriages between people from different cultures (sometimes called "mixed" marriages) were much less common than they are today. In addition, many people felt that musicians were unreliable, disreputable people. Thus, it was pretty unusual for a young American woman to be married to a man like Ricky Ricardo. By presenting these two people in a successful, happy "mixed" marriage, this program presented the argument that it is appropriate for two such people to be married, despite cultural beliefs that suggested the opposite. Most people who watched the *I Love Lucy Show* episode after episode, year after year, would never have thought they were being presented with an argument, and yet, it is very likely that their opinions about inter-cultural marriage, or about musicians, changed because of seeing this program. Arguments such as these are very powerful, largely because they are implicit and not explicit. We are persuaded without even being aware of it. And that is why it is so important to learn to identify and evaluate the arguments that such texts make.

For Practice

1. Can you think of a popular television program of today that goes against the grain of conventional social values? How successful is the program in presenting its argument?

2. Sometimes literary works that are very controversial when they are first published find an audience in later eras. Other works are sometimes banned from the shelves of school libraries as cultural values change. Some very famous books such as *Huckleberry Finn* and *Catcher in the Rye* have been banned at one time or another. Does the act of banning books make more sense to you if you view literature as argument rather than as art? Why or why not?

Using Literary Language

Most professions develop a common language that allows members of the profession to communicate efficiently among themselves. This language, sometimes called *jargon,* consists primarily of a set of terms used to signify the products and processes with which the members of that profession work. Those of us who study language and literature have our own set of terms for talking about what we study. As we talk about how literary texts make arguments, it will help us to be familiar with those terms. In addition to this discussion, you may also refer to the glossary of literary terms at the end of this book.

In creating a text, an author uses certain literary techniques to convey a certain view of the world. It is important to realize that these techniques are, themselves, a kind of argument. How an author creates meaning affects your understanding of that meaning. We will divide our discussion of literary techniques into four categories: Form, Language, Characters, and Situation. You will find, however, from our discussion, that it is not possible to discuss a text only in terms of one of these categories because they are all interrelated. As you read a text, you should look for literary techniques and ask yourself why the author chose to use them. Keep in mind that you will need to apply several of these terms to any given text as you try to interpret its meaning. You should also keep in mind that these factors interact with each other, so that interpreting a literary text is a very complicated endeavor.

Form

There are many different forms of literary texts. The word we use to talk about the form of a text is *genre*. You might find it easier to understand what we mean by the term genre by comparing it to makes and models of vehicles. There are, for example, many different types of vehicles: bicycles, motorcycles, cars, and trucks. Within each of these categories, there are sub-categories. Within the category trucks are sub-categories such as tractor-trailer, light truck, panel van, and moving van, to name a few. The category cars is broken down into sedans, station wagons, compacts, and subcompacts. There are even sub-categories for bicycles and motorcycles. We tend to establish these kinds of categories in order to make thinking and communicating easier. Suppose I want to buy a new car. That process is simplified if I think carefully about what I need to do with my car, decide which sub-category of cars best fits my needs, and then look only at those cars within that sub-category. Think how much more time-consuming a process it would be to look at every single make and model of car to find one that I liked and that suited my needs.

Just as these categories for vehicles makes the process of buying or talking about cars easier, so does the concept of genre make it easier for us to talk about and to produce texts. Suppose for instance, I want to communicate with a manufacturer about a faulty product I have purchased. Should I write them a poem or a letter for this task? Of course, · a letter would be the expected and appropriate means of communication in this instance. And if I want to tell someone about a certain text that I've read or a film that I've seen, it helps to describe it generically. If I say that a film is an action/adventure movie, that communicates a lot of information very efficiently.

Some major textual genres are novels, poetry, drama, and essays. And, of course, there are sub-categories within these major genres. Some of the different types of poems, for example, are sonnets, odes, and epics. Sub-categories of drama are tragedy, comedy, history plays, and romances. And there are many types of novels such as the *bildungsroman* (a coming of age novel), the epistolary novel (made up of a series of letters written between characters), and romances. There are, of course, many other sub-categories of each of these major genres.

What is important to pay attention to is that these categories carry with them certain expectations. If we pick up a novel, we have an expectation that we will be reading a story about some characters who experience a sequence of events. Our expectations for a song are very different. Although some songs tell stories, they certainly can't include the detail that a long novel does. Another way of talking about these expectations is to talk about *literary conventions* associated with each of the different genres. (Perhaps you have heard the word "conventional" used to describe someone who behaves as they are expected to behave, or the word "unconventional" used to describe someone who does the unexpected.) Some conventions of the novel are that it is a long text that is divided into smaller sections like chapters; that it has a plot, a narrator of some sort, and a number of characters. The conventions are what identify a specific genre and they generally coincide with our expectations for that kind of text.

We should keep in mind, then, as we begin to experience a text, what our expectations for this literary form are. As we pick up a text, because of our knowledge of literary conventions, we anticipate a certain kind of experience. The way an author deals with those conventions, or fulfills or fails to fulfill our expectations, is part of how the text works. Just as your experience of life can be very different depending on how people fulfill your expectations, so is your experience of the text conditioned in this way. When an author surprises us by violating literary conventions, we have a certain kind of response to a text. We may feel off-balance or confused. We feel a need to resolve that confusion as we read. But an author can create just as much confusion by following conventions. Murder mysteries, for example, are sometimes so conventional that they lull us into inattentiveness, leading us to overlook the one clue that solves the mystery in the end.

We can see how generic conventions can evoke a certain response by looking at the case of the Renaissance sonnet. A sonnet is a fourteen line poem with a very definite rhyme scheme. It might contain four rhyming quatrains (four-line sections) and end with rhyming couplet (a two-line section), or it might contain an octet (of eight lines) followed by a sestet (of six lines). Obviously, the sonnet is a very tightly controlled form and, generally, it is used to deal very formally with serious subjects such as love or death. You might compare it to the formal atmosphere of a church service where the strict observation of ritual helps to focus the worshipper's mind on serious spiritual matters. Because our expectations for the sonnet form are so strongly determined by the rules governing its form, we are very surprised when the treatment of the subject does not meet our expectations.

During the Renaissance, the sonnet form was conventionally used as part of the courtly love tradition to talk about an unrequited love. The poet, usually a man, would use very elaborate metaphors to describe his lover—her eyes were moonbeams; her lips, a red rose; her teeth, pearls, and so forth. So, when a Renaissance courtier saw a sonnet—and a text could be identified as a sonnet without even reading it, just by observing the poem's structure—he or she would expect to read a poem about the agonies of loving a beautiful but unobtainable lover. Imagine, then, the surprise such a reader would experience upon reading a Shakespearean sonnet which began with the line, "My mistress' eyes are nothing like the sun." Not only is Shakespeare violating the convention of using elaborate metaphors to describe the lover, but he seems to be talking about an actual girlfriend, not some distant and unobtainable woman. In this way, Shakespeare is able to make an argument about the nature of real relationships between men and women.

His audience's experience of this argument is conditioned by the surprise that results from the violation of the sonnet conventions.

This kind of manipulation of formal conventions to condition the argument of a text is not limited to Shakespeare, but happens in all kinds of texts all the time. You might think about a film like *Pulp Fiction*, in which the director, Quentin Tarentino, rearranges the sequence of the plot, creating a degree of uncertainty which only heightens the tension that the audience experiences. As you approach the texts in this book, think about the form of each and analyze your expectations.

For Practice

1. What are some of your expectations for . . .
   - a novel?
   - a rock song?
   - an action/adventure film?
   - an epic poem?
   - a tragedy (play)?
   - a horror movie?
   - a murder mystery?
   - short story?

   Now go to the library and look up as many of these genres as you can in a literary handbook. What does the handbook suggest are the conventions associated with these genres? How do they compare to your own expectations?

2. Consider a movie you have seen more than once, or a story you have read twice. How did your experience change as you became more familiar with that particular work?

3. Look in the Glossary of this book for discussions for the following terms related to the concept of genre: allegory; ballad; conventional form; elegy; epic; essay; free verse/open form; genre; lyric; novel; ode; short story; sonnet.

Language

Many people have said that language is a uniquely human phenomenon and that it is language that distinguishes us from any other species. Whether or not this is the case, language is certainly the means by which we interact with the world and with each other. In ancient cultures, the very act of naming something was seen as a very powerful act in which the namer gained control over the thing or the person who was named. Without language, we cannot communicate with one another, we cannot advance theories, we cannot share our dreams, our tradition, our culture. Language links us to the past and to the future, to one another, and to the world.

Language is a code that we spend our lives learning to interpret. All of us have played with codes at one time or another. Perhaps we used a simple substitution code to send secret messages to our friends. To the extent that words are arbitrary signs that we have assigned to things that exist in the world, it is no more complicated than a simple substitution code. But, of course, it is much more complex than that. Most of us know a lot about this code, particularly about how it is used in interpersonal communication. In this section, we will look at how language code is used to manipulate your experience of a text. In keeping with our purpose, we will be using literary terms as a focus for our discussion.

One way to crack the language code in a text is to examine *diction*, or the way the author uses grammar, vocabulary, and phrasing in a work. One way of thinking about diction is to consider word choices. Words have two types of meanings: *denotative* and *connotative*. Denotative meaning corresponds roughly to the standard dictionary definition; connotative meanings encompass all the subtle nuances that are part of our understanding of a word. Consider, for example, how the word "little" differs in meaning from the word "small." Denotatively, there is virtually no difference between these two words, but connotatively there can be a world of difference. Leona Helmsley, a New York City hotelier who was sent to prison in the 1980s for income tax evasion, became very unpopular because she referred disparagingly to people who couldn't afford to stay in her hotels as "the little people." Somehow, "the small people" doesn't sound so disdainful. Or, can you imagine an Irish storyteller referring to the leprechauns as "the small people"? Slang is another example of how word choice makes a difference in language use. We use slang to indicate that we are part of a group and/or to distinguish ourselves from other groups. So, when an individual chooses to use a word like "cool," or "rad," or "fat," or "bomb" to describe someone they admire, that word choice tells us a lot about the speaker's social or economic background

Diction is also affected by grammatical choices. Speakers often reveal their socio-economic class or their cultural heritage in their grammar. In African American vernacular, for example, the word "be" has a specific and particular meaning that it does not have in other cultures. If someone says, for example, "It be cold in that building," the use of the word "be" indicates that this is a situation that is ongoing and not just an isolated event. The building is always cold, not just cold today. In other social groups, individuals use grammar similar to that in grammar handbooks. We can tell a lot about a person's education and background depending on whether she says, "It's me" or "It is I."

Another element of diction is phrasing. Think about the difference in the effect of hearing short clipped sentences as opposed to long, complex sentences. Ancient orators used to use periodic sentences, long, elaborate sentences in which the point was withheld until the very end. These sentences create a kind of suspense for the reader or listener, but they can be very difficult to read. William Faulkner is known for writing very long sentences that can go on for a page or more. These sentences are a part of Faulkner's art that reveal his view and experience of the world. Among other things, these long sentences capture some of the cadences of southern speech and imitate the meandering path that southern storytellers sometimes follow. We might also consider *rhythm* and *meter* in our discussion of diction as well. Poets may use rhythm and meter to enhance, or sometimes to undercut the literal meaning of their words. Playwrights may use rhythm to imitate the cadences of speech, or help to establish mood.

Another part of the linguistic code of texts is *tone*. We all know what tone is in terms of speech. Who hasn't heard a parent, teacher, or other adult say something like, "Don't take that tone with me, Kid!" In that situation, we know exactly what tone means. We might say that tone is the attitude that accompanies the words in a text. Tone is subjective, in that each of us may interpret tone somewhat differently, and elusive, because it is very difficult to identify the signals that produce a certain tone. Most of us can recognize the tone of "Don't take that tone with me!" because we've experienced that situation. Tone is, perhaps, the most difficult of all literary techniques to explain or to talk about.

One of the identifying characteristics of literary texts is their imaginative or figurative, rather than literal, use of language. As we have said, literary texts make their arguments in very subtle ways. Rather than presenting a logical, reasoned argument, they persuade by evoking moods, by oblique references to cultural values. The use of *figurative language* can be a way of mobilizing our emotions to persuade us. Or, it can be an economical way of making a point. Or, it can be a way of expressing the ineffable, that which cannot easily be expressed.

We can begin talking about figurative language by examining the use of *images* in literary texts. Simply put, images are references within a text to tangible, visible objects. The most obvious use of images is to help a reader paint a visual picture of a scene in the mind's eye. In Robert Browning's poem "My Last Duchess," for example, the Duke uses images to paint a picture of his wife and the life she lived: "the way her mantle laps her wrist," "the flush on her cheek," "a bough of cherries," "the white mule she rode with round the terrace." Through these images we may achieve a sense of what that painting on the wall must look like. Images, however, can do much more in a text than simply describe a scene. The connotations associated with particular images can also evoke a powerful emotional response. In Shakespeare's play *Macbeth,* which is the story of how a Scottish aristocrat murders the king and assumes his throne, one of the most powerful images is blood. The image appears at the very beginning of the play when a blood-covered messenger comes to the king to report the outcome of the battle. In using this image of blood in the opening scene of the play, Shakespeare sets a mood for the whole drama. He intensifies that image throughout the play with images of the bloody assassination of Duncan the king, the slaying of Banquo, and many images of bloody children. After reading this play it is as hard to wash the image of blood from our minds as it was for Lady Macbeth to wash it from her hand. Images which evoke such powerful emotions are often symbolic. In other words, because they stand for something more than themselves. One of the most obvious visual symbols is a flag which stands for a country or state. You can gain a sense of how powerful a *symbol* can be if you think about the animosity generated by the debate about whether to fly the Confederate battle flag. In *Macbeth,* the blood is a symbol for life and death, for inheritance, and, in the case of Lady Macbeth, for her guilt.

Figures of speech are specific uses of figurative language. We most commonly talk about *metaphors* and *similes* as figures of speech. A metaphor is a figure of speech in which a comparison between very different things is implied. If we say, for example, that man is bull-headed, we do not literally mean that he has a bull's head instead of a human one. Rather, we mean that he has certain characteristics which we commonly attribute to bulls, particularly stubbornness. One way of talking about the structure of a metaphor is through the use of the terms *tenor* and *vehicle*. The tenor is the object of the comparison and the vehicle is the thing to which it is compared. In this instance, the man is the tenor while the vehicle is the bull. Closely related to metaphor is the simile, a figure which makes an overt comparison using the word *like*. Shakespeare said, in one of the sonnets, "My love is like a red, red rose."

Metaphors and similes are useful in two ways. First, they stimulate the reader to transfer a whole set of connotative meanings associated with one thing (the vehicle) onto the thing to which it is compared (the tenor). Suppose I say that a woman's beauty is fully blown. The comparison is to a flower which has reached the fullness of its bloom and now can only decay. I have thus transferred to the woman and her beauty, all the emotional responses that we normally associate with flowers, and I have suggested that she will soon begin to age and grow old. Ultimately the message might be that beauty is transient and death is just around the corner. A second important use of metaphor is as a way to express something that is difficult to describe in any other way. How, for example, can you tell someone how angry you are? There are no quantitative measurements for anger. But you can say that you were "mad as a wet hen," that you were so angry you "stormed off," or that you really "blew your top." Metaphor and simile can allow us to express the inexpressible and to speak the unspeakable.

For Practice

1. As you watch an episode of your favorite television show, pay attention to how each of the characters speaks. What does that way of speaking reveal about the character?

2. Make a list of five symbols of American culture. What do you think these symbols stand for? Compare your answer to those of your classmates.

3. Read a poem. What images do you find there? How do those images evoke a scene?

4. Look in the Glossary of this book for discussions of the following: alliteration; archaic language: concrete language; connotation; diction; figurative language; imagery; metaphor; metonymy; onomatopoeia; personification; simile; style; syntax; tone.

Characters

The characters in a story are central to the literary argument. We talk about characters by looking at exposition (how the author describes a character) and character development. Characterization can be the focus of a passage, as in the opening of Charles Dickens' novel *Hard Times,* which begins with a very elaborate description of the bumps and grizzles of Mr. Thomas Gradgrind's head. Or, it can be incidental in the manner of brief descriptive phrases that accompany action: "She ran her fingers through her long blonde hair as she. . . ." Character description is most effectively used in prose (short stories and novels) where expository passages are common. Elaborate descriptions of characters are more awkward in plays where action is the focus of the text. Thus, in drama, characterization is most often achieved through action. How a character behaves usually tells us more about a character than the physical description of a stage note.

In addition to paying attention to how a character is described, we can also note how characters change or do not change. Think, for example, about the Biblical story of Job, who was visited by all kinds of troubles: his family left him, his cattle died, his crops failed, he was afflicted with sores. But throughout all these trials, Job's faith remained strong. The story of Job has become an example of steadfastness and faith. On the other hand, we might consider Charles Dickens' *A Christmas Carol.* As a result of his experiences with the three ghosts, Ebenezer Scrooge changes from a mean and despicable character to one who is generous and loving. Thus, the significance of the degree to which a character changes is related to the story's theme and argument.

For Practice

1. Read a short story and a chapter from a novel. Compare the amount of text that is devoted to character exposition (description). Do you think the genre dictates in some way how character is developed?

2. Look in the Glossary of this book for discussions for the following terms: character; characterization.

The characters who inhabit a text are not the only ones you should consider as you read, however. Another important character is the work's *narrator*. The narrator is the person who tells the story. Sometimes the narrator is a character in a story, sometimes not. Sometimes the narrator is a third person narrator who is not part of the action. Sometimes that narrator is omniscient, knowing everything that goes on in the story, even knowing the minds of all the characters. Other times, the narrator is a character in the story and the point of view is limited to what that character can reasonably know. Still other times, a story is not told by a particular character but is told from the character's perspective. That perspective can shift throughout the course of the narrative. Thus, a reader must constantly pay attention to the narrative *point of view* of a work. One thing that is particularly important to keep in mind is that the story is told from the narrator's perspective, or point of view. We can see how important this is by considering some texts that have more than one narrative. In the 19th century, Robert Browning wrote a long poetic work entitled *The Ring and the Book*. The poem is based on an Italian murder trial of the 17th century and is told by nine different people. Each of the nine versions of the story is quite different. The film *Rashamon* by Japanese filmmaker Akira Kirasawa achieves a similar effect as it tells the story of a murder from several perspectives. These texts remind us that our view of the events of the story is dependent upon the narrator's perspective. It is important, then, that we have some understanding of the narrator's character because it is the one which shapes our view of the events of the narrative. Keep in mind that some narrators, just like some people, are more reliable than others.

For Practice

1. Read a short story. What are some of the techniques the author uses to develop the characters?
2. Look in your Glossary for a discussion of the following terms: antagonist; persona, speaker, or narrator; protagonist.

Finally, as you consider the argument that a text makes, it is helpful to think about the individuals involved in that argument: the author and the audience. As you read a text or view a film or television program, you, the audience, are being addressed by an author who wants to persuade you to accept a certain view of the world. Most readers never meet the author of texts that they read, and yet, after reading a book, they could probably tell you something about what the author "believes" about the world. This "author" that a reader can identify from a text is, of course, not the real person who wrote the book. It is, instead, a persona that is created from the text. Wayne Booth, a literary and rhetorical theorist, has called this author the "implied author." Just as the implied author is not the actual human being who wrote the book, the audience is not precisely the human who reads it, but an audience who is constructed by the text. Wayne Booth provides a helpful way to think about this with his concept of "fields of selves." Every human being has a whole range of personae, or masks, that we put on in response to various relationships. With our parents, we put on the daughter or son persona, while we wear the good student persona with our teachers. The same thing is true with the author/reader relationship. As we read a text, we put on a certain kind of persona or self in response to our developing relationship with the implied author. In this way, we are, in a sense, constructed by the implied author of that text.

The author might want to construct the audience so that they have a different view of other people. Or, the author might want to construct an audience that believes a little differently about patriotism, or racism, or professional sports. As a result of the experience of reading a text or watching a film, we add to our field of selves this new persona. In some slight way, then, we are changed by our encounter with a text. This relationship between the audience and the implied author is at the very heart of the persuasive nature of literary texts. It is what reading literature as argument is all about.

For Practice

1. Think about a book that you have read and really enjoyed. What do you think about the author of that text? What is he or she like? How do you know?

2. Consider a television program like *Seinfeld, Grace Under Fire,* or even *Oprah Winfrey* or *Rosie O'Donnell.* What are these characters like? How do you know? Do you think they are the same at home as they are on these television programs?

3. Each time you read a text, think about the persona you put on in response to it. How are you changed as a result of your experience with this text?

Situation

Finally, we should consider the situation of a text as part of our reading. If we think for just a moment about how the situations in which we find ourselves determine the way we behave, we can understand just how important situation is in our understanding of a text. Suppose, for example, you believe that it is wrong to take the life of another human being. You are drafted into the army during wartime and find yourself on a battlefield, face to face with a soldier from the opposing army. His gun is pointed right at you. How do you think you might respond in this situation? Would your actions be governed by your principled belief in the sanctity of human life, or would your fear for your life cause you to shoot the enemy soldier? Many times, our actions are determined as much by our situations as by our beliefs. In this section, we will look at three kinds of situation that are important to our understanding of a text: the situation within the text; the situation within which the text was written; and the situation in which the text is read.

We can distinguish the situation which exists within a text from those situations in which the text exists by calling it a scene which is made up of setting and plot. *Plot* is simply the sequence of events in a narrative. We should always keep in mind that plots are rarely presented in a simple, linear fashion. Authors often use plot devices such as flashbacks and flash forwards to step outside the temporal sequence of events. Such plot devices are particularly effective in film. Actor/director Orson Welles was one of the first filmmakers to use flashbacks and flash forwards effectively in his highly acclaimed film, *Citizen Kane,* which opens with the lonely death of Kane, a rich and famous newspaper tycoon. Welles then uses the frame story of a journalist researching Kane's life in order to write his obituary to organize even more flashbacks and flash forwards. In this way, Wells is able to use temporal displacements as a way of commenting on the events of Kane's life that led him to die alone and unloved. Such temporal displacements of a plot can be used to emphasize certain actions, or to point out cause and effect relationships between certain events. Sometimes, authors disrupt the temporal sequence of a plot simply to disorient the audience. It is important to pay attention to such temporal shifts and to try to account for them. They are part of the argument of the text.

Setting is the second aspect of the scene of a text. Setting consists of the time, places, and circumstances in which the action of the plot takes place. Setting can determine plot to a large degree. For example, a story set in medieval Europe would not normally include the launch of a telecommunications satellite as an element of its plot. Setting also determines how characters behave just as the situations in which we find ourselves determine how we act. We do not, for example, act the same way in English class as we do at a football game. Finally, setting is an integral part of the mood of a text.

Scene is particularly important in our understanding of texts as arguments because much of the argument of a text consists in the way characters react to the scene. Imagine, for example, a text in which the scene is similar to that experienced by the imaginary draftee at the beginning of this section. That scene could be played out in a number of ways. The draftee could shoot the enemy soldier or be shot by him. The draftee could surrender to the enemy soldier. The war might be a civil war and the draftee might recognize the enemy soldier as a friend or relative. The scene is similar, but the argument of the text would be very different depending upon the actions of the character. In the first scene, where draftee shoots enemy soldier, the argument might be something like "Principles are fine when they aren't challenged, but don't always hold up when they are." In the last scene, the author might be making an argument about the horrors of war.

For Practice

1. Look in the Glossary for discussions of these terms related to the situation within a text: atmosphere, mood, or ambiance; frame story; plot; point of view; setting; situational irony.

In addition to the situation within a text, it is important to consider the situation within which the text was created. We might distinguish this aspect of situation as the rhetorical situation. Paying attention to the circumstances in which a text was produced is a relatively new aspect in contemporary literary studies. For many years, literary theorists insisted that only the text itself was important and that the author's intention for a text could not be known, and should not be considered in our study of it. But, if we approach a literary text as an argument, the author's intention can become very important. This is particularly true for texts which are produced as cultural critique. Many American novelists have produced works intended to criticize the society in which they find themselves. John Steinbeck's novel, *The Grapes of Wrath,* is a scathing criticism of the treatment of migrant workers during the Great Depression. Harriet Beecher Stowe wrote *Uncle Tom's Cabin* as a protest and a call to action to abolish the institution of slavery. To ignore the intent of the author's social critique would make it impossible to appreciate these novels. Not all texts are intended as a rhetorical response to a social situation, but all texts are produced within a particular time and place. Our experience of the text is always enhanced by an understanding of the situation in which it was produced.

Finally, in order to complete our interpretation of a text, it is important to look at the situation in which we experience it. As we said earlier in this chapter, literary texts often tell us much more about the era in which they were written than do contemporary prose accounts. At the same time, however, much is lost over time. As you read *A Midsummer Night's Dream,* the Shakespearean play in this book, you will find that many of the words in the play no longer mean the same thing they did in Shakespeare's time. On the other hand, you will find that much of the action of the play, which dramatizes what fools love makes of us all, is just as meaningful today as it would have been in the 16th century. It is important to try to account for why a text written 400 years ago can still speak to us today. Is it because it is a genuine work of art? Or is it because the contexts in which the text was produced is similar to the one in which you are reading it?

Another aspect of the rhetorical situation of a text is the degree to which it has taken on a cultural life of its own. Remember that we discussed how Shakespeare's play *Romeo and Juliet* had its own cultural identity. Remember also that we said the play was based on an earlier poem and that several versions of the film had been produced. The plot has also been adapted to other settings; *West Side Story,* for example, is an adaptation of the story of Romeo and Juliet. The relationship between all these texts is called *intertextuality*. We might think of it as a conversation between and among these texts. If we pay attention to intertextuality, we examine how the various texts treat the basic elements of plot, setting, and character. Remember how in Browning's poem *The Ring and the Book* the different narrators perceived the events of the murder differently and the differences in perception told us something about the characters themselves. The ways in which each text alters the familiar story of Romeo and Juliet can transform a cultural cliché into a new and unique message.

In the case of texts that transform an old and familiar story, our own knowledge, then, can become part of the situation of the text.

Regardless of which version of *Romeo and Juliet* we see, our own experience of it will be altered if we have seen or read another of the versions. Our expectations for the text will be different each time we experience the story. Thus, interpretation of a text relies as much on the knowledge we bring to the situation as it does on the elements of the text itself.

For Practice

1. Many contemporary films play around with temporal sequence in flashbacks, flash forwards, or even just by repeating a brief action sequence several times. Think about one such film that you've seen. What response did that temporal disjunction evoke in you as an audience member? What do you think the director was trying to accomplish by using this technique?

2. Think of a book you've read in which the setting was memorable. Many horror novels, for instance, have eerie settings. How did the author produce that memorable setting? How does the mood that setting evoked in you function in the argument?

3. Try to think of a film you have seen that is based on a short story, play, or novel that you have read. How were these two versions of the story different? How were they the same? How were your expectations of the second version established by your previous experience with the text?

4. Refer in the Glossary to the discussion of critical approaches to literature. How important are the different situations of a text to the different critical approaches?

Conclusion

In the beginning of this chapter, we talked about literature as *belles lettres,* or as art. We also said that there is a danger that, in designating a text as "art," we tend to begin to view it as a mystery and no longer try to understand the message it delivers or how it delivers that message. As you learn to use the terms in this book to think about literature, you can begin to decipher the messages and arguments that art holds. What is more, you can begin to decide for yourself whether these works of art conform to your own standard of beauty or someone else's. You can make judgments about why they have been chosen to be designated as art. Perhaps you can resurrect the power that James Agee says is stripped from these works when they begin to be called "art."

Putting What You've Learned to Work

Practice using the literary vocabulary you have just learned to analyze this short story. When you have finished, try to answer the questions at the end of the story.

The Story of an Hour

Kate Chopin

Knowing that Mrs. Mallard was afflicted with a heart trouble, great care was taken to break to her as gently as possible the news of her husband's death.

It was her sister Josephine who told her, in broken sentences; veiled hints that revealed in half concealing. Her husband's friend Richards was there, too, near her. It was he who had been in the newspaper office when intelligence of the railroad disaster was received, with Brently Mallard's name leading the list of "killed." He had only taken the time to assure himself of its truth by a second telegram, and had hastened to forestall any less careful, less tender friend in bearing the sad message.

She did not hear the story as many women have heard the same, with a paralyzed inability to accept its significance. She wept at once, with sudden, wild abandonment, in her sister's arms. When the storm of grief had spent itself she went away to her room alone. She would have no one follow her.

There stood, facing the open window, a comfortable, roomy armchair. Into this she sank, pressed down by a physical exhaustion that haunted her body and seemed to reach into her soul.

She could see in the open square before her house the tops of trees that were all aquiver with the new spring life. The delicious breath of rain was in the air. In the street below a peddler was crying his wares. The notes of a distant song which some one was singing reached her faintly, and countless sparrows were twittering in the eaves.

There were patches of blue sky showing here and there through the clouds that had met and piled one above the other in the west facing her window.

She sat with her head thrown back upon the cushion of the chair quite motionless, except when a sob came up into her throat and shook her, as a child who has cried itself to sleep continues to sob in its dreams.

She was young, with a fair, calm face, whose lines bespoke repression and even a certain strength. But now there was a dull stare in her eyes, whose gaze was fixed away off yonder on one of those patches of blue sky. It was not a glance of reflection, but rather indicated a suspension of intelligent thought.

There was something coming to her and she was waiting for it, fearfully. What was it? She did not know; it was too subtle and elusive to name. But she felt it, creeping out of the sky, reaching toward her through the sounds, the scents, the color that filled the air.

Now her bosom rose and fell tumultuously. She was beginning to recognize this thing that was approaching to possess her, and she was striving to beat it back with her will—as powerless as her two white slender hands would have been.

When she abandoned herself a little whispered word escaped her slightly parted lips. She said it over and over under her breath: "free, free, free!" The vacant stare and the look of terror that had followed it went from her eyes. They stayed keen and bright. Her pulses beat fast, and the coursing blood warmed and relaxed every inch of her body.

She did not stop to ask if it were not a monstrous joy that held her. A clear and exalted perception enabled her to dismiss the suggestion as trivial.

She knew that she would weep again when she saw the kind, tender hands folded in death; the face that had never looked save with love upon her, fixed and gray and dead. But she saw beyond that bitter moment a long procession of years to come that would belong to her absolutely. And she opened and spread her arms out to them in welcome.

There would be no one to live for during those coming years; she would live for herself. There would be no powerful will bending hers in that blind persistence with which men and women believe they have a right to impose a private will upon a fellow-creature. A kind intention or a cruel intention made the act seem no less a crime as she looked upon it in that brief moment of illumination.

And yet she had loved him—sometimes. Often she had not. What did it matter! What could love, the unsolved mystery, count for in face of this possession of self-assertion which she suddenly recognized as the strongest impulse of her being!

"Free! Body and soul free!" she kept whispering.

Josephine was kneeling before the closed door with her lips to the keyhole, imploring for admission. "Louise, open the door! I beg; open the door—you will make yourself ill. What are you doing, Louise? For heaven's sake open the door."

"Go away. I am not making myself ill." No; she was drinking in a very elixir of life through that open window.

Her fancy was running riot along those days ahead of her. Spring days, and summer days, and all sorts of days that would be her own. She breathed a quick prayer that life might be long. It was only yesterday she had thought with a shudder that life might be long.

She arose at length and opened the door to her sister's importunities. There was a feverish triumph in her eyes, and she carried herself unwittingly like a goddess of Victory. She clasped her sister's waist, and together they descended the stairs. Richards stood waiting for them at the bottom.

Some one was opening the front door with a latchkey. It was Brently Mallard who entered, a little travel-stained, composedly carrying his gripsack and umbrella. He had been far from the scene of accident, and did not even know there had been one. He stood amazed at Josephine's piercing cry; at Richards' quick motion to screen him from the view of his wife.

But Richards was too late.

When the doctors came they said she had died of heart disease—of joy that kills.

Form

1. Even as short stories go, this is a very short work. How does the briefness of the story reflect the significance of the title?

2. Because the author has chosen to communicate these events using the short story genre, she is limited in her treatment of Mrs. Mallard's life. How does this limitation heighten your understanding of Mrs. Mallard's reaction to her husband's death?

Language

1. How does this author use imagery to reinforce the message of this text?
2. Examine some of the uses of metaphor and simile in the story. Why does the author use them?
3. There is little dialogue in this story. Why is this the case?

Character

1. In what ways does the author describe the character of Mrs. Mallard? Given the description of her character, are you surprised by the ending of the story?
2. Why aren't the other characters in the story described in greater detail?

Situation

1. What is Mrs. Mallard's reaction to the situation in which she finds herself? What in the situation helps you account for this reaction?
2. Read the entry on **plot** in the Glossary. Use Freytag's pyramid to track the plot of this story. What do you think is the climax of the plot? Refer to the discussion of **qualitative progression**. Do you think the climax of this progression is different from that of the plot? If so, how does that difference alter your understanding of the events of the story?
3. Kate Chopin (1851–1904) was born in St. Louis, Missouri, but lived several years in New Orleans, Louisiana, with her husband. Many of her short stories and novels deal with the restrictions that society placed on women's lives. Her last novel, written in 1899, was censured because it dealt frankly with the subject of adulterous love and female sexuality. Can you see a connection between these themes and "The Story of an Hour"? Why do you think Chopin was less explicit in this story than in her later novel?
4. Do you think that "The Story of an Hour" is more or less shocking today than it was when it was printed?

The Argument

1. Try to articulate the argument that this text makes. Does the argument reinforce dominant social values or does it go against them? How do you react to the argument? What literary techniques does the author use to reinforce her argument? How is this argument more effective because it is dramatized as a short story?

Chapter Two

The Structure of Literary Argument

We interpret texts all the time. When we wake up in the morning and look to see what time it is, we interpret the numbers on the clock in order to tell whether it's time to get up. As we walk to class, we interpret the speed of an approaching car in order to decide whether the driver is going to stop at a crosswalk and allow us to cross the street. During class, we listen carefully to our instructor's lecture as we try to determine what information is likely to be on an exam or will help us write an essay. As we perform each of these tasks, our interpretation of these texts is often accompanied by another important activity. In each case, we have to decide between two or more possible actions. When we wake up, we have to decide either to get up or to go back to sleep. As we look at the approaching car, we have to decide whether we should start to cross the street or wait until the car stops or drives by. During class, we have to decide whether to take notes on a given subject or just listen to the instructor's lecture. Each of these decisions involves weighing the possibilities and then deciding which one is in our best interest.

This decision-making process requires us to make an informal argument, a case for one action or another based on the available evidence. If we wake up ten minutes before a class starts, we have to decide whether we would rather stay in bed or go to class. Several factors might influence our decision. The instructor's attendance policy, our current average in the class, the number of times we have missed class before, the weather, and our state of health might all be factors that help us decide. If the instructor takes attendance every day and we have already missed two classes, then we might decide attending class is more important than getting a little more sleep. If we wake up with a cold, feeling miserable might lead us to decide that getting more rest is better than running to class in the rain. In each case, either consciously or unconsciously, we argue with ourselves in order to decide which course of action to pursue.

While we are presented with such informal situations all the time, we are also often required to present our decision-making process to others on a more formal level. For example, let's say that, after waking up late with a cold on a rainy day, you decide not to go to class and when you return a couple of days later you find out that the instructor gave a pop quiz on the day you missed. Now you have to try to persuade your teacher to allow you to make up the quiz. The process that you use to convince this teacher is similar to the one you used to decide to stay in bed. You make a case for a certain course of action, in this case allowing you to make up the quiz you missed due to a cold. However, the circumstances of this situation require that you present your case more formally than when you are simply trying to make up your own mind. For example, simply telling your instructor that you did not come to class and would like to make up the quiz probably will not persuade her to allow you to do so. Telling the teacher that you missed class because you were sick is more likely to sway her, but she may still not be convinced that you missed class for a legitimate reason. The best case might be made by pointing out to the instructor that you have never missed class before and that you are still sneezing and coughing. The first of these reasons demonstrates that you are a responsible student who takes the class seriously. The second one backs up your claim that you were sick.

This chapter discusses the basic elements in making the kinds of arguments that you will be presenting in this class. First, we will examine what an argument is. We will then discuss two forms of reasoning, the syllogism and the enthymeme. The chapter will then present a brief discussion of how writers can use logic, credibility, and emotion to make their appeals. We will conclude by applying all of these concepts to Jonathan Swift's "A Modest Proposal."

Argument 101

At its most fundamental level, an argument is a claim supported by one or more reasons. By "claim" we mean a statement that you believe to be true but whose validity might be questioned by others. For example, if you missed a pop quiz in a class, you might argue that you should be allowed to make up the quiz. In this case, your claim would be:

> I should be allowed to make up the pop quiz.

You believe that this statement is true, but your teacher might not.

However, a claim by itself is not an argument. To be an argument, you also need at least one reason why your teacher should also believe this claim. In this case, your reason might be:

> I was sick and unable to attend the previous class.

Taken together, these two sentences compose a basic argument:

> I should be allowed to make up the pop quiz because
> I was sick and unable to attend the previous class.

For Practice

The first step in making sure that an argument is valid is to check to see that it has a debatable claim. For practice, read each of the following statements. Decide whether you think each one is a claim that someone might question. Be prepared to explain why some of these statements are not claims. For sentences that are claims, be prepared to describe how or why someone might question their validity in class.

1. Bilingual education helps immigrant students assimilate into American culture more quickly by giving them the opportunity to learn in both their native language and in English.

2. Interpreting poetry requires an understanding of literary terminology and techniques.

3. John Sayles's 1996 film *Lone Star* is the best film produced that year.

4. Preventing union members from voting on which political candidates their dues should be used to support is unfair to Republican candidates.

5. The Internet is a useful tool for finding information about nearly any topic.

6. *Lone Star* tells the story of a murder that occurred in a small Texas town many years ago.

7. The United Auto Workers union went on strike yesterday.

8. Pornography is too easily obtainable by children who surf the world-wide web.

9. Bilingual education costs the school district millions of dollars every year.

10. Interpreting poetry is a difficult process.

Reasons

After you check to make sure that an argument's claim is debatable, it is important to make sure that it also has at least one logical reason to support its validity. Many factors influence whether a reason offers valid support for the argument's claim. These include the reason's logical connection to the claim and the rhetorical situation in which the argument is being made.

Checking the Connections

Common sense tells us that every claim must have some reason to support it and that every reason must have some legitimate connection to that claim. For example, the following argument immediately evokes our opposition:

I should be allowed to make up a missed quiz because I'm smart.

This argument immediately raises the question of what being smart has to do with being allowed to make up a quiz. It might also lead the instructor to ask, "If you're so smart, why didn't you make it to class for the quiz?" In this case, being smart does not rationally connect to being allowed to make up the quiz. One might as well say that I should be allowed to make up the quiz because I'm pretty or because I'm a man. These are all biological factors that have nothing to do with whether the teacher should allow you to make up the quiz.

For Practice

The first step in making sure that an argument's reasons are rationally connected to its claim is to subject them to the "common sense test." Read each of the following claims. Using common sense logic, complete each of them with a reason that is rationally connected to claim. Be prepared to explain in class how your reason is connected to the claim.

1. I should be allowed to make up an exam because . . .
2. I deserve a higher grade on this essay because . . .
3. Raising tuition fees will force more students to drop out of school because . . .
4. Requiring all students to take freshman composition improves their ability to perform well in other classes because . . .
5. Teaching sex education in high schools gives students the idea that premarital sex is o.k. because . . .
6. Television violence contributes to the increased amount of violence in our schools because . . .
7. Pornography on the Internet must be regulated by the government because . . .
8. Racial discrimination continues to plague our society today because . . .
9. *The Truman Show* is the best American movie made in 1998 because . . .
10. Gun control won't solve our problems with violence because . . .

Rhetorical Situation

The second factor that influences whether a reason adequately supports a claim is the rhetorical situation in which the argument is made. This rhetorical situation is the contextual situation surrounding the argument. Every argument is made within some rhetorical situation, sometimes it's a classroom, at other times it might be a job situation or a conversation with your parents or friends. To support your claim, you must always choose reasons that make sense in the particular situation in which your argument is being made. For example, going back to the instance where a student is arguing to be allowed to make up a quiz, which of the following arguments is more likely to convince that student's instructor?

> I should be allowed to make up a quiz because having the flu prevented me from attending the previous class.
>
> I should be allowed to make up a quiz because having a hangover prevented me from attending the previous class.

While some teachers will respond differently, most will be more likely to excuse the first absence but not the second one. What is the difference between these two arguments? How is the teacher likely to respond to the second one? Why is the first one more likely to succeed with a teacher than the second one?

Making sure that a reason effectively supports the claim of an argument within a particular rhetorical situation requires that the writer know who his or her audience is. Are you writing for your mother? Your teacher? Your boss? Your roommate? Your boyfriend or girlfriend? Each of these audiences requires a different kind of writing style. For example, in some of these cases you might be very informal. In some you would want to be very professional. Writing a note to your significant other might include more romantic language, while writing a note to your best friend might not even include complete sentences.

For Practice

Write a brief letter or note to each of the following audiences. Your note should briefly ask for the addressee to excuse the fact that you missed a recent appointment (the nature of the appointment is in parentheses). Also explain why you missed the appointment. What kinds of reasons would convince each audience? Be prepared to discuss in class how you tailored each argument to that particular audience. You should also be ready to explain how each of these letters is different from the others.

1. your mother (dinner at your parents' house)
2. your boss (a meeting to discuss a raise)
3. your roommate (coffee at a local coffee shop)
4. your significant other (dinner and a movie)

When a writer knows her audience, she can draw on her knowledge of that audience to make her claims and reasons more effective. Even so, a writer does not always know much about the people who will being reading his work. For example, you do not know as much about your teacher and classmates as you do about your parents, siblings, or friends. Consequently, when a writer constructs an argument, it is often helpful to write that argument for an audience of people predisposed to disagree with it. For example, if you write an essay that argues for gun control, then you might think of the audience for your paper as the members of the NRA. Writing to your opposition forces you to think about your claims and reasons differently than when you write to people who already agree with you.

For Practice

Write a brief paragraph outlining the major reason why you agree with one of the following statements. Write this paragraph for an audience that already agrees with your viewpoint. Write a second paragraph on the same issue, but aim it to an audience that disagrees with your claim. How are these two paragraphs different? Which one was more difficult to write? Why? Which of these paragraphs do you think makes a stronger argument? Why?

1. Congress should pass a law requiring child safety locks on all handguns.
2. Gay marriages should be legalized.
3. Random drug testing in high schools should be implemented in all public schools.
4. Replacing bilingual education with English-only classrooms will improve students' intellectual performance.
5. Teen curfews will help reduce violent crime.
6. Euthanasia should be legalized.
7. Affirmative Action remains a necessary means of helping ethnic minorities achieve social and political equality.
8. Organized prayer at public school functions violates the First Amendment.
9. Children under the age of 18 should not be allowed to play violent computer games.
10. Internet pornography should be banned by the government.

The Enthymeme

While using common sense logic is a good first step in making sure that an argument "works," the next step is to see if the claim and reason make logical sense more formally. One way to check the logic of an argument is to evaluate it as an enthymeme. An enthymeme is a formal structure we have taken from classical Greek philosophers and rhetoricians to expose how we reason with language. It is based on what is called a syllogism, a kind of formula used by logicians to prove a point. Formally, a syllogism works with the factual claims of science whereas an enthymeme works with the probable beliefs of informal arguments. However, we can use the form of the syllogism to explain the kind of reasoning we use in informal arguments and enthymemes. An informal, or rhetorical, syllogism starts with a premise that everyone agrees is true. This statement is called the major premise. It then adds a statement that adds new knowledge to that common belief. This second proposition is called the minor premise. A syllogism ends with a conclusion based on this combined old and new knowledge. Here is an example:

Major premise: Anyone who misses class due to an illness will be allowed to make up any work s/he misses.

Minor premise: I missed class because I had the flu.

Conclusion: I will be allowed to make up the quiz I missed.

If this rhetorical syllogism is valid, it will pass two tests. First, each of its parts will share one term (and only one term) with one of the other statements. In this example, both the major and minor premises share the idea of missing class due to an illness. This is the only element that they share. (If they shared more common ideas, then they would be the same statements!) Both the major premise and the conclusion share the idea that someone will be allowed to make up the quiz. The minor premise and the conclusion share the idea that "I" am the person who is being discussed.

In order to be rhetorically valid, a syllogism's premises must also all be true. The teacher's syllabus probably indicates whether illness is a valid reason for missing class and whether students can make up missed work. Its truth is therefore easy to prove or disprove. The minor premise might be a little more difficult to prove. If the student went to the doctor and was diagnosed with the flu, then she can bring the doctor's prescription to class to prove that she was indeed ill. If the student did not go to the doctor, then she might not be able to prove that she was sick. In this case, the teacher would have to decide whether to accept the student's claim on its own. The conclusion's truth is grounded in the validity of the other two propositions. In some cases, a conclusion's veracity will be affected by the use of such words as "most," "few," "all," or "none."

For Practice

Test whether the conclusions for the following syllogisms are valid. Make sure that each of the premises is true and that all of the statements are logically connected (share one and only one term in common). Be prepared to explain in class why you think each syllogism is either valid or invalid.

1. Everyone who earns a grade of 73 or higher will pass the class.

   John earned a grade of 77.

   John will pass the class.

2. Fish are cold-blooded animals.

   Rattlesnakes are cold-blooded animals.

   Rattlesnakes are fish.

3. First-time performers are nervous.

   Mary Ann is a first-time performer.

   Mary Ann is nervous.

4. Watching violent television shows causes one to act more violently.

   NYPD Blue is a violent television show.

   Watching *NYPD Blue* causes me to act more violently.

5. Murder is wrong.

   Capital punishment is murder.

   Capital punishment is wrong.

6. Heroes save people's lives.

   Jane saved Bill's life.

   Jane is a hero.

7. Great literature critiques important socio-political problems of its time.

   Tolstoy's *Anna Karenina* critiques important socio-political problems of its day.

   Tolstoy's *Anna Karenina* is great literature.

8. Most dramas present a set of characters who interact with one another.

   August Wilson's *The Piano Lesson* is a drama.

   August Wilson's *The Piano Lesson* probably presents a series of characters who interact with one another.

9. Men who write love poems to other men are probably gay.

   Shakespeare addressed several love poems to a handsome young man.

   Shakespeare was probably gay.

10. Poetry is often a powerful expression of human emotions.

    "Sonrisas" is a poem.

    "Sonrisas" is a powerful expression of human emotions.

While syllogisms are excellent ways of checking to make sure that the parts of an argument are logically connected to one another, few people actually talk in syllogisms. Instead, we often start an argument with our "conclusion," the idea that we want to prove. In part, this is due to the fact that syllogisms usually involve statements concerning verifiable truth, things that we can readily prove or disprove. Most arguments on the other hand center around statements of probable truth, claims that we believe to be true but that we cannot prove definitively. For example, when we approach our teacher in order to convince him that we should be allowed to make up a quiz, we usually start the conversation with the claim that "I should be allowed to make up the quiz." This is a statement of belief, not of fact. If the teacher agrees with this statement, then the argument ends here. If he does not agree with this statement, then he will probably ask why we should be allowed to make up the quiz. We might answer, "Because I was sick on Wednesday and was unable to attend class." In most cases, the teacher will then either accept or reject this reason as legitimate support for your argument.

The teacher's decision is based on a third piece of information. If the class syllabus states that illness is a legitimate reason for missing class and that missed work can be made up, then the teacher is likely to accept your argument without further discussion. If the class policy does not allow for work to be made up, then this argument is not likely to convince him. In either case, this third piece of information is unlikely to be discussed, at least initially. Because this information is probably on your syllabus, both you and the teacher assume that you both understand that this policy is the foundation of your argument. Since you both share this knowledge, there is no reason for you to discuss it unless that policy is itself in question. Thus, when you argue that

> **I should be allowed to make up a missed quiz because I was sick on that day and was unable to attend class.**

your argument is grounded in a third, unstated premise:

> **Being sick is an excused absence and work missed due to an excused absence can be made up.**

This kind of argument, one that presents a claim and a reason but also depends on an unstated assumption that both the writer and the audience share, is called an enthymeme. The enthymeme is an organizing statement that draws upon some belief that the audience will already hold in order to arrive at a new consensus concerning some issue which is currently in question. For example, the following statement is an enthymeme:

> **Distributing condoms to high school students weakens the traditional family because providing minors with condoms sends them the message that premarital sex is o.k.**

You can tell that this is an enthymeme because it has three parts: a claim, a reason, and an unstated assumption that ties the two together logically.

Claim: Distributing condoms to high school students weakens the traditional family.

Reason: Providing minors with condoms sends them the message that premarital sex is o.k.

Unstated assumption: Anything that sends minors the message that premarital sex is o.k. weakens the traditional family.

Notice that these three statements can be arranged as a syllogism:

Major premise: Anything that sends minors the message that premarital sex is o.k. weakens the traditional family.

Minor premise: Providing minors with condoms sends them the message that premarital sex is o.k.

Conclusion: Distributing condoms to high school students weakens the traditional family.

Although we often talk in enthymemes, we do not usually interrogate them for their logical consistency. As we have already discussed, testing an argument's logic is an important step in evaluating whether we should be convinced by it. The way to test an enthymeme's logic is to rewrite it as a syllogism and then make sure that each of the premises is true and that all of the statements are logically connected (share one and only one term in common). The first step in this process is to divide the enthymeme into its claim and reason and to divide these statements grammatically (subject, verb, and object). For example, the following enthymeme is divided into its claim and reason and then further divided grammatically.

A	V^1	B
Distributing condoms to high school students	weakens	the traditional family

because

A'	V^2	C
Providing minors with condoms	sends	them the message that premarital sex is o.k.

In this case, "Distributing condoms to high school students" is the subject (A) of the claim. "Weakens" is the claim's verb (V^1). "The traditional family" is its object (B). "Providing minors with condoms" is the subject of the reason (A'). (Notice that the subject of the reason is simply a restatement of the claim's subject. Like the syllogism, an enthymeme's claim and reason must share one and only one term. Using roughly the same subject with different verbs and objects will guarantee that this criterion is met.) "Sends" is the reason's verb (V^2). "Them the message that premarital sex is o.k." is the reason's object (C). (Using letters to designate each part of the enthymeme gives us a quick way to talk about each part, as we will see below.)

For Practice

Divide each of the following enthymemes into their constituent parts. Label each part A (claim's subject), V^1 (claim's verb), B (claim's object), A' (reason's subject, which restated the claim's subject in other words), V^2 (reason's verb), and C (reason's object). (Note: As we will discuss later in this chapter, not all enthymemes are convincing. Some of the following examples might fall into this category.)

1. Abortion is wrong because killing innocent children is murder.

2. Allowing boys to play with dolls teaches them a more positive view of women because changing the usual toys boys play with subverts traditional gender roles.

3. Female characters in NBC's *ER* cannot be divided into "good" and "bad" girls because such characters as Carrie Weaver, Carol Hathaway, and Jeanie Boulet represent a complex range of personality traits.

4. Gay parents cannot raise children properly because single-sex couples cannot model both male and female characteristics for their children.

5. Mark Twain's *Huckleberry Finn* is the best American novel because it depicts the complexity of race relations during the nineteenth century.

Using letters to designate which part of the enthymeme that we are talking about also allows us to figure out what the unstated assumption behind the argument is. You can find the unstated assumption by linking the C and B terms together using the following formula:

Place-holding subject + V^2 + C term + V^1 + B term.

A place-holding subject would be something like "anything that . . ." or "anyone who. . . ." The following statement is the unstated assumption for our enthymeme on condom distribution:

Anything that sends minors the message that premarital sex is o.k. weakens the traditional family.

For Practice

Find the unstated assumption behind each of the enthymemes in the previous exercise. Remember to start this statement with a place-holding subject. Be prepared to discuss your answers in class.

Converting a writer's argument into an enthymeme allows us to test the argument's logical validity. There are several questions we can ask about an enthymeme in order to test its ability to convince its audience.[1]

1. Is the claim a statement with which someone would disagree? (If it isn't, then the writer is not making an argument but rather simply stating a "fact.")

2. Do the claim and reason share only a common subject? (If they do not share a common subject, then they may not be logically related. If they share subjects, verbs, and objects, then they are probably the same basic idea—an argument cannot use its claim to support itself.)

3. Does the reason's restatement of the claim's subject make sense? (For example, in the exercise above, is "killing innocent children" an acceptable rephrasing of the word "abortion"?)

4. Using common sense, does the reason seem to support the argument's claim? (If not, then the argument will never convince anyone of its veracity.)

5. Is the unstated assumption a statement that both the writer and the audience will agree is true? (Remember, the unstated assumption should be based on some knowledge that both the writer and audience share. If not, then the argument is unlikely to be convincing until the assumption itself is proven.)

6. Are there any words in the enthymeme that stand out as hindering its effectiveness? Would adding any qualifiers (most, few, all, none) strengthen the enthymeme's logic?

For Practice

Reread the enthymemes in the exercise above. Using the six questions above, decide which of these enthymemes are more likely to be convincing to an audience that is predisposed to disagree with you. Which are less likely to be convincing? Be prepared to discuss your answers in class.

Ethos, Pathos, and Logos

So far, we have emphasized the importance of logic in evaluating an argument's success. This is not, however, the sole factor in determining whether an argument is likely to convince its audience. Because arguments depend on probable rather than factual proof, the writer's reputation and credibility also influence the audience's acceptance of her claims. Likewise, because one's audience changes in different rhetorical situations, writers often appeal to one audience differently than they might appeal to another one. Classical Greek writers had names for each of these appeals: *logos, ethos,* and *pathos*.

Philosophers such as Aristotle used the word *logos* to describe arguments that depended on logical proof to sway their audience. Such proof might take the form of a syllogism or an enthymeme. These arguments are grounded in "facts," evidence that is used to convince the audience of the claim's probable truth. Our discussion of argument above focuses on the writer's logos.

While most of the arguments that you present this semester will rely on *logos,* logic alone is not always convincing. For example, let's say that the student who missed class because he was ill has already missed 5 other class meetings due to "illness." All of these "illnesses" seem to have struck him only on Fridays. At some point his teacher is likely to begin to suspect the truthfulness of his excuse and might ask for some additional documentation proving that he was indeed ill. At this point, the student's credibility is affecting the persuasiveness of his argument. Let's say that another student, who has never missed class and who has an A average, misses the same quiz. Because she has earned a reputation for being a good student, the teacher might allow her to make up the quiz without even asking her why she missed that class—due to her reputation the instructor assumes that the student had a good reason for missing class. This use of reputation and credibility to affect the outcome of an argument is called *ethos*.

For Practice

Find a work of non-fiction, a newspaper story, a magazine article, a television program, a pamphlet, or a web site. What factors influence the writer's *ethos*, his or her reputation, credibility, persona? What do you know about the writer/speaker that makes the information they are presenting more or less believable? Make a list of these factors and be prepared to discuss them in class.

The third factor that might influence the effectiveness of an argument is *pathos*, the use of emotion to appeal to an audience. These appeals might be blatant or very subtle. For example, if a student approaches his teacher to ask to make up some work and begins crying in the middle of his request, whether he intends it or not, his crying appeals to the instructor's emotions. In this case, the teacher might feel sorry for the student, might suspect his sincerity, or might think that he is being ridiculous crying over a minor quiz. Another student might also approach the same teacher with a more subtle use of emotional appeal. She might begin by talking about how ill she felt the day she missed class. She might then proceed to talk about how she had also had a fight with her boyfriend the day before she got sick and how she is also failing chemistry because she could not make it to a review session and ended up failing an exam. None of this "evidence" directly speaks to whether she qualifies to make up the quiz. Instead, it could slowly gain the teacher's sympathy and makes her feel sorry for the student. This might make it more likely that the student will be allowed to make up the missed work. (Of course an extraneous emotional appeal could also work against the student's argument, creating the impression that the student is irresponsible, damaging his appeal to *ethos*.)

Most arguments are strengthened by keeping all three of these factors in mind. Skillfully combining logic, credibility, and emotion makes an argument much more convincing than using only one of these appeals.

For Practice

Go back to your answers for the exercises in which you wrote brief letters to your mother, your boss, your roommate, and your significant other. Analyze the kinds of appeals, logical, ethical, and emotional, that you used in each case. Are there situations in which one of the appeals seems more convincing than in others? Are there ways to use all three appeals in each case? Be prepared to discuss your answers in class.

Note

1. For a more complete discussion of how to analyze the structure and content of an enthymeme, see John T. Gage's *The Shape of Reason: Argumentative Writing in College*. 2nd ed. New York: Macmillan, 1991.

Putting What You've Learned to Work

Practice using what you've just learned about the structure and content of argument in analyzing this satiric essay by Jonathan Swift. When you've finished try to answer the questions that follow.

A Modest Proposal

Jonathan Swift (1667–1745) was born in Dublin, Ireland, to English parents. Known today as one of the great satirists of the eighteenth century, Swift often explores in his works the antagonisms between the English and the Irish that resulted from the political and social discrimination practiced by the former against the latter. "A Modest Proposal" is an excellent example of this exploration. Written in the vein of many contemporary pamphlets that suggested ways of improving British society, "A Modest Proposal" is a tour-de-force of irony and satire that continues to stir readers today.

A Modest Proposal

Jonathan Swift

FOR Preventing the Children of poor People in Ireland from being a Burden to their Parents or Country, and for making them beneficial to the Public

IT is a melancholy object to those who walk through this great town or travel in the country, when they see the streets, the roads, and cabin doors, crowded with beggars of the female-sex, followed by three, four, or six children, all in rags and importuning every passenger for an alms. These mothers, instead of being able to work for their honest livelihood, are forced to employ all their time in strolling to beg sustenance for their helpless infants, who, as they grow up, either turn thieves for want of work, or leave their dear native country to fight for the Pretender[1] in Spain, or sell them to the Barbadoes.

I think it is agreed by all parties that this prodigious number of children in the arms, or on the backs, or at the heels of their mothers, and frequently of their fathers, is in the present deplorable state of the kingdom, a very great additional grievance; and therefore whoever could find out a fair, cheap, and easy method of making these children sound, useful members of the Commonwealth would deserve so well of the public as to have his statue set up for a preserver of the nation.

But my intention is very far from being confined to provide only for the children of professed beggars; it is of a much greater extent, and shall take in the whole number of infants at a certain age who are born of parents in effect as little able to support them as those who demand our charity in the streets.

As to my own part, having turned my thoughts for many years upon this important subject, and maturely weighed the several schemes of their own protectors, I have always found them grossly mistaken in their computation. It is true, a child just dropped from its dam may be supported by her milk for a solar year, with little other nourishment; at most not above the value of two shillings, which the mother may certainly get, or the value in scraps, by her lawful occupation of begging; and it is exactly at one year old that I propose to provide for them in such a manner as instead of being a charge upon their parents or the parish, or wanting food and raiment for the rest of their lives, they shall on the contrary contribute to the feeding, and partly to the clothing, of many thousands.

There is likewise another great advantage in my scheme, that it will prevent those voluntary abortions, and that horrid practice of women murdering their bastard children, alas, too frequent among us, sacrificing the poor innocent babes, I doubt, more to avoid the expense than the shame, which would move tears and pity in the most savage and inhuman breast.

The number of souls in *Ireland* being usually reckoned one million and a half, of these I calculate there may be about two hundred thousand couple whose wives are breeders; from which number I subtract thirty thousand couples who are able to maintain their own children, although I apprehend there cannot be so many under the present distresses of the kingdom; but this being granted, there will remain a hundred and seventy thousand breeders. I again subtract fifty thousand for those women who miscarry, or whose children die by accident or disease within the year. There only remain an hundred and twenty thousand children of poor parents annually born. The question therefore is, how this number shall be reared and provided for, which as I have already said, under the present situation of affairs, is utterly impossible by all the methods hitherto proposed. For we can neither employ them in handicraft or agriculture; we neither build houses (I mean in the country) nor cultivate land. They can very seldom pick up a livelihood by stealing till they arrive at six years old, except where they are of towardly parts; although I confess they learn the rudiments much earlier, during which time they can however be looked upon only as probationers, as I have been informed by a principal gentleman in the county of Cavan, who protested to me that he never knew above one or two instances under the age of six, even in a part of the kingdom so renowned for the quickest proficiency in that art.

I am assured by our merchants that a boy or a girl before twelve years old is no salable commodity; and even when they come to this age they will not yield above three pounds, or three pounds and half a crown at most on the Exchange; which cannot turn to account either to the parents or the kingdom, the charge of nutriment and rags having been at least four times that value.

I shall now therefore humbly propose my own thoughts, which I hope will not be liable to the least objection.

I have been assured by a very knowing American of my acquaintance in London, that a young healthy child well nursed is at a year old a most delicious, nourishing, and wholesome food, whether stewed, roasted, baked or boiled; and I make no doubt that it will equally serve in a fricassee or ragout.

I do therefore humbly offer it to public consideration that of the hundred and twenty thousand children, already computed, twenty thousand may be reserved for breed, whereof only one fourth part to be males, which is more than we allow to sheep, black cattle, or swine, and my reason is that these children are seldom fruits of marriage, a circumstance not much regarded by our savages, therefore one male will be sufficient to serve four females. That the remaining hundred thousand may at a year old be offered in sale to the persons of quality and fortune through the kingdom, always advising the mother to let them suck plentifully in the last month, so as to render them plump and fat for a good table. A child will make two dishes at an entertainment for friends; and when the family dines alone, the fore or hind quarter will make a reasonable dish, and seasoned with a little pepper or salt will be very good boiled on the fourth day, especially in winter.

I have reckoned upon a medium that a child just born will weigh twelve pounds, and in a solar year if tolerably nursed increaseth to twenty-eight pounds.

I grant this food will be somewhat dear, and therefore very proper for landlords, who, as they have already devoured most of the parents, seem to have the best title to the children.

Infant's flesh will be in season throughout the year, but more plentiful in March, and a little before and after. For we are told by a grave author,[2] an eminent French physician, that fish being a prolific diet, there are more children born in Roman Catholic countries about nine months after Lent than at any other season; therefore, reckoning a year after Lent, the markets will be more glutted than usual, because the number of popish infants is at least three to one in this kingdom; and therefore it will have one other collateral advantage, by lessening the number of Papists among us.

I have already computed the charge of nursing a beggar's child (in which list I reckon all cottagers, laborers, and four fifths of the farmers) to be about two shillings per annum, rags included; and I believe no gentleman would repine to give ten shillings for the carcass of a good fat child, which, as I have said, will make four dishes of excellent nutritive meat, when he hath only some particular friend or his own family to dine with him. Thus the squire will learn to be a good landlord, and grow popular among the tenants; the mother will have eight shillings net profit, and be fit for work till she produces another child.

Those who are more thrifty (as I must confess times require) may flay the carcass; the skin of which artificially dressed will make admirable gloves for ladies, and summer boots for fine gentlemen.

As to our city of Dublin shambles may be appointed for this purpose in the most convenient parts of it, and butchers we may be assured will not be wanting; although I rather recommend buying the children alive, and dressing them hot from the knife as we do roasting pigs.

A very worthy person, a true lover of his country, and whose virtues I highly esteem, was lately pleased in discoursing on this matter to offer a refinement upon my scheme. He said that many gentlemen of his kingdom, having of late destroyed their deer; he conceived that the want of venison might be well supplied by the bodies of young lads and maidens, not exceeding fourteen years of age nor under twelve; so great a number of both sexes in every county being now ready to starve for want of work and service; and these to be disposed of by their parents, if alive, or otherwise by their nearest relations. But with due deference to so excellent a friend and so deserving a patriot, I cannot be altogether in his sentiments. For as to the males, my American acquaintance assured me from frequent experience that their flesh was generally tough and lean, like that of our schoolboys, by continual exercise, and their taste disagreeable; and to fatten them would not answer the charge. Then as to the females, it would, I think with humble submission, be a loss to the public, because they soon would become breeders themselves: and besides, it is not improbable that some scrupulous people might be apt to censure such a practice (although indeed very unjustly) as a little bordering upon cruelty; which, I confess, hath always been with me the strongest objection against any project, how well soever intended.

But in order to justify my friend; he confessed that this expedient was put into his head by the famous Psalmanazar,[3] a native of the island Formosa, who came from thence to London about twenty years ago, and in conversation told my friend that in his country when any young person happened to be put to death, the executioner sold the carcass to persons of quality as a prime dainty; and that in his time the body of a plump girl of fifteen, who was crucified for an attempt to poison the emperor, was sold to his Imperial Majesty's prime minister of state, and other great mandarins of the court, in joints from the gibbet, at four hundred crowns. Neither indeed can I deny that if the same use were made of several plump young girls in this town, who without one single groat to their fortunes cannot stir abroad without a chair, and appear at the play-house and assemblies in foreign fineries which they never will pay for; the kingdom would not be the worse.

Some persons of a desponding spirit are in great concern about that vast number of poor people who are aged, diseased, or maimed, and I have been desired to employ my thoughts what course may be taken to ease the nation of so grievous an encum-brance. But I am not in the least pain upon that matter, because it is very well known that they are every day dying and rotting by cold and famine, and filth and vermin, as fast as can be reasonably expected. And as to the younger laborers, they are now in almost as hopeful a condition. They cannot get work, and consequently pine away for want of nourishment to a degree that if at any time they are accidentally hired to com-mon labor, they have not strength to perform it; and thus the country and themselves are happily delivered from the evils to come.

I have too long digressed, and therefore shall return to my subject. I think the advantages by the proposal which I have made are obvious and many, as well as of the highest importance.

For first, as I have already observed, it would greatly lessen the number of Papists, with whom we are yearly overrun; being the principal breeders of the nation as well as our most dangerous enemies; and who stay at home on purpose to deliver the kingdom to the Pretender; hoping to take their advantage by the absence of so many good Protestants, who have chosen rather to leave their country than to stay at home and pay tithes against their conscience to an Episcopal curate.

Secondly, the poorer tenants will have something valuable of their own, which by law may be made liable to distress, and help to pay their landlord's rent; their corn and cattle being already seized and money a thing unknown.

Thirdly, whereas the maintenance of an hundred thousand children, from two years old and upwards, cannot be computed at less than ten shillings a piece per annum, the nation's stock will be thereby increased fifty thousand pounds per annum, besides the profit of a new dish introduced to the tables of all gentlemen of fortune in the kingdom who have any refinement in taste; and the money will circulate among ourselves, the goods being entirely of our own growth and manufacture.

Fourthly, the constant breeders, besides the gain of eight shillings sterling per annum by the sale of their children, will be rid of the charge of maintaining them after the first year.

Fifthly, this food would likewise bring great custom to taverns, where the vintners will certainly be so prudent as to procure the best receipts for dressing it to perfection; and consequently have their houses frequented by all the fine gentlemen, who justly value themselves upon their knowledge in good eating; and a skillful cook, who under-stands how to oblige his guests, will contrive to make it as expensive as they please.

Sixthly, this would be a great inducement to marriage, which all wise nations have either encouraged by rewards or enforced by laws and penalties. It would increase the care and tenderness of mothers toward their children, when they were sure of a settle-ment for life to the poor babes, provided in some sort by the public, to their annual profit instead of expense. We should see an honest emulation among the married women, which of them could bring the fattest child to the market. Men would become as fond of their wives during the time of their pregnancy as they are now of their mares in foal, their cows in calf, or sows when they are ready to farrow; nor offer to beat or kick them (as is too frequent a practice) for fear of a miscarriage.

Many other advantages might be enumerated. For instance, the addition of some thousand carcasses in our exportation of barreled beef; the propagation of swine's flesh, and improvement in the art of making good bacon; so much wanted among us by the great destruction of pigs, too frequent at our tables, which are no way comparable in taste or magnificence to a well-grown, fat, yearling child; which roasted whole will make a considerable figure at a lord mayor's feast or any other public entertainment. But this and many others I omit, being studious of brevity.

Supposing that one thousand families in this city would be constant customers for infants' flesh; besides others who might have it at merry meetings, particularly weddings and christenings; I compute that Dublin would take off annually about twenty thousand carcasses, and the rest of the kingdom (where probably they will be sold somewhat cheaper) the remaining eighty thousand.

I can think of no one objection that will possibly be raised against this proposal; unless it should be urged that the number of people will be thereby much lessened in the kingdom. This I freely own, and it was indeed one principal design in offering it to the world. I desire the reader will observe, that I calculate my remedy for this one individual kingdom of Ireland and for no other that ever was, is, or I think ever can be upon earth. Therefore let no man talk to me of other expedients: of taxing our absentees at five shillings a pound; of using neither clothes nor household furniture except what is of our own growth and manufacture; of utterly rejecting the materials and instruments that promote foreign luxury; of curing the expensiveness of pride, vanity, idleness, and gaming in our women; of introducing a vein of parsimony, prudence, and temperance; of learning to love our country, in the want of which we differ even from Laplanders and the inhabitants of Topinamboo; of quitting our animosities and factions, nor acting any longer like the Jews, who were murdering one another at the very moment their city was taken; of being, a little cautious not to sell our country and conscience for nothing; of teaching landlords to have at least one degree of mercy toward their tenants; lastly, of putting a spirit of honesty, industry, and skill into our shopkeepers; who, if a resolution could now be taken to buy only our native goods, would immediately unite to cheat and exact upon us in the price, the measure, and the goodness, nor could ever yet be brought to make one fair proposal of just dealing, though often and earnestly invited to it.

Therefore I repeat, let no man talk to me of these and the like expedients, till he hath at least some glimpse of hope that there will ever be some hearty and sincere attempt to put them in practice.

But as to myself, having been wearied out for many years with offering vain, idle, visionary thoughts, and at length utterly despairing of success, I fortunately fell upon this proposal, which, as it is wholly new, so it hath something solid and real, of no expense and little trouble, full in our own power, and whereby we can incur no danger in disobliging England. For this kind of commodity will not bear exportation, the flesh being of too tender a consistence to admit a long continuance in salt, although perhaps I could name a country which would be glad to eat up our whole nation without it.

After all, I am not so violently bent upon my own opinion as to reject any offer proposed by wise men, which shall be found equally innocent, cheap, easy, and effectual. But before something of that kind shall be advanced in contradiction to my scheme, and offering a better, I desire the author or authors will be pleased maturely to consider two points. First, as things now stand, how they will be able to find food and raiment for a hundred thousand useless mouths and backs. And secondly, there being a round million of creatures in human figure throughout this kingdom, whose sole subsistence put into a common stock would leave them in debt two millions of pounds sterling; adding those who are beggars by profession to the bulk of farmers, cottagers, and laborers, with their wives and children who are beggars in effect; I desire those politicians who dislike my overture, and may perhaps be so bold to attempt an answer, that they will first ask the parents of these mortals whether they would not at this day think it a great happiness to have been sold for food at a year old in the manner I prescribe; and thereby have avoided such a perpetual scene of misfortunes as they have since gone through by the oppression of landlords, the impossibility of paying rent without money or trade, the want of common sustenance, with neither house nor clothes to cover them from the inclemencies of the weather, and the most inevitable prospect of entailing the like or greater miseries upon their breed forever.

I profess, in the sincerity of my heart, that I have not the least personal interest in endeavoring to promote this necessary work, having no other motive than the public good of my country, by advancing our trade, providing for infants, relieving the poor, and giving some pleasure to the rich. I have no children by which I can propose to get a single penny; the youngest being nine years old, and my wife past childbearing.

Notes

1. James Stuart, claimant to the throne lost by his father, James II in 1688.
2. Rabelais.
3. George Psalmanazar, the professed author of *An Historical and Geographical Description of Formosa* (London, 1704); a known imposter, he was French by birth, and not the Formosan he claimed to be.

For Practice

1. What is Swift's *literal* thesis in this essay (his "proposal")? How does he support this thesis? What evidence does he give to justify his proposal? Create an enthymeme for his argument.
2. Taken literally, would Swift's proposal solve the problem that he addresses in the first several paragraphs? Why or why not?
3. What is Swift's *real* thesis, his argument concerning the English government's treatment of the Irish? How does he support this thesis? How do we know that this is his actual thesis? Create the real enthymeme behind Swift's essay.
4. "A Modest Proposal" is an ironic satire of English disregard for the suffering of the Irish poor in Dublin. How do we know that his "proposal" is ironic? At what point in the essay do we know that he is being ironic? What gives it away?
5. How does Swift use *logos, pathos,* and *ethos* in this essay? How does his use of these appeals affect his argument?
6. When "A Modest Proposal" was first published, not everyone understood that it was a satire. How does this danger that not everyone will "get it" affect Swift's argument? Does it weaken what he is trying to accomplish? Why or why not?

7. Think back to your reactions to Swift's ideas as you read "A Modest Proposal." What were your reactions? What passages most affected you? Why did these passages affect you? Compare these reactions with your responses to the non-fiction essay, article, television program, or web site that you used in the exercise above. How does reading a text like Swift's differ from reading/watching one of these other texts? Why? How does Swift's use of literary devices, especially irony and satire, make his essay different from these other texts?

Chapter Three
Literature as Argument

Literature has always played an important role in Western culture, but not everyone has always agreed about what that role is. Each of the following writers explains what he or she thinks literature does. Read each of these statements carefully, paying particular attention to what each writer says is the function of literature within society.

> *For not by art does the poet sing, but by divine power; had he learned by rules of art, he would have known how to speak not of one theme only, but of all; and therefore God takes away reason from poets, and uses them as his ministers, as he also uses the pronouncers of oracles and holy prophets, in order that we who hear them may know them to be speaking not of themselves, who utter these priceless words while bereft of reason, but that God himself is the speaker, and that through them he is addressing us.*
>
> *—Plato*
> *from* The Ion

> *I have said that poetry is the spontaneous overflow of powerful feelings: it takes its origin from emotion recollected in tranquillity: the emotion is contemplated till, by a species of reaction, the tranquillity gradually disappears, and an emotion, kindred to that which was before the subject of contemplation, is gradually produced, and does itself actually exist in the mind.*
>
> *—William Wordsworth*
> *from the* Preface *to* Lyrical Ballads

> *Poetry is the way we help give name to the nameless so it can be thought. The farthest external horizons of our hopes and fears are cobbled by our poems, carved from the rock experiences of our daily lives. . . . We can train ourselves to respect our feelings and to discipline (transpose) them into a language that catches those feelings so they can be shared. And where that language does not yet exist, it is our poetry which helps us*

> *to fashion it. Poetry is not only dream or vision, it is the skeleton architecture of our lives.*
>
> —*Audre Lorde*
> *from* Claims for Poetry

What words stand out in each writer's statement? What do these words mean for each writer? (For example, what does Plato mean by the word "art"? How does his definition differ from yours?) Based on these words, how do you think each writer defines the function of literature within the larger culture? Do you share any of these writers' views? What do you think the purpose of literature is?

In one way or another, each of these writers believes that literature provides its readers with new insight into the culture in which it is produced and/or read. Plato argues that artists are prophets who reveal the gods' will and desire. Thus, says this philosopher, poets offer critiques of society's problems and ways to solve those problems. William Wordsworth, a late-eighteenth century poet, contends that literature serves as an emotional outlet that allows us to remember key events in our lives. By giving us this opportunity, says Wordsworth, literature lets us relive the poignancy of life-changing moments. Others who have not shared those moments can learn by feeling the same emotions that the writer evokes. And finally, Audre Lorde believes that literature helps us come to terms with the unknown in life so that we can deal with it effectively. She argues that the imaginative writer shares her experiences with her readers in order to help them understand points of view that they would otherwise never know.

Literature conveys these insights in much the same way that nonfiction writing does: literary works use such appeals as *logos, pathos,* and *ethos* to praise or critique aspects of their societies. For example, literature employs *logos* through the use of conventional forms and genres. Just as an essayist appeals to logic by constructing a well-reasoned enthymeme that draws upon knowledge shared by both the writer and reader, a poet draws upon the conventions of a genre to meet or to thwart the reader's expectations. For instance, a poet who violates the norms of the sonnet form does so in order to draw attention to those violations. In order for this strategy to work, the reader must also be aware of the genre's conventions. Literary works also use *pathos,* emotionally laden language, in order to move their readers to feel a certain way about their subjects. A writer might employ images and symbols which evoke powerful emotional responses in their audience. Or, much as a lawyer attempts to move a jury to pity her client, a novelist might seek to gain the reader's sympathy (or dislike) for a certain character. And finally, literature draws upon *ethos* through its use of characters and narrative personae. Just as a non-fiction writer gains the reader's assent to her argument through the presentation of her credibility, the writer of a short story might undermine a character by giving her moral faults or might lead us to question the narrator's truthfulness by presenting gaps in his knowledge of the story's events.

Discovering the Arguments in Literary Texts

How do we put our knowledge of literature and argument to use in interpreting a text? When we use the word "interpretation," we mean making sense of a text, or decoding the author's message, understanding, and evaluating the argument. It is sometimes helpful to follow a structured plan when undertaking an unfamiliar task of this sort. This section describes an interpretative method which includes four steps: Summary, Analysis, Synthesis, and Evaluation. Read through the description of this SASE process before you put it to work as a tool for interpeting the texts at the end of this chapter. Remember that using this process presumes a thorough and careful reading of the text.

Summary: The summary is perhaps the most difficult part of this method because it requires you to be both detailed and concise. A summary is a brief description of the text and should include, at least, a mention of the genre, the author, the subject or themes of the work, and some discussion of the situation in which it was produced. Naturally, different genres will require that you focus on different aspects of the work. If you are interpreting a novel, for example, you would need to include a very brief plot summary, some mention of the setting, and perhaps the names of main characters. Your summary of a poem, on the other hand, would be more concerned with themes, rhyme scheme and meter, and important images and symbols. You should also give a brief statement of the work's argument. In the summary section, it is important that you identify what is most important or most significant about a text. You can do this in the form of an enthymeme which states the author's thesis.

Analysis: To analyze means to take something apart to see how it works. Your purpose here is to show precisely how the writer constructs the argument. In this section, you should discuss in greater detail the significant aspects of the text that you mentioned in your summary. You should show how different aspects of the text are related. How, for example, does the setting determine plot? How does genre constrain character development? How does a poet use diction, rhythm, rhyme, and metaphors to convey her point? Or, how is a text a reaction to the social conditions at the time it was produced? In short, you should discuss in greater detail how the author uses literary techniques to make an argument.

Synthesis: While analysis means to take things apart, synthesis means to combine them. In this case, you are relating what you read in the article to other information that you already know, or to other texts that you've read. Sometimes the knowledge you bring is factual information; sometimes it is opinion or belief. It is in this step that your own interpretation of the text becomes most clear. This is often a very difficult step because, as we have said throughout these pages, much of what you bring to a text are cultural values and beliefs that you take for granted. In order to synthesize a text fully, you must determine what values and beliefs are at work in the text, then compare them to your own values and beliefs. You might ask yourself what you would do in a similar situation. Or, you might compare the text you are reading with another one which deals with a similar subject or theme. Synthesis requires that you examine the culture that is described in a text and compare it to your own.

Evaluation: In this section, you offer your own opinion about the text. You might critique character development, the use of imagery, or the appropriateness of the setting to the plot. If the work is a poem, you might consider whether the rhythm and meter are appropriate to the subject. If you are reading a play, you might evaluate the playwright's use of dialogue. Most importantly, you should critique the argument itself and the ways in which the writer makes that argument. How does the argument reflect some "truth" about human nature? What does it persuade us to value differently than we did before reading it? Whatever your evaluation, however, you should always have good reasons to support the claims you make.

The SASE process is not the only way to make sense of a text. There are many others. You could devise your own set of questions for examining a literary text. Just remember to focus on both literary terminology and rhetorical strategies.

Now let's test our ability to analyze a poem as an argument. Read the following poem by Pat Mora (b. 1942) carefully. As a Mexican-American writer who lives in El Paso, Texas, Mora's poems frequently examine the interplay between Anglo and Latino culture. As you read the poem, pay particular attention to her use of language in each stanza, as well as to her use of *logos, pathos,* and *ethos.*

Sonrisas

Pat Mora

I live in a doorway
between two rooms, I hear
quiet clicks, cups of black
coffee, *click, click* like facts
   budgets, tenure, curriculum,   5
from careful women in crisp beige
suits, quick beige smiles
that seldom sneak into their eyes.

I peek
in the other room señoras   10
in faded dresses stir sweet
milk coffee, laughter whirls
with steam from fresh *tamales*
   sh, sh, mucho ruido,
they scold one another,   15
press their lips, trap smiles
in their dark, Mexican eyes.

Summary: Briefly describe this work's genre, author, and overall theme. How is the poem divided into parts? Does it use a definite rhyme scheme? What are its major images?

Analysis: As you read this poem, what words stand out? List them on a sheet of paper, divided into whether they come from stanza one or stanza two. These words work together to create both the settings of the poem and the speaker's attitudes about those settings. What is the setting of the first stanza? Which words lead you to this conclusion? What is the setting for the second stanza? Which words lead you to this conclusion? What kind of life does the "I" of lines one and nine live? What might she do for a living? What ethnic background might she have? What leads you to these conclusions?

Look at your list of words that stood out as you read the poem. What connotations do the words from stanza one convey? What connotations do the words from stanza two convey? How do these two connotations differ? (*Mucho ruido* in line 14 means "a lot of noise" in English.) What emotions does each set of words evoke? Compare the affects of such words as "careful women," "crisp beige suits," and "quick beige eyes" with such words as "faded dresses," "sweet milk coffee," and "dark, Mexican eyes."

What are the conventions of most poems? What characteristics do you think of when you think of "poetry?" Does "Sonrisas" follow those expectations? Which ones does it fulfill? Which ones does it defy? What effect does the shortness of line nine have? What does her separation of the poem into two stanzas suggest about the poem's overall theme?

Based on your answers to all of the above questions, what do you conclude is the speaker's attitude toward each of these settings? Does she favor one over the other? What is the poem's argument? Is this argument convincing to you? Why or why not?

Synthesis: How might this poem's argument reflect Mora's own cultural background? Are there ways in which your own experiences parallel Mora's? If so, how? Which part of her life does she seem to value more? Do you also value this portion of your life more than the other part that Mora depicts? Have you read or seen other texts that discuss similar issues? Do those texts make the same argument about the interplay of those spheres as Mora's poem?

Evaluation: How do you evaluate this poem? Is it a "good" poem? (What is a "good" poem in your opinion?) Does her use of imagery, meter, and diction create the desired effect for the reader? Is her argument a sound one in your opinion? Why or why not?

Read the following introduction to Susan Glaspell's one-act play *Trifles* and then use the SASE process to interpret its argument.

Trifles

Susan Glaspell

Susan Glaspell (1882–1948) was born in Davenport, Iowa. After graduating from Drake University, she worked on the staff of the Des Moines Daily News. *In 1911 she moved to New York City, where she married George Cram Cook, a director. The couple founded the Provincetown Playhouse on Cape Cod in 1915. This theater boasted the talents of such well-known writers as Eugene O'Neill, Edna St. Vincent Millay, and John Reed. Glaspell also wrote novels and short stories, including "A Jury of Her Peers," a prose account of the same murder described in* Trifles.*

It was while working for the Des Moines Daily News *that she first reported on this murder case. This play, which draws upon the conventions of the detective story, also reflects Glaspell's interest in the roles and treatment of women in and by society at the turn of the century. As you read this play, pay close attention to the physical actions of each character. How do these actions provide insight into the play's argument?*

S CENE: *The kitchen in the now abandoned farmhouse of* JOHN WRIGHT, *a gloomy kitchen, and left without having been put in order—unwashed pans under the sink, a loaf of bread outside the breadbox, a dish towel on the table—other signs of incompleted work. At the rear the outer door opens, and the* SHERIFF *comes in, followed by the* COUNTY ATTORNEY *and* HALE. *The* SHERIFF *and* HALE *are men in middle life, the* COUNTY ATTORNEY *is a young man; all are much bundled up and go at once to the stove. They are followed by the two women—the* SHERIFF'S WIFE *first; she is a slight wiry woman, a thin nervous face.* MRS. HALE *is larger and would ordinarily be called more comfortable looking, but she is disturbed now and looks fearfully about as she enters. The women have come in slowly and stand close together near the door.*

COUNTY ATTORNEY (*rubbing his hands*): This feels good. Come up to the fire, ladies.

MRS. PETERS (*after taking a step forward*): I'm not—cold.

SHERIFF (*unbuttoning his overcoat and stepping away from the stove as if to mark the beginning of official business*): Now, Mr. Hale, before we move things about, you explain to Mr. Henderson just what you saw when you came here yesterday morning.

COUNTY ATTORNEY: By the way, has anything been moved? Are things just as you left them yesterday?

SHERIFF (*looking about*): It's just the same. When it dropped below zero last night, I thought I'd better send Frank out this morning to make a fire for us—no use getting pneumonia with a big case on; but I told him not to touch anything except the stove—and you know Frank.

COUNTY ATTORNEY: Somebody should have been left here yesterday.

SHERIFF: Oh—yesterday. When I had to send Frank to Morris Center for that man who went crazy—I want you to know I had my hands full yesterday. I knew you could get back from Omaha by today, and as long as I went over everything here myself—

COUNTY ATTORNEY: Well, Mr. Hale, tell just what happened when you came here yesterday morning.

HALE: Harry and I had started to town with a load of potatoes. We came along the road from my place; and as I got here, I said, "I'm going to see if I can't get John Wright to go in with me on a party telephone." I spoke to Wright about it once before, and he put me off, saying folks talked too much anyway, and all he asked was peace and quiet—I guess you know about how much he talked himself; but I thought maybe if I went to the house and talked about it before his wife, though I said to Harry that I didn't know as what his wife wanted made much difference to John—

COUNTY ATTORNEY: Let's talk about that later, Mr. Hale. I do want to talk about that, but tell now just what happened when you got to the house.

HALE: I didn't hear or see anything; I knocked at the door, and still it was all quiet inside. I knew they must be up, it was past eight o'clock. So I knocked again, and I thought I heard somebody say, "Come in." I wasn't sure, I'm not sure yet, but I opened the door—this door (*indicating the door by which the two women are still standing*), and there in that rocker—(*pointing to it*) sat Mrs. Wright. (*They all looked at the rocker*).

COUNTY ATTORNEY: What—was she doing?

HALE: She was rockin' back and forth. She had her apron in her hand and was kind of—pleating it.

COUNTY ATTORNEY: And how did she—look?

HALE: Well, she looked queer.

COUNTY ATTORNEY: How do you mean—queer?

HALE: Well, as if she didn't know what she was going to do next. And kind of done up.

COUNTY ATTORNEY: How did she seem to feel about your coming?

HALE: Why, I don't think she minded—one way or other. She didn't pay much attention. I said, "How do, Mrs. Wright, it's cold, ain't it?" And she said, "Is it?"—and went on kind of pleating at her apron. Well, I was surprised; she didn't ask me to come up to the stove, or set down, but just sat there, not even looking at me, so I said, "I want to see John." And then she laughed. I guess you would call it a laugh. I thought of Harry and the team outside, so I said a little sharp: "Can't I see John?" "No," she says, kind o' dull like. "Ain't he home?" says I. "Yes," says she, "he's home." "Then why can't I see him?" I asked her, out of patience. "Cause he's dead," says she. "*Dead*? says I. She just nodded her head, not getting a bit excited, but rockin' back and forth. "Why—where is he?" says I, not knowing what to say. She just pointed upstairs—like that (*himself pointing to the room above*). I got up, with the idea of going up there. I walked from there to here then I says, "Why, what did he die of?" "He died of a rope around his neck," says she, and just went on pleatin' at her apron. Well, I went out and called Harry. I thought I might—need help. We went upstairs, and there he was lyin'—

COUNTY ATTORNEY: I think I'd rather have you go into that upstairs, where you can point it all out. Just go on now with the rest of the story.

HALE: Well, my first thought was to get that rope off. It looked . . . (*Stops, his face twitches*) . . . but Harry, he went up to him, and he said, "No, he's dead all right, and we'd better not touch anything." So we went back downstairs. She was still sitting that same way. "Has anybody been notified?" I asked. "No," she says, unconcerned. "Who did this, Mrs. Wright?" said Harry. He said it businesslike—and she stopped pleatin' of her apron. "I don't know," she says. "You don't *know*?" says Harry. "No," says she. "Weren't you sleepin' in the bed with him?" says Harry. "Yes," says she, "but I was on the inside." "Somebody slipped a rope round his neck and strangled him and you didn't wake up?" says Harry. "I didn't wake up," she said after him. We must 'a looked as if we didn't see how that could be, for after a minute she said, "I sleep sound." Harry was going to ask her more questions, but I said maybe we ought to let her tell her story first to the coroner, or the sheriff, so Harry went fast as he could to Rivers' place, where there's a telephone.

COUNTY ATTORNEY: And what did Mrs. Wright do when she knew that you had gone for the coroner?

HALE: She moved from that chair to this over here . . . (*Pointing to a small chair in the corner*) . . . and just sat there with her hands held together and looking down. I got a feeling that I ought to make some conversation, so I said I had come in to see if John wanted to put in a telephone, and at that she started to laugh, and then she stopped and looked at me—scared. (*The* COUNTY ATTORNEY, *who has had his notebook out, makes a note.*) I dunno, maybe it wasn't scared. I wouldn't like to say it was. Soon Harry got back, and then Dr. Lloyd came, and you, Mr. Peters, and so I guess that's all I know that you don't.

COUNTY ATTORNEY (*looking around*): I guess we'll go upstairs first—and then out to the barn and around there. (*to the* SHERIFF) You're convinced that there was nothing important here—nothing that would point to any motive?

SHERIFF: Nothing here but kitchen things.

The COUNTY ATTORNEY, *after again looking around the kitchen, opens the door of a cupboard closet. He gets up on a chair and looks on a shelf. Pulls his hand away, sticky.*

COUNTY ATTORNEY: Here's a nice mess.

The women draw nearer.

MRS. PETERS (to the other woman): Oh, her fruit; it did freeze. (*to the* COUNTY ATTORNEY) She worried about that when it turned so cold. She said the fire'd go out and her jars would break.

SHERIFF: Well, can you beat the women! Held for murder and worryin' about her preserves.

COUNTY ATTORNEY: I guess before we're through she may have something more serious than preserves to worry about.

HALE: Well, women are used to worrying over trifles.

The two women move a little closer together.

COUNTY ATTORNEY (*with the gallantry of a young politician*): And yet, for all their worries, what would we do without the ladies? (*The women do not unbend. He goes to the sink, takes a dipperful of water from the pail and, pouring it into a basin, washes his hands. Starts to wipe them on the roller towel, turns it for a cleaner place.*) Dirty towels! (*Kicks his foot against the pans under the sink.*) Not much of a housekeeper, would you say, ladies?

MRS. HALE (*stiffly*): There's a great deal of work to be done on a farm.

COUNTY ATTORNEY: To be sure, and yet . . . (*with a little bow to her*) . . . I know there are some Dickson county farmhouses which do not have such roller towels.

He gives it a pull to expose its full length again.

MRS. HALE: Those towels get dirty awful quick. Men's hands aren't always as clean as they might be.

COUNTY ATTORNEY: Ah, loyal to your sex, I see. But you and Mrs. Wright were neighbors. I suppose you were friends, too.

MRS. HALE (*shaking her head*): I've not seen much of her of late years. I've not been in this house it's more than a year.

COUNTY ATTORNEY: And why was that? You didn't like her?

MRS. HALE: I liked her all well enough. Farmers' wives have their hands full, Mr. Henderson. And then—

COUNTY ATTORNEY: Yes—?

MRS. HALE (*looking about*): It never seemed a very cheerful place.

COUNTY ATTORNEY: No—it's not cheerful. I shouldn't say she had the homemaking instinct.

MRS. HALE: Well, I don't know as Wright had, either.

COUNTY ATTORNEY: You mean that they didn't get on very well?

MRS. HALE: No, I don't mean anything. But I don't think a place'd be any cheerfuller for John Wright's being in it.

COUNTY ATTORNEY: I'd like to talk more of that a little later. I want to get the lay of things upstairs now.

He goes to the left, where three steps lead to a stair door.

SHERIFF: I suppose anything Mrs. Peters does'll be all right. She was to take in some clothes for her, you know, and a few little things. We left in such a hurry yesterday.

COUNTY ATTORNEY: Yes, but I would like to see what you take, Mrs. Peters, and keep an eye out for anything that might be of use to us.

MRS. PETERS: Yes, Mr. Henderson.

The women listen to the men's steps on the stairs, then look about the kitchen.

MRS. HALE: I'd hate to have men coming into my kitchen, snooping around and criticizing.

She arranges the pans under the sink which the COUNTY ATTORNEY *had shoved out of place.*

MRS. PETERS: Of course it's no more than their duty.

MRS. HALE: Duty's all right, but I guess that deputy sheriff that came out to make the fire might have got a little of this on. (*gives the roller towel a pull*) Wish I'd thought of that sooner. Seems mean to talk about her for not having things slicked up when she had to come away in such a hurry.

MRS. PETERS (*Who has gone to a small table in the left rear corner of the room, and lifted one end of a towel that covers a pan*): She had bread set.

Stands still.

MRS. HALE (*eyes fixed on a loaf of bread beside the breadbox, which is on a low shelf at the other side of the room. Moves slowly toward it.*): She was going to put this in there. (*Picks up loaf, then abruptly drops it. In a manner of returning to famil-*

iar things.) It's a shame about her fruit. I wonder if it's all gone. (*gets up on the chair and looks*) I think there's some here that's all right, Mrs. Peters. Yes—here; (*holding it toward the window*) this is cherries, too. (*looking again*) I declare I believe that's the only one. (*Gets down, bottle in her hand. Goes to the sink and wipes it off on the outside.*) She'll feel awful bad after all her hard work in the hot weather. I remember the afternoon I put up my cherries last summer.

She puts the bottle on the big kitchen table, center of the room. With a sigh, is about to sit down in the rocking-chair. Before she is seated she realizes what chair it is; with a slow look at it, steps back. The chair which she has touched rocks back and forth.

MRS. PETERS: Well, I must get those things from the front room closet. (*She goes to the door at the right, but after looking into the other room, steps back.*) You coming with me, Mrs. Hale? You could help me carry them.

They go in the other room; reappear, MRS. PETERS *carrying a dress and skirt,* MRS. HALE *following with a pair of shoes.*

MRS. PETERS: My, it's cold in there.

She puts the clothes on the big table, and hurries to the stove.

MRS. HALE (*examining the skirt*): Wright was close. I think maybe that's why she kept so much to herself. She didn't even belong to the Ladies' Aid. I suppose she couldn't do her part, and then you don't enjoy things when you feel shabby. She used to wear pretty clothes and be lively, when she was Minnie Foster, one of the town girls singing in the choir. But that—oh, that was thirty years ago. This all you was to take in?

MRS. PETERS: She said she wanted an apron. Funny thing to want, for there isn't much to get you dirty in jail, goodness knows. But I suppose just to make her feel more natural. She said they was in the top drawer in this cupboard. Yes, here. And then her little shawl that always hung behind the door. (*opens stair door and looks*) Yes, here it is.

Quickly shuts door leading upstairs.

MRS. HALE (*abruptly moving toward her*): Mrs. Peters?

MRS. PETERS: Yes, Mrs. Hale?

MRS. HALE: Do you think she did it?

MRS. PETERS (*in a frightened voice*): Oh, I don't know.

MRS. HALE: Well, I don't think she did. Asking for an apron and her little shawl. Worrying about her fruit.

MRS. PETERS (*starts to speak, glances up, where footsteps are heard in the room above. In a low voice.*): Mr. Peters says it looks bad for her. Mr. Henderson is awful sarcastic in a speech, and he'll make fun of her sayin' she didn't wake up.

MRS. HALE: Well, I guess John Wright didn't wake when they was slipping that rope under his neck.

MRS. PETERS: No, it's strange. It must have been done awful crafty and still. They say it was such a—funny way to kill a man, rigging it all up like that.

MRS. HALE: That's just what Mr. Hale said. There was a gun in the house. He says that's what he can't understand.

MRS. PETERS: Mr. Henderson said coming out that what was needed for the case was a motive, something to show anger, or—sudden feeling.

MRS. HALE (*who is standing by the table*): Well, I don't see any signs of anger around here. (*She puts her hand on the dish towel which lies on the table, stands looking down at the table, one half of which is clean, the other half messy.*) It's wiped to here. (*Makes a move as if to finish work, then turns and looks at a loaf of bread outside the breadbox. Drops towel. In that voice of coming back to familiar things.*) Wonder how they are finding things upstairs? I hope she had it a little more redd-up up there. You know, it seems kind of *sneaking.* Locking her up in town and then coming out here and trying to get her own house to turn against her.

MRS. PETERS: But Mrs. Hale, the law is the law.

MRS. HALE: I s'pose 'tis. (*unbuttoning her coat*) Better loosen up your things, Mrs. Peters. You won't feel them when you go out.

MRS. PETERS *takes off her fur tippet, goes to hang it on hook at back of room, stands looking at the under part of the small corner table.*

MRS. PETERS: She was piecing a quilt.

She brings the large sewing basket and they look at the bright pieces.

MRS. HALE: It's log cabin pattern. Pretty, isn't it? I wonder if she was goin' to quilt it or just knot it?

Footsteps have been heard coming down the stairs. The SHERIFF *enters, followed by* HALE *and the* COUNTY ATTORNEY.

SHERIFF: They wonder if she was going to quilt it or just knot it!

The men laugh; the women look abashed.

COUNTY ATTORNEY (*rubbing his hands over the stove*): Frank's fire didn't do much up there, did it? Well, let's go out to the barn and get that cleared up.

The men go outside.

MRS. HALE (*resentfully*): I don't know as there's anything so strange, our takin' up our time with little things while we're waiting for them to get the evidence. (*She sits down at the big table, smoothing out a block with decision.*) I don't see as it's anything to laugh about.

MRS. PETERS (*apologetically*): Of course they've got awful important things on their minds.

Pulls up a chair and joins MRS. HALE *at the table.*

MRS. HALE (*examining another block*): Mrs. Peters, look at this one. Here, this is the one she was working on, and look at the sewing! All the rest of it has been so nice and even. And look at this! It's all over the place! Why, it looks as if she didn't know what she was about! (*After she has said this, they look at each other, then start to glance back at the door. After an instant* MRS. HALE *has pulled at a knot and ripped the sewing.*)

MRS. PETERS: Oh, what are you doing, Mrs. Hale?

MRS. HALE (*mildly*): Just pulling out a stitch or two that's not sewed very good. (*threading a needle*) Bad sewing always made me fidgety.

MRS. PETERS (*nervously*): I don't think we ought to touch things.

MRS. HALE: I'll just finish up this end. (*suddenly stopping and leaning forward*) Mrs. Peters?

MRS. PETERS: Yes, Mrs. Hale?

MRS. HALE: What do you suppose she was so nervous about?

MRS. PETERS: Oh—I don't know. I don't know as she was nervous. I sometimes sew awful queer when I'm just tired. (MRS. HALE *starts to say something, looks at* MRS. PETERS, *then goes on sewing.*) Well, I must get these things wrapped up.

They may be through sooner than we think. (*putting apron and other things together*) I wonder where I can find a piece of paper, and string.

MRS. HALE: In that cupboard, maybe.

MRS. PETERS (*looking in cupboard*): Why, here's a birdcage. (*holds it up*) Did she have a bird, Mrs. Hale?

MRS. HALE: Why, I don't know whether she did or not—I've not been here for so long. There was a man around last year selling canaries cheap, but I don't know as she took one; maybe she did. She used to sing real pretty herself.

MRS. PETERS (*glancing around*): Seems funny to think of a bird here. But she must have had one or why should she have a cage? I wonder what happened to it?

MRS. HALE: I s'pose maybe the cat got it.

MRS. PETERS: No, she didn't have a cat. She's got that feeling some people have about cats—being afraid of them. My cat got in her room and she was real upset and asked me to take it out.

MRS. HALE: My sister Bessie was like that. Queer, ain't it.

MRS. PETERS (*examining the cage*): Why, look at this door. It's broke. One hinge is pulled apart.

MRS. HALE (*looking, too*): Looks as if someone must have been rough with it.

MRS. PETERS: Why, yes.

She brings the cage forward and puts it on the table.

MRS. HALE: I wish if they're going to find any evidence they'd be about it. I don't like this place.

MRS. PETERS: But I'm glad you came with me, Mrs. Hale. It would be lonesome for me sitting here alone.

MRS. HALE: It would, wouldn't it? (*dropping her sewing*) But I tell you what I do wish, Mrs. Peters. I wish I had come over sometimes when she was here. I—(*looking around the room*)—wish I had.

MRS. PETERS: But of course you were awful busy, Mrs. Hale—your house and your children.

MRS. HALE: I could've come. I stayed away because it weren't cheerful—and that's why I ought to have come. I—I've never liked this place. Maybe because it's down in a hollow and you don't see the road. I dunno what it is, but it's a lonesome place and always was. I wish I had come over to see Minnie Foster sometimes. I can see now—

Shakes her head.

MRS. PETERS: Well, you mustn't reproach yourself, Mrs. Hale. Somehow we just don't see how it is with other folks until—something comes up.

MRS. HALE: Not having children makes less work—but it makes a quiet house, and Wright out to work all day, and no company when he did come in. Did you know John Wright, Mrs. Peters?

MRS. PETERS: Not to know him; I've seen him in town. They say he was a good man.

MRS. HALE: Yes—good; he didn't drink, and kept his word as well as most, I guess, and paid his debts. But he was a hard man, Mrs. Peters. Just to pass the time of day with him—(*shivers*) Like a raw wind that gets to the bone. (*pauses, her eye falling on the cage*) I should think she would 'a wanted a bird. But what do you suppose went with it?

MRS. PETERS: I don't know, unless it got sick and died.

She reaches over and swings the broken door, swings it again. Both women watch it.

MRS. HALE: You weren't raised round here, were you? (MRS. PETERS *shakes her head.*) You didn't know—her?

MRS. PETERS: Not till they brought her yesterday.

MRS. HALE: She—come to think of it, she was kind of like a bird herself—real sweet and pretty, but kind of timid and—fluttery. How—she—did—change. (*silence; then as if struck by a happy thought and relieved to get back to everyday things*) Tell you what, Mrs. Peters, why don't you take the quilt in with you? It might take up her mind.

MRS. PETERS: Why, I think that's a real nice idea, Mrs. Hale. There couldn't possibly be any objection to it, could there? Now, just what would I take? I wonder if her patches are in here—and her things.

The look in the sewing basket.

MRS. HALE: Here's some red. I expect this has got sewing things in it. (*brings out a fancy box*) What a pretty box. Looks like something somebody would give you. Maybe her scissors are in here. (*Opens box. Suddenly puts her hand to her nose.*) Why—(MRS. *PETERS bends nearer, then turns her face away.*) There's something wrapped up in this piece of silk.

MRS. PETERS: Why, this isn't her scissors.

MRS. HALE (*lifting the silk*): Oh, Mrs. Peters—it's—

MRS. PETERS *bends closer.*

MRS. PETERS: It's the bird.

MRS. HALE (*jumping up*): But Mrs. Peters—look at it. Its neck! Look at its neck! It's all—other side *to.*

MRS. PETERS: Somebody—wrung—its—neck.

Their eyes meet. A look of growing comprehension, of horror. Steps are heard outside. MRS. HALE *slips box under quilt pieces, and sinks into her chair. Enter SHER-IFF and COUNTY ATTORNEY. MRS. PETERS rises.*

COUNTY ATTORNEY (*as one turning from serious things to little pleasantries*): Well, ladies, have you decided whether she was going to quilt it or knot it?

MRS. PETERS: We think she was going to—knot it.

COUNTY ATTORNEY: Well, that's interesting, I'm sure. (*seeing the birdcage*) Has the bird flown?

MRS. HALE (*putting more quilt pieces over the box*): We think the—cat got it.

COUNTY ATTORNEY (*preoccupied*): Is there a cat?

MRS. HALE *glances in a quick covert way at* MRS. PETERS.

MRS. PETERS: Well, not *now.* They're superstitious, you know. They leave.

COUNTY ATTORNEY (*to SHERIFF PETERS, continuing an interrupted conversation*): No sign at all of anyone having come from the outside. Their own rope. Now let's go up again and go over it piece by piece. (*They start upstairs.*) It would have to have been someone who knew just the—

MRS. PETERS *sits down. The two women sit there not looking at one another, but as if peering into something and at the same time holding back. When they talk now, it is in the manner of finding their way over strange ground, as if afraid of what they are saying, but as if they cannot help saying it.*

MRS. HALE: She liked the bird. She was going to bury it in that pretty box.

MRS. PETERS (*in a whisper*): When I was a girl—my kitten—there was a boy took a hatchet, and before my eyes—and before I could get there—(*covers her face an instant*) If they hadn't held me back, I would have (*catches herself, looks upstairs where steps are heard, falters weakly*)—hurt him.

MRS. HALE (*with a slow look around her*): I wonder how it would seem never to have had any children around. (*pause*) No, Wright wouldn't like the bird—a thing that sang. She used to sing. He killed that, too.

MRS. PETERS (*moving uneasily*): We don't know who killed the bird.

MRS. HALE: I knew John Wright.

MRS. PETERS: It was an awful thing was done in this house that night, Mrs. Hale. Killing a man while he slept, slipping a rope around his neck that choked the life out of him.

MRS. HALE: His neck. Choked the life out of him.

Her hand goes out and rests on the birdcage.

MRS. PETERS (*with rising voice*): We don't know who killed him. We don't know.

MRS. HALE (*her own feeling not interrupted*): If there'd been years and years of nothing, then a bird to sing to you, it would be awful still, after the bird was still.

MRS. PETERS (*something within her speaking*): I know what stillness is. When we homesteaded in Dakota, and my first baby died—after he was two years old, and me with no other then—

MRS. HALE (*moving*): How soon do you suppose they'll be through, looking for the evidence?

MRS. PETERS: I know what stillness is. (*pulling herself back*) The law has got to punish crime, Mrs. Hale.

MRS. HALE (*not as if answering that*): I wish you'd seen Minnie Foster when she wore a white dress with blue ribbons and stood up there in the choir and sang. (*a look around the room*) Oh, I *wish* I'd come over here once in a while! That was a crime! That was a crime! Who's going to punish that?

MRS. PETERS (*looking upstairs*): We mustn't—take on.

MRS. HALE: I might have known she needed help! I know how things can be—for women. I tell you, it's queer, Mrs. Peters. We live close together, and we live far apart. We all go through the same things—it's all just a different kind of the same thing. (*brushes her eyes; noticing the bottle of fruit, reaches out for it*) If I was you, I wouldn't tell her her fruit was gone. Tell her it *ain't*. Tell her it's all right. Take this in to prove it to her. She—she may never know whether it was broke or not.

MRS. PETERS (*takes the bottle, looks about for something to wrap it in; takes petticoat from the clothes brought from the other room, very nervously begins winding this around the bottle. In a false voice.*): My, it's a good thing the men couldn't hear us. Wouldn't they just laugh! Getting all stirred up over a little thing like a—dead canary. As if that could have anything to do with—with—wouldn't they *laugh!*

The men are heard coming downstairs.

MRS. HALE (*under her breath*): Maybe they would—maybe they wouldn't.

COUNTY ATTORNEY: No, Peters, it's all perfectly clear except a reason for doing it. But you know juries when it comes to women. If there was some definite thing.

Something to show—something to make a story about—a thing that would connect up with this strange way of doing it.

The women's eyes meet for an instant. Enter HALE *from outer door.*

HALE: Well, I've got the team around. Pretty cold out there.

COUNTY ATTORNEY: I'm going to stay here a while by myself. (*to the* SHERIFF) You can send Frank out for me, can't you? I want to go over everything. I'm not satisfied that we can't do better.

SHERIFF: Do you want to see what Mrs. Peters is going to take in?

The COUNTY ATTORNEY *goes to the table, picks up the apron, laughs.*

COUNTY ATTORNEY: Oh, I guess they're not very dangerous things the ladies have picked up. (*Moves a few things about, disturbing the quilt pieces which cover the box. Steps back.*) No, Mrs. Peters doesn't need supervising. For that matter, a sheriff's wife is married to the law. Ever think of it that way, Mrs. Peters?

MRS. PETERS: Not—just that way.

SHERIFF (*chuckling*): Married to the law. (*moves toward the other room*) I just want you to come in here a minute, George. We ought to take a look at these windows.

COUNTY ATTORNEY (*scoffingly*): Oh, windows!

SHERIFF: We'll be right out, Mr. Hale.

HALE *goes outside.* The SHERIFF *follows the* COUNTY ATTORNEY *into the other room.* Then MRS. HALE *rises, hands tight together, looking intensely at* MRS. PETERS, *whose eyes take a slow turn, finally meeting* MRS. HALE'S. *A moment* MRS. HALE *holds hers, then her own eyes point the way to where the box is concealed. Suddenly* MRS. PETERS *throws back quilt pieces and tries to put the box in the bag she is wearing. It is too big. She opens box, starts to take bird out, cannot touch it, goes to pieces, stands there helpless. Sound of a knob turning in the other room.* MRS. HALE *snatches the box and puts it in the pocket of her big coat. Enter* COUNTY ATTORNEY *and* SHERIFF.

COUNTY ATTORNEY (*facetiously*): Well, Henry, at least we found out that she was not going to quilt it. She was going to—what is it you call it, ladies?

MRS. HALE (*her hand against her pocket*): We call it—knot it, Mr. Henderson.

CURTAIN

For Practice

Now that you have read the play, use skills you have gained through the discussions of literary terminology, argument, and the interpretive process to make sense of this play. Think about the genre, the way Glaspell uses language, the characters and the situation of the play. How does she use these literary strategies rhetorically to create an argument? What is that argument? Use the SASE process, or any other process that works better for you, to put all these elements together. Here are some additional questions to think about as you work through this text.

1. Susan Glaspell wrote about a real life murder case using two genres: the short story and a one-act play. What aspects of this story are highlighted by the fact that it is performed in front of an audience? How does the fact that you are reading the play's script instead of watching it performed affect your understanding of this text?

2. How does the fact that there is no narrator alter your experience of the story? Whose perspective does this work represent? How do you know?

3. The images in a play are both spoken and visual. What images are at work in this play? What kind of rhetorical appeal(s) do they make? What is the symbolic value of these images?

4. The title of Glaspell's short story "A Jury of Her Peers" reflects the historical reality that women did not, at this time, have the right to vote or to serve as members of a jury. Who are Minnie Wright's peers? How do the actions of the two women constitute a kind of judgment? What arguments do the women offer for their decision?

5. What argument does this play make about the ways in which women's lives were controlled by men at this time in history? How is this argument relevant for us today?

UNIT
TWO

Everyday Use

The English poet John Donne wrote that "No man is an island, entire of itself," and that belief is the focus of this section. All the works in this unit address issues of relationships: friendships, romantic relationships, and relationships with family members (including ancestors long dead). Our closest relationships are among the strongest influences in our lives, and they frequently affect other aspects of our behavior. Our personal alliances alter and are altered by the political, religious, and cultural dictates of the society in which we live.

Several readings in this section explore ways in which individuals' personal relationships shape their views of their places in society, as well as their levels of comfort within those positions. Alice Walker's "Everyday Use" examines differing perspectives on a heritage shared by three Southern African-American women. Maxine Hong Kingston makes use of a dramatic yet long-secret family story to begin to explain, both for herself and her readers, what it means to be a Chinese-American caught between two ways of life. Adrienne Rich's sequence of poems explores the difficulty of nurturing a love affair which much of society views as unconventional, and Charlotte Perkins Gilman's short story chronicles the struggle of one nineteenth-century woman to determine her own future in a society suspicious of her fitness for that job.

Likewise crucial to the writers included here are the value of memory and the act of remembrance. For James Agee, it is the remembrance of a childhood surrounded by family love, even though the child does not yet feel secure about his place in the world. For Kingston, the act of memory is an act of rebellion, as she refuses to forget an aunt whose very name has become taboo. For Walker and for Lorraine Hansberry, tangible family heirlooms serve as catalysts for memory and as legacies of all the suffering and triumphs endured, not just by two families, but by generations of African Americans. The important role that the past plays in shaping the present and the future is a vital element in our lives and in these writers' art.

It is important to note that many of the readings included here demonstrate how our relationships can provide valuable encouragement for, or resistance to, our creativity and self-expression. Each of the poets whose work appears in this section aims for new means of expressing age-old feelings in romantic poetry; Pablo Neruda, William Shakespeare, and Adrienne Rich are all aware of the conventional views of love and poetry with which they must struggle to express their special, individual emotions. Authors such as Kingston and Gilman also depict in their work the importance of the writer's art to the writer's self-definition, even when societal norms discourage that effort. Similarly, Walker and Hansberry examine artists whose self-expression emerges not through the written word but through objects passed down through the family from generation to generation. Each writer is noticeably aware that the stories we build through our personal relationships create who we are and are preserved only if expressed through our own unique voices.

As you read through this section, think of the relationships you now hold dear and those you have cherished in the past. How have they shaped you as an individual? How do the relationships shown in the readings here compare with your own relationships? What do the ways in which we relate to others ultimately teach us about ourselves as individuals and as members of large communities? How does literature alter our understanding of our place in our families, our communities, and the human race?

Everyday Use

for Your Grandmama

Alice Walker

Alice Walker (b. 1944) was the youngest of eight children in Eatonton, Georgia. Her father supported this large family by working as a share-cropper, and her mother worked as a domestic. Bashful as a child, Walker nonetheless excelled in school, graduating as valedictorian of her high school. She overcame limited opportunities for poor black women in the South by attending college, first at Spelman College in Atlanta and later at New York's Sarah Lawrence College, where she earned her B.A. While a student at these schools, Walker began her career as an activist for feminist and civil rights causes. She also began to write, and in 1968 her first book, a collection of poems entitled Once, *was published. Since then, Walker has published numerous novels, books of poetry, short stories, and essay collections. Her novel* The Color Purple *(1983) won the National Book Award and a Pulitzer Prize before being adapted into a 1985 film by director Steven Spielburg. Walker now lives and works in northern California.*

The short story "Everyday Use" was originally published in In Love and Trouble: Stories of Black Women *(1973), Walker's first collection of short stories. Written with humor and sensitivity, "Everyday Use" high-lights the complexities involved in defining family heritages and values, especially within African-American families. The story also raises questions of where the line between art and usefulness should be drawn—or whether it can be drawn at all.*

I will wait for her in the yard that Maggie and I made so clean and wavy yesterday afternoon. A yard like this is more comfortable than most people know. It is not just a yard. It is like an extended living room. When the hard clay is swept clean as a floor and the fine sand around the edges lined with tiny, irregular grooves, anyone can come and sit and look up into the elm tree and wait for the breezes that never come inside the house.

Maggie will be nervous until after her sister goes: she will stand hopelessly in corners homely and ashamed of the burn scars down her arms and legs, eyeing her sister with a mixture of envy and awe. She thinks her sister has held life always in the palm of one hand, that "no" is a word the world never learned to say to her.

You've no doubt seen those TV shows where the child who has "made it" is con-fronted, as a surprise, by her own mother and father, tottering in weakly from back-stage. (A pleasant surprise, of course: What would they do if parent and child came on the show only to curse out and insult each other?) On TV mother and child embrace and smile into each other's faces. Sometimes the mother and father weep, the child wraps them in her arms and leans across the table to tell how she would not have made it without their help. I have seen these programs.

Sometimes I dream a dream in which Dee and I are suddenly brought together on a TV program of this sort. Out of a dark and soft-seated limousine I am ushered into a bright room filled with many people. There I meet a smiling, gray, sporty man like Johnny Carson who shakes my hand and tells me what a fine girl I have. Then we are on the stage and Dee is embracing me with tears in her eyes. She pins on my dress a large orchid, even though she has told me once that she thinks orchids are tacky flowers.

In real life I am a large, big-boned woman with rough, man-working hands. In the winter I wear flannel nightgowns to bed and overalls during the day. I can kill and clean a hog as mercilessly as a man. My fat keeps me hot in zero weather. I can work outside all day, breaking ice to get water for washing; I can eat pork liver cooked over the open fire minutes after it comes steaming from the hog. One winter I knocked a bull calf straight in the brain between the eyes with a sledge hammer and had the meat hung up to chill before nightfall. But of course all this does not show on television. I am the way my daughter would want me to be: a hundred pounds lighter, my skin like an uncooked barley pancake. My hair glistens in the hot bright lights. Johnny Carson has much to do to keep up with my quick and witty tongue.

But that is a mistake. I know even before I wake up. Who ever knew a Johnson with a quick tongue? Who can even imagine me looking a strange white man in the eye? It seems to me I have talked to them always with one foot raised in flight, with my head turned in whichever way is farthest from them. Dee, though. She would always look anyone in the eye. Hesitation was not part of her nature.

"How do I look, Mama?" Maggie says, showing just enough of her thin body enveloped in pink skirt and red blouse for me to know she's there, almost hidden by the door.

"Come out into the yard," I say.

Have you ever seen a lame animal, perhaps a dog run over by some careless per-son rich enough to own a car, sidle up to someone who is ignorant enough to be kind to them? That is the way my Maggie walks. She has been like this, chin on chest, eyes on ground, feet in shuffle, ever since the fire that burned the other house to the ground.

Dee is lighter than Maggie, with nicer hair and a fuller figure. She's a woman now, though sometimes I forget. How long ago was it that the other house burned? Ten, twelve years? Sometimes I can still hear the flames and feel Maggie's arms sticking to me, her hair smoking and her dress falling off her in little black papery flakes. Her eyes seemed stretched open, blazed open by the flames reflected in them. And Dee. I see her standing off under the sweet gum tree she used to dig gum out of; a look of concen-tration on her face as she watched the last dingy gray board of the house fall in toward the red-hot brick chimney. Why don't you do a dance around the ashes? I'd wanted to ask her. She had hated the house that much.

I used to think she hated Maggie, too. But that was before we raised the money, the church and me, to send her to Augusta to school. She used to read to us without pity;

forcing words, lies, and other folks' habits, whole lives upon us two, sitting trapped and ignorant underneath her voice. She washed us in a river of make-believe, burned us with a lot of knowledge we didn't necessarily need to know. Pressed us to her with the serious way she read, to shove us away at just the moment, like dimwits, we seemed about to understand.

Dee wanted nice things. A yellow organdy dress to wear to her graduation from high school; black pumps to match a green suit she'd made from an old suit somebody gave me. She was determined to stare down any disaster in her efforts. Her eyelids would not flicker for minutes at a time. Often I fought off the temptation to shake her. At sixteen she had a style of her own: and knew what style was.

I never had an education myself. After second grade the school was closed down. Don't ask me why: in 1927 colored asked fewer questions than they do now. Sometimes Maggie reads to me. She stumbles along good naturedly but can't see well. She knows she is not bright. Like good looks and money, quickness passed her by. She will marry John Thomas (who has mossy teeth in an earnest face) and then I'll be free to sit here and I guess just sing church songs to myself. Although I was never a good singer. Never could carry a tune. I was always better at a man's job. I used to love to milk till I was hooked in the side in '49. Cows are soothing and slow and don't bother you, unless you try to milk them the wrong way.

I have deliberately turned my back on the house. It is three rooms, just like the one that burned, except the roof is tin; they don't make shingle roofs any more. There are no real windows, just some holes cut in the sides, like the portholes in a ship, but not round and not square, with rawhide holding the shutters open on the outside. This house is in a pasture, too, like the other one. No doubt when Dee sees it she will want to tear it down. She wrote me once that no matter where we "choose" to live, she will manage to come see us. But she will never bring her friends. Maggie and I thought about this and Maggie asked me, "Mama, when did Dee ever *have* any friends?"

She had a few. Furtive boys in pink shirts hanging about on washday after school. Nervous girls who never laughed. Impressed with her they worshiped the well-turned phrase, the cute shape, the scalding humor that erupted like bubbles in lye. She read to them.

When she was courting Jimmy T she didn't have much time to pay to us, but turned all her faultfinding power on him. He *flew* to marry a cheap city girl from a family of ignorant flashy people. She hardly had time to recompose herself.

When she comes I will meet—but there they are!

Maggie attempts to make a dash for the house, in her shuffling way, but I stay her with my hand. "Come back here," I say. And she stops and tries to dig a well in the sand with her toe.

It is hard to see them clearly through the strong sun. But even the first glimpse of leg out of the car tells me it is Dee. Her feet were always neat-looking, as if God himself had shaped them with a certain style. From the other side of the car comes a short, stocky man. Hair is all over his head a foot long and hanging from his chin like a kinky mule tail. I hear Maggie suck in her breath. "Uhnnnh," is that what it sounds like. Like when you see the wriggling end of a snake just in front of your foot on the road. "Uhnnnh."

Dee next. A dress down to the ground, in this hot weather. A dress so loud it hurts my eyes. There are yellows and oranges enough to throw back the light of the sun. I feel my whole face warming from the heat waves it throws out. Earrings gold, too, and hanging down to her shoulders. Bracelets dangling and making noises when she moves her arm up to shake the folds of the dress out of her armpits. The dress is loose and flows, and as she walks closer, I like it. I hear Maggie go "Uhnnnh" again. It is her sister's hair. It stands straight up like the wool on a sheep. It is black as night and around the edges are two long pigtails that rope about like small lizards disappearing behind her ears.

"Wa-su-zo-Tean-o!" she says, coming on in that gliding way the dress makes her move. The short stocky fellow with the hair to his navel is all grinning and he follows up with "Asalamalakim, my mother and sister!" He moves to hug Maggie but she falls back, right up against the back of my chair. I feel her trembling there and when I look up I see the perspiration falling off her chin.

"Don't get up," says Dee. Since I am stout it takes something of a push. You can see me trying to move a second or two before I make it. She turns, showing white heels through her sandals, and goes back to the car. Out she peeks next with a Polaroid. She stoops down quickly and lines up picture after picture of me sitting there in front of the house with Maggie cowering behind me. She never takes a shot without making sure the house is included. When a cow comes nibbling around the edge of the yard she snaps it and me and Maggie *and* the house. Then she puts the Polaroid in the back seat of the car, and comes up and kisses me on the forehead.

Meanwhile Asalamalakim is going through motions with Maggie's hand. Maggie's hand is as limp as a fish, and probably as cold, despite the sweat, and she keeps trying to pull it back. It looks like Asalamalakim wants to shake hands but wants to do it fancy. Or maybe he don't know how people shake hands. Anyhow, he soon gives up on Maggie.

"Well," I say. "Dee."

"No Mama," she says. "Not 'Dee,' Wangero Leewanika Kemanjo!"

"What happened to 'Dee'?" I wanted to know.

"She's dead," Wangero said. "I couldn't bear it any longer, being named after the people who oppress me."

"You know as well as me you was named after your aunt Dicie." I said. Dicie is my sister. She named Dee. We called her "Big Dee" after Dee was born.

"But who was *she* named after?" asked Wangero.

"I guess after Grandma Dee," I said.

"And who was she named after?" asked Wangero.

"Her mother," I said, and saw Wangero was getting tired. "That's about as far back as I can trace it," I said. Though, in fact, I probably could have carried it back beyond the Civil War through the branches.

"Well," said Asalamalakim, "there you are."

"Uhnnnh," I heard Maggie say.

"There I was not," I said, "before 'Dicie' cropped up in our family, so why should I try to trace it that far back?"

He just stood there grinning, looking down on me like somebody inspecting a Model A car. Every once in a while he and Wangero sent eye signals over my head.

"How do you pronounce this name?" I asked.

"You don't have to call me by it if you don't want to," said Wangero.

"Why shouldn't I?" I asked. "If that's what you want us to call you, we'll call you."

"I know it might sound awkward at first," said Wangero.

"I'll get used to it," I said. "Ream it out again."

Well, soon as we got the name out of the way, Asalamalakim had a name twice as long and three times as hard. After I tripped over it two or three times he told me to just call him Hakim-a-barber. I wanted to ask him was he a barber, but I didn't really think he was, so I didn't ask.

"You must belong to those beef-cattle peoples down the road," I said. They said "Asalamalakim" when they met you, too, but they didn't shake hands. Always too busy: feeding the cattle, fixing the fences, putting up salt-lick shelters, throwing down hay. When the white folks poisoned some of the herd the men stayed up all night with rifles in their hands. I walked a mile and a half just to see the sight.

Hakim-a-barber said, "I accept some of their doctrines, but farming and raising cattle is not my style." (They didn't tell me, and I didn't ask, whether Wangero [Dee] had really gone and married him.)

We sat down to eat and right away he said he didn't eat collards and pork was unclean. Wangero, though, went on through the chitlins and corn bread, the greens and everything else. She talked a blue streak over the sweet potatoes. Everything delighted her. Even the fact that we still used the benches her daddy made for the table when we couldn't afford to buy chairs.

"Oh, Mama!" she cried. Then turned to Hakim-a-barber. "I never knew how lovely these benches are. You can feel the rump prints," she said running her hands under-neath her and along the bench. Then she gave a sigh and her hand closed over Grandma Dee's butter dish. "That's it!" she said. "I knew there was something I want-ed to ask you if I could have." She jumped up from the table and went over in the cor-ner where the churn stood, the milk in it clabber by now. She looked at the churn and looked at it.

"This churn top is what I need," she said. "Didn't Uncle Buddy whittle it out of a tree you all used to have?"

"Yes," I said.

"Uh huh," she said happily. "And I want the dasher, too."

"Uncle Buddy whittle that, too?" asked the barber.

Dee (Wangero) looked up at me.

"Aunt Dee's first husband whittled the dash," said Maggie so low you almost could-n't hear her. "His name was Henry, but they called him Stash."

"Maggie's brain is like an elephant's," Wangero said, laughing. "I can use the churn top as a centerpiece for the alcove table," she said, sliding a plate over the churn, "and I'll think of something artistic to do with the dasher."

When she finished wrapping the dasher the handle stuck out. I took it for a moment in my hands. You didn't even have to look close to see where hands pushing the dasher up and down to make butter had left a kind of sink in the wood. In fact, there were a lot of small sinks; you could see where thumbs and fingers had sunk into the wood. It was beautiful light yellow wood, from a tree that grew in the yard where Big Dee and Stash had lived.

After dinner Dee (Wangero) went to the trunk at the foot of my bed and started rifling through it. Maggie hung back in the kitchen over the dishpan. Out came Wangero with two quilts. They had been pieced by Grandma Dee and then Big Dee and me had hung them on the quilt frames on the porch and quilted them. One was in the Lone Star pattern. The other was Walk Around the Mountain. In both of them were scraps of dresses Grandma Dee had worn fifty and more years ago. Bits and pieces of Grandpa Jarrell's Paisley shirts. And one teeny faded blue piece, about the size of a penny matchbox, that was from Great Grandpa Ezra's uniform that he wore in the Civil War.

"Mama," Wangero said sweet as a bird. "Can I have these old quilts?"

I heard something fall in the kitchen, and a minute later the kitchen door slammed.

"Why don't you take one or two of the others?" I asked. "These old things was just done by me and Big Dee from some tops your grandma pieced before she died."

"No," said Wangero. "I don't want those. They are stitched around the borders by machine."

"That'll make them last better," I said.

"That's not the point," said Wangero. "These are all pieces of dresses Grandma used to wear. She did all this stitching by hand. Imagine!" She held the quilts securely in her arms, stroking them.

"Some of the pieces, like those lavender ones, come from old clothes her mother handed down to her," I said, moving up to touch the quilts. Dee (Wangero) moved back just enough so that I couldn't reach the quilts. They already belonged to her.

"Imagine!" she breathed again, clutching them closely to her bosom.

"The truth is," I said, "I promised to give them quilts to Maggie, for when she marries John Thomas."

She gasped like a bee had stung her.

"Maggie can't appreciate these quilts!" she said. "She'd probably be backward enough to put them to everyday use."

"I reckon she would," I said. "God knows I've been saving 'em for long enough with nobody using 'em. I hope she will!" I didn't want to bring up how I had offered Dee (Wangero) a quilt when she went away to college. Then she had told me they were old-fashioned, out of style.

"But they're *priceless!*" She was saying now, furiously, for she has a temper. "Maggie would put them on the bed and in five years they'd be in rags. Less than that!"

"She can always make some more," I said. "Maggie knows how to quilt."

Dee (Wangero) looked at me with hatred. "You just will not understand. The point is these quilts, *these* quilts!"

"Well," I said, stumped. "What would *you* do with them?"

"Hang them," she said. As if that was the only thing you *could* do with quilts.

Maggie by now was standing in the door. I could almost hear the sound her feet made as they scraped over each other.

"She can have them, Mama," she said, like somebody used to never winning anything, or having anything reserved for her. "I can 'member Grandma Dee without the quilts."

I looked at her hard. She had filled her bottom lip with checkerberry snuff and it gave her face a kind of dopey, hangdog look. It was Grandma Dee and Big Dee who taught her how to quilt herself. She stood there with her scarred hands hidden in the folds of her skirt. She looked at her sister with something like fear but she wasn't mad at her. This was Maggie's portion. This was the way she knew God to work.

When I looked at her like that something hit me in the top of my head and ran down to the soles of my feet. Just like when I'm in church and the spirit of God touches me and I get happy and shout. I did something I never had done before: hugged Maggie to me, then dragged her on into the room, snatched the quilts out of Miss Wangero's hands and dumped them into Maggie's lap. Maggie just sat there on my bed with her mouth open.

"Take one or two of the others," I said to Dee.

But she turned without a word and went out to Hakim-a-barber.

"You just don't understand," she said, as Maggie and I came out to the car.

"What don't I understand?" I wanted to know.

"Your heritage," she said. And then she turned to Maggie, kissed her, and said, "You ought to try to make something of yourself, too, Maggie. It's really a new day for us. But from the way you and Mama still live you'd never know it."

She put on some sunglasses that hid everything above the tip of her nose and her chin.

Maggie smiled; maybe at the sunglasses, but a real smile, not scared. After we watched the car dust settle I asked Maggie to bring me a dip of snuff. And then the two of us sat there just enjoying, until it was time to go in the house and go to bed.

For Practice

1. Discuss the importance of the setting of the story. What is the setting (time and place) of the story as a whole? Where do the crucial interactions among the central characters take place? How do the atmospheres created by these settings contribute to shaping the main themes and ideas that frame "Everyday Use"?

2. Think about the household objects that the characters call attention to in Walker's story. What do those objects represent for each of the three women in the story? Which object brings about the turning point of the story? Why is that object so important to the story?

3. The conflicts between characters that emerge in works of literature can often be read as conflicts between different values. After reading "Everyday Use," what do you believe are the most important opposing values in this story? What values do you believe the story finally affirms? Explain.

4. Describe Mrs. Johnson's attitudes toward herself and toward each of her daughters in "Everyday Use." Do any of those attitudes change from the beginning to the end of the story? How and why? Has your perspective on your own life changed as a result of reading this text? How and why?

5. What does the title of Walker's story tell you about its main message(s)? Why do you believe the story is dedicated "for your grandmama"?

No Name Woman

Maxine Hong Kingston

Maxine Hong Kingston (b. 1940) was born in Stockton, California, the old-
est child of Chinese immigrants. Her father, a teacher and scholar in
China, moved to America in 1925 and worked variously as a window wash-
er, laundry owner, and manager of illegal gambling houses. Her mother,
who did not follow her husband to America until early 1940, had been
trained as a doctor in China but worked at different times in America as a
maid, a tomato picker, and a cannery worker. Kingston never spoke
English until she started elementary school. In 1962, she earned her bach-
elor's degree in English at the University of California-Berkeley and mar-
ried actor and fellow student Earll Kingston. She currently teaches
English at UC-Berkeley and has published six books, including The
Woman Warrior: Memoirs of a Girlhood Among Ghosts *(1976), a visionary*
autobiography which opens with the essay "No Name Woman." The
Woman Warrior *earned Kingston the 1976 National Book Critics Circle*
Award for nonficiton. In 1980 she received a National Book Award for her
second volume of autobiography, China Men.

"No Name Woman" tells the story of Kingston's aunt, her father's sister,
who suffered severe abuse and ostracism from her family and community in
China after becoming pregnant with an illegitimate child. Her mother broke
a family oath by sharing the story with her daughter as a warning against
extramarital sex, and Kingston in turn shatters the silence permanently by
inscribing her aunt's story in her autobiography. "No Name Woman" also
explores age-old concerns that cross national boundaries: poverty, scape-
goating, the repression of sexual desires, the oppression of women. Kingston
imagines details her mother leaves out of the aunt's story as she works to
give shape to her own identity as a Chinese-American woman by retelling
creatively the stories of her ancestors.

"You must not tell anyone," my mother said, "what I am about to tell
you. In China your father had a sister who killed herself. She jumped
into the family well. We say that your father has all brothers because it is as if she had
never been born.

"In 1924 just a few days after our village celebrated seventeen hurry-up weddings—to make sure that every young man who went 'out on the road' would respon-
sibly come home—your father and his brothers and your grandfather and his brothers

and your aunt's new husband sailed for America, the Gold Mountain. It was your grandfather's last trip. Those lucky enough to get contracts waved good-bye from the decks. They fed and guarded the stowaways and helped them in Cuba, New York, Bali, Hawaii. 'We'll meet in California next year,' they said. All of them sent money home.

"I remember looking at your aunt one day when she and I were dressing; I had not noticed before that she had such a protruding melon of a stomach. But I did not think, 'She's pregnant,' until she began to look like other pregnant women, her shirt pulling and the white tops of her black pants showing. She could not have been pregnant, you see, because her husband had been gone for years. No one said anything. We did not discuss it. In early summer she was ready to have the child, long after the time when it could have been possible.

"The village had also been counting. On the night the baby was to be born the villagers raided our house. Some were crying. Like a great saw, teeth strung with lights, files of people walked zigzag across our land, tearing the rice. Their lanterns doubled in the disturbed black water, which drained away through the broken bunds. As the villagers closed in, we could see that some of them, probably men and women we knew well, wore white masks. The people with long hair hung it over their faces. Women with short hair made it stand up on end. Some had tied white bands around their foreheads, arms, and legs.

"At first they threw mud and rocks at the house. Then they threw eggs and began slaughtering our stock. We could hear the animals scream their deaths—the roosters, the pigs, a last great roar from the ox. Familiar wild heads flared in our night windows; the villagers encircled us. Some of the faces stopped to peer at us, their eyes rushing like searchlights. The hands flattened against the panes, framed heads, and left red prints.

"The villagers broke in the front and the back doors at the same time, even though we had not locked the doors against them. Their knives dripped with the blood of our animals. They smeared blood on the doors and walls. One woman swung a chicken, whose throat she had slit, splattering blood in red arcs about her. We stood together in the middle of our house, in the family hall with the pictures and tables of the ancestors around us, and looked straight ahead.

"At that time the house had only two wings. When the men came back, we would build two more to enclose our courtyard and a third one to begin a second courtyard. The villagers pushed through both wings, even your grandparents' rooms, to find your aunt's, which was also mine until the men returned. From this room a new wing for one of the younger families would grow. They ripped up her clothes and shoes and broke her combs, grinding them underfoot. They tore her from the loom. They scattered the cooking fire and rolled the new weaving in it. We could hear them in the kitchen breaking our bowls and banging the pots. They overturned the great waist-high earthenware jugs; duck eggs, pickled fruits, vegetables burst out and mixed in acrid torrents. The old woman from the next field swept a broom through the air and loosed the spirits-of-the-broom over our heads. 'Pig.' 'Ghost.' 'Pig,' they sobbed and scolded while they ruined our house.

"When they left, they took sugar and oranges to bless themselves. They cut pieces from the dead animals. Some of them took bowls that were not broken and clothes that were not torn. Afterward we swept up the rice and sewed it back up into sacks. But the smells from the spilled preserves lasted. Your aunt gave birth in the pigsty that night. The next morning when I went up for the water, I found her and the baby plugging up the family well.

"Don't let your father know that I told you. He denies her. Now that you have started to menstruate, what happened to her could happen to you. Don't humiliate us. You wouldn't like to be forgotten as if you had never been born. The villagers are watchful."

Whenever she had to warn us about life, my mother told stories that ran like this one, a story to grow up on. She tested our strength to establish realities. Those in the emigrant generations who could not reassert brute survival died young and far from home. Those of us in the first American generations have had to figure out how the invisible world the emigrants built around our childhoods fits in solid America.

The emigrants confused the gods by diverting their curses, misleading them with crooked streets and false names. They must try to confuse their offspring as well, who, I suppose, threaten them in similar ways—always trying to get things straight, always trying to name the unspeakable. The Chinese I know hide their names; sojourners take new names when their lives change and guard their real names with silence.

Chinese-Americans, when you try to understand what things in you are Chinese, how do you separate what is peculiar to childhood, to poverty, insanities, one family, your mother who marked your growing with stories, from what is Chinese? What is Chinese tradition and what is the movies?

If I want to learn what clothes my aunt wore, whether flashy or ordinary, I would have to begin, "Remember Father's drowned-in-the-well sister?" I cannot ask that. My mother has told me once and for all the useful parts. She will add nothing unless powered by Necessity, a riverbank that guides her life. She plants vegetable gardens rather than lawns; she carries the odd-shaped tomatoes home from the fields and eats food left for the gods.

Whenever we did frivolous things, we used up energy; we flew high kites. We children came up off the ground over the melting cones our parents brought home from work and the American movie on New Year's Day—*Oh, You Beautiful Doll* with Betty Grable one year, and *She Wore a Yellow Ribbon* with John Wayne another year. After the one carnival ride each, we paid in guilt; our tired father counted his change on the dark walk home.

Adultery is extravagance. Could people who hatch their own chicks and eat the embryos and the heads for delicacies and boil the feet in vinegar for party food, leaving only the gravel, eating even the gizzard lining—could such people engender a prodigal aunt? To be a woman, to have a daughter in starvation time was a waste enough. My aunt could not have been the lone romantic who gave up everything for sex. Women in the old China did not choose. Some man had commanded her to lie with him and be his secret evil. I wonder whether he masked himself when he joined the raid on her family.

Perhaps she encountered him in the fields or on the mountain where the daughters-in-law collected fuel. Or perhaps he first noticed her in the marketplace. He was not a stranger because the village housed no strangers. She had to have dealings with him other than sex. Perhaps he worked an adjoining field, or he sold her the cloth for the dress she sewed and wore. His demand must have surprised, then terrified her. She obeyed him; she always did as she was told.

When the family found a young man in the next village to be her husband, she stood tractably beside the best rooster, his proxy, and promised before they met that she would be his forever. She was lucky that he was her age and she would be the first wife, an advantage secure now. The night she first saw him, he had sex with her. Then he left for America. She had almost forgotten what he looked like. When she tried to envision him, she only saw the black and white face in the group photograph the men had taken before leaving.

The other man was not, after all, much different from her husband. They both gave orders: she followed. "If you tell your family, I'll beat you. I'll kill you. Be here again next week." No one talked sex, ever. And she might have separated the rapes from the rest of living if only she did not have to buy her oil from him or gather wood in the same forest. I want her fear to have lasted just as long as rape lasted so that the fear could have been contained. Not drawn-out fear. But women at sex hazarded birth and hence lifetimes. The fear did not stop but permeated everywhere. She told the man, "I think I'm pregnant." He organized the raid against her.

On nights when my mother and father talked about their life back home, sometimes they mentioned an "outcast table" whose business they still seemed to be settling, their voices tight. In a commensal tradition, where food is precious, the powerful older people made wrongdoers eat alone. Instead of letting them start separate new lives like the Japanese, who could become samurais and geishas, the Chinese family, faces averted but eyes glowering sideways, hung on to the offenders and fed them leftovers. My aunt must have lived in the same house as my parents and eaten at an outcast table. My mother spoke about the raid as if she had seen it, when she and my aunt, a daughter-in-law to a different household, should not have been living together at all. Daughters-in-law lived with their husband's parents, not their own; a synonym for marriage in Chinese is "taking a daughter-in-law." Her husband's parents could have sold her, mortgaged her, stoned her. But they had sent her back to her own mother and father, a mysterious act hinting at disgraces not told me. Perhaps they had thrown her out to deflect the avengers.

She was the only daughter; her four brothers went with her father, husband, and uncles "out on the road" and for some years became western men. When the goods were divided among the family, three of the brothers took land, and the youngest, my father, chose an education. After my grandparents gave their daughter away to her husband's family, they had dispensed all the adventure and all the property. They expected her alone to keep the traditional ways, which her brothers, now among the barbarians, could fumble without detection. The heavy, deep-rooted women were to maintain the past against the flood, safe for returning. But the rare urge west had fixed upon our family, and so my aunt crossed boundaries not delineated in space.

The work of preservation demands that the feelings playing about in one's guts not to be turned into action. Just watch their passing like cherry blossoms. But perhaps my aunt, my forerunner, caught in a slow life, let dreams grow and fade and after some months or years went toward what persisted. Fear at the enormities of the forbidden kept her desires delicate, wire and bone. She looked at a man because she liked the way the hair was tucked behind his ears, or she liked the question mark line of a long torso curving at the shoulder and straight at the hip. For warm eyes or a soft voice or a slow walk—that's all—a few hairs, a line, a brightness, a sound, a pace, she gave up family. She offered us up for a charm that varnished with tiredness, a pigtail that didn't toss when the wind died. Why, the wrong lighting could erase the dearest thing about him.

It could very well have been, however, that my aunt did not take subtle enjoyment of her friend, but, a wild woman, kept rollicking company. Imagining her free with sex doesn't fit, though. I don't know any women like that, or men either. Unless I see her life branching into mine, she gives me no ancestral help.

To sustain her being in love, she often worked at herself in the mirror, guessing at the colors and shapes that would interest him, changing them frequently in order to hit on the right combination. She wanted him to look back.

On a farm near the sea, a woman who tended her appearance reaped a reputation for eccentricity. All the married women blunt-cut their hair in flaps about their ears or pulled it back in tight buns. No nonsense. Neither style blew easily into heart-catching tangles. And at their weddings they displayed themselves in their long hair for the last time. "It brushed the backs of my knees," my mother tells me. "It was braided, and even so, it brushed the backs of my knees."

At the mirror my aunt combed individuality into her bob. A bun could have been contrived to escape into black streamers blowing in the wind or in quiet wisps about her face, but only the older women in our picture album wear buns. She brushed her hair back from her forehead, tucking the flaps behind her ears. She looped a piece of thread, knotted into a circle between her index fingers and thumbs, and ran the double strand across her forehead. When she closed her fingers as if she were making a pair of shadow geese bite, the string twisted together catching the little hairs. Then she pulled the thread away from her skin, ripping the hairs out neatly, her eyes watering from the needles of pain. Opening her fingers, she cleaned the thread, then rolled it along her hairline and the tops of her eyebrows. My mother did the same to me and my sisters and herself. I used to believe that the expression "caught by the short hairs" meant a captive held with a depilatory string. It especially hurt at the temples, but my mother said we were lucky we didn't have to have our feet bound when we were seven. Sisters used to sit on their beds and cry together, she said, as their mothers or their slave removed the bandages for a few minutes each night and let the blood gush back into their veins. I hope that the man my aunt loved appreciated a smooth brow, that he wasn't just a tits-and-ass man.

Once my aunt found a freckle on her chin, at a spot that the almanac said predestined her for unhappiness. She dug it out with a hot needle and washed the wound with peroxide.

More attention to her looks than these pullings of hairs and pickings at spots would have caused gossip among the villagers. They owned work clothes and good clothes, and they wore good clothes for feasting the new seasons. But since a woman combing her hair hexes beginnings, my aunt rarely found an occasion to look her best. Women looked like great sea snails—the corded wood, babies, and laundry carried were the whorls on their backs. The Chinese did not admire a bent back; goddesses and warriors stood straight. Still there must have been a marvelous freeing of beauty when a worker laid down her burden and stretched and arched.

Such commonplace loveliness, however, was not enough for my aunt. She dreamed of a lover for the fifteen days of New Year's, the time for families to exchange visits, money, and food. She plied her secret comb. And sure enough she cursed the year, the family, the village, and herself.

Even as her hair lured her imminent lover, many other men looked at her. Uncles, cousins, nephews, brothers would have looked, too, had they been home between journeys. Perhaps they had already been restraining their curiosity, and they left, fearful that their glances, like a field of nesting birds, might be startled and caught. Poverty hurt, and that was their first reason for leaving. But another, final reason for leaving the crowded house was the never-said.

She may have been unusually beloved, the precious only daughter, spoiled and mirrorgazing because of the affection the family lavished on her. When her husband left, they welcomed the chance to take her back from the in-laws; she could live like the little daughter for just a while longer. There are stories that my grandfather was different from other people, "crazy ever since the little Jap bayoneted him in the head." He used to put his naked penis on the dinner table, laughing. And one day he brought home a baby girl, wrapped up inside his brown western-style greatcoat. He had traded one of his sons, probably my father, the youngest, for her. My grandmother made him trade back. When he finally got a daughter of his own, he doted on her. They must have all loved her, except perhaps my father, the only brother who never went back to China, having once been traded for a girl.

Brothers and sisters, newly men and women, had to efface their sexual color and present plain miens. Disturbing hair and eyes, a smile like no other, threatened the ideal of five generations living under one roof. To focus blurs, people shouted face to face and yelled from room to room. The immigrants I know have loud voices, unmodulated to American tones even after years away from the village where they called their friendships out across the fields. I have not been able to stop my mother's screams in public libraries or over telephones. Walking erect (knees straight, toes pointed forward, not pigeon-toed, which is Chinese-feminine) and speaking in an inaudible voice, I have tried to turn myself American-feminine. Chinese communication was loud, public. Only sick people had to whisper. But at the dinner table, where the family members came nearest one another, no one could talk, not the outcasts nor any eaters. Every word that falls from the mouth is a coin lost. Silently they gave and accepted food with both hands. A preoccupied child who took his bowl with one hand got a sideways glare. A complete moment of total attention is due everyone alike. Children and lovers have no singularity here, but my aunt used a secret voice, a separate attentiveness.

She kept the man's name to herself throughout her labor and dying; she did not accuse him that he be punished with her. To save her inseminator's name she gave silent birth.

He may have been somebody in her own household, but intercourse with a man outside the family would have been no less abhorrent. All the village were kinsmen, and the titles shouted in loud country voices never let kinship be forgotten. Any man within visiting distance would have been neutralized as a lover— "brother," "younger brother," "older brother"—one hundred and fifteen relationship titles. Parents researched birth charts probably not so much to assure good fortune as to circumvent incest in a population that has but one hundred surnames. Everybody has eight million relatives. How useless then sexual mannerisms, how dangerous.

As if it came from an atavism deeper than fear, I used to add "brother" silently to boys' names. It hexed the boys, who would or would not ask me to dance, and made them less scary and as familiar and deserving of benevolence as girls.

But, of course, I hexed myself also—no dates. I should have stood up, both arms waving, and shouted out across libraries, "Hey, you! Love me back." I had no idea, though, how to make attraction selective, how to control its direction and magnitude. If I made myself American-pretty so that the five or six Chinese boys in the class fell in love with me, everyone else—the Caucasian, Negro, and Japanese boys—would too. Sisterliness, dignified and honorable, made much more sense.

Attraction eludes control so stubbornly that whole societies designed to organize relationships among people cannot keep order, not even when they bind people to one another from childhood and raise them together. Among the very poor and the wealthy, brothers married their adopted sisters, like doves. Our family allowed some romance, paying adult brides' prices and providing dowries so that their sons and daughters could marry strangers. Marriage promises to turn strangers into friendly relatives—a nation of siblings.

In the village structure, spirits shimmered among the live creatures, balanced and held in equilibrium by time and land. But one human being flaring up into violence could open up a black hole, a maelstrom that pulled in the sky. The frightened villagers, who depended on one another to maintain the real, went to my aunt to show her a personal, physical representation of the break she made in the "roundness." Misallying couples snapped off the future, which was to be embodied in true offspring. The villagers punished her for acting as if she could have a private life, secret and apart from them.

If my aunt had betrayed the family at a time of large grain yields and peace, when many boys were born, and wings were being built on many houses, perhaps she might have escaped such severe punishment. But the men—hungry, greedy, tired of planting in dry soil and had been forced to leave the village in order to send food-money home. There were ghost plagues, bandit plagues, wars with the Japanese, floods. My Chinese brother and sister had died of an unknown sickness. Adultery, perhaps only a mistake during good times, became a crime when the village needed food.

The round moon cakes and round doorways, the round tables of graduated size that fit one roundness inside another, round windows and rice bowls—these talismans had lost their power to warn this family of the law: a family must be whole, faithfully keeping the descent line by having sons to feed the old and the dead who in turn look after the family. The villagers came to show my aunt and lover-in-hiding a broken house. The villagers were speeding up the circling of events because she was too short-sighted to see that her infidelity had already harmed the village, that waves of consequences would return unpredictably, sometimes in disguise, as now, to hurt her. This roundness had to be made coin-sized so that she would see its circumference: punish her at the birth of her baby. Awaken her to the inexorable. People who refused fatalism because they could invent small resources insisted on culpability. Deny accidents and wrest fault from the stars.

After the villagers left, their lanterns now scattering in various directions toward home, the family broke their silence and cursed her. "Aiaa, we're going to die. Death is coming. Death is coming. Look what you've done. You've killed us. Ghost! Dead Ghost! Ghost! You've never been born." She ran out into the fields, far enough from the house so that she could no longer hear their voices, and pressed herself against the earth, her own land no more. When she felt the birth coming, she thought that she had been hurt. Her body seized together. "They've hurt me too much," she thought. "This is gall, and it will kill me." With forehead and knees against the earth, her body convulsed and then relaxed. She turned on her back, lay on the ground. The black well of sky and stars went out and out forever; her body and her complexity seemed to disappear. She was one of the stars, a bright dot in blackness, without home, without a companion, in eternal cold and silent. An agoraphobia rose in her, speeding higher and higher, bigger and bigger; she would not be able to contain it; there would be no end to fear.

Flayed, unprotected against space, she felt pain return, focusing her body. This pain chilled her—a cold, steady kind of surface pain. Inside, spasmodically, the other pain, the pain of the child, heated her. For hours she lay on the ground, alternately body and space. Sometimes a vision of normal comfort obliterated reality: she saw the family in the evening gambling at the dinner table, the young people massaging their elders' backs. She saw them congratulating one another, high joy on the mornings the rice shoots came up. When these pictures burst, the stars drew yet further apart. Black space opened.

She got to her feet to fight better and remembered that old-fashioned women gave birth in their pigsties to fool the jealous, pain-dealing gods, who do not snatch piglets. Before the next spasms could stop her, she ran to the pigsty, each step a rushing out into emptiness. She climbed over the fence and knelt in the dirt. It was good to have a fence enclosing her, a tribal person alone.

Laboring, this woman who had carried her child as a foreign growth that sickened her every day, expelled it at last. She reached down to touch the hot, wet, moving mass, surely smaller than anything human, and could feel that it was human after all—fingers, toes, nails, nose. She pulled it up on her belly, and it lay curled there, butt in the air, feet precisely tucked one under the other. She opened her loose shirt and buttoned the child inside. After resting, it squirmed and thrashed and she pushed it up to her breast. It turned its head this way and that until it found her nipple. There, it made little snuffling noises. She clenched her teeth at its preciousness, lovely as a young calf, a piglet, a little dog.

She may have gone to the pigsty as a last act of responsibility: she would protect this child as she had protected its father. It would look after her soul, leaving supplies on her grave. But how would this tiny child without family find her grave when there would be no marker for her anywhere, neither in the earth nor the family hall? No one would give her a family hall name. She had taken the child with her into the wastes. At its birth the two of them had felt the same raw pain of separation, a wound that only the family pressing tight could close. A child with no descent line would not soften her life but only trail after her, ghostlike, begging her to give it purpose. At dawn the villagers on their way to the fields would stand around the fence and look.

Full of milk, the little ghost slept. When it awoke, she hardened her breasts against the milk that crying loosens. Toward morning she picked up the baby and walked to the well.

Carrying the baby to the well shows loving. Otherwise abandon it. Turn its face into the mud. Mothers who love their children take them along. It was probably a girl; there is some hope of forgiveness for boys.

"Don't tell anyone you had an aunt. Your father does not want to hear her name. She has never been born." I have believed that sex was unspeakable and words so strong and fathers so frail that "aunt" would do my father mysterious harm. I have thought that my family, having settled among immigrants who had also been their neighbors in the ancestral land, needed to clean their name, and a wrong word would incite the kinspeople even here. But there is more to this silence: they want me to participate in her punishment. And I have.

In the twenty years since I heard this story I have not asked for details nor said my aunt's name; I do not know it. People who can comfort the dead can also chase after them to hurt them further—a reverse ancestor worship. The real punishment was not the raid swiftly inflicted by the villagers, but the family's deliberately forgetting her. Her betrayal so maddened them, they saw to it that she would suffer forever, even after death. Always hungry, always needing, she would have to beg food from other ghosts, snatch and steal it from those whose living descendants give them gifts. She would have to fight the ghosts massed at crossroads for the buns a few thoughtful citizens leave to decoy her away from village and home so that the ancestral spirits could feast unharassed. At peace, they could act like gods, not ghosts, their descent lines providing them with paper suits and dresses, spirit money, paper houses, paper automobiles, chicken, meat, and rice into eternity—essences delivered up in smoke and flames, steam and incense rising from each rice bowl. In an attempt to make the Chinese care for people outside the family, Chairman Mao encourages us now to give our paper replicas to the spirits of outstanding soldiers and workers, no matter whose ancestors they may be. My aunt remains forever hungry. Goods are not distributed evenly among the dead.

My aunt haunts me—her ghost drawn to me because now, after fifty years of neglect, I alone devote pages of paper to her, though not origamied into houses and clothes. I do not think she always means me well. I am telling on her, and she was a spite suicide, drowning herself in the drinking water. The Chinese are always very frightened of the drowned one, whose weeping ghost, wet hair hanging and skin bloated, waits silently by the water to pull down a substitute.

For Practice

1. "No Name Woman" opens with the sentence, "'You must not tell anyone,' my mother said, 'what I am about to tell you.'" For what reasons might Kingston have begun her essay this way? Why might she have chosen to devote the first nine paragraphs of her essay to quoting from her mother? Do you find the opening to "No Name Woman" to be effective? Why or why not?

2. What parts of the story that Kingston relates appear to be "fact" in your view? What parts appear to be "fiction"? How and why do you make those distinctions?

3. Kingston's aunt chooses to drown herself and her child in the family well. Why does Kingston imagine the child to have been a girl? How does Kingston's identification of the child's gender as female affect your understanding about the aunt's decision to kill herself as well as the child?

4. Kingston has said about the narrator's voice in her autobiographical writing that "'I' am nothing but who 'I' am in relation to other people." What sense can you make of this statement? Use the concepts of implied author and *ethos* that you learned in Chapters 1 and 2 as a way of discussing Kingston's belief about the narrator's voice.

5. After reading "No Name Woman," what is your attitude toward the anonymous aunt? Toward her family? Toward Chinese and American societies? Why? What do you believe is Kingston's attitude toward each of the above? What evidence from the text leads you to these conclusions?

The Yellow Wallpaper

Charlotte Perkins Gilman

Charlotte Perkins Gilman (1860–1935), a prolific author of both fiction and non-fiction, was considered a leading American feminist intellectual at the turn of the century. Having undergone Dr. S. Weir Mitchell's famous "rest cure" in 1887 (very similar to the treatment undergone by the narrator of this story), Gilman wrote "The Yellow Wallpaper" in part as an attempt to effect change in Mitchell's methods. After Gilman tried unsuccessfully for two years to find a publisher, the story finally appeared in 1892 in New England Magazine. *"The Yellow Wallpaper" found early acclaim as a horror story as critics misunderstood Gilman's more practical and realistic goals.*

Since the Feminist Press *reissued it in 1983, "The Yellow Wallpaper" has been reread as a key feminist text, which thematizes the conflict between a woman's private life and career, the struggle for women to maintain autonomy and self-expression within domestic life, and the entrapment of women—both literal and figurative—within certain social systems. Some critics have discussed "The Yellow Wallpaper" as a version of the gothic short story, while others have suggested that it is a semi-autobiographical, intimate account of a breakdown. Still others have approached the story through Gilman's own unhappy childhood in which her father abandoned his family, while her mother, resistant to displaying physical or verbal affection, forbade her daughter from having close friends.*

It is very seldom that mere ordinary people like John and myself secure ancestral halls for the summer.

A colonial mansion, a hereditary estate, I would say a haunted house and reach the height of romantic felicity—but that would be asking too much of fate!

Still I will proudly declare that there is something queer about it.

Else, why should it be let so cheaply? And why have stood so long untenanted?

John laughs at me, of course, but one expects that.

John is practical in the extreme. He has no patience with faith, an intense horror of superstition, and he scoffs openly at any talk of things not to be felt and seen and put down in figures.

John is a physician, and *perhaps*—(I would not say it to a living soul, of course, but this is dead paper and a great relief to my mind)—*perhaps* that is one reason I do not get well faster.

You see, he does not believe I am sick! And what can one do?

If a physician of high standing, and one's own husband, assures friends and relatives that there is really nothing the matter with one but temporary nervous depression—a slight hysterical tendency—what is one to do?

My brother is also a physician, and also of high standing, and he says the same thing.

So I take phosphates or phosphites—whichever it is—and tonics, and air and exercise, and journeys, and am absolutely forbidden to "work" until I am well again.

Personally, I disagree with their ideas.

Personally, I believe that congenial work, with excitement and change, would do me good.

But what is one to do?

I did write for a while in spite of them; but it *does* exhaust me a good deal—having to be so sly about it, or else meet with heavy opposition.

I sometimes fancy that in my condition, if I had less opposition and more society and stimulus—but John says the very worst thing I can do is to think about my condition, and I confess it always makes me feel bad.

So I will let it alone and talk about the house.

The most beautiful place! It is quite alone, standing well back from the road, quite three miles from the village. It makes me think of English places that you read about, for there are hedges and walls and gates that lock, and lots of separate little houses for the gardeners and people.

There is a *delicious* garden! I never saw such a garden—large and shady, full of box-bordered paths, and lined with long grape-covered arbors with seats under them.

There were greenhouses, but they are all broken now.

There was some legal trouble, I believe, something about the heirs and co-heirs; anyhow, the place has been empty for years.

That spoils my ghostliness, I am afraid, but I don't care—there is something strange about the house—I can feel it.

I even said so to John one moonlight evening, but he said what I felt was a draught, and shut the window.

I get unreasonably angry with John sometimes. I'm sure I never used to be so sensitive. I think it is due to this nervous condition.

But John says if I feel so, I shall neglect proper self-control; so I take pains to control myself—before him, at least, and that makes me very tired.

I don't like our room a bit. I wanted one downstairs that opened onto the piazza and had roses all over the window, and such pretty old-fashioned chintz hangings! But John would not hear of it.

He said there was only one window and not room for two beds, and no near room for him if he took another.

He is very careful and loving, and hardly lets me stir without special direction.

I have a schedule prescription for each hour in the day; he takes all care from me, and so I feel basely ungrateful not to value it more.

He said we came here solely on my account, that I was to have perfect rest and all the air I could get. "Your exercise depends on your strength, my dear," said he, "and your food somewhat on your appetite; but air you can absorb all the time." So we took the nursery at the top of the house.

It is a big, airy room, the whole floor nearly, with windows that look all ways, and air and sunshine galore. It was nursery first, and then playroom and gymnasium, I should judge, for the windows are barred for little children, and there are rings and things in the walls.

The paint and paper look as if a boys' school had used it. It is stripped off—the paper—in great patches all around the head of my bed, about as far as I can reach, and in a great place of the other side of the room low down. I never saw a worse paper in my life. One of those sprawling, flamboyant patterns committing every artistic sin.

It is dull enough to confuse the eye in following, pronounced enough constantly to irritate and provoke study, and when you follow the lame uncertain curves for a little distance they suddenly commit suicide—plunge off at outrageous angles, destroy themselves in unheard-of contradictions.

The color is repellent, almost revolting: a smouldering unclean yellow, strangely faded by the slow-turning sunlight. It is a dull yet lurid orange in some places, a sickly sulphur tint in others.

No wonder the children hated it! I should hate it myself if I had to live in this room long.

✦   ✦   ✦

There comes John, and I must put this away—he hates to have me write a word.

We have been here two weeks, and I haven't felt like writing before, since that first day.

I am sitting by the window now, up in this atrocious nursery, and there is nothing to hinder my writing as much as I please, save lack of strength.

John is away all day, and even some nights when his cases are serious.

I am glad my case is not serious!

But these nervous troubles are dreadfully depressing.

John does not know how much I really suffer. He knows there is no reason to suffer, and that satisfies him.

Of course it is only nervousness. It does weigh on me so not to do my duty in any way!

I mean to be such a help to John, such a real rest and comfort, and here I am a comparative burden already!

Nobody would believe what an effort it is to do what little I am able—to dress and entertain, and order things.

It is fortunate Mary is so good with the baby. Such a dear baby!

And yet I *cannot* be with him, it makes me so nervous.

I suppose John never was nervous in his life. He laughs at me so about this wallpaper!

At first he meant to repaper the room, but afterward he said that I was letting it get the better of me, and that nothing was worse for a nervous patient than to give way to such fancies.

He said that after the wallpaper was changed it would be the heavy bedstead, and then the barred windows, and then the gate at the head of the stairs, and so on.

"You know the place is doing you good," he said, "and really, dear, I don't care to renovate the house just for three months' rental."

"Then do let us go downstairs," I said. "There are such pretty rooms there."

Then he took me in his arms and called me a blessed little goose, and said he would go down cellar, if I wished, and have it whitewashed into the bargain.

But he is right enough about the beds and windows and things.

It is as airy and comfortable a room as anyone need wish, and, of course, I would not be so silly as to make him uncomfortable just for a whim.

I'm really getting quite fond of the big room, all but that horrid paper.

Out of one window I can see the garden—those mysterious deep-shaded arbors, the riotous old-fashioned flowers, and bushes and gnarly trees.

Out of another I get a lovely view of the bay and a little private wharf belonging to the estate. There is a beautiful shaded lane that runs down there from the house. I always fancy I see people walking in these numerous paths and arbors, but John has cautioned me not to give way to fancy in the least. He says that with my imaginative power and habit of story-making, a nervous weakness like mine is sure to lead to all manner of excited fancies, and that I ought to use my will and good sense to check the tendency. So I try.

I think sometimes that if I were only well enough to write a little it would relieve the press of ideas and rest me.

But I find I get pretty tired when I try.

It is so discouraging not to have any advice and companionship about my work. When I get really well, John says he will ask Cousin Henry and Julia down for a long visit; but he says he would as soon put fireworks in my pillow-case as to let me have those stimulating people about now.

I wish I could get well faster.

But I must not think about that. This paper looks to me as if it *knew* what a vicious influence it had!

There is a recurrent spot where the pattern lolls like a broken neck and two bulbous eyes stare at you upside down.

I get positively angry with the impertinence of it and the everlastingness. Up and down and sideways they crawl, and those absurd unblinking eyes are everywhere. There is one place where two breadths didn't match, and the eyes go all up and down the line, one a little higher than the other.

I never saw so much expression in an inanimate thing before, and we all know how much expression they have! I used to lie awake as a child and get more entertainment and terror out of blank walls and plain furniture than most children could find in a toy-store.

I remember what a kindly wink the knobs of our big old bureau used to have, and there was one chair that always seemed like a strong friend.

I used to feel that if any of the other things looked too fierce I could always hop into that chair and be safe.

The furniture in this room is no worse than inharmonious, however, for we have had to bring it all from downstairs. I suppose when this was used as a playroom they had to take the nursery things out, and no wonder! I never saw such ravages as the children have made here.

The wallpaper, as I said before, is torn off in spots, and it sticketh closer than a brother—they must have had perseverance as well as hatred.

Then the floor is scratched and gouged and splintered, the plaster itself is dug out here and there, and this great heavy bed, which is all we found in the room, looks as if it had been through the wars.

But I don't mind it a bit—only the paper.

There comes John's sister. Such a dear girl as she is, and so careful of me! I must not let her find me writing.

She is a perfect and enthusiastic housekeeper, and hopes for no better profession. I verily believe she thinks it is the writing which made me sick!

But I can write when she is out, and see her a long way off from these windows.

There is one that commands the road, a lovely shaded winding road, and one that just looks off over the country. A lovely country, too, full of great elms and velvet meadows.

This wallpaper has a kind of sub-pattern in a different shade, a particularly irritating one, for you can only see it in certain lights, and not clearly then.

But in the places where it isn't faded and where the sun is just so—I can see a strange, provoking, formless sort of figure that seems to skulk about behind that silly and conspicuous front design.

There's sister on the stairs!

→ → →

Well, the Fourth of July is over! The people are all gone, and I am tired out. John thought it might do me good to see a little company, so we just had Mother and Nellie and the children down for a week.

Of course I didn't do a thing. Jennie sees to everything now.

But it tired me all the same.

John says if I don't pick up faster he shall send me to Weir Mitchell in the fall.

But I don't want to go there at all. I had a friend who was in his hands once, and she says he is just like John and my brother, only more so!

Besides, it is such an undertaking to go so far.

I don't feel as if it was worthwhile to turn my hand over for anything, and I'm getting dreadfully fretful and querulous.

I cry at nothing, and cry most of the time.

Of course I don't when John is here, or anybody else, but when I am alone.

And I am alone a good deal just now. John is kept in town very often by serious cases, and Jennie is good and lets me alone when I want her to.

So I walk a little in the garden or down that lovely lane, sit on the porch under the roses, and lie down up here a good deal.

I'm getting really fond of the room in spite of the wallpaper. Perhaps *because* of the wallpaper.

It dwells in my mind so!

I lie here on this great immovable bed—it is nailed down, I believe—and follow that pattern about by the hour. It is as good as gymnastics, I assure you. I start, we'll say, at the bottom, down in the corner over there where it has not been touched, and I determine for the thousandth time that I *will* follow that pointless pattern to some sort of conclusion.

I know a little of the principle of design, and I know this thing was not arranged on any laws of radiation, or alternation, or repetition, or symmetry, or anything else that I ever heard of.

It is repeated, of course, by the breadths, but not otherwise.

Looked at in one way, each breadth stands alone; the bloated curves and flourishes—a kind of "debased Romanesque" with delirium tremens—go waddling up and down in isolated columns of fatuity.

But, on the other hand, they connect diagonally, and the sprawling outlines run off in great slanting waves of optic horror, like a lot of wallowing sea-weeds in full chase.

The whole thing goes horizontally, too, at least it seems so, and I exhaust myself trying to distinguish the order of its going in that direction.

They have used a horizontal breadth for a frieze, and that adds wonderfully to the confusion.

There is one end of the room where it is almost intact, and there, when the crosslights fade and the low sun shines directly upon it, I can almost fancy radiation after all—the interminable grotesque seems to form around a common center and rush off in headlong plunges of equal distraction.

It makes me tired to follow it. I will take a nap, I guess.

❖   ❖   ❖

I don't know why I should write this.

I don't want to.

I don't feel able.

And I know John would think it absurd. But I *must* say what I feel and think in some way—it is such a relief!

But the effort is getting to be greater than the relief.

Half of the time now I am awfully lazy, and lie down ever so much.

John says I mustn't lose my strength, and has me take cod liver oil and lots of tonics and things, to say nothing of the ale and wine and rare meat.

Dear John!! He loves me very dearly, and hates to have me sick. I tried to have a real earnest reasonable talk with him the other day, and tell him how I wish he would let me go and make a visit to Cousin Henry and Julia.

But he said I wasn't able to go, nor able to stand it after I got there; and I did not make out a very good case for myself, for I was crying before I had finished.

It is getting to be a great effort for me to think straight. Just this nervous weakness, I suppose.

And dear John gathered me up in his arms, and just carried me upstairs and laid me on the bed, and sat by me and read to me till it tired my head.

He said I was his darling and his comfort and all he had, and that I must take care of myself for his sake, and keep well.

He said not one but myself can help me out of it, that I must use my will and self-control and not let any silly fancies run away with me.

There's one comfort—the baby is well and happy, and does not have to occupy this nursery with the horrid wallpaper.

If we had not used it, that blessed child would have! What a fortunate escape! Why, I wouldn't have a child of mine, an impressionable little thing, live in such a room for worlds.

I never thought of it before, but it is lucky that John kept me here after all; I can stand it so much easier than a baby, you see.

Of course I never mention it to them any more—I am too wise—but I keep watch for it all the same.

There are things in that paper that nobody knows about but me, or ever will.

Behind that outside pattern the dim shapes get clearer every day.

It is always the same shape, only very numerous.

And it is like a woman stooping down and creeping about behind that pattern. I don't like it a bit. I wonder—I begin to think—I wish John would take me away from here!

✦   ✦   ✦

It is so hard to talk with John about my case, because he is so wise, and because he loves me so.

But I tried it last night.

It was moonlight. The moon shines in all around just as the sun does.

I hate to see it sometimes, it creeps so slowly, and always comes in by one window or another.

John was asleep and I hated to waken him, so I kept still and watched the moonlight on that undulating wallpaper till I felt creepy.

The faint figure behind seemed to shake the pattern, just as if she wanted to get out.

I got up softly and went to feel and see if the paper *did* move, and when I came back John was awake.

"What is it, little girl?" he said. "Don't go walking about like that—you'll get cold."

I thought it was a good time to talk, so I told him that I really was not gaining here, and that I wished he would take me away.

"Why, darling!" said he. "Our lease will be up in three weeks, and I can't see how to leave before.

"The repairs are not done at home, and I cannot possibly leave town just now. Of course, if you were in any danger, I could and would, but you really are better, dear, whether you can see it or not. I am a doctor, dear, and I know. You are gaining flesh and color, your appetite is better, I feel really much easier about you."

"I don't weigh a bit more," said I, "nor as much; and my appetite may be better in the evening when you are here but it is worse in the morning when you are away!"

"Bless your little heart!" said he with a big hug. "She shall be as sick as she pleases! But now let's improve the shining hours by going to sleep, and talk about it in the morning!"

"And you won't go away?" I asked gloomily.

"Why, how can I, dear? It is only three weeks more and then we will take a nice little trip for a few days while Jennie is getting the house ready. Really, dear, you are better!"

"Better in body perhaps—" I began, and stopped short, for he sat up straight and looked at me with such a stern, reproachful look that I could not say another word.

"My darling," said he, "I beg of you, for my sake and for our child's sake, as well as for your own, that you will never for one instant let that idea enter your mind! There is nothing so dangerous, so fascinating, to a temperament like yours. It is a false and foolish fancy. Can you not trust me as a physician when I tell you so?"

So of course I said no more on that score, and we went to sleep before long. He thought I was asleep first, but I wasn't, and lay there for hours trying to decide whether that front pattern and the back pattern really did move together or separately.

✦   ✦   ✦

On a pattern like this, by daylight, there is a lack of sequence, a defiance of law, that is a constant irritant to a normal mind.

The color is hideous enough, and unreliable enough, and infuriating enough, but the pattern is torturing.

You think you have mastered it, but just as you get well under way in following, it turns a back-somersault and there you are. It slaps you in the face, knocks you down, and tramples upon you. It is like a bad dream.

The outside pattern is a florid arabesque, reminding one of a fungus. If you can imagine a toadstool in joints, an interminable string of toadstools, budding and sprouting in endless convolutions—why, that is something like it.

That is, sometimes!

There is one marked peculiarity about this paper, a thing nobody seems to notice but myself, and that is that it changes as the light changes.

When the sun shoots in through the east window—I always watch for that first long, straight ray—it changes so quickly that I never can quite believe it.

That is why I watch it always.

By moonlight—the moon shines in all night when there is a moon—I wouldn't know it was the same paper.

At night in any kind of light, in twilight, candlelight, lamplight, and worst of all by moonlight, it becomes bars! The outside pattern, I mean, and the woman behind it is as plain as can be.

I didn't realize for a long time what the thing was that showed behind, that dim sub-pattern, but now I am quite sure it is a woman.

By daylight she is subdued, quiet. I fancy it is the pattern that keeps her so still. It is so puzzling. It keeps me quiet by the hour.

I lie down ever so much now. John says it is good for me, and to sleep all I can.

Indeed he started the habit of making me lie down for an hour after each meal.

It is a very bad habit, I am convinced, for you see, I don't sleep.

And that cultivates deceit, for I don't tell them I'm awake—oh, no!

The fact is I am getting a little afraid of John.

He seems very queer sometimes, and even Jennie has an inexplicable look.

It strikes me occasionally, just as a scientific hypothesis, that perhaps it is the paper!

I have watched John when he did not know I was looking, and come into the room suddenly on the most innocent excuses, and I've caught him several times *looking at the paper!* And Jennie too. I caught Jennie with her hand on it once.

She didn't know I was in the room, and when I asked her in a quiet, a very quiet voice, with the most restrained manner possible, what she was doing with the paper—she turned around as if she had been caught stealing, and looked quite angry—asked me why I should frighten her so!

Then she said that the paper stained everything it touched, that she had found yellow smooches on all my clothes and John's and she wished we would be more careful!

Did not that sound innocent? But I know she was studying the pattern, and I am determined that nobody shall find it out but myself!

→ → →

Life is much more exciting now than it used to be. You see, I have something more to expect, to look forward to, to watch. I really do eat better, and I am more quiet than I was.

John is so pleased to see me improve! He laughed a little the other day, and said I seemed to be flourishing in spite of my wallpaper.

I turned it off with a laugh. I had no intention of telling him it was *because* of the wallpaper—he would make fun of me. He might even want to take me away.

I don't want to leave now until I have found it out. There is a week more, and I think that will be enough.

✦ ✦ ✦

I'm feeling so much better!

I don't sleep much at night, for it is so interesting to watch developments; but I sleep a good deal during the daytime.

In the daytime it is tiresome and perplexing.

There are always new shoots on the fungus, and new shades of yellow all over it. I cannot keep count of them, though I have tried conscientiously.

It is the strangest yellow, that wallpaper! It makes me think of all the yellow things I ever saw—not beautiful ones like buttercups, but old, foul, bad yellow things.

But there is something else about that paper—the smell! I noticed it the moment we came into the room, but with so much air and sun it was not bad. Now we have had a week of fog and rain, and whether the windows are open or not, the smell is here.

It creeps all over the house.

I find it hovering in the dining-room, skulking in the parlor, hiding in the hall, lying in wait for me on the stairs.

It gets into my hair.

Even when I go to ride, if I turn my head suddenly and surprise it—there is that smell!

Such a peculiar odor, too! I have spent hours in trying to analyze it, to find what it smelled like.

It is not bad—at first—and very gentle, but quite the subtlest, most enduring odor I ever met.

In this damp weather it is awful. I wake up in the night and find it hanging over me.

It used to disturb me at first. I thought seriously of burning the house—to reach the smell.

But now I am used to it. The only thing I can think of that it is like is the *color* of the paper! A yellow smell.

There is a very funny mark on this wall, low down, near the mopboard. A streak that runs round the room. It goes behind every piece of furniture, except the bed, a long, straight, even *smooch*, as if it had been rubbed over and over.

I wonder how it was done and who did it, and what they did it for. Round and round and round—round and round and round—it makes me dizzy!

✦ ✦ ✦

I really have discovered something at last.

Through watching so much at night, when it changes so, I have finally found out.

The front pattern *does* move—and no wonder! The woman behind shakes it!

Sometimes I think there are a great many women behind, and sometimes only one, and she crawls around fast, and her crawling shakes it all over.

Then in the very bright spots she keeps still, and in the very shady spots she just takes hold of the bars and shakes them hard.

And she is all the time trying to climb through. But nobody could climb through that pattern—it strangles so; I think that is why it has so many heads.

They get through, and then the pattern strangles them off and turns them upside down, and makes their eyes white!

If those heads were covered or taken off it would not be half so bad.

✦ ✦ ✦

I think that woman gets out in the daytime!

And I'll tell you why—privately—I've seen her!

I can see her out of every one of my windows!

It is the same woman, I know, for she is always creeping, and most women do not creep by daylight.

I see her in that long shaded lane, creeping up and down. I see her in those dark grape arbors, creeping all around the garden.

I see her on that long road under the trees, creeping along, and when a carriage comes she hides under the blackberry vines.

I don't blame her a bit. It must be very humiliating to be caught creeping by daylight!

I always lock the door when I creep by daylight. I can't do it at night, for I know John would suspect something at once.

And John is so queer now that I don't want to irritate him. I wish he would take another room! Besides, I don't want anybody to get that woman out at night but myself.

I often wonder if I could see her out of all the windows at once.

But, turn as fast as I can, I can only see out of one at one time.

And though I always see her, she *may* be able to creep faster than I can turn! I have watched her sometimes away off in the open country, creeping as fast as a cloud shadow in the wind.

If only the top pattern could be gotten off from the under one! I mean to try it, little by little.

✦   ✦   ✦

I have found another funny thing, but I shan't tell it this time! It does not do to trust people too much.

There are only two more days to get this paper off, and I believe John is beginning to notice. I don't like the look in his eyes.

And I heard him ask Jennie a lot of professional questions about me. She had a very good report to give.

She said I slept a good deal in the daytime.

John knows I don't sleep very well at night, for all I'm so quiet!

He asked me all sorts of questions, too, and pretended to be very loving and kind.

As if I couldn't see through him!

Still, I don't wonder he acts so, sleeping under this paper for three months.

It only interests me, but I feel sure John and Jennie are affected by it.

✦   ✦   ✦

Hurrah! This is the last day, but it is enough. John is to stay in town over night, and won't be out until this evening.

Jennie wanted to sleep with me—the sly thing; but I told her I should undoubtedly rest better for a night all alone.

That was clever, for really I wasn't alone a bit! As soon as it was moonlight and that poor thing began to crawl and shake the pattern, I got up and ran to help her.

I pulled and she shook, I shook and she pulled, and before morning we had peeled off yards of that paper.

A strip about as high as my head and half around the room.

And then when the sun came and that awful pattern began to laugh at me, I declared I would finish it today!

We are going away tomorrow, and they are moving all my furniture down again to leave things as they were before.

Jennie looked at the wall in amazement, but I told her merrily that I did it out of pure spite at the vicious thing.

She laughed and said she wouldn't mind doing it herself, but I must not get tired.

How she betrayed herself that time!

But I am here, and no person touches this paper but Me—not *alive!*

She tried to get me out of the room—it was too patent! But I said it was so quiet and empty and clean now that I believed I would lie down again and sleep all I could; and not to wake me even for dinner—I would call when I woke.

So now she is gone, and the servants are gone, and the things are gone, and there is nothing left but that great bedstead nailed down, with the canvas mattress we found on it.

We shall sleep downstairs tonight, and take the boat home tomorrow.

I quite enjoy the room, now it is bare again.

How those children did tear about here!

This bedstead is fairly gnawed!

But I must get to work.

I have locked the door and thrown the key down into the front path.

I don't want to go out, and I don't want to have anybody come in, till John comes.

I want to astonish him.

I've got a rope up here that even Jennie did not find. If that woman does get out, and tries to get away, I can tie her!

But I forgot I could not reach far without anything to stand on!

This bed will *not* move!

I tried to lift and push it until I was lame, and then I got so angry I bit off a little piece at one corner—but it hurt my teeth.

Then I peeled off all the paper I could reach standing on the floor. It sticks horribly and the pattern just enjoys it! All those strangled heads and bulbous eyes and waddling fungus growths just shriek with derision!

I am getting angry enough to do something desperate. To jump out of the window would be admirable exercise, but the bars are too strong even to try.

Besides I wouldn't do it. Of course not. I know well enough that a step like that is improper and might be misconstrued.

I don't like to *look* out the windows even—there are so many of those creeping women, and they creep so fast.

I wonder if they all come out of that wallpaper as I did?

But I am securely fastened now by my well-hidden rope—you don't get *me* out in the road there!

I suppose I shall have to get back behind the pattern when it comes night, and that is hard!

It is so pleasant to be out in this great room and creep around as I please!

I don't want to go outside. I won't even if Jennie asks me to.

For outside you have to creep on the ground, and everything is green instead of yellow.

But here I can creep smoothly on the floor, and my shoulder just fits in that long smooch around the wall, so I cannot lose my way.

Why, there's John at the door!

It is no use, young man, you can't open it.

How he does call and pound!

Now he's crying to Jennie for an axe.

It would be a shame to break down that beautiful door!

"John, dear!" said I in the gentlest voice. "The key is down by the front steps, under a plantain leaf!"

That silenced him for a few moments.

Then he said—very quietly indeed, "Open the door, my darling!"

"I can't," said I. "The key is down by the front door under a plantain leaf!"

And then I said it again, several times, very gently and slowly, and said it so often that he had to go and see, and he got it of course, and came in. He stopped short by the door.

"What is the matter?" he cried. "For God's sake, what are you doing!"

I kept on creeping just the same, but I looked at him over my shoulder.

"I've got out at last," said I, "in spite of you and Jane[.] And I've pulled off most of the paper, so you can't put me back!"

Now why should that man have fainted? But he did, and right across my path by the wall, so that I had to creep over him every time!

Questions

1. Gothic is a literary style characterized by the use of the fantastic or macabre and may include episodes of irrational violence or a desolate or isolate setting. In what ways is this a gothic tale? Does seeing this short story as "gothic" affect your interpretation of it as a feminist text?

2. What clues did you get about the narrator's changing state of mind throughout the story? Is their any moment that seems to you to signal the narrator's break with reality?

3. Think about Gilman's use of a first person narrator for this story. How does this choice help determine the story's effect? What is gained by having the story narrated from the perspective of a woman as she becomes increasingly ill? How would the story be different if it were narrated from the perspective of John? Jennie? An omniscient third person narrator?

4. Examine closely and discuss the many symbols and images in the story: the pattern of the wallpaper itself; the woman in the wallpaper; the arbors and gardens outside; etc. What comparisons can you draw among the woman in the wallpaper, the narrator, and/or women in general? What significance do you find in the fact that the narrator and her husband are sleeping in the home's nursery? Or that the nursery's windows are covered with bars and that the bed is nailed down?

5. When this story appeared in 1892, ideas about illness, both mental and physical, were very different from what they are today. How do you think our culture, specifically current medical practitioners would view the condition of the narrator in this story? How do these different views make our understanding of this story different from that of its original audience?

My Mistress' Eyes Are Nothing Like the Sun (Sonnet 130)

William Shakespeare

William Shakespeare (1564–1616), often cited as the greatest writer in the English language, was born in Stratford-upon-Avon, England, to a middle-class family. Little is known about his early life except that he received a basic education at the local grammar school, was obliged to marry at 18, and eventually headed for London where he achieved fame as an actor and playwright during the 1590s. After twenty years as a dramatist, he retired to Stratford.

Shakespeare's sonnets have been the subject of continued speculation and critical debate since they were first published in 1609. The sonnet sequence consists of 154 poems, divided into three distinct sections. The first group (1–17) addresses a handsome young man with advice to procreate so that the world will not lose his beautiful image. In the second section (18–126), the poet offers to the young man a kind of immortality through his poetry. Much of the critical debate has centered around the identity of the young man and the exact nature of his relationship with the poet. The poems of the final segment (127–154) are addressed to the poet's "dark" mistress, whose identity is also unknown. In Sonnet 130, the narrator uses the unusual method of defining his mistress by contrasting her appearance with that of the Renaissance ideal beauty thereby challenging conventional and contemporary stereotypes. His lover is unique and precious to him precisely because of her unexceptional and unrefined features.

Sonnet 130

My mistress' eyes are nothing like the sun;
Coral is far more red than her lips' red:
If snow be white, why then her breasts are dun;
If hairs be wires, black wires grow on her head.
I have seen roses damask'd, red and white,   5
But no such roses see I in her cheeks;
And in some perfumes is there more delight

Than in the breath that from my mistress reeks.
I love to hear her speak, yet well I know
That music hath a far more pleasing sound: 10
I grant I never saw a goddess go;
My mistress, when she walks, treads on the ground:
  And yet, by heaven, I think my love as rare
  As any she belied with false compare.

For Practice

1. This sonnet satirizes the ideal of beauty that is conventionally found in Renaissance love poetry. Working backward from Shakespeare's description, what sort of images do you think poets used to praise their lovers? What do these images reveal about how women were valued in Renaissance culture?

2. Given sorts of images that you identified in question one, what do you think was the Renaissance vision of the "ideal" woman? How does this courtly love "ideal" compare with today's notions of the "ideal" woman?

3. This poem is an example of the English or Shakespearean sonnet. Describe the rhyme scheme. How many stanzas does the poem have? (You can refer to the Glossary for precise definitions of these terms.) How does Shakespeare use these formal aspects as part of his argument?

4. What do you think is the message of Shakespeare's poem? Is it meant to criticize his mistress or to praise her? Does he intend it only as a poem to his mistress, or is it also a comment on the love poems of his contemporary poets? Give reasons for your answer.

5. How does this Shakespearean sonnet change your own perspectives on relationships?

You Must Know That I Do Not Love and That I Love You
(Sonnet XLIV)

Pablo Neruda

Pablo Neruda (1904–1973) born in Chile as Ricardo Eliezar Neftali Reyes y Basoalto, is widely respected as one of the most influential Latin American poets of the twentieth century. A prolific writer, Neruda published fifty-seven volumes of poetry as well as various essays, short stories, a drama, and a collection of his memoirs. He received the Nobel Prize for literature in 1971. In addition to his accomplishments as a writer, Neruda was active in leftist Chilean politics, serving at different points in his political career as a diplomat in Mexico, a member of the Chilean Senate, an ambassador to France, and a nominee for the Chilean presidency in 1970. The old poet in the recent academy-award winning film, Il Postino, *was a fictionalized version of Pablo Neruda.*

Although much of his poetry is political in nature, Neruda is perhaps best known as a crafter of powerful love poetry. His Cien Sonetos de Amor (One Hundred Love Sonnets), *which includes the following poem, appeared in 1959. The sequence of poems was inspired by and dedicated to Matilde Urrutia, who was to become Neruda's second wife in 1966. Like many of the* Cien Sonetos de Amor, *this poem uses language creatively to express the vastness of the poet's love in seemingly understated ways. Neruda celebrates the beauty of a love that he suggests could never exist without its rough edges.*

You must know that I do not love *and* that I love you,
because everything alive has its two sides;
a word is one wing of the silence,
fire has its cold half.

I love you in order to begin to love you,   5
to start infinity again

and never to stop loving you:
that's why I do not love you yet.

I love you, and I do not love you, as if I held
keys in my hand: to a future of joy—   10
a wretched, muddled fate—

My love has two lives, in order to love you:
that's why I love you when I do not love you,
and also why I love you when I do.

For Practice

1. What was your initial reaction upon reading the first line of the poem? Upon reading the entire poem? Read the poem again. How does the first line strike you now?

2. The speaker uses several oppositions to describe love in this poem. What are they? What does this use of opposition say about the nature of romantic love?

3. Review the characteristics of a sonnet in the Glossary of this book. The English version of the poem does not exhibit the strict control of rhyme that we expect, although the Spanish version does. What does this tell you about the limitations of translation? What do you think might be lost in the translation of this poem? How does this affect the argument?

4. State the message of the poem as an argument by writing a one-sentence paraphrase (prose, not poetry) of each stanza. Does your paraphrase reveal anything new about the speaker's particular experience of love as described in the sonnet? How does the emotional tone of the poem affect the argument?

5. In what ways, if any, has your own attitude toward love been changed as a result of reading this poem?

Twenty-One Love Poems

Adrienne Rich

Adrienne Rich (b. 1929) is a native of Baltimore, Maryland, and graduated from Radcliffe College in 1951. Her first volume of poetry, A Change of World, *was selected for publication by W. H. Auden in the Yale Younger Poets series. A prolific writer of poetry and nonfiction, Rich received the 1974 National Book Award for her collection* Diving into the Wreck. *In a statement written with Audre Lorde and Alice Walker, she rejected the award as an individual, but accepted it in the name of all women. Since 1970, Rich has identified herself as a lesbian and has actively participated in the feminist movement.*

First published in a limited edition of 1000 books in 1976, Twenty-One Love Poems *was Rich's first explicit poetic treatment of a lesbian relationship. Rich adapts the structure and conventions of a traditional sonnet sequence to chronicle this relationship, which is not traditionally addressed in sonnets. These poems were later included as the central section of Rich's* The Dream of a Common Language: Poems 1974–1977.

I
Wherever in this city, screens flicker
with pornography, with science-fiction vampires,
victimized hirelings bending to the lash,
we also have to walk . . . if simply as we walk
through the rainsoaked garbage, the tabloid cruelties   5
of our own neighborhoods.
We need to grasp our lives inseparable
from those rancid dreams, that blurt of metal, those disgraces,
and the red begonia perilously flashing
from a tenement sill six stories high,   10
or the long-legged young girls playing ball
in the junior highschool playground.
No one has imagined us. We want to live like trees,
sycamores blazing through the sulfuric air,
dappled with scars, still exuberantly budding,   15
our animal passion rooted in the city.

II

I wake up in your bed. I know I have been dreaming.
Much earlier, the alarm broke us from each other,
you've been at your desk for hours. I know what I dreamed:
our friend the poet comes into my room
where I've been writing for days,   5
drafts, carbons, poems are scattered everywhere,
and I want to show her one poem
which is the poem of my life. But I hesitate,
and wake. You've kissed my hair
to wake me. *I dreamed you were a poem,*   10
I say, *a poem I wanted to show someone . . .*
and I laugh and fall dreaming again
of the desire to show you to everyone I love,
to move openly together
in the pull of gravity, which is not simple,   15
which carries the feathered grass a long way down the upbreathing air.

III

Since we're not young, weeks have to do time
for years of missing each other. Yet only this odd warp
in time tells me we're not young.
Did I ever walk the morning streets at twenty,
my limbs streaming with a purer joy?   5
did I lean from any window over the city
listening for the future
as I listen here with nerves tuned for your ring?
And you, you move toward me with the same tempo.
Your eyes are everlasting, the green spark   10
of the blue-eyed grass of early summer,
the green-blue wild cress washed by the spring.
At twenty, yes: we thought we'd live forever.
At forty-five, I want to know even our limits.
I touch you knowing we weren't born tomorrow,   15
and somehow, each of us will help the other live,
and somewhere, each of us must help the other die.

IV

I come home from you through the early light of spring
flashing off ordinary walls, the Pez Dorado,
the Discount Wares, the shoe-store . . . I'm lugging my sack
of groceries, I dash for the elevator
where a man, taut, elderly, carefully composed   5
lets the door almost close on me.—*For god's sake hold it!*
I croak at him.—*Hysterical,*—he breathes my way.
I let myself into the kitchen, unload my bundles,
make coffee, open the window, put on Nina Simone
singing *Here comes the sun . . .* I open the mail,   10
drinking delicious coffee, delicious music,

my body still both light and heavy with you. The mail
lets fall a Xerox of something written by a man
aged 27, a hostage, tortured in prison:
My genitals have been the object of such a sadistic display   15
they keep me constantly awake with the pain . . .
Do whatever you can to survive.
You know, I think that men love wars . . .
And my incurable anger, my unmendable wounds
break open further with tears, I am crying helplessly,   20
and they still control the world, and you are not in my arms.

V

This apartment full of books could crack open
to the thick jaws, the bulging eyes
of monsters, easily: Once open the books, you have to face
the underside of everything you've loved—
the rack and pincers held in readiness, the gag   5
even the best voices have had to mumble through,
the silence burying unwanted children—
women, deviants, witnesses—in desert sand.
Kenneth tells me he's been arranging his books
so he can look at Blake and Kafka while he types;   10
yes; and we still have to reckon with Swift
loathing the woman's flesh while praising her mind,
Goethe's dread of the Mothers, Claudel vilifying Gide,
and the ghosts—their hands clasped for centuries—
of artists dying in childbirth, wise-women charred at the stake,   15
centuries of books unwritten piled behind these shelves;
and we still have to stare into the absence
of men who would not, women who could not, speak
to our life—this still unexcavated hole
called civilization, this act of translation, this half-world.   20

VI

Your small hands, precisely equal to my own—
only the thumb is larger, longer—in these hands
I could trust the world, or in many hands
like these, handling power-tools or steering-wheel
or touching a human face . . . Such hands could turn   5
the unborn child rightways in the birth canal
or pilot the exploratory rescue-ship
through icebergs, or piece together
the fine, needle-like sherds of a great krater-cup
bearing on its sides   10
figures of esctatic women striding
to the sibyl's den or the Eleusinian cave—
such hands might carry out an unavoidable violence
with such restraint, with such a grasp

of the range and limits of violence   15
that violence ever after would be obsolete.

VII
What kind of beast would turn its life into words?
What atonement is this all about?
—and yet, writing words like these, I'm also living.
Is all this close to the wolverines' howled signals,
that modulated cantata of the wild?   5
or, when away from you I try to create you in words,
am I simply using you, like a river or a war?
And how have I used rivers, how have I used wars
to escape writing of the worst thing of all—
not the crimes of others, not even our own death,   10
but the failure to want our freedom passionately enough
so that blighted elms, sick rivers, massacres would seem
mere emblems of that desecration of ourselves?

VIII
I can see myself years back at Sunion,
hurting with an infected foot, Philoctetes
in woman's form, limping the long path,
lying on a headland over the dark sea,
looking down the red rocks to where a soundless curl   5
of white told me a wave had struck,
imagining the pull of that water from that height,
knowing deliberate suicide wasn't my métier,
yet all the time nursing, measuring that wound.
Well, that's finished. The woman who cherished   10
her suffering is dead. I am her descendant.
I love the scar-tissue she handed on to me,
but I want to go on from here with you
fighting the temptation to make a career of pain.

IX
Your silence today is a pond where drowned things live
I want to see raised dripping and brought into the sun.
It's not my own face I see there, but other faces,
even your face at another age.
Whatever's lost there is needed by both of us—   5
a watch of old gold, a water-blurred fever chart,
a key . . . Even the silt and pebbles of the bottom
deserve their glint of recognition. I fear this silence,
this inarticulate life. I'm waiting
for a wind that will gently open this sheeted water   10
for once, and show me what I can do
for you, who have often made the unnameable
nameable for others, even for me.

X

Your dog, tranquil and innocent, dozes through
our cries, our murmured dawn conspiracies
our telephone calls. She knows—what can she know?
If in my human arrogance I claim to read
her eyes, I find there only my own animal thoughts: 5
that creatures must find each other for bodily comfort,
that voices of the psyche drive through the flesh
further than the dense brain could have foretold,
that the planetary nights are growing cold for those
on the same journey, who want to touch   10
one creature-traveler clear to the end;
that without tenderness, we are in hell.

XI

Every peak is a crater. This is the law of volcanoes,
making them eternally and visibly female.
No height without depth, without a burning core,
though our straw soles shred on the hardened lava.
I want to travel with you to every sacred mountain   5
smoking within like the sibyl stooped over his tripod,
I want to reach for your hand as we scale the path,
to feel your arteries glowing in my clasp,
never failing to note the small, jewel-like flower
unfamiliar to us, nameless till we rename her,   10
that clings to the slowly altering rock—
that detail outside ourselves that brings us to ourselves,
was here before us, knew we would come, and sees beyond us.

XII

Sleeping, turning in turn like planets
rotating in their midnight meadow:
a touch is enough to let us know
we're not alone in the universe, even in sleep:
the dream-ghosts of two worlds   5
walking their ghost-towns, almost address each other.
I've wakened to your muttered words
spoken light—or dark-years away
as if my own voice had spoken.
But we have different voices, even in sleep,   10
and our bodies, so alike, are yet so different
and the past echoing through our bloodstreams
is freighted with different language, different meanings—
though in any chronicle of the world we share
it could be written with new meaning   15
we were two lovers of one gender,
we were two women of one generation.

XIII

The rules break like a thermometer,
quicksilver spills across the charted systems,
we're out in a country that has no language
no laws, we're chasing the raven and the wren
through gorges unexplored since dawn   5
whatever we do together is pure invention
the maps they gave us were out of date
by years . . . we're driving through the desert
wondering if the water will hold out
the hallucinations turn to simple villages   10
the music on the radio comes clear—
neither *Rosenkavalier* nor *Gotterdammerung*
but a woman's voice singing old songs
with new words, with a quiet bass, a flute
plucked and fingered by women outside the law.   15

XIV

It was your vision of the pilot
confirmed my vision of you: you said, *He keeps*
on steering headlong into the waves, on purpose
while we crouched in the open hatchway
vomiting into plastic bags   5
for three hours between St. Pierre and Miquelon.
I never felt closer to you.
In the close cabin where the honeymoon couples
huddled in each other's laps and arms
I put my hand on your thigh   10
to comfort both of us, your hand came over mine,
we stayed that way, suffering together
in our bodies, as if all suffering
were physical, we touched so in the presence
of strangers who knew nothing and cared less   15
vomiting their private pain
as if all suffering were physical.

(The Floating Poem, Unnumbered)

Whatever happens with us, your body
will haunt mine—tender, delicate
your lovemaking, like the half-curled frond
of the fiddlehead fern in forests
just washed by sun. Your traveled, generous thighs   5
between which my whole face has come and come—
the innocence and wisdom of the place my tongue has found there—
the live, insatiate dance of your nipples in my mouth—
your touch on me, firm, protective, searching
me out, your strong tongue and slender fingers   10
reaching where I had been waiting years for you
in my rose-wet cave—whatever happens, this is.

XV

If I lay on that beach with you
white, empty, pure green water warmed by the Gulf Stream
and lying on that beach we could not stay
because the wind drove fine sand against us
as if it were against us   5
if we tried to withstand it and we failed—
if we drove to another place
to sleep in each other's arms
and the beds were narrow like prisoners' cots
and we were tired and did not sleep together   10
and this was what we found, so this is what we did—
was the failure ours?
If I cling to circumstances I could feel
not responsible. Only she who says
she did not choose, is the loser in the end.   15

XVI

Across a city from you, I'm with you,
just as an August night
moony, inlet-warm, seabathed, I watched you sleep,
the scrubbed, sheenless wood of the dressing-table
cluttered with our brushes, books, vials in the moonlight—   5
or a salt-mist orchard, lying at your side
watching red sunset through the screendoor of the cabin,
G minor Mozart on the tape-recorder,
falling asleep to the music of the sea.
This island of Manhattan is wide enough   10
for both of us, and narrow:
I can hear your breath tonight, I know how your face
lies upturned, the halflight tracing
your generous, delicate mouth
where grief and laughter sleep together.   15

XVII

No one's fated or doomed to love anyone.
The accidents happen, we're not heroines,
they happen in our lives like car crashes,
books that change us, neighborhoods
we move into and come to love.   5
Tristan und Isolde is scarcely the story,
women at least should know the difference
between love and death. No poison cup,
no penance. Merely a notion that the tape-recorder
should have caught some ghost of us: that tape-recorder   10
not merely played but should have listened to us,
and could instruct those after us:
this we were, this is how we tried to love,

and these are the forces they had ranged against us,
and these are the forces we had ranged within us,   15
within us and against us, against us and within us.

XVIII

Rain on the West Side Highway,
red light at Riverside:
the more I live the more I think
two people together is a miracle.
You're telling the story of your life   5
for once, a tremor breaks the surface of your words.
The story of our lives becomes our lives.
Now you're in fugue across what some I'm sure
Victorian poet called the *salt estranging sea.*
Those are the words that come to mind.   10
I feel estrangement, yes. As I've felt dawn
pushing toward daybreak. Something: a cleft of light—?
Close between grief and anger, a space opens
where I am Adrienne alone. And growing colder.

XIX

Can it be growing colder when I begin
to touch myself again, adhesions pull away?
When slowly the naked face turns from staring backward
and looks into the present,
the eye of winter, city, anger, poverty, and death   5
and the lips part and say: *I mean to go on living?*
Am I speaking coldly when I tell you in a dream
or in this poem, *There are no miracles?*
(I told you from the first I wanted daily life,
this island of Manhattan was island enough for me.)   10
If I could let you know—
two women together is a work
nothing in civilization has made simple,
two people together is a work
heroic in its ordinariness,   15
the slow-picked, halting traverse of a pitch
where the fiercest attention becomes routine
—look at the faces of those who have chosen it.

XX

That conversation we were always on the edge
of having, runs on in my head,
at night the Hudson trembles in New Jersey light
polluted water yet reflecting even
sometimes the moon   5
and I discern a woman
I loved, drowning in secrets, fear wound round her throat

and choking her like hair. And this is she
with whom I tried to speak, whose hurt, expressive head
turning aside from pain, is dragged down deeper   10
where it cannot hear me,
and soon I shall know I was talking to my own soul.

XXI

The dark lintels, the blue and foreign stones
of the great round rippled by stone implements
the midsummer night light rising from beneath
the horizon—when I said "a cleft of light"
I meant this. And this is not Stonehenge   5
simply nor any place but the mind
casting back to where her solitude,
shared, could be chosen without loneliness,
not easily nor without pains to stake out
the circle, the heavy shadows, the great light.   10
I choose to be a figure in that light,
half-blotted by darkness, something moving
across that space, the color of stone
greeting the moon, yet more than stone:
a woman. I choose to walk here. And to draw this circle.   15

For Practice

1. The sonnet sequence is a literary tradition that flourished during the Renaissance and slowly became less common over the next couple of centuries. Typically, the poems in a sonnet sequence all address a common theme, and show some change in the treatment of that theme throughout. Why do you think Rich elected to address the theme of a lesbian relationship in such a traditional form?

2. What tone does the first poem set for the series as a whole? Why does Rich emphasize the coexistence of the poem's "we" and the "tabloid cruelties of our own neighborhoods?"

3. Examine Rich's use of pronouns in these poems, particularly the frequent references to "we" and "they." Compare the use of these pronouns in two or more of the poems (IV and XIII are particularly good choices). To whom does "they" refer? What about "we"? Does the pronoun reference change? Why do you think Rich has left these pronoun references ambiguous?

4. Notice that there are actually twenty-two poems here rather than twenty-one. Why is the "Floating Poem, Unnumbered" 'floating' and unnumbered? What does this suggest about the sentiments experssed in this poem and the relationship of these to the sentiments expressed in the other poems?

5. Throughout this poem cycle, Rich utilizes water imagery (see for example, poems IX, XV, XVIII, and XX). Analyze her use of these images, explaining the changing significance of water in these poems.

6. In poems II, V, and VII, Rich specifically addresses issues of writing and writers: the clash of the desire for privacy with the writer's need for self-expres-

sion; the violence that texts can commit or communicate; the immortality that writing can impart to a love affair. Does Rich resolve these different visions of the power of language, or does she leave them unresolved?

7. Identify the argument behind the sonnet sequence. How does this argument affect your own perspective?

Knoxville: Summer 1915

James Agee

James Agee (1909–1955) was born in Knoxville, Tennessee, and lived there until 1919 when his mother enrolled him in St. Andrew's, a boarding school near Sewanee, Tennessee. He again lived in Knoxville while he attended high school in 1924–25. Agee received his college education at Harvard. He worked primarily as a journalist, writing feature stories and film criticism, but also published poetry and fiction. His most famous works are Let Us Now Praise Famous Men, *a non-fiction work about cotton sharecroppers in Alabama during the Great Depression, and his novel,* A Death in the Family, *which received the Pulitzer Prize in 1957, two years after Agee's premature death from a heart attack.*

Agee's father was killed in an automobile accident in 1916 when the boy was six years old. A Death in the Family *chronicles this death and its effects on Agee and his family. This essay, which is usually reprinted as a prologue to the novel, was originally written during the winter of 1935–36 and was published in the* Partisan Review *in 1938. In this essay, Agee was attempting to come to terms, through his writing, with his Knoxville experiences and with the death of his father.*

We are talking now of summer evenings in Knoxville, Tennessee, in the time that I lived there so successfully disguised to myself as a child. It was a little bit mixed sort of block, fairly solidly lower middle class, with one or two juts apiece on either side of that. The houses corresponded: middle-sized gracefully fretted wood houses built in the late nineties and early nineteen hundreds, with small front and side and more spacious back yards, and trees in the yards, and porches. These were softwooded trees, poplars, tulip trees, cottonwoods. There were fences around one or two of the houses, but mainly the yards ran into each other with only now and then a low hedge that wasn't doing very well. There were few good friends among the grown people, and they were not poor enough for the other sort of intimate acquaintance, but everyone nodded and spoke, and even might talk short times, trivially, and at the two extremes of the general or the particular, and ordinarily next door neighbors talked quite a bit when they happened to run into each other, and never paid calls. The men were mostly small businessmen, one or two very modestly executives, one or two worked with their hands, most of them clerical, and most of them between thirty and forty-five.

But it is of these evenings, I speak.

Supper was at six and was over by half past. There was still daylight, shining soft-ly and with a tarnish, like the lining of a shell; and the carbon lamps lifted at the cor-ners were on in the light, and the locusts were started, and the fire flies were out, and a few frogs were flopping in the dewy grass, by the time the fathers and the children came out. The children ran out first hell bent and yelling those names by which they were known; then the fathers sank out leisurely in crossed suspenders, their collars removed and their necks looking tall and shy. The mothers stayed back in the kitchen washing and drying, putting things away, recrossing their traceless footsteps like the lifetime journeys of bees, measuring out the dry cocoa for breakfast. When they came out they had taken off their aprons and their skirts were dampened and they sat in rockers on their porches quietly.

It is not of the games children play in the evening that I want to speak now, it is of a contemporaneous atmosphere that has little to do with them: that of the fathers of families, each in his space of lawn, his shirt fishlike pale in the unnatural light and his face nearly anonymous, hosing their lawns. The hoses were attached at spiggots that stood out of the brick foundations of the houses. The nozzles were variously set but usually so there was a long sweet stream of spray, the nozzle wet in the hand, the water trickling the right forearm and the peeled-back cuff, and the water whishing out a long loose and low-curved cone, and so gentle a sound. First an insane noise of violence in the nozzle, then the still irregular sound of adjustment, then the smoothing into steadiness and a pitch as accurately tuned to the size and style of stream as any violin. So many qualities of sound out of one hose: so many choral differences out of those several hoses that were in earshot. Out of any one hose, the almost dead silence of the release, and the short still arch of the separate big drops, silent as a held breath, and the only noise the flattering noise on leaves and the slapped grass at the fall of each big drop. That, and the intense hiss with the intense stream; that, and that same intensity not growing less but growing more quiet and delicate with the turn of the nozzle, up to that extreme tender whisper when the water was just a wide bell of film. Chiefly, though, the hoses were set much alike, in a compromise between distance and ten-derness of spray (and quite surely a sense of art behind this compromise, and a quiet deep joy, too real to recognize itself), and the sounds therefore were pitched much alike; pointed by the snorting start of a new hose; decorated by some man playful with the nozzle; left empty, like God by the sparrow's fall, when any single one of them desists: and all, though near alike, of various pitch; and in this unison. These sweet pale streamings in the light lift out their pallors and their voices all together, mothers hushing their children, the hushing unnaturally prolonged, the men gentle and silent and each snail-like withdrawn into the quietude of what he singly is doing, the urina-tion of huge children stood loosely military against an invisible wall, and gentle happy and peaceful, tasting the mean goodness of their living like the last of their suppers in their mouths; while the locusts carry on this noise of hoses on their much higher and sharper key. The noise of the locust is dry, and it seems not to be rasped or vibrated but urged from him as if through a small orifice by a breath that can never give out. Also there is never one locust but an illusion of at least a thousand. The noise of each locust is pitched in some classic locust range out of which none of them varies more than two full tones: and yet you seem to hear each locust discrete from all the rest, and there is a long, slow, pulse in their noise, like the scarcely defined arch of a long and high set bridge. They are all around in every tree, so that the noise seems to come from nowhere and everywhere at once, from the whole shell heaven, shivering in your flesh and teasing your eardrums, the boldest of all the sounds of night. And yet it is habitual to summer nights, and is of the great order of noises, like the noises of the sea and of the blood her precocious grandchild, which you realize you are hearing only when you catch yourself listening. Meantime from low in the dark, just outside the swaying horizons of the hoses, conveying always grass in the damp of dew and its strong green-black smear of smell, the regular yet spaced noises of the crickets, each a sweet cold silver noise threenoted, like the slipping each time of three matched links of a small chain.

But the men by now, one by one, have silenced their hoses and drained and coiled them. Now only two, and now only one, is left, and you see only ghostlike shirt with the sleeve garters, and sober mystery of his mild face like the lifted face of large cattle enquiring of your presence in a pitchdark pool of meadow; and now he too is gone; and it has become that time of evening when people sit on their porches, rocking gently and talking gently and watching the street and the standing up into their sphere of possession of the trees, of birds hung havens, hangars. People go by; things go by. A horse, drawing a buggy, breaking his hollow iron music on the asphalt; a loud auto; a quiet auto; people in pairs, not in a hurry, scuffling, switching their weight of aestival body, talking casually, the taste hovering over them of vanilla, strawberry, pasteboard and starched milk, the image upon them of lovers and horsemen, squared with clowns in hueless amber. A street car raising its iron moan; stopping, belling and starting; stertorous; rousing and raising again its iron increasing moan and swimming its gold windows and straw seats on past and past and past, the bleak spark crackling and cursing above it like a small malignant spirit set to dog its tracks; the iron whine rises on rising speed; still risen, faints; halts; the faint stinging bell; rises again, still fainter; fainter, lifting, lifts, faints foregone: forgotten. Now is the night one blue dew.

Now is the night one blue dew, my father has drained, he has coiled the hose.

Low on the length of lawns, a frailing of fire who breathes.

Content, silver, like peeps of light, each cricket makes his comment over and over in the drowned grass.

A cold toad thumpily flounders.

Within the edges of damp shadows of side yards are hovering children nearly sick with joy of fear, who watch the unguarding of a telephone pole.

Around white carbon corner lamps bugs of all sizes are lifted elliptic, solar systems. Big hardshells bruise themselves, assailant: he is fallen on his back, legs squiggling.

Parents on porches: rock and rock: From damp strings morning glories: hang their ancient faces.

The dry and exalted noise of the locusts from all the air at once enchants my eardrums.

On the rough wet grass of the back yard my father and mother have spread quilts. We all lie there, my mother, my father, my uncle, my aunt, and I too am lying there. First we were sitting up, then one of us lay down, and then we all lay down, on our stomachs, or on our sides, or on our backs, and they have kept on talking. They are not talking much, and the talk is quiet, of nothing in particular, of nothing at all in particular, of nothing at all. The stars are wide and alive, they seem each like a smile of great sweetness, and they seem very near. All my people are larger bodies than mine, quiet, with voices gentle and meaningless like the voices of sleeping birds. One is an artist, he is living at home. One is a musician, she is living at home. One is my mother who is good to me. One is my father who is good to me. By some chance, here they are, all on this earth; and who shall ever tell the sorrow of being on this earth, lying, on quilts, on the grass, in a summer evening, among the sounds of the night. May God bless my people, my uncle, my aunt, my mother, my good father, oh, remember them kindly in their time of trouble; and in the hour of their taking away.

After a little I am taken in and put to bed. Sleep, soft smiling, draws me unto her: and those receive me, who quietly treat me, as one familiar and well-beloved in that home: but will not, oh, will not, not now, not ever; but will not ever tell me who I am.

For Practice

1. More than many writers, Agee blurs the boundaries between fiction and non-fiction and between poetry and prose. Point to some ways that he uses literary techniques in this essay. How does his use of these techniques challenge the distinctions we normally make between reality and fiction? Between autobiography and fiction?

2. Look at Agee's many descriptions of the sounds of his neighborhood at dusk: both sounds of nature—frogs, locusts, and crickets—and the sounds of a busy city—a street car, a horse and buggy, and strolling couples. Why do you think Agee includes all this descriptive detail, and why does he concentrate so much on sound?

3. What is the significance of the long description of the fathers watering their lawns? Why does Agee concentrate on such an everyday occurrence?

4. Reread the last two paragraphs in which the narrator recalls lying on the lawn surrounded by his family. How would the writer's memories of this childhood scene (set in 1915) be affected by his awareness of his father's death in 1916? How is this awareness conveyed through the mood of the scene? What can you point to in the language of this passage that communicates the complexity of this memory?

5. What does Agee mean in the first sentence when the narrator recalls "the time that I lived there so successfully disguised to myself as a child"? How does this line relate to the last line in which the narrator says that those who treat him "as one familiar and well-beloved in that home . . . will not ever tell me who I am"?

6. What does Agee's personal exploration tell us about our own lives?

A Raisin in the Sun

Lorraine Hansberry

Lorraine Hansberry (1930–1965) was born into a middle-class family in Chicago. As a child, she was relatively sheltered from the harsher aspects of racial discrimination until her family attempted to move into a restricted white neighborhood when she was about seven or eight years old. The family was subjected to intimidation, threats, and violence, and it took a Supreme Court ruling to insure their right to remain in their home. Hansberry first became active in the theater while still in high school and continued her interest while in college at the University of Wisconsin. She later studied painting in Chicago and abroad; she wrote for Paul Robeson's Freedom Magazine; *and she began writing drama in 1957. Lorraine Hansberry died from cancer at the age of thirty-four.*

A Raisin in the Sun *was the first of Hansberry's four plays. It is the first play written by a black woman to be produced on Broadway, and, at the time, the first to be directed by a black director in more than fifty years. Hansberry was the youngest writer and the first black author to receive the New York Drama Critics Circle Award. The play enjoyed a successful run, playing from 1959 until the day she died in 1965, and was turned into a major motion picture in 1961.*

CHARACTERS
(In order of appearance)

RUTH YOUNGER	JOSEPH ASAGAI
TRAVIS YOUNGER	GEORGE MURCHISON
WALTER LEE YOUNGER (BROTHER)	KARL LINDNER
BENEATHA YOUNGER	BOBO
LENA YOUNGER (MAMA)	MOVING MEN

The action of the play is set in Chicago's Southside, sometime between World War II and the present.

ACT I

Scene One: Friday morning.
Scene Two: The following morning.

ACT II

Scene One: Later, the same day.
Scene Two: Friday night, a few weeks later.
Scene Three: Moving day, one week later.

ACT III

An hour later.

ACT I
Scene I

The YOUNGER *living room would be a comfortable and well-ordered room if it were not for a number of indestructible contradictions to this state of being. Its furnishings are typical and undistinguished and their primary feature now is that they have clearly had to accommodate the living of too many people for too many years—and they are tired. Still, we can see that at some time, a time probably no longer remembered by the family (except perhaps for* MAMA*), the furnishings of this room were actually selected with care and love and even hope—and brought to this apartment and arranged with taste and pride.*

That was a long time ago. Now the once loved pattern of the couch upholstery has to fight to show itself from under acres of crocheted doilies and couch covers which have themselves finally come to be more important than the upholstery. And here a table or a chair has been moved to disguise the worn places in the carpet; but the carpet has fought back by showing its weariness, with depressing uniformity, elsewhere on its surface.

Weariness has, in fact, won in this room. Everything has been polished, washed, sat on, used, scrubbed too often. All pretenses but living itself have long since vanished from the very atmosphere of this room.

Moreover, a section of this room, for it is not really a room unto itself, though the landlord's lease would make it seem so, slopes backward to provide a small kitchen area, where the family prepares the meals that are eaten in the living room proper, which must also serve as dining room. The single window that has been provided for these "two" rooms is located in this kitchen area. The sole natural light the family may enjoy in the course of a day is only that which fights its way through this little window.

At left, a door leads to a bedroom which is shared by MAMA *and her daughter,* BENEATHA. *At right, opposite, is a second room (which in the beginning of the life of this apartment was probably a breakfast room) which serves as a bedroom for* WALTER *and his wife,* RUTH.

Time: *Sometime between World War II and the present.*

Place: *Chicago's Southside.*

At Rise: *It is morning dark in the living room.* TRAVIS *is asleep on the make-down bed at center. An alarm clock sounds from within the bedroom at right, and presently* RUTH *enters from that room and closes the door behind her. She crosses sleepily toward the window. As she passes her sleeping son she reaches down and shakes him a little. At the window she raises the shade and a dusky Southside morning light comes in feebly. She fills a pot with water and puts it on to boil. She calls to the boy, between yawns, in a slightly muffled voice.*

RUTH *is about thirty. We can see that she was a pretty girl, even exceptionally so, but now it is apparent that life has been little that she expected, and disappointment has already begun to hang in her face. In a few years, before thirty-five even, she will be known among her people as a "settled woman."*

She crosses to her son and gives him a good, final, rousing shake.

RUTH: Come on now, boy, it's seven thirty! *(Her son sits up at last, in a stupor of sleepiness.)* I say hurry up, Travis! You ain't the only person in the world got to use a bathroom! *(The child, a sturdy, handsome little boy of ten or eleven, drags himself out of the bed and almost blindly takes his towels and "today's clothes" from drawers and a closet and goes out to the bathroom, which is in an outside hall and which is shared by another family or families on the same floor.* RUTH *crosses to the bedroom door at right and opens it and calls in to her husband)* Walter Lee! . . . It's after seven thirty! Lemme see you do some waking up in there now! *(She waits)* You better get up from there, man! It's after seven thirty I tell you. *(She waits again)* All right, you just go ahead and lay there and next thing you know Travis be finished and Mr. Johnson'll be in there and you'll be fussing and cussing round here like a madman! And be late too! *(She waits, at the end of patience)* Walter Lee—it's time for you to GET UP!

(She waits another second and then starts to go into the bedroom, but is apparently satisfied that her husband has begun to get up. She stops, pulls the door to, and returns to the kitchen area. She wipes her face with a moist cloth and runs her fingers through her sleep-disheveled hair in a vain effort and ties an apron around her housecoat. The bedroom door at right opens and her husband stands in the doorway in his pajamas, which are rumpled and mismatched. He is a lean, intense young man in his middle thirties, inclined to quick nervous movements and erratic speech habits—and always in his voice there is a quality of indictment)

WALTER: Is he out yet?

RUTH: What you mean *out*? He ain't hardly got in there good yet.

WALTER *(wandering in, still more oriented to sleep than to a new day):* Well, what was you doing all that yelling for if I can't even get in there yet? *(Stopping and thinking)* Check coming today?

RUTH: They *said* Saturday and this is just Friday and I hopes to God you ain't going to get up here first thing this morning and start talking to me 'bout no money— 'cause I 'bout don't want to hear it.

WALTER: Something the matter with you this morning?

RUTH: No—I'm just sleepy as the devil. What kind of eggs you want?

WALTER: Not scrambled. *(*RUTH *starts to scramble eggs)* Paper come? *(*RUTH *points impatiently to the rolled up Tribune on the table, and he gets it and spreads it out and vaguely reads the front page)* Set off another bomb yesterday.

RUTH *(maximum indifference):* Did they?

WALTER *(looking up):* What's the matter with you?

RUTH: Ain't nothing the matter with me. And don't keep asking me that this morning.

WALTER: Ain't nobody bothering you. *(Reading the news of the day absently again)* Say Colonel McCormick is sick.

RUTH (*affecting tea-party interest*): Is he now? Poor thing.

WALTER (*sighing and looking at his watch*): Oh, me. (*He waits*) Now what is that boy doing in that bathroom all this time? He just going to have to start getting up earlier. I can't be being late to work on account of him fooling around in there.

RUTH (*turning on him*): Oh, no, he ain't going to be getting up earlier no such thing! It ain't his fault that he can't get to bed no earlier nights 'cause he got a bunch of crazy good-for-nothing clowns sitting up running their mouths in what is supposed to be his bedroom after ten o'clock at night . . .

WALTER: That's what you mad about, ain't it? The things I want to talk about with my friends just couldn't be important in your mind, could they?

(*He rises and finds a cigarette in her handbag on the table and crosses to the little window and looks out, smoking and deeply enjoying this first one*)

RUTH (*almost matter of factly, a complaint too automatic to deserve emphasis*): Why you always got to smoke before you eat in the morning?

WALTER (*at the window*): Just look at 'em down there . . . Running and racing to work . . . (*He turns and faces his wife and watches her a moment at the stove, and then, suddenly*) You look young this morning, baby.

RUTH (*indifferently*): Yeah?

WALTER: Just for a second—stirring them eggs. It's gone now—just for a second it was—you looked real young again. (*He reaches for her; she crosses away. Then, drily*) It's gone now—you look like yourself again.

RUTH: Man, if you don't shut up and leave me alone.

WALTER (*looking out to the street again*): First thing a man ought to learn in life is not to make love to no colored woman first thing in the morning. You all some eeeevil people at eight o'clock in the morning. (TRAVIS *appears in the hall doorway, almost fully dressed and quite wide awake now, his towels and pajamas across his shoulders. He opens the door and signals for his father to make the bathroom in a hurry*)

TRAVIS (*watching the bathroom*): Daddy, come on!

(WALTER *gets his bathroom utensils and flies out to the bathroom*)

RUTH: Sit down and have your breakfast, Travis.

TRAVIS: Mama, this is Friday. (*Gleefully*) Check coming tomorrow, huh?

RUTH: You get your mind off money and eat your breakfast.

TRAVIS (*eating*): This is the morning we supposed to bring the fifty cents to school.

RUTH: Well, I ain't got no fifty cents this morning.

TRAVIS: Teacher say we have to.

RUTH: I don't care what teacher say. I ain't got it. Eat your breakfast, Travis.

TRAVIS: I *am* eating.

RUTH: Hush up now and just eat!

(*The boy gives her an exasperated look for her lack of understanding, and eats grudgingly*)

TRAVIS: You think Grandmama would have it?

RUTH: No! And I want you to stop asking your grandmother for money, you hear me?

TRAVIS (*outraged*): Gaaaleee! I don't ask her, she just gimme it sometimes!

RUTH: Travis Willard Younger—I got too much on me this morning to be—

TRAVIS: Maybe Daddy—

RUTH: Travis!

(The boy hushes abruptly. They are both quiet and tense for several seconds)

TRAVIS *(presently):* Could I maybe go carry some groceries in front of the supermarket for a little while after school then?

RUTH: Just hush, I said. *(TRAVIS jabs his spoon into his cereal bowl viciously, and rests his head in anger upon his fists)* If you through eating, you can get over there and make up your bed.

(The boy obeys stiffly and crosses the room, almost mechanically, to the bed and more or less carefully folds the covering. He carries the bedding into his mother's room and returns with his books and cap)

TRAVIS *(sulking and standing apart from her unnaturally):* I'm gone.

RUTH *(looking up from the stove to inspect him automatically):* Come here. *(He crosses to her and she studies his head)* If you don't take this comb and fix this here head, you better! *(TRAVIS puts down his books with a great sigh of oppression, and crosses to the mirror. His mother mutters under her breath about his "stubbornness")* 'Bout to march out of here with that head looking just like chickens slept in it! I just don't know where you get your stubborn ways . . . And get your jacket, too. Looks chilly out this morning.

TRAVIS *(with conspicuously brushed hair and jacket):* I'm gone.

RUTH: Get carfare and milk money—*(Waving one finger)*—and not a single penny for no caps, you hear me?

TRAVIS *(with sullen politeness):* Yes'm.

(He turns in outrage to leave. His mother watches after him as in his frustration he approaches the door almost comically. When she speaks to him, her voice has become a very gentle tease)

RUTH *(mocking; as she thinks he would say it):* Oh, Mama makes me so mad sometimes, I don't know what to do! *(She waits and continues to his back as he stands stock-still in front of the door)* I wouldn't kiss that woman good-bye for nothing in this world this morning! *(The boy finally turns around and rolls his eyes at her, knowing the mood has changed and he is vindicated; he does not, however, move toward her yet)* Not for nothing in this world! *(She finally laughs aloud at him and holds out her arms to him and we see that it is a way between them, very old and practiced. He crosses to her and allows her to embrace him warmly but keeps his face fixed with masculine rigidity. She holds him back from her presently and looks at him and runs her fingers over the features of his face. With utter gentleness—)* Now—whose little old angry man are you?

TRAVIS *(the masculinity and gruffness start to fade at last):* Aw gaalee—Mama . . .

RUTH *(Mimicking):* Aw—gaaaaalleeeee, Mama! *(She pushes him, with rough playfulness and finality, toward the door)* Get on out of here or you going to be late.

TRAVIS *(In the face of love, new aggressiveness):* Mama, could I *please* go carry groceries?

RUTH: Honey, it's starting to get so cold evenings.

WALTER *(Coming in from the bathroom and drawing a make-believe gun from a make-believe holster and shooting at his son):* What is it he wants to do?

RUTH: Go carry groceries after school at the supermarket.

WALTER: Well, let him go . . .

TRAVIS *(quickly, to the ally):* I have to—she won't gimme the fifty cents . . .

WALTER *(to his wife only):* Why not?

RUTH *(simply, and with flavor):* 'Cause we don't have it.

WALTER *(To* RUTH *only):* What you tell the boy things like that for? *(Reaching down into his pants with a rather important gesture)* Here, son—

(He hands the boy the coin, but his eyes are directed to his wife's. TRAVIS *takes the money happily)*

TRAVIS: Thanks, Daddy. *(He starts out.* RUTH *watches both of them with murder in her eyes. Walter stands and stares back at her with defiance, and suddenly reaches into his pocket again on an afterthought)*

WALTER *(without even looking at his son, still staring hard at his wife):* In fact, here's another fifty cents . . . Buy yourself some fruit today—or take a taxicab to school or something!

TRAVIS: Whoopee—

(He leaps up and clasps his father around the middle with his legs, and they face each other in mutual appreciation; slowly WALTER LEE *peeks around the boy to catch the violent rays from his wife's eyes and draws his head back as if shot)*

WALTER: You better get down now—and get to school, man.

TRAVIS *(at the door):* O.K. Good-bye.

(He exits)

WALTER *(after him, pointing with pride):* That's *my* boy. *(She looks at him in disgust and turns back to her work)* You know what I was thinking 'bout in the bathroom this morning?

RUTH: No.

WALTER: How come you always try to be so pleasant!

RUTH: What is there to be pleasant 'bout!

WALTER: You want to know what I was thinking 'bout in the bathroom or not!

RUTH: I know what you thinking 'bout.

WALTER *(ignoring her):* 'Bout what me and Willy Harris was talking about last night.

RUTH *(immediately—a refrain):* Willy Harris is a good-for-nothing loudmouth.

WALTER: Anybody who talks to me has got to be a good-for-nothing loud mouth, ain't he? And what you know about who is just a good-for-nothing loudmouth? Charlie Atkins was just a "good-for-nothing loud mouth" too, wasn't he! When he wanted me to go in the dry-cleaning business with him. And now—he's grossing a hundred thousand a year. A hundred thousand dollars a year! You still call *him* a loudmouth!

RUTH *(Bitterly):* Oh, Walter Lee . . . *(She folds her head on her arms over the table)*

WALTER *(Rising and coming to her and standing over her):* You tired, ain't you? Tired of everything. Me, the boy, the way we live—this beat-up hole—everything. Ain't you? *(She doesn't look up, doesn't answer)* So tired—moaning and groaning all the time, but you wouldn't do nothing to help, would you? You couldn't be on my side that long for nothing, could you?

RUTH: Walter, please leave me alone.

WALTER: A man needs for a woman to back him up . . .

RUTH: Walter—

WALTER: Mama would listen to you. You know she listen to you more than she do me and Bennie. She think more of you. All you have to do is just sit down with her when you drinking your coffee one morning and talking 'bout things like you do and—*(He sits down beside her and demonstrates graphically what he thinks her methods and tone should be)*—you just sip your coffee, see, and say easy like that you been thinking 'bout that deal Walter Lee is so interested in, 'bout the store and all, and sip some more coffee, like what you saying ain't really that important to you—And the next thing you know, she be listening good and asking you questions and when I come home—I can tell her the details. This ain't no fly-by-night proposition, baby. I mean we figured it out, me and Willy and Bobo.

RUTH *(with a frown):* Bobo?

WALTER: Yeah. You see, this little liquor store we got in mind cost seventy-five thousand and we figured the initial investment on the place be 'bout thirty thousand, see. That be ten thousand each. Course, there's a couple of hundred you got to pay so's you don't spend your life just waiting for them clowns to let your license get approved —

RUTH: You mean graft?

WALTER *(frowning impatiently):* Don't call it that. See there, that just goes to show you what women understand about the world. Baby, don't *nothing* happen for you in this world 'less you pay *somebody* off!

RUTH: Walter, leave me alone! *(She raises her head and stares at him vigorously—then says, more quietly)* Eat your eggs, they gonna be cold.

WALTER *(straightening up from her and looking off):* That's it. There you are. Man say to his woman: I got me a dream. His woman say: Eat your eggs. *(Sadly, but gaining in power)* Man say: I got to take hold of this here world, baby! And a woman will say: Eat your eggs and go to work. *(Passionately now)* Man say: I got to change my life, I'm choking to death, baby! And his woman say—*(In utter anguish as he brings his fists down on his thighs)*—Your eggs is getting cold!

RUTH *(softly):* Walter, that ain't none of our money.

WALTER *(not listening at all or even looking at her):* This morning, I was lookin' in the mirror and thinking about it . . . I'm thirty-five years old; I been married eleven years and I got a boy who sleeps in the living room—*(Very, very quietly)*—and all I got to give him is stories about how rich white people live.

RUTH: Eat your eggs, Walter.

WALTER *(slams the table and jumps up):* DAMN MY EGGS . . . DAMN ALL THE EGGS THAT EVER WAS!

RUTH: Then go to work.

WALTER *(looking up at her):* See—I'm trying to talk to you 'bout myself—*(Shaking his head with the repetition)*—and all you can say is eat them eggs and go to work.

RUTH *(wearily):* Honey, you never say nothing new. I listen to you every day, every night and every morning, and you never say nothing new. *(Shrugging)* So you would rather *be* Mr. Arnold than be his chauffeur. So—I would *rather* be living in Buckingham Palace.

WALTER: That is just what is wrong with the colored woman in this world . . . Don't understand about building their men up and making 'em feel like they somebody. Like they can do something.

RUTH *(drily, but to hurt):* There *are* colored men who do things.

WALTER: No thanks to the colored woman.

RUTH: Well, being a colored woman, I guess I can't help myself none.

(She rises and gets the ironing board and sets it up and attacks a huge pile of rough-dried clothes, sprinkling them in preparation for the ironing and then rolling them into tight fat balls.)

WALTER *(mumbling):* We one group of men tied to a race of women with small minds.

(His sister BENEATHA *enters. She is about twenty, as slim and intense as her brother. She is not as pretty as her sister-in-law, but her lean, almost intellectual face has a handsomeness of its own. She wears a bright-red flannel nightie, and her thick hair stands wildly about her head. Her speech is a mixture of many things; it is different from the rest of the family's insofar as education has permeated her sense of English—and perhaps the Midwest rather than the South has finally—at last—won out in her inflection; but not altogether, because over all of it is a soft slurring and transformed use of vowels which is the decided influence of the Southside. She passes through the room without looking at either* RUTH *or* WALTER *and goes to the outside door and looks, a little blindly, out to the bathroom. She sees that it has been lost to the Johnsons. She closes the door with a sleepy vengeance and crosses to the table and sits down a little defeated.)*

BENEATHA: I am going to start timing those people.

WALTER: You should get up earlier.

BENEATHA *(her face in her hands. She is still fighting the urge to go back to bed):* Really—would you suggest dawn? Where's the paper?

WALTER *(pushing the paper across the table to her as he studies her almost clinically, as though he has never seen her before):* You a horrible-looking chick at this hour.

BENEATHA *(drily):* Good morning, everybody.

WALTER *(senselessly):* How is school coming?

BENEATHA *(in the same spirit):* Lovely. Lovely. And you know, biology is the greatest. *(Looking up at him)* I dissected something that looked just like you yesterday.

WALTER: I just wondered if you've made up your mind and everything.

BENEATHA *(gaining in sharpness and impatience):* And what did I answer yesterday morning—and the day before that?

RUTH *(from the ironing hoard, like someone disinterested and old):* Don't be so nasty, Bennie.

Beneatha *(still to her brother):* And the day before that and the day before that!

WALTER *(defensively):* I'm interested in you. Something wrong with that? Ain't many girls who decide—

WALTER and BENEATHA *(in unison):*—"to be a doctor."

(Silence)

WALTER: Have we figured out yet just exactly how much medical school is going to cost?

RUTH: Walter Lee, why don't you leave that girl alone and get out of here to work?

BENEATHA *(exits to the bathroom and bangs on the door):* Come on out of there, please! *(She comes back into the room)*

WALTER *(looking at his sister intently):* You know the check is coming tomorrow.

BENEATHA *(turning on him with a sharpness all her own):* That money belongs to Mama, Walter, and it's for her to decide how she wants to use it. I don't care if she wants to buy a house or a rocket ship or just nail it up somewhere and look at it. It's hers. Not ours—*hers.*

WALTER *(bitterly):* Now ain't that fine! You just got your mother's interest at heart, ain't you, girl? You such a nice girl—but if Mama got that money she can always take a few thousand and help you through school too—can't she?

BENEATHA: I have never asked anyone around here to do anything for me!

WALTER: No! And the line between asking and just accepting when the time comes is big and wide—ain't it!

BENEATHA *(with fury):* What do you want from me, Brother—that I quit school or just drop dead, which!

WALTER: I don't want nothing but for you to stop acting holy 'round here. Me and Ruth done made some sacrifices for you—why can't you do something for the family?

RUTH: Walter, don't be dragging me in it.

WALTER: You are in it—Don't you get up and go work in somebody's kitchen for the last three years to help put clothes on her back?

RUTH: Oh, Walter—that's not fair . . .

WALTER: It ain't that nobody expects you to get on your knees and say thank you, Brother; thank you, Ruth; thank you, Mama—and thank you, Travis, for wearing the same pair of shoes for two semesters —

BENEATHA *(dropping to her knees):* Well—I *do*—all right?—thank everybody . . . and forgive me for ever wanting to be anything at all *(Pursuing him on her knees across the floor)* FORGIVE ME, FORGIVE ME, FORGIVE ME!

RUTH: Please stop it! Your mama'll hear you.

WALTER: Who the hell told you you had to be a doctor? If you so crazy 'bout messing 'round with sick people—then go be a nurse like other women—or just get married and be quiet . . .

BENEATHA: Well—you finally got it said . . . It took you three years but you finally got it said. Walter, give up; leave me alone—it's Mama's money.

WALTER: *He was my father, too!*

BENEATHA: So what? He was mine, too—and Travis' grandfather—but the insurance money belongs to Mama. Picking on me is not going to make her give it to you to invest in any liquor stores—*(Under breath, dropping into a chair)*—and I for one say, God bless Mama for that!

WALTER *(to Ruth):* See—did you hear? Did you hear!

RUTH: Honey, please go to work.

WALTER: Nobody in this house is ever going to understand me.

BENEATHA: Because you're a nut.

WALTER: Who's a nut?

BENEATHA: You—you are a nut. Thee is mad, boy.

WALTER *(looking at his wife and his sister from the door, very sadly):* The world's most backward race of people, and that's a fact.

BENEATHA *(Turning slowly in her chair):* And then there are all those prophets who would lead us out of the wilderness—Walter *(slams out of the house)*—into the swamps!

RUTH: Bennie, why you always gotta be pickin' on your brother? Can't you be a little sweeter sometimes? *(Door opens.* WALTER *walks in). (He fumbles with his cap, starts to speak, clears his throat, looks everywhere but at* RUTH. *Finally:)*

WALTER *(to* RUTH*):* I need some money for carfare.

RUTH *(looks at him, then warms; teasing, but tenderly):* Fifty cents? *(She goes to her bag and gets money)* Here, take a taxi.

*(*WALTER *exits.* MAMA *enters. She is a woman in her early sixties, full-bodied and strong. She is one of those women of a certain grace and beauty who wear it so unobtrusively that it takes a while to notice. Her dark-brown face is surrounded by the total whiteness of her hair, and, being a woman who has adjusted to many things in life and overcome many more, her face is full of strength. She has, we can see, wit and faith of a kind that keep her eyes lit and full of interest and expectancy. She is, in a word, a beautiful woman. Her bearing is perhaps most like the noble bearing of the*

women of the Heroes of Southwest Africa—rather as if she imagines that as she walks she still bears a basket or a vessel upon her head. Her speech, on the other hand, is as careless as her carriage is precise—she is inclined to slur everything—but her voice is perhaps not so much quiet as simply soft)

MAMA: Who that 'round here slamming doors at this hour?

(She crosses through the room, goes to the window, opens it, and brings in a feeble little plant growing doggedly in a small pot on the window sill. She feels the dirt and puts it back out)

RUTH: That was Walter Lee. He and Bennie was at it again.

MAMA: My children and they tempers. Lord, if this little old plant don't get more sun than it's been getting it ain't never going to see spring again. *(She turns from the window)* What's the matter with you this morning, Ruth? You looks right peaked. You aiming to iron all them things? Leave some for me. I'll get to 'em this afternoon. Bennie honey, it's too drafty for you to be sitting 'round half dressed. Where's your robe?

BENEATHA: In the cleaners.

MAMA: Well, go get mine and put it on.

BENEATHA: I'm not cold, Mama, honest.

MAMA: I know—but you so thin . . .

BENEATHA *(irritably):* Mama, I'm not cold.

MAMA: *(Seeing the make-down bed as* TRAVIS *has left it).* Lord have mercy, look at that poor bed. Bless his heart—he tries, don't he?

(She moves to the bed TRAVIS *has sloppily made up)*

RUTH: No—he don't half try at all 'cause he knows you going to come along behind him and fix everything. That's just how come he don't know how to do nothing right now—you done spoiled that boy so.

MAMA *(folding bedding):* Well—he's a little boy. Ain't supposed to know 'bout housekeeping. My baby, that's what he is. What you fix for his breakfast this morning?

RUTH *(angrily):* I feed my son, Lena!

MAMA: I ain't meddling—*(Under breath; busy-bodyish)* I just noticed all last week he had cold cereal, and when it starts getting this chilly in the fall a child ought to have some hot grits or something when he goes out in the cold—

RUTH *(furious):* I gave him hot oats—is that all right!

MAMA: I ain't meddling. *(Pause)* Put a lot of nice butter on it? *(*RUTH *shoots her an angry look and does not reply)* He likes lots of butter.

RUTH *(Exasperated):* Lena—

MAMA: *(To* BENEATHA. MAMA *is inclined to wander conversationally sometimes):* What was you and your brother fussing 'bout this morning?

BENEATHA: It's not important, Mama.

(She gets up and goes to look out at the bathroom, which is apparently free, and she picks up her towels and rushes out)

MAMA: What was they fighting about?

RUTH: Now you know as well as I do.

MAMA *(shaking her head):* Brother still worrying hisself sick about that money?

RUTH: You know he is.

MAMA: You had breakfast?

RUTH: Some coffee.

MAMA: Girl, you better start eating and looking after yourself better. You almost thin as Travis.

RUTH: Lena—

MAMA: Uh-hunh?

RUTH: What are you going to do with it?

MAMA: Now don't you start, child. It's too early in the morning to be talking about money. It ain't Christian.

RUTH: It's just that he got his heart set on that store —

MAMA: You mean that liquor store that Willy Harris want him to invest in?

RUTH: Yes—

MAMA: We ain't no business people, Ruth. We just plain working folks.

RUTH: Ain't nobody business people till they go into business. Walter Lee say colored people ain't never going to start getting ahead till they start gambling on some different kinds of things in the world—investments and things.

MAMA: What done got into you, girl? Walter Lee done finally sold you on investing.

RUTH: No. Mama, something is happening between Walter and me. I don't know what it is—but he needs something—something I can't give him any more. He needs this chance, Lena.

MAMA *(frowning deeply):* But liquor, honey—

RUTH: Well—like Walter say—I spec people going to always be drinking themselves some liquor.

MAMA: Well—whether they drinks it or not ain't none of my business. But whether I go into business selling it to 'em *is*, and I don't want that on my ledger this late in life. *(Stopping suddenly and studying her daughter-in-law)* Ruth Younger, what's the matter with you today? You look like you could fall over right there.

RUTH: I'm tired.

MAMA: Then you better stay home from work today.

RUTH: I can't stay home. She'd be calling up the agency and screaming at them, "My girl didn't come in today—send me somebody! My girl didn't come in!" Oh, she just have a fit . . .

MAMA: Well, let her have it. I'll just call her up and say you got the flu —

RUTH *(laughing):* Why the flu?

MAMA: 'Cause it sounds respectable to 'em. Something white people get, too. They know 'bout the flu. Otherwise they think you been cut up or something when you tell 'em you sick.

RUTH: I got to go in. We need the money.

MAMA: Somebody would of thought my children done all but starved to death the way they talk about money here late. Child, we got a great big old check coming tomorrow.

RUTH *(sincerely, but also self-righteously):* Now that's your money. It ain't got nothing to do with me. We all feel like that—Walter and Bennie and me—even Travis.

MAMA: *(thoughtfully, and suddenly very far away):* Ten thousand dollars—

RUTH: Sure is wonderful.

MAMA: Ten thousand dollars.

RUTH: You know what you should do, Miss Lena? You should take yourself a trip somewhere. To Europe or South America or someplace—

MAMA *(throwing up her hands at the thought):* Oh, child!

RUTH: I'm serious. Just pack up and leave! Go on away and enjoy yourself some. Forget about the family and have yourself a ball for once in your life—

MAMA *(Drily):* You sound like I'm just about ready to die. Who'd go with me? What I look like wandering 'round Europe by myself?

RUTH: Shoot—these here rich white women do it all the time. They don't think nothing of packing up they suitcases and piling on one of them big steamships and—swoosh!—they gone, child.

MAMA: Something always told me I wasn't no rich white woman.

RUTH: Well—what are you going to do with it then?

MAMA: I ain't rightly decided. *(Thinking. She speaks now with emphasis)* Some of it got to be put away for Beneatha and her schoolin'—and ain't nothing going to touch that part of it. Nothing. *(She waits several seconds, trying to make up her mind about something, and looks at* RUTH *a little tentatively before going on)* Been thinking that we maybe could meet the notes on a little old two-story somewhere, with a yard where Travis could play in the summertime, if we use part of the insurance for a down payment and everybody kind of pitch in. I could maybe take on a little day work again, few days a week—

RUTH *(studying her mother-in-law furtively and concentrating on her ironing, anxious to encourage without seeming to):* Well, Lord knows, we've put enough rent into this here rat trap to pay for four houses by now . . .

MAMA *(Looking up at the words "rat trap" and then looking around and leaning back and sighing—in a suddenly reflective mood—):* "Rat trap"—yes, that's all it is. *(Smiling)* I remember just as well the day me and Big Walter moved in here. Hadn't been married but two weeks and wasn't planning on living here no more than a year. *(She shakes her head at the dissolved dream)* We was going to set away, little by little, don't you know, and buy a little place out in Morgan Park. We had even picked out the house. *(Chuckling a little)* Looks right dumpy today. But Lord, child, you should know all the dreams I had 'bout buying that house and fixing it up and making me a little garden in the back—*(She waits and stops smiling)* And didn't none of it happen. *(Dropping her hands in a futile gesture)*

RUTH *(keeps her head down, ironing):* Yes, life can be a barrel of disappointments, sometimes.

MAMA: Honey, Big Walter would come in here some nights back then and slump down on that couch there and just look at the rug, and look at me and look at the rug and then back at me —and I'd know he was down then . . . really down. *(After a second very long and thoughtful pause; she is seeing back to times that only she can see)* And then, Lord, when I lost that baby—little Claude—I almost thought I was going to lose Big Walter too. Oh, that man grieved hisself! He was one man to love his children.

RUTH: Ain't nothin' can tear at you like losin' your baby.

MAMA: I guess that's how come that man finally worked hisself to death like he done. Likely he was fighting his own war with this here world that took his baby from him.

RUTH: He sure was a fine man, all right. I always liked Mr. Younger.

MAMA: Crazy 'bout his children! God knows there was plenty wrong with Walter Younger—hard-headed, mean, kind of wild with women—plenty wrong with him. But he sure loved his children. Always wanted them to have something—be something. That's where Brother gets all these notions, I reckon. Big Walter used to say, he'd get right wet in the eyes sometimes, the water standing in his eyes and say,

"Seems like God didn't see fit to give the black man nothing but dreams—but He did give us children to make them dreams seem worth while." *(She smiles)* He could talk like that, don't you know.

RUTH: Yes, he sure could. He was a good man, Mr. Younger.

MAMA: Yes, a fine man—just couldn't never catch up with his dreams, that's all.

(BENEATHA comes in, brushing her hair and looking up to the ceiling, where the sound of a vacuum cleaner has started up)

BENEATHA: What could be so dirty on that woman's rugs that she has to vacuum them every single day?

RUTH: I wish certain young women 'round here who I could name would take inspiration about certain rugs in a certain apartment I could also mention.

BENEATHA *(shrugging):* How much cleaning can a house need, for Christ's sakes?

MAMA *(not liking the Lord's name used thus):* Bennie!

RUTH: Just listen to her—just listen!

BENEATHA: Oh, God!

MAMA: If you use the Lord's name just one more time —

BENEATHA *(a bit of a whine):* Oh, Mama —

RUTH: Fresh—just fresh as salt, this girl!

BENEATHA *(drily):* Well—if the salt loses its savor—

MAMA: Now that will do. I just ain't going to have you 'round here reciting the scriptures in vain—you hear me?

BENEATHA: How did I manage to get on everybody's wrong side by just walking into a room?

RUTH: If you weren't so fresh —

BENEATHA: Ruth, I'm twenty years old.

MAMA: What time you be home from school today?

BENEATHA: Kind of late. *(With enthusiasm)* Madeline is going to start my guitar lessons today.

(MAMA and RUTH look up with the same expression)

MAMA: Your *what* kind of lessons?

BENEATHA: Guitar.

RUTH: Oh, Father!

MAMA: How come you done taken it in your mind to learn to play the guitar?

BENEATHA: I just want to, that's all.

MAMA *(smiling):* Lord, child, don't you know what to do with yourself? How long it going to be before you get tired of this now—like you got tired of that little play-acting group you joined last year? *(Looking at RUTH)* And what was it the year before that?

RUTH: The horseback-riding club for which she bought that fifty-five-dollar riding habit that's been hanging in the closet ever since!

MAMA *(to BENEATHA):* Why you got to flit so from one thing to another, baby?

BENEATHA *(sharply):* I just want to learn to play the guitar. Is there anything wrong with that?

MAMA: Ain't nobody trying to stop you. I just wonders sometimes why you has to flit so from one thing to another all the time. You ain't never done nothing with all that camera equipment you brought home —

BENEATHA: I don't flit! I—I experiment with different forms of expression—

RUTH: Like riding a horse?

BENEATHA: —People have to express themselves one way or another.

MAMA: What is it you want to express?

BENEATHA *(angrily):* Me! (MAMA *and* RUTH *look at each other and burst into raucous laughter)* Don't worry—I don't expect you to understand.

MAMA *(to change the subject.)* Who you going out with tomorrow night?

BENEATHA *(with displeasure):* George Murchison again.

MAMA *(pleased):* Oh—you getting a little sweet on him?

RUTH: You ask me, this child ain't sweet on nobody but herself—*(Underbreath)* Express herself!

(They laugh)

BENEATHA: Oh—I like George all right, Mama. I mean I like him enough to go out with him and stuff, but—

RUTH *(for devilment):* What does *and stuff* mean?

BENEATHA: Mind your own business.

MAMA: Stop picking at her now, Ruth. *(She chuckles—then a suspicious sudden look at her daughter as she turns in her chair for emphasis)* What DOES it mean?

BENEATHA *(wearily):* Oh, I just mean I couldn't ever really be serious about George. He's—he's so shallow.

RUTH: Shallow—what do you mean he's shallow? He's *Rich!*

MAMA: Hush, Ruth.

BENEATHA: I know he's rich. He knows he's rich, too.

RUTH: Well—what other qualities a man got to have to satisfy you, little girl?

BENEATHA: You wouldn't even begin to understand. Anybody who married Walter could not possibly understand.

MAMA *(outraged):* What kind of way is that to talk about your brother?

BENEATHA: Brother is a flip—let's face it.

MAMA *(to* RUTH, *helplessly)* What's a flip?

RUTH *(glad to add kindling):* She's saying he's crazy.

BENEATHA: Not crazy. Brother isn't really crazy yet—he—he's an elaborate neurotic.

MAMA: Hush your mouth!

BENEATHA: As for George. Well. George looks good—he's got a beautiful car and he takes me to nice places and, as my sister-in-law says, he is probably the richest boy I will ever get to know and I even like him sometimes—but if the Youngers are sitting around waiting to see if their little Bennie is going to tie up the family with the Murchisons, they are wasting their time.

RUTH: You mean you wouldn't marry George Murchison if he asked you someday? That pretty, rich thing? Honey, I knew you was odd —

BENEATHA: No, I would not marry him if all I felt for him was what I feel now. Besides, George's family wouldn't really like it.

MAMA: Why not?

BENEATHA: Oh, Mama—The Murchisons are honest-to-God-real-*live*-rich colored people, and the only people in the world who are more snobbish than rich white people are rich colored people. I thought everybody knew that. I've met Mrs. Murchison. She's a scene!

MAMA: You must not dislike people 'cause they well off, honey.

BENEATHA: Why not? It makes just as much sense as disliking people 'cause they are poor, and lots of people do that.

RUTH *(a wisdom-of-the-ages manner. To* MAMA.*)* Well, she'll get over some of this—

BENEATHA: Get over it? What are you talking about, Ruth? Listen, I'm going to be a doctor. I'm not worried about who I'm going to marry yet—if I ever get married.

MAMA *and* RUTH: *If!*

MAMA: Now, Bennie—

BENEATHA: Oh, I probably will . . . but first I'm going to be a doctor, and George, for one, still thinks that's pretty funny. I couldn't be bothered with that. I am going to be a doctor and everybody around here better understand that!

MAMA *(kindly):* 'Course you going to be a doctor, honey, God willing.

BENEATHA *(drily):* God hasn't got a thing to do with it.

MAMA: Beneatha—that just wasn't necessary.

BENEATHA: Well—neither is God. I get sick of hearing about God.

MAMA: Beneatha!

BENEATHA: I mean it! I'm just tired of hearing about God all the time. What has He got to do with anything? Does he pay tuition?

MAMA: You 'bout to get your fresh little jaw slapped!

RUTH: That's just what she needs, all right!

BENEATHA: Why? Why can't I say what I want to around here, like everybody else?

MAMA: It don't sound nice for a young girl to say things like that—you wasn't brought up that way. Me and your father went to trouble to get you and Brother to church every Sunday.

BENEATHA: Mama, you don't understand. It's all a matter of ideas, and God is just one idea I don't accept. It's not important. I am not going out and be immoral or commit crimes because I don't believe in God. I don't even think about it. It's just that I get tired of Him getting credit for all the things the human race achieves through its own stubborn effort. There simply is no blasted God—there is only man and it is He who makes miracles!

(MAMA absorbs this speech, studies her daughter and rises slowly and crosses to BENEATHA and slaps her powerfully across the face. After, there is only silence and the daughter drops her eyes from her mother's face, and MAMA is very tall before her)

MAMA: Now—you say after me, in my mother's house there is still God. *(There is a long pause and BENEATHA stares at the floor wordlessly. MAMA repeats the phrase with precision and cool emotion)* In my mother's house there is still God.

BENEATHA: In my mother's house there is still God.

(A long pause)

MAMA *(walking away from BENEATHA too disturbed for triumphant posture. Stopping and turning back to her daughter):* There are some ideas we ain't going to have in this house. Not long as I am at the head of this family.

BENEATHA: Yes, ma'am.

(MAMA walks out of the room)

RUTH *(almost gently, with profound understanding):* You think you a woman, Bennie—but you still a little girl. What you did was childish—so you got treated like a child.

BENEATHA: I see. *(Quietly)* I also see that everybody thinks it's all right for Mama to be a tyrant. But all the tyranny in the world will never put a God in the heavens!

(She picks up her books and goes out)

RUTH *(Goes to MAMA 's door):* She said she was sorry.

MAMA: *(coming out, going to her plant):* They frightens me, Ruth. My children.

RUTH: You got good children, Lena. They just a little off sometimes—but they're good.

MAMA: No—There's something come down between me and them that don't let us understand each other and I don't know what it is. One done almost lost his mind thinking 'bout money all the time and the other done commence to talk about things I can't seem to understand in no form or fashion. What is it that's changing, Ruth.

RUTH *(soothingly, older than her years):* Now . . . you taking it all too seriously. You just got strong-willed children and it takes a strong woman like you to keep 'em in hand.

MAMA *(looking at her plant and sprinkling a little water on it):* They spirited all right, my children. Got to admit they got spirit—Bennie and Walter. Like this little old plant that ain't never had enough sunshine or nothing—and look at it . . .

(She has her back to RUTH, who has had to stop ironing and lean against something and put the back of her hand to her forehead)

RUTH *(Trying to keep MAMA from noticing):* You . . . sure . . . loves that little old thing, don't you? . . .

MAMA: Well, I always wanted me a garden like I used to see sometimes at the back of the houses down home. This plant is close as I ever got to having one. *(She looks out of the window as she replaces the plant)* Lord, ain't nothing as dreary as the view from this window on a dreary day, is there? Why ain't you singing this morning, Ruth? Sing that "No Ways Tired." That song always lifts me up so —*(She turns at last to see that RUTH has slipped quietly to the floor, in a state of semiconsciousness)* Ruth! Ruth honey—what's the matter with you . . . Ruth!

Curtain

Scene II

It is the following morning; a Saturday morning, and house cleaning is in progress at the YOUNGERS. Furniture has been shoved hither and yon and MAMA is giving the kitchen-area walls a washing down. BENEATHA, in dungarees, with a handkerchief tied around her face, is spraying insecticide into the cracks in the walls. As they work, the radio is on and a Southside disk-jockey program is inappropriately filling the house with a rather exotic saxophone blues. TRAVIS, the sole idle one, is leaning on his arms, looking out of the window.

TRAVIS: Grandmama, that stuff Bennie is using smells awful. Can I go downstairs, please?

TRAVIS: Did you get all them chores done already? I ain't seen you doing much.

TRAVIS: Yes'm— finished early. Where did Mama go this morning?

MAMA *(looking at BENEATHA):* She had to go on a little errand.

(The phone rings. BENEATHA runs to answer it and reaches it before WALTER, who has entered from the bedroom.)

TRAVIS: Where?

MAMA: To tend to her business.

BENEATHA: Haylo . . . *(Disappointed)* Yes, he is. *(She tosses the phone to WALTER, who barely catches it)* It's Willie Harris again.

WALTER *(as privately as possible under MAMA 's gaze):* Hello, Willie. Did you get the papers from the lawyer? . . . No, not yet. I told you the milkman doesn't get here till ten-thirty . . . No, I'll come there . . . Yeah! Right away. *(He bangs up and goes for his coat)*

BENEATHA: Brother, where did Ruth go?

WALTER *(as he exits):* How should I know!

TRAVIS: Aw come on, Grandma. Can I go outside?

MAMA: Oh, I guess so. You better stay right in front of the house, though, and keep a good lookout for the postman.

TRAVIS: Yes'm. *(He darts into bedroom for stickball and bat, reenters, and sees* BENEATHA *on her knees spraying under sofa with behind upraised. He edges closer to the target, takes aim, and lets her have it. She screams)* Leave them poor little old cockroaches alone, they ain't bothering you none. *(He runs as she swings the spray gun at him both viciously and playfully)*: Grandma! Grandma!

MAMA: Look out there, girl, before you be spilling some of that stuff on that child!

TRAVIS *(safely behind the bastion of* MAMA*):* That's right—look out now! *(He exits)*

Beneatha *(drily):* I can't imagine that it would hurt him—it has never hurt the roaches.

MAMA: Well, little boys' hides ain't as tough as Southside roaches. You better get over there behind the bureau. I seen one marching out of there like Napoleon yesterday.

BENEATHA: There's really only one way to get rid of them, Mama—

MAMA: How?

BENEATHA: Set fire to this building! Mama, where did Ruth go?

MAMA: *(looking at her with meaning):* To the doctor, I think.

BENEATHA: The doctor? What's the matter? *(They exchange glances)* You don't think—

MAMA: *(with her sense of drama):* Now I ain't saying what I think. But I ain't never been wrong 'bout a woman neither.

(The phone rings)

BENEATHA *(At the phone):* Hay-lo . . . *(Pause, and a moment of recognition)* Well—when did you get back! . . . And how was it? . . . Of course I've missed you—in my way . . . This morning? No . . . house cleaning and all that and Mama hates it if I let people come over when the house is like this . . . You *have?* Well, that's different . . . What is it—Oh, what the hell, come on over . . . Right, see you then. Arrividerci.

(She hangs up)

MAMA: *(who has listened vigorously, as is her habit):* Who is that you inviting over here with this house looking like this? You ain't got the pride you was born with!

BENEATHA: Asagai doesn't care how houses look, Mama—he's an intellectual.

MAMA: *Who?*

BENEATHA: Asagai—Joseph Asagai. He's an African boy I met on campus. He's been studying in Canada all summer.

MAMA: What's his name?

BENEATHA: Asagai, Joseph. Ah-sah-guy . . . He's from Nigeria.

MAMA: Oh, that's the little country that was founded by slaves way back . . .

BENEATHA: No, Mama—that's Liberia.

MAMA: I don't think I never met no African before.

BENEATHA: Well, do me a favor and don't ask him a whole lot of ignorant questions about Africans. I mean, do they wear clothes and all that—

MAMA: Well, now, I guess if you think we so ignorant 'round here maybe you shouldn't bring your friends here —

BENEATHA: It's just that people ask such crazy things. All anyone seems to know about when it comes to Africa is Tarzan—

MAMA *(indignantly):* Why should I know anything about Africa?

BENEATHA: Why do you give money at church for the missionary work?

MAMA: Well, that's to help save people.

BENEATHA: You mean save them from *heathenism*—

MAMA *(innocently):* Yes.

BENEATHA: I'm afraid they need more salvation from the British and the French.

(RUTH *comes in forlornly and pulls off her coat with dejection. They both turn to look at her)*

RUTH *(dispiritedly):* Well, I guess from all the happy faces—everybody knows.

BENEATHA: You pregnant?

MAMA: Lord have mercy, I sure hope it's a little old girl. TRAVIS ought to have a sister.

(BENEATHA *and* RUTH *give her a hopeless look for this grandmotherly enthusiasm)*

BENEATHA: How far along are you?

RUTH: Two months.

BENEATHA: Did you mean to? I mean did you plan it or was it an accident?

MAMA: What do you know about planning or not planning?

BENEATHA: Oh, Mama.

RUTH *(wearily):* She's twenty years old, Lena.

BENEATHA: Did you plan it, Ruth?

RUTH: Mind your own business.

BENEATHA: It is my business—where is he going to live, on the *roof? (There is silence following the remark as the three women react to the sense of it)* Gee—I didn't mean that, Ruth, honest. Gee, I don't feel like that at all. I—I think it is wonderful.

RUTH *(dully):* Wonderful.

BENEATHA: Yes—really.

MAMA *(looking at* RUTH, *worried):* Doctor say everything going to be all right?

RUTH *(far away):* Yes—she says everything is going to be fine . . .

MAMA *(immediately suspicious):* "She"—What doctor you went to?

(RUTH *folds over, near hysteria)*

MAMA: *(Worriedly hovering over* RUTH*):* Ruth, honey—what's the matter with you—you sick?

(RUTH *has her fists clenched on her thighs and is fighting hard to suppress a scream that seems to be rising in her)*

BENEATHA: What's the matter with her, Mama?

MAMA: *(working her fingers in* RUTH*'s shoulder to relax her):* She be all right. Women gets right depressed sometimes when they get her way. *(Speaking softly, expertly, rapidly)* Now you just relax. That's right . . . just lean back, don't think 'bout nothing at all . . . nothing at all —

RUTH: I'm all right . . .

(The glassy-eyed look melts and then she collapses into a fit of heavy sobbing. The bell rings)

BENEATHA: Oh, my God—that must be Asagai.

MAMA *(to* RUTH*):* Come on now, honey. You need to lie down and rest awhile . . . then have some nice hot food.

(They exit, RUTH*'s weight on her mother-in-law.* BENEATHA *herself profoundly disturbed, opens the door to admit a rather dramatic-looking young man with a large package)*

ASAGAI: Hello, Alaiyo—

BENEATHA *(Holding the door open and regarding him with pleasure):* Hello . . . *(Long pause)* Well—come in. And please excuse everything. My mother was very upset about my letting anyone come here with the place like this.

ASAGAI *(coming into the room):* You look disturbed too . . . Is something wrong?

BENEATHA *(still at the door, absently):* Yes . . . we've all got acute ghetto-itus. *(She smiles and comes toward him, finding a cigarette and sitting)* So—sit down! No! Wait! *(She whips the spraygun off sofa where she had left it and puts the cushions back. At last perches on arm of sofa. He sits)* So, how was Canada?

ASAGAI *(a sophisticate):* Canadian.

BENEATHA *(looking at him):* Asagai, I'm very glad you are back.

ASAGAI *(Looking back at her in turn):* Are you really?

BENEATHA: Yes—very.

ASAGAI: Why?—you were quite glad when I went away. What happened?

BENEATHA: You went away.

ASAGAI: Ahhhhhhhh.

BENEATHA: Before—you wanted to be so serious before there was time.

ASAGAI: How much time must there be before one knows what one feels?

BENEATHA *(stalling this particular conversation. Her hands pressed together, in a deliberately childish gesture):* What did you bring me?

ASAGAI *(handing her the package):* Open it and see.

BENEATHA *(eagerly opening the package and drawing out some records and the colorful robes of a Nigerian woman):* Oh, Asagai! . . . You got them for me! . . . How beautiful . . . and the records too! *(She lifts out the robes and runs to the mirror with them and holds the drapery up in front of herself)*

ASAGAI *(coming to her at the mirror):* I shall have to teach you how to drape it properly. *(He flings the material about her for the moment and stands back to look at her)* Ah—*Oh-pay-gay-day, oh-ghah-mu-shay. (A Yoruba exclamation for admiration)* You wear it well . . . very well . . . mutilated hair and all.

BENEATHA *(Turning suddenly):* My hair—what's wrong with my hair?

ASAGAI *(shrugging):* Were you born with it like that?

BENEATHA *(Reaching up to touch it):* No. . . of course not.

(She looks back to the mirror, disturbed)

ASAGAI: *(Smiling)* How then?

BENEATHA: You know perfectly well how . . . as crinkly as yours . . . that's how.

ASAGAI: And it is ugly to you that way?

BENEATHA *(quickly):* Oh, no—not ugly . . . *(More slowly, apologetically)* But it's so hard to manage when it's, well—raw.

ASAGAI: And so to accommodate that—you mutilate it every week?

BENEATHA: It's not mutilation!

ASAGAI *(laughing aloud at her seriousness):* Oh . . . please! I am only teasing you because you are so very serious about these things. *(He stands back from her and folds his arms across his chest as he watches her pulling at her hair and frowning in the mirror)* Do you remember the first time you met me at school? . . . *(He laughs)* You came up to me and said—and I thought you were the most serious little thing I had ever seen—you said: *(He imitates her)* "Mr. Asagai—I want very much to talk with you. About Africa. You see, Mr. Asagai, I am looking for my *identity!*"

(He laughs)

BENEATHA *(turning to him, not laughing):* Yes —

(Her face is quizzical, profoundly disturbed)

ASAGAI *(still teasing and reaching out and taking her face in his hands and turning her profile to him):* Well . . . it is true that this is not so much a profile of a Hollywood queen as perhaps a queen of the Nile—*(A mock dismissal of the importance of the question)* But what does it matter? Assimilationism is so popular in your country.

BENEATHA *(wheeling, passionately, sharply):* I am not an assimilationist!

ASAGAI *(the protest hangs in the room for a moment and* ASAGAI *studies her, his laughter fading):* Such a serious one. *(There is a pause)* So—you like the robes? You must take excellent care of them—they are from my sister's personal wardrobe.

BENEATHA *(with incredulity):* You—you sent all the way home—for me?

ASAGAI *(with charm):* For you—I would do much more . . . Well, that is what I came for. I must go.

BENEATHA: Will you call me Monday?

ASAGAI: Yes . . . We have a great deal to talk about. I mean about identity and time and all that.

BENEATHA: Time?

ASAGAI: Yes. About how much time one needs to know what one feels.

BENEATHA: You see! You never understood that there is more than one kind of feeling which can exist between a man and a woman—or, at least, there should be.

ASAGAI *(shaking his head negatively but gently):* No. Between a man and a woman there need be only one kind of feeling. I have that for you . . . Now even . . . right this moment . . .

BENEATHA: I know—and by itself—it won't do. I can find that anywhere.

ASAGAI: For a woman it should be enough.

BENEATHA: I know—because that's what it says in all the novels that men write. But it isn't. Go ahead and laugh—but I'm not interested in being someone's little episode in America or—*(With feminine vengeance)*—one of them! *(*ASAGAI *has burst into laughter again)* That's funny as hell, huh!

ASAGAI: It's just that every American girl I have known has said that to me. White—black—in this you are all the same. And the same speech, too!

BENEATHA *(angrily):* Yuk, yuk, yuk!

ASAGAI: It's how you can be sure that the world's most liberated women are not liberated at all. You all talk about it too much!

*(*MAMA *enters and is immediately all social charm because of the presence of a guest)*

BENEATHA: Oh—Mama—this is Mr. Asagai.

MAMA: How do you do?

ASAGAI *(total politeness to an elder):* How do you do, Mrs. Younger. Please forgive me for coming at such an outrageous hour on a Saturday.

MAMA: Well, you are quite welcome. I just hope you understand that our house don't always look like this. *(Chatterish)* You must come again. I would love to hear all about—*(Not sure of the name)*—your country. I think it's so sad the way our American Negroes don't know nothing about Africa 'cept Tarzan and all that. And all that money they pour into these churches when they ought to be helping you people over there drive out them French and Englishmen done taken away your land.

(The mother flashes a slightly superior look at her daughter upon completion of the recitation)

ASAGAI *(taken aback by this sudden and acutely unrelated expression of sympathy):* Yes . . . yes . . .

MAMA *(smiling at him suddenly and relaxing and looking him over):* How many miles is it from here to where you come from?

ASAGAI: Many thousands.

MAMA *(looking at him as she would* WALTER*):* I bet you don't half look after yourself, being away from your mama either. I spec you better come 'round here from time to time and get yourself some decent home-cooked meals . . .

ASAGAI *(moved):* Thank you. Thank you very much. *(They are all quiet, then—)* Well . . . I must go. I will call you Monday, Alaiyo.

MAMA: What's that he call you?

ASAGAI: Oh—"Alaiyo." I hope you don't mind. It is what you would call a nickname, I think. It is a Yoruba word. I am a Yoruba.

MAMA *(looking at* BENEATHA*):* I—I thought he was from—*(Uncertain)*

ASAGAI *(understanding):* Nigeria is my country. Yoruba is my tribal origin—

BENEATHA: You didn't tell us what Alaiyo means . . . for all I know, you might be calling me Little Idiot or something . . .

ASAGAI: Well . . . let me see . . . I do not know how just to explain it . . . The sense of a thing can be so different when it changes languages.

BENEATHA: You're evading.

ASAGAI: No—really it is difficult . . . *(Thinking)* It means . . . it means One for Whom Bread—Food—Is Not Enough. *(He looks at her)* Is that all right?

BENEATHA *(understanding, softly):* Thank you.

MAMA *(looking from one to the other and not understanding any of it):* Well . . .that's nice . . . You must come see us again—Mr.——

ASAGAI: Ah-sah-guy . . .

MAMA: Yes . . . Do come again.

ASAGAI: Good-bye.

(He exits)

MAMA *(after him):* Lord, that's a pretty thing just went out here! *(Insinuatingly, to her daughter)* Yes, I guess I see why we done commence to get so interested in Africa 'round here. Missionaries my aunt Jenny!

(She exits)

BENEATHA: Oh, Mama! . . .

(She picks up the Nigerian dress and holds it up to her in front of the mirror again. She sets the headdress on haphazardly and then notices her hair again and clutches at it and then replaces the headdress and frowns at herself. Then she starts

to wriggle in front of the mirror as she thinks a Nigerian woman might. TRAVIS *enters and stands regarding her)*

TRAVIS: What's the matter, girl, you cracking up?

BENEATHA: Shut up.

(She pulls the headdress off and looks at herself in the mirror and clutches at her hair again and squinches her eyes as if trying to imagine something. Then, suddenly, she gets her raincoat and kerchief and hurriedly prepares for going out)

MAMA *(coming back into the room):* She's resting now. Travis, baby, run next door and ask Miss Johnson to please let me have a little kitchen cleanser. This here can is empty as Jacob's kettle.

TRAVIS: I just came in.

MAMA: Do as you told. *(He exits and she looks at her daughter)* Where you going?

BENEATHA *(halting at the door):* To become a queen of the Nile!

(She exits in a breathless blaze of glory. RUTH *appears in the bedroom doorway)*

MAMA: Who told you to get up?

RUTH: Ain't nothing wrong with me to be lying in no bed for. Where did Bennie go?

MAMA *(drumming her fingers):* Far as I could make out—to Egypt. *(*RUTH *just looks at her)* What time is it getting to?

RUTH: Ten twenty. And the mailman going to ring that bell this morning just like he done every morning for the last umpteen years.

*(*TRAVIS *comes in with the cleanser can)*

TRAVIS: She say to tell you that she don't have much.

MAMA *(angrily):* Lord, some people I could name sure is tight-fisted! *(Directing her grandson)* Mark two cans of cleanser down on the list there. If she that hard up for kitchen cleanser, I sure don't want to forget to get her none!

RUTH: Lena—maybe the woman is just short on cleanser—

MAMA *(not listening):*—Much baking powder as she done borrowed from me all these years, she could of done gone into the baking business!

(The bell sounds suddenly and sharply and all three are stunned—serious—and silent—mid-speech. In spite of all the other conversation and distractions of the morning, this is what they have been waiting for, even TRAVIS, *who looks helplessly from his mother to his grandmother.* RUTH *is the first to come to life again)*

RUTH *(to* TRAVIS*):* Get down them steps, boy! *(*TRAVIS *snaps to life and flies out to get the mail)*

MAMA *(Her eyes wide, her hand to her breast):* You mean it done really come?

RUTH *(excited):* Oh, Miss Lena!

MAMA *(collecting herself):* Well . . . I don't know what we all so excited about 'round here for. We known it was coming for months.

RUTH: That's a whole lot different from having it come and being able to hold it in your hands . . . a piece of paper worth ten thousand dollars . . . *(*TRAVIS *bursts back into the room. He holds the envelope high above his head, like a little dancer, his face is radiant and he is breathless. He moves to his grandmother with sudden slow ceremony and puts the envelope into her hands. She accepts it, and then merely holds it and looks at it)* Come on! Open it . . . Lord have mercy, I wish Walter Lee was here!

TRAVIS: Open it, Grandmama!

MAMA *(staring at it):* Now you all be quiet. It's just a check.

RUTH: Open it . . .

MAMA *(still staring at it):* Now don't act silly . . . We ain't never been no people to act silly 'bout no money—

RUTH *(swiftly):* We ain't never had none before—OPEN IT!

(MAMA *finally makes a good strong tear and pulls out the thin blue slice of paper and inspects it closely. The boy and his mother study it raptly over* MAMA's *shoulders)*

MAMA: *Travis! (She is counting off with doubt)* Is that the right number of zeros?

TRAVIS: Yes'm . . . ten thousand dollars. Gaalee, Grandmama, you rich.

MAMA *(she holds the check away from her, still looking at it. Slowly her face sobers into a mask of unhappiness):* Ten thousand dollars. *(She hands it to* RUTH*)* Put it away somewhere, Ruth. *(She does not look at* RUTH; *her eyes seem to be seeing something somewhere very far off)* Ten thousand dollars they give you. Ten thousand dollars.

TRAVIS *(to his mother, sincerely):* What's the matter with Grandmama—don't she want to be rich?

RUTH *(distractedly):* You go on out and play now, baby. *(*TRAVIS *exits.* MAMA *starts wiping dishes absently, humming intently to herself.* RUTH *turns to her, with kind exasperation)* You've gone and got yourself upset.

MAMA *(not looking at her):* I spec if it wasn't for you all . . . I would just put that money away or give it to the church or something.

RUTH: Now what kind of talk is that. Mr. Younger would just be plain mad if he could hear you talking foolish like that.

MAMA *(stopping and staring off):* Yes . . . he sure would. *(Sighing)* We got enough to do with that money, all right. *(She halts then, and turns and looks at her daughter-in-law hard;* RUTH *avoids her eyes and* MAMA *wipes her hands with finality and starts to speak firmly to* RUTH*)* Where did you go today, girl?

RUTH: To the doctor.

MAMA: *(impatiently):* Now, Ruth . . . you know better than that. Old Doctor Jones is strange enough in his way but there ain't nothing 'bout him make somebody slip and call him "she"—like you done this morning.

RUTH: Well, that's what happened—my tongue slipped.

MAMA: You went to see that woman, didn't you?

RUTH *(defensively, giving herself away):* What woman you talking about?

MAMA *(angrily):* That woman who—

(WALTER *enters in great excitement)*

WALTER: Did it come?

MAMA *(quietly):* Can't you give people a Christian greeting before you start asking about money?

WALTER *(to* RUTH*):* Did it come? *(*RUTH *unfolds the check and lays it quietly before him, watching him intently with thoughts of her own.* WALTER *sits down and grasps it close and counts off the zeros)* Ten thousand dollars—*(He turns suddenly, frantically to his mother and draws some papers out of his breast pocket)* Mama—look. Old Willy Harris put everything on paper—

MAMA: Son—I think you ought to talk to your wife . . . I'll go on out and leave you alone if you want—

WALTER: I can talk to her later—Mama, look—

MAMA: Son—

WALTER: WILL SOMEBODY PLEASE LISTEN TO ME TODAY!

MAMA *(quietly):* I don't 'low no yellin' in this house, Walter Lee, and you know it—
(WALTER *stares at them in frustration and starts to speak several times)* And there
ain't going to be no investing in no liquor stores.

WALTER: But, Mama, you ain't even looked at it.

MAMA: I don't aim to have to speak on that again.

(A long pause)

WALTER: . . . you don't aim to have to speak on that again? You ain't even looked at it
and you have decided—*(Crumpling his papers)* Well, *you* tell that to my boy
tonight when you put him to sleep on the living-room couch . . . *(Turning to* MAMA
and speaking directly to her) Yeah—and tell it to my wife, Mama, tomorrow when
she has to go out of here to look after somebody else's kids. And tell it to *me*,
Mama, every time we need a new pair of curtains and I have to watch *you* go out
and work in somebody's kitchen. Yeah, you tell me then!

*(*WALTER *starts out)*

RUTH: Where you going?

WALTER: I'm going out!

RUTH: Where?

WALTER: Just out of this house somewhere —

RUTH *(getting her coat):* I'll come too.

WALTER: I don't want you to come!

RUTH: I got something to talk to you about, Walter.

WALTER: That's too bad.

MAMA *(still quietly):* Walter Lee—*(She waits and he finally turns and looks at her)* Sit
down.

WALTER: I'm a grown man, Mama.

MAMA: Ain't nobody said you wasn't grown. But you still in my house and my presence.
And as long as you are—you'll talk to your wife civil. Now sit down.

RUTH *(suddenly):* Oh, let him go on out and drink himself to death! He makes me sick
to my stomach! *(She flings her coat against him and exits to the bedroom)*

WALTER *(violently):* And you turn mine, too baby! *(The door slams behind her.)* That
was my greatest mistake—

MAMA *(still quietly):* Walter, what is the matter with you?

WALTER: Matter with me? Ain't nothing the matter with *me!*

MAMA: Yes there is. Something eating you up like a crazy man. Something more than
me not giving you this money. The past few years I been watching it happen to you.
You get all nervous acting and kind of wild in the eyes—*(*WALTER *jumps up impatiently at her words)* I said sit there now, I'm talking to you!

WALTER: Mama—I don't need no nagging at me today.

MAMA: Seem like you getting to a place where you always tied up in some kind of knot
about something. But if anybody ask you 'bout it you just yell at 'em and bust out
the house and go out and drink somewheres. Walter Lee, people can't live with
that. Ruth's a good, patient girl in her way—but you getting to be too much. Boy,
don't make the mistake of driving that girl away from you.

WALTER: Why—what she do for me?

MAMA: She loves you.

WALTER: Mama—I'm going out. I want to go off somewhere and be by myself for a while.

MAMA: I'm sorry 'bout your liquor store, son. It just wasn't the thing for us to do. That's what I want to tell you about—

WALTER: I got to go out, Mama—

(He rises)

MAMA: It's dangerous, son.

WALTER: What's dangerous?

MAMA: When a man goes outside his home to look for peace.

WALTER *(beseechingly):* Then why can't there never be no peace in this house then?

MAMA: You done found it in some other house?

WALTER: No—there ain't no woman! Why do women always think there's a woman somewhere when a man gets restless. *(Picks up the check)* Do you know what this money means to me? Do you know what this money can do for us? *(Puts it back)* Mama—Mama—I want so many things . . .

MAMA: Yes, son—

WALTER: I want so many things that they are driving me kind of crazy . . . Mama—look at me.

MAMA: I'm looking at you. You a good-looking boy. You got a job, a nice wife, a fine boy and—

WALTER: A job. *(Looks at her)* Mama, a job? I open and close car doors all day long. I drive a man around in his limousine and I say, "Yes, sir; no, sir; very good, sir; shall I take the Drive, sir?" Mama, that ain't no kind of job . . . that ain't nothing at all. *(Very quietly)* Mama, I don't know if I can make you understand.

MAMA: Understand what, baby?

WALTER *(Quietly):* Sometimes it's like I can see the future stretched out in front of me—just plain as day. The future, Mama. Hanging over there at the edge of my days. Just waiting for me—a big, looming blank space—full of *nothing*. Just waiting for *me*. *(Pause. Kneeling bedside her chair)* Mama—sometimes when I'm downtown and I pass them cool, quiet-looking restaurants where them white boys are sitting back and talking 'bout things . . . sitting there turning deals worth millions of dollars . . . sometimes I see guys don't look much older than me—

MAMA: Son—how come you talk so much 'bout money?

WALTER *(With immense passion):* Because it is life, Mama!

Mama *(quietly):* Oh—*(Very quietly)* So now it's life. Money is life. Once upon a time freedom used to be life—now it's money. I guess the world really do change . . .

WALTER: No—it was always money, Mama. We just didn't know about it.

MAMA: No . . . something has changed. *(She looks at him)* You something new, boy. In my time we was worried about not being lynched and getting to the North if we could and how to stay alive and still have a pinch of dignity too . . . Now here come you and Beneatha—talking 'bout things we ain't never even thought about hardly, me and your daddy. You ain't satisfied or proud of nothing we done. I mean that you had a home; that we kept you out of trouble till you was grown; that you don't have to ride to work on the back of nobody's streetcar—You my children—but how different we done become.

WALTER *(a long beat. He pats her hand and gets up):* You just don't understand, Mama, you just don't understand.

MAMA: Son—do you know your wife is expecting another baby? *(WALTER stands, stunned, and absorbs what his mother has said)* That's what she wanted to talk to you about. *(WALTER sinks down into a chair)* This ain't for me to be telling—but you ought to know. *(She waits)* I think Ruth is thinking 'bout getting rid of that child.

WALTER *(slowly understanding):* No—no—Ruth wouldn't do that.

MAMA: When the world gets ugly enough—a woman will do anything for her family. *The part that's already living.*

WALTER: You don't know Ruth, Mama, if you think she would do that.

(RUTH opens the bedroom door and stands there a little limp)

RUTH *(beaten):* Yes I would too, Walter. *(Pause)* I gave her a five-dollar down payment.

(There is total silence as the man stares at his wife and the mother stares at her son)

MAMA *(presently):* Well—*(tightly)* Well—son, I'm waiting to hear you say something . . . *(She waits)* I'm waiting to hear how you be your father's son. Be the man he was . . . *(Pause. The silence shouts)* Your wife say she going to destroy your child. And I'm waiting to hear you talk like him and say we a people who give children life, not who destroys them—*(She rises)* I'm waiting to see you stand up and look like your daddy and say we done give up one baby to poverty and that we ain't going to give up nary another one . . . I'm waiting.

WALTER: Ruth—*(He can say nothing)*

MAMA: If you a son of mine, tell her! *(WALTER picks up his keys and his coat and walks out. She continues, bitterly)* You . . . you are a disgrace to your father's memory. Somebody get me my hat!

Curtain

ACT II
Scene I

Time: *Later the same day.*

At rise: RUTH *is ironing again. She has the radio going. Presently* BENEATHA's *bedroom door opens and* RUTH's *mouth falls and she puts down the iron in fascination.*

RUTH: What have we got on tonight!

BENEATHA *(emerging grandly from the doorway so that we can see her thoroughly robed in the costume* ASAGAI *brought):* You are looking at what a well-dressed Nigerian woman wears—*(She parades for* RUTH, *her hair completely hidden by the headdress; she is coquettishly fanning herself with an ornate oriental fan, mistakenly more like Butterfly than any Nigerian that ever was)* Isn't it beautiful? *(She promenades to the radio and, with an arrogant flourish, turns off the good loud blues that is playing)* Enough of this assimilationist junk! *(RUTH follows her with her eyes as she goes to the phonograph and puts on a record and turns and waits ceremoniously for the music to come up. Then with a shout)*—OCOMOGOSIAY!

(RUTH jumps. The music comes up, a lovely Nigerian melody. BENEATHA *listens, enraptured, her eyes far away—"back to the past." She begins to dance.* RUTH *is dumbfounded)*

RUTH: What kind of dance is that?

BENEATHA: A folk dance.

RUTH *(Pearl Bailey):* What kind of folks do that, honey?

BENEATHA: It's from Nigeria. It's a dance of welcome.

RUTH: Who you welcoming?

BENEATHA: The men back to the village.

RUTH: Where they been?

BENEATHA: How should I know—out hunting or something. Anyway, they are coming back now . . .

RUTH: Well, that's good.

BENEATHA *(With the record):* Alundi, alundi Alundi alunya

Jop pu àjeepua

Ang gu soooooooooo

Ai yai yae . . .

Ayehaye—alundi . . .

(WALTER comes in during this performance; he has obviously been drinking. He leans against the door heavily and watches his sister, at first with distaste. Then his eyes look off—"back to the past"—as he lifts both his fists to the roof, screaming)

WALTER: YEAH . . . AND ETHIOPIA STRETCH FORTH HER HANDS AGAIN! . . .

RUTH *(drily, looking at him):* Yes—and Africa sure is claiming her own tonight. *(She gives them both up and starts ironing again)*

WALTER *(All in a drunken, dramatic shout):* Shut up! . . . I'm digging them drums . . . them drums move me! . . . *(He makes his weaving way to his wife's face and leans in close to her)* In my heart of hearts—*(He thumps his chest)*—I am much warrior!

RUTH *(without even looking up):* In your heart of hearts you are much drunkard.

WALTER *(coming away from her and starting to wander around the room, shouting):* Me and Jomo . . . *(Intently, in his sister's face. She has stopped dancing to watch him in this unknown mood)* That's my man, Kenyatta. *(Shouting and thumping his chest)* FLAMING SPEAR! HOT DAMN! *(He is suddenly in possession of an imaginary spear and actively spearing enemies all over the room)* OCOMOGOSIAY . . . THE LION IS WAKING . . .

(He pulls his shirt open and leaps up on the table and gestures with his spear. The bell rings. RUTH goes to answer)

BENEATHA *(To encourage WALTER, thoroughly caught up with this side of him):* OCOMOGOSIAY, FLAMING SPEAR!

WALTER: THE LION IS WAKING . . . OWIMOWEH!

(He pulls his shirt open and leaps up on the table and gestures with his spear)

BENEATHA: OWIMOWEH!

WALTER *(on the table, very far gone, his eyes pure glass sheets. He sees what we cannot, that he is a leader of his people, a great chief, a descendant of Chaka, and that the hour to march has come):* Listen, my black brothers—

BENEATHA: OCOMOGOSIAY!

WALTER:—Do you hear the waters rushing against the shores of the coastlands—

BENEATHA: OCOMOGOSIAY!

WALTER:—Do you hear the screeching of the cocks in yonder hills beyond where the chiefs meet in council for the coming of the mighty war—

BENEATHA: OCOMOGOSIAY!

(And now the lighting shifts subtly to suggest the world of WALTER's imagination, and the mood shifts from pure comedy. It is the inner WALTER speaking: the Southside chauffeur has assumed an unexpected majesty)

WALTER:—Do you hear the beating of the wings of the birds flying low over the mountains and the low places of our land—

BENEATHA: OCOMOGOSIAY!

WALTER:—Do you hear the singing of the women, singing the war songs of our fathers to the babies in the great houses. Singing the sweet war songs? *(The doorbell rings)* OH, DO YOU HEAR, MY BLACK BROTHERS?

BENEATHA *(completely gone):* We hear you, Flaming Spear—

(RUTH opens the door, GEORGE MURCHSION enters)

WALTER: Telling us to prepare for the GREATNESS OF TIME—*(Lights back to normal. He turns and sees GEORGE)* Black Brother!

(He extends his hand for the fraternal clasp)

GEORGE: Black Brother, hell!

RUTH *(having had enough, and embarrassed for the family):* Beneatha, you got company—what's the matter with you? Walter Lee Younger, get down off that table and stop acting like a fool . . .

(WALTER comes down off the table suddenly and makes a quick exit to the bathroom)

RUTH: He's had a little to drink . . . I don't know what her excuse is.

GEORGE *(To BENEATHA):* Look honey, we're going *to* the theatre—we're not going to be *in* it . . . so go change, huh?

(BENEATHA looks at him and slowly, ceremoniously, lifts her hands and pulls off the headdress. Her hair is close-cropped and unstraightened. GEORGE freezes mid-sentence and RUTH's eyes all but fall out of her head)

GEORGE: What in the name of—

RUTH *(touching BENEATHA's hair):* Girl, you done lost your natural mind!? Look at your head!

GEORGE: What have you done to your head—I mean your hair!

BENEATHA: Nothing—except cut it off.

RUTH: Now that's the truth—it's what ain't been done to it! You expect this boy to go out with you with your head all nappy like that?

BENEATHA *(looking at GEORGE):* That's up to George. If he's ashamed of his heritage —

GEORGE: Oh, don't be so proud of yourself, Bennie—just because you look eccentric.

BENEATHA: How can something that's natural be eccentric?

GEORGE: That's what being eccentric means—being natural. Get dressed.

BENEATHA: I don't like that, George.

RUTH: Why must you and your brother make an argument out of everything people say?

BENEATHA: Because I hate assimilationist Negroes!

RUTH: Will somebody please tell me what assimila-who-ever means!

GEORGE: Oh, it's just a college girl's way of calling people Uncle Toms—but that isn't what it means at all.

RUTH: Well, what does it mean?

BENEATHA *(cutting GEORGE off and staring at him as she replies to RUTH):* It means someone who is willing to give up his own culture and submerge himself completely in the dominant, and in this case, *oppressive* culture!

GEORGE: Oh, dear, dear, dear! Here we go! A lecture on the African past! On our Great West African Heritage! In one second we will hear all about the great Ashanti empires; the great Songhay civilizations; and the great sculpture of Bénin—and then some poetry in the Bantu—and the whole monologue will end with the word *heritage! (Nastily)* Let's face it, baby, your heritage is nothing but a bunch of raggedy-assed spirituals and some grass huts!

BENEATHA: GRASS HUTS! *(RUTH crosses to her and forcibly pushes her toward the bedroom)* See there . . . you are standing there in your splendid ignorance talking about people who were the first to smelt iron on the face of the earth! *(RUTH is pushing her through the door)* The Ashanti were performing surgical operations when the English—*(RUTH pulls the door to, with* BENEATHA *on the other side, and smiles graciously at* GEORGE. BENEATHA *opens the door and shouts the end of the sentence defiantly at* GEORGE*)*—were still tattooing themselves with blue dragons . . . *(She goes back inside)*

RUTH: Have a seat, George. *(They both sit.* RUTH *folds her hands rather primly on her lap, determined to demonstrate the civilization of the family)* Warm, ain't it? I mean for September. *(Pause)* Just like they always say about Chicago weather: If it's too hot or cold for you, just wait a minute and it'll change. *(She smiles happily at this cliché of clichés)* Everybody say it's got to do with them bombs and things they keep setting off. *(Pause)* Would you like a nice cold beer?

GEORGE: No, thank you. I don't care for beer. *(He looks at his watch)* I hope she hurries up.

RUTH: What time is the show?

GEORGE: It's an eight-thirty curtain. That's just Chicago, though. In New York standard curtain time is eight forty.

(He is rather proud of this knowledge)

RUTH *(properly appreciating it):* You get to New York a lot?

GEORGE *(off hand):* Few times a year.

RUTH: Oh—that's nice. I've never been to New York.

(WALTER enters. We feel he has relieved himself, but the edge of unreality is still with him)

WALTER: New York ain't got nothing Chicago ain't. Just a bunch of hustling people all squeezed up together—being "Eastern."

(He turns his face into a screw of displeasure)

GEORGE: Oh—you've been?

WALTER: *Plenty* of times.

RUTH *(shocked at the lie):* Walter Lee Younger!

WALTER *(staring her down):* Plenty! *(Pause)* What we got to drink in this house? Why don't you offer this man some refreshment. *(To* GEORGE*)* They don't know how to entertain people in this house, man.

GEORGE: Thank you— I don't really care for anything.

WALTER *(feeling his head; sobriety coming):* Where's Mama?

RUTH: She ain't come back yet.

WALTER *(looking* MURCHISON *over from head to toe, scrutinizing his carefully casual tweed sports jacket over cashmere V-neck sweater over soft eyelet shirt and tie, and soft slacks, finished off with white buckskin shoes):* Why all you college boys wear them faggoty-looking white shoes?

RUTH: Walter Lee! *(*GEORGE MURCHISON *ignores the remark)*

WALTER *(to* RUTH*):* Well, they look crazy as hell—white shoes, cold as it is.

RUTH *(crushed):* You have to excuse him—

WALTER: No he don't! Excuse me for what? What you always excusing me for! I'll excuse myself when I needs to be excused! *(A pause)* They look as funny as them black knee socks Beneatha wears out of here all the time.

RUTH: It's the college *style*, Walter.

WALTER: Style, hell. She looks like she got burnt legs or something!

RUTH: Oh, Walter—

WALTER *(an irritable mimic):* Oh, Walter! Oh, Walter! *(To* MURCHISON*)* How's your old man making out? I understand you all going to buy that big hotel on the Drive? *(He finds a beer in the refrigerator, wanders over to* MURCHISON, *sipping and wiping his lips with the back of his hand, and straddling a chair backwards to talk to the other man)* Shrewd move. Your old man is all right, man. *(Tapping his head and half winking for emphasis)* I mean he knows how to operate. I mean he thinks *big*, you know what I mean, I mean for a *home*, you know? But I think he's kind of running out of ideas now. I'd like to talk to him. Listen, man, I got some plans that could turn this city upside down. I mean I think like he does. *Big*. Invest big, gamble big, hell, lose *big* if you have to, you know what I mean. It's hard to find a man on this whole Southside who understands my kind of thinking—you dig? *(He scrutinizes* MURCHISON *again, drinks his beer, squints his eyes and leans in close, confidential, man to man)* Me and you ought to sit down and talk sometimes, man. Man, I got me some ideas . . .

MURCHISON *(With boredom):* Yeah—sometimes we'll have to do that, Walter.

WALTER *(Understanding the indifference, and offended):* Yeah—well, when you get the time, man. I know you a busy little boy.

RUTH: Walter, please—

WALTER *(Bitterly, hurt):* I know ain't nothing in this world as busy as you colored college boys with your fraternity pins and white shoes . . .

RUTH *(Covering her face with humiliation):* Oh, Walter Lee—

WALTER: I see you all all the time—with the books tucked under your arms—going to your *(British A—a mimic)* "clahsses." And for what! What the hell you learning over there? Filling up your heads—*(Counting off on his fingers)*—with the sociology and the psychology—but they teaching you how to be a man? How to take over and run the world? They teaching you how to run a rubber plantation or a steel mill? Naw—just to talk proper and read books and wear them faggoty-looking white shoes . . .

GEORGE *(looking at him with distaste, a little above it all):* You're all wacked up with bitterness, man.

WALTER *(intently, almost quietly, between the teeth, glaring at the boy):* And you—ain't you bitter, man? Ain't you just about had it yet? Don't you see no stars gleaming that you can't reach out and grab? You happy?—You contented son-of-a-bitch—you happy? You got it made? Bitter? Man, I'm a volcano. Bitter? Here I am a giant—surrounded by ants! Ants who can't even understand what it is the giant is talking about.

RUTH *(passionately and suddenly):* Oh, Walter—ain't you with nobody!

WALTER *(violently):* No! 'Cause ain't nobody with me! Not even my own mother!

RUTH: Walter, that's a terrible thing to say!

*(*BENEATHA *enters, dressed for the evening in a cocktail dress and earrings, hair natural)*

GEORGE: Well—hey—*(Crosses to* BENEATHA; *thoughtful, with emphasis, since this is a reversal)* You look great!

WALTER *(seeing his sister's hair for the first time):* What's the matter with your head?

BENEATHA *(tired of the jokes now):* I cut it off, Brother.

WALTER *(coming closer to inspect it and walking around her):* Well, I'll be damned. So that's what they mean by the African bush . . .

BENEATHA: Ha ha. Let's go, George.

GEORGE *(looking at her):* You know something? I like it. It's sharp. I mean it really is. *(Helps her into her wrap)*

RUTH: Yes—I think so, too. *(She goes to the mirror and starts to clutch at her hair)*

Walter: Oh no! You leave yours alone, baby. You might turn out to have a pin-shaped head or something!

BENEATHA: See you all later.

RUTH: Have a nice time.

GEORGE: Thanks. Good night. *(Half out the door, he reopens it. To* WALTER, *sarcastically)* Good night, Prometheus.

*(*BENEATHA *and* GEORGE *exit)*

WALTER *(to* RUTH*):* Who is Prometheus?

RUTH: I don't know. Don't worry about it.

WALTER *(in fury, pointing after* GEORGE*):* See there—they get to a point where they can't insult you man to man—they got to go talk about something ain't nobody never heard of!

RUTH: How do you know it was an insult? *(To humor him)* Maybe Prometheus is a nice fellow.

WALTER: Prometheus! I bet there ain't even no such thing! I bet that simple-minded clown—

RUTH: Walter—

(She stops what she is doing and looks at him)

WALTER *(yelling):* Don't start!

RUTH: Start what?

WALTER: Your nagging! Where was I? Who was I with? How much money did I spend?

RUTH *(Plaintively):* Walter Lee—why don't we just try to talk about it . . .

WALTER *(not listening):* I been out talking with people who understand me. People who care about the things I got on my mind.

RUTH *(wearily):* I guess that means people like Willy Harris.

WALTER: Yes, people like Willy Harris.

RUTH *(with a sudden flash of impatience):* Why don't you all just hurry up and go into the banking business and stop talking about it!

WALTER: Why? You want to know why? 'Cause we all tied up in a race of people that don't know how to do nothing but moan, pray and have babies!
(The line is too bitter even for him and he looks at her and sits down)

RUTH: Oh, Walter . . . *(Softly)* Honey, why can't you stop fighting me?

WALTER *(Without thinking):* Who's fighting you? Who even cares about you? *(This line begins the retardation of his mood)*

RUTH: Well—*(She waits a long time, and then with resignation starts to put away her things)* I guess I might as well go on to bed *(More or less to herself)* I don't know where we lost it . . . but we have . . . *(Then, to him)* I—I'm sorry about this new baby, Walter. I guess maybe I better go on and do what I started . . . I guess I just didn't realize how bad things was with us . . . I guess I just didn't really realize— *(She starts out to the bedroom and stops)* You want some hot milk?

WALTER: Hot milk?

RUTH: Yes—hot milk.

WALTER: Why hot milk?

RUTH: 'Cause after all that liquor you come home with you ought to have something hot in your stomach.

WALTER: I don't want no milk.

RUTH: You want some coffee then?

WALTER: No, I don't want no coffee. I don't want nothing hot to drink. *(Almost plaintively)* Why you always trying to give me something to eat?

RUTH *(standing and looking at him helplessly):* What *else* can I give you, Walter Lee Younger?

(She stands and looks at him and presently turns to go out again. He lifts his head and watches her going away from him in a new mood which began to emerge when he asked her "Who cares about you?")

WALTER: It's been rough, ain't it, baby? *(She hears and stops but does not turn around and he continues to her back)* I guess between two people there ain't never as much understood as folks generally thinks there is. I mean like between me and you—*(She turns to face him)* How we gets to the place where we scared to talk softness to each other. *(He waits, thinking hard himself)* Why you think it got to be like that? *(He is thoughtful, almost as a child would be)* Ruth, what is it gets into people ought to be close?

RUTH: I don't know, honey. I think about it a lot.

WALTER: On account of you and me, you mean? The way things are with us. The way something done come down between us.

RUTH: There ain't so much between us, Walter . . . Not when you come to me and try to talk to me. Try to be with me . . . a little even.

WALTER *(total honesty):* Sometimes . . . sometimes . . . I don't even know how to try.

RUTH: Walter—

WALTER: Yes?

RUTH *(coming to him, gently and with misgiving, but coming to him):* Honey . . . life don't have to be like this. I mean sometimes people can do things so that things are better . . . You remember how we used to talk when Travis was born . . . about the way we were going to live . . . the kind of house . . . *(She is stroking his head)* Well, it's all starting to slip away from us . . .

(He turns her to him and they look at each other and kiss, tenderly and hungrily. The door opens and MAMA enters—WALTER breaks away and jumps up. A beat)

WALTER: Mama, where have you been?

MAMA: My—them steps is longer than they used to be. Whew! *(She sits down and ignores him)* How you feeling this evening, RUTH!

(RUTH shrugs, disturbed some at having been prematurely interrupted and watching her husband knowingly)

WALTER: Mama, where have you been all day?

MAMA: *(Still ignoring him and leaning on the table and changing to more comfortable shoes):* Where's Travis?

RUTH: I let him go out earlier and he ain't come back yet. Boy, is he going to get it!

WALTER: Mama!

MAMA *(As if she has heard him for the first time):* Yes, son?

WALTER: Where did you go this afternoon?

MAMA: I went downtown to tend to some business that I had to tend to.

WALTER: What kind of business?

MAMA: You know better than to question me like a child, Brother.

WALTER *(rising and bending over the table):* Where were you, Mama? *(Bringing his fists down and shouting)* Mama, you didn't go do something with that insurance money, something crazy?

(The front door opens slowly, interrupting him, and TRAVIS *peeks his head in, less than hopefully)*

TRAVIS *(to his mother):* Mama, I—

RUTH: "Mama I" nothing! You're going to get it, boy! Get on in that bedroom and get yourself ready!

TRAVIS: But I—

MAMA: Why don't you all never let the child explain hisself.

RUTH: Keep out of it now, Lena.

*(*MAMA *clamps her lips together, and* RUTH *advances toward her son menacingly)*

RUTH: A thousand times I have told you not to go off like that—

MAMA *(Holding out her arms to her grandson):* Well—at least let me tell him something. I want him to be the first one to hear . . . Come here, Travis. *(The boy obeys, gladly)* TRAVIS—*(She takes him by the shoulder and looks into his face)*—you know that money we got in the mail this morning?

TRAVIS: Yes'm—

MAMA: Well—what you think your grandmama gone and done with that money?

TRAVIS: I don't know, Grandmama.

MAMA *(putting her finger on his nose for emphasis):* She went out and she bought you a house! *(The explosion comes from* WALTER *at the end of the revelation and he jumps up and turns away from all of them in a fury.* MAMA *continues, to* TRAVIS*)* You glad about the house? It's going to be yours when you get to be a man.

TRAVIS: Yeah—I always wanted to live in a house.

MAMA: All right, gimme some sugar then— *(*TRAVIS *puts his arms around her neck as she watches her son over the boy's shoulder. Then, to* TRAVIS, *after the embrace)* Now when you say your prayers tonight, you thank God and your grandfather— 'cause it was him who give you the house—in his way.

RUTH *(taking the boy from* MAMA *and pushing him toward the bedroom):* Now you get out of here and get ready for your beating.

TRAVIS: Aw, Mama—

RUTH: Get on in there—*(Closing the door behind him and turning radiantly to her mother-in-law)* So you went and did it!

MAMA *(quietly, looking at her son with pain):* Yes, I did.

RUTH *(raising both arms classically):* PRAISE GOD! *(Looks at* WALTER *a moment, who says nothing. She crosses rapidly to her husband)* Please, honey—let me be glad . . . you be glad too. *(She has laid her hands on his shoulders, but he shakes himself free of her roughly, without turning to face her)* Oh, Walter . . . a home . . . *a home. (She comes back to* MAMA*)* Well—where is it? How big is it? How much it going to cost?

MAMA: Well—

RUTH: When we moving?

MAMA *(smiling at her):* First of the month.

RUTH *(throwing back her head with jubilance):* Praise God!

MAMA *(tentatively, still looking at her son's back turned against her and* RUTH*):* It's—it's a nice house too . . . *(She cannot help speaking directly to him. An imploring quality in her voice, her manner, makes her almost like a girl now)* Three bedrooms— nice big one for you and Ruth . . . Me and Beneatha still have to share our room, but TRAVIS have one of his own —and *(With difficulty)* I figure if the—new baby—is a boy, we could get one of them double-decker outfits . . . And there's a yard with a little patch of dirt where I could maybe get to grow me a few flowers . . . And a nice big basement . . .

RUTH: Walter honey, be glad —

MAMA *(still to his back, fingering things on the table):* 'Course I don't want to make it sound fancier than it is . . . It's just a plain little old house—but it's made good and solid—and it will be *ours.* Walter Lee—it makes a difference in a man when he can walk on floors that belong to *him* . . .

RUTH: Where is it?

MAMA *(Frightened at this telling):* Well—well—it's out there in Clybourne Park—

(RUTH*'s radiance fades abruptly, and* WALTER *finally turns slowly to face his mother with incredulity and hostility)*

RUTH: Where?

MAMA *(matter-of-factly):* Four o six Clybourne Street, Clybourne Park.

RUTH: Clybourne Park? Mama, there ain't no colored people living in Clybourne Park.

MAMA *(almost idiotically):* Well, I guess there's going to be some now.

WALTER *(bitterly):* So that's the peace and comfort you went out and bought for us today!

MAMA *(raising her eyes to meet his finally):* Son—I just tried to find the nicest place for the least amount of money for my family.

RUTH *(trying to recover from the shock):* Well—well—'course I ain't one never been 'fraid of no crackers, mind you—but—well, wasn't there no other houses nowhere?

MAMA: Them houses they put up for colored in them areas way out all seem to cost twice as much as other houses. I did the best I could.

RUTH *(struck senseless with the news, in its various degrees of goodness and trouble, she sits a moment, her fists propping her chin in thought, and then she starts to rise, bringing her fists down with vigor, the radiance spreading from cheek to cheek again):* Well—well!—All I can say is—if this is my time in life—*MY TIME*— to say goodbye—*(And she builds with momentum as she starts to circle the room with an exuberant, almost tearfully happy release)*—to these Goddamned cracking walls!—*(She pounds the walls)*—and these marching roaches!—*(She wipes at an imaginary army of marching roaches)*—and this cramped little closet which ain't now or never was no kitchen! . . . then I say it loud and good, HALLELUJAH! and GOOD-BYE MISERY . . . I DON'T NEVER WANT TO SEE YOUR UGLY FACE AGAIN! *(She laughs joyously, having practically destroyed the apartment, and flings her arms up and lets them come down happily, slowly, reflectively, over her abdomen, aware for the first time perhaps that the life therein pulses with happiness and not despair)* Lena?

MAMA *(moved, watching her happiness):* Yes, honey?

RUTH *(looking off):* Is there—is there a whole lot of sunlight?

MAMA *(understanding):* Yes, child, there's a whole lot of sunlight.

(Long pause)

RUTH *(collecting herself and going to the door of the room* TRAVIS *is in):* Well—I guess I better see 'bout TRAVIS. *(To* MAMA*)* Lord, I sure don't feel like whipping nobody today!

(She exits)

MAMA *(the mother and son are left alone now and the mother waits a long time, considering deeply, before she speaks):* Son—you—you understand what I done, don't you? *(*WALTER *is silent and sullen)* I —I just seen my family falling apart today . . . just falling to pieces in front of my eyes . . . We couldn't of gone on like we was today. We was going backwards 'stead of forwards—talking 'bout killing babies and wishing each other was dead . . . When it gets like that in life—you just got to do something different, push on out and do something bigger . . . *(She waits)* I wish you say something, son . . . I wish you'd say how deep inside you you think I done the right thing—

WALTER *(crossing slowly to his bedroom door and finally turning there and speaking measuredly):* What you need me to say you done right for? *You* the head of this family. You run our lives like you want to. It was your money and you did what you wanted with it. So what you need for me to say it was all right for? *(Bitterly, to hurt her as deeply as he knows is possible)* So you butchered up a dream of mine— you—who always talking 'bout your children's dreams . . .

MAMA: Walter Lee—

(He just closes the door behind him. MAMA *sits alone, thinking heavily)*

Curtain

Scene II

Time: Friday night. A few weeks later.

At rise: Packing crates mark the intention of the family to move. BENEATHA *and* GEORGE *come in, presumably from an evening out again*

GEORGE: O.K. . . . O.K., whatever you say . . . *(They both sit on the couch. He tries to kiss her. She moves away)* Look, we've had a nice evening; let's not spoil it, huh? . . .

(He again turns her head and tries to nuzzle in and she turns away from him, not with distaste but with momentary lack of interest; in a mood to pursue what they were talking about)

BENEATHA: I'm trying to talk to you.

GEORGE: We always talk.

BENEATHA: Yes—and I love to talk.

GEORGE *(exasperated; rising):* I know it and I don't mind it sometimes . . . I want you to cut it out, see—The moody stuff, I mean. I don't like it. You're a nice-looking girl . . . all over. That's all you need, honey, forget the atmosphere. Guys aren't going to go for the atmosphere—they're going to go for what they see. Be glad for that. Drop the Garbo routine. It doesn't go with you. As for myself, I want a nice— *(Groping)*—simple *(Thoughtfully)*—sophisticated girl . . . not a poet—O.K.? *(He starts to kiss her, she rebuffs him again and he jumps up)*

BENEATHA: Why are you angry, George?

GEORGE: Because this is stupid! I don't go out with you to discuss the nature of "quiet desperation" or to hear all about your thoughts—because the world will go on thinking what it thinks regardless—

BENEATHA: Then why read books? Why go to school?

GEORGE *(with artificial patience, counting on his fingers):* It's simple. You read books—to learn facts—to get grades—to pass the course—to get a degree. That's all—it has nothing to do with thoughts.

(A long pause)

BENEATHA: I see. *(He starts to sit)* Good night, George.

*(*GEORGE *looks at her a little oddly, and starts to exit. He meets* MAMA *coming in)*

GEORGE: Oh—hello, Mrs. Younger.

MAMA: Hello, George, how you feeling?

GEORGE: Fine—fine, how are you?

MAMA: Oh, a little tired. You know them steps can get you after a day's work. You all have a nice time tonight?

GEORGE: Yes—a fine time.

MAMA: Well, good night.

GEORGE: Good night. *(He exits.* MAMA *closes the door behind her)* Hello, honey. What you sitting like that for?

BENEATHA: I'm just sitting.

MAMA: Didn't you have a nice time?

BENEATHA: No.

MAMA: No? What's the matter?

BENEATHA: Mama, George is a fool—honest. (She rises)

MAMA (hustling around unloading the packages she has entered with. She stops): Is he, baby?

BENEATHA: Yes.

*(*BENEATHA *makes up* TRAVIS' *bed as she talks)*

MAMA: You sure?

BENEATHA: Yes.

MAMA: Well—I guess you better not waste your time with no fools.

*(*BENEATHA *looks up at her mother, watching her put groceries in the refrigerator. Finally she gathers up her things and starts into the bedroom. At the door she stops and looks back at her mother)*

BENEATHA: Mama—

MAMA: Yes, baby—

BENEATHA: Thank you.

MAMA: For what?

BENEATHA: For understanding me this time.

(She exits quickly and the mother stands, smiling a little, looking at the place where BENEATHA *had stood.* RUTH *enters)*

RUTH: Now don't you fool with any of this stuff, Lena—

MAMA: Oh, I just thought I'd sort a few things out. Is Brother here?

RUTH: Yes.

MAMA *(with concern):* Is he—

RUTH *(reading her eyes):* Yes.

(MAMA *is silent and someone knocks on the door.* MAMA *and* RUTH *exchange weary and knowing glances and* RUTH *opens it to admit the neighbor,* MRS. JOHNSON,* *who is a rather squeaky wide-eyed lady of no particular age, with a newspaper under her arm)*

MAMA *(changing her expression to acute delight and a ringing cheerful greeting):* Oh—hello there, Johnson.

JOHNSON *(This is a woman who decided long ago to be enthusiastic about EVERY-THING in her life and she is inclined to wave her wrist vigorously at the height of her exclamatory comments):* Hello there, yourself! H'you this evening, Ruth?

RUTH (not much of a deceptive type): Fine, Mis' Johnson, h'you?

JOHNSON: Fine. *(Reaching out quickly, playfully, and patting* RUTH's *stomach)* Ain't you starting to poke out none yet! *(She mugs with delight at the over-familiar remark and her eyes dart around looking at the crates and packing preparation;* MAMA's *face is a cold sheet of endurance)* Oh, ain't we getting ready round here, though! Yessir! Lookathere! I'm telling you the Youngers is really getting ready to "move on up a little higher!"—Bless God!

MAMA *(a little drily, doubting the total sincerity of the Blesser):* Bless God.

JOHNSON: He's good, ain't He?

MAMA: Oh yes, He's good.

JOHNSON: I mean sometimes He works in mysterious ways . . . but He works, don't He!

MAMA *(the same):* Yes, he does.

JOHNSON: I'm just soooooo happy for y'all. And this here child—*(About* RUTH*)* looks like she could just pop open with happiness, don't she. Where's all the rest of the family?

MAMA: Bennie's gone to bed—

JOHNSON: Ain't no . . . *(The implication is pregnancy)* sickness done hit you—I hope . . . ?

MAMA: No—she just tired. She was out this evening.

JOHNSON *(all is a coo, an emphatic coo):* Aw—ain't that lovely. She still going out with the little Murchison boy?

MAMA *(drily):* Ummmm huh.

JOHNSON: That's lovely. You sure got lovely children, Younger. Me and Isaiah talks all the time 'bout what fine children you was blessed with. We sure do.

MAMA: Ruth, give Mis' Johnson a piece of sweet popato pie and some milk.

JOHNSON: Oh honey, I can't stay hardly a minute—I just dropped in to see if there was anything I could do. *(Accepting the food easily)* I guess y'all seen the news what's all over the colored paper this week . . .

MAMA: No—didn't get mine yet this week.

JOHNSON *(lifting her head and blinking with the spirit of catastrophe):* You mean you ain't read 'bout them colored people that was bombed out their place out there?

(RUTH straightens with concern and takes the paper and reads it. JOHNSON *notices her and feeds commentary)*

JOHNSON: Ain't it something how bad these here white folks is getting here in Chicago! Lord, getting so you think you right down in Mississippi! *(With a tremendous and rather insincere sense of melodrama)* 'Course I thinks it's wonderfull how our folks keeps on pushing out. You hear some of these Negroes round here talking 'bout how they don't go where they ain't wanted and all that—but not me, honey! *(This is a lie)* Wilhemenia Othella Johnson goes anywhere, any time she feels like it! *(With head movement for emphasis)* Yes I do! Why if we left it up to these here crackers, the poor niggers wouldn't have nothing—*(She clasps her hand over her mouth)* Oh, I always forgets you don't 'low that word in your house.

MAMA *(quietly, looking at her):* No—I don't 'low it.

JOHNSON *(vigorously again):* Me neither! I was just telling Isaiah yesterday when he come using it in front of me—I said, "Isaiah, it's just like Mis' Younger says all the time—"

MAMA: Don't you want some more pie?

JOHNSON: No—no thank you; this was lovely. I got to get on over home and have my midnight coffee. I hear some people say it don't let them sleep but I finds I can't close my eyes right lessen I done had that laaaast cup of coffee . . . *(She waits. A beat. Undaunted)* My Goodnight coffee, I calls it!

MAMA *(with much eye-rolling and communication between herself and* RUTH): Ruth, why don't you give Mis' Johnson some coffee.

*(*RUTH *gives* MAMA *an unpleasant look for her kindness)*

JOHNSON *(accepting the coffee):* Where's Brother tonight?

MAMA: He's lying down.

JOHNSON: MMmmmmm, he sure gets his beauty rest, don't he? Good-looking man. Sure is a good-looking man! *(Reaching out to pat* RUTH's *stomach again)* I guess that's how come we keep on having babies around here. *(She winks at* MAMA*)* One thing 'bout Brother, he always know how to have a *good* time. And sooooo ambitious! I bet it was his idea y'all moving out to Clybourne Park. Lord—I bet this time next month y'all's names will have been in the papers plenty—*(Holding up her hands to mark off each word of the headline she can see in front of her)* "NEGROES INVADE CLYBROUNE PARK—BOMBED!"

MAMA *(she and* RUTH *look at the woman in amazement):* We ain't exactly moving out there to get bombed.

JOHNSON: Oh, honey—you know I'm praying to God every day that don't nothing like that happen! But you have to think of life like it is—and these here Chicago peckerwoods is some baaaad peckerwoods.

*(*BENEATHA *comes out of the bedroom in her robe and passes through to the bathroom.* MRS. JOHNSON *turns)*

JOHNSON: Hello there, Bennie!

BENEATHA *(crisply):* Hello, Mrs. Johnson.

Johnson: How is school?

BENEATHA *(crisply):* Fine, thank you. *(She goes out.)*

JOHNSON *(insulted):* Getting so she don't have much to say to nobody.

MAMA: The child was on her way to the bathroom.

JOHNSON: I know—but sometimes she act like ain't got time to pass the time of day with nobody ain't been to college. Oh—I ain't criticizing her none. It's just—you know some of our young people gets when they get a little education. *(*MAMA *and* RUTH *say nothing, just look at her)* Yes—well. Well, I guess I better get on home. *(Unmoving)* 'Course I can understand how she must be proud and everything—being the only one in the family to make something of herself. I know just being a chauffeur ain't never satisfied Brother none. He shouldn't feel like that, though. Ain't nothing wrong with being a chauffeur.

MAMA: There's plenty wrong with it.

JOHNSON: What?

MAMA: Plenty. My husband always said being any kind of a servant wasn't a fit thing for a man to have to be. He always said a man's hands was made to make things, or to turn the earth with—not to drive nobody's car for 'em—or—*(She looks at her own hands)* carry they slop jars. And my boy is just like him—he wasn't meant to wait on nobody.

JOHNSON *(rising, somewhat offended):* Mmmmmmmmm. The Youngers is too much for me! *(She looks around)* You sure one proud-acting bunch of colored folks. Well—I always thinks like Booker T. Washington said that time—"Education has spoiled many a good plow hand"—

MAMA: Is that what old Booker T. said?

JOHNSON: He sure did.

MAMA: Well, it sounds like him. The fool.

JOHNSON *(indignantly):* Well—he was one of our great men.

MAMA: Who said so?

JOHNSON *(nonplussed):* You know, me and you ain't never agreed about some things, Lena Younger. I guess I better be going—

RUTH *(quickly):* Good night.

JOHNSON: Good night. Oh—*(Thrusting it at her)* You can keep the paper! *(With a trill)* 'Night.

MAMA: Good night, Mis' Johnson.

*(*MRS. JOHNSON *exits)*

RUTH: If ignorance was gold . . .

MAMA: Shush. Don't talk about folks behind their backs.

RUTH: You do.

MAMA: I'm old and corrupted. *(*BENEATHA *enters)* You was rude to Mis' Johnson, Beneatha, and I don't like it at all.

BENEATHA *(at her door):* Mama, if there are two things we, as a people, have got to overcome, one is the Ku Klux Klan—and the other is Mrs. Johnson. *(She exits)*

(The phone rings)

RUTH: I'll get it.

MAMA: Lord, ain't this a popular place tonight.

RUTH *(at the phone):* Hello—just a minute. *(Goes to door)* Walter, it's Mrs. Arnold. *(Waits. Goes back to the phone. Tense)* Hello. Yes, this is his wife speaking . . . He's lying down now. Yes . . . well, he'll be in tomorrow. He's been very sick. Yes—I know we should have called, but we were so sure he'd be able to come in today. Yes—yes, I'm very sorry. Yes . . . Thank you very much. *(She hangs up.* WALTER *is standing in the doorway of the bedroom behind her)* That was Mrs. Arnold.

WALTER *(indifferently):* Was it?

RUTH: She said if you don't come in tomorrow that they are getting a new man . . .

WALTER: Ain't that sad—ain't that crying sad.

RUTH: She said Mr. Arnold has had to take a cab for three days . . . Walter, you ain't been to work for three days! *(This is a revelation to her)* Where you been, Walter Lee Younger? *(*WALTER *looks at her and starts to laugh)* You're going to lose your job.

WALTER: That's right . . . *(He turns on the radio)*

RUTH: Oh, Walter, and with your mother working like a dog every day—

(A steamy, deep blues pours into the room)

WALTER: That's sad too—Everything is sad.

MAMA: What you been doing for these three days, son?

WALTER: Mama—you don't know all the things a man what got leisure can find to do in this city . . . What's this—Friday night? Well—Wednesday I borrowed Willy Harris' car and I went for a drive . . . just me and myself and I drove and drove . . . Way out . . . way past South Chicago, and I parked the car and I sat and looked at the steel mills all day long. I just sat in the car and looked at them big black chimneys for hours. Then I drove back and I went to the Green Hat. *(Pause)* And Thursday— Thursday I borrowed the car again and I got in it and I pointed it the other way and I drove the other way—for hours—way, way up to Wisconsin, and I looked at the farms. I just drove and looked at the farms. Then I drove back and I went to the Green Hat. *(Pause)* And today—today I didn't get the car. Today I just walked. All over the Southside. And I looked at the Negroes and they looked at me and finally I just sat down on the curb at Thirty-ninth and South Parkway and I just sat there and watched the Negroes go by. And then I went to the Green Hat. You all sad? You all depressed? And you know where I am going right now—

*(*RUTH *goes out quietly)*

MAMA: Oh, Big Walter, is this the harvest of our days?

WALTER: You know what I like about the Green Hat? I like this little cat they got there who blows a sax . . . He blows. He talks to me. He ain't but 'bout five feet tall and he's got a conked head and his eyes is always closed and he's all music —

MAMA *(rising and getting some papers out of her handbag):* Walter—

WALTER: And there's this other guy who plays the piano . . . and they got a sound. I mean they can work on some music . . . They got the best little combo in the world in the Green Hat . . . You can just sit there and drink and listen to them three men play and you realize that don't nothing matter worth a damn, but just being there —

MAMA: I've helped do it to you, haven't I, son? Walter, I been wrong.

WALTER: Naw—you ain't never been wrong about nothing, Mama.

MAMA: Listen to me, now. I say I been wrong, son. That I been doing to you what the rest of the world been doing to you. *(She turns off the radio. She stops and he looks up slowly at her and she meets his eyes pleadingly)* What you ain't understood is that I ain't got nothing, don't own nothing, ain't never really wanted nothing that wasn't for you. There ain't nothing as precious to me . . . There ain't nothing worth holding on to, money, dreams, nothing else—if it means—if it means it's going to destroy my boy. *(She takes an envelope out of her handbag and puts it in front of him and he watches her without speaking or moving)* I paid the man thirty-five hundred dollars down on the house. That leaves sixty-five hundred dollars. Monday morning I want you to take this money and take three thousand dollars and put it in a savings account for Beneatha's medical schooling. The rest you put in a checking account—with your name on it. And from now on any penny that come out of it or that go in it is for you to look after. For you to decide. *(She drops her hands a little helplessly)* It ain't much, but it's all I got in the world and I'm putting it in your hands. I'm telling you to be the head of this family from now on like you supposed to be.

WALTER *(stares at the money):* You trust me like that, Mama?

MAMA: I ain't never stop trusting you. Like I ain't never stop loving you.

(She goes out, and WALTER *sits looking at the money on the table. Finally, in a decisive gesture, he gets up, and, in mingled joy and desperation, picks up the money. At the same moment,* TRAVIS *enters for bed)*

TRAVIS: What's the matter, Daddy? You drunk?

WALTER *(sweetly, more sweetly than we have ever known him):* No, Daddy ain't drunk. Daddy ain't going to never be drunk again. . . .

TRAVIS: Well, good night, Daddy.

(The father has come from behind the couch and leans over, embracing his son)

WALTER: Son, I feel like talking to you tonight.

TRAVIS: About what?

WALTER: Oh, about a lot of things. About you and what kind of man you going to be when you grow up. . . . Son—son, what do you want to be when you grow up?

TRAVIS: A bus driver.

WALTER *(laughing a little):* A what? Man, that ain't nothing to want to be!

TRAVIS: Why not?

WALTER: 'Cause, man—it ain't big enough—you know what I mean.

TRAVIS: I don't know then. I can't make up my mind. Sometimes Mama asks me that too. And sometimes when I tell her I just want to be like you—she says she don't want me to be like that and sometimes she says she does. . . .

WALTER *(gathering him up in his arms):* You know what, Travis? In seven years you going to be seventeen years old. And things is going to be very different with us in seven years, Travis . . . One day when you are seventeen I'll come home—home from my office downtown somewhere—

TRAVIS: You don't work in no office, Daddy.

WALTER: No—but after tonight. After what your daddy gonna do tonight, there's going to be offices—a whole lot of offices. . . .

TRAVIS: What you gonna do tonight, Daddy?

WALTER: You wouldn't understand yet, son, but your daddy's gonna make a transaction . . . a business transaction that's going to change our lives . . . That's how come one day when you 'bout seventeen years old I'll come home and I'll be pretty tired, you know what I mean, after a day of conferences and secretaries getting things wrong the way they do . . . 'cause an executive's life is hell, man—*(The more he talks the farther away he gets)* And I'll pull the car up on the driveway . . . just a plain black Chrysler, I think, with white walls—no—black tires. More elegant. Rich people don't have to be flashy . . . though I'll have to get something a little sportier for Ruth—maybe a Cadillac convertible to do her shopping in. . . . And I'll come up the steps to the house and the gardener will be clipping away at the hedges and he'll say, "Good evening, Mr. Younger." And I'll say, "Hello, Jefferson, how are you this evening?" And I'll go inside and Ruth will come downstairs and meet me at the door and we'll kiss each other and she'll take my arm and we'll go up to your room to see you sitting on the floor with the catalogues of all the great schools in America around you. . . . All the great schools in the world! And—and I'll say, all right son—it's your seventeenth birthday, what is it you've decided? . . . Just tell me where you want to go to school and you'll *go.* Just tell me, what it is you want to be—and you'll be it. . . . Whatever you want to be—Yessir! *(He holds his arms open for* TRAVIS*)* You just name it, son . . . *(*TRAVIS *leaps into them)* and I hand you the world!

(WALTER's voice has risen in pitch and hysterical promise and on the last line he lifts TRAVIS high)

Blackout

Scene III

Time: *Saturday, moving day, one week later.*

Before the curtain rises, RUTH's voice, a strident, dramatic church alto, cuts through the silence.

It is, in the darkness, a triumphant surge, a penetrating statement of expectation: "Oh, Lord, I don't feel no ways tired! Children, oh, glory hallelujah!"

As the curtain rises we see that RUTH is alone in the living room, finishing up the family's packing. It is moving day. She is nailing crates and tying cartons. BENEATHA enters, carrying a guitar case, and watches her exuberant sister-in-law.

RUTH: Hey!

BENEATHA *(putting away the case):* Hi.

RUTH *(pointing at a package):* Honey— look in that package there and see what I found on sale this morning at the South Center. *(RUTH gets up and moves to the package and draws out some curtains)* Lookahere—hand-turned hems!

BENEATHA: How do you know the window size out there?

RUTH *(who hadn't thought of that):* Oh—Well, they bound to fit something in the whole house. Anyhow, they was too good a bargain to pass up. *(RUTH slaps her head, suddenly remembering something)* Oh, Bennie—I meant to put a special note on that carton over there. That's your mama's good china and she wants 'em to be very careful with it.

BENEATHA: I'll do it.

(BENEATHA finds a piece of paper and starts to draw large letters on it)

RUTH: You know what I'm going to do soon as I get in that new house?

BENEATHA: What?

RUTH: Honey—I'm going to run me a tub of water up to here . . . *(With her fingers practically up to her nostrils)* And I'm going to get in it— and I am going to sit . . . and sit . . . and sit in that hot water and the first person who knocks to tell *me* to hurry up and come out—

BENEATHA: Gets shot at sunrise.

RUTH *(laughing happily):* You said it, sister! *(Noticing how large BENEATHA is absentmindedly making the note)* Honey, they ain't going to read that from no airplane.

BENEATHA *(laughing herself):* I guess I always think things have more emphasis if they are big, somehow.

RUTH *(looking up at her and smiling):* You and your brother seem to have that as a philosophy of life. Lord, that man—done changed so 'round here. You know—you know what we did last night? Me and Walter Lee?

BENEATHA: What?

RUTH *(smiling to herself):* We went to the movies. *(Looking at BENEATHA to see if she understands)* We went to the movies. You know the last time me and WALTER went to the movies together?

BENEATHA: No.

RUTH: Me neither. That's how long it been. *(Smiling again)* But we went last night. The picture wasn't much good, but that didn't seem to matter. We went—and we held hands.

BENEATHA: Oh, Lord!

RUTH: We held hands—and you know what?

BENEATHA: What?

RUTH: When we come out of the show it was late and dark and all the stores and things was closed up . . . and it was kind of chilly and there wasn't many people on the streets . . . and we was still holding hands, me and Walter.

BENEATHA: You're killing me.

(WALTER enters with a large package. His happiness is deep in him; he cannot keep still with his new-found exuberance. He is singing and wiggling and snapping his fingers. He puts his package in a corner and puts a phonograph record, which he has brought in with him, on the record player. As the music comes up he dances over to RUTH and tries to get her to dance with him. She gives in at last to his raunchiness and in a fit of giggling allows herself to be drawn into his mood. They dip and she melts into his arms in a classic, body-melding "slow drag")

BENEATHA *(regarding them a long time as they dance, then drawing in her breath for a deeply exaggerated comment which she does not particularly mean)*: Talk about—olddddddddddd-fashionedddddddd-Negroes!

WALTER *(stopping momentarily)*: What kind of Negroes? *(He says this in fun. He is not angry with her today, nor with anyone. He starts to dance with his wife again)*

BENEATHA: Old-fashioned.

WALTER *(as he dances with RUTH)*: You know, when these *New Negroes* have their convention—*(Pointing at his sister)*—that is going to be the chairman of the Committee on Unending Agitation. *(He goes on dancing, then stops)* Race, race, race! . . . Girl, I do believe you are the first person in the history of the entire human race to successfully brainwash yourself. *(BENEATHA breaks up and he goes on dancing. He stops again, enjoying his tease)* Damn, even the N double A C P takes a holiday sometimes! *(BENEATHA and RUTH laugh. He dances with RUTH some more and starts to laugh and stops and pantomimes someone over an operating table)* I can just see that chick someday looking down at some poor cat on an operating table before she starts to slice him, she says . . . *(Pulling his sleeves back maliciously)* "By the way, what are your views on civil rights down there? . . ."

(He laughs at her again and starts to dance happily. The bell sounds)

BENEATHA: Sticks and stones may break my bones but . . . words will never hurt me!

(BENEATHA goes to the door and opens it as WALTER and RUTH go on with the clowning. BENEATHA is somewhat surprised to see a quiet-looking middle-aged white man in a business suit holding his hat and a briefcase in his hand and consulting a small piece of paper)

MAN: Uh—how do you do, miss. I am looking for a Mrs.— *(He looks at the slip of paper)* Mrs. Lena Younger? *(He stops short, struck dumb at the sight of the oblivious WALTER and RUTH.)*

BENEATHA *(smoothing her hair with slight embarrassment)*: Oh—yes, that's my mother. Excuse me. *(She closes the door and turns to quiet the other two)* Ruth! Brother! Somebody's here. *(Enunciating precisely but soundlessly: "There's a white man at the door!" They stop dancing, RUTH cuts off the phonograph. She opens the door. The man casts a curious quick glance at all of them)* Uh—come in please.

MAN *(Coming in):* Thank you.

BENEATHA: My mother isn't here just now. Is it business?

MAN: Yes . . . well, of a sort.

WALTER *(freely, the Man of the House):* Have a seat. I'm Mrs. Younger's son. I look after most of her business matters.

> *(RUTH and BENEATHA exchange amused glances)*

MAN *(Regarding WALTER, and sitting):* Well—My name is Karl Lindner . . .

WALTER *(Stretching out his hand):* Walter Younger. This is my wife—*(RUTH nods politely)*—and my sister.

LINDNER: How do you do.

WALTER *(Amiably, as he sits himself easily on a chair, leaning forward on his knees with interest and looking expectantly into the newcomer's face):* What can we do for you, Mr. Lindner!

LINDNER *(Some minor shuffling of the hat and briefcase on his knees):* Well—I am a representative of the Clybourne Park Improvement Association—

WALTER *(Pointing):* Why don't you sit your things on the floor?

LINDNER: Oh—yes. Thank you. *(He slides the briefcase and hat under the chair)* And as I was saying—I am from the Clybourne Park Improvement Association and we have had it brought to our attention at the last meeting that you people—or at least your mother—has bought a piece of residential property at— *(He digs for the slip of paper again)*—four o six Clybourne Street . . .

WALTER: That's right. Care for something to drink? Ruth, get Mr. Lindner a beer.

LINDNER *(Upset for some reason):* Oh—no, really. I mean thank you very much, but no thank you.

RUTH *(Innocently):* Some coffee?

LINDNER: Thank you, nothing at all.

> *(BENEATHA is watching the man carefully)*

LINDNER: Well, I don't know how much you folks know about our organization. *(He is a gentle man; thoughtful and somewhat labored in his manner)* It is one of these community organizations set up to look after—oh, you know, things like block upkeep and special projects and we also have what we call our New Neighbors Orientation Committee . . .

BENEATHA *(drily):* Yes —and what do they do?

LINDNER *(turning a little to her and then returning the main force to WALTER):* Well—it's what you might call a sort of welcoming committee, I guess. I mean they, we—I'm the chairman of the committee—go around and see the new people who move into the neighborhood and sort of give them the lowdown on the way we do things out in Clybourne Park.

BENEATHA *(With appreciation of the two meanings, which escape RUTH and WALTER):* Uh-huh.

LINDNER: And we also have the category of what the association calls—*(He looks elsewhere)*—uh—special community problems . . .

BENEATHA: Yes—and what are some of those?

WALTER: Girl, let the man talk.

LINDNER *(with understated relief):* Thank you. I would sort of like to explain this thing in my own way. I mean I want to explain to you in a certain way.

WALTER: Go ahead.

LINDNER: Yes. Well. I'm going to try to get right to the point. I'm sure we'll all appreciate that in the long run.

BENEATHA: Yes.

WALTER: Be still now!

LINDNER: Well—

RUTH *(still innocently):* Would you like another chair—you don't look comfortable.

LINDNER *(more frustrated than annoyed):* No, thank you very much. Please. Well —to get right to the point I—*(A great breath, and he is off at last)* I am sure you people must be aware of some of the incidents which have happened in various parts of the city when colored people have moved into certain areas—*(*BENEATHA *exhales heavily and starts tossing a piece of fruit up and down in the air)* Well—because we have what I think is going to be a unique type of organization in American community life—not only do we deplore that kind of thing—but we are trying to do something about it. *(*BENEATHA *stops tossing and turns with a new and quizzical interest to the man)* We feel—*(gaining confidence in his mission because of the interest in the faces of the people he is talking to)*—we feel that most of the trouble in this world, when you come right down to it—*(He hits his knee for emphasis)*—most of the trouble exists because people just don't sit down and talk to each other.

RUTH *(nodding as she might in church, pleased with the remark):* You can say that again, mister.

LINDNER *(more encouraged by such affirmation):* That we don't try hard enough in this world to understand the other fellow's problem. The other guy's point of view.

RUTH: Now that's right.

*(*BENEATHA *and* WALTER *merely watch and listen with genuine interest)*

LINDNER: Yes—that's the way we feel out in Clybourne Park. And that's why I was elected to come here this afternoon and talk to you people. Friendly like, you know, the way people should talk to each other and see if we couldn't find some way to work this thing out. As I say, the whole business is a matter of caring about the other fellow. Anybody can see that you are a nice family of folks, hard working and honest I'm sure. *(*BENEATHA *frowns slightly, quizzically, her head tilted regarding him)* Today everybody knows what it means to be on the outside of *something.* And of course, there is always somebody who is out to take advantage of people who don't always understand.

WALTER: What do you mean?

LINDNER: Well—you see our community is made of people who've worked hard as the dickens for years to build up that little community. They're not rich and fancy people; just hard-working, honest people who don't really have much but those little homes and a dream of the kind of community they want to raise their children in. Now, I don't say we are perfect and there is a lot wrong in some of the things they want. But you've got to admit that a man, right or wrong, has the right to want to have the neighborhood he lives in a certain kind of way. And at the moment the overwhelming majority of our people out there feel that people get along better, take more of a common interest in the life of the community, when they share a common background. I want you to believe me when I tell you that race prejudice simply doesn't enter into it. It is a matter of the people of Clybourne Park believing, rightly or wrongly, as I say, that for the happiness of all concerned that our Negro families are happier when they live in their *own* communities.

BENEATHA *(with a grand and bitter gesture):* This, friends, is the Welcoming Committee!

WALTER *(dumbfounded, looking at* LINDNER*):* Is this what you came marching all the way over here to tell us?

LINDNER: Well, now we've been having a fine conversation. I hope you'll hear me all the way through.

WALTER *(tightly):* Go ahead, man.

LINDNER: You see—in the face of all things I have said, we are prepared to make your family a very generous offer . . .

BENEATHA: Thirty pieces and not a coin less!

WALTER: Yeah?

LINDNER *(putting on his glasses and drawing a form out of the briefcase):* Our association is prepared, through the collective effort of our people, to buy the house from you at a financial gain to your family.

RUTH: Lord have mercy, ain't this the living gall!

WALTER: All right, you through?

LINDNER: Well, I want to give you the exact terms of the financial arrangement—

WALTER: We don't want to hear no exact terms of no arrangements. I want to know if you got any more to tell us 'bout getting together?

LINDNER *(taking off his glasses):* Well—I don't suppose that you feel . . .

WALTER: Never mind how I feel—you got any more to say 'bout how people ought to sit down and talk to each other? . . . Get out of my house, man.

(He turns his back and walks to the door)

LINDNER *(Looking around at the hostile faces and reaching and assembling his hat and briefcase):* Well—I don't understand why you people are reacting this way. What do you think you are going to gain by moving into a neighborhood where you just aren't wanted and where some elements—well—people can get awful worked up when they feel that their whole way of life and everything they've ever worked for is threatened.

WALTER: Get out.

LINDNER *(at the door, holding a small card):* Well—I'm sorry it went like this.

WALTER: Get out.

LINDNER *(almost sadly regarding* WALTER*):* You just can't force people to change their hearts, son.

(He turns and put his card on a table and exits. WALTER *pushes the door to with stinging hatred, and stands looking at it.* RUTH *just sits and* BENEATHA *just stands. They say nothing.* MAMA *and* TRAVIS *enter)*

MAMA: Well—this all the packing got done since I left out of here this morning. I testify before God that my children got all the energy of the *dead!* What time the moving men due?

BENEATHA: Four o'clock. You had a caller, Mama.

(She is smiling, teasingly)

MAMA: Sure enough—who?

BENEATHA *(her arms folded saucily):* The Welcoming Committee.

*(*WALTER *and* RUTH *giggle)*

MAMA: *(innocently):* Who?

BENEATHA: The Welcoming Committee. They said they're sure going to be glad to see you when you get there.

WALTER *(devilishly):* Yeah, they said they can't hardly wait to see your face.

(Laughter)

MAMA *(sensing their facetiousness):* What's the matter with you all?

WALTER: Ain't nothing the matter with us. We just telling you 'bout the gentleman who came to see you this afternoon. From the Clybourne Park Improvement Association.

MAMA: What he want?

RUTH *(in the same mood as* BENEATHA *and* WALTER*):* To welcome you, honey.

WALTER: He said they can't hardly wait. He said the one thing they don't have, that they just dying to have out there is a fine family of colored people! (To RUTH and BENEATHA) Ain't that right!

RUTH *(mockingly):* Yeah! He left his card in case—

BENEATHA *(handing card to* MAMA*):* In case.

*(*MAMA *reads the card, and picks it up and throws it on the floor—understanding and looking off as she draws her chair up to the table on which she has put her plant and some sticks and some cord)*

MAMA: Father, give us strength. *(knowingly—and without fun)* Did he threaten us?

BENEATHA: Oh—Mama—they don't do it like that any more. He talked Brotherhood. He said everybody ought to learn how to sit down and hate each other with good Christian fellowship.

(She and WALTER *shake hands to ridicule the remark)*

MAMA *(sadly):* Lord, protect us . . .

RUTH: You should hear the money those folks raised to buy the house from us. All we paid and then some.

BENEATHA: What they think we going to do—eat 'em?

RUTH: No, honey, marry 'em.

Mama *(shaking her head):* Lord, Lord, Lord . . .

RUTH: Well—that's the way the crackers crumble. *(A beat)* Joke.

BENEATHA *(laughingly noticing what her mother is doing):* Mama, what are you doing?

MAMA: Fixing my plant so it won't get hurt none on the way . . .

BENEATHA: Mama, you going to take *that* to the new house?

MAMA: Un-huh—

BENEATHA: That raggedy-looking old thing?

MAMA: *(stopping and looking at her):* It expresses me.

RUTH *(With delight, to* BENEATHA*):* So there, Miss Thing!

*(*WALTER *comes to* MAMA *suddenly and bends down behind her and squeezes her in his arms with all his strength. She is overwhelmed by the suddenness of it and, though delighted, her manner is like that of* RUTH *with* TRAVIS*)*

MAMA: Look out now, boy! You make me mess up my thing here!

WALTER *(his face lit, he slips down on his knees beside her, his arms still about her):* Mama . . . you know what it means to climb up in the chariot?

Mama *(gruffly, very happy):* Get on away from me now . . .

RUTH *(near the gift-wrapped package, trying to catch* WALTER*'s eye):* Psst—

WALTER: What the old song say, Mama . . .

RUTH: Walter—Now?

(She is pointing at the package)

WALTER *(Speaking the lines, sweetly, playfully, in his mother's face):* I got wings . . . you got wings . . . All God's children got wings . . .

MAMA: Boy—get out of my face and do some work . . .

WALTER: When I get to heaven gonna put on my wings, Gonna fly all over God's heaven . . .

BENEATHA *(teasingly, from across the room):* Everybody talking 'bout heaven ain't going there!

WALTER *(to* RUTH, *who is carrying the box across to them):* I don't know, you think we ought to give her that . . . Seems to me she ain't been very appreciative around here.

MAMA *(eyeing the box, which is obviously a gift):* What is that?

WALTER *(taking it from* RUTH *and putting it on the table in front of* MAMA*):* Well—what you all think? Should we give it to her?

RUTH: Oh—she was pretty good today.

MAMA: I'll good you—

(She turns her eyes to the box again)

BENEATHA: Open it, Mama.

(She stands up, looks at it, turns and looks at all of them, and then presses her hands together and does not open the package)

WALTER *(Sweetly):* Open it, Mama. It's for you. (MAMA *looks in his eyes. It is the first present in her life without its being Christmas. Slowly she opens her package and lifts out, one by one, a brand-new sparkling set of gardening tools.* WALTER *continues, prodding)* Ruth made up the note—read it . . .

MAMA *(picking up the card and adjusting her glasses):* "To our own Mrs. Miniver—Love from Brother, Ruth and Beneatha." Ain't that lovely . . .

TRAVIS *(tugging at his father's sleeve):* Daddy, can I give her mine now?

WALTER: All right, son. *(*TRAVIS *flies to get his gift)*

MAMA: Now I don't have to use my knives and forks no more . . .

WALTER: Travis didn't want to go in with the rest of us, Mama. He got his own. *(Somewhat amused)* We don't know what it is . . .

TRAVIS *(racing back in the room with a large hatbox and putting it in front of his grandmother):* Here!

MAMA: Lord have mercy, baby. You done gone and bought your grandmother a hat?

TRAVIS *(very proud):* Open it!

(She does and lifts out an elaborate, but very elaborate, wide gardening hat, and all the adults break up at the sight of it)

RUTH: Travis, honey, what is that?

TRAVIS *(who thinks it is beautiful and appropriate):* It's a gardening hat! Like the ladies always have on in the magazines when they work in their gardens.

BENEATHA *(giggling fiercely):* Travis—we were trying to make Mama Mrs. Miniver—not Scarlet O'Hara!

MAMA *(indignantly):* What's the matter with you all! This here is a beautiful hat! *(Absurdly)* I always wanted me one just like it!

(She pops it on her head to prove it to her grandson, and the hat is ludicrous and considerably oversized)

RUTH: Hot dog! Go, Mama!

WALTER *(doubled over with laughter):* I'm sorry, Mama—but you look like you ready to go out and chop you some cotton sure enough!

(They all laugh except MAMA *out of deference to* TRAVIS'S *feelings)*

MAMA *(gathering the boy up to her):* Bless your heart—this is the prettiest hat I ever owned—*(*WALTER, RUTH *and* BENEATHA *chime in noisily, festively and insincerely congratulating* TRAVIS *on his gift)* What are we all standing around here for? We ain't finished packing yet. Bennie, you ain't packed one book.

(The bell rings)

BENEATHA: That couldn't be the movers . . . it's not hardly two o'clock yet—

*(*BENEATHA *goes into her room.* MAMA *starts for door)*

WALTER *(turning, stiffening):* Wait—wait—I'll get it.

(He stands and looks at the door)

MAMA: You expecting company, son?

WALTER *(just looking at the door):* Yeah—yeah . . . *(*MAMA *looks at* RUTH, *and they exchange innocent and unfrightened glances)*

MAMA *(Not understanding):* Well, let them in, son.

BENEATHA *(from her room):* We need some more string.

MAMA: Travis—you run to the hardware and get me some string cord.

*(*MAMA *goes out and* WALTER *turns and looks at* RUTH: TRAVIS *goes to a dish for money)*

RUTH: Why don't you answer the door, man?

WALTER *(suddenly bounding across the floor to her):* 'Cause sometimes it hard to let the future begin!

(Stooping down in her face)

> I got wings! You got wings!
> All God's children got wings!

(He crosses to the door and throws it open. Standing there is a very slight little man in a not too prosperous business suit and with haunted frightened eyes and a hat pulled down tightly, brim up, around his forehead. TRAVIS *passes between the men and exits.* WALTER *leans deep in the man's face, still in his jubilance)*

> When I get to heaven gonna put on my wings,
> Gonna fly all over God's heaven . . .

(The little man just stares at him)

> Heaven—

(Suddenly he stops and looks past the little man into the empty hallway) Where's Willy, man?

BOBO: He ain't with me.

WALTER *(not disturbed):* Oh—come on in. You know my wife.

BOBO *(Dumbly, taking off his hat):* Yes—h'you, Miss Ruth.

RUTH *(quietly, a mood apart from her husband already, seeing Bobo):* Hello, Bobo.

WALTER: You right on time today . . . Right on time. That's the way! *(He slaps* BOBO *on his back)* Sit down . . . . lemme hear.

*(*RUTH *stands stiffly and quietly in back of them, as though somehow she senses death, her eyes fixed on her husband)*

BOBO *(His frightened eyes on the floor, his hat in his hands):* Could I please get a drink of water, before I tell you about it, Walter Lee?

(WALTER does not take his eyes off the man. RUTH goes blindly to the tap and gets a glass of water and brings it to BOBO)

WALTER: There ain't nothing wrong, is there?

BOBO: Lemme tell you—

WALTER: Man—didn't nothing go wrong?

BOBO: Lemme tell you—Walter Lee. *(Looking at RUTH and talking to her more than to WALTER)* You know how it was. I got to tell you how it was. I mean first I got to tell you how it was all the way . . . I mean about the money I put in, Walter Lee . . .

WALTER *(with taut agitation now):* What about the money you put in?

BOBO: Well—it wasn't much as we told you—me and Willy—(He stops) I'm sorry, Walter. I got a bad feeling about it. I got a real bad feeling about it . . .

WALTER: Man, what you telling me about all this for? . . . Tell me what happened in Springfield . . .

BOBO: Springfield.

RUTH *(like a dead woman):* What was supposed to happen in Springfield?

BOBO *(to her):* This deal that me and Walter went into with Willy—Me and Willy was going to go down to Springfield and spread some money 'round so's we wouldn't have to wait so long for the liquor license . . . That's what we were going to do. Everybody said that was the way you had to do, you understand, Miss Ruth?

WALTER: Man—what happened down there?

BOBO *(a pitiful man, near tears):* I'm trying to tell you, Walter.

WALTER *(screaming at him suddenly):* THEN TELL ME, GODDAMMIT . . . WHAT'S THE MATTER WITH YOU?

BOBO: Man . . . I didn't go to no Springfield, yesterday.

WALTER *(halted, life hanging in the moment):* Why not?

BOBO *(the long way, the hard way to tell):* 'Cause I didn't have no reasons to . . .

WALTER: Man, what are you talking about!

BOBO: I'm talking about the fact that when I got to the train station yesterday morning—eight o'clock like we planned . . . Man—*Willy didn't never show up.*

WALTER: Why . . . where was he . . . where is he?

BOBO: That's what I'm trying to tell you . . . I don't know . . . I waited six hours . . . I called his house . . . and I waited . . . six hours . . . I waited in that train station six hours . . . *(Breaking into tears)* That was all the extra money I had in the world . . . *(Looking up at WALTER with the tears running down his face)* Man, *Willy is gone.*

WALTER: Gone, what you mean Willy is gone? Gone where? You mean he went by himself. You mean he went off to Springfield by himself—to take care of getting the license—*(Turns and looks anxiously at RUTH)* You mean maybe he didn't want too many people in on the business down there? *(Looks to RUTH again, as before)* You know Willy got his own ways. *(Looks back to BOBO)* Maybe you was late yesterday and he just went on down there without you. Maybe—maybe—he's been callin' you at home tryin' to tell you what happened or something. Maybe—maybe—he just got sick. He's somewhere—he's got to be somewhere. We just got to find him—me and you got to find him. *(Grabs BOBO senselessly by the collar and starts to shake him)* We got to!

BOBO *(in sudden angry, frightened agony):* What's the matter with you, Walter! When a cat take off with your money he don't leave you no road maps!

WALTER *(Turning madly, as though he is looking for WILLY in the very room):* Willy! . . . Willy . . . don't do it . . . Please don't do it . . . Man, not with that money . . .

Man, please, not with that money . . . Oh, God . . . Don't let it be true . . . *(He is wandering around, crying out for* WILLY *and looking for him or perhaps for help from God)* Man . . . I trusted you . . . Man, I put my life in your hands . . . *(He starts to crumple down on the floor as* RUTH *just covers her face in horror.* MAMA *opens the door and comes into the room, with* BENEATHA *behind her)* Man . . . *(He starts to pound the floor with his fists, sobbing wildly)* THAT MONEY IS MADE OUT OF MY FATHER'S FLESH—

BOBO *(standing over him helplessly):* I'm sorry, Walter . . . *(Only* WALTER's *sobs reply.* BOBO *puts on his hat)* I had my life staked on this deal, too . . .

(He exits)

MAMA: *(To* WALTER*):* Son—*(She goes to him, bends down to him, talks to his bent head)* Son . . . Is it gone? Son, I gave you sixty-five hundred dollars. Is it gone? All of it? Beneatha's money too?

WALTER *(lifting his head slowly):* Mama . . . I never . . . went to the bank at all . . .

MAMA: *(not wanting to believe him):* You mean . . . your sister's school money . . . you used that too . . . Walter? . . .

WALTER: Yessss! . . . All of it . . . It's all gone . . .

(There is total silence. RUTH *stands with her face covered with her hands;* BENEATHA *leans forlornly against a wall, fingering a piece of red ribbon from the mother's gift. Mama stops and looks at her son without recognition and then, quite without thinking about it, starts to beat him senselessly in the face.* BENEATHA *goes to them and stops it)*

BENEATHA: Mama!

*(*MAMA *stops and looks at both of her children and rises slowly and wanders vaguely, aimlessly away from them)*

MAMA: I seen . . . him . . . night after night . . . come in . . . and look at that rug . . . and then look at me . . . the red showing in his eyes . . .the veins moving in his head . . . I seen him grow thin and old before he was forty . . . working and working and working like somebody's old horse . . . killing himself . . . and you—you give it all away in a day . . .

(She raises her arms to strike him again)

BENEATHA: Mama—

MAMA: Oh, God . . . *(She looks up to Him)* Look down here—and show me the strength.

BENEATHA: Mama—

MAMA *(folding over):* Strength . . .

BENEATHA *(plaintively):* Mama . . .

MAMA: Strength!

Curtain

ACT III

An hour later

At curtain, there is a sullen light of gloom in the living room, gray light not unlike that which began the first scene of Act One. At left we can see WALTER *within his room, alone with himself. He is stretched out on the bed, his shirt out and open, his arms under his head. He does not smoke, he does not cry out, he merely lies there, looking up at the ceiling, much as if he were alone in the world.*

In the living room BENEATHA *sits at the table, still surrounded by the now almost ominous packing crates. She sits looking off. We feel that this is a mood struck perhaps an hour before, and it lingers now, full of the empty sound of profound disappointment. We see on a line from her brother's bedroom the sameness of their attitudes. Presently the bell rings and* BENEATHA *rises without ambition or interest in answering. It is* ASAGAI, *smiling broadly, striding into the room with energy and happy expectation and conversation.*

ASAGAI: I came over . . . I had some free time. I thought I might help with the packing. Ah, I like the look of packing crates! A household in preparation for a journey! It depresses some people . . . but for me . . . it is another feeling. Something full of the flow of life, do you understand? Movement, progress . . . It makes me think of Africa.

BENEATHA: Africa!

ASAGAI: What kind of a mood is this? Have I told you how deeply you move me?

BENEATHA: He gave away the money, Asagai . . .

ASAGAI: Who gave away what money?

BENEATHA: The insurance money. My brother gave it away.

ASAGAI: Gave it away?

BENEATHA: He made an investment with a man even Travis wouldn't have trusted with his most worn-out marbles.

ASAGAI: And it's gone?

BENEATHA: Gone!

ASAGAI: I'm very sorry . . . And you, now?

BENEATHA: Me? . . . Me? . . . Me, I'm nothing . . . Me. When I was very small . . . we used to take our sleds out in the wintertime and the only hills we had were the ice-covered stone steps of some houses down the street. And we used to fill them in with snow and make them smooth and slide down them all day . . . and it was very dangerous, you know . . . far too steep . . . and sure enough one day a kid named Rufus came down too fast and hit the sidewalk and we saw his face just split open right there in front of us . . . And I remember standing there looking at his bloody open face thinking that was the end of Rufus. But the ambulance came and they took him to the hospital and they fixed the broken bones and they sewed it all up . . . and the next time I saw Rufus he just had a little line down the middle of his face . . . I never got over that . . .

ASAGAI: What?

BENEATHA: That that was what one person could do for another, fix him up— sew up the problem, make him all right again. That was the most marvelous thing in the world . . . I wanted to do that. I always thought it was the one concrete thing in the world that a human being could do. Fix up the sick, you know—and make them whole again. This was truly being God . . .

ASAGAI: You wanted to be God?

BENEATHA: No—I wanted to cure. It used to be so important to me. I wanted to cure. It used to matter. I used to care. I mean about people and how their bodies hurt . . .

ASAGAI: And you've stopped caring?

BENEATHA: Yes—I think so.

ASAGAI: Why?

BENEATHA *(bitterly)*: Because it doesn't seem deep enough, close enough to what ails mankind! It was a child's reaction to the world. I thought that doctors had the secret to all the hurts . . . That's the way a child way of seeing things—or an idealist's.

ASAGAI: Children see things very well sometimes—and idealists even better.

BENEATHA: I know that's what you think. Because you are still where I left off. You with all your talk and dreams about Africa! You still think you can patch up the world. Cure the Great Sore of Colonialism—*(Loftily, mocking it)* with the Penicillin of Independence—!

ASAGAI: Yes!

BENEATHA: Independence *and then what?* What about all the crooks and thieves and just plain idiots who will come into power and steal and plunder the same as before— only now they will be black and do it in the name of the new Independence— WHAT ABOUT THEM?!

ASAGAI: That will be the problem for another time. First we must get there.

BENEATHA: And where does it end?

ASAGAI: End? Who even spoke of an end? To life? To living?

BENEATHA: An end to misery! To stupidity! Don't you see there isn't any real progress, Asagai, there is only one large circle that we march in, around and around, each of us with our own little picture in front of us—our own little mirage that we think is the future.

ASAGAI: That is the mistake.

BENEATHA: What?

ASAGAI: What you just said—about the circle. It isn't a circle—it is simply a long line— as in geometry, you know, one that reaches into infinity. And because we cannot see the end—we also cannot see how it changes. And it is very odd but those who see the changes—who dream, who will not give up—are called idealists . . . and those who see only the circle—we call *them* the "realists"!

BENEATHA: Asagai, while I was sleeping in that bed in there, people went out and took the future right out of my hands! And nobody asked me, nobody consulted me— they just went out and changed my life!

ASAGAI: Was it your money?

BENEATHA: What?

ASAGAI: Was it your money he gave away?

BENEATHA: It belonged to all of us.

ASAGAI: But did you earn it? Would you have had it at all if your father had not died?

BENEATHA: No.

ASAGAI: Then isn't there something wrong in a house—in a world—where all dreams, good or bad, must depend on the death of a man? I never thought to see *you* like this, Alaiyo. You! Your brother made a mistake and you are grateful to him so that now you can give up the ailing human race on account of it! You talk about what good is struggle, what good is anything! Where are we all going and why are we bothering!

BENEATHA: AND YOU CANNOT ANSWER IT!

ASAGAI *(shouting over her): I LIVE THE ANSWER! (Pause)* In my village at home it is the exceptional man who can even read a newspaper . . . or who ever sees a book at all. I will go home and much of what I will have to say will seem strange to the people of my village. But I will teach and work and things will happen, slowly and swiftly. At times it will seem that nothing changes at all . . . and then again the sudden dramatic events which make history leap into the future. And then quiet again. Retrogression even. Guns, murder, revolution. And I even will have moments when I wonder if the quiet was not better than all that death and hatred. But I will look about my village at the illiteracy and disease and ignorance and I will not wonder long. And perhaps . . . perhaps I will be a great man . . . I mean perhaps I will hold on to the substance of truth and find my way always with the right course . . . and perhaps for it I will be butchered in my bed some night by the servants of empire . . .

BENEATHA: *The martyr!*

ASAGAI *(he smiles):* . . . or perhaps I shall live to be a very old man, respected and esteemed in my new nation . . . And perhaps I shall hold office and this is what I'm trying to tell you, Alaiyo; perhaps the things I believe now for my country will be wrong and outmoded, and I will not understand and do terrible things to have things my way or merely to keep my power. Don't you see that there will be young men and women—not British soldiers then, but my own black countrymen—to step out of the shadows some evening and slit my then useless throat? Don't you see they have always been there . . . that they always will be. And that such a thing as my own death will be an advance? They who might kill me even . . . actually replenish all that I was.

BENEATHA: Oh, Asagai, I know all that.

ASAGAI: Good! Then stop moaning and groaning and tell me what you plan to do.

BENEATHA: Do?

ASAGAI: I have a bit of a suggestion.

BENEATHA What?

ASAGAI *(rather quietly for him):* That when it is all over—that you come home with me—

BENEATHA *(staring at him and crossing away):* Oh—Asagai—at this moment you decide to be romantic!

ASAGAI *(quickly understanding the misunderstanding):* My dear, young creature of the New World—I do not mean across the city—I mean across the ocean; home—to Africa.

BENEATHA *(slowly understanding and turning to him with murmured amazement):* To Africa?

ASAGAI: Yes! . . . *(Smiling and lifting his arms playfully)* Three hundred years later the African Prince rose up out of the seas and swept the maiden back across the middle passage over which her ancestors had come—

BENEATHA *(unable to play):* To—to Nigeria?

ASAGAI: Nigeria. Home. *(Coming to her with genuine romantic flippancy)* I will show you our mountains and our stars; and give you cool drinks from gourds and teach you the old songs and the ways of our people—and, in time, we will pretend that— *(Very softly)*—you have only been away for a day—Say that you'll come—*(He swings her around and takes her full in his arms in a long embrace which proceeds to passion)*

BENEATHA *(pulling away):* You're getting me all mixed up—

ASAGAI: Why?

BENEATHA: Too many things—too many things have happened today. I must sit down and think. I don't know what I feel about anything right this minute.

(She promptly sits down and props her chin on her fist)

ASAGAI *(charmed):* All right, I shall leave you. No—don't get up. *(Touching her, gently, sweetly)* Just sit awhile and think . . . Never be afraid to sit awhile and think. *(He goes to door and looks at her)* How often I have looked at you and said, "Ah—so this is what the New World hath finally wrought. . .

(He exits. BENEATHA sits on alone. Presently WALTER enters from his room and starts to rummage through things, feverishly looking for something. She looks up and turns in her seat)

BENEATHA *(hissingly):* Yes—just look at what the New World hath wrought! . . . just look! *(She gestures with bitter disgust)* There he is! Monsieur le petit bourgeois noir—himself! There he is—Symbol of a Rising Class! Entrepreneur! Titan of the system! *(WALTER ignores her completely and continues frantically and destructively looking for something and hurling things to the floor and tearing things out of their place in his search. BENEATHA ignores the eccentricity of his actions and goes on with the monologue of insult)* Did you dream of yachts on Lake Michigan, Brother? Did you see yourself on that Great Day sitting down at the Conference Table, surrounded by all the mighty bald-headed men in America? All halted, waiting, breathless, waiting for your pronouncements on industry? Waiting for you—Chairman of the Board! *(WALTER finds what he is looking for—a small piece of white paper—and pushes it in his pocket and puts on his coat and rushes out without ever having looked at her. She shouts after him)* I look at you and I see the final triumph of stupidity in the world!

(The door slams and she returns to just sitting again. RUTH comes quickly out of MAMA's room)

RUTH: Who was that?

BENEATHA: Your husband.

RUTH: Where did he go?

BENEATHA: Who knows—maybe he has an appointment at U.S. Steel.

RUTH *(anxiously, with frightened eyes):* You didn't say nothing bad to him, did you?

BENEATHA: Bad? Say anything bad to him? No—I told him he was a sweet boy and full of dreams and everything is strictly peachy keen, as the ofay kids say!

(MAMA enters from her bedroom. She is lost, vague, trying to catch hold, to make some sense of her former command of the world, but it still eludes her. A sense of waste overwhelms her gait; a measure of apology rides on her shoulders. She goes to her plant, which has remained on the table, looks at it, picks it up and takes it to the window sill and sets it outside, and she stands and looks at it a long moment. Then she closes the window, straightens her body with effort and turns around to her children)

MAMA: Well—ain't it a mess in here, though? (A false cheerfulness, a beginning of something) I guess we all better stop moping around and get some work done. All this unpacking and everything we got to do. *(RUTH raises her head slowly in response to the sense of the line; and BENEATHA in similar manner turns very slowly to look at her mother)* One of you all better call the moving people and tell 'em not to come.

RUTH: Tell 'em not to come?

MAMA: Of course, baby. Ain't no need in 'em coming all the way here and having to go back. They charges for that too. *(She sits down, fingers to her brow, thinking)* Lord, ever since I was a little girl, I always remembers people saying, "Lena—Lena Eggleston, you aims too high all the time. You needs to slow down and see life a little more like it is. Just slow down some." That's what they always used to say down home—"Lord, that Lena Eggleston is a high-minded thing. She'll get her due one day!"

RUTH: No, Lena . . .

MAMA: Me and Big Walter just didn't never learn right.

RUTH: Lena, no! We gotta go. Bennie—tell her . . . *(She rises and crosses to* BENEATHA *with her arms outstretched.* BENEATHA *doesn't respond)* Tell her we can still move . . . the notes ain't but a hundred and twenty-five a month. We got four grown people in this house—we can work . . .

MAMA *(to herself)*: Just aimed too high all the time—

RUTH *(turning and going too fast—the words pouring out with urgency and desperation)*: Lena—I'll work . . . I'll work twenty hours a day in all the kitchens in Chicago . . . I'll strap my baby on my back if I have to and scrub all the floors in America and wash all the sheets in America if I have to—but we got to MOVE! We got to get OUT OF HERE!!

*(*MAMA *reaches out absently and pats* RUTH's *hand)*

MAMA: No—I sees things differently now. Been thinking 'bout some of the things we could do to fix this place up some. I seen a second-hand bureau over on Maxwell Street just the other day that could fit right there. *(She points to where the new furniture might go.* RUTH *wanders away from her)* Would need some new handles on it and then a little varnish and then it look like something brand-new. And— we can put up them new curtains in the kitchen . . . Why this place be looking fine. Cheer us all up so that we forget trouble ever came . . . *(To* RUTH*)* And you could get some nice screens to put up in your room round the baby's bassinet . . . *(She looks at both of them, pleadingly)* Sometimes you just got to know when to give up some things . . . and hold on to what you got.

*(*WALTER *enters from the outside, looking spent and leaning against the door, his coat hanging from him)*

MAMA: Where you been, son?

WALTER *(breathing hard)*: Made a call.

MAMA: To who, son?

WALTER: To The Man. *(He heads for his room)*

MAMA: What man, baby?

WALTER *(stops in the door)*: The Man, Mama. Don't you know who The Man is?

RUTH: Walter Lee?

WALTER: *The Man.* Like the guys in the street say—The Man. Captain Boss—Mistuh Charley . . . Old Cap'n Please Mr. Bossman . . .

BENEATHA *(suddenly)*: Lindner!

WALTER: That's right! That's good. I told him to come right over.

BENEATHA *(fiercely, understanding)*: For what? What do you want to see him for?

WALTER *(looking at his sister)*: We are going to do business with him.

MAMA: What you talking 'bout, son?

WALTER: Talking 'bout life, Mama. You all always telling me to see life like it is. Well—I laid in there on my back today . . . and I figured it out. Life just like it is. Who gets and who don't get. *(He sits down with his coat on and laughs)* Mama, you know it's all divided up. Life is. Sure enough. Between the takers and the "tooken." *(He laughs)* I've figured it out finally. *(He looks around at them)* Yeah. Some of us always getting "tooken." *(He laughs)* People like Willy Harris, they don't never get "tooken." And you know why the rest of us do? 'Cause we all mixed up. Mixed up bad. We get to looking 'round for the right and the wrong; and we worry about it and cry about it and stay up nights trying to figure out 'bout the wrong and the right of things all the time . . . And all the time, man, them takers is out there operating, just taking and taking. Willy Harris? Shoot—Willy Harris don't even count. He don't even count in the big scheme of things. But I'll say one thing for old Willy Harris . . . he's taught me something. He's taught me to keep my eye on what counts in this world. Yeah—*(Shouting out a little)* Thanks, Willy!

RUTH: What did you call that man for, Walter Lee!

WALTER: Called him to tell him to come on over to the show. Gonna put on a show for the man. Just what he wants to see. You see, Mama, the man came here today and he told us that them people out there where you want us to move—well they so upset they willing to pay us *not* to move out there. *(He laughs again)* And—and oh, Mama—you would of been proud of the way me and Ruth and Bennie acted. We told him to get out . . . Lord have mercy! We told the man to get out! Oh, we was some proud folks this afternoon, yeah. *(He lights a cigarette)* We were still full of that old-time stuff . . .

RUTH *(coming toward him slowly):* You talking 'bout taking them people's money to keep us from moving in that house?

WALTER: I ain't just talking 'bout it, baby—I'm telling you that's what's going to happen.

BENEATHA: Oh, God! Where is the bottom! Where is the real honest-to-God bottom so he can't go any farther!

WALTER: See—that's the old stuff. You and that boy that was here today. You all want everybody to carry a flag and a spear and sing some marching songs, huh? You wanna spend your life looking into things and trying to find the right and the wrong part, huh? Yeah. You know what's going to happen to that boy someday—he'll find himself sitting in a dungeon, locked in forever—and the takers will have the key! Forget it, baby! There ain't no causes—there ain't nothing but taking in this world, and he who takes most is smartest—and it don't make a damn bit of difference how.

MAMA: You making something inside me cry, son. Some awful pain inside me.

WALTER: Don't cry, Mama. Understand. That white man is going to walk in that door able to write checks for more money than we ever had. It's important to him and I'm going to help him . . . I'm going to put on the show, Mama.

MAMA: Son—I come from five generations of people who was slaves and sharecroppers—but ain't nobody in my family never let nobody pay 'em no money that was a way of telling us we wasn't fit to walk the earth. We ain't never been that poor. *(Raising her eyes and looking at him)* We ain't never been that—dead inside.

BENEATHA: Well—we are dead now. All the talk about dreams and sunlight that goes on in this house. It's all dead now.

WALTER: What's the matter with you all! I didn't make this world! It was give to me this way! Hell, yes, I want me some yachts someday! Yes, I want to hang some real pearls 'round my wife's neck. Ain't she supposed to wear no pearls? Somebody tell me—tell me, who decides which women is suppose to wear pearls in this world. I tell you I am a *man*—and I think my wife should wear some pearls in this world!

(This last line hangs a good while and WALTER *begins to move about the room. The word "Man" has penetrated his consciousness; he mumbles it to himself repeatedly between strange agitated pauses as he moves about)*

MAMA: Baby, how you going to feel on the inside?

WALTER: Fine! . . . Going to feel fine . . . a man . . .

MAMA: You won't have nothing left then, Walter Lee.

WALTER *(coming to her):* I'm going to feel fine, Mama. I'm going to look that son-of-a-bitch in the eyes and say—*(He falters)*—and say, "All right, Mr. Lindner—*(He falters even more)*—that's *your* neighborhood out there. You got the right to keep it like you want! You got the right to have it like you want. Just write the check and—the house is yours." And—and I am going to say—*(His voice almost breaks)* "And you—you people just put the money in my hand and you won't have to live next to this bunch of stinking niggers! . . ." *(He straightens up and moves away from his mother, walking around the room)* And maybe—maybe I'll just get down on my black knees . . . *(He does so;* RUTH *and* BENNIE *and* MAMA *watch him in frozen horror)* Captain, Mistuh, Bossman—*(Groveling and grinning and wringing his hands in profoundly anguished imitation of the slow-witted movie stereotype)* A-hee-hee-hee! Yasssssuh! Great white—*(Voice breaking, he forces himself to go on)*—Father, just gi' ussen de money, fo' God's sake, and we's—we's ain't gwine come out deh and dirty up yo' white folks neighborhood . . . *(He breaks down completely)* And I'll feel fine! Fine! FINE! *(He gets up and goes into the bedroom)*

BENEATHA: That is not a man. That is nothing but a toothless rat.

MAMA: Yes—death done come in this here house. *(She is nodding, slowly, reflectively)* Done come walking in my house—on the lips of my children. You what supposed to be my beginning again. You—what supposed to be my harvest. *(To* BENEATHA*)* You—you mourning your brother?

BENEATHA: He's no brother of mine.

MAMA: What you say?

BENEATHA: I said that that individual in that room is no brother of mine.

MAMA: That's what I thought you said. You feeling like you better than he is today? *(*BENEATHA *does not answer)* Yes? What you tell him a minute ago? That he wasn't a man? Yes? You give him up for me? You done wrote his epitaph too—like the rest of the world? Well, who give you the privilege?

BENEATHA: Be on my side for once! You saw what he just did, Mama! You saw him—down on his knees. Wasn't it you who taught me—to despise any man who would do that? Do what he's going to do?

MAMA: Yes—I taught you that. Me and your daddy. But I thought I taught you something else too . . . I thought I taught you to love him.

BENEATHA: Love him? There is nothing left to love.

MAMA: There is *always* something left to love. And if you ain't learned that, you ain't learned nothing. *(Looking at her)* Have you cried for that boy today? I don't mean for yourself and for the family 'cause we lost the money. I mean for him; what he been through and what it done to him. Child, when do you think is the time to love somebody the most? When they done good and made things easy for everybody? Well then, you ain't through learning—because that ain't the time at all. It's when he's at his lowest and can't believe in hisself 'cause the world done whipped him so! When you starts measuring somebody, measure him right, child, measure him right. Make sure you done taken into account what hills and valleys he come through before he got to wherever he is.

(TRAVIS bursts into the room at the end of the speech, leaving the door open)

TRAVIS: Grandmama—the moving men are downstairs! The truck just pulled up.

MAMA *(turning and looking at him):* Are they, baby? They downstairs?

(She sighs and sits. LINDNER appears in the doorway. He peers in and knocks lightly, to gain attention, and comes in. All turn to look at him)

LINDNER *(hat and briefcase in hand):* Uh-hello . . .

(RUTH crosses mechanically to the bedroom door and opens it and lets it swing open freely and slowly as the lights come up on WALTER within, still in his coat, sitting at the far corner of the room. He looks up and out through the room to LINDNER)

RUTH: He's here.

(A long minute passes and WALTER slowly gets up)

LINDNER *(coming to the table with efficiency, putting his briefcase on the table and starting to unfold papers and unscrew fountain pens):* Well, I certainly was glad to hear from you people. *(WALTER has begun the trek out of the room, slowly and awkwardly, rather like a small boy, passing the back of his sleeve across his mouth from time to time)* Life can really be so much simpler than people let it be most of the time. Well—with whom do I negotiate? You, Mrs. Younger, or your son here? *(MAMA sits with her hands folded on her lap and her eyes closed as WALTER advances. TRAVIS goes close to LINDNER and looks at the papers curiously)* Just some official papers, sonny.

RUTH: Travis, you go downstairs—

MAMA *(opening her eyes and looking into WALTER's):* No. Travis, you stay right here. And you make him understand what you doing, Walter Lee. You teach him good. Like Willy Harris taught you. You show where our five generations done come to. *(WALTER looks from her to the boy, who grins at him innocently)* Go ahead, son— (She folds her hands and closes her eyes) Go ahead.

WALTER *(at last crosses to LINDNER, who is reviewing the contrast):* Well, Mr. Lindner. *(BENEATHA turns away)* We called you—*(There is a profound, simple groping quality in his speech)*—because, well, me and my family *(He looks around and shifts from one foot to the other)* Well—we are very plain people . . .

LINDNER: Yes—

WALTER: I mean—I have worked as a chauffeur most of my life—and my wife here, she does domestic work in people's kitchens. So does my mother. I mean—we are plain people . . .

LINDNER: Yes, Mr. Younger—

WALTER *(really like a small boy, looking down at his shoes and then up at the man):* And—uh—well, my father, well, he was a laborer most of his life. . .

LINDNER *(absolutely confused):* Uh, yes—yes, I understand. *(He turns back to the contract)*

WALTER *(a beat; staring at him):* And my father—*(With sudden intensity)* My father almost *beat a man to death* once because this man called him a bad name or something, you know what I mean?

LINDNER *(looking up, frozen):* No, no, I'm afraid I don't.

WALTER *(a beat. The tension hangs; then* WALTER *steps back from it):* Yeah. Well—what I mean is that we come from people who had a lot of *pride.* I mean—we are very proud people. And that's my sister over there and she's going to be a doctor—and we are very proud—

LINDNER: Well—I am sure that is very nice, but—

WALTER *(Signaling to* TRAVIS*):* Travis, come here. *(*TRAVIS *crosses and* WALTER *draws him before him facing the man)* What I am telling you is that we called you over here to tell you that we are very proud and that this—this is my son, who makes the sixth generation of our family in this country. And we have all thought about your offer—

LINDNER: Well, good . . . good—

WALTER: And we have decided to move into our house because my father—my father— he earned it for us brick by brick. *(*MAMA *has her eyes closed and is rocking back and forth as though she were in church, with her head nodding the Amen yes)* We don't want to make no trouble for nobody or fight no causes, and we will try to be good neighbors and that's *all* we got to say about that. *(He looks the man absolutely in the eyes)* We don't want your money. *(He turns and walks away)*

LINDNER *(looking around at all of them)*: I take it then—that you have decided to occupy . . .

BENEATHA: That's what the man said.

LINDNER *(To* MAMA *in her reverie):* Then I would like to appeal to you, Mrs. Younger. You are older and wiser and understand things better I am sure . . .

MAMA: I am afraid you don't understand. My son said we was going to move and there ain't nothing left for me to say. *(Briskly)* You know how these young folks is nowadays, mister. Can't do a thing with 'em. *(As he opens his mouth, she rises)* Good-bye.

LINDNER *(folding up his materials):* Well—if you are that final about it . . . there is nothing left for me to say. *(He finishes. He is almost ignored by the family, who are concentrating on* WALTER LEE. *At the door* LINDNER *halts and looks around)* I sure hope you people know what you're getting into.

(He shakes his head and exits)

RUTH *(looking around and coming to life):* Well, for God's sake—if the moving men are here—LET'S GET THE HELL OUT OF HERE!

MAMA *(into action):* Ain't it the truth! Look at all this here mess. Ruth, put Travis' good jacket on him . . . Walter Lee, fix your tie and tuck your shirt in, you look just like somebody's hoodlum. Lord have mercy, where is my plant? *(She flies to get it amid the general bustling of the family, who are deliberately trying to ignore the nobility of the past moment)* You all start on down . . . Travis child, don't go empty-handed . . . Ruth, where did I put that box with my skillets in it? I want to be in charge of it myself . . . I'm going to make us the biggest dinner we ever ate tonight . . . Beneatha, what's the matter with them stockings? Pull them things up, girl . . .

(The family starts to file out as two moving men appear and begin to carry out the heavier pieces of furniture, bumping into the family as they move about)

BENEATHA: Mama, Asagai—asked me to marry him today and go to Africa—

MAMA *(In the middle of her getting-ready activity):* He did? You ain't old enough to marry nobody—*(Seeing the moving men lifting one of her chairs precariously)* Darling, that ain't no bale of cotton, please handle it so we can sit in it again. I had that chair twenty-five years . . .

(The movers sigh with exasperation and go on with their work)

BENEATHA *(girlishly and unreasonably trying to pursue the conversation):* To go to Africa, Mama—be a doctor in Africa . . .

MAMA *(Distracted):* Yes, baby—

WALTER: *Africa!* What he want you to go to Africa for?

BENEATHA: To practice there . . .

WALTER: Girl, if you don't get all them silly ideas out your head! You better marry yourself a man with some loot . . .

BENEATHA *(angrily, precisely as in the first scene of the play):* What have you got to do with who I marry!

WALTER: Plenty. Now I think George Murchison—

(WALTER and BENEATHA go out yelling at each other vigorously and the anger is loud and real till their voices diminish. RUTH stands at the door and turns to MAMA and smiles knowingly)

BENEATHA: George Murchison! I wouldn't marry him if he was Adam and I was Eve!

MAMA *(fixing her hat at last):* Yeah—they something all right, my children . . .

RUTH: Yeah—they're something. Let's go, Lena.

MAMA: *(stalling, starting to look around at the house):* Yes—I'm coming. Ruth—

RUTH: Yes?

MAMA *(quietly, woman to woman):* He finally come into his manhood today, didn't he? Kind of like a rainbow after the rain . . .

RUTH *(biting her lip lest her own pride explode in front of MAMA):* Yes, Lena.

(WALTER's voice calls for them raucously)

WALTER *(off stage):* Y'all come on! These people charges by the hour, you know!

MAMA *(Waving RUTH out vaguely):* All right, honey—go on down. I be down directly.

(RUTH hesitates, then exits. MAMA stands, at last alone in the living room, her plant on the table before her as the lights start to come down. She looks around at all the walls and ceilings and suddenly, despite herself, while the children call below, a great heaving thing rises in her and she puts her fist to her mouth to stifle it, takes a final desperate look, pulls her coat about her, pats her hat and goes out. The lights dim down. The door opens and she comes back in, grabs her plant, and goes out for the last time)

Curtain

—1958

For Practice

1. Stage directions (the parts of a script that describe the play's setting, actions, and special effects for the director, actors, and readers) can range from practically nonexistent to very detailed. The stage directions in this play are remarkable for their specificity. Re-read the stage directions at the beginning of the play. Which aspects of these instructions seem to convey information that is necessary for the literal staging of this play? What aspects seem to convey additional information? What is the nature of this additional information? What is its usefulness? To whom is it useful? Why?

2. This play was written before the greatest achievements of the civil rights movement in the 1960s. Blacks in America were only beginning to take their seats at the "table" of American culture and politics. How is *A Raisin in the Sun* a call to action within this political context? What is its political message(s)?

3. Popular revolutions taking place in Africa during the 1950s helped to motivate the increased participation of black people in American society and during the time this play was written. These revolutions led many black Americans of African descent to reconstruct their ancestral heritage. How does Beneatha's friendship with Asagai awaken her own desire to learn about African culture? How does this heritage help to lessen the tension between her and her brother? How does it affect her relationships with the other members of her family?

4. Hansberry uses many symbols in this play, including the check, the new home, Mama's plant, and Beneatha's hairdo. How do the characters' dreams for the future affect their interpretations of these objects? How do these differing interpretations serve to increase or decrease the tension among the family members? What might such symbols mean in your own family?

5. The Younger family only comes together as a family in response to a threat from outside forces. What does this say about the nature of families? What does it say about relationships between husbands and wives? Between parents and children? Between brothers and sisters? Between family members and non-family members?

6. The title of this play is taken from Langston Hughes's poem, "Dream Deferred." Find a copy of the poem and read it. Does the poem alter your understanding of the play? Do you find that your reading of the poem is conditioned by having read the play?

7. In the 1990s, many people think that the battles of the civil rights movement have been won, while others still pursue the struggle. How does the experience of reading *A Raisin in the Sun* change your own perspective on the struggle for civil rights in this country?

Creating Your Own Arguments

1. Several readings in this section make use of memory to craft individual and group identities. Select two or more texts in this section and discuss ways in which the writers and/or the narrators use memory to shape identity.

2. Think of an important family story of your own that you know only by word-of-mouth and not by witnessing the events personally. Write two versions of that story: first a story that records only the details told to you, and second, a story in which you use your imagination and creativity to fill in the gaps from your point of view, to explain what goes unexplained or unmentioned in the original version. Which story was more difficult to write? Why?

3. How do you define words like "heritage" and "tradition"? (You may want to think about—and even write about—certain family heirlooms or sentimental objects that have come to stand for these ideas in your view.) How do you believe these concepts might help people in shaping their identities as individuals and as family or community members? Compare your answers to these questions to those proposed in two works in this unit. Is it valuable to explore this question? Why or why not?

4. Both "Everyday Use" and *A Raisin in the Sun* portray African-American families in conflict with themselves and with their pasts. In what ways are these stuggles similar in both texts? In what ways are they different? How are these depictions of African-American experience different from the experiences of Asian families or families from other racial or ethnic groups? In what ways might these experiences be similar? What is most valuable—exploring similarites or differences?

5. This section contains love sonnets by William Shakespeare, Pablo Neruda, and Adrienne Rich. How do these poets adapt the sonnet conventions to their own purposes? How are the poets' messages and strategies for communicating their messages similar? How are they different?

6. Several readings in this section focus on the influence of a particular place and/or time on crucial interactions between and among family members and other loved ones. Select any two texts in this unit in which you believe the setting plays an important role in communicating the texts' meanings. How do the authors use these settings to develop the argument(s) of the texts?

7. Many of these authors have relied upon the imagery of water as a way to approach the topic of memory. Focusing on the works of Kingston, Agee, and Rich, notice the different ways in which water is used to embody the operations or effects of memory. How does this imagery change within individual works, and how is it similar or different?

8. How do the authors in this unit depict the importance of self-expression? Do they present this activity differently? Does the self-expression meet different levels of resistance? If so, why? Do any of the arguments suggest ways in which we, as a culture, should change?

UNIT
THREE

"Happily Ever After? . . .":
Lives of Fantasy
and Reality

Beginning with our childhood, we are surrounded by storytelling and fantasy. Our parents reassure us that Santa Claus is "real," we go to bed listening to the story of Snow White's wicked stepmother, and Walt Disney's cinematic versions of fairy tales are often the first movies we remember seeing. As we grow older, we begin to see these stories as "childish." This unit asks if the narratives of our adulthood are any less fantastic. If we stop to think about it for a moment, television, film, and advertising all bombard us with images that create and encourage desires which are no more realistic than Cinderella's Fairy Godmother.

Our attraction to these images reflects the seemingly timeless impulse to tell stories. What might explain the enduring nature of the fantastic tales we continue to tell each other? One way to approach this question might be to look at fairy tales and myths, the two types of narratives that are blatantly unrealistic yet which might also be seen to have practical purposes. As Bruno Bettelheim speculates in *The Uses of Enchantment,* we might think that primitive cultures created myths to explain phenomena that were unexplainable; for example, the story of Demeter and Persephone offered a reason for the changing seasons. Even Old Testament narratives might be seen to serve a similar function; the Tower of Babel explains the existence of different languages. For Bettelheim, children are like these primitive cultures in that they lack the capacity to comprehend the world around them in rational terms, so mythical explanations like the "stork" are given to make their world more ordered. Fairy tales often explicitly teach children "lessons" such as don't walk into the woods alone and don't trust strangers; less overtly but even more importantly, these tales teach cultural expectations such as what behavior is needed to be a good husband or wife.

This practical explanation for fantastic narratives ignores an important factor, however: as we grow older, we don't stop telling each other fantastic stories. The selection of "urban myths" by Jan Harold Brunvand reveals that our modern technological culture continues to tell itself powerfully fantastic stories and the fact that we do continue to tell these tales should attest to the staying power of myth. Rather than see mythmaking as a primitive activity, we might examine our own culture for the very powerful myths and stories we continue to tell ourselves everyday and ask ourselves why we tell them. Even in our everyday lives, when significant or "fantastic" things happen to us, we find ourselves telling and re-telling those events again and again. Often, we create different versions of these events for different situations and different audiences. For example, if you were describing the events of a Saturday night, how might the narrative you tell your grandmother differ from the version you tell to your roommate? Which is the "true" story? Regarded from this perspective, everything we do is linked to storytelling.

For adults, perhaps our most compelling fantasy narratives are those concerning romance and beauty. From the goddess' beauty contest that leads to the abduction of Helen and sparks the Trojan War to the obsession of Snow White's wicked stepmother with the question "who's the fairest one of all?" to the great romances of the Golden Age of Hollywood like *Gone with the Wind*, we are fascinated by the paradigms of beauty and love provided by these narratives. To examine this fascination with fantastic narratives of beauty we have selected readings which explore the myths that fashion our desires for beauty and love. The "Beauty and the Beast" tale, first published in an eighteenth-century conduct manual, may teach that appearances are not as important as a person's "inner self," but the blond-haired, blue-eyed Prince that the Beast becomes at the end of the Disney film makes us pause: would Belle have married the Beast? Would the Beast have wanted Belle if she had not been beautiful? Likewise, the set of poems beginning with Marge Piercy's satirical "Barbie Doll" and moving to the earlier poems by Herrick and Swift demonstrate both the continuing power of the "beauty myth," and in the case of Piercy and Swift, the impossibility of achieving that ideal. For Piercy, this ideal is destructive; for Swift, who examines the reality behind the powdered, perfumed, and beribboned facade of cosmetic beauty, the ideal beauty is deconstructed into the grotesque (evidencing a rather sexist attitude, perhaps, but the poem is a fitting attack at the early signs of what has become a multi-billion dollar cosmetic industry).

The last set of readings examines the power of fantasy in our everyday lives, particularly in the arena of romance. Chaucer's knights face a set of physical battles, but their real struggle lies in their rather unknightly quest for satisfaction with their own situations as they unfavorably contrast the ideal or idyllic demands of "romance" with their own positions. Browning's Duke of Ferrara, in order to maintain his highly valued control over his wife, must have her smiles "stopped" in real life but preserved in a portrait so that only those he chooses can see her face. Oates explores the effects of consumer/suburban culture on our fantasy lives, in particular, those of a teenaged girl surrounded and immersed in popular culture; these fantasies can be liberating, but also destructive. Finally, Mason's "Shiloh" examines a couple who attempts to cope with their changing perceptions of one another. The story's ending raises questions about the possibility of transcending our often romanticized impressions of our significant other; can we ever really escape our own histories?

While fantasy may emerge from our primitive impulses, as Bettelheim's essay contends, the continuing persistence of these myths in our "civilized" culture attests to their power and this is why we must study and learn from these narratives to understand how they shape our lives.

The Child's Need for Magic

Bruno Bettelheim

Born in Vienna, Austria, child psychologist Bruno Bettelheim (1903–1990) studied under Sigmund Freud before being captured by the Nazis in 1938. After spending time in two concentration camps, Bettelheim was released in 1939 and came to the United States, where he became a citizen in 1944. He taught at the University of Chicago and worked with disturbed children at the Orthogenic School. In addition to his numerous publications on child psychology, his interests in psychoanalytic theory and developmental psychology resulted in his best-known work, The Uses of Enchantment *(1976). Bettelheim died in 1990, apparently from suicide. A recent biography by Richard Pollack,* The Creation of Dr. B: A Biography of Bruno Bettelheim *(1997), reveals another side to Bettelheim, however. While Pollack's charges of academic fraud, abuse, and deception are well-documented (he interviewed Bettelheim's colleagues at the Orthogenic School, his wife, and two of his children), the fact that Pollack's brother, a patient of Bettelheim's, died at the age of six under mysterious circumstances obviously affects the author's motivations for writing the book. Whatever the recent revelations about Bettelheim's darker side, his theories about fairy tales continue to influence the research on this subject.*

The Uses of Enchantment analyzes the psychological importance of fairy tales, particularly for children, and "show[s] what kind of repressed or otherwise unconscious material underlies myths and fairy tales." Bettelheim believes that the fairy tale offers optimistic solutions for the "everyman" depicted in these tales. The text also evidences the influence of Swiss psychologist Jean Piaget, for the period of development in which children are most affected by fairy tales would be what Piaget describes as the "period of concrete operations," when children learn language and drawing abilities, then begin to think logically. According to Bettelheim's theory in "The Child's Need for Magic," it is after the child begins to conceptualize abstract issues (around age eleven) that he no longer needs the "explanations" of fairy tales to give meaning to those aspects of the world which seem incomprehensible to children.

Myths and fairy stories both answer the eternal questions: What is the world really like? How am I to live my life in it? How can I truly be myself? The answers given by myths are definite, while the fairy tale is suggestive; its messages may imply solutions, but it never spells them out. Fairy tales leave to the child's fantasizing whether and how to apply to himself what the story reveals about life and human nature.

The fairy tale proceeds in a manner which conforms to the way a child thinks and experiences the world; this is why the fairy tale is so convincing to him. He can gain much better solace from a fairy tale than he can from an effort to comfort him based on adult reasoning and viewpoints. A child trusts what the fairy story tells, because its world view accords with his own.

Whatever our age, only a story conforming to the principles underlying our thought processes carries conviction for us. If this is so for adults, who have learned to accept that there is more than one frame of reference for comprehending the world—although we find it difficult if not impossible truly to think in any but our own—it is exclusively true for the child. His thinking is animistic.

Like all preliterate and many literate people, "the child assumes that his relations to the inanimate world are of one pattern with those to the animate world of people: he fondles as he would his mother the pretty thing that pleased him; he strikes the door that has slammed on him." It should be added that he does the first because he is convinced that this pretty thing loves to be petted as much as he does; and he punishes the door because he is certain that the door slammed deliberately, out of evil intention.

As Piaget has shown, the child's thinking remains animistic until the age of puberty. His parents and teachers tell him that things cannot feel and act; and as much as he may pretend to believe this to please these adults, or not to be ridiculed, deep down the child knows better. Subjected to the rational teachings of others, the child only buries his "true knowledge" deeper in his soul and it remains untouched by rationality; but it can be formed and informed by what fairy tales have to say.

To the eight-year-old (to quote Piaget's examples), the sun is alive because it gives light (and, one may add, it does that because it wants to). To the child's animistic mind, the stone is alive because it can move, as it rolls down a hill. Even a twelve-and-a-half-year-old is convinced that a stream is alive and has a will, because its water is flowing. The sun, the stone, and the water are believed to be inhabited by spirits very much like people, so they feel and act like people.

To the child, there is no clear line separating objects from living things; and whatever has life has life very much like our own. If we do not understand what rocks and trees and animals have to tell us, the reason is that we are not sufficiently attuned to them. To the child trying to understand the world, it seems reasonable to expect answers from those objects which arouse his curiosity. And since the child is self-centered, he expects the animal to talk about the things which are really significant to him, as animals do in fairy tales, and as the child himself talks to his real or toy animals. A child is convinced that the animal understands and feels with him, even though it does not show it openly.

Since animals roam freely and widely in the world, how natural that in fairy tales these animals are able to guide the hero in his search which takes him into distant places. Since all that moves is alive, the child can believe that the wind can talk and carry the hero to where he needs to go, as in "East of the Sun and West of the Moon." In animistic thinking, not only animals feel and think as we do, but even stones are alive; so to be turned into stone simply means that the being has to remain silent and unmoving for a time. By the same reasoning, it is entirely believable when previously silent objects begin to talk, give advice, and join the hero on his wanderings. And since everything is inhabited by a spirit similar to all other spirits (namely, that of the child who has projected his spirit into all these things), because of this inherent sameness it is believable that man can change into animal, or the other way around, as in "Beauty and the Beast" or "The Frog King." Since there is no sharp line drawn between living and dead things, the latter, too, can come to life.

When, like the great philosophers, children are searching for the solutions to the first and last questions—"Who am I? How ought I to deal with life's problems? What must I become?"—they do so on the basis of their animistic thinking. But since the child is so uncertain of what his existence consists, first and foremost comes the question "Who am I?"

As soon as a child begins to move about and explore, he begins to ponder the problem of his identity. When he spies his mirror image, he wonders whether what he sees is really he, or a child just like him standing behind this glassy wall. He tries to find out by exploring whether this other child is really, in all ways, like him. He makes faces, turns this way or that, walks away from the mirror and jumps back in front of it to ascertain whether this other one has moved away or is still there. Though only three years old, the child is already up against the difficult problem of personal identity.

The child asks himself: "Who am I? Where did I come from? How did the world come into being? Who created man and all the animals? What is the purpose of life?" True, he ponders these vital questions not in the abstract, but mainly as they pertain to him. He worries not whether there is justice for individual man, but whether he will be treated justly. He wonders who or what projects him into adversity, and what can prevent this from happening to him. Are there benevolent powers in addition to his parents? Are his parents benevolent powers? How should he form himself, and why? Is there hope for him, though he may have done wrong? Why has all this happened to him? What will it mean for his future? Fairy tales provide answers to these pressing questions, many of which the child becomes aware of only as he follows the stories.

From an adult point of view and in terms of modern science, the answers which fairy stories offer are fantastic rather than true. As a matter of fact, these solutions seem so incorrect to many adults—who have become estranged from the ways in which young people experience the world—that they object to exposing children to such "false" information. However, realistic explanations are usually incomprehensible to children, because they lack the abstract understanding required to make sense of them. While giving a scientifically correct answer makes adults think they have clarified things for the child, such explanations leave the young child confused, overpowered, and intellectually defeated. A child can derive security only from the conviction that he understands now what baffled him before—never from being given facts which create *new* uncertainties. Even as the child accepts such an answer, he comes to doubt that he has asked the right question. Since the explanation fails to make sense to him, it must apply to some unknown problem—not the one he asked about.

It is therefore important to remember that only statements which are intelligible in terms of the child's existing knowledge and emotional preoccupations carry conviction for him. To tell a child that the earth floats in space, attracted by gravity into circling around the sun, but that the earth doesn't fall to the sun as the child falls to the ground, seems very confusing to him. The child knows from his experience that everything has to rest on something, or be held up by something. Only an explanation based on that knowledge can make him feel he understands better about the earth in space.

More important, to feel secure on earth, the child needs to believe that this world is held firmly in place. Therefore he finds a better explanation in a myth that tells him that the earth rests on a turtle, or is held up by a giant.

If a child accepts as true what his parents tell him—that the earth is a planet held securely on its path by gravity—then the child can only imagine that gravity is a string. Thus the parents' explanation has led to no better understanding or feeling of security. It requires considerable intellectual maturity to believe that there can be stability to one's life when the ground on which one walks (the firmest thing around, on which everything rests) spins with incredible speed on an invisible axis; that in addition it rotates around the sun; and furthermore hurtles through space with the entire solar system. I have never yet encountered a prepubertal youngster who could comprehend all these combined movements, although I have known many who could repeat this information. Such children parrot explanations which according to their own experience of the world are lies, but which they must believe to be true because some adult has said so. The consequence is that children come to distrust their own experience, and therefore themselves and what their minds can do for them.

In the fall of 1973, the comet *Kohoutek* was in the news. At that time a competent science teacher explained the comet to a small group of highly intelligent second-and third-graders. Each child had carefully cut out a paper circle and had drawn on it the course of the planets around the sun; a paper ellipse, attached by a slit to the paper circle, represented the course of the comet. The children showed me the comet moving along at an angle to the planets. When I asked them, the children told me that they were holding the comet in their hands, showing me the ellipse. When I asked how the comet which they were holding in their hands could also be in the sky, they were all nonplussed.

In their confusion, they turned to their teacher, who carefully explained to them that what they were holding in their hands, and had so diligently created, was only a model of the planets and the comet. The children all agreed that they understood this, and would have repeated it if questioned further. But whereas before they had regarded proudly this circle-cum-ellipse in their hands, they now lost all interest. Some crumpled the paper up, others dropped the model in the wastepaper basket. When the pieces of paper had been the comet to them, they had all planned to take the model home to show their parents, but now it no longer had meaning for them.

In trying to get a child to accept scientifically correct explanations, parents all too frequently discount scientific findings of how a child's mind works. Research on the child's mental processes, especially Piaget's, convincingly demonstrates that the young child is not able to comprehend the two vital abstract concepts of the permanence of quantity, and of reversibility—for instance, that the same quantity of water rises high in a narrow receptacle and remains low in a wide one; and that subtraction reverses the process of addition. Until he can understand abstract concepts such as these, the child can experience the world only subjectively.

Scientific explanations require objective thinking. Both theoretical research and experimental exploration have shown that no child below school age is truly able to grasp these two concepts, without which abstract understanding is impossible. In his early years, until age eight or ten, the child can develop only highly personalized concepts about what he experiences. Therefore it seems natural to him, since the plants which grow on this earth nourish him as his mother did from her breast, to see the earth as a mother or a female god, or at least as her abode.

Even a young child somehow knows that he was created by his parents; so it makes good sense to him that, like himself, all men and where they live were created by a superhuman figure not very different from his parents—some male or female god. Since his parents watch over the child and provide him with his needs in his home, then naturally he also believes that something like them, only much more powerful, intelligent, and reliable a guardian angel—will do so out in the world.

A child thus experiences the world order in the image of his parents and of what goes on within the family. The ancient Egyptians, as a child does, saw heaven and the sky as a motherly figure (Nut) who protectively bent over the earth, enveloping it and them serenely. Far from preventing man from later developing a more rational explanation of the world, such a view offers security where and when it is most needed—a security which, when the time is ripe, allows for a truly rational world view. Life on a small planet surrounded by limitless space seems awfully lonely and cold to a child—just the opposite of what he knows life ought to be. This is why the ancients needed to feel sheltered and warmed by an enveloping mother figure. To depreciate protective imagery like this as mere childish projections of an immature mind is to rob the young child of one aspect of the prolonged safety and comfort he needs.

True, the notion of a sheltering sky-mother can be limiting to the mind if clung to for too long. Neither infantile projections nor dependence on imaginary protectors—such as a guardian angel who watches out for one when one is asleep, or during Mother's absence—offers true security; but as long as one cannot provide complete security for oneself, imaginings and projections are far preferable to no security. It is such (partly imagined) security which, when experienced for a sufficient length of time, permits the child to develop that feeling of confidence in life which he needs in order to trust himself—a trust necessary for his learning to solve life's problems through his own growing rational abilities. Eventually the child recognizes that what he has taken as literally true—the earth as a mother—is only a symbol.

A child, for example, who has learned from fairy stories to believe that what at first seemed a repulsive, threatening figure can magically change into a most helpful friend is ready to believe that a strange child whom he meets and fears may also be changed from a menace into a desirable companion. Belief in the "truth" of the fairy tale gives him courage not to withdraw because of the way this stranger appears to him at first. Recalling how the hero of many a fairy tale succeeded in life because he dared to befriend a seemingly unpleasant figure, the child believes he may work the same magic.

I have known many examples where, particularly in late adolescence, years of belief in magic are called upon to compensate for the person's having been deprived of it prematurely in childhood, through stark reality having been forced on him. It is as if these young people feel that now is their last chance to make up for a severe deficiency in their life experience; or that without having had a period of belief in magic, they will be unable to meet the rigors of adult life. Many young people who today suddenly seek escape in drug-induced dreams, apprentice themselves to some guru, believe in astrology, engage in practicing "black magic," or who in some other fashion escape from reality into daydreams about magic experiences which are to change their life for the better, were prematurely pressed to view reality in an adult way. Trying to evade reality in such ways has its deeper cause in early formative experiences which prevented the development of the conviction that life can be mastered in realistic ways.

What seems desirable for the individual is to repeat in his life span the process involved historically in the genesis of scientific thought. For a long time in his history man used emotional projections—such as gods—born of his immature hopes and anxieties to explain man, his society, and the universe; these explanations gave him a feeling of security. Then slowly, by his own social, scientific, and technological progress, man freed himself of the constant fear for his very existence. Feeling more secure in the world, and also within himself, man could now begin to question the validity of the images he had used in the past as explanatory tools. From there man's "childish" projections dissolved and more rational explanations took their place. This process, however, is by no means without vagaries. In intervening periods of stress and scarcity, man seeks for comfort again in the "childish" notion that he and his place of abode are the center of the universe.

Translated in terms of human behavior, the more secure a person feels within the world, the less he will need to hold on to "infantile" projections—mythical explanations or fairy-tale solutions to life's eternal problems—and the more he can afford to seek rational explanations. The more secure a man is within himself, the more he can afford to accept an explanation which says his world is of minor significance in the cosmos. Once man feels truly significant in his human environment, he cares little about the importance of his planet within the universe. On the other hand, the more insecure a man is in himself and his place in the immediate world, the more he withdraws into himself because of fear, or else moves outward to conquer for conquest's sake. This is the opposite of exploring out of a security which frees our curiosity.

For these same reasons a child, as long as he is not sure his immediate human environment will protect him, needs to believe that superior powers, such as a guardian angel, watch over him, and that the world and his place within it are of paramount importance. Here is one connection between a family's ability to provide basic security and the child's readiness to engage in rational investigations as he grows up.

As long as parents fully believed that Biblical stories solved the riddle of our existence and its purpose, it was easy to make a child feel secure. The Bible was felt to contain the answers to all pressing questions: the Bible told man all he needed to know to understand the world, how it came into being, and how to behave in it. In the Western world the Bible also provided prototypes for man's imagination. But rich as the Bible is in stories, not even during the most religious of times were these stories sufficient for meeting all the psychic needs of man.

Part of the reason for this is that while the Old and New Testaments and the histories of the saints provided answers to the crucial questions of how to live the good life, they did not offer solutions for the problems posed by the dark sides of our personalities. The Biblical stories suggest essentially only one solution for the asocial aspects of the unconscious: repression of these (unacceptable) strivings. But children, not having their ids in conscious control, need stories which permit at least fantasy satisfaction of these "bad" tendencies, and specific models for their sublimation.

Explicitly and implicitly, the Bible tells of God's demands on man. While we are told that there is greater rejoicing about a sinner who reformed than about the man who never erred, the message is still that we ought to live the good life, and not, for example, take cruel revenge on those whom we hate. As the story of Cain and Abel shows, there is no sympathy in the Bible for the agonies of sibling rivalry—only a warning that acting upon it has devastating consequences.

But what a child needs most, when beset by jealousy of his sibling, is the permission to feel that what he experiences is justified by the situation he is in. To bear up under the pangs of his envy, the child needs to be encouraged to engage in fantasies of getting even someday; then he will be able to manage at the moment, because of the conviction that the future will set things aright. Most of all, the child wants support for his still very tenuous belief that through growing up, working hard, and maturing he will one day be the victorious one. If his present sufferings will be rewarded in the future, he need not act on his jealousy of the moment, the way Cain did.

Like Biblical stories and myths, fairy tales were the literature which edified everybody—children and adults alike—for nearly all of man's existence. Except that God is central, many Bible stories can be recognized as very similar to fairy tales. In the story of Jonah and the whale, for example, Jonah is trying to run away from his superego's (conscience's) demand that he fight against the wickedness of the people of Nineveh. The ordeal which tests his moral fiber is, as in so many fairy tales, a perilous voyage in which he has to prove himself.

Jonah's trip across the sea lands him in the belly of a great fish. There, in great danger, Jonah discovers his higher morality, his higher self, and is wondrously reborn, now ready to meet the rigorous demands of his superego. But the rebirth alone does not achieve true humanity for him: to be a slave neither to the id and the pleasure principle (avoiding arduous tasks by trying to escape from them) nor to the superego (wishing destruction upon the wicked city) means true freedom and higher selfhood. Jonah attains his full humanity only when he is no longer subservient to either institution of his mind, but relinquishes blind obedience to both id and superego and is able to recognize God's wisdom in judging the people of Nineveh not according to the rigid structures of their human frailty.

For Practice

1. Why, according to Bettelheim, do children "need" myths and fairy tales? Do fairy tales fulfill a need that other children's fiction does not? Do we ever outgrow this need? How might a "contemporary" fairy tale which appeals to adults like *The Wizard of Oz* (1900) fit into his paradigm?

2. Who is the audience for Bettelheim's book? Parents? Scholars? Why do you think he wrote it?

3. Fairy tales are, obviously, unrealistic. How does this lack of realism contribute to (or detract from) their message?

4. What is the comfort in the "happily ever after" ending of most fairy tales? What message do we get from fairy tales that do not end happily?

5. "The Child's Need for Magic" suggests that fairy tales are comforting to children since they provide them with a framework for understanding the world around them. Considering the often violent nature of fairy tales (like "Hansel and Gretel" and "Little Red Riding Hood"), do you agree with this? What are other possible functions of fairy tales? What lessons might "Little Red Riding Hood" teach, for example?

Curses! Broiled Again!

Jan Harold Brunvand

*Jan Harold Brunvand is one of the leading authorities on folklore in the
United States. He received his bachelor's degree in journalism at Michigan
State University, but his interest in folklore led him to accept a position at
the University of Utah in the English department. He began his academic
career publishing studies of folklore such as* Folklore: A Study and
Research Guide *(1976), and his most recent work on the subject is the
comprehensive* The Study of American Folklore: an Introduction *(1998).
However, he became interested in urban legends, which he describes as
"contemporary folklore," because of what these stories can tell us about
modern society. These "myths" are the stories you hear from friends
which they swear to be true, but which they have no documentation to
prove: the girl who fries her insides at the tanning bed, the man who wakes
up in a hotel room after a night of passion to find a kidney missing, the
assumption (proven by no student guide book) that if your roommate dies,
you will get a 4.0 for the semester. He published his first book on urban
myths,* The Vanishing Hitchhiker: American Urban Legends and Their
Meaning, *in 1981, and he began writing a syndicated newspaper column,
"Urban Legends," in 1987.* Curses! Broiled Again! *(1989) collects articles
from this column. Testimonies to the interest in urban myths are the
numerous letters Brunvand receives, many of them detailing a story the
writer swears is "true," and Brunvand's own appearances on talk shows
like "Late Night with David Letterman."*

*Like fairy tales, these stories often have a "lesson": the tanning bed
myth, which Brunvand analyzes in* Curses! Broiled Again!, *offers a
reminder about the dangers of vanity, for the girl (and a girl is always the
victim in these stories) is often bronzing herself to prepare for the prom.
The tale also manifests the fear of female "insides," for a horrible smell is
the first sign that the girl has "fried" herself.*

I like to designate the most popular urban legend of the time as "the hottest
story going," and this one was certainly hot during the summer of 1987.
In fact, it's *still* hot (would I give you old news?). Read on.

The basis of the story is that a young woman wants a dark tan and somehow contrives to schedule extra sessions at a tanning salon. The result of her indiscreet vanity
is that she cooks her insides.

First credit for telling me this shocker goes to my University of Utah colleague, Professor Robert Steensma. When he came back to town in mid-August 1987 from a summer-school teaching stint at Augustana College in Sioux Falls, South Dakota, Steensma told me two versions he had heard there.

In one, a girl wanting to look nice and tan repeatedly visited the same salon at different times of day. Soon she began feeling ill, and she consulted a doctor. He told her that she had cooked her insides. Version 2 from South Dakota claimed that she fried a muscle in an arm and that limb had to be amputated.

Later the same day, a student from my summer folklore class reported a story she had heard the night before. This supposedly happened, she said, to the wife of the cousin of the man who had told it to a woman friend of hers who then told her. Something like that.

This time the tanning salon had a rule to protect customers from overexposure: a thirty-minutes-per-day limit. But this girl—friend of a friend of a friend—circumvented that by signing up at four different salons, thus getting four times the recommended dosage.

Her husband began to notice that she "smelled funny," and her doctor gave her the bad news. Cooked insides and certain death. "It's funny," I commented, "that such a dramatic event never made the Salt Lake City papers."

My student had discussed the story with another friend, who claimed that the tanning-salon roasting had really happened to a girl who was tanning herself into shape to be a swell-looking bridesmaid for her best pal.

So I'm sitting in my office in the second stage of folkloristic research (first, collection; second, classification; third, analysis). I'm labeling a file folder "Cooked Alive: New Legend?" when the telephone rings. The caller, a local person, reads my column in the *Deseret News,* and she had just heard this awful story from someone at work and was delegated to call and ask whether I thought it was an urban legend.

In her version, a young lady from the small northern Utah town of Tremonton needed a good tan to take to summer cheerleader camp at Utah State University over in Logan. So she signed up at several different tanning salons and went in four or five times per day.

Again, the bad smell developed, and she showered, then showered again. The smell didn't go away, and when her mother noticed it, she rushed her daughter to the doctor. The diagnosis was "microwaved insides." Another cooked goose, just for wanting a fast tan.

At that point, I wrote one of my newspaper columns on the story of the girl who was sizzled medium rare in the tanning salon. When the Salt Lake City *Deseret News* ran the column on Friday, September 18, they assigned it the wonderful headline that provides the title to this book: "Curses! Broiled Again!" Then the following Tuesday, September 22, in publishing the regular "Dear Abby" column for that day, the *DN* added the note, "Other variations on the following tanning salon story appeared in last Friday's 'Urban Legends' column by Jan Harold Brunvand."

Oddly enough, the cooked-goose legend came to Abby from the city of Provo in the state of Utah, via Springfield, Oregon. A concerned mother of a Brigham Young University student had written to ask Abby to warn her readers about the fate of a seventeen-year-old girl that her daughter had described in a letter. The teenager had supposedly fried herself under the tanning lamps and was said to be lying "totally blind" in the Utah Valley Regional Medical Center in Provo with an estimated twenty-six days to live.

Abby was suspicious about that precise figure of "twenty-six days" and called the medical center. She learned that there was no such patient being treated, though the story was known to the center spokesperson. In fact, Joann Cox, the secretary who answered the telephone, told Abby's staff that she had also heard the same story told recently in Pocatello, Idaho.

Dozens of my readers clipped Dear Abby's column for that day and forwarded it to me along with the versions they had heard in Pennsylvania, New York, Ohio, and even Florida. (Why do they need tanning salons in Florida?) Noting the emphasis on Utah in the two column versions, one folklorist sent me the "Dear Abby" clipping with the scribbled "Is Utah now the center of new urban legends?"

Actually, I had wondered the same thing at first. Practically everyone I spoke to in Utah for the next few months tried to tell me a new variation on the legend. My favorite was from a caller in the city of West Jordan who said the doctor had told the victim, "To cure this condition would be like frying a steak and then trying to bring it back to life." Huh? You couldn't bring a *raw* steak back to life, could you?

Anyway, there are at least two interesting questions here. First, did the story just develop out of the blue in the middle of the summer of '87? Second, had it, perhaps, actually happened somewhere, possibly in the West or Midwest, where many of the versions I collected came from?

But coming "out of the blue" seemed too simple, and I soon found that the story was older and more widespread than I suspected. The first publication of it that I have uncovered, however, was still from the Midwest. A news story on July 16, 1987, bylined Ross Bielema, in the *Dubuque* (Iowa) *Telegraph Herald*, described and debunked several local versions of the story. The young woman was said to be seventeen, worked at Hartig Drug store, was a student at Loras College, needed the tan for a wedding; she had a bad smell, got the bad news, etc.—the works. Bielema did a nice job on the story, incidentally, and (I must admit it) he scooped both Abby and me by a month.

Meanwhile, I learned that just about the same time that I was beginning to hear the story told in Utah, the same legend had been posted to the nationwide computer hookup "ARPANET" on August 10 by a subscriber at Stanford University. (Why do they need tanning salons in California?)

"Curses! Broiled Again!" was obviously an appealing story that summer more because of its horror content and warning function than because of any actual gruesome medical case that any of the informants knew about firsthand. In other words, the cardinal rule of urban legends definitely applies here: The truth never stands in the way of a good story. But where does a story like this come from?

I would trace one theme in the legend to an earlier rumor about home tanning lamps, which always carry important safety warnings and require certain precautions. Last summer, a man in Ohio wrote me this: "About six years ago when I was shopping for a sun lamp, the appliance salesman emphasized the reliable timer on one model. Then he recounted as a fact that a woman using a lesser product fell asleep and had her contact lenses fused to her eyeballs."

The fused-cornea-and-contact story, you may remember, is an urban legend usually associated with an imaginary welding accident that somehow generates microwaves that allegedly dry up the fluids in the eye.

Another connection here is the specialized horror stories about microwaved pets and babies, which are part of the lore warning against modern technology and product misuse. While accidents with appliances do happen, these horror stories floating around in different versions in oral tradition almost certainly did *not* happen. In some of them, as in the tanning-salon story, it sounds like people are confusing ultraviolet tanning rays with the microwaves used in cooking.

What could follow from overuse of a home sunlamp or extra tanning sessions is serious burns to the skin. That's just good old-fashioned sunburn, which doesn't smell bad, unless you count the ointments used to soothe the ache.

There's another growing fear expressed in this story: the mounting evidence that too much tanning will increase your risk of skin cancer. Nearly everyone knows by now of the danger from too much sun, but nearly everyone seems willing to catch a few extra rays anyway.

"It can't happen to me" is the assumption, though it might happen to some silly young thing like this girl in the story. So far I have heard only of females suffering this particular fate, but it may be that male versions of the cooked-insides story just have not yet made their way to me.

The tanning-salon-accident story has not died out; in fact, it seems to have held on through the winter and revived strongly the following summer. In January 1988, for example, I got the story again from Bill Kestell of New Holstein, Wisconsin, who says his secretary heard it from a girlfriend who was told it by a friend at work who was supposed to have been in the same wedding party as the victim. In March, a graduate student in English at Iowa State University, Ames, reported the legend being told by her roommate who heard it from a friend who thought she may have read it in *Glamour* magazine. Could be, I suppose, though I have not found it there.

The following month I got a report from Pacifica, California. This victim was a bride, not a bridesmaid, and the storyteller asserted that the lamps at tanning salons really do emit microwaves, as this story proves. I thought it was the other way around, that the lack of microwaves in tanning lamps proves that the story is false.

The latest versions of "Curses! Broiled Again!" came in the mail during the summer of 1988, about a year after I first heard it from Bob Steensma. Here's a report from Christine A. Lehman, writing from Santa Ana, California, whose letter demonstrates one way that the story may be inserted into conversations: "I was looking at a newspaper ad for a tanning parlor and mentioned to one of my co-workers that I might go check it out. She got a very serious look on her face. 'Oh, you better be real careful. I just heard the most awful story about those places from my cousin. Her best friend was about to get married, and she decided she wanted to have a real dark tan. . . .'"

Need I continue this sad story? The moral it teaches, of course, is "Curses! Broiled Again!"

Most recently, I have been hearing what might be called "The General Health and Fitness Version" of the legend. For example, Lynda M. Sholly of Granger, Indiana, wrote me in July 1988 about the story as she heard it, concerning "a young woman who was physically active in exercise . . . always very careful regarding her appearance and bodily habits. She strove to always look and smell her best."

There is nothing whatever in this version about brides or bridesmaids, cheerleaders, trips to Hawaii, or even deliberate overuse of tanning salons. But when the inevitable bad smell develops, the fitness freak's doctor asks whether she has been going to a tanning salon. When she replies in the affirmative, he warns her, "There's really nothing I can do. You wanted this artificial tan, and now you are paying for it, but you are rotting away from the inside, and eventually you'll die from the rotting." (In a similar version of the story sent from Illinois, the doctor explains that his patient's body is unable to clear itself of dead cells caused internally by excessive expo-sure to the tanning lamps and that his patient will be dead in six months.)

It would seem, in the final analysis, that "Curses! Broiled Again!" is partly a warn-ing against overdoing a health routine in general, rather than merely against tanning salons in particular.

Postscript: In October 1988, I received a letter from a woman in Orem, Utah, who had just heard at her hairdressers about a girl, "probably a BYU coed," who had cooked her insides by visiting several tanning salons in one day. The woman commented, "This sounds too bizarre to be true. Do you know if it is fact or legend?" I sent a one-word answer to her question—the L-word, if you know what I mean.

This is where I came in with this particular urban legend.

For Practice

1. Compare the variations on the tanning bed incident that Brunvand describes. Why do you think there are so many different versions of this myth?

2. What seem to be some common characteristics of the urban myth? Note the attention to precise details (the number of tanning beds a woman goes to, the particular organs affected by the tanning bed, the circumstances under which the woman needed a quick tan).

3. Why do you think the "victim" in this myth is always a female? What might this say about our society's assumptions about women and vanity?

4. Brunvand suggests that the tanning bed myth could be seen as the expres-sion of a contemporary fear of technology, a fear which emerges in myths about microwaves and other appliances as well. How might this particular myth differ from other ones concerning technology (like the pets who are microwaved by their owners in order to dry them, a myth nicely parodied in the film *Gremlins*)?

5. How might you use Bettelheim's discussion of fairy tales to understand the function of urban myth? How is the purpose of these myths different from fairy tales?

6. Think of an urban myth you have heard and analyze its "message."

Beauty and the Beast

Mme. Le Prince de Beaumont

Although known today primarily for her fairy tales, Mme. Le Prince de Beaumont (1711–1780) published at least seventy volumes during her lifetime and is also believed to be the first woman to write and edit a magazine, Magasin des Enfants. *She was also a teacher both in her native France and in England. Although education for girls was generally considered unnecessary for much of the eighteenth century, de Beaumont strongly advocated education for young women, believing that knowledge would help them to be more virtuous, rather than the opposite as some people believed.*

De Beaumont used fairy tales such as "Beauty and the Beast," published in 1757, to instruct her female students. She would often begin a lesson with a fairy tale and then encourage the young girls to discover its moral through a process of asking them questions. This tale then is meant to teach a moral lesson, a lesson aimed particularly at young women of the eighteenth century. As you read the tale, you should consider what kind of virtues are valued in the tale and what moral lessons de Beaumont might have been advocating with it. This translation was made by Sabine Baring-Gould in 1895.

There was a merchantman once, who was very rich. He had three daughters, and he spared no expense to provide them with an excellent education.

His daughters were beautiful; but the youngest so excelled her sisters that, from earliest childhood, she was called the Beauty, and afterwards this name slipped into, simply, Beauty.

But the real cause why she was so much more admired than her sisters was that she was amiable and they were not; and the sweetness of her disposition shone out in her face and made it doubly sweet. No frown ever spoiled her fair brow; no pout was ever on her pleasant lips. She possessed the charm of good temper which makes even a plain face agreeable.

The merchant's elder daughters were idle, ill-humoured, and proud; and people did not consider them as beautiful, because they saw only the bad temper that was in the expression of their faces. The pride of the young ladies was so great that they despised all such as were of their own rank in life, and wished to be the friends of noble ladies and princesses. They hunted after grand acquaintances, and met with many mortifications accordingly. They gave themselves great airs, and, to show the world how high in life they were, they held up their noses. Their whole time was spent in balls, operas, and visiting and driving about.

Meanwhile, Beauty kept to her books; and, when not at work, she loved in kindly way to go among the sick and poor, and comfort them. Thus it came about that she was as much beloved by the poor as she was admired by the rich.

As it was well known that their father was a well-to-do man, many merchants asked the girls in marriage; but all these offers were refused, because the two eldest had set their minds on marrying only nobles, and the youngest had no wish to be married at all.

Beauty's great desire was to be with her father when he was old and feeble, and to be then his comfort.

One unhappy day the merchant returned home, very downcast, to inform his children that his ships had been wrecked, his head clerk had defrauded him, and that the firms which owed him money were bankrupt. He was, therefore, a ruined man. Beauty wept because her father was unfortunate and unhappy, and asked him what was to be done.

'Alack, dear child!' he replied, 'I must sell this house, and go to live in a cottage in the country; and we shall have to work with our hands to put bread into our mouths.'

'Well, father,' said Beauty, 'I can spin and knit and sew very neatly. I daresay I shall be able to help you.'

The elder daughters said nothing, but resolved to marry such of their rejected lovers as were richest. They speedily found, however, that their rejected lovers rejected all their advances, now that they were poor.

On the other hand, such as had admired Beauty pressed their services on her, and would gladly have shared their fortunes with her. She, however, could not think of deserting her father when he was reduced to low estate. She felt she must abide by him, and work for him.

Very soon, the grand house in town was sold, as well as all the rich furniture, and the merchant and his daughters retired into the country.

Beauty now rose at four o'clock every morning. She cleaned the house, laid and lighted the fires, prepared the breakfast, and put flowers on the table. Then she cooked the dinner, and made the house tidy. She was happy, and sang like a lark over her work, and slept peacefully, and had pleasant dreams.

Meanwhile, her sisters grew peevish, dissatisfied, and miserable. They would not work; and, as they had no occupation and no amusement, the days dragged along and seemed as though they would never end. They did nothing but regret the past, and grumble over the present. As they had no one to admire them, they neglected their personal appearance and became veritable dowdies.

Perhaps they perceived that the contrast between their sister and themselves was not to their advantage, for they became spiteful in their manner to Beauty, and held up their hands and declared that she had always been fit only to be a servant.

'It is clear as daylight,' said they to Beauty; 'that Nature made you to occupy a menial position, and now you are in your proper place. As for us, we are ladies. We can't soil our fingers, we can't dust the furniture, we can't scrub the floor. We are above such things.'

The merchant heard, after a while, that there was some chance of retrieving part of his fortune if he made a journey to a country where one of his richest vessels had been wrecked. He must claim what had been recovered from the sea. Accordingly, he bade his daughters farewell, and he did so in a hopeful spirit, for he believed he would get back enough to make their life more comfortable. Before leaving, he asked his daughters what they would desire him to bring for them on his return, as a little token that he remembered them.

The eldest asked for a diamond necklace. The second wished for a whole suite of pearls. The youngest said? 'Dear father, bring me a white rose.'

So the father kissed all his daughters, and departed. He was successful; and had recovered so much of his property that he hoped to reopen his business, and in time recover all that was lost. When he prepared to return home, he remembered the requests of his daughters, and bought diamonds for the eldest and pearls for the second; but he sought everywhere in vain for a white rose. This distressed him greatly as his youngest daughter was his favourite child.

Now, as he was on his way home, he lost his way in a wood. Night was closing in, and as the merchant was aware that there were wolves, bears, and wild boars in that country, he was very anxious to find a shelter for the night.

Presently he perceived in the distance a twinkling light, and he urged his horse in that direction. But, to his surprise, instead of coming to a woodman's hut, he found himself in front of a magnificent castle, to which led a stately avenue, composed of orange and lemon-trees hung with fruit.

He did not hesitate to pass down this avenue, and, at the end, he came to the steps leading to the front gate, and through the open door shone the light that had attracted him.

He entered, having first knocked at the door, and looked round him expecting to see servants. But no one responded to his knock, and the hall was wholly deserted. He passed through several galleries and empty rooms—all illuminated and all empty—and finally stayed his course in a smaller apartment where a fire was burning, and a couch was prepared as if for some one to lie on it. Being very tired and cold, he cast himself down on the couch and fell asleep.

After a pleasant and refreshing slumber he awoke, and found he was still alone; but a little table stood by him, and on it was spread a delicious repast. As he was extremely hungry, he sat at the table, and partook of all the good things on it. Then he threw himself on the couch again, and again fell asleep.

When he awoke, the morning sun shone into the room, the little table was still at his side, but on it was now spread an excellent breakfast.

The merchant began now to be very uneasy at the intense stillness of the house, and perplexed at seeing no one. He left the little room and entered the garden, which was beautifully laid out, and was full of flowers. 'Well,' said the merchant to himself, 'this wonderful place seems to have no master. I will go home and bring my daughters to it, and we shall be able to claim it as our home; for I discovered it, and it belongs, as far as I can see, to no one.'

He then went to fetch his horse, and, as he turned down the path to the stable, he saw a hedge of white roses on each side of it. Thereat the merchant remembered the request of his youngest daughter, and he plucked one to take to her.

Immediately he was alarmed by hearing a horrible noise. Turning in the direction of the sound, he saw a frightful Beast, which seemed to be very angry, and which exclaimed—

'Who gave you permission to gather my roses? Was it not enough that I suffered you to lie on my couch, and warm yourself at my fire, and eat my supper and breakfast? Your insolence shall not go unpunished.'

The merchant, terrified at these words and threats, dropped the rose, and casting himself on his knees, cried: 'Forgive me, sir; I am sincerely grateful for your hospitality, which was so profuse that I hardly thought you would grudge me one rose.'

The Beast's anger was not mitigated by this speech. ' I pay no regard to your excuses,' said he. 'You shall most certainly die.'

'Alas!' exclaimed the merchant. 'Oh, Beauty! Beauty! why did you ask this fatal thing of me ? The white rose you desired will be the death of your father.'

The Beast asked the merchant the meaning of this exclamation, and the merchant then related the story of his misfortunes, and of the requests made by his daughters. 'It cost me nearly all I recovered of my fortune,' said he, 'to buy the diamonds and pearls for my eldest girls; I did not think I was doing any harm in plucking the poor little white rose for my youngest.'

The Beast considered for a while, and then said—'I will pardon you on one condition, that is, that you will give me one of your daughters.'

'Oh!' exclaimed the merchant. 'If I were so cruel as to buy my own life at the expense of one of my children, what excuse could I make to bring her here?'

'No excuse is needed,' answered the Beast. 'If she comes at all, she will come willingly. Let me see if any one of them be brave enough, and loves you dearly enough, to come here and save your life. You seem to be an honest man. I give you a month in which to return home and propose to one of your daughters to come here to me. If none of them be willing, then I expect you, on your honour, to return here to your death. Say goodbye to them for ever.'

The merchant reluctantly accepted this proposal. He did not think any of his daughters would come; but it reprieved him for one month, and gave him an opportunity of saying farewell to them, and of settling his affairs.

He promised to return at the appointed time, and then asked permission to set off at once.

But the Beast would not allow this till the next day. 'Then,' said he, 'you will find a horse ready for you. Go in, and eat your dinner, and await my further orders.'

The poor merchant, more dead than alive, went back into the palace, and into the same room in which he had rested before. There he found a most delicious meal prepared for him. He was, however, in no mood to eat; and if he swallowed a few mouthfuls, it was only lest he should anger the Beast by refusing all food from his table. When he had finished, he heard a trampling in the passages, and, shortly, the monstrous Beast appeared, who repeated the terms of the agreement they had made; and he added—

'Do not get up to-morrow until after sunrise, and till you have heard a bell ring. Then you will find your breakfast prepared for you here, and the horse you are to ride will be ready in the courtyard. He will bring you back again when you come with your daughter a month hence. Farewell! take a white rose for Beauty; and remember your engagement.'

The merchant was only too glad when the Beast went away, and though he could not sleep for sadness of heart, yet he lay down on the couch. Next morning, after a hasty breakfast, he went to gather the rose for Beauty, mounted the horse, and rode swiftly away.

The gloomy thoughts that weighed on his mind were not dispersed when he drew up at his cottage door. His daughters, who had been uneasy at his long absence, were prodigal of their embraces, and, seeing him ride home on such a splendid horse, they felt quite sure that he had been successful in his journey. He gave his elder daughters the gems and pearls they had desired, and, as he handed the rose to Beauty, he sadly said, 'You little know, my darling, what this has cost me.'

This saying greatly excited the curiosity of his children, and they gave him no rest till he had told them the whole story from beginning to end.

The elder daughters urged him to break his promise and remain at the cottage; but their father said that a promise was a promise, whether made to a king or a pauper, a man or a beast, and that he must fulfil it. Then the two eldest were very angry with Beauty, and told her that it was all her fault. If she had asked for something sensible this would not have happened.

'If it be my fault,' answered Beauty meekly, 'it is only fitting that I should suffer for it. I will, therefore, go back with my father to the palace of the Beast.'

At first her father would not hear of this, but Beauty was firm.

As the time drew near she divided all her little possessions between her sisters, and said good-bye to all she loved.

Now, it must be told, that when Beauty had received the white rose she put it in water, and when she had heard how it was won, and what it entailed, she had wept nightly over it, and her tears falling on it seemed to have preserved it in its beauty, for at the end of the month it was as fresh as when first picked; and the scent was so sweet that it perfumed the whole house. She put the white rose in her bosom, when the day came for departure, and she mounted on a pillion behind her father to depart.

The horse seemed to fly rather than gallop; and Beauty would have enjoyed the journey if it were not for the dreadful prospect of the Beast at the end of it. Her father constantly urged her to dismount and turn back, but she would not hearken to this.

At last they reached the avenue of orange trees, and then a wonderful sight was seen. Every orange was like a globe of light; the oranges were deep yellow, and the lemons pale yellow, and all shone like lamps. Moreover, beautiful lights played about the palace, and sweet music murmured among the trees.

'The Beast must be very hungry,' said Beauty, 'if he makes such rejoicing over getting such a little mouthful as myself.'

The horse now stopped at the foot of the flight of steps leading to the gate, and when she had dismounted, her father led her through the halls and galleries to the little room in which he had rested and been regaled when there on his former visit. Again the fire was burning, and on the table a lavish supper was spread.

The merchant knew that this was meant for them; and Beauty, who was rather less frightened now that she had passed through so many rooms without seeing the Beast, was willing to begin, for her long ride had made her hungry.

They had hardly finished eating, before they heard tramp, tramp! stump, stump! It was the sound of the Beast approaching; and Beauty clung to her father in terror, which was heightened when she saw how greatly alarmed he was.

But when the Beast entered, like a brave and a courteous girl she stood up, mastered her fear, and, making a low courtesy, said: 'I thank you, Mr. Beast, for my pretty white rose.'

Then the Beast was pleased. He saw the little flower in her bosom, looking white and fresh as when first picked; and he said, somewhat gently—

'Did you come quite willingly, Beauty?'

'Yes, Mr. Beast,' said Beauty, and dropped another courtesy.

'And will you be willing to remain with me, when your father is gone? I will not eat you—my food is only crystallised rose and violet leaves. I eat nothing more solid or less aesthetic.'

'Yes, Mr. Beast,' answered Beauty; and the thought that she was not to be eaten revived her courage, and she dropped another little courtesy.

'I am well pleased with you,' said the Beast. 'You shall stay. As for you,' he now turned to the merchant, 'at sunrise, to-morrow, you must depart. When the bell rings, rise quickly and eat your breakfast, and you will find the same horse waiting to take you home; but remember, you must never venture to seek my palace again.'

Then, turning to Beauty, he said: 'Take your father into the next room, and help him to choose presents for your sisters. There are two portmanteaus there. Fill them with whatever you like to send home. All are yours, and at your disposal.'

Then the Beast made a clumsy bow, put his paw to his heart, and said: 'Good-bye, Beauty; good-bye, merchantman.'

Beauty was very sorrowful to have to part with her father, and much dismayed at the thought of being left alone in the great palace with no one but the Beast. However, she promptly obeyed his orders. The room they entered was full of the costliest objects, the most splendid dresses, and the richest jewelry. After making a selection, she put them in the portmanteau which she intended to contain the presents for her sisters. Then she found a trunk full of gold coins, and with them she stuffed the second portmanteau, which was for her father.

But Beauty and her father much doubted whether the horse could carry the load. However, on reaching the courtyard, there they saw two horses beside that on which the merchant had ridden. They moved the portmanteaus down, and strapped them on the pack-horses' backs. Then the merchant bade his daughter a tender farewell with many tears, and rode away.

Then Beauty wept bitterly, and wandered sadly back to the room in which she had eaten. She soon found herself so sleepy that she threw herself on the couch and closed her eyes, and was at once in the world of dreams.

Now, in her dreams, she saw something very strange. She thought that there stood before her a Prince, handsomer than any man she had ever seen, wearing a crown of white roses on his head. He said to her: 'Beauty! your fate is not as forlorn as you suppose. Be true-hearted as you are beautiful, and all will be well in the end.'

Beauty awoke, after a long sleep, much refreshed. She then began to explore the palace. The first room she entered was lined with looking-glasses, and Beauty saw herself reflected on every side. Then she saw a bracelet hanging down from a chandelier. She took it, looked at it, and saw that from it hung a locket, and in this locket was the portrait of the very Prince she had seen in her dream.

The next room she entered was tapestried round with foliage, and it was full of musical instruments. Beauty knew how to play some of them; and she amused herself for some time trying them, and playing the different ballad tunes that came into her head. First she sang—

> There was a fair maiden, all forlorn,
> With hey! with ho! for the rain;
> And she sat herself down all under a thorn,
> The poppies are red in the grain.

Next she sang—

> There rode a knight when the moon shone bright,
> He rode to the lady's hall;
> He sang her a lay, bade her come away,

> And follow him at his call.
> He courted her many a long winter night,
> And many a short winter day,
> And he laid in wait, both early and late,
> For to take her sweet life away.

Then she sang—

> There came an earl a-riding by,
> A gipsy maid espied he;
> O nut-brown maid, to her he said,
> I prithee, come away with me.
> I'll take you up, I'll carry you home,
> I'll put a safeguard over you;
> Your slippers shall be of Spanish leather,
> And silken stockings all of blue.

And last of all she sang—

> Green gravel! Green gravel!
> The grass is so green,
> The fairest young damsel
> That ever was seen.
> O Beauty! O Beauty!
> Your true love is dead,
> He sends you a letter
> To turn round your head.

Then Beauty was tired of singing and playing, and she went into the next room, which was a library, and it was full of books. She pulled down several and looked at them, and thought that surely it would take her all her life to read the books she saw there.

Then she walked in the garden, and wondrous were the flowers and the fruit there. Never had she seen so many and such beautiful flowers; never had she tasted such delicious fruit.

At last day declined, and she came indoors. A brilliant light illumined all the rooms; she found supper prepared for her, and she seated herself to eat.

Then she heard, tramp, tramp! stump, stump! and in came the Beast.

He asked her if she thought she could be happy in his palace; and Beauty answered, that everything was so beautiful that she would be very hard to please if she could not be happy. Then he asked if he might sit down and eat his meal with her.

'Oh! what shall I say?' cried Beauty, for she knew that she could not eat in comfort, with him munching crystallised rose-leaves and violets out of a bon-bon box on the other side of the table.

'Say exactly what you think,' he replied.

'Oh! no, Beast!' said Beauty, hastily.

'Since you will not—good-night, Beauty,' he said; and she responded: 'good-night, Beast.'

When she was asleep she again dreamed of the mysterious Prince.

Next day she found a room in which were silks and canvas and needles, and all sorts of articles for embroidery.

Then she entered an aviary full of beautiful birds, which were so tame that they flew to Beauty as soon as they saw her, and perched on her shoulder and hands.

The day passed a little more heavily than the last, and Beauty began to long for some one to talk to, and even was pleased when at supper she heard the tramp, tramp! stump, stump! of the Beast coming along the passages.

She now put a chair on the side of the table opposite her, and when the Beast said, 'May I sit down and eat with you, Beauty?' she answered, 'Oh! please do, Beast!'

That night she dreamed of the Prince again, and he smiled at her and looked pleased.

Next day she walked in the woods, and she saw deer there, fleet and graceful; and she came on fish-ponds in which were gold and silver fish. She went to the music-room and tried to play and sing, but became tired of her loneliness, and wished greatly for supper, when the Beast would appear and she could talk with him, and hear him talk.

When day declined, and the palace was lighted up for supper, then she waited impatiently for the tramp, tramp! stump, stump! and when the Beast came in she ran to meet him, dropped a courtesy, and said, 'Please, Beast, can you play and sing?'

'Yes, Beauty.'

'Would you play and sing with me, sometimes?' she asked.

'Certainly, Beauty! if you wish it.'

Next day when she entered the music-room, the Beast was there, and she found that not only could he play very charmingly on many instruments, but also could sing a rich bass. They made together quite a charming little concert, singing duets and playing different instruments, and this wore the morning away.

In the afternoon, Beauty was quite dull by herself. She wandered in the library, looking at one book after another, and she could not choose which to read.

So at supper she ran along the gallery to meet the Beast directly when she heard his tramp, tramp! stump, stump! and, dropping a little courtesy, she said: 'Please, Beast! will you tell me what books to read?'

'Certainly, Beauty!' he answered; and next day she found him in the library, and he read with her, and explained to her difficult passages, and so a very pleasant morning was passed.

In the afternoon, Beauty walked in the garden, admiring the flowers, and wishing that she knew their names. At supper, when she heard the tramp, tramp! stump, stump! of the Beast, she ran to meet him, and, taking one of his paws in her hand, said: 'Please, Beast! will you walk in the garden with me?'

'Certainly, Beauty!' he answered; and next day when she went into the garden there he was, and he was able to tell her all about the flowers, their names and their properties, and whence they came.

That evening, at supper, she said to the Beast: 'Please, Beast! may I make you a pair of slippers?' 'Certainly, Beauty!' he answered. 'But my feet are very big and clumsy.'

'Oh!' said she, 'not half so big and clumsy as those of an elephant.'

So she amused herself in embroidering for the Beast a pair of slippers. The ground was turquoise blue, and on it were white roses, with stamens of gold, and the pods for seed were scarlet. Never before or after were such beautiful slippers made.

That night she dreamed that she saw the Prince. He looked at her, smiling, and showed that he wore her slippers—which she had made for the Beast—and they had shrunk to the size of his finely-formed feet.

One day she was in the forest, and she thought: 'Oh! how nice it would be to ride out hunting, but how dull to ride all alone!'

So that evening at supper, she ran to the Beast, when she heard his tramp, tramp! stump, stump! and, catching hold of both his paws, she said:

'Please, Beast! will you go hunting with me?'

'Certainly, Beauty!' he answered.

Next day there was a fine hunt, and Beauty enjoyed herself vastly.

One day, when Beauty was walking in the garden with the Beast, she passed with him by the hedge of white rose, and she put out her hand and picked one. Then he said to her: 'Beauty, will you marry me? If so—give me the white rose.'

'Oh! what shall I say?' cried Beauty; for she was sorry to offend the Beast, who had been so kind to her, and such an agreeable companion, and so eager to forestall all her wishes; but, at the same time—he was a Beast.

He said, seeing her hesitation: 'Say just what you think.'

Then Beauty answered hastily, 'Oh! no, Beast!'

That night she dreamed of her Prince, and that he looked sad and wobegone.

So everything went on for a time, until at last, happy as she was, Beauty began to long for the sight of her father and sisters; and one evening, seeing her look very sad, and her eyes red, the Beast asked her what was the matter.

Beauty had quite ceased to be afraid of him. She knew that he was gentle and kind in spite of his ferocious appearance; and clever and learned in spite of his being such an animal; and quite dainty and courteous in his manners, though a Beast.

She answered, that she was longing to see her home once more.

Upon hearing this, the Beast seemed greatly affected. He sighed, and said: 'Ah! Beauty, will you desert your poor Beast like this? Is it because you hate me that you want to leave me?'

'No, dear Beast,' answered Beauty, softly. 'Indeed I do not hate you, and it would make me very unhappy if I thought I should never see and talk with you again. But I do long greatly to see my father. Let me go, if only for two months, and I promise to return to you, and stay with you the rest of my life.'

The Beast said: 'I can refuse you nothing, and that you well know. Take the four boxes; you will find in the room next your own, and fill them with whatever you like to take away with you. But remember your promise, and return when two months have expired, or you will find your faithful Beast dead. You will not need any carriage to bring you back. Only say good-bye to your father and sisters the night before you come away, and then, in your room, turn this ring I give you on your finger, and say: "I wish to be with my Beast again."'

As soon as Beauty was by herself, she hastened to fill the boxes with all the rare and precious things she saw about her. Then she went to bed, but could hardly sleep for joy. And when at last she did begin to dream of her beloved Prince, she saw him lying stretched on the grass, sad and weeping.

When she opened her eyes, she could hardly believe her senses. She was in a very different place from the palace of the Beast. The room was neat and comfortable, but not splendid. Where could she be? She dressed herself hastily, and then saw that the boxes she had packed were in the room.

Whilst she was wondering where she was, she heard her father's voice. She at once left the room, and, seeing him, threw herself into his arms. She was, in fact, in the new house to which her father had removed from the cottage, when his fortunes were improved. Her sisters were greatly astonished to see her. All embraced her with demonstrations of the greatest joy, but her sisters were not in heart glad to see her. Their jealousy was not extinguished.

She was made to tell her story, and it filled all with astonishment. But when she said that her stay with them was limited to two months, then her father was sorrowful, but her sisters secretly rejoiced.

Her father had much to tell her, and her sisters had made many acquaintances, and the time was spent in going about making visits and in receiving company. Nevertheless, somehow, Beauty did not feel as happy as she had been with her Beast. The time had come at last when she ought to return; but her father was so sorrowful when she spoke of departure, and there was always something arranged for the next day for which she was expected to remain, so that she did not fulfil her promise exactly. Besides, she so loved her father that she could not make up her mind to bid him good-bye.

One night she had a dreadful dream. She thought she was back again in the Beast's palace, and that she was walking through the rooms seeking him. Not finding him anywhere, she went into the garden and called him, but received no answer. At last, having reached a portion of the shrubberies that was allowed to run wild, she heard groans issuing from a cave.

She penetrated into it, and found the Beast prostrate on the ground, and apparently dying. He reproached her with having forgotten him and broken her promise, and reminded her of what he had said, that her absence protracted beyond the two months allotted to her would be death to him. Beauty was so terrified by this dream that she sprang from her bed, hastily clothed herself, ran to her father's room, roused him, said farewell; then she did the same to her sisters, and, still agitated with the thoughts of the dying Beast, turned her ring and wished herself back again in his palace.

Hardly had she done this before she was again in the little chamber in which she had spent so many agreeable hours. She looked about; no Beast was there. Then, although it was night, she ran out into the garden, calling him and seeking him. She was still searching for him when the grey of dawn appeared. Then she was able to find her way, and she sought the wilderness she had been in, in her dream, and at last lit on the cavern of which she had dreamed.

In fact, from this now issued the most lamentable sighs and groans.

She ran in and saw the poor Beast stretched on earth, and evidently exceedingly weak and suffering.

'O Beast! Beast!' she cried; 'I am so sorry! So heartily sorry that I have delayed my return. Oh tell me you will recover!'

'Nothing now will restore me but one thing,' he answered in a faint voice.

'Tell me what that is, and it is yours.'

'The rose,' he answered—'the white rose. You will find it growing over the mouth of this cave. But, remember—if you give me that, you give me yourself with it. You accept me as your husband.' In a moment, without speaking, Beauty sprang out of the cave and hastily plucked a beautiful white rose that hung down over the mouth.

Returning to the poor Beast, she gave it him, and said: 'Dear Beast!—indeed I am yours. I love you with all my heart.'

'Will you kiss me on my snout?' asked the Beast. 'Indeed—indeed I will,' answered Beauty.

At that moment the sun rose and poured its golden beams into the cave, and made the walls glitter and twinkle like a cave of rainbow, and indeed they were all of ruby, carbuncle, amethyst, topaz, emerald, and every imaginable stone.

The reflection was so dazzling that Beauty having kissed the Beast covered her eyes. When she drew her hands away he had disappeared. In his place stood her long-dreamed-of, beautiful Prince. Then he took her by the hand, and said: 'Dear Beauty, to you, to your faithfulness and goodness, I owe my delivery. I have been bewitched by a cruel fairy, who said I should remain in the form of a hideous monster until some maiden would consent to be my wife, and in token of her consent give me a white rose, and kiss me on the mouth. This is my palace, I have an immense kingdom and innumerable treasures. You shall be my queen, and we will make your father happy, and, if possible, your sisters shall be made contented. I shall never forget what you have done for me, and all my life shall be devoted to rendering you happy.'

For Practice

1. What kind of virtues are valued in this tale? What moral lessons might de Beaumont have been advocating with it? For example, this fairy tale, as many others, ends with a marriage. Yet, since this tale is offered as a moral lesson for young girls, it is helpful to think about what the story says about marriage in more depth. What makes for a happy marriage in this work? What role do things such as money and beauty play in the construction of a happy marriage?

2. How are the daughters described in the story? How do the "elder daughters" compare with Beauty? What qualities do they possess? What qualities does Beauty possess? What "lesson" is offered through these comparisons?

3. Why does Beauty ask for a rose? What does the rose reveal about her character? Why does the rose get the father in trouble?

4. What is the Beast like? What qualities does he possess? What is it that makes him a beast in this tale?

5. Watch a film version of this fairy tale, such as Jean Cocteau's 1946 *Beauty and the Beast* or the 1991 Disney film by the same name. How are the films similar and/or different from the original tale? What do the changes reveal about the cultures/times in which these films were produced?

The Tiger's Bride

Angela Carter

From the publication of her first novel, Shadow Dance *(1965), Angela Carter (1940–1992) has been recognized as one of the most original and talented British writers of postmodern fiction. The author of nine novels and four collections of short stories, as well as several collections of non-fiction, Carter has been awarded a number of prizes, including the Cheltenham Festival of Literature Award for* The Bloody Chamber *(1979) from which this selection is taken. Carter's novels often contain fantastical elements that are treated in a realistic manner, a technique known as magic realism. Her use of fantastical elements may help to explain the attraction fairy tales held for Carter throughout her life; in fact, at the time of her death, Carter was editing a volume of international fairy tales titled* Strange Things Sometimes Still Happen *(1993).*

In The Bloody Chamber, *Carter revises some of the most familiar fairy tales, such as "Little Red Riding Hood." "The Tiger's Bride" is one of two (re)tellings of "Beauty and the Beast" that appear in the work. As with most of the tales in* The Bloody Chamber, *this story is retold from a contemporary perspective that examines the codes for gender behavior advocated in the original and revises the story from a more feminist perspective. Therefore, as you read this tale compare it with the original version contained in this chapter. Consider what the changes in this tale reveal about each work and the themes the authors want to develop.*

My father lost me to The Beast at cards.

There's a special madness strikes travellers from the North when they reach the lovely land where the lemon trees grow. We come from countries of cold weather; at home, we are at war with nature but here, ah! you think you've come to the blessed plot where the lion lies down with the lamb. Everything flowers; no harsh wind stirs the voluptuous air. The sun spills fruit for you. And the deathly, sensual lethargy of the sweet South infects the starved brain; it gasps: 'Luxury! more luxury!' But then the snow comes, you cannot escape it, it followed us from Russia as if it ran behind our carriage, and in this dark, bitter city has caught up with us at last, flocking against the windowpanes to mock my father's expectations of perpetual pleasure as the veins in his forehead stand out and throb, his hands shake as he deals the Devil's picture books.

The candles dropped hot, acrid gouts of wax on my bare shoulders. I watched with the furious cynicism peculiar to women whom circumstances force mutely to witness folly, while my father, fired in his desperation by more and yet more draughts of the firewater they call 'grappa', rids himself of the last scraps of my inheritance. When we left Russia, we owned black earth, blue forest with bear and wild boar, serfs, cornfields, farmyards, my beloved horses, white nights of cool summer, the fireworks of the northern lights. What a burden all those possessions must have been to him, because he laughs as if with glee as he beggars himself; he is in such a passion to donate all to The Beast.

Everyone who comes to this city must play a hand with the *grand seigneur;* few come. They did not warn us at Milan, or, if they did, we did not understand them—my limping Italian, the bewildering dialect of the region. Indeed, I myself spoke up in favour of this remote, provincial place, out of fashion two hundred years, because, oh irony, it boasted no casino. I did not know that the price of a stay in its Decembral solitude was a game with Milord.

The hour was late. The chill damp of this place creeps into the stones, into your bones, into the spongy pith of the lungs; it insinuated itself with a shiver into our parlour, where Milord came to play in the privacy essential to him. Who could refuse the invitation his valet brought to our lodging? Not my profligate father, certainly; the mirror above the table gave me back his frenzy, my impassivity, the withering candles, the emptying bottles, the coloured tide of the cards as they rose and fell, the still mask that concealed all the features of The Beast but for the yellow eyes that strayed, now and then, from his unfurled hand towards myself.

'La Bestia!' said our landlady, gingerly fingering an envelope with his huge crest of a tiger rampant on it, something of fear, something of wonder in her face. And I could not ask her why they called the master of the place, 'La Bestia'—was it to do with that heraldic signature?—because her tongue was so thickened by the phlegmy, bronchitic speech of the region I scarcely managed to make out a thing she said except, when she saw me: 'Che bella!'

Since I could toddle, always the pretty one, with my glossy, nut-brown curls, my rosy cheeks. And born on Christmas Day—her 'Christmas rose', my English nurse called me. The peasants said: 'The living image of her mother,' crossing themselves out of respect for the dead. My mother did not blossom long; bartered for her dowry to such a feckless sprig of the Russian nobility that she soon died of his gaming, his whoring, his agonizing repentances. And The Beast gave me the rose from his own impeccable if outmoded buttonhole when he arrived, the valet brushing the snow off his black coat. This white rose, unnatural, out of season, that now my nervous fingers ripped, petal by petal, apart as my father magnificently concluded the career he had made of catastrophe.

This is a melancholy, introspective region; a sunless, featureless landscape, the sullen river sweating fog, the shorn, hunkering willows. And a cruel city; the sombre piazza, a place uniquely suited to public executions, under the beetling shadow of that malign barn of a church. They used to hang condemned men in cages from the city walls; unkindness comes naturally to them, their eyes are set too close together, they have thin lips. Poor food, pasta soaked in oil, boiled beef with sauce of bitter herbs. A funeral hush about the place, the inhabitants huddled up against the cold so you can hardly see their faces. And they lie to you and cheat you, innkeepers, coachmen, everybody. God, how they fleeced us!

The treacherous South, where you think there is no winter but forget you take it with you.

My senses were increasingly troubled by the fuddling perfume of Milord, far too potent a reek of purplish civet at such close quarters in so small a room. He must bathe himself in scent, soak his shirts and underlinen in it; what can he smell of, that needs so much camouflage?

I never saw a man so big look so two-dimensional, in spite of the quaint elegance of The Beast, in the old-fashioned tailcoat that might, from its looks, have been bought in those distant years before he imposed seclusion on himself; he does not feel the need to keep up with the times. There is a crude clumsiness about his outlines, that are on the ungainly, giant side; and he has an odd air of self-imposed restraint, as if fighting a battle with himself to remain upright when he would far rather drop down on all fours. He throws our human aspirations to the godlike sadly awry, poor fellow; only from a distance would you think The Beast not much different from any other man, although he wears a mask with a man's face painted most beautifully on it. Oh, yes, a beautiful face; but one with too much formal symmetry of feature to be entirely human: one profile of his mask is the mirror image of the other, too perfect, uncanny. He wears a wig, too, false hair tied at the nape with a bow, a wig of the kind you see in old-fashioned portraits. A chaste silk sock stuck with a pearl hides his throat. And gloves of blond kid that are yet so huge and clumsy they do not seem to cover hands.

He is a carnival figure made of papier mache and crepe hair; and yet he has the Devil's knack at cards.

His masked voice echoes as from a great distance as he stoops over his hand and he has such a growling impediment in his speech that only his valet, who understands him, can interpret for him, as if his master were the clumsy doll and he the ventrilo-quist.

The wick slumped in the eroded wax, the candles guttered. By the time my rose had lost all its petals, my father, too, was left with nothing.

'Except the girl.'

Gambling is a sickness. My father said he loved me yet he staked his daughter on a hand of cards. He fanned them out; in the mirror, I saw wild hope light up his eyes. His collar was unfastened, his rumpled hair stood up on end, he had the anguish of a man in the last stages of debauchery. The draughts came out of the old walls and bit me, I was colder than I'd ever been in Russia, when nights are coldest there.

A queen, a king, an ace. I saw them in the mirror. Oh, I know he thought he could not lose me; besides, back with me would come all he had lost, the unravelled fortunes of our family at one blow restored. And would he not win, as well, The Beast's heredi-tary palazzo outside the city; his immense revenues; his lands around the river; his rents, his treasure chest, his Mantegnas, his Giulio Romanos, his Cellini salt-cellars, his titles . . . the very city itself.

You must not think my father valued me at less than a king's ransom; but, at *no more* than a king's ransom.

It was cold as hell in the parlour. And it seemed to me, child of the severe North, that it was not my flesh but, truly, my father's soul that was in peril.

My father, of course, believed in miracles; what gambler does not? In pursuit of just such a miracle as this, had we not travelled from land of bears and shooting stars?

So we teetered on the brink.

The Beast bayed; laid down all three remaining aces.

The indifferent servants now glided smoothly forward as on wheels to douse the candles one by one. To look at them you would think that nothing of any moment had occurred. They yawned a little resentfully; it was almost morning, we had kept them out of bed. The Beast's man brought his cloak. My father sat amongst these preparations for departure, staring on at the betrayal of his cards upon the table.

The Beast's man informed me crisply that he, the valet, would call for me and my bags tomorrow, at ten, and conduct me forthwith to The Beast's palazzo. Capisco? So shocked was I that I scarcely did 'capisco'; he repeated my orders patiently, he was a strange, thin, quick little man who walked with an irregular, jolting rhythm upon splayed feet in curious, wedge-shaped shoes.

Where my father had been red as fire, now he was white as the snow that caked the window-pane. His eyes swam; soon he would cry.

"'Like the base Indian,'" he said; he loved rhetoric. "'One whose hand,/Like the base Indian, threw a pearl away/Richer than all his tribe . . .'" I have lost my pearl, my pearl beyond price.'

At that, the Beast made a sudden, dreadful noise, halfway between a growl and a roar; the candles flared. The quick valet, the prim hypocrite, interpreted unblinking: 'My master says: If you are so careless of your treasures, you should expect them to be taken from you.'

He gave us the bow and smile his master could not offer us and they departed.

I watched the snow until, just before dawn, it stopped falling; a hard frost settled, next morning there was a light like iron.

The Beast's carriage, of an elegant if antique design, was black as a hearse and it was drawn by a dashing black gelding who blew smoke from his nostrils and stamped upon the packed snow with enough sprightly appearance of life to give me some hope that not all the world was locked in ice, as I was. I had always held a little towards Gulliver's opinion, that horses are better than we are, and, that day, I would have been glad to depart with him to the kingdom of horses, if I'd been given the chance.

The valet sat up on the box in a natty black and gold livery, clasping, of all things, a bunch of his master's damned white roses as if a gift of flowers would reconcile a woman to any humiliation. He sprang down with preternatural agility to place them ceremoniously in my reluctant hand. My tear-beslobbered father wants a rose to show that I forgive him. When I break off a stem, I prick my finger and so he gets his rose all smeared with blood.

The valet crouched at my feet to tuck the rugs about me with a strange kind of unflattering obsequiousness yet he forgot his station sufficiently to scratch busily beneath his white periwig with an over-supple index finger as he offered me what my old nurse would have called an 'old-fashioned look', ironic, sly, a smidgen of disdain in it. And pity? No pity. His eyes were moist and brown, his face seamed with the innocent cunning of an ancient baby. He had an irritating habit of chattering to himself under his breath all the time as he packed up his master's winnings. I drew the curtains to conceal the sight of my father's farewell; my spite was sharp as broken glass.

Lost to The Beast! And what, I wondered, might be the exact nature of his 'beastliness'? My English nurse once told me about a tiger-man she saw in London, when she was a little girl, to scare me into good behaviour, for I was a wild wee thing and she could not tame me into submission with a frown or the bribe of a spoonful of jam. If you don't stop plaguing the nursemaids, my beauty, the tiger-man will come and take you away. They'd brought him from Sumatra, in the Indies, she said; his hinder parts were all hairy and only from the head downwards did he resemble a man.

And yet The Beast goes always masked; it cannot be his face that looks like mine.

But the tiger-man, in spite of his hairiness, could take a glass of ale in his hand like a good Christian and drink it down. Had she not seen him do so, at the sign of The George, by the steps of Upper Moor Fields when she was just as high as me and lisped and toddled, too. Then she would sigh for London, across the North Sea of the lapse of years. But, if this young lady was not a good little girl and did not eat her boiled beet-root, then the tiger-man would put on his big black travelling cloak lined with fur, just like your daddy's, and hire the Erl-King's galloper of wind and ride through the night straight to the nursery and—

Yes, my beauty! GOBBLE YOU UP!

How I'd squeal in delighted terror, half believing her, half knowing that she teased me. And there were things I knew that I must not tell her. In our lost farmyard, where the giggling nursemaids initiated me into the mysteries of what the bull did to the cows, I heard about the waggoner's daughter. Hush, hush, don't let on to your nursie we said so; the waggoner's lass, hare-lipped, squint-eyed, ugly as sin, who would have taken her? Yet, to her shame, her belly swelled amid the cruel mockery of the ostlers and her son was born of a bear, they whispered. Born with a full pelt and teeth; that proved it. But, when he grew up, he was a good shepherd, although he never married, lived in a hut outside the village and could make the wind blow any way he wanted to besides being able to tell which eggs would become cocks, which hens.

The wondering peasants once brought my father a skull with horns four inches long on either side of it and would not go back to the field where their poor plough disturbed it until the priest went with them; for this skull had the jaw-bone of a *man*, had it not?

Old wives' tales, nursery fears! I knew well enough the reason for the trepidation I costly titillated with superstitious marvels of my childhood on the day my childhood ended. For now my own skin was my sole capital in the world and today I'd make my first investment.

We had left the city far behind us and were now traversing a wide, flat dish of snow where the mutilated stumps of the willows flourished their ciliate heads athwart frozen ditches; mist diminished the horizon, brought down the sky until it seemed no more than a few inches above us. As far as eye could see, not one thing living. How starveling, how bereft the dead season of this spurious Eden in which all the fruit was blighted by cold! And my frail roses, already faded. I opened the carriage door and tossed the defunct bouquet into the rucked, frost-stiff mud of the road. Suddenly a sharp, freezing wind arose and pelted my face with a dry rice of powdered snow. The mist lifted sufficiently to reveal before me an acreage of half-derelict facades of sheer red brick, the vast man-trap, the megalomaniac citadel of his palazzo.

It was a world in itself but a dead one, a burned-out planet. I saw The Beast bought solitude, not luxury, with his money.

The little black horse trotted smartly through the figured bronze doors that stood open to the weather like those of a barn and the valet handed me out of the carriage on to the scarred tiles of the great hall itself, into the odorous warmth of a stable, sweet with hay, acrid with horse dung. An equine chorus of neighings and soft drumming of hooves broke out beneath the tall roof, where the beams were scabbed with last summer's swallows' nests; a dozen gracile muzzles lifted from their mangers and turned towards us, ears erect. The Beast had given his horses the use of the dining room. The walls were painted, aptly enough, with a fresco of horses, dogs and men in a wood where fruit and blossom grew on the bough together.

The valet tweaked politely at my sleeve. Milord is waiting.

Gaping doors and broken windows let the wind in everywhere. We mounted one staircase after another, our feet clopping on the marble. Through archways and open doors, I glimpsed suites of vaulted chambers opening one out of another like systems of Chinese boxes into the infinite complexity of the innards of the place. He and I and the wind were the only things stirring; and all the furniture was under dust sheets, the chandeliers bundled up in cloth, pictures taken from their hooks and propped with their faces to the walls as if their master could not bear to look at them. The palace was dismantled, as if its owner were about to move house or had never properly moved in; The Beast had chosen to live in an uninhabited place.

The valet darted me a reassuring glance from his brown, eloquent eyes, yet a glance with so much queer superciliousness in it that it did not comfort me, and went bounding ahead of me on his bandy legs, softly chattering to himself. I held my head high and followed him; but, for all my pride, my heart was heavy.

Milord has his eyrie high above the house, a small, stifling, darkened room; he keeps his shutters locked at noon. I was out of breath by the time we reached it and returned to him the silence with which he greeted me. I will not smile. He cannot smile.

In his rarely disturbed privacy, The Beast wears a garment of Ottoman design, a loose, dull purple gown with gold embroidery round the neck that falls from his shoulders to conceal his feet. The feet of the chair he sits in are handsomely clawed. He hides his hands in his ample sleeves. The artificial masterpiece of his face appals me. A small fire in a small grate. A rushing wind rattles the shutters.

The valet coughed. To him fell the delicate task of transmitting to me his master's wishes.

'My master—'

A stick fell in the grate. It made a might clatter in that dreadful silence; the valet started; lost his place in his speech, began again.

'My master has but one desire.'

The thick, rich, wild scent with which Milord had soaked himself the previous evening hangs all about us, ascends in cursive blue from the smoke of a precious Chinese pot.

'He wishes only—'

Now, in the face of my impassivity, the valet twittered, his ironic composure gone, for the desire of a master, however trivial, may yet sound unbearably insolent in the mouth of a servant and his role of go-between clearly caused him a good deal of embarrassment. He gulped; he swallowed, at last contrived to unleash an unpunctuated flood.

'My master's sole desire is to see the pretty young lady unclothed nude without her dress and that only for the one time after which she will be returned to her father undamaged with bankers' orders for the sum which be lost to my master at cards and also a number of fine presents such as furs, jewels and horses—'

I remained standing. During this interview, my eyes were level with those inside the mask that now evaded mine as if, to his credit, he was ashamed of his own request even as his mouthpiece made it for him. Agitato, molto agitato, the valet wrung his white-gloved hands.

'Desnuda—'

I could scarcely believe my ears. I let out a raucous guffaw; no young lady laughs like that! my old nurse used to remonstrate. But I did. And do. At the clamour of my heartless mirth, the valet danced backwards with perturbation, palpitating his fingers as if attempting to wrench them off, expostulating, wordlessly pleading. I felt that I owed it to him to make my reply in as exquisite a Tuscan as I could master.

'You may put me in a windowless room, sir, and I promise you I will pull my skirt up to my waist, ready for you. But there must be a sheet over my face, to hide it; though the sheet must be laid over me so lightly that it will not choke me. So I shall be covered completely from the waist upwards, and no lights. There you can visit me once, sir, and only the once. After that I must be driven directly to the city and deposited in the public square, in front of the church. If you wish to give me money, then I should be pleased to receive it. But I must stress that you should give me only the same amount of money that you would give to any other woman in such circumstances. However, if you choose not to give me a present, then that is your right.'

How pleased I was to see I struck The Beast to the heart! For, after a baker's dozen heartbeats, one single tear swelled, glittering, at the corner of the masked eye. A tear! A tear, I hoped, of shame. The tear trembled for a moment on an edge of painted bone, then tumbled down the painted cheek to fall, with an abrupt tinkle, on the tiled floor.

The valet, ticking and clucking to himself, hastily ushered me out of the room. A mauve cloud of his master's perfume billowed out into the chill corridor with us and dissipated itself on the spinning winds.

A cell had been prepared for me, a veritable cell, windowless, airless, lightless, in the viscera of the palace. The valet lit a lamp for me; a narrow bed, a dark cupboard with fruit and flowers carved on it bulked out of the gloom..

'I shall twist a noose out of my bed linen and hang myself with it,' I said.

'Oh, no, said the valet, fixing upon me wide and suddenly melancholy eyes. 'Oh, no, you will not. You are a woman of honour.'

And what was *he* doing in my bedroom, this jigging caricature of a man? Was he to be my warder until I submitted to The Beast's whim or he to mine? Am I in such reduced circumstances that I may not have a lady's maid? As if in reply to my unspoken demand, the valet clapped his hands.

'To assuage your loneliness, madame . . .'

A knocking and clattering behind the door of the cupboard; the door swings open and out glides a soubrette from an operetta, with glossy, nut-brown curls, rosy cheeks, blue, rolling eyes; it takes me a moment to recognize her, in her little cap, her white stockings, her frilled petticoats. She carries a looking glass in one hand and a powder puff in the other and there is a musical box where her heart should be; she tinkles as she rolls towards me on her tiny wheels.

'Nothing human lives here,' said the valet.

My maid halted, bowed; from a split seam at the side of her bodice protrudes the handle of a key. She is a marvellous machine, the most delicately balanced system of cords and pulleys in the world.

'We have dispensed with servants,' the valet said. 'We surround ourselves, instead, for utility and pleasure, with simulacra and find it no less convenient than do most gentlemen.

This clockwork twin of mine halted before me, her bowels churning out a settecento minuet, and offered me the bold carnation of her smile. Click, click—she raises her arm and busily dusts my cheeks with pink, powdered chalk that makes me cough; then thrusts towards me her little mirror.

I saw within it not my own face but that of my father, as if I had put on his face when I arrived at The Beast's palace as the discharge of his debt. What, you self-deluding fool, are you crying still? And drunk, too. He tossed back his grappa and hurled the tumbler away.

Seeing my astonished fright, the valet took the mirror away from me, breathed on it, polished it with the ham of his gloved fist, handed it back to me. Now all I saw was myself, haggard from a sleepless night, pale enough to need my maid's supply of rouge.

I heard the key turn in the heavy door and the valet's footsteps patter down the stone passage. Meanwhile, my double continued to powder the air, emitting her jangling tune but, as it turned out, she was not inexhaustible; soon she was powdering more and yet more languorously, her metal heart slowed in imitation of fatigue, her musical box ran down until the notes separated themselves out of the tune and plopped little single raindrops and, as if sleep had overtaken her, at last she moved no longer. As she succumbed to sleep, I had no option but to do so, too. I dropped on that narrow bed as if felled.

Time passed but I do not know how much; then the valet woke me with rolls and honey. I gestured the tray away but he set it down firmly beside the lamp and took from it a little shagreen box, which he offered to me.

I turned away my head.

'Oh, my lady!' Such hurt cracked his high-pitched voice! He dexterously unfastened the gold clasp; on a bed of crimson velvet lay a single diamond earring, perfect as a tear.

I snapped the box shut and tossed it into a corner. This sudden, sharp movement must have disturbed the mechanism of the doll; she jerked her arm almost as if to reprimand me, letting out a rippling fart of gavotte. Then was still again.

'Very well,' said the valet, put out. And indicated it was time for me to visit my host again. He did not let me wash or comb my hair. There was so little natural light in the interior of the palace that I could not tell whether it was day or night.

You would not think The Beast had budged an inch since I last saw him; he sat in his huge chair, with his hands in his sleeves, and the heavy air never moved. I might have slept an hour, a night, or a month, but his sculptured calm, the stilling air remained just as it had been. The incense rose from the pot, still traced the same signature on the air. The same fire burned.

Take off my clothes for you, like a ballet girl? Is that all you want of me?

'The sight of a young lady's skin that no man has seen before—'stammered the valet.

I wished I'd rolled in the hay with every lad on my father's farm, to disqualify myself from this humiliating bargain. That he should want so little was the reason why I could not give it; I did not need to speak for The Beast to understand me.

A tear came from his other eye. And then he moved; he buried his cardboard carnival head with its ribboned weight of false hair in, I would say, his arms; he withdrew his, I might say, hands from his sleeves and I saw his furred pads, his excoriating claws.

The dropped tear caught upon his fur and shone. And in my room for hours I hear those paws pad back and forth outside my door.

When the valet arrived again with his silver salver, I had a pair of diamond earrings of the finest water in the world; I threw the other into the corner where the first one lay. The valet twittered with aggrieved regret but did not offer to lead me to The Beast again. Instead, he smiled ingratiatingly and confided: 'My master, he say: invite the young lady to go riding.'

'What's this?'

He briskly mimicked the action of a gallop and, to my amazement, tunelessly croaked: 'Tantivy! tantivy! a-hunting we will go!'

'I'll run away, I'll ride to the city.'

'Oh, no,' he said. 'Are you not a woman of honour?'

He clapped his hands and my maidservant clicked and jangled into the imitation of life. She rolled towards the cupboard where she had come from and reached inside it to fetch out over her synthetic arm my riding habit. Of all things. My very own riding habit; that I'd left behind me in a trunk in a loft in that country house outside Petersburg that we'd lost long ago, before, even, we set out this wild pilgrimage to the cruel South. Either the riding habit my old nurse had sewn for me or else a copy of it perfect to the lost button on the right sleeve, the ripped hem held up for a pin. I turned the worn cloth about in my hands, looking for a clue. The wind that sprinted through the palace made the door tremble in its frame; had the north wind blown my garments across Europe to me? At home, the bear's son directed the winds at his pleasure; what democracy of magic held this palace and the fir forest in common? Or, should I be prepared to accept it as proof of the axiom my father had drummed into me: that, if you have enough money, anything is possible?

'Tantivy,' suggested the now twinkling valet, evidently charmed at the pleasure mixed with my bewilderment. The clockwork maid held my jacket out to me and I allowed myself to shrug into it as if reluctantly, although I was half mad to get out into the open air, away from this deathly palace, even in such company.

The doors of the hall let the bright day in; I saw that it was morning. Our horses, saddled and bridled, beasts in bondage, were waiting for us, striking sparks from the tiles with their impatient hooves while their stablemates lolled at ease among the straw, conversing with one another in the mute speech of horses. A pigeon or two, feathers puffed to keep out the cold, strutted about, pecking at ears of corn. The little black gelding who had brought me here greeted me with a ringing neigh that resonated inside the misty roof as in a sounding box and I knew he was meant for me to ride.

I always adored horses, noblest of creatures, such wounded sensitivity in their wise eyes, such rational restraint of energy at their high-strung hindquarters. I lirruped and hurrumphed to my shining black companion and he acknowledged my greeting with a kiss on the forehead from his soft lips. There was a little shaggy pony nuzzling at the *trompe l'ceil* foliage beneath the hooves of the painted horses on the wall, into whose saddle the valet sprang with a flourish as of the circus. Then The Beast, wrapped in a black fur-lined cloak, came to heave himself aloft a grave grey mare. No natural horseman he; he clung to her mane like a shipwrecked sailor to a spar.

Cold, that morning, yet dazzling with the sharp winter sunlight that wounds the retina. There was a scurrying wind about that seemed to go with us, as if the masked, immense one who did not speak carried it inside his cloak and let it out at his pleasure, for it stirred the horses' manes but did not lift the lowland mists.

A bereft landscape in the sad browns and sepias of winter lay all about us, the marshland drearily protracting itself towards the wide river. Those decapitated willows. Now and then, the swoop of a bird, its irreconcilable cry.

A profound sense of strangeness slowly began to possess me. I knew my two companions were not, in any way, as other men, the simian retainer and the master for whom he spoke, the one with clawed forepaws who was in a plot with the witches who let the winds out of their knotted handkerchiefs up towards the Finnish border. I knew they lived according to a different logic than I had done until my father abandoned me to the wild beasts by his human carelessness. This knowledge gave me a certain fearfulness still; but, I would say, not much . . . I was a young girl, a virgin, and therefore men denied me rationality just as they denied it to all those who were not exactly like themselves, in all their unreason. If I could see not one single soul in that wilderness of desolation all around me, then the six of us—mounts and riders, both—could boast amongst us not one soul, either, since all the best religions in the world state categorically that not beasts nor women were equipped with the flimsy, insubstantial things when the good Lord opened the gates of Eden and let Eve and her familiars tumble out. Understand, then, that though I would not say I privately engaged in metaphysical speculation as we rode through the reedy approaches to the river, I certainly meditate on the nature of my own state, how I had been bought and sold, passed from hand to hand. That clockwork girl who powdered my cheeks for me; had I not been allotted only the same kind of imitative life amongst men that the doll-maker had given her?

Yet, as to the true nature of the being of this clawed magus who rode his pale horse in a style that made me recall how Kublai Khan's leopards went out hunting on horseback, of that I had no notion.

We came to the bank of the river that was so wide we could not see across it, so still with winter that it scarcely seemed to flow. The horses lowered their heads to drink. The valet cleared his throat, about to speak; we were in a place of perfect privacy, beyond a brake of winter-bare rushes, a hedge of reeds.

'If you will not let him see you without your clothes—'

I involuntarily shook my head—

'—you must, then, prepare yourself for the sight of my master, naked.'

The river broke on the pebbles with a diminishing sigh. My composure deserted me; all at once I was on the brink of panic. I did not think that I could bear the sight of him, whatever he was. The mare raised her dripping muzzle and looked at me keenly, as if urging me. This river broke again at my feet. I was far from home.

'You,' said the valet, 'must.'

When I saw how scared he was I might refuse, I nodded.

The reed bowed down in a sudden snarl of wind that brought with it a gust of the heavy odour of his disguise. The valet held out his master's cloak to screen him from me as he removed the mask. The horses stirred.

The tiger will never lie down with the lamb; he acknowledges no pact that is not reciprocal. The lamb must learn to run with the tigers.

A great, feline, tawny shape whose pelt was barred with a savage geometry of bars the colour of burned wood. His domed, heavy head, so terrible he must hide it. How subtle the muscles, how profound the tread. The annihilating vehemence of his eyes, like twin suns.

I felt my breast ripped apart as if I suffered a marvellous wound.

The valet moved forward as if to cover up his master now the girl had acknowledged him, but I said: 'No.' The tiger sat still as a heraldic breast, in the pact he had made with his own ferocity to do me no harm. He was far larger than I could have imagined, from the poor, shabby things I'd seen once, in the Czar's menagerie at Petersburg, the golden fruit of their eyes dimming, withering in the far North of captivity. Nothing about him reminded me of humanity.

I therefore, shivering, now unfastened my jacket, to show him I would do him no harm. Yet I was clumsy and blushed a little, for no man had seen me naked and I was a proud girl. Pride it was, not shame, that thwarted my fingers so; and a certain trepidation lest this frail little article of human upholstery before him might not be, in itself, ground enough to satisfy his expectations of us, since those, for all I knew, might have grown infinite during the endless time he had been waiting. The wind clattered in the rushes, pulled and eddied in the river.

I showed his grave silence my white skin, my red nipples, and the horses turned their heads to watch me, as if they, too, were courteously curious as to the fleshly nature of women. Then The Beast lowered his massive head; Enough! said the valet with a gesture. The wind died down, all was still again.

Then they went off together, the valet on his pony, the tiger running before him like a hound, and I walked along the river bank for a while. I felt I was at liberty for the first time in my life. Then the winter sun began to tarnish, a few flakes of snow drifted from the darkening sky and, when I returned to the horses, I found The Beast mounted again on his grey mare, cloaked and masked and once more, to all appearances, a man, while the valet had a fine catch of waterfowl dangling from his hand and the corpse of a young roebuck slung behind his saddle. I climbed up on the black gelding in silence and so we returned to the palace as the snow fell more and more heavily, obscuring the tracks that we had left behind us.

The valet did not return me to my cell but, instead, to an elegant, if old-fashioned boudoir with sofas of faded pink brocade, a jinn's treasury of Oriental carpets, tintinnabulation of cut-glass chandeliers. Candles in antlered holders struck rainbows from the prismatic heart of my diamond earrings, that lay on my new dressing table at which my attentive maid stood ready with her powder puff and mirror. Intending to fix the ornaments in my ears, I took the looking glass from her hand, but it was in the midst of one of its magic fits again and I did not see my own face in it but that of my father; at first I thought he smiled at me. Then I saw he was smiling with pure gratification.

He sat, I saw, in the parlour of our lodgings, at the very table where he had lost me, but now he was busily engaged in counting out a tremendous pile of banknotes. My father's circumstances had changed already; well-shaven, neatly barbered, smart new clothes. A frosted glass of sparkling wine sat convenient to his hand beside an ice bucket. The Beast had clearly paid cash on the nail for his glimpse of my bosom, and paid up promptly, as if it had not been a sight I might have died of showing. Then I saw my father's trunks were packed, ready for departure. Could he so easily leave me here?

There was a note on the table with the money, in a fine hand. I could read it quite clearly. 'The young lady will arrive immediately.' Some harlot with whom he'd briskly negotiated a liaison on the strength of his spoils? Not at all. For, at that moment, the valet knocked at my door to announce that I might leave the palace at any time hereafter, and he bore over his arm a handsome sable cloak, my very own little gratuity, the Beast's morning gift, in which he proposed to pack me up and send me off.

When I looked at the mirror again, my father had disappeared and all I saw was a pale, hollow-eyed girl whom I scarcely recognized. The valet asked politely when he should prepare the carriage, as if he did not doubt that I would leave with my booty at the first opportunity while my maid, whose face was no longer the spit of my own, continued bonnily to beam. I will dress her in my own clothes, wind her up, send her back to perform the part of my fathers daughter.

'Leave me alone,' I said to the valet.

He did not need to lock the door, now. I fixed the earrings in my ears. They were very heavy. Then I took off my riding habit, left it where it lay on the floor. But, when I got down to my shift, my arms dropped to my sides. I was unaccustomed to nakedness. I was so unused to my own skin that to take off all my clothes involved a kind of flaying. I thought The Beast had wanted a little thing compared with what I was prepared to give him; but it is not natural for humankind to go naked, not since first we hid our loins with fig leaves. He had demanded the abominable. I felt as much atrocious pain as if I was stripping off my own underpelt and the smiling girl stood poised in the oblivion of her balked simulation of life, watching me peel down to the cold, white meat of contract and, if she did not see me, then so much more like the market place, where the eyes that watch you take no account of your existence.

And it seemed my entire life, since I had left the North, had passed under the indifferent gaze of eyes like hers.

Then I was flinching stark, except for his irreproachable tears.

I huddled in the furs I must return to him, to keep me from the lacerating winds that raced along the corridors. I knew the way to his den without the valet to guide me.

No response to my tentative rap on his door.

Then the wind blew the valet whirling along the passage. He must have decided that, if one should go naked, then all should go naked; without his livery, he revealed himself, as I had suspected, a delicate creature, covered with silken moth-grey fur, brown fingers supple as leather, chocolate muzzle, the gentlest creature in the world. He gibbered a little to see my fine furs and jewels as if I were dressed up for the opera and, with a great deal of tender ceremony, removed the sables from my shoulders. The sables thereupon resolved themselves into a pack of black, squeaking rats that rattled immediately down the stairs on their hard little feet and were lost to sight.

The valet bowed me inside The Beast's room.

The purple dressing gown, the mask, the wig, were laid out on his chair; a glove was planted on each arm. The empty house of his appearance was ready for him but he had abandoned it. There was a reek of fur and piss; the incense pot lay broken in pieces on the floor. Half-burned sticks were scattered from the extinguished fire. A candle stuck by its own grease to the mantlepiece lit two narrow flames in the pupils of the tiger's eyes.

He was pacing backwards and forwards, backwards and forwards, the tip of his heavy tail twitching as he paced out the length and breadth of his imprisonment between the gnawed and bloody bones.

He will gobble you up.

Nursery fears made flesh and sinew; earliest and most archaic of fears, fear of devourment. The beast and his carnivorous bed of bone and I, white, shaking, raw, approaching him as if offering, in myself, the key to a peaceable kingdom in which his appetite need not be my extinction.

He went still as stone. He was far more frightened of me than I was of him.

I squatted on the wet straw and stretched out my hand. I was now within the field of force of his golden eyes. He growled at the back of his throat, lowered his head, sank on to his forepaws, snarled, showed me his red gullet, his yellow teeth. I never moved. He snuffed the air, as if to smell my fear; he could not.

Slowly, slowly he began to drag his heavy, gleaming weight across the floor towards me.

A tremendous throbbing, as of the engine that makes the earth turn, filled the little room; he had begun to purr.

The sweet thunder of this purr shook the old walls, made the shutters batter the windows until they burst apart and let in the white light of the snowy moon. Tiles came crashing down from the roof; I heard them fall into the courtyard far below. The reverberations of his purring rocked the foundations of the house, the walls began to dance. I thought: 'It will all fall, everything will disintegrate.'

He dragged himself closer and closer to me, until I felt the harsh velvet of his head against my hand, then a tongue, abrasive as sandpaper. 'He will lick the skin off me!'

And each stroke of his tongue ripped off skin after successive skin, all the skins of a life in the world, and left behind a nascent patina of shining hairs. My earrings turned back to water and trickled down my shoulders; I shrugged the drops off my beautiful fur.

For Practice

1. What is the effect of the opening line of the story? Does this line conform to the normal construction of fairy tales? Why or why not?

2. Roses are a common symbol in fairy tales. How does Carter use roses as a symbol in this work? What do they symbolize? Why is that significant for understanding the work itself?

3. What is it that the Master wants from her? Why? What is she willing to give him? Which of these things is the greater sacrifice? Why? What finally causes her to give him what he asks for? How does this exchange connect with the overall theme of the work?

4. What happens at the end of the story? How does this ending differ from the typical fairy tale ending in a marriage followed by the promise that "they lived happily ever after"?

5. As a child, the narrator's nurse has told her the story of the tiger-man she has seen as a way of getting her to behave. What does this reveal about the punitive value of fairy tales? How is this fairy tale a response to such understandings of fairy tales?

6. Compare/contrast this version of the tale with any of the film versions discussed in the de Beaumont section or with the original tale itself. What do each of these works reveal about the cultures in which they were written? Since de Beaumont's tale is meant to teach a lesson to young girls about how they should behave and what they should value, students may want to consider how these changes alter that message (if indeed they do) and the effect of making such alterations on the theme/moral of the story itself.

7. In "The Child's Need for Magic," Bettelheim claims that fairy tales help children understand aspects of the world they are not yet able to comprehend and that as we grow up we no longer need fairy tales and begin to think logically. Does Carter's fairy tale function in this way? Does it support or contradict Bettelheim's understanding of fairy tales and their place in our development? By revising this fairy tale as she does has Carter altered the place of "magic" in our lives?

Barbie Doll

Marge Piercy

Marge Piercy (b. 1936) is an award winning poet and novelist. Recipient of such awards as a 1978 National Endowment of the Arts award and the Orion Scott Award in the Humanities, Piercy is known as a feminist writer who uses personal experiences to convey social and political messages. The daughter of a labor activist, Piercy uses her poetry to reveal aspects of society that she feels have been hidden or silenced. The prominence of political themes in Piercy's works led some early critics to view her work as politics rather than art, but the originality of her subjects and the power of her use of language have challenged such reactions and given her a place of importance among contemporary poets. In addition to feminist themes, Piercy often writes about nature and her Jewish background.

"Barbie Doll" (1973) is a poem that reflects Piercy's commitment to feminist issues; in this poem, she takes on a familiar icon of American culture and uses it to discuss the gender identity of young women. Although this poem is not as directly autobiographical as some of her works, Piercy is using a seemingly personal voice to convey a "universal" theme. As you read this poem, think about her choice of Barbie to tell the story of this young woman.

This girlchild was born as usual
and presented dolls that did pee-pee
and miniature GE stoves and irons
and wee lipsticks the color of cherry candy.
Then in the magic of puberty, a classmate said: 5
You have a great big nose and fat legs.

She was healthy, tested intelligent,
possessed strong arms and back,
abundant sexual drive and manual dexterity.
She went to and fro apologizing.   10
Everyone saw a fat nose on thick legs.

She was advised to play coy,
exhorted to come on hearty,
exercise, diet, smile and wheedle.
Her good nature wore out like a fan belt.   15

So she cut off her nose and her legs
and offered them up.

In the casket displayed on satin she lay
with the undertaker's cosmetics painted on,
a turned-up putty nose,   20
dressed in a pink and white nightie.
Doesn't she look pretty? everyone said.
Consummation at last
To every woman a happy ending.

For Practice

1. Why does Piercy title the poem "Barbie Doll"? What role does Barbie play in this poem? In what ways is this girl like or not like a Barbie doll?

2. What is the girl of the poem like? What good qualities does she have? What are her weaknesses? How important are physical flaws? Why? How does Piercy indicate this in the work itself?

3. What does the word "consummation" mean in this poem? Why does Piercy choose this word? What does it reveal about the theme of the poem? What irony is represented in her choice of this word?

4. In the Spring of 1997, it was announced that Barbie would be remodeled so that her proportions were more "realistic." This announcement seems to be in response to a number of complaints about the negative impact Barbie may have on young girls' impressions of their own bodies. Look at recent discussions of this change and our response to it. Compare/contrast the issues involved in this discussion with Piercy's poem. How does her poem reflect or revise these issues?

Delight in Disorder

Robert Herrick

The son of a prosperous goldsmith, Robert Herrick (1591–1674) reluc-
tantly became a priest in 1623. For men of his station, becoming a priest
meant being able to pursue the leisured life of academic study and casual
poetic experimentation. In Herrick's case, it also meant gaining access to
many of the most important intellectual and political figures of his day,
including Ben Jonson, one of King James I's favorite poets and play-
wrights. Herrick was one of the so-called "Sons of Ben," an informal
"school" of poetry centered around Jonson that stressed urbane "wit" and
natural grace over complexity and difficulty. Their conceptions of man-
nered and decorous behavior in poetry also corresponded to a belief that
living, eating, thinking, and writing well will translate into living ethical-
ly well. This group also thought that mannered, decorous, and beautiful
behaviors indicated a correspondent inner beauty. As you read "Delight in
Disorder" (1648) you might ask yourself how well the categories of beau-
ty Herrick espouses pertain to our modern conceptions of beauty.

A sweet disorder in the dress
  Kindles in clothes a wantonness.
A lawn about the shoulders thrown
Into a fine distraction;
An erring lace, which here and there   5
Enthralls the crimson stomacher,
A cuff neglectful, and thereby
Ribbands to flow confusedly;
A winning wave, deserving note,
In the tempestuous petticoat;   10
A careless shoestring, in whose tie
I see a wild civility
Do more bewitch me than when art
Is too precise in every part.

For Practice

1. How does Herrick define *beauty*? What are the criteria for beautiful
   behaviors?

2. What does Herrick mean by the word "art" in line 13? What does it mean for this art to be "too precise?"

3. Most descriptions of beauty describe the female body. What do you make of the fact that Herrick concentrates on this woman's clothes and not her person? (A "lawn" is a scarf made out of linen. A "stomacher" covers a woman's lower torso.)

4. Review Shakespeare's sonnet from the previous unit. How does Herrick's vision of beauty compare with Shakespeare's? Do these two poets reject the same vision of beauty?

5. Herrick praises the beauty of "sprezzatura," or the appearance of "careless grace," in his mistress. Yet, this appearance of artful carelessness might just be another kind of the "precise art" that he is critiquing. This raises the possibility of acting or behaving "outside" of conventions. For example, is it possible to be "alternative" or do alternative behaviors really just imply a reaction against an established convention (and are by extension similarly conventional)? When asked to introduce a set of so-called "alternative" music during a guest appearance on MTV's "120 Minutes," Henry Rollins bemusedly wondered that "alternative" bands were an "alternative to what?" Is there a way to behave "outside" of conventions and stereotypes?

The Lady's Dressing Room

Jonathan Swift

Perhaps most famous for his creation of Lemuel Gulliver, Jonathan Swift (1667–1745) is the great satirist in an age of complex and difficult satire. Living in a political milieu which crossed national and religious boundaries, the specific politics of Swift's satire can be difficult for the modern student unfamiliar with the intricacies of eighteenth-century politics. Swift's satire left almost no important target of his day unscathed.

While considered coarse by some members of both his contemporary audience and modern audiences, Swift's focus on the ways in which the realities of the female body conflict with ideal conceptions of beauty continues to raise important questions for society today. As you read "The Lady's Dressing Room" (1730), you might compare Swift's view of cosmetic beauty with our own. Also note Swift's use of couplets (pairs of rhyming lines).

Five Hours, (and who can do it less in?)
By haughty *Celia* spent in Dressing;
The Goddess from her Chamber issues,
Array'd in Lace, Brocades and Tissues.
    Strephon, who found the Room was void,   5
And *Betty*, otherwise employ'd;
Stole in, and took a strict Survey,
Of all the Litter as it lay;
Whereof, to make the Matter clear,
An Inventory follows here.   10
    And first a dirty Smock appear'd,
Beneath the Arm-pits well besmear'd.
Strephon, the Rogue, display'd it wide,
And turn'd it round on every Side.
On such a Point few Words are best,   15
And *Strephon* bids us guess the rest;
But swears how damnably the Men lie,
In calling *Celia* sweet and cleanly.
Now listen while he next produces,
The various Combs for various Uses,   20
Fill'd up with Dirt so closely fixt,

No Brush could force a Way betwixt.
A Paste of Composition rare,
Sweat Dandriff Powder Lead and Hair;
A Forehead Cloth with Oyl upon't   25
To smooth the Wrinkles on her Front;
Here Allum Flower to stop the Steams
Exhal'd from sour unsavoury Streams
There Night-gloves made of *Tripsy's* Hide,
Bequeath'd by *Tripsy* when she dy'd   30
With Puppy Water Beauty's Help
Distill'd from *Tripsy's* darling Whelp;
Here Gallypots and Vials plac'd
Some fill'd with Washes some with Paste,
Some with Pomatum Paints and Slops,   35
And Ointments good for scabby Chops.
Hard by a filthy Bason stands,
Fowl'd with the Scouring of her Hands;
The Bason takes whatever comes
The Scrapings of her Teeth and Gums   40
A nasty Compound of all Hues,
For here she spits and here she spues.
But oh! it turn'd poor *Strephon's* Bowels,
When he beheld and smelt the Towels,
Begumm'd bematter'd and beslim'd   45
With Dirt, and Sweat, and Ear-Wax grim'd.
No Object *Strephon's* Eye escapes,
Here Pettycoats in frowzy Heaps;
Nor be the Handkerchiefs forgot
All varnish'd o'er with Snuff and Snot.   50
The Stockings, why shou'd I expose,
Stain'd with the Marks of stinking Toes;
Or greasy Coifs and Pinners reeking,
Which *Celia* slept at least a Week in?
A Pair of Tweezers next he found   55
To pluck her Brows in Arches round,
Or Hairs that sink the Forehead low,
Or on her Chin like Bristles grow.
     The Virtues we must not let pass
Of *Celia's* magnifying Glass.   60
When frighted *Strephon* cast his Eye on't
It shew'd the Visage of a Gyant.
A Glass that can to Sight disclose,
The smallest Worm in *Celia's* Nose,
And faithfully direct her Nail   65
To squeeze it out from Head to Tail;
For catch it nicely by the Head,
It must come out alive or dead.
     Why *Strephon* will you tell the rest?

And must you needs describe the Chest?   70
That careless Wench! No Creature warn her
To move it out from yonder Corner;
But leave it standing full in Sight
For you to exercise your Spight.
In vain, the Workman shew'd his Wit   75
With Rings and Hinges counterfeit
To make it seem in this Disguise,
A Cabinet to vulgar Eyes;
For *Strephon* ventur'd to look in,
Resolv'd to go thro' thick and thin;   80
He lifts the Lid, there needs no more,
He smelt it all the Time before.
As from within *Pandora's* Box,
When *Epimetheus* op'd the Locks,
A sudden universal Crew   85
Of humane Evils upwards flew;
he still was comforted to find
That *Hope* at last remain'd behind;
So *Strephon* lifting up the Lid,
To view what in the Chest was hid.   90
The Vapours flew from out the Vent,
But *Strephon* cautious never meant
The Bottom of the Pan to grope,
And fowl his Hands in Search of *Hope*.
O never say such vile Machine   95
Be once in *Celia's* Chamber seen!
O may she better learn to keep
Those "secrets of the hoary Deep!"
        As Mutton Cutlets, Prime of Meat,
Which tho' with Art you salt and beat,   100
As Laws of Cookery require,
And toast them at the clearest Fire;
If from adown the hopeful Chops
The Fat upon a Cinder drops,
To stinking Smoak it turns the Flame   105
Pois'ning the flesh from whence it came;
And up exhales a greasy Stench,
For which you curse the careless Wench;
So Things, which must not be exprest,
When plumpt into the reeking Chest;   110
Send up an excremental Smell
To taint the Parts from whence they fell.
The Pettycoats and Gown perfume,
Which waft a Stink round every Room.
        Thus finishing his grand Survey,   115
Disgusted *Strephon* stole away
Repeating in his amorous Fits,

Oh! *Celia Celia Celia* shits!
　　But Vengeance, Goddess never sleeping
Soon punished *Strephon* for his Peeping;   120
His foul Imagination links
Each Dame he sees with all her Stinks:
And if unsav'ry Odours fly
Conceives a Lady standing by:
All Women his Description fits,   125
And both Idea's jump like Wits:
By vicious Fancy coupled fast,
And still appearing in Contrast.
I pity wretched *Strephon* blind
To all the Charms of Female Kind;   130
Should I the Queen of Love refuse,
Because she rose from stinking Ooze?
To him that looks behind the Scene,
Statira's but some pocky Quean.
When *Celia* in her Glory shows,   135
If *Strephon* would but stop his Nose;
(Who now so impiously blasphemes
Her Ointments, Daubs and Paints and Creams,
Her Washes Slops and every Clout
With which he makes so foul a Rout;)   140
He soon would learn to think like me,
And bless his ravisht Sight to see
Such Order from Confusion sprung,
Such gaudy Tulips rais'd from Dung.

For Practice

1. The names *Celia* and *Strephon* are commonly used for the main characters in pastoral poetry. What aspects of this poem seem pastoral? How does drawing upon the pastoral tradition help Swift make his point?

2. Compare the litany of cosmetic and hygienic products used by Celia to modern cosmetics. Despite the fact that Swift writes in an era before such things as indoor plumbing and the flush toilet, is this a world totally foreign to us or one very familiar?

3. What is the "tone" of the poem? Is it angry or bemused? What words contribute to the construction of this tone?

4. What is the argument the poem makes about "beauty" and cosmetic enhancement of beauty? Is Celia or Strephon the target of Swift's satire? Why?

The Knight's Tale

Geoffrey Chaucer

As the son of a London vinter, Geoffrey Chaucer (c.1342–1400) spent his whole life negotiating his position between economic classes. Despite having something like "middle class" status, Chaucer married above his station to the sister of John of Gaunt's third wife, an economic and political accomplishment that might not be fully appreciated in our own time, and enjoyed the patronage of Gaunt for his entire life. Chaucer assumed numerous political and diplomatic posts which allowed him to travel the European continent and exposed him to the Italian Renaissance, perhaps even bringing him on a journey to Genoa in 1372 and into personal contact with Petrarch and Boccaccio (whose Teseida *is a source for "The Knight's Tale"). As a new class of civil servant, Chaucer transcended his birth and rose to the rank of esquire, yet we might see Chaucer as an outsider looking in on the upper class. He enjoyed their patronage and served in their courts, but his memory of his own background might be one of the reasons his works show the necessary (and amused) detachment required to make valuable observations and judgements on his society. To read* The Canterbury Tales *(begun in 1386 and never completed) and hear their famous pilgrims tell their tales is to take a vivid trip back in time, but it is a trip where this vivid observation is also tinged with social critique and satire.*

Once on a time, as old histories tell us,
There was a duke whose name was Theseus,
Who was of Athens lord and governor,
And in his day so great a conqueror
There was none mightier beneath the sun.
Many a wealthy kingdom he had won;
What with his generalship and bravery
He'd conquered all the land of Femeny,
Realm of the Amazons, once called Scythia,
And married there its Queen Hippolyta, 10
And brought her home with him to his country
With splendour, pomp, and solemn pageantry,
And also her young sister Emily.
And thus with music and in victory

I'll leave this noble duke, and let him ride
To Athens with his armed host at his side.
    And trust me, were it not too long to hear,
I would have told you fully the manner
In which the kingdom of Femeny
Was won by Theseus and his cavalry;   20
Especially the great battle fought between
The Amazons and the Athenian men;
And of the siege laid to Hippolyta,
The beautiful fierce Queen of Scythia;
And of the feast they held for the wedding,
The storm that blew up on the voyage home;
But all these things I must pass over now.
I have, the Lord knows, a large field to furrow,
Weak oxen in the team to draw my plough.
The remainder of the tale is long enough.   30
I'll not get in the way of anyone:
Let every fellow tell his tale in turn,
And now let's see which of us is to win
The dinner—where I left off, I'll begin.
    This duke of whom I'm speaking, having come
Almost to the approaches of the town,
In the height of all his triumph and his joy
Perceived out of the corner of his eye
There kneeling in the highway, two by two,
A company of ladies in a row;   40
In clothes of black each one of them was clad.
But such a cry, such clamouring they made
That in this world there is no creature living
That ever heard the like of their lamenting;
Nor of their clamour would they stint, until
One of them clutched the reins of his bridle.
    'Who may you be, that at my homecoming
Disturb the celebration with your crying?
Have you such jealousy,' said Theseus,
'Of these my honours, that you lament thus?   50
And who's menaced you? or has done you hurt?
And now tell me if it may be put right,
And why you are all clad in black like this.'
Whereupon, fainting, with a deathlike face,
So it was pitiful to see and hear,
The eldest lady of the group made answer:
'My lord, you to whom Fortune has assigned
Victory and a conqueror's garland,
We grudge you neither glory nor honour,
But we beseech your mercy and succour.   60
Have mercy on our woe and our distress!
On us poor women, in your nobleness

Of heart, let but one drop of pity fall!
Indeed, sir, there is none amongst us all
Who was not once a duchess or a queen,
And is now destitute, as may be seen,
Since Fortune and her fickle wheel makes sure
That no prosperity can be secure.
And truly, lord, to watch your coming, we
In this the temple of Divine Pity   70
Have waited a whole fortnight for you here.
Now help us, sir, since it lies in your power.
　　　'I who weep and wail in misery like this
Was once the wife of King Capaneus
Who died at Thebes—a curse upon that day!
And all of us who are dressed as you see,
We who are making all this lamentation,
Have each of us lost husbands in that town,
Killed in the siege. And now the ancient Creon
Who is, alas, the lord now of the city,   80
Brimful of anger and iniquity,
Out of tyrannic malice has defiled
The bodies of our husbands who were killed,
And dragged them all together in a heap;
And he will neither vouchsafe nor permit
Either their burial or burning, but
Has given them over to the dogs to eat.'
　　　And with these words, as soon as they were spoken,
They fell upon their faces, sadly crying
'Have some compassion on us wretched women!   90
And let our sorrow sink into your heart.'
With a breast filled with pity, the good duke
Leapt from his war-horse when he heard them speak.
It seemed to him as if his heart must break,
Seeing them so forlorn and desolate,
Who formerly had been of high estate;
And in his arms he raised up each of them
And tried to give them comfort; there and then
He swore upon his honour as a knight
He would put forth the utmost of his might   100
So to avenge them on the tyrant Creon
All Greece would talk about his overthrowing
By Theseus, and say he had been served
As one whose death had richly been deserved.
And thereupon his banner he displayed
And, delaying no longer, forth he rode
Toward the town of Thebes with his host.
He would not go near Athens, nor would rest
And take his ease for even half a day,
But pushed on, lodging that night on the way,   110

Having sent, with Hippolyta the queen,
Her sister Emily, so fair and young,
On to the town of Athens, there to stay
While he rode on; there is no more to say.
    The red image of Mars with spear and shield
Gleams in his broad white standard till the fields
Seem lit on all sides with its glittering.
And borne next to his banner is his pennon
Of richest gold, embroidered with a great
Head of the Minotaur which he killed in Crete.   120
Thus rode this conquering duke; among the flower
Of chivalry he rode, in his armed power
To Thebes; where in splendour he drew up
Upon a field where he purposed to fight.
But, not to make too long a tale of this,
He fought with Creon, who was King of Thebes,
And killed him, as befits a valiant knight,
In fair combat, and put his men to flight;
And after that he took the town by storm,
And wall and beam and rafter he tore down,   130
And to the ladies he restored again
The bodies of their husbands who were slain
For funeral rites, as was the custom then.
But to describe it would take all too long—
The lamentation and the din of mourning
That went up from the ladies at the burning
Of the dead bodies, and the great honour
Duke Theseus, that noble conqueror,
Paid to the ladies when they took their leave—
For it is my intention to be brief.   140
    And now this noble duke, this Theseus,
With Creon slain, and Thebes taken thus,
Quietly rested in the field all night,
All Creon's kingdom lying at his feet.
    The pillagers went busily to work
After the battle and the Theban rout,
To rummage in the pile of slaughtered men
And strip the armour and the clothes from them.
Among the heap of corpses there they found
Pierced through and through with many a deep wound,   150
Two young knights lying bleeding side by side,
Both in the same expensive armour clad;
One of the two was Arcita by name,
The other knight was known as Palamon.
They were not quite alive nor wholly dead;
Seeing their coat-of-arms, the heralds said
That they were cousins of the royal blood
Of Thebes: that two sisters gave them birth.

Out of the heap of dead they were dragged forth.
Gently the looters bore them to the tent   160
Of Theseus; who thereupon had them sent
At once to Athens, to remain in prison
For ever, for he would not hear of ransom.
Then the great duke, so soon as this was done,
Gathered his host together and rode home
Crowned with the laurel of a conqueror,
And there lives on in happiness and honour
For ever after; what more need I say?
And Palamon and his friend Arcita
Are in a tower, in misery and grief   170
For evermore; no gold can buy release.
     So time passed, year by year and day by day,
Till it so happened, in the month of May,
That Emily, lovelier to look upon
Than is the lily on its stalk of green,
And fresher than the May with flowers new—
For with the rose's colour strove her hue,
Nor can I tell the lovelier of the two—
Well before day, as she was wont to do,
Was risen and dressed and ready to go out,   180
For, as you know, the nights are not for sleep
In May. The season stirs in every heart
That's noble, and from slumber rouses it,
Saying, 'Get up, pay homage to the spring!'
And therefore Emily was remembering
To rise and celebrate the month of May.
Picture her clad in colours fresh and gay:
Her yellow hair was plaited in a tress
Behind her back, a yard in length I'd guess.
And in the garden, while the sun uprises,   190
She wanders here and there, and as she pleases
Goes gathering flowers, mixing white and red,
To weave a graceful garland for her head;
And like an angel out of heaven sang.
     The great tower, that was so thick and strong,
Which was the castle's principal dungeon
Wherein the two knights languished in prison
Who were and are the subject of my tale,
Adjoined exactly to the garden wall
Where Emily was used to take her pleasure.   200
Bright was the sun that morning, bright and clear,
And Palamon, that wretched prisoner,
As was his way, by leave of his gaoler,
Was up, and roaming in an upper room
From which the noble city could be seen,
Also the garden, filled with greenery,

In which the fair and radiant Emily
Was wandering, and walking up and down.
This wretched prisoner, this Palamon
Walks in his chamber, pacing to and fro,   210
And to himself complaining of his woe
And wishing that he never had been born.
It chanced, as fate or luck would have it then,
That through a window, fenced with iron bars
Solid and big as any wooden beam,
He cast his eye upon Emilia:
At which he started back with a loud cry,
As though he had been bitten to the heart.
And at that cry Arcita leapt up
And said, 'Why do you look so deathly pale?   220
What is the matter, cousin? Are you ill?
Who has upset you? Why did you cry out?
I beg you, for the love of God, submit
With patience to our gaol, since it must be.
Fortune has dealt us this adversity:
Some malign aspect or disposition
Of Saturn in some adverse position
Has brought it on us; nothing's to be done:
It stood thus in our stars when we were born;
The long and short of it is this: Endure.'   230
      And to that, Palamon said in reply,
'Truly, cousin, you have the wrong idea.
Prison was not the reason for my cry,
For I was hurt just now, pierced through the eye
Right to the heart; the wound is killing me.
The beauty of that lady whom I see
There in that garden wandering to and fro,
Made me cry out; she's cause of all my woe.
I don't know if she's woman or goddess,
But it is really Venus, I would guess.'   240
With that Palamon fell upon his knees,
Exclaiming: 'Venus, if it be your wish
Thus to transform yourself in this garden
For me, a sorrowful and wretched man,
Will you not help us to escape from prison?
And if it be my destiny to die
As foreordained by eternal decree
In prison, then at least bestow compassion
Upon our house, brought low by tyranny!'
But while he talked, Arcita cast his eye   250
To where the lady wandered to and fro;
And at the sight, her beauty hurt him so
That if Palamon has been wounded sore,
Arcita is as badly hurt, or more.

And with a sigh, dejectedly he spoke:
'Beauty so fresh destroys me, as I look
On her who wanders yonder in that place.
Unless I win her mercy and her grace
That I at least may see her every day,
I'm better dead; what more is there to say?'   260
        Hearing those words, his cousin Palamon
Looked black, and angrily replied to him:
'Do you say that in earnest or in jest?'
'No, on my oath,' said Arcita, 'in earnest.
So help me God, I'm in no mood to clown.'
Knitting his brows together, Palamon
Retorted, 'It would do you no great honour
Did you prove either faithless or a traitor
To me who am your cousin, and sworn brother,
Each bound by solemn oaths, one to the other,   270
That even if it means we die by torture,
Neither of us would ever cross the other
In love or any other thing, dear brother,
Till death shall part the two of us for ever!
No, you must always come to my support
As loyally as I must come to yours:
This was your solemn oath, and mine also,
Which you dare not deny, as I well know.
Thus you're in my confidence, there's no doubt,
And like a traitor you are now about   280
To begin to make love to my own lady
Whom I must love and serve until I die!
No, you shall not, be sure of that, you liar!
I loved her first, and told you my desire
As to my confidant, to one who swore
To lend support, as I have said before;
Therefore you are committed, as a knight,
To help me on, if it lies in your might,
Or else I dare aver you are forsworn.'
        And Arcita disdainfully answered him: 290
'You'll be forsworn', said he, 'sooner than I;
Forsworn I tell you, forsworn utterly!
For I loved her first, and as a woman too.
What can you say? You can't tell even now
Whether she is a goddess or a woman.
Yours is no more than a religious feeling:
Mine is real love, love of a human being;
I told you what happened to me for that reason,
As to my cousin, as to my sworn brother.
        'But, granted that you loved her earlier,   300
Have you forgot the old philosophic saw
That goes like this, "All's fair in love and war"?

Love is a mightier law, upon my soul,
Than any made by any mortal rule;
For love, all man-made laws are broken by
Folk of all kinds, all day and every day.
A man is bound to love, against all reason.
Though it should cost his life, there's no escaping,
Whether she's a maid, a widow, or a wife.
What's more, you are not likely, all your life,   310
To win her favour, any more than I;
For as you yourself know too certainly,
Both you and I have been condemned to prison
For ever; and for us there's no escaping.
We bicker like the two dogs for a bone;
They fought all day for it, and yet got none;
For while they quarrelled, a kite came along,
And from between them both bore off the bone.
And therefore, brother, as in politics,
Each for himself—there isn't any choice.   320
Love if you wish; I love, and ever shall.
And truly, my dear brother, one thing's sure:
Here in this prison we must both endure,
And each of us must take his chance, that's all.'
        Bitter and long the strife between the two,
Which, had I leisure, I'd depict for you;
But to the point: it happened—if I may
Make a long story shorter—that one day
A noble duke, whose name was Perotheus,
Who'd been a friend of the Duke Theseus   330
Since they were boys together, came to pay
A visit to his friend, and holiday
In Athens, as he often used to do;
There was no man on earth whom he loved so—
And Theseus loved him just as tenderly.
So great was their love, ancient writers say,
That when one of them came at last to die,
His friend went down and looked for him in hell.
But that's a tale I have no wish to tell.
        Duke Perotheus loved Arcita well,   340
And had known him in Thebes for many a year.
And finally, at the request and prayer
Of Perotheus, and without ransom,
Duke Theseus let Arcita out of prison,
Free to go as it pleased him anywhere
On certain terms: I'll tell you what they were.
        This, set down in plain language, was the pact
Between Theseus and Arcita: that
If so be Arcita were ever found
Alive by night or day on Theseus' land   350

And Arcita were caught, it was agreed
His head was to be cut off with the sword.
There was no other choice or help for it
But to take leave, and go home with all speed.
He'd better watch out, now his neck's forfeit!
　　　How sharp the agony Arcita suffers now!
He feels death itself pierce his heart right through.
He weeps, he wails, he laments pitifully,
Watches a chance to kill himself secretly.
He cried, 'Alas, the day that I was born!　　　　　　　　360
For I'm in a worse prison than before.
Now it's my fate eternally to dwell
Not in a purgatory, but in hell!
Alas that ever I knew Perotheus!
Otherwise I'd have stayed with Theseus
Fettered for ever in his prison.
Then Happiness and not misery had been mine.
Though I may never win nor yet deserve
Her favour, yet the sight of her I serve
Would have sufficed to have contented me.　　　　　　370
O my dear cousin Palamon!' cried he,
'It seems that in this case you've come out best,
How happily in prison you may rest!
In prison—no indeed, but paradise!
Yours is the luck in this throw of the dice,
For you have sight of her, I the absence.
It's possible, being in her presence,
And since you are a doughty knight, and able,
That by some chance—since Fortune is changeable—
You'll sooner or later attain your desire　　　　　　　380
While I, who am exiled and in despair,
So barren of hope that there's no living creature
That's formed of earth or water, flame or air,
That can yield comfort or a cure for this—
Well may I die in despair and distress!
Farewell my life, my joy, my happiness!
　　　'Alas, why is it that most folk complain
So much of God's providence, or Fortune,
That often grants them, in so many ways,
Far better favours than they could devise?　　　　　　390
Here's someone wishes for enormous wealth,
And this leads to his murder, or ill-health;
Here's someone longing to get out of prison,
Whose servants murder him when he gets home.
Infinite harms from this would seem to flow;
We don't know what we pray for here below,
But, like a man drunk as a wheelbarrow,
Who knows he's got a home where he can go,

But doesn't know which is the right road thither—
For when you're drunk, then every road's a slither.   400
Yes, in this world, that's how it goes with us;
All frantically seeking happiness,
But oftener than not in the wrong place.
There's no doubt we can all of us say so.
Especially I, who conceived a great notion
That if I only could escape from prison
Then joy and perfect happiness must be mine,
Whereas I'm exiled from my well-being.
For since I cannot see you, Emily,
I might as well be dead; no cure for me.'   410
     Upon the other hand, when Palamon
Came to realize that Arcita had gone,
He created such an outcry, the great tower
Resounded with his bellowings and clamour.
The very fetters round his shins were wet
With the salt bitter tears Palamon shed.
'Alas,' he cried, 'God knows you've gained the day
In this our quarrel, cousin Arcita!
Now you're at large in Thebes, walking free
And caring little for my misery.   420
You may, since you are resolute and shrewd,
Assemble all our kinsfolk and kindred,
And make so fierce an assault on this city
That by some chance, or through some kind of treaty,
You may gain her for your lady and your wife,
She for whose sake I needs must lose my life.
For, when one weighs the chances, one can see,
As you're at large, no prisoner but free,
And a prince too, how great is your advantage:
Greater than mine, here dying in a cage.   430
For I must weep and wail while I'm alive,
With all that prison brings with it of grief;
And with the added pangs of love also,
Which doubles all my torment and my woe.'
With that the fire of jealousy awoke
Within his breast, and took hold of his heart
So furiously, that Palamon turned white,
The white of boxwood or of cold dead ash.
     Then he cried, 'O you cruel gods, who rule
This world, and bind it with your eternal   440
Decree, and on the adamantine tablet
Inscribe your will and your eternal fiat,
What's mankind to you? Of no more esteem
Than is the sheep that cowers in the pen?
For man dies, just like any animal,
Suffers imprisonment and gaol as well,
Endures great adversity and sickness;

Often as not he's innocent, alas!
What governing mind is in such prescience
That so torments the guiltless innocent?   450
And, what makes all my tribulation worse,
Man is bound to observe the divine laws,
And for the love of God must curb his will,
Whereas no restraint curbs the animal.
And when a beast is dead, it feels no hurt,
But after death man has to weep and wail,
Despite his cares and sorrows while on earth.
There isn't any doubt it may be so.
I leave it to theologians to reply,
But well I know this world's a misery.   460
Alas! I see some viper, or thief, who's done
Mischief enough to many an honest man,
At large, free to go where it pleases him:
But I must stay in prison, for Saturn
And Juno too, have in their jealous rage
Almost destroyed the whole lineage
Of Thebes, whose broad walls desolate lie.
And Venus undoes me in another way,
With fear and jealousy of that Arcita.'

    Now I will pause and let Palamon rest,   470
Leave him to wait in silence in his gaol,
Turn to Arcita, and resume his tale.

    The summer passes, and the nights are long,
Increasing and redoubling love's keen sting
For both the lover and the prisoner.
I don't know which of them has more to bear—
To put it in a nutshell, Palamon
Is condemned to perpetual prison,
In chains and fetters till the day he dies;
Arcita is on pain of death exiled   480
For evermore from Theseus' territory,
Never to look again upon his lady.

    Now all you lovers, let me pose the question:
Who's worse off, Arcita or Palamon?
The one may see his lady every day,
But is shut up in prison for always;
Whereas the other, free to go or come,
May never see his Emily again.
Now make your choice between them, if you can;
I'll go on with the tale as I began.   490

Part Two

Now when Arcita at last reached Thebes,
He fainted half the day, and cried, 'Alas!'
For he would never see his lady again.

And, to sum up in a few words his pain,
Such grief was never felt by any creature
That was or will be while the world endures.
Bereft of food, of drink, and of his sleep,
Arcita grew thin, dry as a stick;
His eyes were hollow, horrible to look at,
Sallow and pale his colour, like cold ash;   500
And he was always solitary and alone.
And bewailing his woes the whole night long;
If he heard the sound of music, or a song,
The tears came, and he could not leave off weeping.
So enfeebled were his spirits, and so low,
So changed was he, that nobody would know
His voice and speech for Arcita's, though he heard it.
So changed was he, Arcita went about
For all the world as if not merely lovesick,
But actually manic, suffering from   510
Some melancholic humour in his forehead,
Which is the seat of imagination.
All things, in short, had been turned upside-down
Both in the character and disposition
Of the lover Arcita, that sorrowful man.
      But why go on all day about his pain?
When he had endured for a year or two
This cruel torment and this pain and woe
In Thebes (his native land, as I explained)
One night, as there he lay asleep, it seemed   520
To him as if Mercury, the winged god,
Appeared before him, bidding him take heart.
He bore erect his drowsy caduceus
And wore a helmet on his glorious
Hair—for he noted that he was arrayed
As when he lulled Argus the hundred-eyed.
And the god said: 'To Athens you must go,
There waits the destined ending of your woe.
At this Arcita gave a start, and woke.
'For sure, however heavy be the cost,   530
I'll go to Athens, and right now,' said he,
'No fear of death is likely to deter me
From seeing her whom I love and obey.
If I'm with her, what matter if I die?'
      And as he spoke, he picked up a large mirror,
And saw how his complexion had changed colour,
And that his countenance was now wholly changed.
Right then it came into Arcita's mind
That, since his visage was so much disfigured
By the affliction that he had endured,   540
Were he to keep a low profile, he might

Live quite unknown in Athens all his life,
And see his lady almost every day.
Whereupon Arcita changed, without delay,
His clothes for those of a poor labourer,
Then, all alone—save only for a squire
To whom he had confided his whole story,
And was disguised as shabbily as he—
Set off for Athens by the shortest route.
And so one day he turned up at the court   550
And offered his services at the gate,
To fetch and carry, any kind of work;
And, to cut short a tale already long,
He got a job under a chamberlain
Whose office was to work for Emily;
A cunning fellow who kept a sharp eye
On every servant serving his mistress.
As Arcita was young, strong as an ox,
And tall as well, and big-boned, he was good
At drawing water and at hewing wood,   560
And doing any job that he was asked.
He spent a year or two in this service
As chamber-page to the fair Emily;
Philostrate was the name they called him by.
But never was a person of his class
Half so beloved as he, in the whole court.
So gentlemanly was his disposition
All Theseus' palace rang with his renown.
They said that it would be a gracious act
If Theseus were to raise him up a step,   570
And find for him a worthier employment,
Where he might better exercise his talent.
So great his reputation grew in time,
Both for his helpfulness and courteous tongue,
That the Duke Theseus, to have him near,
Appointed Arcita a chamber-squire,
With money to maintain his new position.
And people also brought to him his income
From his own country yearly, on the quiet;
But his spending was so prudent and discreet   580
That no one wondered how he came by it.
So for three years he led his life like this,
And did his job so well, in peace and war,
There was no man whom Theseus valued more.
Let's leave him in this happiness; and I'll
Speak of Palamon for a little while.
      Buried in his impregnable prison,
In darkness and in horror, Palamon
These seven years has worn himself away

In anguish and distress. And who but he   590
Feels twofold grief and pain? Love stings him so
That he's gone clean out of his wits for sorrow.
And, more than that, he is a prisoner
Not just for one year, but for evermore.
        Who could rhyme rightly in the English tongue
His torment? To be sure I'm not the man;
So I will skip the matter, if I may.
        It happened in the seventh year, in May,
On the third night, as ancient writers tell
Who give the fullest version of this tale,   600
Whether by accident or destiny
—For when a thing is fated, it must be—
That not long after midnight, Palamon,
Helped by a friend, broke out of his prison,
And, fast as he could go, fled from the city.
He'd given his gaoler such a dose of clarry
(A narcotic made of a certain wine
Spiked with the finest Theban opium),
The gaoler slept, no matter how they shook him,
The whole night long, and could not be awoken;   610
And off Palamon goes, fast as he can.
        The night was short and day was near at hand,
So at all costs Palamon had to hide;
And to a nearby wood, with fearful tread,
And stealthy foot, there tiptoed Palamon;
To cut it short, he thought it his best plan
To hide himself within the wood all day,
And then when night had come to make his way
Homeward to Thebes, and there beg assistance
From friends to go to war with Theseus;   620
And, in a word, he'd either lose his life
Or else win Emily to be his wife.
Such was his purpose, and such was his plan.
        And now I'll turn to Arcita again,
Who little guessed how close he was to mishap,
Till Fortune chose her time to spring the trap.
        The busy lark, the messenger of day,
With song is saluting the morning grey,
While burning Phoebus, rising up so bright
That all the east is laughing in the light,   630
Is with his long beams drying in the groves
The silver drops still hanging on the leaves.
And Arcita, who in the royal palace
Is now chief squire to the Duke Theseus,
Rises and looks out on the cheerful day:
And to pay homage to the month of May,
Yet thinking all the while of his desire,

On a horse prancing like a flame of fire
Rides to amuse himself, out to the fields
A mile or two beyond the palace walls;   640
And by some chance begins to shape his course
Towards the very wood of which I spoke,
To make himself a garland from the groves
Either of woodbine or of hawthorn leaves;
And in the sunlight he sings lustily,
'May, with all your flowers and greenery,
Welcome to you, fresh and lovely May!
I hope to garner some green leaf or spray.'
       And, leaping from his horse lightheartedly,
He swiftly thrusts his way into the wood.   650
Along a path he wanders up and down,
As chance would have it, near where Palamon
Lay hidden in a thicket out of sight,
Lurking in mortal terror of his life.
Who it could be, Palamon had no notion;
He would have thought Arcita the last person—
But it's been truly said, these many years,
That 'Fields have eyes, and even woods have ears'.
It's best a man should keep his wits about him,
For people turn up when you least expect them.   660
How little did Arcita imagine
His friend was near, to hear what he was saying,
For he crouched in the thicket very still.
       When Arcita had tired of wandering,
And ended was the joyful song he sang,
He suddenly began to muse, and fell
In a brown study, as these lovers will,
Now high in heaven, and now deep in hell,
Now up, now down, a bucket in a well;
Just like a Friday, if the truth be spoken,   670
One moment, sunshine; the next, pouring down;
Just so does Venus overcloud and darken
Her followers' hearts; just as her day is fickle
(Friday's her day), so is her mood changeable;
There's no day of the week that's quite like Friday.
       His song done, Arcita began to sigh,
And without more ado sat himself down.
'Alas!' he cried, 'that ever I was born!
For how long, Juno, pitiless goddess,
Will you continue to wage war on Thebes?   680
Alas! it's been brought to destruction,
The royal blood of Cadmus and Amphion,
Of royal Cadmus, first to build and plan
Thebes, and the first founder of the town—
Cadmus, who was the city's first crowned king.

Of his lineage am I, and his offspring
By the true line, and of the blood royal;
And now I am a serf, so miserable
A slave, that as a menial squire I
Serve him who is my mortal enemy.   690
Yet Juno heaps upon me still more shame,
For I dare not be known by my own name;
Am no more Arcita, but Philostrate,
Am Arcita no more, but Fiddlestick!
Alas, Juno! Alas, relentless Mars!
All of our line have perished through your wrath
Except for me and wretched Palamon,
Whom Theseus martyrs in a dungeon.
On top of all, to break me utterly,
Love with his burning arrow has pierced me   700
And so scorched through my true and troubled heart,
My death was sewn for me before my shirt.
From one look of your eyes, O Emily!
I perish; and because of you I die.
All the rest of my misery and care
I'd count as nothing, as not worth a straw,
If I could only please you, Emily.'
With that he swooned, and for a long time lay
Senseless upon the ground; and then leapt up.
        Palamon felt as if a cold sword slid   710
Suddenly through his heart; and shuddering
With anger, could remain no longer hidden,
But, when he'd heard all that Arcita said,
Sprang like a madman with face pale and dead
Out of the thick bushes, crying, 'Liar!
You foul, black, lying traitor, Arcita!
I've got you, you who love my lady so,
For whom I suffer so much grief and pain;
You, my blood brother, sworn confidant too,
As I've told you before, time and again;   720
You who have made a dupe of Theseus
And changed your name dishonestly like this—
All I can say is, one of us must die!
You shall not love my lady Emily,
None shall love her but I, and only I;
For I am Palamon, your enemy!
Though here, as luck will have it, I've no weapon,
For I am only just escaped from prison,
Never you fear, it's either you must die,
Or else give up your love for Emily.   730
Now take your choice, for you shan't escape.'
        Then Arcita, with hatred in his heart
When he'd recognized Palamon, and heard

His tale, fierce as a lion drew his sword,
And thus replied: 'By God in heaven above,
If it weren't that you're sick and crazed with love,
And if you were not here without a sword,
You'd never walk a step out of this wood
Alive, but die instead, here by my hand!
For I disown the covenant and bond   740
Which you have made, or so you say, with me.
Get this into your head, fool: Love is free,
And I will love her still, in your despite!
But seeing that you are a noble knight,
And ready to decide your claim in battle,
My word on it, tomorrow I'll not fail,
None knowing, to be here, as I'm a knight;
And I'll bring arms enough for you and me:
Choose you the best, and leave the worst for me.
Tonight I'll bring you enough food and drink,   750
And bedding too; and if so be you win
And kill me in this wood that we are in,
She shall be yours, as far as I'm concerned.'
    'My hand on that,' was Palamon's response.
And so they separated till the morrow,
Each having pledged himself to meet the other.
    O Cupid, lacking in all charity,
Allowing none to share thy rule with thee!
It's a true saying, neither Love nor Power
Willingly brooks a rival or compeer,   760
As Arcita and Palamon have found.
Now Arcita rides straight back to the town,
And in the morning, before daylight, he
Prepares two sets of armour secretly,
Fit and sufficient for them to settle
Their difference upon the field of battle;
And on his horse, alone as he was born,
He carries all his gear in front of him.
Within this wood, at the set time and place,
Both Arcita and Palamon are met.   770
And then the colour of their faces change
Like those of Thracian huntsmen when they stand
Guarding a gap in covert with the spear
When hunting for the lion, or the bear,
And hear the beast come rushing through the groves,
And breaking through the branches and the leaves,
And think, 'Here comes a deadly enemy!
No question, one of us has got to die;
For I must either kill it breaking cover,
Or it must do me in, if I should blunder.'   780
It happened so with them; they altered hue,

So well each knight the other's prowess knew.
    And there was no 'Good-day' or other greeting;
With no preliminaries, or word spoken,
Each of them helped the arming of the other,
As friendly as a brother helping brother;
And then with sharp strong spears each thrust at each,
So long it was a wonder it could last.
To see them fight, you'd have thought Palamon
Had been a raging ravenous lion;   790
And Arcita a cruel ruthless tiger.
They ran against each other, mad with ire,
Like wild boars frothing white foam, till they stood
Fighting up to the ankles in their blood.
And, fighting thus, I'll leave them for a while,
For it's of Theseus that I have to tell.
    Destiny, paramount minister
That in this world executes everywhere
God's predetermined providence, is so strong
Things thought impossible by everyone,   800
Things which you'd swear could never ever be,
Shall yet be brought to pass, though on a day
That happens once a thousand years or so.
For certainly our passions here below,
Whether of war or peace, or hate or love,
Are governed by the providence above.
    All this bears on the great Duke Theseus,
Who is so keen and eager for the chase,
And most of all in May to hunt the stag,
That no day dawns that finds him in his bed,   810
But up and dressed, in readiness to ride
With horn and hounds and huntsman at his side.
For Theseus takes such delight in hunting,
The killing of the stag is his great passion;
Forsaking Mars, the mighty god of war,
He follows now the huntress Diana.
As I have said, the day was fine and clear
When Theseus set out, joyous and gay,
With fair Hippolyta, his lovely queen,
And Emily, all of them clad in green,   820
Riding to hunt in royallest array.
Making his way straight on towards a wood
Hard by, where he'd been told there was a stag,
Duke Theseus rode directly to a glade
Where, as he knew, a stag would often break
From cover, leap the brook, and so away.
It was his hope to try a course or two
With hounds he had selected for the work.
    Now, having come into the glade, the duke,

Shading his eyes from the still rising sun,   830
Caught sight of Arcita and Palamon.
They might have been two boars, furiously clashing;
Back and forth the bright swords flickered, flashing
So fearsomely, it seemed their lightest stroke
Would be enough to fell the stoutest oak.
But who they were, he had no clue whatever.
The duke clapped spurs that instant to his courser,
And at a bound he was between the pair
With sword pulled out, and crying, 'Stop! No more!
Who strikes another blow must lose his head!   840
By Mars, the next man I see move is dead!
But tell me now what manner of men you are
Who've the audacity to duel here
With no umpire or other officer,
As if it were a royal tournament?'
        To which Palamon answered the next moment,
Saying, 'My lord, what needs it to waste breath?
We both of us deserve no less than death.
We are two unhappy creatures, two captives,
Already overburdened with our lives;   850
And as you are a lawful prince, and judge,
Grant to us neither mercy nor refuge.
But kill me first, for holy charity,
And kill this fellow here as well as me.
Or first kill him, for little do you know
That this is Arcita, your deadly foe,
Banished on pain of death from your country,
For which alone he well deserves to die.
For this is he who turned up at your gate
And, saying that his name was Philostrate,   860
Has made a fool of you year after year;
And you have gone and made him your chief squire,
And he's the man in love with Emily!
And, as the day has come when I must die,
I may as well make a full confession:
I am that miserable Palamon
Unlawfully escaped from your prison.
I am your deadly enemy; it is I
Who burn with love for lovely Emily,
And in her sight, this instant, I would die!   870
I ask for sentence, and for death, therefore.
But at the same time kill this fellow here,
Since both of us deserve death at your hand.'
        'That's about it,' the noble duke returned,
'By this confession, out of your own mouth
You stand condemned; which sentence I confirm;
No need for torture to make you confess!
By red almighty Mars, for you it's death!'

But then the queen, in womanly sympathy,
Began to weep, and so did Emily, 880
And all the ladies in the company.
Greatest of pities it would be, they thought,
That such a fate should ever be their lot;
For noble birth was theirs, and high estate,
And love alone the matter at debate.
They saw their bleeding wounds, so deep and wide,
And all together as one woman cried,
'Have pity, sir, upon us women all!'
And then upon their bare knees down they fell,
And would have kissed his feet, there where he stood; 890
Till his wrath slackened, altering his mood,
For pity soon repairs to noble hearts.
Though anger made him shake with rage at first,
He briefly reconsidered what they'd done,
Summed up the causes of their transgression,
And, although in his wrath they stood accused,
Yet by his reason they were both excused.
For, so he argued, in love there's not a man
Who will not give himself what help he can;
No less will he endeavour to break prison. 900
And in his heart too he took pity on
The women, for they never ceased from weeping.
And in his noble heart he thought again,
And to himself, under his breath, he said,
'Shame on the ruler who has no compunction
But acts the lion, both in word and deed,
With those who are repentant and afraid,
As well as with the proud and scornful, those
Who persist in the error of their ways.
He's not got much discernment if he is 910
Unable to discriminate in such cases,
But treats alike humility and pride.'
And when his anger had thus passed away
He looked up, and a gleam was in his eye
As he spoke aloud; and this is what he said:
    'The god of love indeed! Now God bless me,
How great, how powerful a prince is he!
His might prevails against all obstacles,
He's a real god: look at his miracles:
For in his own way he can always make 920
Just what he likes of every human heart.
    'Look at Arcita here, and Palamon,
Escaping scot-free out of my prison
To Thebes, where they could have lived like kings,
And, knowing that I am their mortal foe,
And that their lives are in my hands also—

In spite of all this, Love none the less brings
Both of them here with open eyes, to die!
Now isn't that the very height of folly?
What bigger fool than he who is in love?   930
Just look at them, by God in heaven above!
Look at the state they're in! See how they bleed!
That's how the god of love, their master, paid
Their fees and wages for their services!
Yet they suppose themselves, these devotees
Of Love, to be completely rational!
But just you wait, here's the best joke of all:
The cause of all their horseplay, this young lady,
Has no more reason to thank them than I;
And of these fiery goings-on knows no more,   940
God save us, than a cuckoo or March hare.
But we'll try anything once, hot or cold;
A man must be a young fool, or an old—
That's what I found myself, in days long gone:
I was one of Love's servants in my time.
And therefore, since I too have felt the sting
Of Love, and know how it can hurt a man,
As one who's been caught often in that noose,
I here forgive you wholly your trespass,
At request of the queen, who's kneeling here,   950
And also Emily, my sister dear.
Now both of you must swear an oath to me,
That you will never do my country harm,
And never war upon me, night or day,
But be my friends in every way you can.
And I forgive you wholly this trespass.'
    And, as he asked, they swore in proper form;
As overlord they asked for his protection,
Which Theseus granted. Then he said to them:
'Even though she were a queen or a princess,   960
Both of you are eligible, of course,
As far as royal blood and riches go,
To marry her some day; but none the less
—It's of my sister Emily I speak,
The cause of all your jealousy and strife—
Though you fought for ever, it remains the truth,
As yourselves know, she cannot marry both.
Like it or leave it, one of you, therefore,
Of necessity must go whistle for her.
In other words she can't have both at once;   970
It's no use being angry or jealous.
And therefore I will order matters so
That each of you shall win what destiny
May have decreed for him. Let me explain—
Here is your part in what I shall arrange.

'To put an end to it once and for all,
Without more argument, this is my will,
Like it or lump it, each of you is free,
And without ransom or impediment,
To go wherever he may wish to go,   980
And this day twelvemonth, and no later, he
Shall bring along with him a hundred knights
Armed at all points, and equipped for the lists,
And ready to make good his claim to her
In battle; and I promise on my honour,
And as I am a knight, that without fail
That whichever is able to prevail,
In other words, whichever of the two
Can, with his hundred I spoke of just now,
Kill or drive from the lists his adversary,   990
I shall then give in marriage Emily
To whomsoever Fortune favours so.
I'll build the lists here; and so help me God
I'll prove a fair and even-handed judge.
This is the only outcome I'll permit:
One of you must be killed or made captive.
And if what I have said seems good to you,
Say so, and count yourselves fortunate too.
For both of you the matter's at an end.'
　　　Who looks happier now than Palamon?   1000
Who but Arcita leaps up in delight?
What tongue is there to tell, what pen to write
Of the joy thus created by the generous
Gesture made there by the Duke Theseus?
Down on their knees they fell, all sorts of folk,
To render thanks with all their hearts and might,
And the two Thebans thanked him oftenest;
Then, with light hearts, and filled with cheerfulness
And hope, rode homeward after their farewells,
To Thebes with its broad and ancient walls.   1010

Part Three

No doubt I'd be accounted most remiss
Did I neglect to tell how Theseus
Spared no expense, as he went busily
To work to build the lists right royally;
And nowhere in the world, I dare aver,
Was to be seen a finer amphitheatre.
A mile in radius was the circuit,
Entirely walled with stone, and ditched without,
As round as any circle was its shape,
Filled with tiered seats rising to sixty feet,   1020
And so designed, that in whichever row

You sat, you'd not obstruct your neighbour's view.
    At the eastern end stood a white marble gate,
And at the west its fellow opposite.
In the whole world there was no place like it,
Considering how quickly it was built;
For there was not a craftsman in the land
Skilled in mathematics, no artisan,
No portrait-painter, carver of images,
Whom Theseus did not pay with board and wages   1030
To build and decorate his amphitheatre.
Above the eastern gate he'd raised an altar
And temple for his rites and sacrifices
In Venus' honour, who is Love's goddess;
And for Mars another like it, on the west,
Which cost a wagonload of gold at least.
Then, in a turret on the northern wall,
He'd set up a resplendent sanctuary
 Of white alabaster and red coral,
A rich, magnificent oratory   1040
For Diana, goddess of chastity.
    But I'd almost forgotten to rehearse
The splendid carvings, sculptures, and pictures,
The forms, the shapes, the faces and figures,
That were contained in these three oratories.
    First, in the temple of Venus you saw unfold,
Set on the walls, and moving to behold,
The broken sleeps, the shuddering and cold
Sighs, the sacred tears, and doleful wailings,
The fiery stings, the longings and desirings,   1050
That all Love's servants in this life endure;
The oaths that bind and make their vows secure;
Pleasure, Hope, Desire, and Foolhardiness,
Beauty and Youth, and Laughter and Largesse;
Potions and Force, Falsehood and Flattery,
Extravagance, Intrigue, and Jealousy
With yellow marigolds for a garland
And with a cuckoo perched upon her hand;
Feasts, Music, Songs, and Joy and Display,
And Dances; all of Love's phenomena   1060
That I have told you of and mean to tell,
Were painted in their order on the wall,
And many more than I can mention here.
For indeed, the whole hill of Cytherea
Where Venus has her principal residence,
Was figured on the walls in fresco-paint,
With all its garden and its gaiety.
Nor was the porter, Idleness, passed by,
Nor beautiful Narcissus, of times gone;

Nor yet the folly of King Solomon,   1070
Nor the enormous strength of Hercules,
Medea and Circe with their witcheries,
Nor the proud-hearted Turnus' stern courage,
Nor wealthy Croesus as a wretched slave.
As you can see, not Wisdom nor Riches,
Strength nor Beauty, Cunning nor Boldness,
Can ever hold a candle to Venus,
Who steers the entire world just as she pleases.
You see, these folk were so caught in her noose,
Time and again they'd cry out in distress,   1080
As one or two examples here will show,
Although I could provide a thousand more.
    The image of Venus was marvellous.
She naked, floating on a boundless sea,
And all was hidden, from the navel down,
With green waves bright as glass; and a cithern
Was held in her right hand, while fluttering
Above a lovely garland of fresh scented
Roses that she was wearing, her doves circled.
In front of her stood her son Cupid, who   1090
Was winged, as he is often shown; blind too.
He bore sharp shining arrows and a bow.
    Why should I not tell you as well of all
The frescoes that were painted on the wall
Inside the temple of red Mars the great,—
Frescoed throughout its entire length and breadth,
Like the interior of that dismal place
That's known as the Great Temple of Mars, in Thrace,
In that most frigid, cold, and icy region
Wherein Mars has his principal mansion?   1100
    First on the wall was painted a forest
Inhabited by neither man nor beast,
And filled with knotted, gnarled, old barren trees,
Jagged broken stumps, rotten and hideous,
Through which there ran a rumble and a sough,
As if a gale were breaking every bough.
And half-way down a hill, under a slope,
There stood the temple of Mars Armipotent,
All built of burnished steel; its entrance was
Exiguous, long, and dismal to look at.   1110
From it there came a rush, a furious blast
Of air, so strong it made the whole gate shake.
And through the doors a wintry glimmer shone,
For the wall had no window—no, not one
Through which a glimpse of light might enter in.
The door was of eternal adamant;
Lengthwise and crosswise it was double-clenched
With toughest iron; and, to make all strong,

Each pillar that the temple stood upon
Was barrel-thick, and made of gleaming iron.   1120
    There you could see the dark imaginings
Of Treachery, and all its contrivings;
And cruel Anger, red as burning coal;
The pickpocket; and Fear with visage pale;
The smiler with the knife beneath his cloak;
The farmstead burning under the black smoke;
The perfidy of the murder in the bed;
Stark War, with open wounds, all bebloodied;
Discord, with dripping knife and direful face.
And full of screeching was that gruesome place.   1130
The killer of himself you could see there,
With his own heart's blood drenching all his hair;
The driven nail that split the sleeping head;
Stark Death upon his back, with mouth agape.
In the middle of the temple sat Mischance,
With comfortless and dismal countenance.
And you saw Madness, laughing in his rage,
Armed Revolt, Hue and Cry, and fierce Outrage;
The carcass with slit throat flung in a bush;
A thousand dead, and they not killed by plague;   1140
The tyrant with the plunder he had reft;
The town obliterated and laid waste.
You saw the reeling ships burn on the sea;
The wild bears crush the hunter; and the sow
Devour the child right in the very cradle;
The cook scalded, for all his length of ladle;
All the misfortune that to Mars belongs—
Run over by his cart, the carter pinned
And lying on the ground beneath its wheel.
Also there were, among those Mars protects,   1150
The barber, and the butcher, and the smith
Who forges on his anvil the sharp sword.
And high above, depicted on a tower,
You saw Conquest, seated in great splendour,
With the sharp sword-blade hung above his head
Suspended by a thin and slender thread.
Caesar's and Nero's murders were portrayed,
And Mark Anthony's, albeit none of these
Had yet been born; but none the less their deaths
And the foreseen malignancy of Mars   1160
Were there, told by these paintings, as the stars
Tell who is to be killed, or die, for love.
One example taken from legend should serve;
Even if I wished, I could not tell them all.
    Mars' effigy, with dire and maniacal
Regard, stood armed upon a chariot;
And over his head two starry figures shone,

Which ancient books of geomancy name,
The one Puella, the other Rubeus;
The god of war was represented thus. 1170
A wolf stood at his feet in front of him,
Eyes glowering, about to eat a man;
Subtle the pencil that portrayed this story
In reverence of Mars, and of his glory.
    Now I shall speed as quickly as I may
To the holy temple of chaste Diana
To give you a description of it all.
A painted fresco covered every wall:
Scenes of the hunt, or shamefaced chastity.
There you could see sorrowful Callisto 1180
Who, when she had offended Diana,
Was transformed from a woman to a bear,
And after that became the northern star;
So it was pictured; I can tell no more.
Her son's a star as well, as you can see.
Again, a little further on, you saw
How Atalanta hunted the wild boar
With Meleager and others; Diana
Plagued him for this, and he was made to pay
And many another scene as wonderful, 1190
Which I'll not trouble memory to recall.
    High on a stag the goddess had her seat.
And there was Dana, turned into a tree;
No, I don't mean the goddess Diana,
But Penneus' daughter, who was called Dana.
And there was Actaeon, turned into a stag
For punishment; he'd seen Diana naked;
And there you saw how his own deerhounds caught
And ate him up, because they knew him not.
With small hounds playing round about her feet; 1200
Beneath her feet was set a waxing moon,
Waxing at present, but about to wane.
Her effigy was clothed in green, with bow
In hand, and arrows in a quiver. Low
The eyes were cast, bent in the direction
Of Pluto and his dark dominion.
Before her was a woman, labouring
In travail, with a child too long unborn,
Who plaintively was calling on her name,
Crying for help: 'For only you alone 1210
May help me'—and whoever painted it
Grudged not a penny on the colours, but
Knew how to paint the life, and knew his job.
    At last the lists were ready. Theseus,
Who had provided, at no little cost,

The temples and the arena with all
Their furnishings down to the last detail,
Was wonderfully pleased when it was done.
But that's enough of Theseus; it's time
To speak of Arcita and Palamon.   1220
The day of their returning is at hand,
      When each of them must bring a hundred knights
To settle all by battle in the lists.
And so to Athens each of them has brought,
In order that their covenant might be kept,
A hundred knights, all well armed and equipped.
Indeed it was maintained, by many a man,
That never, since the world itself began,
Had so few ever made, on sea or land,
So far as knightly prowess is concerned,   1230
So noble and renowned a company;
For all who took delight in chivalry,
And meant to make themselves a famous name,
Had begged and prayed to take part in that game;
And any who was chosen was in luck.
You know, if such an event were set up
—Either in England or no matter where—
Tomorrow, every able-bodied knight
And lover would be eager to be there,—
To battle for a lady, Lord bless me!   1240
A sight worth seeing, that's what it would be!
      And such were those who came with Palamon.
For many were the knights who rode with him,
Some armed with breastplate and habergeon
With a light tunic under; others wore
Steel plates, or else full suits of body-armour;
One carried a buckler, one a Prussian shield;
One cased his legs in armour, and would wield
A battleaxe; another, a steel mace;
New weapons; but on older models based.   1250
Thus everyone was armed as he thought best,
As I have told.
               And there you might have seen
Riding in company with Palamon,
Lycurgus himself, the great King of Thrace.
Black was his beard, and powerful his face;
And the round rolling eyeballs in his head
Gleamed with a light half yellow and half red;
With beetling shaggy brows he looked about him
As if he were an eagle-headed gryphon;   1260
Huge were his limbs, and his thews hard and strong,
His shoulders broad, arms muscular and long.
As was the custom of his native country

High on a chariot of gold stood he,
Four white bulls in the traces; and he wore
Instead of surcoat over his armour,
A bearskin turned by age as black as coal,
Its yellow claws gilded as bright as gold.
And combed behind his back, his flowing hair
Was black and shining like a raven's feather   1270
Under a wreath of gold upon his head,
Of immense weight, thick as your arm; all set
With gleaming jewels—rubies, diamonds.
Round and about his chariot, white wolfhounds,
Twenty and more, each one big as a steer,
And trained to hunt the lion and the deer,
Were following him with tightly fastened muzzles,
Filed leash-rings fitted to their golden collars.
A hundred lords came with him in his train;
All excellently armed, stout-hearted men.   1280
    According to legend, with Arcita
The great Emetrius, King of India,
Upon a bay horse accoutred in steel,
And covered with a diapered cloth of gold,
Came riding, like the god of weapons, Mars.
His surcoat was of purple silk from Tars
And overlaid with white pearls, huge and round;
His saddle was of fine new-beaten gold;
A sleeveless cloak was hanging from his shoulder,
Swarming with rubies, red as sparkling fire;   1290
His hair was curling, and arranged in rings—
Yellow they were, and glittered in the sun.
A high nose; eyes the colour of citron;
Full rounded lips; a florid complexion;
He'd a few freckles sprinkled on his face,
Some yellow, and some shading into black,
And gazed about him glaring like a lion.
His age was twenty-five, or so I reckon.
His beard had sprouted, and was well begun;
His voice was like a trumpet thundering.   1300
Upon his head he wore a gay green garland
Of laurel, fresh and pleasing to the eye.
For sport, he carried perched upon his hand
A falcon, tamed and whiter than a lily.
He had a hundred nobles with him there,
Bareheaded, but all armed with richest gear,
Fully equipped in every kind of way.
For, take it from me, dukes and earls and king
Had gathered in this splendid company
For love and the advance of chivalry.   1310
You saw, on every side about the king,

Tame lions and tame leopards gambolling.
And in this style these nobles, one and all,
Came on the Sunday to the citadel
About nine, and there alighted in the town.
    And when that valiant knight, Duke Theseus,
Had brought them all to Thebes, his city,
And had, according to rank and degree,
Found lodging for the whole great company,
He laboured for the comfort of his guests,   1320
Regaling them with banquets and with feasts,
Till no one could have shown, so people said,
A better judgement, or improved on it.
    The music, service at the feast, and how
Great gifts were presented to high and low,
The splendid spectacle of Theseus' palace,
Who sat first, and who last, upon the dais,
Which ladies were the loveliest, or danced best,
Or which of them could best dance and sing,
Or which could speak of love with most feeling,   1330
What hawks were sitting on the perch above,
What dogs were lying on the floor below,
Of all these things I shall say nothing now,
But give the gist of it; I think that's best.
But to the point—so listen, if you please.
    That Sunday night, before the break of day,
Palamon heard the lark begin its lay—
Although it was two hours before the dawn,
Yet the lark sang—and up rose Palamon,
In highest spirits and with devout heart   1340
Ready to go upon his pilgrimage
To Cytherea, the blessed and benign—
I mean, to Venus and her honoured shrine.
In the hour ruled by her, he slowly trod
Towards the lists, where Venus' temple stood,
And kneeling down, with humble demeanour
And a full heart, he prayed as you shall hear:
    'Fairest of the fair, daughter to Jupiter,
And bride of Vulcan, O my lady Venus,
You who bring joy to mount Cytherea,   1350
By that love which you bore for Adonis,
Take pity on my bitter smarting tears,
And take into your heart my humble prayer.
Alas, I have no words with which to tell
The nature or the torment of my hell;
My heart's not able to reveal its woe;
I am so confused I can only say,
"Take pity, radiant Lady, for you know
My thought, and see the wounds that hurt me so.

Think of all this, take pity on my sorrow,   1360
And evermore, so far as lies in me,
Your true and faithful servant I shall be,
And wage eternal war on chastity."
If you will help me, this shall be my vow.
I have no wish to brag of feats of arms,
Nor that tomorrow should bring victory,
Nor for renown, nor for the hollow glory
Of honour won, trumpeted up and down;
But what I want is the sole possession
Of Emily, and to die serving you.   1370
Do you devise the means, and show me how.
Whether the victory is theirs or mine
Means nothing, makes no difference to me,
So that I have my lady in my arms.
Though it be true that Mars is god of arms,
Your power is so great in heaven above,
That, if you wish, I'll surely gain my love.
I'll worship in your temple ever after:
Wherever I may go, upon your altar
I shall make sacrifice, and light the flame;   1380
If this be not your will, sweet Lady, then
I beg you let Arcita drive a spear
Straight through my heart tomorrow. I won't care,
It will mean nothing when I've lost my life,
If Arcita should win her for his wife.
This is the sum and total of my prayer:
Give me my love, O blissful Lady dear.'
      His prayer being ended, Palamon
Made sacrifice with all due rites, although
I shall not tell of his devotions now.   1390
But in the end the statue of Venus shook,
And made a sign; and this Palamon took
To mean his prayer had been heard that day.
For though the sign betokened a delay,
He was quite sure his boon was granted him;
And so with cheerful heart he hastened home.
      Three hours after Palamon set forth
To visit the temple of divine Venus,
Up rose the sun, and up rose Emily,
And to Diana's temple made her way.   1400
The maidens whom she took with her had brought
With them the fire, all ready and prepared;
The vestments and incense, and all the rest
That appertains to making sacrifice;
The horns filled full of mead, as custom was;
Nothing was lacking for her sacrifice.
The temple, smoking with incense, was full

Of splendid hangings; with light heart, Emily
Washes herself in water from a well;
How she performed that rite, I dare not tell,   1410
Unless it be in a most general way;
And yet it would be fun to hear it all.
For men of goodwill, such things are no harm;
But they're best left to the imagination.
Her shining hair was combed, untressed and loose;
A coronal of evergreen oakleaves
Was on her head, neatly and meetly set.
Two fires upon the altar being lit,
She then performed those rites which you may read
In old books such as Statius' *Thebiad*.   1420
Then she began, when she had lit the fire,
To pray to Diana, as you shall hear:
      'O you chaste goddess of the greenwood, you
Who look upon earth, heaven, and the sea,
Queen of Pluto's dark kingdom there below,
Goddess of virgins, who for many a year
Have understood my heart, known my desire,
O keep me from your vengeance and anger,
From which Actaeon suffered long ago.
O you chaste goddess, you know well that I   1430
Desire to be a virgin all my life,
Never to be a mistress or a wife.
You know I'm still one of your company,
A virgin, and a lover of the chase,
Who would far rather roam the forests wild
Than ever be a wife, or be with child.
I'll never be companioned with a man.
Now help me, Lady, since you may and can
By virtue of your threefold deity.
For Palamon, who has such love for me,   1440
And Arcita, whose passion hurts him so,
This favour, and no more, I beg from you:
Set peace and amity between the two,
And from me let their hearts be turned away,
Till all their burning love and hot desire,
And all their feverish torment and fire
Be quite put out, or else turned otherwhere.
But if it happens you won't grant this favour,
Or if my destiny be ordained so
That needs must I must have one of the two,   1450
Send me the one that most desires me.
Behold, O goddess of chaste purity,
These bitter tears upon my cheeks falling.
And since you are a virgin, and our guardian,
Do you defend and guard my maidenhood,
And while I live I'll serve you as a maid.'

The fires were burning clear upon the altar
While Emily was thus engaged in prayer.
But suddenly she saw a curious sight:
For all at once one of the fires went out,   1460
And caught again; immediately after that,
The other fire dimmed and extinguished;
And as it went out, it began a whistling,
Making a noise like wet branches burning,
And there, out of the end of every faggot,
Ran blood, or what seemed blood, drop after drop;
At which Emily, all but terrified
Out of her wits and senses, gave a cry:
But it was only out of shock she cried,
Having no notion what it signified;   1470
And she wept pitiably. But Diana
Chose at this very moment to appear
Clothed like a huntress, with her bow in hand,
And spoke: 'Dry your tears, daughter; understand
Among the gods on high it is affirmed,
The eternal word is set down and confirmed,
That you shall marry one of these two men
Who suffer so for you; but which of them,
I may not say. And now farewell, for I
May stay no longer. But the fires that burn   1480
Upon my altar shall in time make plain
Before you leave here, what your destiny
In this affair may be.' And thereupon
Her arrows clattered in their case and rang;
The goddess vanished. Emily, amazed,
Exclaimed aloud, 'What can this mean, alas?
I place myself in your protecting care,
To dispose as you wish, O Diana!'
And home she went, taking the shortest way;
And that was all—there is no more to say.   1490
    An hour after this—the hour of Mars—
Arcita strode to the fierce god of war's
Grim temple, to perform his sacrifice
With all due pagan rites and ceremonies.
With deep devotion, and with suppliant heart,
He made his prayer thus, direct to Mars:
    'O you strong god, honoured in the cold
Regions of Thrace, and there accounted lord,
Who hold in every kingdom, every land,
The bridle-reins of war firm in your hand,   1500
You who can sway their fortunes as you please,
Accept of me my humble sacrifice.
And if you think my youth may so deserve,
And that my strength is sufficient to serve

Your godhead; if you count me as your man,
I pray you to take pity on my pain.
By those same pangs, and by that scorching fire,
Those flames in which you once burned with desire
When Venus' beauty was all yours to use,
Young, lovely Venus, fresh and generous;   1510
And when at will you had her in your arms—
Although things fell out badly for you once,
That time when Vulcan caught you in his net,
And found you lying with his wife, alack!
For all the pain that then was in your heart,
Take pity too, I pray, on my sore hurt.
For I am young and ignorant, as you know,
More racked and torn with love, as I suppose,
Than any living creature ever was;
For she for whom I suffer all this pain   1520
Cares not a button if I sink or swim.
Before she'll promise me her heart, it's plain
I must by main strength win her in the lists;
And well I know that without help or grace
From you, my lord, my strength will not avail.
Then give me aid tomorrow in the battle,
For that fire that once burned you long ago,
As well as for that fire that burns me now,
So that tomorrow brings me victory—
Let mine be all the doing, yours the glory!   1530
Above all other places I shall honour
Your sovereign temple; I shall ever labour
For your delight in your hard trade of war;
And I shall hang my banner in your fane,
With all the weapons of my company,
And ever after, till the day I die,
Feed an eternal fire there for you.
I bind myself, moreover, with this vow:
My beard, and these long hanging locks of hair,
As yet untouched by razor or by shears,   1540
To you I dedicate; and I shall be
Your true and faithful servant till I die.;
Take pity on my burning sorrows, Lord;
Give me the victory; I ask no more.'
    When strong Arcita had ceased his prayer,
The rings that hung upon the temple door
Clattered together; the doors clanged as well;
At which Arcita flinched. The altar fires
Blazed up until they lighted the whole temple,
And from the ground emanated a sweet smell.   1550
Arcita lifted up his hand, to cast
More incense on the fire; until at last

After more and other rites, the carven
Statue of Mars made its steel hauberk ring;
And with that sound he heard a murmuring,
Very low and soft; and it said, 'Victory!'
To Mars he gave the honour and the glory,
Then, full of hope that all will turn out well,
Arcita heads for home; he is as joyful
And glad as the birds are of the bright sun.   1560
    But in a trice a furious row began
Over this granted boon, in heaven above,
As between Venus, the goddess of love,
And Mars, the cruel god armipotent.
Jupiter was kept busy making peace
Till bleak old Saturn, versed in stratagems,
Was able, from his long experience,
To find an answer satisfying both.
The old, in fact, have a great advantage:
Wisdom, experience, belong to age.   1570
You can outdo the old, but not outwit.
Though it's not Saturn's nature to discourage
Terror and contention, he was quick
To find a remedy for the whole dispute.
    'My dear daughter Venus,' said Saturn,
'Mine is the widest orbit round the sun,
And so my power is greater than men suppose;
Mine are all drownings in the gloomy seas,
Mine is the prison in the dark dungeon;
Mine are all stranglings, hangings by the throat,   1580
The mutter and rebellion of the mob,
All discontents and clandestine poisonings;
When I am in the sign of Leo, mine
Is vengeance, mine is fell retribution.
Mine is the ruin of high palaces,
The falling of the walls and of the towers
Upon the miner and the carpenter.
For I killed Samson, shaking. the pillar;
To me belong all deadly sicknesses,
Black treacheries, deceits, conspiracies;   1590
The pestilence is fathered by my glance.
Now weep no more; I'll use all diligence
To see that your own knight, your Palamon,
Shall win his lady as you promised him.
Though Mars must help his man, yet none the less
Between you two there must some time be peace,
Albeit your temperaments are opposed,
From which these endless squabbles take their rise.
I am your grandfather, ready to command;
So dry your tears, I'll do what you demand.'   1600

Now that's enough about the gods above,
Of Mars, and Venus the goddess of love;
And I'll tell you, as plainly as I can,
The outcome of the tale that I began.

Part Four

Great junketings were going on that day
In Athens, while the joyous month of May
So lifted up the spirits, thus enhancing
The general gaiety, that people passed
All of the Monday jousting, or in dancing,
Or else spent it in Venus' high service.   1610
But, needing to rise early for the fight,
Early they took themselves to bed that night.
And in the morning, when the dawn was breaking,
In all the inns about there was a clattering
Of horses and armour. Bands and companies
Of noblemen on stallions and palfreys
Rode to Theseus' palace. You'd have seen there
Much preparing of marvellous armour,
Well-wrought and rich; steelwork, embroidery,
And goldsmithry; the glittering shields, and steel   1620
Headpieces, trappings, golden helmets, mail,
And coats-of-arms; princes on war-horses,
Robed splendidly; attendant knights, and squires
Nailing the spearheads fast, and buckling on
The helmets; strapping shields with leather thongs;
With so much to be done there, none was idle.
You'd see the horses foam, champ the gold bridle;
You'd see the armourers spurring to and fro
With file and hammer, fast as they could go;
Yeomen-on foot, commoners by the thousand,   1630
All of them armed with short staves, thickly crowding;
Pipes, trumpets, kettledrusus, and clarions
That howl for blood in battle and in war;
The palace filled with people everywhere,
In knots of two or three, or nine or ten,
Debating back and forth, and speculating
About the Theban knights; some of them saying
One thing, and some another; others laying
Wagers on different knights—some backing Blackbeard,
Some Baldhead, while yet others were for Thatch-haired,   1640
'That one looks tough, he'll put up a good fight!'
'That axe of his is twenty pounds in weight!'
—Thus the whole hall was full of speculation
A long time after that day's sun had risen.
    The great Duke Theseus, from sleep aroused
By the music and the hubbub of the crowd

Outside his palace gates, kept to his chamber,
Till—for they treated them with equal honour—
They brought the Theban knights to the palace.
Duke Theseus was at a window seat,   1650
Just like a god in splendour on his throne.
Thither the press of people hurried in
To see him, and to pay due homage, and
Listen to his directives and commands.
'Ho there!' a herald on a scaffold shouted
Until the noise of the crowd abated,
And silence having fallen on them all.
He then announced the great Duke Theseus' will:
      'The prince has, in his prudence and wisdom,
Concluded that it would be mere destruction   1660
Of noble blood, if this affair were fought
In terms of mortal combat, to the death.
And therefore he desires to modify
His first proposal, so that none shall die.
No man, therefore, upon pain of death,
May bring with him, or have sent to the lists,
Any kind of arrow, poleaxe, or short knife;
No short, sharp-pointed sword for stabbing with
May any draw, nor carry at his side.
And at the tournament no man may ride   1670
More than one charge against his opponent
With spear unblunted; but for self-defence,
Thrusting on foot's permitted; any man
Who's down, must not be killed, but must be taken,
Brought to the stake that's fixed on either side,
Forcibly carried there, and there abide.
And should it chance that either of the captains
Is captured, or else kills his opponent,
That is the finish of the tournament.
And now, Godspeed! Forward, and lay on hard!   1680
Fight your fill, gentlemen, with mace and sword!
Go ahead and begin: the prince has spoken.'
      The people's voice rose to the roof of heaven,
So loud they cried, with so joyous a note:
And their cry was, 'God save so good a duke!
He'll have no wholesale spilling of good blood!'
Up go the trumpets, and the fanfares shrilled,
And in due order the whole company
Goes riding to the lists, through the great city
Hung with no plainer stuff than cloth-of-gold.   1690
      In princely state the noble Theseus rides
With the two Thebans upon either side;
Behind them rode the queen, and Emily,
And after them, another company

Of various folk, in order of degree.
And in this way they passed through the city
Until they reached the lists with time in hand.
It was still early in the morning, when
Theseus took his seat in state on high,
With Queen Hippolyta, and Emily,   1700
And other ladies, each in their degree.
Meanwhile, a great crowd presses to the seats.
At the west end, there enters through the gates
Of Mars, Arcita with red banner and
The hundred knights belonging to his band;
And at the selfsame moment Palamon
Enters by the gates of Venus at the east,
With a white banner and defiant face.
No matter where you looked, you'd never find
Anywhere in the world two companies   1710
So equally matched at every point as these;
None might, no matter how expert, contend
That any, in either, held an advantage
In years, in birth or rank, or in courage,
So evenly had each of them been chosen.
In two trim rows they ranged themselves. And when
The roll was called, and every name was read,
Their numbers checked to ensure no deceit,
Then were the gates shut, and up goes the cry:
'Now do your duty, show your mettle, knights!'   1720
        The heralds leave off spurring up and down;
Now the loud trumpets, and the clarion
Ring out; and on the east side and the west
In go the spears, couched firm for the attack,
In go the spurs, sharp in the horse's side.
We'll soon see who can joust, and who can ride!
There on thick shields the shafts shiver and split.
One of them through the breast-bone feels the thrust.
Twenty feet in the air the spears leap up;
Out come the swords, like silver is their flash;   1740
They hew at helms, and hack them all to bits;
And out in harsh red floods the blood now spurts;
Under their heavy maces the bones smash.
This one thrusts through the thickest of the press
Where strongest horses stumble; down go all;
One's rolling underfoot, just like a ball;
And one, on foot, thrusts with his broken shaft,
Another with his horse comes crashing down;
And one is wounded through the body, taken,
Manhandled to the stake, furiously fighting;   1750
There he, according to the rules, must bide.
Another's captured on the other side.

From time to time Theseus makes them rest
To take refreshment, drink if they so wish.
Often have these two Thebans met in combat,
And each has done his opponent a mischief,
And both have been unhorsed by one another.
No tiger in the vale of Gargophia
Reft of its cub and turning on the hunter,
Could have been queller than Arcita   1760
Is in his jealous rage to Palamon.
And there's no lion hunted in Benmarin
More fell, more hunger-frenzied for its prey
And thirsty for its blood, than Palamon
Out to kill Arcita, his enemy.
The eager blows rain down and bite
Their helmets; and the red blood gushes out.
But soon or late, all things must have an end.
Before the sun went down, the mighty King
Emetrius had at length contrived to catch   1770
Palamon fighting Arcita; his sword bit
Deep into Palamon's flesh; whom it took
Twenty to drag, unyielding, to the stake.
In coming to the aid of Palamon
The mighty King Lycurgus was knocked down,
While King Emetrius, for all his strength,
Was thrown out of his saddle a sword's length
By Palamon's last blow, so hard he hit;
But all for nothing—he's dragged to the stake.
Of no avail his courageous heart: 1780
There he must stay now that he has been caught,
Held there by force, and by the rules agreed on.
      Now who is in worse case than Palamon,
Since he may not go out again to fight?
And when Duke Theseus had seen it happen,
To everyone there fighting he called out:
'Ho there! No more! All's over now and done!
I'll be an honest judge, no partisan: 1790
Arcita of Thebes shall have Emily,
The luck's with him, she has been fairly won.'
At once there rose a shout from one and all
For joy at this, so loud and thunderous
It seemed the very lists themselves would fall.
      Now what can Venus do, in heaven above?
What can she do or say, the Queen of Love,
But weep because she cannot have her wish,
Until her tears rain down upon the lists?
Cried she, 'Now I am thoroughly disgraced!'   1800
      But Saturn answered, 'Daughter, hold your tongue!
Mars has his way, his knight has got his boon,

And, as I live, you'll be contented soon.'
    The trumpeters and the loud music blare;
Loudly the heralds yell and shout and cry
Happy as larks for the Prince Arcita.
But bear with me, and don't anticipate,
You'll hear what kind of miracle happened next.
    Noble Arcita, having taken off
His helmet, so that he can show his face,   1810
Spurs the whole length of the great arena
All the while looking up at Emily,
Who casts on him, in turn, a friendly eye,
(For, generally speaking, all women
Follow whoever's favoured by Fortune)
And she was all his heart's delight and joy.
    Out of the ground there bursts a hellborn Fury,
From Pluto sent at request of Saturn,
At which his frightened horse begins to shy,
And leap aside, and stumble in leaping;   1820
And before Arcita can react, he
Has been thrown off and pitched upon his head,
And lies in the arena as if dead,
With his chest smashed in by his saddle-bow.
Turning as black as coal, black as a crow,
He lay there, the blood rushing to his face.
Quickly they carried him out of the place
With heavy hearts, to Theseus' palace.
They cut the laces of his armour, then
Put him to bed without the least delay,   1830
For he was conscious still, and still alive,
And calling all the while for Emily.
    And now Duke Theseus and his guests arrive
Back home at Athens, with great pomp and joy.
Despite what happened, he'd not cast a gloom
If he could help it, over everyone;
Besides, they said Arcita would not die,
But must recover from his injury.
They were as pleased about another thing:
Not one of all their number had been slain,   1840
Though some were badly wounded, like the man
Who'd been thrust with a spear through the breast-bone.
As for their other wounds and broken arms,
Some of them had ointments, some had charms;
They also drank infusions and herb-medicines
To help regain the full use of their limbs;
For which the noble duke, as best he can,
Comforts and honours every one of them,
Holding high revel all the livelong night
For the foreign lords and princes, as was right.   1850

No thought was there of victory or defeat
Any more than at a tournament or joust,
For, really, there was no disgrace. A fall
Need not be counted, it's incidental;
And to be hauled by main force to the stake
Unyielding, captured by a score of knights,
One man all on his own, and harried so,
Pulled and propelled with arm and foot and toe,
And his horse driven off with stave and cudgel
By yeomen, men on foot, and boys as well: 1860
There's nobody would count that as disgrace,
Or who would dare to call it cowardice!
It was proclaimed, by order of the duke,
To put a stop to rancour and malice,
That neither side did better than the other,
But each matched each, as brother matches brother.
He gave appropriate gifts to one and all,
And for three days he held high festival,
And honourably escorted the two kings
As far as a day's travel from Athens.   1870
Then every man went home the shortest way:
It was all over, bar 'Good luck! Goodbye!'
About the tournament I'll say no more,
But tell of Palamon and Arcita.
        Swollen and swelling is Arcita's breast,
The pain about his heart grows worse and worse.
The clotted blood, for all the doctors' skill
Corrupts and festers in his belly, till
Bleeding and cupping are no help for him,
Nor herbal draughts, nor any medicine.   1880
For the expelling, or 'animal' power
Can neither eliminate nor expel
The venom from the other, 'natural', power.
The vessels of his lungs begin to swell
And every muscle, deep down in his chest,
With poison and with gangrene is corrupt.
Nothing is any use to save his life,
For he can neither vomit nor excrete.
Broken and shattered is that part of him,
And Nature now has no domination.   1890
All you can say, where Nature will not work,
Is, 'Goodbye, doctor! Take the man to church!'
The long and short of it is, he must die;
And so Arcita sends for Emily,
And for his dearest cousin, Palamon.
And this is what Arcita said to them:
'The heavy heart that is within my breast
May not declare a tithe of my sharp grief

To you, my lady, whom I love the best;
But I bequeath the service of my ghost   1900
To you above all created beings, for
I know my life no longer may endure.
Alas the woe! Alas the bitter pain
That I have suffered for you for so long!
And alas death! Alas, my Emily!
Alas, the parting of our company!
Alas, queen of my heart! Alas, my bride!
Lady of my heart, and causer of my death!
What is this world? What does man ask to have?
Now with his love, now in the chilling grave,   1910
Alone, and with no kind of company!
Sweet enemy, farewell, my Emily!
Hold and fold me in your two arms gently
For love of God, and hear what I shall say.
      'For love of you there's been contention
Between me and my cousin Palamon,
Rancour and jealousy for many a day.
Now may wise Jupiter direct my heart
Fittingly and faithfully to portray
A lover's attributes and qualities,   1920
Such as faith, wisdom, honour, chivalry,
Rank, birth, humility, magnanimity,
And all that's needed for the lover's art.
As I look to Jupiter for salvation,
In the whole world there isn't anyone
So worthy to be loved as Palamon,
Who serves you, and will serve you all his life.
And if you ever think to be a wife,
Do not forget the noble Palamon.
And with these words, his speech began to fail,   1930
For from his feet up to his breast there came
The chill of death, so that it vanquished him,
While in his arms the vital power dispersed.
The intellect that lived in his sick breast
Failed only when the heart was touched by death.
And then, with darkening eyes and flagging breath,
Upon his lady he still cast his eye.
His last word was, 'Have pity, Emily!'
His spirit changed its house and went on—where
I cannot say, for I was never there.   1940
I'll shut up; I'm no theologian;
There's nothing about souls in the volume
I found my story in; it's not my line
To talk about such theories, although
Much has been written about where they go.
Arcita's cold; may Mars direct his soul:

It is of Emily I have to tell.
Emily shrieks; Palamon groans; and soon,
His sister having fallen in a swoon
Beside the corpse, the duke leads her away.   1950
But what's the use of wasting precious time
In telling how she wept both night and day?
In cases like this women feel such sorrow
When they have lost their husbands, most of them
Will mourn and grieve and lament in this way,
Or very likely fall in a decline
So deep that in the end they're bound to die.
    Unending were the laments, and the tears
Shed by the old, and those of tender years,
For the dead Theban, throughout the city.   1960
The whole town wept for him, both man and boy;
Be sure there was not half the lamentation
When Hector, newly killed, was brought back home
To Troy. What a mourning there was here!
Scratching of cheeks, and tearing of the hair!
And women crying, 'O why did you die,
Had you not gold enough, and Emily?'
    There was no man could comfort Theseus,
Excepting his old father, Aegeus,
Who understood the world's transmutations,   1970
Having seen so many of its ups and downs,
Joy after woe, grief after happiness;
He gave examples of such happenings.
    'Just as no man has ever died,' said he,
'Who has not lived in this world in some way,
Just so there never lived a man,' he said,
'Anywhere on earth, but at some time was dead.
This world is but a thoroughfare of woe,
And we are pilgrims, travelling to and fro.   —
All earthly troubles have an end in death.'   1980
And he said much more to the same effect,
Exhorting people to be comforted.
    Duke Theseus then gave the most careful thought
To finding the best place to build the tomb
Of good Arcita: one to honour him,
Appropriate to his rank and position.
At length he came to the conclusion
That where Arcita and Palamon
Had first fought one another for their love,
There in that very grove so fresh and green,   1990
Where Arcita had felt the burning flame
Of love, and amorous desires, and sung
His complaint, there he would erect a pyre
Where all the funeral rites could be performed.

Then he commanded them to hack and hew
The ancient oaks, and lay them in a row
Of faggots, properly disposed to burn.
So on swift feet the duke's officers run
At his command. Next, Theseus bids them bring
A funeral bier, and over it he spread   2000
A cloth-of-gold, the richest that he had.
And he had Arcita swathed in the same
Material, with white gloves on his hands,
His head wreathed with a fresh green laurel crown,
A keen and gleaming sword set in his hand.
He laid him, face uncovered, on the bier,
Then wept, till it would break your heart to hear.
When day broke, that it might be seen by all
He had the body brought into the hall,
Which echoed with the din of lamentation.   2010
     Then the heart-broken Theban, Palamon,
Came with bedraggled beard, ash-matted hair,
In clothes of black, bespotted with his tears,
And, weeping more than any, Emily,
The saddest there of the whole company.
As Arcita was of the blood royal,
To dignify and enrich the funeral
Duke Theseus commanded them to bring
Three horses, all harnessed in glittering
Steel, covered with the arms of Arcita.   2020
Each of these huge white horses had a rider,
One of them carrying the dead man's shield,
While high aloft another man upheld
His spear, and the third bore his Turkish bow
(Its quiver burnished gold, the trappings too),
And they rode sadly at a walking pace
Towards the greenwood grove, as you shall hear.
And following them the noblest of the Greeks
Bore on their shoulders Prince Arcita's bier
With even steps, with their eyes red and wet,   2030
Across the city, along its main street
Spread with black draperies, hung from on high,
And draped with the same colour all the way.
On the right hand there walked old Aegeus,
And on the other side, Duke Theseus,
With vessels in their hands of finest gold,
All full of wine and honey, milk and blood;
Palamon next, with a great company,
And these were followed by poor Emily,
Bearing the fire—the custom in those days—   2040
For her part in the funeral service.
     Splendid the work and preparation for

The funeral, and building of the pyre;
The green top of the pyre reached the sky,
Its base spread twenty fathoms—that's to say
The branches and the logs reached out that far.
First, they laid down load after load of straw—
But how they built the pyre as high as heaven,
How the trees were felled, or what their names were even,
—Oak, fir, beech, aspen, elder, flex, hazel,   2050
Willow, elm, plane, ash, box, poplar, lime, laurel,
Maple, thorn, beech, yew, dogwood, and chestnut—
Are things I'm not proposing to relate;
Nor how the demigods ran up and down,
Disinherited of their habitation,
In which they'd lived in quietness and peace,
Nymphs, dryads, fauns, and hamadryades;
Nor how the animals and birds all fled
In panic terror, when they felled the wood;
Nor how the ground blenched, aghast at the bright   2060
Sun, being unaccustomed to the light;
Nor how the pyre was first laid with straw,
Then with dry sticks, and faggots split in three,
Then with green wood, and then with spicery,
Then cloth-of-gold, and gems and jewellery,
And then with garlands hung with many flowers,
With myrrh and incense, and all sweet odours;
Nor how Arcita lay amidst all this,
Nor what the treasure piled around him was;
Nor how Emily, according to usage,   2070
Thrust in the funeral torch, and lit the blaze;
Nor how she fainted when the fire built up,
Nor even what she said, nor what she thought,
Nor what the Jewels were that people cast
Into the fire when the flames blazed up;
I'll not tell how some threw in shield and spear,
Others the very clothing that they wore,
And goblets full of wine, and milk, and blood,
Into the roaring flames that blazed white-hot;
Nor how the Greeks, in a great band together,   2080
Faced to the left, then with a loud shouting
Galloped their horses thrice around the pyre,
And round it thrice again, with spears clattering;
Nor how three times the women made their keen;
Nor how Emily was at last led home;
Nor how Arcita burned to ashes cold;
Nor shall I tell you how his wake was held,
The livelong night; nor how the Greeks contested
The funeral games, for I'm not interested
In who wrestled best, his body oiled and naked,   2090

Or who made the best showing, though bested.
I will not even tell how they went home
To Athens, once the funeral games were done;
But make an end of my long story, and
Come to the point as quickly as I can.
    In time, after the passage of some years,
Ended at length the mourning and the tears
Of all the Greeks, by tacit agreement.
Then it appears they held a parliament
At Athens, to talk over various   2100
Affairs and issues; among which there was
Some talk of making foreign alliances,
And of compelling Theban allegiance.
And therefore the good Theseus lost no time
In sending for the noble Palamon.
Not knowing for what cause he came, or why,
Dressed in his clothes of black, sorrowfully
Prince Palamon has hastened to obey.
Thereupon Theseus sent for Emily.
When all were seated, and the place was hushed,   2110
For a short space of time Theseus paused.
Before speaking from the wisdom of his heart
He let his eyes rove over them. His face
Was serious. Then with a quiet sigh
He spoke his mind to the whole assembly:
    'When the First Mover, the First Cause above,
First created the great chain of love,
Great was His purpose, great the consequence.
He knew all whys and wherefores when He bent
With that great chain of love, water and land,   2120
And air and fire, within fixed certain bounds
They may not go beyond. And that same Prince
And Mover', he continued, 'established
Here in this miserable world below
For all things that are engendered on earth,
Fixed seasons, days, durations, beyond which
They may last no longer, not a day; although
That period they may easily abridge.
There is no need to cite authorities;
Experience proves it; all I want to do   2130
Is to make clear just what my meaning is.
Then from this divine order it is plain
The Mover is eternal, does not change.
It's clear to anyone, except a fool,
That every part derives from a great Whole,
For Nature did not take its beginning
From any part or portion of a thing,
But from a being perfect and immutable,
Descending thence to become corruptible.

And therefore in His provident foresight 2140
He has so ordered His creation that
Things of all kinds, all processes, survive
By continual succession, do not live
For ever and ever. And this is no lie,
As anyone can see with half an eye.
Look at the oak, that has so long a growth
From the time it first begins to germinate,
And has so long a life, as is well known,
But in the end decays; the tree falls down.

    'Likewise consider how the hardest stone 2150
Under our feet, the stone we tread upon
As it lies on the road, is worn away.
In time the broadest river will run dry;
Great cities we have seen decline and fall;
Thus we may see that an end comes to all.

    'In the case of men and women, it's clear also
That at one time or another, they must go;
That is to say, in either youth or age
Die you must, whether you be king or page;
One dies in bed, another in the sea, 2160
Another on dry land, it's plain to see;
It can't be helped, for all go the same way.
And so I can affirm all things must die.
'Who contrives this but Jupiter the King,
Who is the Prince and Cause of everything,
Who converts all back to its proper source
From which, in very truth, it first arose?
And against this it's useless, in the end,
For any living creature to contend.

    'It's common sense, or so it seems to me, 2170
To make a virtue of necessity,
Take what we can't avoid with a good grace,
Especially what's due to all of us.
Whoever mutters at this is a fool,
And rebellious to Him Who governs all.
The man who dies in his life's prime and flower
While sure of his good name, wins most honour,
For in that case he brings no shame to either
Himself or friends. And his friend ought to be
Gladder of his death when it's with honour he 2180
Yields up his latest breath, than when his name
Has faded in the course of age and time,
When all his former prowess is forgotten.
And so it's best, as regards his good name,
To die when he is at the height of fame.

    'Now to deny this is perversity.
Then why should we repine or be downcast
That good Arcita, flower of chivalry,

Has departed with honour and repute
Out of the foul prison of this life?   2190
And why should these, his cousin and his wife,
Lament his happiness, who loved them well?
Would he thank them? Not on your life: his soul
And themselves they offend, yet are no happier.
    'What conclusion is there for me to draw
From this long argument, save to advise
We should let gladness follow upon sadness,
And then thank Jupiter for all his goodness?
And now, before departing from this place,
I think that of two sorrows we should make   2200
One perfect joy that will always last.
And look: there where we find the deepest sorrow,
There shall we first of all begin the cure.
    'Sister,' said he, 'it has my full consent,
And is confirmed here by my parliament,
That noble Palamon, your own true knight,
Who's served you with his whole soul, heart, and might,
As he has always done since first you knew him,
Deserves your favour, so take pity on him,
And take him for your lord and your husband.   2210
We have agreed on this; give me your hand.
And now let's see your womanly compassion!
For after all, he's a king's brother's son;
Even if he were no knight, but a poor squire,
As he has loved and served you year by year,
And suffered for you such adversity,
That ought to be considered, for, believe me,
Noble compassion should outweigh justice.'
Then he addressed the knight, Palamon, thus:
'I take it there needs little arguing   2220
To obtain your agreement to this thing.
Come here and take your lady by the hand.'
And so between them both was sealed the bond
Of matrimony, which some folk term marriage,
By the whole council and the baronage.
And thus with joy and with minstrelsy
Palamon has wedded Emily.
May God, Who created this world so wide,
Grant him His love, for he has dearly paid;
For Palamon from now on all is bliss,   2230
He lives in wealth and health and happiness,
And Emily loves him so tenderly,
And he loves and serves her so devotedly,
That between those two was never spoken
A jealous word, nor so much as a cross one.
No more of Palamon and Emily,
And God save all this noble company!

For Practice

1. What do you see as the central problem in "The Knight's Tale"? Is it the romance between the knights and Emily or is it something else? What is that "something else"?

2. What is the role of Theseus? Is he a good leader? During the course of the tale Theseus must make many decisions. Are they all good ones? Does Theseus change and learn along the way or is he a consistent ruler?

3. What does the story seem to suggest about "unity"? Does the story move inevitably towards one single conclusion, suggesting that fate is ordained for these characters? Or, does the story seem to suggest that individuals have the ability to change their own destiny and the destiny of others? What about happiness along the way? Are characters most happy when they attain their goals or when they are in the process of attaining them? What does this seem to say about human motivation and desire?

4. On first reading, we might be tempted to skim over the lengthy descriptions of the temples dedicated to love and war. Look again at those descriptions. What are the examples of "love" that are enshrined in the temple to Venus? What does this suggest about romantic love? If you know something about the conventions of medieval romance narratives (like the Arthurian myths) how does this story seem to talk about that type of "romance"?

5. Look at the character of the two knights. Is there something disturbing about their knightly behavior? How does their behavior seem to suggest a critique of knighthood? (For an interesting discussion of the dubious role of knights in English history you might see Terry's Jones' *Chaucer's Knight*).

My Last Duchess

Robert Browning

One of the most famous poets of Victorian England, Robert Browning (1812–1889) was born in a suburb of London to parents whose love of painting, rare books, and music fostered his poetic talent. He began publishing his poetry in 1833 and his last collection of poems, Parleyings with Certain People of Importance in Their Day, *was published two years before his death in Venice. His personal life, especially his courtship and marriage to fellow poet Elizabeth Barrett Browning, has been almost as responsible for his enduring popularity as his poems' brilliant insights into human nature.*

Most critics consider Browning's most important collections to be Dramatic Lyrics *(1842),* Men and Women *(1855), and* Dramatis Personae *(1864). His masterpiece is* The Ring and the Book *(1868–69), a series of monologues offering conflicting perspectives on a murder. "My Last Duchess" was first published in the* Dramatic Lyrics *collection and is considered one of his best "dramatic monologues," a form that particularly fascinated Browning. Similar to the drama's soliloquy, the dramatic monologue presents someone speaking to an unheard audience. Unlike the soliloquy, in which the speaker offers the truth to the best of his ability, the speaker of the dramatic monologue is usually lying or trying to manipulate his auditor through rhetorical strategies, as the Duke of Ferrara does in this poem.*

Ferrara

That's my last Duchess painted on the wall,
Looking as if she were alive, I call
That piece of a wonder, now: Frà Pandolf's hands
Worked busily a day, and there she stands.
Will't please you sit and look at her? I said   5
"Frà Pandolf" by design, for never read
Strangers like you that pictured countenance,
The depth and passion of its earnest glance,
But to myself they turned (since none puts by
The curtain I have drawn for you, but I)   10

And seemed as they would ask me, if they durst,
How such a glance came there; so, not the first
Are you to turn and ask thus. Sir, 'twas not
Her husband's presence only, called that spot
Of joy into the Duchess' cheek: perhaps   15
Frà Pandolf chanced to say "Her mantle laps
Over my lady's wrist too much," or "Paint
Must never hope to reproduce the faint
Half-flush that dies along her throat": such stuff
Was courtesy, she thought, and cause enough   20
For calling up that spot of joy. She had
A heart—how shall I say?—too soon made glad,
Too easily impressed; she liked whate'er
She looked on, and her looks went everywhere.
Sir, 'twas all one! My favor at her breast,   25
The dropping of the daylight in the West,
The bough of cherries some officious fool
Broke in the orchard for her, the white mule
She rode with round the terrace—all and each
Would draw from her alike the approving speech,   30
Or blush, at least. She thanked men,—good! but thanked
Somehow—I know not how—as if she ranked
My gift of a nine-hundred-years-old name
With anybody's gift. Who'd stoop to blame
This sort of trifling? Even had you skill   35
In speech—which I have not—to make your will
Quite clear to such an one, and say, "Just this
Or that in you disgusts me; here you miss,
Or there exceed the mark"—and if she let
Herself be lessoned so, nor plainly set   40
Her wits to yours, forsooth, and made excuse,
—E'en then would be some stooping; and I choose
Never to stoop. Oh sir, she smiled, no doubt,
Whene'er I passed her; but who passed without
Much the same smile? This grew; I gave commands;   45
Then all smiles stopped together. There she stands
As if alive. Will't please you rise? We'll meet
The company below, then. I repeat,
The Count your master's known munificence
Is ample warrant that no just pretense   50
Of mine for dowry will be disallowed;
Though his fair daughter's self, as I avowed
At starting, is my object. Nay, we'll go
Together down, sir. Notice Neptune, though,
Taming a sea-horse, thought a rarity,   55
Which Claus of Innsbruck cast in bronze for me!

1842

For Practice

1. "My Last Duchess" is set in sixteenth-century Italy. Browning often set his dramatic monologues in distant times and foreign places; how might this particular setting, as well as the Duke's social standing and "nine-hundred-years-old name," be important to the poem?

2. What attitude does the Duke have towards his first wife? What does his careful guardianship of the painting, as well as the statue of Neptune "taming a sea-horse," suggest about his attitude towards women in general?

3. What was the first Duchess like? What regard did she have for social conventions and hierarchies? Why was the Duke so angry with her, especially since the man who did her portrait, Fra Pandolf, was a monk? What does "I gave commands/Then all smiles stopped" suggest happened to the first Duchess?

4. How do we see the conventions of the dramatic monologue at work here? Why is it only the Duke who speaks? Who is he speaking to, and what would be his reasons for wanting to manipulate this listener?

5. This poem, like much of Shakespeare's drama, is in iambic pentameter, the poetic meter most like human speech patterns. However, the enjambed line endings disguise the fact that this poem is not in blank verse; Browning uses rhymed couplets. How might this suggest an artificiality in the Duke's manner? Has this scene been staged? Why?

Where Are You Going, Where Have You Been?

For Bob Dylan

Joyce Carol Oates

Joyce Carol Oates (b. 1938) is one of America's most prolific and acclaimed writers. She has published more than 20 novels, including With Shuddering Fall *(1964),* You Must Remember This *(1987), and* Because It Is Bitter, and Because It Is My Heart *(1991), and hundreds of short stories, plays, and essays on a wide variety of subjects. The recipient of numerous writing awards such as the National Book Award, she is currently an English professor and artist-in-residence at Princeton University.*

"Where Are You Going, Where Have You Been?", first published in Epoch *in 1966, is her most frequently anthologized story, perhaps because it encompasses so many of the themes that pervade her fiction. Often defined as "neorealism" because of the frequent infusion of the supernatural or gothic into the otherwise mundane, her work focuses on ordinary characters whose lives are threatened by patriarchal culture; she repeatedly confronts the dangers to women in supposedly "safe" suburbs. Arnold Friend tells Connie, "This place you are now—inside your daddy's house—is nothing but a cardboard box I can knock down at any time." The threat of violence hovers around the margins of her fiction.*

Critical commentaries on "Where Are You Going, Where Have You Been?" differ dramatically. Some read Connie's story as a coming-of-age narrative, others as a critique of popular culture (or an homage to it, since the story is dedicated to Bob Dylan) or a reenactment of Satan's temptation of Eve. Choosing to perceive the story as realistic or allegorical often depends upon one's interpretation of Arnold Friend. This bizarre character, who embodies both the traditions of the rock star and the demon lover, is a frightening reminder of the dangers of sexuality, and the flirtatious Connie cannot control this manifestation of her romantic fantasies.

Her name was Connie. She was fifteen and she had a quick nervous giggling habit of craning her neck to glance into mirrors, or checking other people's faces to make sure her own was all right. Her mother, who noticed everything and knew everything and who hadn't much reason any longer to look at her own face, always scolded Connie about it. "Stop gawking at yourself, who are you? You think you're so pretty?" she would say. Connie would raise her eyebrows at these familiar complaints and look right through her mother, into a shadowy vision of herself as she was right at that moment: she knew she was pretty and that was everything. Her mother had been pretty once too, if you could believe those old snapshots in the album, but now her looks were gone and that was why she was always after Connie.

"Why don't you keep your room clean like your sister? How've you got your hair fixed—what the hell stinks? Hair spray? You don't see your sister using that junk."

Her sister June was twenty-four and still lived at home. She was a secretary in the high school Connie attended, and if that wasn't bad enough—with her in the same building—she was so plain and chunky and steady that Connie had to hear her praised all the time by her mother and her mother's sisters. June did this, June did that, she saved money and helped clean the house and cooked and Connie couldn't do a thing, her mind was all filled with trashy daydreams. Their father was away at work most of the time and when he came home he wanted supper and he read the newspaper at supper and after supper he went to bed. He didn't bother talking much to them, but around his bent head Connie's mother kept picking at her until Connie wished her mother was dead and she herself was dead and it was all over. "She makes me want to throw up sometimes," she complained to her friends. She had a high, breathless, amused voice which made everything she said sound a little forced, whether it was sincere or not.

There was one good thing; June went places with girl friends of hers, girls who were just as plain and steady as she, and so when Connie wanted to do that her mother had no objections. The father of Connie's best girl friend drove the girls the three miles to town and left them off at a shopping plaza, so that they could walk through the stores or go to a movie, and when he came to pick them up again at eleven he never bothered to ask what they had done.

They must have been familiar sights, walking around that shopping plaza in their shorts and flat ballerina slippers that always scuffed the sidewalk, with charm bracelets jingling on their thin wrists; they would lean together to whisper and laugh secretly if someone passed by who amused or interested them. Connie had long dark blond hair that drew anyone's eye to it, and she wore part of it pulled up on her head and puffed out and the rest of it she let fall down her back. She wore a pull-over jersey blouse that looked one way when she was at home and another way when she was away from home. Everything about her had two sides to it, one for home and one for anywhere that was not home: her walk that could be childlike and bobbing, or languid enough to make anyone think she was hearing music in her head, her mouth which was pale and smirking most of the time, but bright and pink on these evenings out, her laugh which was cynical and drawing at home—"Ha, ha, very funny"—but high-pitched and nervous anywhere else, like the jingling of the charms on her bracelet.

Sometimes they did go shopping or to a movie, but sometimes they went across the highway, ducking fast across the busy road, to a drive-in restaurant where older kids hung out. The restaurant was shaped like a big bottle, though squatter than a real bottle, and on its cap was a revolving figure of a grinning boy who held a hamburger aloft. One night in mid-summer they ran across, breathless with daring, and right away someone leaned out a car window and invited them over, but it was just a boy from high school they didn't like. It made them feel good to be able to ignore him. They went up through the maze of parked and cruising cars to the bright-lit, fly-infested restaurant, their faces pleased and expectant as if they were entering a sacred building that loomed out of the night to give them what haven and what blessing they yearned for. They sat at the counter and crossed their legs at the ankles, their thin shoulders rigid with excitement, and listened to the music that made everything so good: the music was always in the background like music at a church service, it was something to depend upon.

A boy named Eddie came in to talk with them. He sat backwards on his stool, turning himself jerkily around in semi-circles and then stopping and turning again, and after a while he asked Connie if she would like something to eat. She said she did and so she tapped her friend's arm on her way out—her friend pulled her face up into a brave droll look—and Connie said she would meet her at eleven, across the way. "I just hate to leave her like that," Connie said earnestly, but the boy said that she wouldn't be alone for long. So they went out to his car and on the way Connie couldn't help but let her eyes wander over the windshields and faces all around her, her face gleaming with a joy that had nothing to do with Eddie or even this place; it might have been the music. She drew her shoulders up and sucked in her breath with the pure pleasure of being alive, and just at that moment she happened to glance at a face just a few feet from hers. It was a boy with shaggy black hair, in a convertible jalopy painted gold. He stared at her and then his lips widened into a grin. Connie slit her eyes at him and turned away, but she couldn't help glancing back and there he was still watching her. He wagged a finger and laughed and said, "Gonna get you, baby," and Connie turned away again without Eddie noticing anything.

She spent three hours with him, at the restaurant where they ate hamburgers and drank Cokes in wax cups that were always sweating, and then down an alley a mile or so away, and when he left her off at five to eleven only the movie house was still open at the plaza. Her girl friend was there, talking with a boy. When Connie came up the two girls smiled at each other and Connie said, "How was the movie?" and the girl said, "*You* should know." They rode off with the girl's father, sleepy and pleased, and Connie couldn't help but look at the darkened shopping plaza with its big empty parking lot and its signs that were faded and ghostly now, and over at the drive-in restaurant where cars were still circling tirelessly. She couldn't hear the music at this distance.

Next morning June asked her how the movie was and Connie said, "So-so."

She and that girl and occasionally another girl went out several times a week that way, and the rest of the time Connie spent around the house—it was summer vacation—getting in her mother's way and thinking, dreaming, about the boys she met. But all the boys fell back and dissolved into a single face that was not even a face, but an idea, a feeling, mixed up with the urgent insistent pounding of the music and the humid night air of July. Connie's mother kept dragging her back to the daylight by finding things for her to do or saying, suddenly, "What's this about the Pettinger girl?"

And Connie would say nervously, "Oh, her. That dope." She always drew thick clear lines between herself and such girls, and her mother was simple and kindly enough to believe her. Her mother was so simple, Connie thought, that it was maybe cruel to fool her so much. Her mother went scuffling around the house in old bedroom slippers and complained over the telephone to one sister about the other, then the other called up and the two of them complained about the third one. If June's name was mentioned her mother's tone was approving, and if Connie's name was mentioned it was disapproving. This did not really mean she disliked Connie and actually Connie thought that her mother preferred her to June because she was prettier, but the two of them kept up a pretense of exasperation, a sense that they were tugging and struggling over something of little value to either of them. Sometimes, over coffee, they were almost friends, but something would come up—some vexation that was like a fly buzzing suddenly around their heads—and their faces went hard with contempt.

One Sunday Connie got up at eleven—none of them bothered with church—and washed her hair so that it could dry all day long, in the sun. Her parents and sister were going to a barbecue at an aunt's house and Connie said no, she wasn't interested, rolling her eyes to let her mother know just what she thought of it. "Stay home alone then," her mother said sharply. Connie sat out back in a lawn chair and watched them drive away, her father quiet and bald, hunched around so that he could back the car out, her mother with a look that was still angry and not at all softened through the windshield, and in the back seat poor old June all dressed up as if she didn't know what a barbecue was, with all the running yelling kids and the flies. Connie sat with her eyes closed in the sun, dreaming and dazed with the warmth about her as if this were a kind of love, the caresses of love, and her mind slipped over onto thought of the boy she had been with the night before and how nice he had been, how sweet it always was, not the way someone like June would suppose but sweet, gentle, the way it was in movies and promised in songs; and when she opened her eyes she hardly knew where she was, the back yard ran off into weeds and a fence-line of trees and behind it the sky was perfectly blue and still. The asbestos "ranch house" that was now three years old startled her—it looked small. She shook her head as if to get awake.

It was too hot. She went inside the house and turned on the radio to drown out the quiet. She sat on the edge of her bed, barefoot, and listened for an hour and a half to a program called XYZ Sunday Jamboree, record after record of hard, fast, shrieking songs she sang along with, interspersed by exclamations from "Bobby King": "An' look here you girls at Napoleon's—Son and Charley want you to pay real close attention to this song coming up!"

And Connie paid close attention herself, bathed in a glow of slow-pulsed joy that seemed to rise mysteriously out of the music itself and lay languidly about the airless little room, breathed in and breathed out with each gentle rise and fall of her chest.

After a while she heard a car coming up the drive. She sat up at once, startled, because it couldn't be her father so soon. The gravel kept crunching all the way in from the road—the driveway was long—and Connie ran to the window. It was a car she didn't know. It was an open jalopy, painted a bright gold that caught the sunlight opaquely. Her heart began to pound and her fingers snatched at her hair, checking it, and she whispered "Christ, Christ," wondering how bad she looked. The car came to a stop at the side door and the horn sounded four short taps as if this were a signal Connie knew.

She went into the kitchen and approached the door slowly, then hung out the screen door, her bare toes curling down off the step. There were two boys in the car and now she recognized the driver: he had shaggy, shabby black hair that looked crazy as a wig and he was grinning at her.

"I ain't late, am I?" he said.

"Who the hell do you think you are?" Connie said.

"Toldja I'd be out, didn't I?"

"I don't even know who you are."

She spoke sullenly, careful to show no interest or pleasure, and he spoke in a fast bright monotone. Connie looked past him to the other boy, taking her time. He had fair brown hair, with a lock that fell onto his forehead. His sideburns gave him a fierce, embarrassed look, but so far he hadn't even bothered to glance at her. Both boys wore sunglasses. The driver's glasses were metallic and mirrored everything in miniature.

"You wanta come for a ride?" he said.

Connie smirked and let her hair fall loose over one shoulder.

"Don'tcha like my car? New paint job," he said. "Hey."

"What?"

"You're cute."

She pretended to fidget, chasing flies away from the door.

"Don'tcha believe me, or what?" he said.

"Look, I don't even know who you are," Connie said in disgust.

"Hey, Ellie's got a radio, see. Mine's broke down." He lifted his friend's arm and showed her the little transistor the boy was holding, and now Connie began to hear the music. It was the same program that was playing inside the house.

"Bobby King?" she said.

"I listen to him all the time. I think he's great."

"He's kind of great," Connie said reluctantly.

"Listen, that guy's *great*. He knows where the action is."

Connie blushed a little, because the glasses made it impossible for her to see just what this boy was looking at. She couldn't decide if she liked him or if he was just a jerk, and so she dawdled in the doorway and wouldn't come down or go back inside. She said "What's all that stuff painted on your car?"

"Can'tcha read it?" He opened the door very carefully, as if he was afraid it might fall off. He slid out just as carefully, planting his feet firmly on the ground, the tiny metallic world in his glasses slowing down like gelatine hardening and in the midst of it Connie's bright green blouse. "This here is my name, to begin with," he said. ARNOLD FRIEND was written in tarlike black letters on the side, with a drawing of a round grinning face that reminded Connie of a pumpkin, except it wore sunglasses. "I wanta introduce myself, I'm Arnold Friend and that's my real name and I'm gonna be your friend, honey, and inside the car's Ellie Oscar, he's kinda shy." Ellie brought his transistor radio up to his shoulder and balanced it there. "Now these numbers are a secret code, honey," Arnold Friend explained. He read off the numbers 33, 19, 17 and raised his eyebrows at her to see what she thought of that, but she didn't think much of it. The left rear fender had been smashed and around it was written, on the gleaming gold background: DONE BY CRAZY WOMAN DRIVER. Connie had to laugh at that. Arnold Friend was pleased at her laughter and looked up at her. "Around the other side's a lot more—you wanta come and see them?"

"No."

"Why not?"

"Why should I?"

"Don'tcha wanta see what's on the car? Don'tcha wanta go for a ride?"

"I don't know."

"Why not?"

"I got things to do."

"Like what?"

"Things."

He laughed as if she had said something funny. He slapped his thighs. He was standing in a strange way, leaning back against the car as if he were balancing himself. He wasn't tall, only an inch or so taller than she would be if she came down to him.

Connie liked the way he was dressed, which was the way all of them dressed: tight faded jeans stuffed into black, scuffed boors, a belt that pulled his waist in and showed how lean he was, and a white pull-over shirt that was a little soiled and showed the hard small muscles of his arms and shoulders. He looked as if he probably did hard work, lifting and carrying things. Even his neck looked muscular. And his face was a familiar face, somehow: the jaw and chin and cheeks slightly darkened, because he hadn't shaved for a day or two, and the nose long and hawk-like, sniffing as if she were a treat he was going to gobble up and it was all a joke.

"Connie, you ain't telling the truth. This is your day set aside for a ride with me and you know it," he said, still laughing. The way he straightened and recovered from his fit of laughing showed that it had been all fake.

"How do you know what my name is?" she said suspiciously.

"It's Connie."

"Maybe and maybe not."

"I know my Connie," he said, wagging his finger. Now she remembered him even better, back at the restaurant, and her cheeks warmed at the thought of how she sucked in her breath just at the moment she passed him—how she must have looked to him. And he had remembered her. "Ellie and I come out here especially for you," he said. "Ellie can sit in back. How about it?"

"Where?"

"Where what?"

"Where're we going?"

He looked at her. He took off the sunglasses and she saw how pale the skin around his eyes was, like holes that were not in shadow but instead in light. His eyes were chips of broken glass that catch the light in an amiable way. He smiled. It was as if the idea of going for a ride somewhere, to some place, was a new idea to him.

"Just for a ride, Connie sweetheart."

"I never said my name was Connie," she said.

"But I know what it is. I know your name and all about you, lots of things," Arnold Friend said. He had not moved yet but stood still leaning back against the side of his jalopy. "I took a special interest in you, such a pretty girl, and found out all about you like I know your parents and sister are gone somewheres and I know where and how long they're going to be gone, and I know who you were with last night, and your best girl friend's name is Betty. Right?"

He spoke in a simple lilting voice, exactly as if he were reciting the words to a song. His smile assured her that everything was fine. In the car, Ellie turned up the volume on his radio and did not bother to look around at them.

"Ellie can sit in the back seat," Arnold Friend said. He indicated his friend with a casual jerk of his chin, as if Ellie did not count and she should not bother with him.

"How'd you find out all that stuff?" Connie said.

"Listen: Betty Schultz and Tony Fitch and Jimmy Pettinger and Nancy Pettinger," he said, in a chant. "Raymond Stanley and Bob Hutter—"

"Do you know all those kids?"

"I know everybody."

"Look, you're kidding. You're not from around here."

"Sure."

"But—how come we never saw you before?"

"Sure you saw me before," he said. He looked down at his boots, as if he were a little offended. "You just don't remember."

"I guess I'd remember you," Connie said.

"Yeah?" He looked up at this, beaming. He was pleased. He began to mark time with the music from Ellie's radio, tapping his fists lightly together. Connie looked away from his smile to the car, which was painted so bright it almost hurt her eyes to look at it. She looked at that name, ARNOLD FRIEND. And up at the front fender was an expression that was familiar—MAN THE FLYING SAUCERS. It was an expression kids had used the year before, but didn't use this year. She looked at it for a while as if the words meant something to her that she did not yet know.

"What're you thinking about? Huh?" Arnold Friend demanded. "Not worried about your hair blowing around in the car, are you?"

"No."

"Think I maybe can't drive good?"

"How do I know?"

"You're a hard girl to handle. How come?" he said. "Don't you know I'm your friend? Didn't you see me put my sign in the air when you walked by?"

"What sign?"

"My sign." And he drew an X in the air, leaning out toward her. They were maybe ten feet apart. After his hand fell back to his side the X was still in the air, almost visible. Connie let the screen door close and stood perfectly still inside it, listening to the music from her radio and the boy's blend together. She stared at Arnold Friend. He stood there so stiffly relaxed, pretending to be relaxed, with one hand idly on the door handle as if he were keeping himself up that way and had no intention of ever moving again. She recognized most things about him, the tight jeans that showed his thighs and buttocks and the greasy leather boots and the tight shirt, and even that slippery friendly smile of his, that sleepy dreamy smile that all the boys used to get across ideas they didn't want to put into words. She recognized all this and also the singsong way he talked, slightly mocking, kidding, but serious and a little melancholy, and she recognized the way he tapped one fist against the other in homage to the perpetual music behind him. But all these things did not come together.

She said suddenly, "Hey, how old are you?"

His smile faded. She could see then that he wasn't a kid, he was much older—thirty, maybe more. At this knowledge her heart began to pound faster.

"That's a crazy thing to ask. Can'tcha see I'm your own age?"

"Like hell you are."

"Or maybe a couple years older, I'm eighteen."

"Eighteen?" she said doubtfully.

He grinned to reassure her and lines appeared at the corners of his mouth. His teeth were big and white. He grinned so broadly his eyes became slits and she saw how thick the lashes were, thick and black as if painted with a black tarlike material. Then he seemed to become embarrassed, abruptly, and looked over his shoulder at Ellie. "*Him,* he's crazy," he said. "Ain't he a riot, he's a nut, a real character." Ellie was still listening to the music. His sunglasses told nothing about what he was thinking. He wore a bright orange shirt unbuttoned halfway to show his chest, which was a pale, bluish chest and not muscular like Arnold Friend's. His shirt collar was turned up all around and the very tips of the collar pointed out past his chin as if they were protecting him. He was pressing the transistor radio up against his ear and sat there in a kind of daze, right in the sun.

"He's kinda strange," Connie said.

"Hey, she says you're kinda strange! Kinda strange!" Arnold Friend cried. He pounded on the car to get Ellie's attention. Ellie turned for the first time and Connie saw with shock that he wasn't a kid either—he had a fair, hairless face, cheeks reddened slightly as if the veins grew too close to the surface of his skin, the face of a forty-year-old baby. Connie felt a wave of dizziness rise in her at this sight and she stared at him as if waiting for something to change the shock of the moment, make it all right again. Ellie's lips kept shaping words, mumbling along, with the words blasting in his ear.

"Maybe you two better go away," Connie said faintly.

"What? How come?" Arnold Friend cried. "We come out here to take you for a ride. It's Sunday." He had the voice of a man on the radio now. It was the same voice, Connie thought. "Don'tcha know it's Sunday all day and honey, no matter who you were with last night today you're with Arnold Friend and don't you forget it!—Maybe you better step out here," he said, and this last was in a different voice. It was a little flatter, as if the heat was finally getting to him.

"No. I got things to do."

"Hey."

"You two better leave."

"We ain't leaving until you come with us."

"Like hell I am—"

"Connie, don't fool around with me. I mean, I mean, don't fool *around*," he said, shaking his head. He laughed incredulously. He placed his sunglasses on top of his head, carefully, as if he were indeed wearing a wig, and brought the stems down behind his ears. Connie stared at him, another wave of dizziness and fear rising in her so that for a moment he wasn't even in focus but was just a blur, standing there against his gold car, and she had the idea that he had driven up the driveway all right but had come from nowhere before that and belonged nowhere and that everything about him and even about the music that was so familiar to her was only half real.

"If my father comes and sees you—"

"He ain't coming. He's at a barbecue."

"How do you know that?"

"Aunt Tillie's. Right now they're—uh—they're drinking. Sitting around," he said vaguely, squinting as if he were staring all the way to town and over to Aunt Tillie's backyard. Then the vision seemed to get clear and he nodded energetically. "Yeah. Sitting around. There's your sister in a blue dress, huh? And high heels, the poor sad bitch—nothing like you, sweetheart! And your mother's helping some fat woman with the corn, they're cleaning the corn—husking the corn—"

"What fat woman?" Connie cried.

"How do I know what fat woman. I don't know every goddam fat woman in the world!" Arnold Friend laughed.

"Oh, that's Mrs. Hornby. . . . Who invited her?" Connie said. She felt a little light-headed. Her breath was coming quickly.

"She's too fat. I don't like them fat. I like them the way you are, honey," he said, smiling sleepily at her. They stared at each other for awhile, through the screen door. He said softly, "Now what you're going to do is this: you're going to come out that door. You're going to sit up front with me and Ellie's going to sit in the back, the hell with Ellie, right? This isn't Ellie's date. You're my date. I'm your lover, honey."

"What? You're crazy—"

"Yes, I'm your lover. You don't know what that is but you will," he said. "I know that too. I know all about you. But look: it's real nice and you couldn't ask for nobody better than me, or more polite. I always keep my word. I'll tell you how it is, I'm always nice at first, the first time. I'll hold you so tight you won't think you have to try to get away or pretend anything because you'll know you can't. And I'll come inside you where it's all secret and you'll give in to me and you'll love me—"

"Shut up! You're crazy!" Connie said. She backed away from the door. She put her hands against her ears as if she'd heard something terrible, something not meant for her. "People don't talk like that, you're crazy," she muttered. Her heart was almost too big now for her chest and its pumping made sweat break out all over her. She looked out to see Arnold Friend pause and then take a step toward the porch lurching. He almost fell. But, like a clever drunken man, he managed to catch his balance. He wobbled in his high boots and grabbed hold of one of the porch posts.

"Honey?" he said. "You still listening?"

"Get the hell out of here!"

"Be nice, honey. Listen."

"I'm going to call the police—"

He wobbled again and out of the side of his mouth came a fast spat curse, an aside not meant for her to hear. But even this "Christ!" sounded forced. Then he began to smile again. She watched this smile come, awkward as if he were smiling from inside a mask. His whole face was a mask, she thought wildly, tanned down onto his throat but then running out as if he had plastered make-up on his face but had forgotten about his throat.

"Honey—? Listen, here's how it is. I always tell the truth and I promise you this: I ain't coming in that house after you."

"You better not! I'm going to call the police if you—if you don't—"

"Honey," he said, talking right through her voice, "honey, I'm not coming in there but you are coming out here. You know why?"

She was panting. The kitchen looked like a place she had never seen before, some room she had run inside but which wasn't good enough, wasn't going to help her. The kitchen window had never had a curtain, after three years, and there were dishes in the sink for her to do—probably—and if you ran your hand across the table you'd probably feel something sticky there.

"You listening, honey? Hey?"

"—going to call the police—"

"Soon as you touch the phone I don't need to keep my promise and can come inside. You won't want that."

She rushed forward and tried to lock the door. Her fingers were shaking. "But why lock it," Arnold Friend said gently, talking right into her face. "It's just a screen door. It's just nothing." One of his boots was at a strange angle, as if his foot wasn't in it. It pointed out to the left, bent at the ankle. "I mean, anybody can break through a screen door and glass and wood and iron or anything else if he needs to, anybody at all and specially Arnold Friend. If the place got lit up with a fire honey you'd come running out into my arms, right into my arms and safe at home—like you knew I was your lover and'd stopped fooling around. I don't mind a nice shy girl but I don't like no fooling around." Part of those words were spoken with a slight rhythmic lilt, and Connie somehow recognized them—the echo of a song from last year, about a girl rushing into her boy friend's arms and coming home again—

Connie stood barefoot on the linoleum floor, staring at him. "What do you want?" she whispered.

"I want you," he said.

"What?"

"Seen you that night and thought, that's the one, yes sir. I never needed to look any more."

"But my father's coming back. He's coming to get me. I had to wash my hair first—"

She spoke in a dry, rapid voice, hardly raising it for him to hear.

"No, your daddy is not coming and yes, you had to wash your hair and you washed it for me. It's nice and shining and all for me, I thank you, sweetheart," he said, with a mock bow, but again he almost lost his balance. He had to bend and adjust his boots. Evidently his feet did not go all the way down; the boots must have been stuffed with something so that he would seem taller. Connie stared out at him and behind him Ellie in the car, who seemed to be looking off toward Connie's right, into nothing. This Ellie said, pulling the words out of the air one after another as if he were just discovering them, "You want me to pull out the phone?"

"Shut your mouth and keep it shut," Arnold Friend said, his face red from bending over or maybe from embarrassment because Connie had seen his boots. "This ain't none of your business."

"What—what are you doing? What do you want?" Connie said. "If I call the police they'll get you, they'll arrest you—"

"Promise was not to come in unless you touch that phone, and I'll keep that promise," he said. He sounded like a hero in a movie, declaring something important. He spoke too loudly and it was as if he were speaking to someone behind Connie. "I ain't made plans for coming in that house where I don't belong but just for you to come out to me, the way you should. Don't you know who I am?"

"You're crazy," she whispered. She backed away from the door but did not want to go into another part of the house, as if this would give him permission to come through the door. "What do you . . . You're crazy, you . . ."

"Huh? What're you saying, honey?"

Her eyes darted everywhere in the kitchen. She could not remember what it was, this room.

"This is how it is, honey: you come out and we'll drive away, have a nice ride. But if you don't come out we're gonna wait till your people come home and then they're all going to get it."

"You want that telephone pulled out?" Ellie said. He held the radio away from his ear and grimaced, as if without the radio the air was too much for him.

"I toldja shut up, Ellie," Arnold Friend said, "you're deaf, get a hearing aid, right? Fix yourself up. This little girl's no trouble and's gonna be nice to me, so Ellie keep to yourself, this ain't your date—right? Don't hem in on me. Don't hog. Don't crush. Don't bird dog. Don't trail me," he said in a rapid meaningless voice, as if he were running through all the expressions he'd learned but was no longer sure which one of them was in style, then rushing on to new ones, making them up with his eyes closed, "Don't crawl under my fence, don't squeeze in my chipmunk hole, don't sniff my glue, suck my popsicle, keep your own greasy fingers on yourself!" He shaded his eyes and peered in at Connie, who was backed against the kitchen table. "Don't mind him honey he's just a creep. He's a dope. Right? I'm the boy for you and like I said you come out here nice like a lady and give me your hand, and nobody else gets hurt, I mean, your nice old bald-headed daddy and your mummy and your sister in her high heels. Because listen: why bring them in this?"

"Leave me alone," Connie whispered.

"Hey, you know that old woman down the road, the one with the chickens and stuff—you know her?"

"She's dead!"

"Dead? What? You know her?" Arnold Friend said.

"She's dead—"

"Don't you like her?"

"She's dead—she's—she isn't here any more—"

"But don't you like her, I mean, you got something against her? Some grudge or something?" Then his voice dipped as if he were conscious of a rudeness. He touched the sunglasses perched on top of his head as if to make sure they were still there. "Now you be a good girl."

"What are you going to do?"

"Just two things, or maybe three," Arnold Friend said. "But I promise it won't last long and you'll like me that way you get to like people you're close to. You will. It's all over for you here, so come on out. You don't want your people in any trouble, do you?"

She turned and bumped against a chair or something, hurting her leg, but she ran into the back room and picked up the telephone. Something roared in her ear, a tiny roaring, and she was so sick with fear that she could do nothing but listen to it—the telephone was clammy and very heavy and her fingers groped down to the dial but were too weak to touch it. She began to scream into the phone, into the roaring. She cried out, she cried for her mother, she felt her breath start jerking back and forth in her lungs as if it were something Arnold Friend were stabbing her with again and again with no tenderness. A noisy sorrowful wailing rose all about her and she was locked inside it the way she was locked inside the house.

After a while she could hear again. She was sitting on the floor with her wet back against the wall.

Arnold Friend was saying from the door, "That's a good girl. Put the phone back."

She kicked the phone away from her.

"No, honey. Pick it up. Put it back right."

She picked it up and put it back. The dial tone stopped.

"That's a good girl. Now come outside."

She was hollow with what had been fear, but what was now just an emptiness. All that screaming had blasted it out of her. She sat, one leg cramped under her, and deep inside her brain was something like a pinpoint of light that kept going and would not let her relax. She thought, I'm not going to see my mother again. She thought, I'm not going to sleep in my bed again. Her bright green blouse was all wet.

Arnold Friend said, in a gentle-loud voice that was like a stage voice, "The place where you came from ain't there any more, and where you had in mind to go is cancelled out. This place you are now—inside your daddy's house—is nothing but a cardboard box I can knock down any time. You know that and always did know it. You hear me?"

She thought, I have got to think. I have to know what to do.

"We'll go out to a nice field, out in the country here where it smells so nice and it's sunny," Arnold Friend said. "I'll have my arms around you so you won't need to try to get away and I'll show you what love is like, what it does. The hell with this house! It looks solid all right," he said. He ran a fingernail down the screen and the noise did not make Connie shiver, as it would have the day before. "Now put your hand on your heart, honey. Feel that? That feels solid too but we know better, be nice to me, be sweet like you can because what else is there for a girl like you but to be sweet and pretty and give in?—and get away before her people come back?"

She felt her pounding heart. Her hand seemed to enclose it. She thought for the first time in her life that it was nothing that was hers, that belonged to her, but just a pounding, living thing inside this body that wasn't really hers either.

"You don't want them to get hurt," Arnold Friend went on. "Now get up, honey. Get up all by yourself."

She stood up.

"Now turn this way. That's right. Come over here to me—Ellie, put that away, didn't I tell you? You dope. You miserable creepy dope," Arnold said. His words were not angry but only part of an incantation. The incantation was kindly. "Now come out through the kitchen to me honey and let's see a smile, try it, you're a brave sweet little girl and now they're eating corn and hotdogs cooked to bursting over an outdoor fire, and they don't know one thing about you and never did and honey you're better than them because not a one of them would have done this for you."

Connie felt the linoleum under her feet; it was cool. She brushed her hair back out of her eyes. Arnold Friend let go of the post tentatively and opened his arms for her, his elbows pointing in toward each other and his wrists limp, to show that this was an embarrassed embrace and a little mocking, he didn't want to make her self-conscious.

She put out her hand against the screen. She watched herself push the door slowly open as if she were safe back somewhere in the other doorway, watching this body and this head of long hair moving out into the sunlight where Arnold Friend waited.

"My sweet little blue-eyed girl," he said, in a half-sung sigh that had nothing to do with her brown eyes but was taken up just the same by the vast sunlit reaches of the land behind him and on all sides of him, so much land that Connie had never seen before and did not recognize except to know that she was going to it.

For Practice

1. How does popular culture shape Connie's conception of "romance"? How do these perceptions color her initial impressions of Friend?

2. How does Oates characterize Connie? Compare the depiction of Connie to other accounts of teenage behavior in film and television; are we supposed to see her as a typical teenager, or is she unusually vain? What comment is Oates making about women brought up in a consumer-oriented culture? In what ways is this story about the end of Connie's innocence? Was she "innocent" before her encounter with Friend?

3. Who or what is Arnold Friend? The physical descriptions of him, especially his clothing, invoke the "rebel without a cause" popular in the 1950s, but how might the myth of the "demon lover," popularized by films like Francis Ford Coppola's Bram Stoker's *Dracula*, help us to understand Friend? Does he seduce Connie? What suggestions does Oates offer that he is "otherworldly?"

4. How does the transition from the traditional realism of the first part of the story to the "gothic" horror in the conclusion affect our perception of the encounter between Friend and Connie?

5. One of the most puzzling "clues" in the story is the set of numbers on Friend's car: 33, 19, 17. These correspond to Judges 19:17, an Old Testament narrative in which a Levite travels to Bethlehem to retrieve his concubine, who is later killed by a group of "base fellows" who threaten the house where they have been given shelter for the night. The title of the story can be found in this narrative, and the threat of violence to women at a moment when they are seemingly safe in a domestic space (the concubine is "given" to the men so that they will leave everyone else in the house alone) is a theme echoed by Oates. How might this Biblical text help us to understand the Oates story?

Shiloh

Bobbie Ann Mason

The daughter of a dairy farmer, Bobbie Ann Mason (b. 1940) grew up in Kentucky. After graduating from the University of Kentucky in 1962, she moved to New York and worked in the publishing industry. She returned to school, receiving a master's degree from SUNY-Binghamton in 1966 and a Ph.D. from the University of Connecticut in 1972. The New Yorker published her first story in 1980, and her first collection of short stories, Shiloh and Other Stories, *was published in 1982. That collection won the Ernest Hemingway Foundation Award and was a finalist for the National Book Critics Circle Award. She has since published another collection of short stories,* Love Life *(1989), a novel,* In Country *(1985), and a novella,* Spence and Lila *(1988). She now lives in rural Pennsylvania.*

Mason's stories return again and again to the South of her upbringing, focusing on characters who might at first be characterized as "white trash," but who, upon closer examination, lead much more complex lives than the stereotype acknowledges. In "Shiloh," Leroy and Norma Jean Moffitt must come to terms with not only their own pasts, but the complicated past of the South itself. As you read this story, think about the ways in which the journey to the famous Civil War battleground in Tennessee allows Leroy and Norma Jean a chance for redemption.

Leroy Moffitt's wife, Norma Jean, is working on her pectorals. She lifts three-pound dumbbells to warm up, then progresses to a twenty-pound barbell. Standing with her legs apart, she reminds Leroy of Wonder Woman.

"I'd give anything if I could just get these muscles to where they're real hard," says Norma Jean. "Feel this arm. It's not as hard as the other one."

"That's 'cause you're right-handed," says Leroy, dodging as she swings the barbell in an arc.

"Do you think so?"

"Sure."

Leroy is a truckdriver. He injured his leg in a highway accident four months ago, and his physical therapy, which involves weights and a pulley, prompted Norma Jean to try building herself up. Now she is attending a body-building class. Leroy has been collecting temporary disability since his tractor-trailer jackknifed in Missouri, badly twisting his left leg in its socket. He has a steel pin in his hip. He will probably not be able to drive his rig again. It sits in the backyard, like a gigantic bird that has flown home to roost. Leroy has been home in Kentucky for three months, and his leg is almost healed, but the accident frightened him and he does not want to drive any more long hauls. He is not sure what to do next. In the meantime, he makes things from craft kits. He started by building a miniature log cabin from notched Popsicle sticks. He varnished it and placed it on the TV set, where it remains. It reminds him of a rustic Nativity scene. Then he tried string art (sailing ships on black velvet), a macramé owl kit, a snap-together B-17 Flying Fortress, and a lamp made out of a model truck, with a light fixture screwed in the top of the cab. At first the kits were diversions, something to kill time, but now he is thinking about building a full-scale log house from a kit. It would be considerably cheaper than building a regular house, and besides, Leroy has grown to appreciate how things are put together. He has begun to realize that in all the years he was on the road he never took time to examine anything. He was always flying past scenery.

"They won't let you build a log cabin in any of the new subdivisions," Norma Jean tells him.

"They will if I tell them it's for you," he says, teasing her. Ever since they were married, he has promised Norma Jean he would build her a new home one day. They have always rented, and the house they live in is small and nondescript. It does not even feel like a home, Leroy realizes now.

Norma Jean works at the Rexall drugstore, and she has acquired an amazing amount of information about cosmetics. When she explains to Leroy the three stages of complexion care, involving creams, toners, and moisturizers, he thinks happily of other petroleum products—axle grease, diesel fuel. This is a connection between him and Norma Jean. Since he has been home, he has felt unusually tender about his wife and guilty over his long absences. But he can't tell what she feels about him. Norma Jean has never complained about his traveling; she has never made hurt remarks, like calling his truck a "widow-maker." He is reasonably certain she has been faithful to him, but he wishes she would celebrate his permanent homecoming more happily. Norma Jean is often startled to find Leroy at home, and he thinks she seems a little disappointed about it. Perhaps he reminds her too much of the early days of their marriage, before he went on the road. They had a child who died as an infant, years ago. They never speak about their memories of Randy, which have almost faded, but now that Leroy is home all the time, they sometimes feel awkward around each other, and Leroy wonders if one of them should mention the child. He has the feeling that they are waking up out of a dream together—that they must create a new marriage, start afresh. They are lucky they are still married. Leroy has read that for most people losing a child destroys the marriage—or else he heard this on *Donahue*. He can't always remember where he learns things anymore.

At Christmas, Leroy bought an electric organ for Norma Jean. She used to play the piano when she was in high school. "It don't leave you," she told him once. "It's like riding a bicycle."

The new instrument had so many keys and buttons that she was bewildered by it at first. She touched the keys tentatively, pushed some buttons, then pecked out "Chop-sticks." It came out in an amplified fox-trot rhythm, with marimba sounds.

"It's an orchestra!" she cried.

The organ had a pecan-look finish and eighteen preset chords, with optional flute, violin, trumpet, clarinet, and banjo accompaniments. Norma Jean mastered the organ almost immediately. At first she played Christmas songs. Then she bought *The Sixties*

Songbook and learned every tune in it, adding variations to each with the rows of brightly colored buttons.

"I didn't like these old songs back then," she said. "But I have this crazy feeling I missed something."

"You didn't miss a thing," said Leroy.

Leroy likes to lie on the couch and smoke a joint and listen to Norma Jean play "Can't Take My Eyes Off You" and "I'll Be Back." He is back again. After fifteen years on the road, he is finally settling down with the woman he loves. She is still pretty. Her skin is flawless. Her frosted curls resemble pencil trimmings.

Now that Leroy has come home to stay, he notices how much the town has changed. Subdivisions are spreading across western Kentucky like an oil slick. The sign at the edge of town says "Pop: 11,500"—only seven hundred more than it said twenty years before. Leroy can't figure out who is living in all the new houses. The farmers who used to gather around the courthouse square on Saturday afternoons to play checkers and spit tobacco juice have gone. It has been years since Leroy has thought about the farmers, and they have disappeared without his noticing.

Leroy meets a kid named Stevie Hamilton in the parking lot at the new shopping center. While they pretend to be strangers meeting over a stalled car, Stevie tosses an ounce of marijuana under the front seat of Leroy's car. Stevie is wearing orange jogging shoes and a T-shirt that says CHATTAHOOCHEE SUPER-RAT. His father is a prominent doctor who lives in one of the expensive subdivisions in a new white-columned brick house that looks like a funeral parlor. In the phone book under his name there is a separate number, with the listing "Teenagers."

"Where do you get this stuff?" asks Leroy. "From your pappy?"

"That's for me to know and you to find out," Stevie says. He is slit-eyed and skinny.

"What else you got?"

"What you interested in?"

"Nothing special, just wondered."

Leroy used to take speed on the road. Now he has to go slowly. He needs to be mellow. He leans back against the car and says, "I'm aiming to build me a log house, soon as I get time. My wife, though, I don't think she likes the idea."

"Well, let me know when you want me again," Stevie says. He has a cigarette in his cupped palm, as though sheltering it from the wind. He takes a long drag, then stomps it on the asphalt and slouches away.

Stevie's father was two years ahead of Leroy in high school. Leroy is thirty-four. He married Norma Jean when they were both eighteen, and their child Randy was born a few months later, but he died at the age of four months and three days. He would be about Stevie's age now. Norma Jean and Leroy were at the drive-in, watching a double feature (*Dr. Strangelove* and *Lover Come Back*), and the baby was sleeping in the back seat. When the first movie ended, the baby was dead. It was the sudden infant death syndrome. Leroy remembers handing Randy to a nurse at the emergency room, as though he were offering her a large doll as a present. A dead baby feels like a sack of flour. "It just happens sometimes," said the doctor, in what Leroy always recalls as a nonchalant tone. Leroy can hardly remember the child anymore, but he still sees vividly a scene from *Dr. Strangelove* in which the President of the United States was talking in a folksy voice on the hot line to the Soviet premier about the bomber accidentally headed toward Russia. He was in the War Room, and the world map was lit up.

Leroy remembers Norma Jean standing catatonically beside him in the hospital and himself thinking: Who is this strange girl? He had forgotten who she was. Now scientists are saying that crib death is caused by a virus. Nobody knows anything, Leroy thinks. The answers are always changing.

When Leroy gets home from the shopping center, Norma Jean's mother, Mabel Beasley, is there. Until this year, Leroy has not realized how much time she spends with Norma Jean. When she visits, she inspects the closets and then the plants, informing Norma Jean when a plant is droopy or yellow. Mabel calls the plants "flowers," although there are never any blooms. She always notices if Norma Jean's laundry is piling up. Mabel is a short, overweight woman whose tight, brown-dyed curls look more like a wig than the actual wig she sometimes wears. Today she has brought Norma Jean an off-white dust ruffle she made for the bed; Mabel works in a custom-upholstery shop.

"This is the tenth one I made this year," Mabel says. "I got started and couldn't stop."

"It's real pretty," says Norma Jean.

"Now we can hide things under the bed," says Leroy, who gets along with his mother-in-law primarily by joking with her. Mabel has never really forgiven him for disgracing her by getting Norma Jean pregnant. When the baby died, she said that fate was mocking her.

"What's that thing?" Mabel says to Leroy in a loud voice, pointing to a tangle of yarn on a piece of canvas.

Leroy holds it up for Mabel to see. "It's my needlepoint," he explains. "This is a *Star Trek* pillow cover."

"That's what a woman would do," says Mabel. "Great day in the morning!"

"All the big football players on TV do it," he says.

"Why, Leroy, you're always trying to fool me. I don't believe you for one minute. You don't know what to do with yourself—that's the whole trouble. Sewing!"

"I'm aiming to build us a log house," says Leroy. "Soon as my plans come."

"Like *heck* you are," says Norma Jean. She takes Leroy's needlepoint and shoves it into a drawer. "You have to find a job first. Nobody can afford to build now anyway."

Mabel straightens her girdle and says, "I still think before you get tied down y'all ought to take a little run to Shiloh."

"One of these days, Mama," Norma Jean says impatiently.

Mabel is talking about Shiloh, Tennessee. For the past few years, she has been urging Leroy and Norma Jean to visit the Civil War battleground there. Mabel went there on her honeymoon—the only real trip she ever took. Her husband died of a perforated ulcer when Norma Jean was ten, but Mabel, who was accepted into the United Daughters of the Confederacy in 1975, is still preoccupied with going back to Shiloh.

"I've been to kingdom come and back in that truck out yonder," Leroy says to Mabel, "but we never yet set foot in that battleground. Ain't that something? How did I miss it?"

"It's not even that far," Mabel says.

After Mabel leaves, Norma Jean reads to Leroy from a list she has made. "Things you could do," she announces. "You could get a job as a guard at Union Carbide, where they'd let you set on a stool. You could get on at the lumberyard. You could do a little carpenter work, if you want to build so bad. You could—"

"I can't do something where I'd have to stand up all day."

"You ought to try standing up all day behind a cosmetics counter. It's amazing that I have strong feet, coming from two parents that never had strong feet at all." At the moment Norma Jean is holding on to the kitchen counter, raising her knees one at a time as she talks. She is wearing two-pound ankle weights.

"Don't worry," says Leroy. "I'll do something."

"You could truck calves to slaughter for somebody. You wouldn't have to drive any big old truck for that."

"I'm going to build you this home," says Leroy. "I want to make you a real home."

"I don't want to live in any log cabin."

"It's not a cabin. It's a house."

"I don't care. It looks like a cabin."

"You and me together could lift those logs. It's just like lifting weights."

Norma Jean doesn't answer. Under her breath, she is counting. Now she is marching through the kitchen. She is doing goose steps.

Before his accident, when Leroy came home he used to stay in the house with Norma Jean, watching TV in bed and playing cards. She would cook fried chicken, picnic ham, chocolate pie—all his favorites. Now he is home alone much of the time. In the mornings, Norma Jean disappears, leaving a cooling place in the bed. She eats a cereal called Body Buddies, and she leaves the bowl on the table, with the soggy tan balls floating in a milk puddle. He sees things about Norma Jean that he never realized before. When she chops onions, she stares off into a corner, as if she can't bear to look. She puts on her house slippers almost precisely at nine o'clock every evening and nudges her jogging shoes under the couch. She saves bread heels for the birds. Leroy watches the birds at the feeder. He notices the peculiar way goldfinches fly past the window. They close their wings, then fall, then spread their wings to catch and lift themselves. He wonders if they close their eyes when they fall. Norma Jean closes her eyes when they are in bed. She wants the lights turned out. Even then, he is sure she closes her eyes.

He goes for long drives around town. He tends to drive a car rather carelessly. Power steering and an automatic shift make a car feel so small and inconsequential that his body is hardly involved in the driving process. His injured leg stretches out comfortably. Once or twice he has almost hit something, but even the prospect of an accident seems minor in a car. He cruises the new subdivisions, feeling like a criminal rehearsing for a robbery. Norma Jean is probably right about a log house being inappropriate here in the new subdivisions. All the houses look grand and complicated. They depress him.

One day when Leroy comes home from a drive he finds Norma Jean in tears. She is in the kitchen making a potato and mushroom-soup casserole, with grated-cheese topping. She is crying because her mother caught her smoking.

"I didn't hear her coming. I was standing here puffing away pretty as you please," Norma Jean says, wiping her eyes.

"I knew it would happen sooner or later," says Leroy, putting his arm around her.

"She don't know the meaning of the word 'knock,'" says Norma Jean. "It's a wonder she hadn't caught me years ago."

"Think of it this way," Leroy says. "What if she caught me with a joint?"

"You better not let her!" Norma Jean shrieks. "I'm warning you, Leroy Moffitt!"

"I'm just kidding. Here, play me a tune. That'll help you relax."

Norma Jean puts the casserole in the oven and sets the timer. Then she plays a ragtime tune, with horns and banjo, as Leroy lights up a joint and lies on the couch, laughing to himself about Mabel's catching him at it. He thinks of Stevie Hamilton— a doctor's son pushing grass. Everything is funny. The whole town seems crazy and small. He is reminded of Virgil Mathis, a boastful policeman Leroy used to shoot pool with. Virgil recently led a drug bust in a back room at a bowling alley, where he seized ten thousand dollars' worth of marijuana. The newspaper had a picture of him holding up the bags of grass and grinning widely. Right now, Leroy can imagine Virgil breaking down the door and arresting him with a lungful of smoke. Virgil would probably have been alerted to the scene because of all the racket Norma Jean is making. Now she sounds like a hard-rock band. Norma Jean is terrific. When she switches to a Latin-rhythm version of "Sunshine Superman," Leroy hums along. Norma Jean's foot goes up and down, up and down.

"Well, what do you think?" Leroy says, when Norma Jean pauses to search through her music.

"What do I think about what?"

His mind has gone blank. Then he says, "I'll sell my rig and build us a house." That wasn't what he wanted to say. He wanted to know what she thought—what she *really* thought—about them.

"Don't start in on that again," says Norma Jean. She begins playing "Who'll Be the Next in Line?"

Leroy used to tell hitchhikers his whole life story—about his travels, his hometown, the baby. He would end with a question: "Well, what do you think?" It was just a rhetorical question. In time, he had the feeling that he'd been telling the same story over and over to the same hitchhikers. He quit talking to hitchhikers when he realized how his voice sounded—whining and self-pitying, like some teenage-tragedy song. Now Leroy has the sudden impulse to tell Norma Jean about himself, as if he had just met her. They have known each other so long they have forgotten a lot about each other. They could become reacquainted. But when the oven timer goes off and she runs to the kitchen, he forgets why he wants to do this.

The next day, Mabel drops by. It is Saturday and Norma Jean is cleaning. Leroy is studying the plans of his log house, which have finally come in the mail. He has them spread out on the table—big sheets of stiff blue paper, with diagrams and numbers printed in white. While Norma Jean runs the vacuum, Mabel drinks coffee. She sets her coffee cup on a blueprint.

"I'm just waiting for time to pass," she says to Leroy, drumming her fingers on the table.

As soon as Norma Jean switches off the vacuum, Mabel says in a loud voice, "Did you hear about the datsun dog that killed the baby?"

Norma Jean says, "The word is 'dachshund.'"

"They put the dog on trial. It chewed the baby's legs off. The mother was in the next room all the time." She raises her voice. "They thought it was neglect."

Norma Jean is holding her ears. Leroy manages to open the refrigerator and get some Diet Pepsi to offer Mabel. Mabel still has some coffee and she waves away the Pepsi.

"Datsuns are like that," Mabel says. "They're jealous dogs. They'll tear a place to pieces if you don't keep an eye on them."

"You better watch out what you're saying, Mabel," says Leroy.

"Well, facts is facts."

Leroy looks out the window at his rig. It is like a huge piece of furniture gathering dust in the backyard. Pretty soon it will be an antique. He hears the vacuum cleaner. Norma Jean seems to be cleaning the living room rug again.

Later, she says to Leroy, "She just said that about the baby because she caught me smoking. She's trying to pay me back."

"What are you talking about?" Leroy says, nervously shuffling blueprints.

"You know good and well," Norma Jean says. She is sitting in a kitchen chair with her feet up and her arms wrapped around her knees. She looks small and helpless. She says, "The very idea, her bringing up a subject like that! Saying it was neglect."

"She didn't mean that," Leroy says.

"She might not have *thought* she meant it. She always says things like that. You don't know how she goes on."

"But she didn't really mean it. She was just talking."

Leroy opens a king-sized bottle of beer and pours it into two glasses, dividing it carefully. He hands a glass to Norma Jean and she takes it from him mechanically. For a long time, they sit by the kitchen window watching the birds at the feeder.

Something is happening. Norma Jean is going to night school. She has graduated from her six-week body-building course and now she is taking an adult-education course in composition at Paducah Community College. She spends her evenings out-lining paragraphs.

"First you have a topic sentence," she explains to Leroy. "Then you divide it up. Your secondary topic has to be connected to your primary topic."

To Leroy, this sounds intimidating. "I never was any good in English," he says.

"It makes a lot of sense."

"What are you doing this for, anyhow?"

She shrugs. "It's something to do." She stands up and lifts her dumbbells a few times.

"Driving a rig, nobody cared about my English."

"I'm not criticizing your English."

Norma Jean used to say, "If I lose ten minutes' sleep, I just drag all day." Now she stays up late, writing compositions. She got a B on her first paper—a how-to theme on soup-based casseroles. Recently Norma Jean has been cooking unusual foods—tacos, lasagna, Bombay chicken. She doesn't play the organ anymore, though her second paper was called "Why Music Is Important to Me." She sits at the kitchen table, con-centrating on her outlines, while Leroy plays with his log house plans, practicing with a set of Lincoln Logs. The thought of getting a truckload of notched, numbered logs scares him, and he wants to be prepared. As he and Norma Jean work together at the kitchen table, Leroy has the hopeful thought that they are sharing something, but he knows he is a fool to think this. Norma Jean is miles away. He knows he is going to lose her. Like Mabel, he is just waiting for time to pass.

One day, Mabel is there before Norma Jean gets home from work, and Leroy finds himself confiding in her. Mabel, he realizes, must know Norma Jean better than he does.

"I don't know what's got into that girl," Mabel says. "She used to go to bed with the chickens. Now you say she's up all hours. Plus her a-smoking. I like to died."

"I want to make her this beautiful home," Leroy says, indicating the Lincoln Logs. "I don't think she even wants it. Maybe she was happier with me gone."

"She don't know what to make of you, coming home like this."

"Is that it?"

Mabel takes the roof off his Lincoln Log cabin. "You couldn't get *me* in a log cabin," she says. "I was raised in one. It's no picnic, let me tell you."

"They're different now," says Leroy.

"I tell you what," Mabel says, smiling oddly at Leroy.

"What?"

"Take her on down to Shiloh. Y'all need to get out together, stir a little. Her brain's all balled up over them books."

Leroy can see traces of Norma Jean's features in her mother's face. Mabel's worn face has the texture of crinkled cotton, but suddenly she looks pretty. It occurs to Leroy that Mabel has been hinting all along that she wants them to take her with them to Shiloh.

"Let's all go to Shiloh," he says. "You and me and her. Come Sunday."

Mabel throws up her hands in protest. "Oh, no, not me. Young folks want to be by theirselves."

When Norma Jean comes in with groceries, Leroy says excitedly, "Your mama here's been dying to go to Shiloh for thirty-five years. It's about time we went, don't you think?"

"I'm not going to butt in on anybody's second honeymoon," Mabel says.

"Who's going on a honeymoon, for Christ's sake?" Norma Jean says loudly.

"I never raised no daughter of mine to talk that-a-way," Mabel says.

"You ain't seen nothing yet," says Norma Jean. She starts putting away boxes and cans, slamming cabinet doors.

"There's a log cabin at Shiloh," Mabel says. "It was there during the battle. There's bullet holes in it."

"When are you going to *shut up* about Shiloh, Mama?" asks Norma Jean.

"I always thought Shiloh was the prettiest place, so full of history," Mabel goes on. "I just hoped y'all could see it once before I die, so you could tell me about it." Later, she whispers to Leroy, "You do what I said. A little change is what she needs."

"Your name means 'the king,'" Norma Jean says to Leroy that evening. He is trying to get her to go to Shiloh, and she is reading a book about another century.

"Well, I reckon I ought to be right proud."

"I guess so."

"Am I still king around here?"

Norma Jean flexes her biceps and feels them for hardness. "I'm not fooling around with anybody, if that's what you mean," she says.

"Would you tell me if you were?"

"I don't know."

"What does *your* name mean?"

"It was Marilyn Monroe's real name."

"No kidding!"

"Norma comes from the Normans. They were invaders," she says. She closes her book and looks hard at Leroy. "I'll go to Shiloh with you if you'll stop staring at me."

On Sunday, Norma Jean packs a picnic and they go to Shiloh. To Leroy's relief, Mabel says she does not want to come with them. Norma Jean drives, and Leroy, sitting beside her, feels like some boring hitchhiker she has picked up. He tries some conversation, but she answers him in monosyllables. At Shiloh, she drives aimlessly through the park, past bluffs and trails and steep ravines. Shiloh is an immense place, and Leroy cannot see it as a battleground. It is not what he expected. He thought it would look like a golf course. Monuments are everywhere, showing through the thick clusters of trees. Norma Jean passes the log cabin Mabel mentioned. It is surrounded by tourists looking for bullet holes.

"That's not the kind of log house I've got in mind," says Leroy apologetically.

"I know *that*."

"This is a pretty place. Your mama was right."

"It's O.K.," says Norma Jean. "Well, we've seen it. I hope she's satisfied."

They burst out laughing together.

At the park museum, a movie on Shiloh is shown every half hour, but they decide that they don't want to see it. They buy a souvenir Confederate flag for Mabel, and then they find a picnic spot near the cemetery. Norma Jean has brought a picnic cooler, with pimiento sandwiches, soft drinks, and Yodels. Leroy eats a sandwich and then smokes a joint, hiding it behind the picnic cooler. Norma Jean has quit smoking altogether. She is picking cake crumbs from the cellophane wrapper, like a fussy bird.

Leroy says, "So the boys in gray ended up in Corinth. The Union soldiers zapped 'em finally, April 7, 1862."

They both know that he doesn't know any history. He is just talking about some of the historical plaques they have read. He feels awkward, like a boy on a date with an older girl. They are still just making conversation.

"Corinth is where Mama eloped to," says Norma Jean.

They sit in silence and stare at the cemetery for the Union dead and, beyond, at a tall cluster of trees. Campers are parked nearby, bumper to bumper, and small children in bright clothing are cavorting and squealing. Norma Jean wads up the cake wrapper and squeezes it tightly in her hand. Without looking at Leroy, she says, "I want to leave you."

Leroy takes a bottle of Coke out of the cooler and flips off the cap. He holds the bottle poised near his mouth but cannot remember to take a drink. Finally he says, "No, you don't."

"Yes, I do."

"I won't let you."

"You can't stop me."

"Don't do me that way."

Leroy knows Norma Jean will have her own way. "Didn't I promise to be home from now on?" he says.

"In some ways, a woman prefers a man who wanders," says Norma Jean. "That sounds crazy, I know."

"You're not crazy."

Leroy remembers to drink from his Coke. Then he says, "Yes, you *are* crazy. You and me could start all over again. Right back at the beginning."

"We *have* started all over again," says Norma Jean. "And this is how it turned out."

"What did I do wrong?"

"Nothing."

"Is this one of those women's lib things?" Leroy asks.

"Don't be funny."

The cemetery, a green slope dotted with white markers, looks like a subdivision site. Leroy is trying to comprehend that his marriage is breaking up, but for some reason he is wondering about white slabs in a graveyard.

"Everything was fine till Mama caught me smoking," says Norma Jean, standing up. "That set something off."

"What are you talking about?"

"She won't leave me alone—*you* won't leave me alone." Norma Jean seems to be crying, but she is looking away from him. "I feel eighteen again. I can't face that all over again." She starts walking away. "No, it *wasn't* fine. I don't know what I'm saying. Forget it."

Leroy takes a lungful of smoke and closes his eyes as Norma Jean's words sink in. He tries to focus on the fact that thirty-five hundred soldiers died on the grounds around him. He can only think of that war as a board game with plastic soldiers. Leroy almost smiles, as he compares the Confederates' daring attack on the Union camps and Virgil Mathis's raid on the bowling alley. General Grant, drunk and furious, shoved the Southerners back to Corinth, where Mabel and Jet Beasley were married years later, when Mabel was still thin and good-looking. The next day, Mabel and Jet visited the battleground, and then Norma Jean was born, and then she married Leroy and they had a baby, which they lost, and now Leroy and Norma Jean are here at the same battleground. Leroy knows he is leaving out a lot. He is leaving out the insides of history. History was always just names and dates to him. It occurs to him that building a house out of logs is similarly empty—too simple. And the real inner workings of a marriage, like most of history, have escaped him. Now he sees that building a log house is the dumbest idea he could have had. It was clumsy of him to think Norma Jean would want a log house. It was a crazy idea: He'll have to think of something else, quickly. He will wad the blueprints into tight balls and fling them into the lake. Then he'll get moving again. He opens his eyes. Norma Jean has moved away and is walking through the cemetery, following a serpentine brick path.

Leroy gets up to follow his wife, but his good leg is asleep and his bad leg still hurts him. Norma Jean is far away, walking rapidly toward the bluff by the river, and he tries to hobble toward her. Some children run past him, screaming noisily. Norma Jean has reached the bluff, and she is looking out over the Tennessee River. Now she turns toward Leroy and waves her arms. Is she beckoning to him? She seems to be doing an exercise for her chest muscles. The sky is unusually pale—the color of the dust ruffle Mabel made for their bed.

For Practice

1. What is the point of view in this story? What is the tone of the narrator towards the Moffitts?

2. What kind of marriage do Leroy and Norma Jean have? What details does Mason give us about their day-to-day existence? How does Leroy's injury change their lifestyle?

3. Compare the depiction of suburban life in "Shiloh" to that found in "Where Are You Going, Where Have You Been?" How are they similar? How are they different?

4. Do Leroy and Norma Jean romanticize their lives the way Connie does? Why does Leroy want to build his wife a log house? Why does Norma Jean want to improve herself by going to school? How does Norma Jean's mother react to the changes in her daughter? How does Leroy react to the changes in his wife?

5. Why do the Moffitts go to Shiloh? What effect does the trip have on them and why? What do you think the end of the story means?

Writing Your Own Arguments

1. In "The Child's Need for Magic," Bettelheim suggests that we leave behind the "childish" stories of our youth as we grow older. However, many of our childhood rituals set up expectations that carry into adulthood. How do the texts in this unit support or refute Bettelheim's thesis? How do you characterize the function of fantasy/myth/fairy tales in our adult lives? You might want to look at some of the current debates about Barbie or a discussion on film such as the one found in Susan Faludi's *Backlash* for some insight about the ways in which popular culture affects our society's constructions of beauty and romance.

2. Write an essay analyzing the relationship between a "classic" fairy tale (you could look at the versions of Charles Perrault or the Grimm Brothers) and a modern revision of that fairy tale. What do the changes in the tale suggest about culture/time from which each version came? Some suggestions:

   "Cinderella" and *Pretty Woman* or *Working Girl*
   "Beauty and the Beast" and the films of the same name by Disney or Cocteau
   "Beauty and the Beast" and *Wolf*
   "Hansel and Gretel" and Robert Coover's "The Gingerbread House"
   Anne Sexton's poems that are revisions of fairy tales
   "Little Red Riding Hood" and *The Company of Wolves*
   "Bluebeard" and *The Secret Beyond the Door* (a 1940s film)

3. "Shiloh" and "Where Are You Going, Where Have You Been?" are only two examples of contemporary stories which examine the impact of fantasy on our everyday lives. Like Marge Piercy's use of the Barbie Doll, these authors look at popular/consumer culture's influence on our fantasy life. How are movies, songs, and popular fiction like romance novels similar to fairy tales in the ways that they shape our conceptions of romance? Analyze the message about popular culture in either of these stories. Are they reinforcing old ideals? Creating new ones? In what ways do they suggest that fantasy is liberating and suburbia is restricting? Some other texts that you might look at: Robert Coover's "The Babysitter," John Cheever's "The Country Husband," John Updike's "A & P," Richard Linklater's *Suburbia*, Susan Seidelman's *Desperately Seeking Susan,* or Peter Bogdanovich's *The Last Picture Show.*

4. *Pretty Woman* is, in many ways, a parody or critique of the "Cinderella" story. While at one point the two female characters even discuss the ridiculousness of the story's "happily ever after" ending and the false promises this makes to women, the ending of the film follows the conventional romantic formula: the prostitute and the businessman live "happily ever after." Examine how a particular text critiques or reinforces romantic ideals about courtship and marriage. What constitutes a "good" marriage? How do fantastic narratives like fairy tales or romantic films shape our (and the characters in these stories) view of marriage? How do certain stories critique the idealization of marriage? Two plays that you might want to read for this question are Harold Pinter's *The Lover* and Edward Albee's *Who's Afraid of Virginia Woolf?* Both explicitly deal with the ways in which fantasy destroys the "real" in a marriage.

5. In *The Beauty Myth,* Naomi Wolf analyzes the importance of "beauty" in contemporary American culture. She stresses the fact that "beauty" is not a universal standard; instead it is "a currency system . . . determined by politics" and changes depending on particular cultural values and other circumstances. For example, in the late 1950s Marilyn Monroe's size 12 was viewed as a model of perfection, whereas today the size 2 "waif" models are considered "beautiful." What causes these different standards? Using the texts in this unit, examine how these standards have changed over the last few centuries. How have they remained the same?

6. Several of the works in this unit examine relationships between men and women and argue that these relationships are often stifling for women. Many of the works also deal with the differences between fantasy and reality in these relationships. What are the fantasies in these relationships? How do they differ from reality? Do you think that these works argue that such fantasies inevitable? Do you agree? Why or why not?

UNIT
FOUR

*And Justice for All?
Literature and the
Struggle for an
Equitable Society*

When you were in grade school, did you recite the Pledge of Allegiance each day? It contains a familiar definition of America: "one nation under God, indivisible, with liberty and justice for all." The values of unity, equality, and fairness expressed in the Pledge are central to the American vision of how society should function. One does not have to look very hard at our history, however, to realize that justice is much harder to attain than to talk about. Workers have fought to gain safe working conditions and reasonable pay; women struggled for decades to gain the right to vote which gives them a voice in American democracy; everyone has argued about when and how America should go to war. Perhaps the most crucial question of justice in American history, though, is found in the area of race relations. After all, we came very close to dissolving our "one nation" over this issue, and ever since the Civil War debates have raged over how to ensure that African-Americans and those of other racial backgrounds are treated fairly. These examples show that the American ideal of "justice for all" is actually something each generation labors to achieve, sometimes succeeding, sometimes not. America is not unique in its continuous struggle for social justice. Every society faces similar problems and responds to them within the context of its own history and culture.

Literature thus has much to teach us about how other cultures wrestle with the problems of justice.

Given the fact that so much effort and attention are applied to resolving problems of justice, it is only natural that literature reflects and comments upon specific instances where standards of justice are called into question. In *Antigonê*, a text written more than 2000 years ago, we see people who are very different from us in terms of their politics, lifestyle, and religion confronting an apparently universal dilemma: Should individuals follow the written laws composed by humans, or is there a divine law which transcends them? We continue to struggle with this question, as did seventeenth-century Puritans seeking a "city on a hill," and African-Americans fighting for civil rights. While the issue remains constant, its expression varies across time and cultures.

In fact, literature can be a powerful tool for helping readers understand and sympathize with others who are being denied fair treatment. Readers who learn to sympathize with those facing injustice will naturally desire to see their situation improved and might even be inspired to try to correct it themselves. Authors wishing to change some aspect of society therefore play upon the emotional power of literature to call readers to action. William Blake's poetic dramatization of the plight of children forced into labor as chimney sweeps evokes our sympathy and calls for action to remedy such conditions. Blake's call for action might now be mobilized in service of a similar situation in our own day—children of third-world countries who work in factories to produce consumer goods for first-world markets.

In questions of justice there is not always an easy answer. When you read the selections in this chapter, as well as others in this anthology, you should keep in mind that the authors are writing from a certain viewpoint which may not correspond with yours. It is important that, while you should be open to a full understanding of the author's intent in a given work, you also retain a healthy degree of skepticism about the views it presents. Is the author accurately representing the lives of those who are oppressed and those who are the oppressors? Are there other important ways of viewing the situation which the author neglects to portray? Is the author really seeking justice or just substituting one tyranny for another? Asking questions like these will help you avoid blindly accepting every author's notion of justice. On the contrary, they will help you test literary works against your own experience and ethical perspective, and doing so is a powerful way to refine your sense of what justice is and how it can be best achieved.

Antigonê

Sophocles

Sophocles (ca. 496/95–406 B.C.E.) was one of the three great 5th-century Greek tragedians (the other two being Aeschylus and Euripides). Though only seven of his plays survive, Sophocles composed more than 120 plays and won 18 victories at the City Dionysia, the most prestigious theatrical competition in Athens. Antigonê (ca. 442/41 B.C.E.) was part of one of those victories.

At the heart of Antigonê *are conflicting definitions of law (nomos) and debates regarding the authority of the city-state (polis) and its representatives. Antigonê, Ismenê, Eteoclês and Polyneicês are the children of Oedipus, former king of Thebes, who brought ruin to the state of Thebes when he (unwittingly) fulfilled a prophecy that he would kill his father and marry his own mother. Previous to the action of the play, Eteoclês banished Polyneicês who then amassed an army to attack his brother. Both brothers died in the battle, and the Theban throne went to Creon, uncle of the children of Oedipus. The initiating event of* Antigonê *is Creon's decree that Eteoclês be buried with full rites as a hero while Polyneicês is to be left unburied as a traitor. Furthermore, any violation of this edict would be punishable by death.*

As you read this play, you should consider carefully Antigonê's reasons for her actions. How should the individual act when the laws of the state come into conflict with family tradition and religious laws?

(an English version by Dudley Fitts and Robert Fitzgerald)

CHARACTERS

ANTIGONÊ	TEIRESIAS
ISMENÊ	A SENTRY
EURYDICÊ	A MESSENGER
CREON	CHORUS
HAIMON	

Scene: *Before the palace of* CREON, *King of Thebes. A central double door, and two lateral doors. A platform extends the length of the façade, and from this platform three steps lead down into the "orchestra" or chorus-ground.*

Time: *Dawn of the day after the repulse of the Argive army from the assault on Thebes.*

PROLOGUE

ANTIGONÊ *and* ISMENÊ *enter from the central door of the palace.*

ANTIGONÊ: Ismenê, dear sister,
    You would think that we had already suffered enough
    For the curse on Oedipus.°
    I cannot imagine any grief
    That you and I have not gone through. And now—   5
    Have they told you of the new decree of our King Creon?
ISMENÊ: I have heard nothing: I know
    That two sisters lost two brothers, a double death
    In a single hour; and I know that the Argive army
    Fled in the night; but beyond this, nothing.   10
ANTIGONÊ: I thought so. And that is why I wanted you
    To come out here with me. There is something we must do.
ISMENÊ: Why do you speak so strangely?
ANTIGONÊ: Listen, Ismenê.
    Creon buried our brother Eteoclês   15
    With military honors, gave him a soldier's funeral,
    And it was right that he should; but Polyneicês,
    Who fought as bravely and died as miserably,—
    They say that Creon has sworn
    No one shall bury him, no one mourn for him,   20
    But his body must lie in the fields, a sweet treasure
    For carrion birds to find as they search for food.
    That is what they say, and our good Creon is coming here
    To announce it publicly; and the penalty—
    Stoning to death in the public square!   25
                               There it is,
    And now you can prove what you are:
    A true sister, or a traitor to your family.
ISMENÊ: Antigonê, you are mad! What could I possibly do?
ANTIGONÊ: You must decide whether you will help me or not.   30
ISMENÊ: I do not understand you. Help you in what?
ANTIGONÊ: Ismenê, I am going to bury him. Will you come?
ISMENÊ: Bury him! You have just said the new law forbids it.
ANTIGONÊ: He is my brother. And he is your brother, too.
ISMENÊ: But think of the danger! Think what Creon will do!   35
ANTIGONÊ: Creon is not strong enough to stand in my way.
ISMENÊ: Ah sister!
    Oedipus died, everyone hating him
    For what his own search brought to light, his eyes
    Ripped out by his own hand; and Iocastê died,   40
    His mother and wife at once she twisted the cords

3 Oedipus, former King of Thebes, father of Antigonê and Ismenê, and of Polyneicês, and Eteoclês, their brothers. Oedipus unwittingly killed his father, Laïos, and married his mother, Iocastê. When he learned what he had done, he blinded himself and left Thebes. Eteoclês and Polyneicês quarreled; Polyneicês was defeated but returned to assault Thebes. Both brothers were killed in battle; Creon ordered that Polyneicês remain unburied.

That strangled her life; and our two brothers died,
Each killed by the other's sword. And we are left:
But oh, Antigonê,
Think how much more terrible than these
Our own death would be if we should go against Creon   45
And do what he has forbidden! We are only women,
We cannot fight with men, Antigonê!
The law is strong, we must give in to the law
In this thing, and in worse. I beg the Dead
To forgive me, but I am helpless: I must yield   50
To those in authority. And I think it is dangerous business
To be always meddling.

ANTIGONÊ: If that is what you think,
I should not want you, even if you asked to come.
You have made your choice, you can be what you want to be.
But I will bury him; and if I must die,   55
I say that this crime is holy: I shall lie down
With him in death, and I shall be as dear
To him as he to me.
                              It is the dead,
Not the living, who make the longest demands:
We die for ever . . .
                              You do as you like,   60
Since apparently the laws of the gods mean nothing to you.

ISMENÊ: They mean a great deal to me; but I have no strength
To break laws that were made for the public good.

ANTIGONÊ: That must be your excuse, I suppose. But as for me,
I will bury the brother I love.

ISMENÊ: Antigonê,   65
I am so afraid for you!

ANTIGONÊ: You need not be:
You have yourself to consider, after all.

ISMENÊ: But no one must hear of this, you must tell no one!
I will keep it a secret, I promise!

ANTIGONÊ: Oh tell it! Tell everyone!
Think how they'll hate you when it all comes out   70
If they learn that you knew about it all the time!

ISMENÊ: So fiery! You should be cold with fear.

ANTIGONÊ: Perhaps. But I am doing only what I must.

ISMENÊ: But can you do it? I say that you cannot.

ANTIGONÊ: Very well: when my strength gives out,
I shall do no more.   75

ISMENÊ: Impossible things should not be tried at all.

ANTIGONÊ: Go away, Ismenê:
I shall be hating you soon, and the dead will too,
For your words are hateful. Leave me my foolish plan:
I am not afraid of the danger; if it means death,   80
It will not be the worst of deaths—death without honor.

ISMENÊ: Go then, if you feel that you must.
    You are unwise,
    But a loyal friend indeed to those who love you.

    Exit into the Palace. ANTIGONÊ *goes off, left. Enter the* CHORUS.

PARODOS

Strophe 1

CHORUS: Now the long blade of the sun, lying
    Level east to west, touches with glory
    Thebes of the Seven Gates. Open, unlidded
    Eye of golden day! O marching light
    Across the eddy and rush of Dircê's stream,°   5
    Striking the white shields of the enemy
    Thrown headlong backward from the blaze of morning!
CHORAGOS:° Polyneicês their commander
    Roused them with windy phrases,
    He the wild eagle screaming   10
    Insults above our land,
    His wings their shields of snow,
    His crest their marshalled helms.

Antistrophe 1

CHORUS: Against our seven gates in a yawning ring
    The famished spears came onward in the night;   15
    But before his jaws were sated with our blood,
    Or pinefire took the garland of our towers,
    He was thrown back; and as he turned, great Thebes—
    No tender victim for his noisy power—
    Rose like a dragon behind him, shouting war.   20
CHORAGOS: For God hates utterly
    The bray of bragging tongues;
    And when he beheld their smiling,
    Their swagger of golden helms,
    The frown of his thunder blasted   25
    Their first man from our walls.

Strophe 2

CHORUS: We heard his shout of triumph high in the air
    Turn to a scream; far out in a flaming arc
    He fell with his windy torch, and the earth struck him.
    And others storming in fury no less than his   30
    Found shock of death in the dusty joy of battle.
CHORAGOS: Seven captains at seven gates
    Yielded their clanging arms to the god
    That bends the battle-line and breaks it.
    These two only, brothers in blood,   35

---

5 Dircê's stream—river near Thebes.   8 Choragos—leader of the chorus.

Face to face in matchless rage,
Mirroring each the other's death,
Clashed in long combat.

Antistrophe 2

CHORUS: But now in the beautiful morning of victory
    Let Thebes of the many chariots sing for joy!   40
    With hearts for dancing we'll take leave of war:
    Our temples shall be sweet with hymns of praise,
    And the long night shall echo with our chorus.

SCENE I

CHORAGOS: But now at last our new King is coming:
    Creon of Thebes, Menoikeus' son.
    In this auspicious dawn of his reign
    What are the new complexities
    That shifting Fate has woven for him?   5
    What is his counsel? Why has he summoned
    The old men to hear him?

Enter CREON *from the palace, center. He addresses the* CHORUS *from the top step.*

CREON: Gentlemen: I have the honor to inform you that our Ship of State, which recent storms have threatened to destroy, has come safely to harbor at last, guided by the merciful wisdom of Heaven. I have summoned you here this 10 morning because I know that I can depend upon you: your devotion to King Laïos was absolute; you never hesitated in your duty to our late ruler Oedipus; and when Oedipus died, your loyalty was transferred to his children. Unfortunately, as you know, his two sons, the princes Eteoclês and Polyneicês, have killed each other in battle; and I, as the next in blood, have succeeded to 15 the full power of the throne.

    I am aware, of course, that no Ruler can expect complete loyalty from his subjects until he has been tested in office. Nevertheless, I say to you at the very outset that I have nothing but contempt for the kind of Governor who is afraid, for whatever reason, to follow the course that he knows is best for the State; 20 and as for the man who sets private friendship above the public welfare,—I have no use for him, either. I call God to witness that if I saw my country headed for ruin, I should not be afraid to speak out plainly; and I need hardly remind you that I would never have any dealings with an enemy of the people. No one values friendship more highly than I; but we must remember that friends made at 25 the risk of wrecking our Ship are not real friends at all.

    These are my principles, at any rate, and that is why I have made the following decision concerning the sons of Oedipus: Eteoclês, who died as a man should die, fighting for his country, is to be buried with full military honors, with all the ceremony that is usual when the greatest heroes die; but his broth- 30 er Polyneicês, who broke his exile to come back with fire and sword against his native city and the shrines of his fathers' gods, whose one idea was to spill the blood of his blood and sell his own people into slavery—Polyneicês, I say, is to have no burial: no man is to touch him or say the least prayer for him; he shall lie on the plain, unburied; and the birds and the scavenging dogs can do with 35 him whatever they like.

This is my command, and you can see the wisdom behind it. As long as I
am King, no traitor is going to be honored with the loyal man. But whoever
shows by word and deed that he is on the side of the State,—he shall have my
respect while he is living and my reverence when he is dead.   40
CHORAGOS: If that is your will, Creon son of Menoikeus,
   You have the right to enforce it: we are yours.
CREON: That is my will. Take care that you do your part.
CHORAGOS: We are old men: let the younger ones carry it out.
CREON: I do not mean that: the sentries have been appointed.   45
CHORAGOS: Then what is it that you would have us do?
CREON: You will give no support to whoever breaks this law.
CHORAGOS: Only a crazy man is in love with death!
CREON: And death it is; yet money talks, and the wisest
   Have sometimes been known to count a few coins too many.   50

Enter SENTRY *from left.*

SENTRY : I'll not say that I'm out of breath from running, King, because every time
   I stopped to think about what I have to tell you, I felt like going back. And all
   the time a voice kept saying, "You fool, don't you know you're walking straight
   into trouble?"; and then another voice: "Yes, but if you let somebody else get   55
   the news to Creon first, it will be even worse than that for you!" But good sense
   won out, at least I hope it was good sense, and here I am with a story that makes
   no sense at all; but I'll tell it anyhow, because, as they say, what's going to hap-
   pen's going to happen, and—
CREON: Come to the point. What have you to say?   60
SENTRY : I did not do it. I did not see who did it. You must not punish me for what
   someone else has done.
CREON: A comprehensive defense! More effective, perhaps,
   If I knew its purpose. Come: what is it?   65
SENTRY : A dreadful thing . . . I don't know how to put it—
CREON: Out with it!
SENTRY: Well, then;
   The dead man—
                  Polyneicês—   70

Pause. The SENTRY *is overcome, fumbles for words.* CREON *waits impassively.*

            out there—
                    someone,—
   New dust on the slimy flesh!

            Pause. No sign from CREON.

   Someone has given it burial that way, and   75
   Gone . . .

            Long pause. CREON *finally speaks with deadly control:*

CREON: And the man who dared do this?
SENTRY :   I swear I
   Do not know! You must believe me!
   Listen: 80
   The ground was dry, not a sign of digging, no,
   Not a wheeltrack in the dust, no trace of anyone.

It was when they relieved us this morning: and one of them,
The corporal, pointed to it.

                 There it was,   85

The strangest—

        Look:

The body, just mounded over with light dust: you see?
Not buried really, but as if they'd covered it
Just enough for the ghost's peace. And no sign   90
Of dogs or any wild animal that had been there,
And then what a scene there was! Every man of us
Accusing the other: we all proved the other man did it,
We all had proof that we could not have done it.
We were ready to take hot iron in our hands,   95
Walk through fire, swear by all the gods,
It was not I!
I do not know who it was, but it was not I!

      CREON's *rage has been mounting steadily, but the* SENTRY *is*
         too intent upon his story to notice it.

And then, when this came to nothing, someone said
A thing that silenced us and made us stare   100
Down at the ground: you had to be told the news,
And one of us had to do it! We threw the dice,
And the bad luck fell to me. So here I am,
No happier to be here than you are to have me:
Nobody likes the man who brings bad news.   105

CHORAGOS: I have been wondering, King: can it be that the gods have done this?

CREON: *(furiously)* Stop!

Must you doddering wrecks
Go out of your heads entirely? "The gods"!
Intolerable!   110
The gods favor this corpse? Why? How had he served them?
Tried to loot their temples, burn their images,
Yes, and the whole State, and its laws with it!
Is it your senile opinion that the gods love to honor bad men?
A pious thought!—   115

          No, from the very beginning
There have been those who have whispered together,
Stiff-necked anarchists, putting their heads together,
Scheming against me in alleys. These are the men,
And they have bribed my own guard to do this thing.   120
(Sententiously.) Money!
There's nothing in the world so demoralizing as money.
Down go your cities,
Homes gone, men gone, honest hearts corrupted,
Crookedness of all kinds, and all for money!

        (To SENTRY*)*

          But you—!

I swear by God and by the throne of God,   125
The man who has done this thing shall pay for it!
Find that man, bring him here to me, or your death
Will be the least of your problems: I'll string you up
Alive, and there will be certain ways to make you
Discover your employer before you die;   120
And the process may teach you a lesson you seem to have missed:
The dearest profit is sometimes all too dear:
That depends on the source. Do you understand me?
A fortune won is often misfortune.

SENTRY: King, may I speak?   125
CREON: Your very voice distresses me.
SENTRY: Are you sure that it is my voice, and not your conscience?
CREON: By God, he wants to analyze me now!
SENTRY: It is not what I say, but what has been done, that hurts you.
CREON: You talk too much.   130
SENTRY: Maybe; but I've done nothing.
CREON: Sold your soul for some silver: that's all you've done.
SENTRY: How dreadful it is when the right judge judges wrong!
CREON: Your figures of speech
May entertain you now; but unless you bring me the man,   135
You will get little profit from them in the end.

        Exit CREON *into the palace.*

SENTRY: "Bring me the man"—!
I'd like nothing better than bringing him the man!
But bring him or not, you have seen the last of me here.   140
At any rate, I am safe!

        Exit SENTRY.

        ODE I

Strophe 1

CHORUS: Numberless are the world's wonders, but none
    More wonderful than man; the stormgray sea
    Yields to his prows, the huge crests bear him high;
    Earth, holy and inexhaustible, is graven
    With shining furrows where his plows have gone   5
    Year after year, the timeless labor of stallions.

Antistrophe I

    The lightboned birds and beasts that cling to cover,
    The lithe fish lighting their reaches of dim water,
    All are taken, tamed in the net of his mind;
    The lion on the hill, the wild horse windy-maned,   10
    Resign to him; and his blunt yoke has broken
    The sultry shoulders of the mountain bull.

Strophe 2

    Words also, and thought as rapid as air,
    He fashions to his good use; statecraft is his,

And his the skill that deflects the arrows of snow,   15
The spears of winter rain: from every wind
He has made himself secure—from all but one:
In the late wind of death he cannot stand.

Antistrophe 2

O clear intelligence, force beyond all measure!
O fate of man, working both good and evil!   20
When the laws are kept, how proudly his city stands!
When the laws are broken, what of his city then?
Never may the anárchic man find rest at my hearth,
Never be it said that my thoughts are his thoughts.

SCENE II

Reenter SENTRY *leading* ANTIGONÊ.

CHORAGOS: What does this mean? Surely this captive woman
Is the Princess, Antigonê. Why should she be taken?
Sentry: Here is the one who did it! We caught her
In the very act of burying him.—Where is Creon?
CHORAGOS: Just coming from the house.   5

Enter CREON, *center.*

CREON: What has happened?
Why have you come back so soon?
SENTRY: *(Expansively).*   O King,
A man should never be too sure of anything:
I would have sworn   10
That you'd not see me here again: your anger
Frightened me so, and the things you threatened me with;
But how could I tell then
That I'd be able to solve the case so soon?
No dice-throwing this time: I was only too glad to come!
Here is this woman. She is the guilty one: 15
We found her trying to bury him.
Take her, then; question her; judge her as you will.
I am through with the whole thing now, and glad of it.
CREON: But this is Antigonê! Why have you brought her here?
SENTRY: She was burying him, I tell you!   20
CREON: *(severely).*   Is this the truth?
SENTRY: I saw her with my own eyes. Can I say more?
CREON: The details: come, tell me quickly!
SENTRY: It was like this:
After those terrible threats of yours, King,   25
We went back and brushed the dust away from the body.
The flesh was soft by now, and stinking,
So we sat on a hill to windward and kept guard.
No napping this time! We kept each other awake.
But nothing happened until the white round sun   30
Whirled in the center of the round sky over us:

Then, suddenly,
A storm of dust roared up from the earth, and the sky
Went out, the plain vanished with all its trees
In the stinging dark. We closed our eyes and endured it.
The whirlwind lasted a long time, but it passed;   35
And then we looked, and there was Antigonê!
I have seen
A mother bird come back to a stripped nest, heard
Her crying bitterly a broken note or two
For the young ones stolen. Just so, when this girl   40
Found the bare corpse, and all her love's work wasted,
She wept, and cried on heaven to damn the hands
That had done this thing.
                  And then she brought more dust
And sprinkled wine three times for her brother's ghost.   45
We ran and took her at once. She was not afraid,
Not even when we charged her with what she had done.
She denied nothing.
             And this was a comfort to me,
And some uneasiness: for it is a good thing   50
To escape from death, but it is no great pleasure
To bring death to a friend.
              Yet I always say
There is nothing so comfortable as your own safe skin!
CREON: *(slowly, dangerously).* And you, Antigonê,   55
   You with your head hanging,—do you confess this thing?
ANTIGONÊ: I do. I deny nothing.
CREON: *(to* SENTRY*)*   You may go.

                (Exit SENTRY.*)*

(To ANTIGONÊ*)* Tell me, tell me briefly:
   Had you heard my proclamation touching this matter?   60
ANTIGONÊ: It was public. Could I help hearing it?
CREON: And yet you dared defy the law.
ANTIGONÊ: I dared.
   It was not God's proclamation. That final Justice
   That rules the world below makes no such laws.   65

   Your edict, King, was strong,
   But all your strength is weakness itself against
   The immortal unrecorded laws of God.
   They are not merely now: they were, and shall be,
   Operative for ever, beyond man utterly.   70

   I knew I must die, even without your decree:
   I am only mortal. And if I must die
   Now, before it is my time to die,
   Surely this is no hardship: can anyone
   Living, as I live, with evil all about me,   75
   Think Death less than a friend? This death of mine

Is of no importance; but if I had left my brother
Lying in death unburied, I should have suffered.
Now I do not.
              You smile at me. Ah Creon,   80
Think me a fool, if you like; but it may well be
That a fool convicts me of folly.
CHORAGOS: Like father, like daughter: both headstrong, deaf to reason!
    She has never learned to yield.
CREON: She has much to learn.   85
    The inflexible heart breaks first, the toughest iron
    Cracks first, and the wildest horses bend their necks
    At the pull of the smallest curb.
    Pride? In a slave?
    This girl is guilty of a double insolence,   90
    Breaking the given laws and boasting of it.
    Who is the man here,
    She or I, if this crime goes unpunished?
    Sister's child, or more than sister's child,
    Or closer yet in blood—she and her sister   95
    Win bitter death for this!

                (To SERVANTS.*)*
              Go, some of you,
    Arrest Ismenê. I accuse her equally.
    Bring her: you will find her sniffling in the house there.

    Her mind's a traitor: crimes kept in the dark   100
    Cry for light, and the guardian brain shudders;
    But how much worse than this
    Is brazen boasting of barefaced anarchy!
ANTIGONÊ: Creon, what more do you want than my death?
CREON: Nothing.
    That gives me everything.   105
    ANTIGONÊ: Then I beg you: kill me.
    This talking is a great weariness: your words
    Are distasteful to me, and I am sure that mine
    Seem so to you. And yet they should not seem so:
    I should have praise and honor for what I have done.   110
    All these men here would praise me
    Were their lips not frozen shut with fear of you.
    (Bitterly.) Ah the good fortune of kings,
    Licensed to say and do whatever they please!
CREON: You are alone here in that opinion.   115
ANTIGONÊ: No, they are with me. But they keep their tongues in leash.
CREON: Maybe. But you are guilty, and they are not.
ANTIGONÊ: There is no guilt in reverence for the dead.
CREON: But Eteoclês—was he not your brother too?
ANTIGONÊ: My brother too.   120
CREON: And you insult his memory?
ANTIGONÊ: *(softly).* The dead man would not say that I insult it.

CREON: He would: for you honor a traitor as much as him.

ANTIGONÊ: His own brother; traitor or not, and equal in blood.

CREON: He made war on his country. Eteoclês defended it.   125

ANTIGONÊ: Nevertheless, there are honors due all the dead.

CREON: But not the same for the wicked as for the just.

ANTIGONÊ: Ah Creon, Creon,

    Which of us can say what the gods hold wicked?

CREON: An enemy is an enemy, even dead.   130

ANTIGONÊ: It is my nature to join in love, not hate.

CREON *(finally losing patience)*. Go join them, then; if you must have your love,

    Find it in hell!

CHORAGOS: But see, Ismenê comes:

             Enter ISMENÊ, *guarded.*

    Those tears are sisterly, the cloud   135

    That shadows her eyes rains down gentle sorrow.

CREON: You too, Ismenê,

    Snake in my ordered house, sucking my blood

    Stealthily—and all the time I never knew

    That these two sisters were aiming at my throne!   140

                     Ismenê,

    Do you confess your share in this crime, or deny it?

    Answer me.

ISMENÊ: Yes, if she will let me say so. I am guilty.

ANTIGONÊ *(coldly)*. No, Ismenê. You have no right to say so.   145

    You would not help me, and I will not have you help me.

ISMENÊ: But now I know what you meant; and I am here

    To join you, to take my share of punishment.

ANTIGONÊ: The dead man and the gods who rule the dead

    Know whose act this was. Words are not friends.   150

ISMENÊ: Do you refuse me, Antigonê? I want to die with you:

    I too have a duty that I must discharge to the dead.

ANTIGONÊ: You shall not lessen my death by sharing it.

ISMENÊ: What do I care for life when you are dead?

ANTIGONÊ: Ask Creon. You're always hanging on his opinions.   155

ISMENÊ: You are laughing at me. Why, Antigonê?

ANTIGONÊ: It's a joyless laughter, Ismenê.

ISMENÊ: But can I do nothing?

ANTIGONÊ: Yes. Save yourself. I shall not envy you.

    There are those who will praise you; I shall have honor, too.   160

ISMENÊ: But we are equally guilty!

ANTIGONÊ: No more, Ismenê.

    You are alive, but I belong to Death.

CREON *(to the chorus)*. Gentlemen, I beg you to observe these girls:

    One has just now lost her mind; the other,   165

    It seems, has never had a mind at all.

ISMENÊ: Grief teaches the steadiest minds to waver, King.

CREON: Yours certainly did, when you assumed guilt with the guilty!

ISMENÊ: But how could I go on living without her?

CREON: You are.   170
    She is already dead.
ISMENÊ: But your own son's bride!
CREON: There are places enough for him to push his plow.
    I want no wicked women for my sons!
ISMENÊ: O dearest Haimon, how your father wrongs you!   175
CREON: I've had enough of your childish talk of marriage!
CHORAGOS: Do you really intend to steal this girl from your son?
CREON: No; Death will do that for me.
CHORAGOS: Then she must die?
CREON *(ironically)* You dazzle me.   180
             —But enough of this talk!
    (To GUARDS.*)* You, there, take them away and guard them well:
    For they are but women, and even brave men run
    When they see Death coming.

            Exeunt ISMENÊ, ANTIGONÊ, *and* GUARDS

ODE II

Strophe 1

CHORUS: Fortunate is the man who has never tasted God's vengeance!
    Where once the anger of heaven has struck, that house is shaken
    For ever: damnation rises behind each child
    Like a wave cresting out of the black northeast,
    When the long darkness under sea roars up   5
    And bursts drumming death upon the windwhipped sand.

Antistrophe 1

    I have seen this gathering sorrow from time long past
    Loom upon Oedipus' children: generation from generation
    Takes the compulsive rage of the enemy god.
    So lately this last flower of Oedipus' line   10
    Drank the sunlight! but now a passionate word
    And a handful of dust have closed up all its beauty.

Strophe 2

        What mortal arrogance
        Transcends the wrath of Zeus?
    Sleep cannot lull him, nor the effortless long months   15
    Of the timeless gods: but he is young for ever,
    And his house is the shining day of high Olympos.
        All that is and shall be,
        And all the past, is his.
    No pride on earth is free of the curse of heaven.   20

Antistrophe 2

    The straying dreams of men
        May bring them ghosts of joy:
    But as they drowse, the waking embers burn them;
    Or they walk with fixed eyes as blind men walk.
    But the ancient wisdom speaks for our own time: 25

Fate works most for woe
With Folly's fairest show.
Man's little pleasure is the spring of sorrow.

SCENE III

CHORAGOS: But here is Haimon, King, the last of all your sons.
    Is it grief for Antigonê that brings him here,
    And bitterness at being robbed of his bride?

Enter HAIMON.

CREON: We shall soon see, and no need of diviners.

—Son,   5

    You have heard my final judgment on that girl:
    Have you come here hating me, or have you come
    With deference and with love, whatever I do?
HAIMON: I am your son, father. You are my guide.
    You make things clear for me, and I obey you.   10
    No marriage means more to me than your continuing wisdom.
CREON: Good. That is the way to behave: subordinate
    Everything else, my son, to your father's will.
    This is what a man prays for, that he may get
    Sons attentive and dutiful in his house,   15
    Each one hating his father's enemies,
    Honoring his father's friends. But if his sons
    Fail him, if they turn out unprofitably,
    What has he fathered but trouble for himself
    And amusement for the malicious?   20

So you are right

    Not to lose your head over this woman.
    Your pleasure with her would soon grow cold, Haimon,
    And then you'd have a hellcat in bed and elsewhere.
    Let her find her husband in Hell!   25
    Of all the people in this city, only she
    Has had contempt for my law and broken it.

    Do you want me to show myself weak before the people?
    Or to break my sworn word? No, and I will not.
    The woman dies.   30
    I suppose she'll plead "family ties." Well, let her.
    If I permit my own family to rebel,
    How shall I earn the world's obedience?
    Show me the man who keeps his house in hand,
    He's fit for public authority.   35

I'll have no dealings

    With law-breakers, critics of the government:
    Whoever is chosen to govern should be obeyed—
    Must be obeyed, in all things, great and small,
    Just and unjust! O Haimon,   40
    The man who knows how to obey, and that man only,
    Knows how to give commands when the time comes.

You can depend on him, no matter how fast
The spears come: he's a good soldier, he'll stick it out.

Anarchy, anarchy! Show me a greater evil!   45
This is why cities tumble and the great houses rain down,
This is what scatters armies!
No, no: good lives are made so by discipline.
We keep the laws then, and the lawmakers,
And no woman shall seduce us. If we must lose,   50
Let's lose to a man, at least! Is a woman stronger than we?
CHORAGOS: Unless time has rusted my wits,
    What you say, King, is said with point and dignity.
HAIMON *(boyishly earnest).* Father:
    Reason is God's crowning gift to man, and you are right.   55
To warn me against losing mine. I cannot say—
I hope that I shall never want to say!—that you
Have reasoned badly. Yet there are other men
Who can reason, too; and their opinions might be helpful.
You are not in a position to know everything   60
That people say or do, or what they feel:
Your temper terrifies them—everyone
Will tell you only what you like to hear.
But I, at any rate, can listen; and I have heard them
Muttering and whispering in the dark about this girl.   65
They say no woman has ever, so unreasonably,
Died so shameful a death for a generous act:
"She covered her brother's body. Is this indecent?
She kept him from dogs and vultures. Is this a crime?
Death?—She should have all the honor that we can give her!"   70
This is the way they talk out there in the city.

You must believe me:
Nothing is closer to me than your happiness.
What could be closer? Must not any son
Value his father's fortune as his father does his?   75
I beg you, do not be unchangeable:
Do not believe that you alone can be right.
The man who thinks that,
The man who maintains that only he has the power
To reason correctly, the gift to speak, the soul—
A man like that, when you know him, turns out empty.   80

It is not reason never to yield to reason!

In flood time you can see how some trees bend,
And because they bend, even their twigs are safe,
While stubborn trees are torn up, roots and all.
And the same thing happens in sailing: 85
Make your sheet fast, never slacken,—and over you go,
Head over heels and under: and there's your voyage.
Forget you are angry! Let yourself be moved!
I know I am young; but please let me say this:

The ideal condition 90
Would be, I admit, that men should be right by instinct;
But since we are all too likely to go astray,
The reasonable thing is to learn from those who can teach.

CHORAGOS: You will do well to listen to him, King,
If what he says is sensible. And you, Haimon, 95
Must listen to your father.—Both speak well.

CREON: You consider it right for a man of my years and experience
To go to school to a boy?

HAIMON: It is not right
If I am wrong. But if I am young, and right, 100
What does my age matter?

CREON: You think it right to stand up for an anarchist?

HAIMON: Not at all. I pay no respect to criminals.

CREON: Then she is not a criminal?

HAIMON: The City would deny it, to a man. 105

CREON: And the City proposes to teach me how to rule?

HAIMON: Ah. Who is it that's talking like a boy now?

CREON: My voice is the one voice giving orders in this City!

HAIMON: It is no City if it takes orders from one voice.

CREON: The State is the King! 110

HAIMON: Yes, if the State is a desert.

Pause.

CREON: This boy, it seems, has sold out to a woman.

HAIMON: If you are a woman: my concern is only for you.

CREON: So? Your "concern"! In a public brawl with your father!

HAIMON: How about you, in a pubic brawl with justice? 115

CREON: With justice, when all that I do is within my rights?

HAIMON: You have no right to trample on God's right.

CREON *(completely out of control.)* Fool, adolescent fool! Taken in by a woman!

HAIMON: You'll never see me taken in by anything vile.

CREON: Every word you say is for her!

Haimon *(quietly, darkly).*   And for you. 120
And for me. And for the gods under the earth.

CREON: You'll never marry her while she lives.

HAIMON: Then she must die.—But her death will cause another.

CREON: Another?
Have you lost your senses? Is this an open threat? 125

HAIMON: There is no threat in speaking to emptiness.

CREON: I swear you'll regret this superior tone of yours!
You are the empty one!

HAIMON: If you were not my father, I'd say you
were perverse. 130

CREON: You girlstruck fool, don't play at words with me!

HAIMON: I am sorry. You prefer silence.

CREON: Now, by God—!
I swear, by all the gods in heaven above us,
You'll watch it, I swear you shall! 135

(To the SERVANTS*)*

Bring her out! 140
Bring the woman out! Let her die before his eyes!
Here, this instant, with her bridegroom beside her!
HAIMON: Not here, no; she will not die here, King.
And you will never see my face again.
Go on raving as long as you've a friend to endure you. 145

(Exit HAIMON.*)*

CHORAGOS: Gone, gone.
Creon, a young man in a rage is dangerous!
CREON: Let him do, or dream to do, more than a man can.
He shall not save these girls from death.
CHORAGOS: These girls? 150
You have sentenced them both?
CREON: No, you are right.
I will not kill the one whose hands are clean.
CHORAGOS: But Antigonê?
Creon *(somberly).* I will carry her far away 155
Out there in the wilderness, and lock her
Living in a vault of stone. She shall have food,
As the custom is, to absolve the State of her death.
And there let her pray to the gods of hell:
They are her only gods: 160
Perhaps they will show her an escape from death,
Or she may learn,
though late,
That piety shown the dead is pity in vain.

(Exit CREON.*)*

ODE III

Strophe

CHORUS: Love, unconquerable
Waster of rich men, keeper
Of warm lights and all-night vigil
In the soft face of a girl:
Sea-wanderer, forest-visitor! 5
Even the pure Immortals cannot escape you,
And mortal man, in his one day's dusk,
Trembles before your glory.

Antistrophe

Surely you swerve upon ruin
The just man's consenting heart, 10
As here you have made bright anger
Strike between father and son—
And none has conquered but Love!
A girl's glánce wórking the will of heaven:

Pleasure to her alone who mocks us,   15
Merciless Aphroditê.°

SCENE IV

CHORAGOS *(as* ANTIGONÊ *enters guarded)*. But I can no longer stand
    in awe of this,
Nor, seeing what I see, keep back my tears.
Here is Antigonê, passing to that chamber
Where all find sleep at last.

Strophe I

ANTIGONÊ: Look upon me, friends, and pity me   5
    Turning back at the night's edge to say
    Good-by to the sun that shines for me no longer;
    Now sleepy Death
    Summons me down to Acheron,° that cold shore:
    There is no bridesong there, nor any music.   10
CHORUS: Yet not unpraised, not without a kind of honor,
    You walk at last into the underworld;
    Untouched by sickness, broken by no sword.
    What woman has ever found your way to death?

Antistrophe 1

ANTIGONÊ: How often I have heard the story of Niobê,   15
    Tantalos' wretched daughter, how the stone
    Clung fast about her, ivy-close: and they say
    The rain falls endlessly
    And sifting soft snow; her tears are never done.
    I feel the loneliness of her death in mine.   20
CHORUS: But she was born of heaven, and you
    Are woman, woman-born. If her death is yours,
    A mortal woman's, is this not for you
    Glory in our world and in the world beyond?

Strophe 2

ANTIGONÊ: You laugh at me. Ah, friends, friends,   25
    Can you not wait until I am dead? O Thebes,
    O men many-charioted, in love with Fortune,
    Dear springs of Dircê, sacred Theban grove,
    Be witnesses for me, denied all pity,
    Unjustly judged! and think a word of love   30
    For her whose path turns
    Under dark earth, where there are no more tears.
CHORUS: You have passed beyond human daring and come at last
    Into a place of stone where Justice sits.
    I cannot tell   35
    What shape of your father's guilt appears in this.

16 Aphroditê—goddess of love.   9 Acheron—a river of the underworld.

Antistrophe 2

ANTIGONÊ: You have touched it at last: that bridal bed
    Unspeakable, horror of son and mother mingling:
    Their crime, infection of all our family!
    O Oedipus, father and brother!   40
    Your marriage strikes from the grave to murder mine.
    I have been a stranger here in my own land:
    All my life
    The blasphemy of my birth has followed me.
CHORUS: Reverence is a virtue, but strength   45
    Lives in established law: that must prevail.
    You have made your choice,
    Your death is the doing of your conscious hand.

Epode

ANTIGONÊ: Then let me go, since all your words are bitter,   50
    And the very light of the sun is cold to me.
    Lead me to my vigil, where I must have
    Neither love nor lamentation; no song, but silence.

                    CREON *interrupts impatiently.*

CREON: If dirges and planned lamentations could put off death,
    Men would be singing for ever.

                    (To the SERVANTS*).*

                                    Take her, go!
    You know your orders: take her to the vault   55
    And leave her alone there. And if she lives or dies,
    That's her affair, not ours: our hands are clean.
ANTIGONÊ: O tomb, vaulted bride-bed in eternal rock,
    Soon I shall be with my own again
    Where Persephone° welcomes the thin ghosts underground: 60
    And I shall see my father again, and you, mother,
    And dearest Polyneicês—
                        dearest indeed
    To me, since it was my hand
    That washed him clean and poured the ritual wine:
    And my reward is death before my time!   65

    And yet, as men's hearts know, I have done no wrong.
    I have not sinned before God. Or if I have,
    I shall know the truth in death. But if the guilt
    Lies upon Creon who judged me, then, I pray,
    May his punishment equal my own.
CHORAGOS: O passionate heart,   70
    Unyielding, tormented still by the same winds!
CREON: Her guards shall have good cause to regret their delaying.
ANTIGONÊ: Ah! That voice is like the voice of death!

60 Persephonê—queen of the underworld.

CREON: I can give you no reason to think you are mistaken.
ANTIGONÊ: Thebes, and you my fathers' gods,   75
    And rulers of Thebes, you see me now, the last
    Unhappy daughter of a line of kings,
    Your kings, led away to death. You will remember
    What things I suffer, and at what men's hands,
    Because I would not transgress the laws of heaven.   80
    (To the GUARDS, *simply).* Come: let us wait no longer.

            (Exit ANTIGONÊ, *left, guarded.)*

ODE IV

Strophe 1

CHORUS: All Danaê's beauty was locked away
    In a brazen cell where the sunlight could not come:
    A small room, still as any grave, enclosed her.
    Yet she was a princess too,
    And Zeus in a rain of gold poured love upon her.   5
    O child, child,
    No power in wealth or war
    Or tough sea-blackened ships
    Can prevail against untiring Destiny!

Antistrophe 1

    And Dryas' son° also, that furious king,   10
    Bore the god's prisoning anger for his pride:
    Sealed up by Dionysos in deaf stone,
    His madness died among echoes.
    So at the last he learned what dreadful power
    His tongue had mocked: 15
    For he had profaned the revels,
    And fired the wrath of the nine
    Implacable Sisters° that love the sound of the flute.

Strophe 2

    And old men tell a half-remembered tale
    Of horror where a dark ledge splits the sea   20
    And a double surf beats on the gray shores:
    How a king's new woman,° sick
    With hatred for the queen he had imprisoned,
    Ripped out his two sons' eyes with her bloody hands
    While grinning Arês° watched the shuttle plunge   25
    Four times: four blind wounds crying for revenge.

Antistrophe 2

    Crying, tears and blood mingled.—Piteously born,
    Those sons whose mother was of heavenly birth!

10 Dryas' son—Lycurgus, King of Thrace.   18 Implacable Sisters—The Muses.   22 King's new woman—Eidothea, second wife of King Phineas, blinded her stepsons after the King had imprisoned their mother in a cave.   25 Arês—god of war.

Her father was the god of the North Wind
And she was cradled by gales,
She raced with young colts on the glittering hills
And walked untrammeled in the open light:
But in her marriage deathless Fate found means
To build a tomb like yours for all her joy.

SCENE V

Enter blind TEIRESIAS, *led by a boy. The opening speeches of*
TEIRESIAS *should be in singsong contrast to the realistic lines of* CREON.

TEIRESIAS: This is the way the blind man comes, Princes, Princes,
　　Lock-step, two heads lit by the eyes of one.
CREON: What new thing have you to tell us, old Teiresias?
TEIRESIAS: I have much to tell you: listen to the prophet, Creon.
CREON: I am not aware that I have ever failed to listen.
TEIRESIAS: Then you have done wisely, King, and ruled well.
CREON: I admit my debt to you. But what have you to say?
TEIRESIAS: This, Creon: you stand once more on the edge of fate.
CREON: What do you mean? Your words are a kind of dread.
TEIRESIAS: Listen, Creon:
　　I was sitting in my chair of augury, at the place
　　Where the birds gather about me. They were all a-chatter,
　　As is their habit, when suddenly I heard
　　A strange note in their jangling, a scream, a
　　Whirring fury; I knew that they were fighting,
　　Tearing each other, dying
　　In a whirlwind of wings clashing. And I was afraid.
　　I began the rites of burnt-offering at the altar,
　　But Hephaistos° failed me: instead of bright flame,
　　There was only the sputtering slime of the fat thigh flesh
　　Melting: the entrails dissolved in gray smoke,
　　The bare bone burst from the welter. And no blaze!
　　This was a sign from heaven. My boy described it,
　　Seeing for me as I see for others.

　　I tell you, Creon, you yourself have brought
　　This new calamity upon us. Our hearths and altars
　　Are stained with the corruption of dogs and carrion birds
　　That glut themselves on the corpse of Oedipus' son.
　　The gods are deaf when we pray to them, their fire
　　Recoils from our offering, their birds of omen
　　Have no cry of comfort, for they are gorged
　　With the thick blood of the dead.
　　　　　　　　　　　　　O my son,
　　These are no trifles! Think: all men make mistakes,
　　But a good man yields when he knows his course is wrong,

19 Hephaistos—god of fire.

And repairs the evil. The only crime is pride.

Give in to the dead man, then: do not fight with a corpse—
What glory is it to kill a man who is dead?
Think, I beg you: 40
It is for your own good that I speak as I do.
You should be able to yield for your own good.
CREON: It seems that prophets have made me their special province.
All my life long
I have been a kind of butt for the dull arrows   45
Of doddering fortune-tellers!
                                             · No, Teiresias:
If your birds—if the great eagles of God himself
Should carry him stinking bit by bit to heaven,
I would not yield. I am not afraid of pollution: 50
No man can defile the gods.
                                             Do what you will,
Go into business, make money, speculate
In India gold or that synthetic gold from Sardis,
Get rich otherwise than by my consent to bury him.   55
Teiresias, it is a sorry thing when a wise man
Sells his wisdom, lets out his words for hire!
TEIRESIAS: Ah Creon! Is there no man left in the world—
CREON: To do what?—Come, let's have the aphorism!
TEIRESIAS: No man who knows that wisdom outweighs any wealth?   60
CREON: As surely as bribes are baser than any baseness.
TEIRESIAS: You are sick, Creon! You are deathly sick!
CREON: As you say: it is not my place to challenge a prophet.
TEIRESIAS: Yet you have said my prophecy is for sale.
CREON: The generation of prophets has always loved gold.   65
TEIRESIAS: The generation of kings has always loved brass.
CREON: You forget yourself! You are speaking to your King.
TEIRESIAS: I know it. You are a king because of me.
CREON: You have a certain skill; but you have sold out.
TEIRESIAS: King, you will drive me to words that—   70
CREON: Say them, say them!
Only remember: I will not pay you for them.
TEIRESIAS: No, you will find them too costly.
CREON: No doubt. Speak:
Whatever you say, you will not change my will.   75
TEIRESIAS: Then take this, and take it to heart!
The time is not far off when you shall pay back
Corpse for corpse, flesh of your own flesh.
You have thrust the child of this world into living night,
You have kept from the gods below the child that is theirs: 80
The one in a grave before her death, the other,
Dead, denied the grave. This is your crime:
And the Furies and the dark gods of Hell
Are swift with terrible punishment for you.

Do you want to buy me now, Creon?   85
Not many days,
And your house will be full of men and women weeping,
And curses will be hurled at you from far
Cities grieving for sons unburied, left to rot
Before the walls of Thebes.   90

These are my arrows, Creon: they are all for you.

(To BOY.*)* But come, child: lead me home.
Let him waste his fine anger upon younger men.
Maybe he will learn at last
To control a wiser tongue in a better head.

(Exit TEIRESIAS.*)*

CHORAGOS: The old man has gone, King, but his words   95
    Remain to plague us. I am old, too,
    But I cannot remember that he was ever false.
CREON: That is true . . . It troubles me.
    Oh it is hard to give in! but it is worse
    To risk everything for stubborn pride.
CHORAGOS: Creon: take my advice.   100
CREON: What shall I do?
CHORAGOS: Go quickly: free Antigonê from her vault
    And build a tomb for the body of Polyneicês.
CREON: You would have me do this?
CHORAGOS: Creon, yes!   105
    And it must be done at once: God moves
    Swiftly to cancel the folly of stubborn men.
CREON: It is hard to deny the heart! But I
    Will do it: I will not fight with destiny.
CHORAGOS: You must go yourself, you cannot leave it to others.   110
CREON: I will go.
                   —Bring axes, servants:
    Come with me to the tomb. I buried her, I
    Will set her free.
                   Oh quickly!   115
    My mind misgives—
    The laws of the gods are mighty, and a man must serve them
    To the last day of his life!

(Exit CREON.*)*

PAEAN°

Strophe 1

CHORAGOS: God of many names
CHORUS: O Iacchos°
                  son
    of Kadmeian Sémelê°

Paean—a hymn.   1 Iacchos—Bacchos or Dionysos, god of wine and revelry.   2 Sémelê—mother
of Iacchos, consort of Zeus.

5

              O born of the Thunder!

Guardian of the West

              Regent

of Eleusis' plain

              O Prince of Maenad° Thebes

and the Dragon Field by rippling Ismenós.°   10

Antistrophe 1

CHORAGOS: God of many names

CHORUS: the flame of torches

    flares on our hills

              the nymphs of Iacchos

    dance at the spring of Castalia:°   15

    From the vine-close mountain

              come ah come in ivy:

    Evohé evohé! sings through the streets of Thebes

Strophe 2

CHORAGOS: God of many names

CHORUS: Iacchos of Thebes   20

    heavenly Child

              of Sémelê bride of the Thunderer!

    The shadow of plague is upon us:

                     come

    with clement feet   25

              oh come from Parnasos

    down the long slopes

              across the lamenting water

Antistrophe 2

CHORAGOS: Iô Fire! Chorister of the throbbing stars!

    O purest among the voices of the night!   30

    Thou son of God, blaze for us!

    CHORUS: Come with choric rapture of circling Maenads

    Who cry *Iô Iacche!*

               God of many names!

EXODOS

Enter MESSENGER, *left.*

MESSENGER: Men of the line of Kadmos,° you who live

    Near Amphion's citadel,°

              I cannot say

    Of any condition of human life "This is fixed,

    This is clearly good, or bad". Fate raises up,   5

    And Fate casts down the happy and unhappy alike:

---

9 maenad—female worshipper, attendant of Iacchos.   10 Ismenós—a river near Thebes where, according to legend, dragon's teeth were sown from which sprang the ancestors of Thebes.   15 Castalia—a spring on Mount Parnasos.   1 Kadmos—sowed the dragon's teeth; founded Thebes. 2 Amphion's citadel—Amphion's lyre playing charmed stones to form a wall around Thebes.

No man can foretell his Fate.
Take the case of Creon:
Creon was happy once, as I count happiness:
Victorious in battle, sole governor of the land,   10
Fortunate father of children nobly born.
And now it has all gone from him! Who can say
That a man is still alive when his life's joy fails?
He is a walking dead man. Grant him rich,
Let him live like a king in his great house: 15
If his pleasure is gone, I would not give
So much as the shadow of smoke for all he owns.
CHORAGOS: Your words hint at sorrow: what is your news for us?
MESSENGER: They are dead. The living are guilty of their death.
CHORAGOS: Who is guilty? Who is dead? Speak!   20
MESSENGER: Haimon.
Haimon is dead; and the hand that killed him
Is his own hand.
CHORAGOS: His father's? or his own?
MESSENGER: His own, driven mad by the murder his father had done.   25
CHORAGOS: Teiresias, Teiresias, how clearly you saw it all!
Messenger: This is my news: you must draw what conclusions you can from it.
CHORAGOS: But look: Eurydicê, our Queen:
Has she overheard us?

Enter EURYDICÊ from the palace, center.

EURYDICÊ: I have heard something, friends:
As I was unlocking the gate of Pallas' shrine,   25
For I needed her help today, I heard a voice
Telling of some new sorrow. And I fainted
There at the temple with all my maidens about me.
But speak again: whatever it is. I can bear it:
Grief and I are no strangers.   30
MESSENGER: Dearest Lady,
I will tell you plainly all that I have seen.
I shall not try to comfort you: what is the use,
Since comfort could lie only in what is not true?
The truth is always best.   35
I went with Creon
To the outer plain where Polyneicês was lying,
No friend to pity him, his body shredded by dogs.
We made our prayers in that place to Hecatê
And Pluto, that they would be merciful. And we bathed   40
The corpse with holy water, and we brought
Fresh-broken branches to burn what was left of it,
And upon the urn we heaped up a towering barrow
Of the earth of his own land.
When we were done, we ran   45
To the vault where Antigonê lay on her couch of stone.
One of the servants had gone ahead,

And while he was yet far off he heard a voice
Grieving within the chamber, and he came back
And told Creon. And as the King went closer, 50
The air was full of wailing, the words lost,
And he begged us to make all haste. "Am I a prophet?"
He said, weeping, "And must I walk this road,
The saddest of all that I have gone before?
My son's voice calls me on. Oh quickly, quickly! 55
Look through the crevice there, and tell me
If it is Haimon, or some deception of the gods!"

We obeyed; and in the cavern's farthest corner
We saw her lying:
She had made a noose of her fine linen veil 60
And hanged herself. Haimon lay beside her,
His arms about her waist, lamenting her,
His love lost under ground, crying out
That his father had stolen her away from him.

When Creon saw him the tears rushed to his eyes 65
And he called to him: "What have you done, child?
      Speak to me.
What are you thinking that makes your eyes so strange?
O my son, my son, I come to you on my knees!"
But Haimon spat in his face. He said not a word, 70
Staring—
      And suddenly drew his sword
And lunged. Creon shrank back, the blade missed; and the boy,
Desperate against himself, drove it half its length
Into his own side, and fell. And as he died 75
He gathered Antigonê close in his arms again,
Choking, his blood bright red on her white cheek.
And now he lies dead with the dead, and she is his
At last, his bride in the house of the dead.

Exit EURYDICÊ *into the palace.*

CHORAGOS: She has left us without a word. What can this mean? 80
MESSENGER: It troubles me, too; yet she knows what is best,
      Her grief is too great for public lamentation,
      And doubtless she has gone to her chamber to weep
      For her dead son, leading her maidens in his dirge.

Pause.

CHORAGOS: It may be so: but I fear this deep silence. 85
MESSENGER: I will see what she is doing. I will go in.

Exit MESSENGER *into the palace.*

Enter CREON *with attendants, bearing* HAIMON's *body.*

CHORAGOS: But here is the king himself: oh look at him,
      Bearing his own damnation in his arms.
CREON: Nothing you say can touch me any more.

My own blind heart has brought me   90
From darkness to final darkness. Here you see
The father murdering, the murdered son—
And all my civic wisdom!

Haimon my son, so young, so young to die,
I was the fool, not you; and you died for me.   95
CHORAGOS: That is the truth; but you were late in learning it.
CREON: This truth is hard to bear. Surely a god
    Has crushed me beneath the hugest weight of heaven,
    And driven me headlong a barbaric way
    To trample out the thing I held most dear.

    The pains that men will take to come to pain!   100

Enter MESSENGER *from the palace.*

MESSENGER: The burden you carry in your hands is heavy,
    But it is not all: you will find more in your house.
CREON: What burden worse than this shall I find there?
MESSENGER: The Queen is dead.
CREON: O port of death, deaf world,   105
    Is there no pity for me? And you, Angel of evil,
    I was dead, and your words are death again.
    Is it true, boy? Can it be true?
    Is my wife dead? Has death bred death?
MESSENGER: You can see for yourself.   110

The doors are opened, and the body of EURYDICÊ *is disclosed within.*

CREON: Oh pity!
    All true, all true, and more than I can bear!
    O my wife, my son!
MESSENGER: She stood before the altar, and her heart
    Welcomed the knife her own hand guided,   115
    And a great cry burst from her lips for Megareus dead,
    And for Haimon dead, her sons; and her last breath
    Was a curse for their father, the murderer of her sons.
    And she fell, and the dark flowed in through her closing eyes.
CREON: O God, I am sick with fear.   120
    Are there no swords here? Has no one a blow for me?
MESSENGER: Her curse is upon you for the deaths of both.
CREON: It is right that it should be. I alone am guilty.
    I know it, and I say it. Lead me in,
    Quickly, friends.   125
    I have neither life nor substance. Lead me in.
CHORAGOS: You are right, if there can be right in so much wrong.
    The briefest way is best in a world of sorrow.
CREON: Let it come,
    Let death come quickly, and be kind to me.   130
    I would not ever see the sun again.
CHORAGOS: All that will come when it will; but we, meanwhile,
    Have much to do. Leave the future to itself.

CREON: All my heart was in that prayer!

CHORAGOS: Then do not pray any more: the sky is deaf.   135

CREON: Lead me away. I have been rash and foolish.

    I have killed my son and my wife.

    I look for comfort; my comfort lies here dead.

    Whatever my hands have touched has come to nothing.

    Fate has brought all my pride to a thought of dust.   140

               As CREON *is being led into the house, the*
        CHORAGOS *advances and speaks directly to the audience.*

CHORAGOS: There is no happiness where there is no wisdom;

    No wisdom but in submission to the gods.

    Big words are always punished,

    And proud men in old age learn to be wise.

For Practice

1. In ancient Greece, dramas such as Antigonê were staged in large annual competitions and were considered very important public events. They dealt with important cultural issues such as law, tradition, and religion. Do we have any comparable events today? Why or why not?

2. The Chorus, while it was an integral part of Greek drama, has no real counterpart in contemporary drama. The Chorus functions in several ways in this play. What do you think some of its purposes are? Would you consider the Chorus equivalent to another character? to an omniscient narrator?

3. Who makes a better case regarding what should be done with Polynices's body, Antigonê or Creon? Summarize the reasoning of each character. You might also look at arguments made by other characters, such as Ismenê, Haimon, and Teiresias. In the debate between Creon and Haimon regarding the punishment of Antigonê, who makes the better argument?

4. In Antigonê there is an opposition between governmental law, on the one hand, and religious law and duty to one's family on the other. When these forces are in conflict, which should win out? Should a government always defer to religious practice or family interests? Consider a contemporary conflict between a governmental body and religion or family interests. Develop arguments for each side. In the specific situation you have selected, which side is more convincing?

5. How does *Antigonê* affect your own perspective on contemporary issues in which civil law is at odds with morality or family tradition?

Impressions of an Indian Childhood and *The School Days of an Indian Girl*

Gertrude Bonnin (Zitkala-Sa)

Gertrude Bonnin (1876–1938), whose Yankton Sioux name was Zitkala-Sa, devoted her life to the struggle for Native American rights. She taught, wrote, and studied violin in her early adulthood but quickly turned her energies to activism. In addition to editing the American Indian Magazine, *she founded the National Council of American Indians in 1926 and was a leading proponent of the Indian Citizenship Act of 1924.*

The following selections from "Impressions of an Indian Childhood" and "The School Days of an Indian Girl," both originally published in Atlantic Magazine *in 1900, reveal Bonnin's isolation from both the Sioux culture she left at age eight and the white American culture whose religion, customs, attitudes toward nature, and lack of respect for other cultures she finds terrifying. Though these pieces depict some of the indignities suffered by Native Americans in the 19th century, Bonnin's experiences can also be related to those of millions of immigrants to the United States who have been pressured to assimilate and thus abandon much of their cultural heritage.*

from *Impressions of an Indian Childhood*

The Big Red Apples

The first turning away from the easy, natural flow of my life occurred in an early spring. It was in my eighth year; in the month of March, I afterward learned. At this age I knew but one language, and that was my mother's native tongue.

From some of my playmates I heard that two paleface missionaries were in our village. They were from that class of white men who wore big hats and carried large hearts, they said. Running direct to my mother, I began to question her why these two strangers were among us. She told me, after I had teased much, that they had come to take away Indian boys and girls to the East. My mother did not seem to want me to talk about them. But in a day or two, I gleaned many wonderful stories from my playfellows concerning the strangers.

"Mother, my friend Judéwin is going home with the missionaries. She is going to a more beautiful country than ours; the palefaces told her so!" I said wistfully, wishing in my heart that I too might go.

Mother sat in a chair, and I was hanging on her knee. Within the last two seasons my big brother Dawée had returned from a three years' education in the East, and his coming back influenced my mother to take a farther step from her native way of living. First it was a change from the buffalo skin to the white man's canvas that covered our wigwam. Now she had given up her wigwam of slender poles, to live, a foreigner, in a home of clumsy logs.

"Yes, my child, several others besides Judéwin are going away with the palefaces. Your brother said the missionaries had inquired about his little sister," she said, watching my face very closely.

My heart thumped so hard against my breast, I wondered if she could hear it.

"Did he tell them to take me, mother?" I asked, fearing lest Dawée had forbidden the palefaces to see me, and that my hope of going to the Wonderland would be entirely blighted.

With a sad, slow smile, she answered: "There! I knew you were wishing to go, because Judéwin has filled your ears with the white men's lies. Don't believe a word they say! Their words are sweet, but, my child, their deeds are bitter. You will cry for me, but they will not even soothe you. Stay with me, my little one! Your brother Dawée says that going East, away from your mother, is too hard an experience for his baby sister."

Thus my mother discouraged my curiosity about the lands beyond our eastern horizon; for it was not yet an ambition for Letters that was stirring me. But on the following day the missionaries did come to our very house. I spied them coming up the footpath leading to our cottage. A third man was with them, but he was not my brother Dawée. It was another, a young interpreter, a paleface who had a smattering of the Indian language. I was ready to run out to meet them, but I did not dare to displease my mother. With great glee, I jumped up and down on our ground floor. I begged my mother to open the door, that they would be sure to come to us. Alas! They came, they saw, and they conquered!

Judéwin had told me of the great tree where grew red, red apples; and how we could reach out our hands and pick all the red apples we could eat. I had never seen apple trees. I had never tasted more than a dozen red apples in my life; and when I heard of the orchards of the East, I was eager to roam among them. The missionaries smiled into my eyes, and patted my head. I wondered how mother could say such hard words against them.

"Mother, ask them if little girls may have all the red apples they want, when they go East," I whispered aloud, in my excitement.

The interpreter heard me, and answered: "Yes, little girl, the nice red apples are for those who pick them; and you will have a ride on the iron horse if you go with these good people."

I had never seen a train, and he knew it.

"Mother, I'm going East! I like big red apples, and I want to ride on the iron horse! Mother, say yes!" I pleaded.

My mother said nothing. The missionaries waited in silence; and my eyes began to blur with tears, though I struggled to choke them back. The corners of my mouth twitched, and my mother saw me.

"I am not ready to give you any word," she said to them. "Tomorrow I shall send you my answer by my son."

With this they left us. Alone with my mother, I yielded to my tears, and cried aloud, shaking my head so as not to hear what she was saying to me. This was the first time I had ever been so unwilling to give up my own desire that I refused to hearken to my mother's voice.

There was a solemn silence in our home that night. Before I went to bed I begged the Great Spirit to make my mother willing I should go with the missionaries.

The next morning came, and my mother called me to her side. "My daughter, do you still persist in wishing to leave your mother?" she asked.

"Oh, mother, it is not that I wish to leave you, but I want to see the wonderful Eastern land," I answered.

My dear old aunt came to our house that morning, and I heard her say, "Let her try it."

I hoped that, as usual, my aunt was pleading on my side. My brother Dawée came for mother's decision. I dropped my play, and crept close to my aunt.

"Yes, Dawée, my daughter, though she does not understand what it all means, is anxious to go. She will need an education when she is grown, for then there will be fewer real Dakotas, and many more palefaces. This tearing her away, so young, from her mother is necessary, if I would have her an educated woman. The palefaces, who owe us a large debt for stolen lands, have begun to pay a tardy justice in offering some education to our children. But I know my daughter must suffer keenly in this experiment. For her sake, I dread to tell you my reply to the missionaries. Go, tell them that they may take my little daughter, and that the Great Spirit shall not fail to reward them according to their hearts."

Wrapped in my heavy blanket, I walked with my mother to the carriage that was soon to take us to the iron horse. I was happy. I met my playmates, who were also wearing their best thick blankets. We showed one another our new beaded moccasins, and the width of the belts that girdled our new dresses. Soon we were being drawn rapidly away by the white man's horses. When I saw the lonely figure of my mother vanish in the distance, a sense of regret settled heavily upon me. I felt suddenly weak, as if I might fall limp to the ground. I was in the hands of strangers whom my mother did not fully trust. I no longer felt free to be myself, or to voice my own feelings. The tears trickled down my cheeks, and I buried my face in the folds of my blanket. Now the first step, parting me from my mother, was taken, and all my belated tears availed nothing.

Having driven thirty miles to the ferryboat, we crossed the Missouri in the evening. Then riding again a few miles eastward, we stopped before a massive brick building. I looked at it in amazement, and with a vague misgiving, for in our village I had never seen so large a house. Trembling with fear and distrust of the palefaces, my teeth chattering from the chilly ride. I crept noiselessly in my soft moccasins along the narrow hall, keeping very close to the bare wall. I was a frightened and bewildered as the captured young of a wild creature.

from *The School Days of an Indian Girl*

I The Land of Red Apples

There were eight in our party of bronzed children who were going East with the missionaries. Among us were three young braves, two tall girls, and we three little ones, Judéwin, Thowin, and I.

We had been very impatient to start on our journey to the Red Apple Country, which, we were told, lay a little beyond the great circular horizon of the Western prairie. Under a sky of rosy apples we dreamt of roaming as freely and happily as we had chased the cloud shadows on the Dakota plains. We had anticipated much pleasure from a ride on the iron horse, but the throngs of staring palefaces disturbed and troubled us.

On the train, fair women, with tottering babies on each arm, stopped their haste and scrutinized the children of absent mothers. Large men, with heavy bundles in their hands, halted near by, and riveted their glassy blue eyes upon us.

I sank deep into the corner of my seat, for I resented being watched. Directly in front of me, children who were no longer than I hung themselves upon the backs of their seats, with their bold white faces toward me. Sometimes they took their forefingers out of their mouths and pointed at my moccasined feet. Their mothers, instead of reproving such rude curiosity, looked closely at me, and attracted their children's further notice to my blanket. This embarrassed me, and kept me constantly on the verge of tears.

I sat perfectly still, with my eyes downcast, daring only now and then to shoot long glances around me. Chancing to turn to the window at my side, I was quite breathless upon seeing one familiar object. It was the telegraph pole which strode by at short paces. Very near my mother's dwelling, along the edge of a road thickly bordered with wild sunflowers, some poles like these had been planted by white men. Often I had stopped, on my way down the road, to hold my ear against the pole, and, hearing its low moaning, I used to wonder what the paleface had done to hurt it. Now I sat watching for each pole that glided by to be the last one.

In this way I had forgotten my uncomfortable surroundings, when I heard one of my comrades call out my name. I saw the missionary standing very near, tossing candies and gums into our midst. This amused us all, and we tried to see who could catch the most of the sweet-meats. The missionary's generous distribution of candies was impressed upon my memory by a disastrous result which followed. I had caught more than my share of candies and gums, and soon after our arrival at the school I had a chance to disgrace myself, which, I am ashamed to say, I did.

Though we rode several days inside of the iron horse, I do not recall a single thing about our luncheons.

It was night when we reached the school grounds. The lights from the windows of the large buildings fell upon some of the icicled trees that stood beneath them. We were led toward an open door, where the brightness of the lights within flooded out over the heads of the excited palefaces who blocked the way. My body trembled more from fear than from the snow I trod upon.

Entering the house, I stood close against the wall. The strong glaring light in the large whitewashed room dazzled my eyes. The noisy hurrying of hard shoes upon a bare wooden floor increased the whirring in my ears. My only safety seemed to be in keeping next to the wall. As I was wondering in which direction to escape from all this confusion, two warm hands grasped me firmly, and in the same moment I was tossed high in midair. A rosy-cheeked paleface woman caught me in her arms. I was both frightened and insulted by such trifling. I stared into her eyes, wishing her to let me stand on my own feet, but she jumped me up and down with increasing enthusiasm. My mother had never made a plaything of her wee daughter. Remembering this I began to cry aloud.

They misunderstood the cause of my tears, and placed me at a white table loaded with food. There our party were united again. As I did not hush my crying, one of the older ones whispered to me, "Wait until you are alone in the night."

It was very little I could swallow besides my sobs, that evening.

"Oh, I want my mother and my brother Dawée! I want to go to my aunt!" I pleaded; but the ears of the palefaces could not hear me.

From the table we were taken along an upward incline of wooden boxes, which I learned afterward to call a stairway. At the top was a quiet hall, dimly lighted. Many narrow beds were in one straight line down the entire length of the wall. In them lay sleeping brown faces, which peeped just out of the coverings. I was tucked into bed with one of the tall girls, because she talked to me in my mother tongue and seemed to soothe me.

I had arrived in the wonderful land of rosy skies, but I was not happy, as I had thought I should be. My long travel and the bewildering sights had exhausted me. I fell asleep, heaving deep, tired sobs. My tears were left to dry themselves in streaks, because neither my aunt not my mother was near to wipe them away.

II The Cutting of My Long Hair

The first day in the land of apples was a bitter-cold one: for the snow still covered the ground, and the trees were bare. A large bell rang for breakfast, its loud metallic voice crashing through the belfry overhead and into our sensitive ears. The annoying clatter of shoes on bare floors gave us no peace. The constant clash of harsh noises, with an undercurrent of many voices murmuring an unknown tongue, made a bedlam within which I was securely tied. And though my spirit tore itself in struggling for its lost freedom, all was useless.

A paleface woman, with white hair, came up after us. We were placed in a line of girls who were marching into the dining room. These were Indian girls, in stiff shoes and closely clinging dresses. The small girls wore sleeved aprons and shingled hair. As I walked noiselessly in my soft moccasins, I felt like sinking to the floor, for my blanket had been stripped from my shoulders. I looked hard at the Indian girls, who seemed not to care that they were even more immodestly dressed than I, in their tightly fitting clothes. While we marched in, the boys entered at an opposite door. I watched for the three young braves who came in our party. I spied them in the rear ranks, looking as uncomfortable as I felt.

A small bell was tapped, and each of the pupils drew a chair from under the table. Supposing this act meant they were to be seated, I pulled out mine and at once slipped into it from one side. But when I turned my head, I saw that I was the only one seated, and all the rest at our table remained standing. Just as I began to rise, looking shyly around to see how chairs were to be used, a second bell was sounded. All were seated at last, and I had to crawl back into my chair again. I heard a man's voice at one end of the hall, and I looked around to see him. But all the others hung their heads over their plates. As I glanced at the long chain of tables, I caught the eyes of a paleface woman upon me. Immediately I dropped my eyes, wondering why I was so keenly watched by the strange woman. The man ceased his mutterings, and then a third bell was tapped. Every one picked up his knife and fork and began eating. I began crying instead, for by this time I was afraid to venture anything more.

But this eating by formula was not the hardest trial in that first day. Late in the morning, my friend Judéwin gave me a terrible warning. Judéwin knew a few words of English; and she had overheard the paleface woman talk about cutting our long, heavy hair. Our mothers had taught us that only unskilled warriors who were captured had their hair shingled by the enemy. Among our people, short hair was worn by mourners, and shingled hair by cowards!

We discussed our fate some moments, and when Judéwin said, "We have to submit, because they are strong." I rebelled.

"No, I will not submit! I will struggle first!" I answered.

I watched my chance, and when no one noticed I disappeared. I crept up the stairs as quietly as I could in my squeaking shoes,—my moccasins had been exchanged for shoes. Along the hall I passed, without knowing whither I was going. Turning aside to an open door, I found a large room with three white beds in it. The windows were covered with dark green curtains, which made the room very dim. Thankful that no one was there, I directed my steps toward the corner farthest from the door. On my hands and knees I crawled under the bed, and cuddled myself in the dark corner.

From my hiding place I peered out, shuddering with fear whenever I heard footsteps near by. Though in the hall loud voices were calling my name, and I knew that even Judéwin was searching for me, I did not open my mouth to answer. Then the steps were quickened and the voices became excited. The sounds came nearer and nearer. Women and girls entered the room. I held my breath, and watched them open closet doors and peep behind large trunks. Some one threw up the curtains, and the room was filled with sudden light. What caused them to stoop and look under the bed I do not know. I remember being dragged out, though I resisted by kicking and scratching wildly. In spite of myself, I was carried downstairs and tied fast in a chair.

I cried aloud, shaking my head all the while until I felt the cold blades of the scissors against my neck, and heard them gnaw off one of my thick braids. Then I lost my spirit. Since the day I was taken from my mother I had suffered extreme indignities. People had stared at me. I had been tossed about in the air like a wooden puppet. And now my long hair was shingled like a coward's! In my anguish I moaned for my mother, but no one came to comfort me. Not a soul reasoned with me, as my own mother used to do: for now I was only one of many little animals driven by a herder.

III The Snow Episode

A short time after our arrival we three Dakotas were playing in the snowdrifts. We were all still deaf to the English language, excepting Judéwin, who always heard such puzzling things. One morning we learned through her ears that we were forbidden to fall lengthwise in the snow, as we had been doing, to see our own impressions. However, before many hours we had forgotten the order, and were having great sport in the snow, when a shrill voice called us. Looking up, we saw an imperative hand beckoning us into the house. We shook the snow off ourselves, and started toward the woman as slowly as we dared.

Judéwin said: "Now the paleface is angry with us. She is going to punish us for falling into the snow. If she looks straight into your eyes and talks loudly, you must wait until she stops. Then, after a tiny pause, say, 'No.'" The rest of the way we practiced upon the little word "no."

As it happened, Thowin was summoned to judgment first. The door shut behind her with a click.

Judéwin and I stood silently listening at the keyhole. The paleface woman talked in very severe tones. Her words fell from her lips like crackling embers, and her inflection ran up like the small end of a switch. I understood her voice better than the things she was saying. I was certain we had made her very impatient with us. Judéwin heard enough of the words to realize all too late that she had taught us the wrong reply.

"Oh, poor Thowin!" she gasped, as she put both hands over her ears.

Just then I heard Thowin's tremulous answer, "No."

With an angry exclamation, the woman gave her a hard spanking. Then she stopped to say something. Judéwin said it was this: "Are you going to obey my word the next time?"

Thowin answered again with the only word at her command, "No."

This time the woman meant her blows to smart, for the poor frightened girl shrieked at the top of her voice. In the midst of the whipping the blows ceased abruptly, and the woman asked another question: "Are you going to fall in the snow again?"

Thowin gave her bad password another trial. We heard her say feebly, "No! No!"

With this the woman hid away her half-worn slipper, and led the child out, stroking her black shorn head. Perhaps it occurred to her that brute force is not the solution for such a problem. She did nothing to Judéwin nor to me. She only returned to us our unhappy comrade, and left us alone in the room.

During the first two or three seasons misunderstandings as ridiculous as this one of the snow episode frequently took place, bringing unjustifiable frights and punishments into our little lives.

Within a year I was able to express myself somewhat in broken English. As soon as I comprehended a part of what was said and done, a mischievous spirit of revenge possessed me. One day I was called in from my play for some misconduct. I had disregarded a rule which seemed to me very needlessly binding. I was sent into the kitchen to mash the turnips for dinner. It was noon, and steaming dishes were hastily carried into the dining room. I hated turnips, and their odor which came from the brown jar was offensive to me. With fire in my heart, I took the wooden tool that the paleface woman held out to me. I stood upon a step, and, grasping the handle with both hands, I bent in hot rage over the turnips. I worked my vengeance upon them. All were so busily occupied that no one noticed me. I saw that the turnips were in a pulp, and that further beating could not improve them; but the order was, "Mash these turnips," and mash them I would! I renewed my energy; and as I sent the masher into the bottom of the jar, I felt a satisfying sensation that the weight of my body had gone into it.

Just here a paleface woman came up to my table. As she looked into the jar, she shoved my hands roughly aside. I stood fearless and angry. She placed her red hands upon the rim of the jar. Then she gave one lift and a stride away from the table. But lo! the pulpy contents fell through the crumbled bottom to the floor! She spared me no scolding phrases that I had earned. I did not heed them. I felt triumphant in my revenge, though deep within me I was a wee bit sorry to have broken the jar.

As I sat eating my dinner, and saw that no turnips were served, I whooped in my heart for having once asserted the rebellion within me. . . .

VI Four Strange Summers

After my first three years in school, I roamed again in the Western country through four strange summers.

During this time I seemed to hang in the heart of chaos, beyond the touch or voice of human aid. My brother, being almost ten years my senior, did not quite understand my feelings. My mother had never gone inside of a schoolhouse, and so she was not capable of comforting her daughter who could read and write. Even nature seemed to have no place for me. I was neither a wee girl nor a tall one; neither a wild Indian nor a tame one. This deplorable situation was the effect of my brief course in the East, and the unsatisfactory "teenth" in a girl's years.

It was under these trying conditions that, one bright afternoon, as I sat restless and unhappy in my mother's cabin, I caught the sound of the spirited step of my brother's pony on the road which passed by our dwelling. Soon I heard the wheels of a light buckboard, and Dawée's familiar "Ho!" to his pony. He alighted upon the bare ground in front of our house. Tying his pony to one of the projecting corner logs of the low-roofed cottage, he stepped upon the wooden doorstep.

I met him there with a hurried greeting, and, as I passed by, he looked a quiet "What?" into my eyes.

When he began talking with my mother, I slipped the rope from the pony's bridle. Seizing the reins and bracing my feet against the dashboard, I wheeled around in an instant. The pony was ever ready to try his speed. Looking backward, I saw Dawée waving his hand to me. I turned with the curve in the road and disappeared. I followed the winding road which crawled upward between the bases of little hillocks. Deep water-worn ditches ran parallel on either side. A strong wind blew against my cheeks and fluttered my sleeves. The pony reached the top of the highest hill, and began an even race on the level lands. There was nothing moving within that great circular horizon of the Dakota prairies save the tall grasses, over which the wind blew and rolled off in long, shadowy waves.

Within this vast wigwam of blue and green I rode reckless and insignificant. It satisfied my small consciousness to see the white foam fly from the pony's mouth.

Suddenly, out of the earth a coyote came forth at a swinging trot that was taking the cunning thief toward the hills and the village beyond. Upon the moment's impulse, I gave him a long chase and a wholesome fright. As I turned away to go back to the village, the wolf sank down upon his haunches for rest, for it was a hot summer day; and as I drove slowly homeward, I saw his sharp nose still pointed at me, until I vanished below the margin of the hilltops.

In a little while I came in sight of my mother's house. Dawée stood in the yard, laughing at an old warrior who was pointing his forefinger, and again waving his whole hand, toward the hills. With his blanket drawn over one shoulder, he talked and motioned excitedly. Dawée turned the old man by the shoulder and pointed me out to him.

"Oh, han!" (Oh, yes) the warrior muttered, and went his way. He had climbed the top of his favorite barren hill to survey the surrounding prairies, when he spied my chase after the coyote. His keen eyes recognized the pony and driver. At once uneasy for my safety, he had come running to my mother's cabin to give her warning. I did not appreciate his kindly interest, for there was an unrest gnawing at my heart.

As soon as he went away, I asked Dawée about something else.

"No, my baby sister. I cannot take you with me to the party to-night," he replied. Though I was not far from fifteen, and I felt that before long I should enjoy all the privileges of my tall cousin, Dawée persisted in calling me his baby sister.

That moonlight night, I cried in my mother's presence when I heard the jolly young people pass by our cottage. They were no more young braves in blankets and eagle plumes, nor Indian maids with prettily painted cheeks. The young men wore the white man's coat and trousers, with bright neckties. The girls wore tight muslin dresses, with ribbons at neck and waist. At these gatherings they talked English. I could speak English almost as well as my brother, but I was not properly dressed to be taken along. I had no hat, no ribbons, and no close-fitting gown. Since my return from school I had thrown away my shoes, and wore again the soft moccasins.

While Dawée was busily preparing to go I controlled my tears. But when I heard him bounding away on his pony, I buried my face in my arms and cried hot tears.

My mother was troubled by my unhappiness. Coming to my side, she offered me the only printed matter we had in our home. It was an Indian Bible, given her some years ago by a missionary. She tried to console me. "Here, my child, are the white man's papers. Read a little from them," she said most piously.

I took it from her hand, for her sake; but my enraged spirit felt more like burning the book, which afforded me no help, and was a perfect delusion to my mother. I did not read it, but laid it unopened on the floor, where I sat on my feet. The dim yellow light of the braided muslin burning in a small vessel of oil flickered and sizzled in the awful silent storm which followed my rejection of the Bible.

Now my wrath against the fates consumed my tears before they reached my eyes. I sat stony, with a bowed head. My mother threw a shawl over her head and shoulders, and stepped out into the night.

After an uncertain solitude, I was suddenly aroused by a loud cry piercing the night. It was my mother's voice wailing among the barren hills which held the bones of buried warriors. She called aloud for her brothers' spirits to support her in her helpless misery. My fingers grew icy cold, as I realized that my unrestrained tears had betrayed my suffering to her, and she was grieving for me.

Before she returned, though I knew she was on her way, for she had ceased her weeping, I extinguished the light, and leaned my head on the window sill.

Many schemes of running away from my surroundings hovered about in my mind. A few more moons of such a turmoil drove me away to the Eastern school. I rode on the white man's iron steed, thinking it would bring me back to my mother in a few winters, when I should be grown tall, and there would be congenial friends awaiting me.

VII Incurring My Mother's Displeasure

In the second journey to the East I had not come without some precautions. I had a secret interview with one of our best medicine men, and when I left his wigwam I carried securely in my sleeve a tiny bunch of magic roots. This possession assured me of friends wherever I should go. So absolutely did I believe in its charms that I wore it through all the school routine for more than a year. Then, before I lost my faith in the dead roots, I lost the little buckskin bag containing all my good luck.

At the close of this second term of three years I was the proud owner of my first diploma. The following autumn I ventured upon a college career against my mother's will.

I had written for her approval, but in her reply I found no encouragement. She called my notice to her neighbors' children, who had completed their education in three years. They had returned to their homes, and were then talking English with the frontier settlers. Her few words hinted that I had better give up my slow attempt to learn the white man's ways, and be content to roam over the prairies and find my living upon wild roots. I silenced her by deliberate disobedience.

Thus, homeless and heavy-hearted, I began anew my life among strangers.

As I hid myself in my little room in the college dormitory, away from the scornful and yet curious eyes of the students, I pined for sympathy. Often I wept in secret, wishing I had gone West, to be nourished by my mother's love, instead of remaining among a cold race whose hearts were frozen hard with prejudice.

During the fall and winter seasons I scarcely had a real friend, though by that time several of my classmates were courteous to me at a safe distance.

My mother had not yet forgiven my rudeness to her, and I had no moment for letterwriting. By daylight and lamplight, I spun with reeds and thistles, until my hands were tired from their weaving, the magic design which promised me the white man's respect.

At length, in the spring term, I entered an oratorical contest among the various classes. As the day of competition approached, it did not seem possible that the event was so near at hand, but it came. In the chapel the classes assembled together, with their invited guests. The high platform was carpeted, and gayly festooned with college colors. A bright white light illumined the room, and outlined clearly the great polished beams that arched the domed ceiling. The assembled crowds filled the air with pulsating murmurs. When the hour for speaking arrived all were hushed. But on the wall the old clock which pointed out the trying moment ticked calmly on.

One after another I saw and heard the orators. Still, I could not realize that they longed for the favorable decision of the judges as much as I did. Each contestant received a loud burst of applause, and some were cheered heartily. Too soon my turn came, and I paused a moment behind the curtains for a deep breath. After my concluding words, I heard the same applause that the others had called out.

Upon my retreating steps, I was astounded to receive from my fellow-students a large bouquet of roses tied with flowing ribbons. With the lovely flowers I fled from the stage. This friendly token was a rebuke to me for the hard feelings I had borne them.

Later, the decision of the judges awarded me the first place. Then there was a mad uproar in the hall, where my classmates sang and shouted my name at the top of their lungs; and the disappointed students howled and brayed in fearfully dissonant tin trumpets. In this excitement, happy students rushed forward to offer their congratulations. And I could not conceal a smile when they wished to escort me in a procession to the students' parlor, where all were going to calm themselves. Thanking them for the kind spirit which prompted them to make such a proposition, I walked alone with the night to my own little room.

A few weeks afterward, I appeared as the college representative in another contest. This time the competition was among orators from different colleges in our State. It was held at the State capital, in one of the largest opera houses.

Here again was a strong prejudice against my people. In the evening, as the great audience filled the house, the student bodies began warring among themselves. Fortunately, I was spared witnessing any of the noisy wrangling before the contest began. The slurs against the Indian that stained the lips of our opponents were already burning like a dry fever within my breast.

But after the orations were delivered a deeper burn awaited me. There, before that vast ocean of eyes, some college rowdies threw out a large white flag, with a drawing of a most forlorn Indian girl on it. Under this they had printed in bold black letters words that ridiculed the college which was represented by a "squaw." Such worse than barbarian rudeness embittered me. While we waited for the verdict of the judges, I gleamed fiercely upon the throngs of palefaces. My teeth were hard set, as I saw the white flag still floating insolently in the air.

Then anxiously we watched the man carry toward the stage the envelope containing the final decision.

There were two prizes given, that night, and one of them was mine!

The evil spirit laughed within me when the white flag dropped out of sight, and the hands which hurled it hung limp in defeat.

Leaving the crowd as quickly as possible, I was soon in my room. The rest of the night I sat in an armchair and gazed into the crackling fire. I laughed no more in triumph when thus alone. The little taste of victory did not satisfy a hunger in my heart. In my mind I saw my mother far away on the Western plains, and she was holding a charge against me.

For Practice

1. Bonnin's essays, which are very critical of white American culture, first appeared in *Atlantic Magazine*. Why do you think the magazine would publish these articles? Do you think the fact that they were published in a magazine of white America affect the audience's understanding of Zitkala's message?

2. List everything that troubles Bonnin during her voyage east and at the missionary school. Why do these events disturb the child? What differences do they indicate between Sioux and white American culture?

3. Bonnin describes an extreme case of "culture clash." Is it possible for multiple cultures to exist within the United States, or in any country, without one culture dominating the others? How do you think Bonnin would answer this question? How could a balance among multiple cultures be achieved?

4. Several elements from fairy tales of European origin appear in Bonnin's recollections. Why would she describe her childhood experiences as if they were part of a fairy tale? Might she be using fairy tale images, language, and structures as a means of resistance?

5. Have these excerpts from the work of Gertrude Bonnin (Zitkala-Sa) changed your mind about the ethics of the treatment of native Americans by white society? In what ways?

Chimney Sweeper I & II

William Blake

Now considered one of the great English poets, William Blake (1757–1827) was not well known during his lifetime. He earned a meager living as an engraver, and his expertise in this area led him to create illustrated poems, which he composed, engraved, printed, and colored himself. These remarkable works of art present a detailed mythology, which Blake devised to explain why human beings find themselves in a degraded condition and how they might recover their innocence through the use of imagination. Though Blake's mythological verses are very challenging to the reader, the "Chimney Sweep" poems are among his most accessible works. The first version was published in Blake's 1789 volume Songs of Innocence, *and the second appeared in the expanded 1794 edition entitled* Songs of Innocence and Experience Shewing the Two Contrary States of the Human Soul.*

The subtitle of this last work is revealing: Blake presents "innocence" and "experience" as two contrasting, mutually satirical modes of looking at life. In the case of the "Chimney Sweep" poems, Blake shows us the lives of young boys who were sold by their families into a dangerous and difficult job. He felt that since the poems express the perspectives of "innocent" and "experience," neither contains a complete view of the truth. As you read them, you can decide whether you accept Blake's interpretation, or if one poem sounds particularly true to you.

The Chimney Sweeper

When my mother died I was very young,
And my father sold me while yet my tongue
Could scarcely cry "'weep! 'weep! 'weep! 'weep!'"
So your chimneys I sweep & in soot I sleep.   4

There's little Tom Dacre, who cried when his head
That curl'd like a lamb's back, was shav'd, so I said,
"Hush, Tom! never mind it, for when your head's bare,
You know that the soot cannot spoil your white hair."   8

And so he was quiet, & that very night,
As Tom was a-sleeping he had such a sight!
That thousands of sweepers, Dick, Joe, Ned, & Jack,
Were all of them lock'd up in coffins of black;   12

And by came an Angel who had a bright key,
And he open'd the coffins & set them all free;
Then down a green plain, leaping, laughing they run,
And wash in a river and shine in the Sun.   16

Then naked & white, all their bags left behind,
They rise upon clouds, and sport in the wind.
And the Angel told Tom, if he'd be a good boy,
He'd have God for his father & never want joy.   20

And so Tom awoke; and we rose in the dark
And got with our bags & our brushes to work.
Tho' the morning was cold, Tom was happy & warm;
So if all do their duty, they need not fear harm.   24
                                                                 1789

The Chimney Sweeper

A little black thing among the snow
Crying "'weep, 'weep," in notes of woe!
"Where are thy father & mother? say?"
"They are both gone up to the church to pray.   4

"Because I was happy upon the heath,
And smil'd among the winter's snow;
They clothed me in the clothes of death,
And taught me to sing the notes of woe.   8

"And because I am happy, & dance & sing,
They think they have done me no injury,
And are gone to praise God & his Priest & King,
Who make up a heaven of our misery."   12
                                                           1790–92, 1794

For Practice

1. Blake was among the first writers to use poetry as a way of making a radical political statement. How effective are the chimney sweep poems as calls for social action? What kind of rhetorical appeal does the poem use to stimulate the reader to act?

2. What symbols and images do these poems contain? Is one poem more heavily symbolic than the other? Why?

3. The first "Chimney Sweeper" poem is narrated by one speaker, but in the second, Blake uses an impersonal, third-person speaker as well as the young boy. What is the effect of these choices of narrator?

4. Do you agree with Blake that innocence and experience are only partial approaches to truth? If so, how does this complicate questions of social justice?

5. In America today there are laws protecting children from the conditions described in the "Chimney Sweep" poems, yet children still suffer in other ways. What sort of argument might Blake make today about the social injustices experienced by children?

A Rose for Emily

William Faulkner

No writer has recorded the culture of the American South more fully than has William Faulkner (1897–1962). Drawing on his experience growing up in a prominent family from Oxford, Mississippi, Faulkner created the fictional world of Yoknapatawpha county which served as the setting for novels such as The Sound and the Fury, Light in August, *and* Absalom, Absalom! *Faulkner's writing is often experimental in form, combining numerous narrative fragments to create a mosaic of perspectives on one central story. Faulkner won the Nobel Prize for literature in 1950 and the National Book Award for his* Collected Stories *in the following year.*

"A Rose for Emily" (1931) is one of Faulkner's most popular stories. Carefully employing shifts in time, Faulkner not only creates a powerful suspense story, but also provides a picture of Southern society in two different eras. The younger characters in the story have difficulty in dealing with Miss Emily, who holds firmly to older social patterns in which decisions were made, not according to the letter of the law, but by the dictates of honor and tradition. This extends to the area of justice, for Miss Emily manages to evade the law by steadfastly ignoring it all her life. Not many readers can sympathize with Miss Emily, and Faulkner seems to enjoy bringing out her eccentricity; yet the story stands as a tribute, his "rose" for her.

When Miss Emily Grierson died, our whole town went to her funeral: the men through a sort of respectful affection for a fallen monument, the women mostly out of curiosity to see the inside of her house, which no one save an old manservant—a combined gardener and cook—had seen in at least ten years.

It was a big, squarish frame house that had once been white, decorated with cupolas and spires and scrolled balconies in the heavily lightsome style of the seventies, set on what had once been our most select street. But garages and cotton gins had encroached and obliterated even the august names of that neighborhood; only Miss Emily's house was left, lifting its stubborn and coquettish decay above the cotton wagons and the gasoline pumps—an eyesore among eyesores. And now Miss Emily had gone to join the representatives of those august names where they lay in the cedar-bemused cemetery among the ranked and anonymous graves of Union and Confederate soldiers who fell at the battle of Jefferson.

Alive, Miss Emily had been a tradition, a duty, and a care; a sort of hereditary obligation upon the town, dating from that day in 1894 when Colonel Sartoris, the mayor—he who fathered the edict that no Negro woman should appear on the streets without an apron—remitted her taxes, the dispensation dating from the death of her father on into perpetuity. Not that Miss Emily would have accepted charity. Colonel Sartoris invented an involved tale to the effect that Miss Emily's father had loaned money to the town, which the town, as a matter of business, preferred this way of repaying. Only a man of Colonel Sartoris' generation and thought could have invented it and only a woman could have believed it.

When the next generation, with its more modern ideas, became mayors and aldermen, this arrangement created some little dissatisfaction. On the first of the year they mailed her a tax notice. February came, and there was no reply. They wrote her a formal letter, asking her to call at the sheriff's office at her convenience. A week later the mayor wrote her himself, offering to call or to send his car for her, and received in reply a note on paper of an archaic shape, in a thin, flowing calligraphy in faded ink, to the effect that she no longer went out at all. The tax notice was also enclosed, without comment.

They called a special meeting of the Board of Aldermen. A deputation waited upon her, knocked at the door through which no visitor had passed since she ceased giving china painting lessons eight or ten years earlier. They were admitted by the old Negro into a dim hall from which a stairway mounted into still more shadow. it smelled of dust and disuse—a close, dank smell. The Negro led them into the parlor. It was furnished in heavy, leather-covered furniture. When the Negro opened the blinds of one window, they could see that the leather was cracked; and when they sat down, a faint dust rose sluggishly about their thighs, spinning with slow motes in the single sun-ray. On a tarnished gilt easel before the fireplace stood a crayon portrait of Miss Emily's father.

They rose when she entered—a small, fat woman in black, with a thin gold chain descending to her waist and vanishing into her belt, leaning on an ebony cane with a tarnished gold head. Her skeleton was small and spare; perhaps that was why what would have been merely plumpness in another was obesity in her. She looked bloated, like a body long submerged in motionless water, and of that pallid hue. Her eyes, lost in the fatty ridges of her face, looked like two small pieces of coal pressed into a lump of dough as they moved from one face to another while the visitors stated their errand.

She did not ask them to sit. She just stood in the door and listened quietly until the spokesman came to a stumbling halt. Then they could hear the invisible watch ticking at the end of the gold chain.

Her voice was dry and cold. "I have no taxes in Jefferson. Colonel Sartoris explained it to me. Perhaps one of you can gain access to the city records and satisfy yourselves."

"But we have. We are the city authorities, Miss Emily. Didn't you get a notice from the sheriff, signed by him?"

"I received a paper, yes," Miss Emily said. "Perhaps he considers himself the sheriff. . . . I have no taxes in Jefferson."

"But there is nothing on the books to show that, you see. We must go by the—"

"See Colonel Sartoris. I have no taxes in Jefferson."

"But, Miss Emily—"

"See Colonel Sartoris." (Colonel Sartoris had been dead almost ten years.) "I have no taxes in Jefferson. Tobe!" The Negro appeared. "Show these gentlemen out."

II

So she vanquished them, horse and foot, just as she had vanquished their fathers thirty years before about the smell. That was two years after her father's death and a short time after her sweetheart—the one we believed would marry her—had deserted her. After her father's death she went out very little; after her sweetheart went away, people hardly saw her at all. A few of the ladies had the temerity to call, but were not received, and the only sign of life about the place was the Negro man—a young man then—going in and out with a market basket.

"Just as if a man—any man—could keep a kitchen properly," the ladies said; so they were not surprised when the smell developed. It was another link between the gross, teeming world and the high and mighty Griersons.

A neighbor, a woman, complained to the mayor, Judge Stevens, eighty years old.

"But what will you have me do about it, madam?" he said.

"Why, send her word to stop it," the woman said. "Isn't there a law?"

"I'm sure that won't be necessary," Judge Stevens said. "It's probably just a snake or a rat that nigger of hers killed in the yard. I'll speak to him about it."

The next day he received two more complaints, one from a man who came in diffident deprecation. "We really must do something about it, Judge. I'd be the last one in the world to bother Miss Emily, but we've got to do something." That night the Board of Aldermen met—three graybeards and one younger man, a member of the rising generation.

"It's simple enough," he said. "Send her word to have her place cleaned up. Give her a certain time to do it in, and if she don't. . . ."

"Dammit, sir," Judge Stevens said, "will you accuse a lady to her face of smelling bad?"

So the next night, after midnight, four men crossed Miss Emily's lawn and slunk about the house like burglars, sniffing along the base of the brickwork and at the cellar openings while one of them performed a regular sowing motion with his hand out of a sack slung from his shoulder. They broke open the cellar door and sprinkled lime there, and in all the outbuildings. As they recrossed the lawn, a window that had been dark was lighted and Miss Emily sat in it, the light behind her, and her upright torso motionless as that of an idol. They crept quietly across the lawn and into the shadow of the locusts that lined the street. After a week or two the smell went away.

That was when people had begun to feel really sorry for her. People in our town, remembering how old lady Wyatt, her great-aunt, had gone completely crazy at last, believed that the Griersons held themselves a little too high for what they really were. None of the young men were quite good enough for Miss Emily and such. We had long thought of them as a tableau, Miss Emily a slender figure in white in the background, her father a spraddled silhouette in the foreground, his back to her and clutching a horsewhip, the two of them framed by the back-flung front door. So when she got to be thirty and was still single, we were not pleased exactly, but vindicated; even with insanity in the family she wouldn't have turned down all of her chances if they had really materialized.

When her father died, it got about that the house was all that was left to her; and in a way, people were glad. At last they could pity Miss Emily. Being left alone, and a pauper, she had become humanized. Now she too would know the old thrill and the old despair of a penny more or less.

The day after his death all the ladies prepared to call at the house and offer con-dolence and aid, as is our custom. Miss Emily met them at the door, dressed as usual and with no trace of grief on her face. She told them that her father was not dead. She did that for three days, with the ministers calling on her, and the doctors, trying to per-suade her to let them dispose of the body. Just as they were about to resort to law and force, she broke down, and they buried her father quickly.

We did not say she was crazy then. We believed she had to do that. We remembered all the young men her father had driven away, and we knew that with nothing left, she would have to cling to that which had robbed her, as people will.

III

She was sick for a long time. When we saw her again, her hair was cut short, mak-ing her look like a girl, with a vague resemblance to those angels in colored church windows—sort of tragic and serene.

The town had just let the contracts for paving the sidewalks, and in the summer after her father's death they began the work. The construction company came with nig-gers and mules and machinery, and a foreman named Homer Barron, a Yankee—a big, dark, ready man, with a big voice and eyes lighter than his face. The little boys would follow in groups to hear him cuss the niggers, and the niggers singing in time to the rise and fall of picks. Pretty soon he knew everybody in town. Whenever you heard a lot of laughing anywhere about the square, Homer Barron would be in the center of the group. Presently we began to see him and Miss Emily on Sunday afternoons dri-ving in the yellow-wheeled buggy and the matched team of bays from the livery stable.

At first we were glad that Miss Emily would have an interest, because the ladies all said, "Of course a Grierson would not think seriously of a Northerner, a day laborer." But there were still others, older people, who said that even grief could not cause a real lady to forget *noblesse oblige*—without calling it *noblesse oblige*. They just said, "Poor Emily. Her kinsfolk should come to her." She had some kin in Alabama; but years ago her father had fallen out with them over the estate of old lady Wyatt, the crazy woman, and there was no communication between the two families. They had not even been represented at the funeral.

And as soon as the old people said, "Poor Emily," the whispering began. "Do you suppose it's really so?" they said to one another. "Of course it is. What else could. . . ." This behind their hands; rustling of craned silk and satin behind jalousies closed upon the sun of Sunday afternoon as the thin, swift clop-clop-clop of the matched team passed: "Poor Emily."

She carried her head high enough—even when we believed that she was fallen. It was as if she demanded more than ever the recognition of her dignity as the last Grierson; as if it had wanted that touch of earthiness to reaffirm her imperviousness. Like when she bought the rat poison, the arsenic. That was over a year after they had begun to say "Poor Emily," and while the two female cousins were visiting her.

"I want some poison," she said to the druggist. She was over thirty then, still a slight woman, though thinner than usual, with cold, haughty black eyes in a face the flesh of which was strained across the temples and about the eyesockets as you imag-ine a lighthouse-keeper's face ought to look. "I want some poison," she said.

"Yes, Miss Emily. What kind? For rats and such? I'd recom—"

"I want the best you have. I don't care what kind."

The druggist named several. "They'll kill anything up to an elephant. But what you want is—"

"Arsenic," Miss Emily said. "Is that a good one?"

"Is . . . arsenic? Yes, ma'am. But what you want—"

"I want arsenic."

The druggist looked down at her. She looked back at him, erect, her face like a strained flag. "Why, of course," the druggist said. "If that's what you want. But the law requires you to tell what you are going to use it for."

Miss Emily just stared at him, her head tilted back in order to look him eye for eye, until he looked away and went and got the arsenic and wrapped it up. The Negro delivery boy brought her the package; the druggist didn't come back. When she opened the package at home there was written on the box, under the skull and bones: "For rats."

IV

So the next day we all said, "She will kill herself"; and we said it would be the best thing. When she had first begun to be seen with Homer Barron, we had said, "She will marry him." Then we said, "She will persuade him yet," because Homer himself had remarked—he liked men, and it was known that he drank with the younger men in the Elks' Club—that he was not a marrying man. Later we said, "Poor Emily" behind the jalousies as they passed on Sunday afternoon in the glittering buggy, Miss Emily with her head high and Homer Barron with his hat cocked and a cigar in his teeth, reins and whip in a yellow glove.

Then some of the ladies began to say that it was a disgrace to the town and a bad example to the young people. The men did not want to interfere, but at last the ladies forced the Baptist minister—Miss Emily's people were Episcopal—to call upon her. He would never divulge what happened during that interview, but he refused to go back again. The next Sunday they again drove about the streets, and the following day the minister's wife wrote to Miss Emily's relations in Alabama.

So she had blood-kin under her roof again and we sat back to watch developments. At first nothing happened. Then we were sure that they were to be married. We learned that Miss Emily had been to the jeweler's and ordered a man's toilet set in silver, with the letters H. B. on each piece. Two days later we learned that she had bought a complete outfit of men's clothing, including a nightshirt, and we said, "They are married." We were really glad. We were glad because the two female cousins were even more Grierson than Miss Emily had ever been.

So we were not surprised when Homer Barron—the streets had been finished some time since—was gone. We were a little disappointed that there was not a public blowing-off, but we believed that he had gone on to prepare for Miss Emily's coming, or to give her a chance to get rid of the cousins. (By that time it was a cabal, and we were all Miss Emily's allies to help circumvent the cousins.) Sure enough, after another week they departed. And, as we had expected all along, within three days Homer Barron was back in town. A neighbor saw the Negro man admit him at the kitchen door at dusk one evening.

And that was the last we saw of Homer Barron. And of Miss Emily for some time. The Negro man went in and out with the market basket, but the front door remained closed. Now and then we would see her at a window for a moment, as the men did that night when they sprinkled the lime, but for almost six months she did not appear on the streets. Then we knew that this was to be expected too; as if that quality of her father which had thwarted her woman's life so many times had been too virulent and too furious to die.

When we next saw Miss Emily, she had grown fat and her hair was turning gray. During the next few years it grew grayer and grayer until it attained an even pepper-and-salt iron-gray, when it ceased turning. Up to the day of her death at seventy-four it was still that vigorous iron-gray, like the hair of an active man.

From that time on her front door remained closed, save for a period of six or seven years, when she was about forty, during which she gave lessons in china-painting. She fitted up a studio in one of the downstairs rooms, where the daughters and grand-daughters of Colonel Sartoris' contemporaries were sent to her with the same regularity and in the same spirit that they were sent on Sundays with a twenty-five-cent piece for the collection plate. Meanwhile her taxes had been remitted.

Then the newer generation became the backbone and the spirit of the town, and the painting pupils grew up and fell away and did not send their children to her with boxes of color and tedious brushes and pictures cut from the ladies' magazines. The front door closed upon the last one and remained closed for good. When the town got free postal delivery, Miss Emily alone refused to let them fasten the metal numbers above her door and attach a mailbox to it. She would not listen to them.

Daily, monthly, yearly we watched the Negro grow grayer and more stooped, going in and out with the market basket. Each December we sent her a tax notice, which would be returned by the post office a week later, unclaimed. Now and then we would see her in one of the downstairs windows—she had evidently shut up the top floor of the house—like the carven torso of an idol in a niche, looking or not looking at us, we could never tell which. Thus she passed from generation to generation—dear, inescapable, impervious, tranquil, and perverse.

And so she died. Fell ill in the house filled with dust and shadows, with only a doddering Negro man to wait on her. We did not even know she was sick; we had long since given up trying to get any information from the Negro. He talked to no one, probably not even to her, for his voice had grown harsh and rusty, as if from disuse.

She died in one of the downstairs rooms, in a heavy walnut bed with a curtain, her gray head propped on a pillow yellow and moldy with age and lack of sunlight.

V

The Negro met the first of the ladies at the front door and let them in, with their hushed, sibilant voices and their quick, curious glances, and then he disappeared. He walked right through the house and out the back and was not seen again.

The two female cousins came at once. They held the funeral on the second day, with the town coming to look at Miss Emily beneath a mass of bought flowers, with the crayon face of her father musing profoundly above the bier and the ladies sibilant and macabre; and the very old men—some in their brushed confederate uniforms—on the porch and the lawn, talking of Miss Emily as if she had been a contemporary of theirs, believing that they had danced with her and courted her perhaps, confusing time with its mathematical progression, as the old do, to whom all the past is not a diminishing road, but, instead, a huge meadow which no winter ever quite touches, divided from them now by the narrow bottleneck of the most recent decade of years.

Already we knew that there was one room in that region above stairs which no one had seen in forty years, and which would have to be forced. They waited until Miss Emily was decently in the ground before they opened it.

The violence of breaking down the door seemed to fill this room with pervading dust. A thin, acrid pall as of the tomb seemed to lie everywhere upon this room decked and furnished as for a bridal: upon the valance curtains of faded rose color, upon the rose-shaded lights, upon the dressing table, upon the delicate array of crystal and the man's toilet things backed with tarnished silver, silver so tarnished that the monogram was obscured. Among them lay a collar and tie, as if they had just been removed, which, lifted, left upon the surface a pale crescent in the dust. Upon the chair hung the suit, carefully folded; beneath it the two mute shoes and the discarded socks.

The man himself lay in the bed.

For a long while we just stood there, looking down at the profound and fleshless grin. The body had apparently once lain in the attitude of an embrace, but now the long sleep that outlasts love, that conquers even the grimace of love, had cuckolded him. What was left of him, rotted beneath what was left of the nightshirt, had become inextricable from the bed in which he lay; and upon him and upon the pillow beside him lay that even coating of the patient and biding dust.

Then we noticed that in the second pillow was the indentation of a head. One of us lifted something from it, and leaning forward, that faint and invisible dust dry and acrid in the nostrils, we saw a long strand of iron-gray hair.

For Practice

1. Faulkner enhances the suspense of this story by using a series of flashbacks to control the pattern in which the reader learns vital pieces of information. At what points in the story did you suddenly gain insight into what was going on? What clues helped you to do so? Try plotting on a piece of paper all of the shifts in time that take place in the story; Faulkner gives dates for some events, so use those to help make your time scheme as specific as possible.

2. Why do the townspeople have so much trouble dealing with Miss Emily? You may want to use your timeline from the previous question and consider what was happening in the American South during those years.

3. Who is the narrator? Is he or she speaking for Faulkner? What do you think Faulkner's attitude is toward Emily? Why?

4. Emily clearly violates the law in several instances in this story, yet she is not the only character whose conduct is suspect. Analyze the characters in the story according to their degree of guilt: who is most culpable? Who, if anyone, is completely innocent?

5. What do you think is at issue in this story? What kind of argument is Faulkner trying to make?

Desiree's Baby

Kate Chopin

Katherine O'Flaherty Chopin (1851–1904) was a native of St. Louis, but her fiction reflects the 14 years she spent in Louisiana with her husband. Married to Oscar Chopin at age 19, Kate lived with him in New Orleans in the Cane River district until his death in 1882, at which she returned with their six children to St. Louis. When she began to write, it was not about her native St. Louis, but the New Orleans of the Creoles and Acadians that animated her fiction. Chopin's novel, The Awakening, *first published in 1899, was proclaimed by critics to be scandalous and morbid. In the 1970's,* The Awakening *was rediscovered and is now considered a masterpiece of American realism.*

On January 4, 1893, Chopin published what was to become one of her most famous stories, "Desiree's Baby," in Vogue *magazine. This story was later included in* Bayou Folk, *a collection of 23 stories and sketches published in 1894. "Desiree's Baby" depicts the deep-rooted caste system in Creole society and the tragic consequences that can result from adherence to such an unjust system.*

As the day was pleasant, Madame Valmondé drove over to L'Abri to see Désirée and the baby.

It made her laugh to think of Désirée with a baby. Why, it seemed but yesterday that Désirée was little more than a baby herself; when Monsieur in riding through the gateway of Valmondé had found her lying asleep in the shadow of the big stone pillar.

The little one awoke in his arms and began to cry for "Dada." That was as much as she could do or say. Some people thought she might have strayed there of her own accord, for she was of the toddling age. The prevailing belief was that she had been purposely left by a party of Texans, whose canvas-covered wagon, late in the day, had crossed the ferry that Coton Maïs kept, just below the plantation. In time Madame Valmondé abandoned every speculation but the one that Désirée had been sent to her by a beneficent Providence to be the child of her affection, seeing that she was without child of the flesh. For the girl grew to be beautiful and gentle, affectionate and sincere,—the idol of Valmondé.

It was no wonder, when she stood one day against the stone pillar in whose shadow she had lain asleep, eighteen years before, that Armand Aubigny riding by and seeing her there, had fallen in love with her. That was the way all the Aubignys fell in love, as if struck by a pistol shot. The wonder was that he had not loved her before; for he had known her since his father brought him home from Paris, a boy of eight, after his mother died there. The passion that awoke in him that day, when he saw her at the gate, swept along like an avalanche, or like a prairie fire, or like anything that drives headlong over all obstacles.

Monsieur Valmondé grew practical and wanted things well considered: that is, the girl's obscure origin. Armand looked into her eyes and did not care. He was reminded that she was nameless. What did it matter about a name when he could giver her one of the oldest and proudest in Louisiana? He ordered the *corbeille* from Paris, and contained himself with what patience he could until it arrived; then they were married.

Madame Valmondé had not seen Désirée and the baby for four weeks. When she reached L'Abri she shuddered at the first sight of it, as she always did. It was a sad looking place, which for many years had not known the gentle presence of a mistress, old Monsieur Aubigny having married and buried his wife in France, and she having loved her own land too well ever to leave it. The roof came down steep and black like a cowl, reaching out beyond the wide galleries that encircled the yellow stuccoed house. Big, solemn oaks grew close to it, and their thick-leaved, far-reaching branches shadowed it like a pall. Young Aubigny's rule was a strict one, too, and under it his negroes had forgotten how to be gay, as they had been during the old master's easy-going and indulgent lifetime.

The young mother was recovering slowly, and lay full length, in her soft white muslins and laces, upon a couch. The baby was beside her, upon her arm, where he had fallen asleep, at her breast. The yellow nurse woman sat beside a window fanning herself.

Madame Valmondé bent her portly figure over Désirée and kissed her, holding her an instant tenderly in her arms. Then she turned to the child.

"This is not the baby!" she exclaimed, in startled tones. French was the language spoken at Valmondé in those days.

"I knew you would be astonished," laughed Désirée, "at the way he has grown. The little *cochon de lait*! Look at his legs, mamma, and his hands and fingernails,—real fingernails. Zandrine had to cut them this morning. Isn't it true, Zandrine?"

The woman bowed her turbaned head majestically, "Mais si, Madame."

"And the way he cries," went on Désirée, "is deafening. Armand heard him the other day as far away as La Blanche's cabin."

Madame Valmondé had never removed her eyes from the child. She lifted it and walked with it over to the window that was lightest. She scanned the baby narrowly, then looked as searchingly at Zandrine, whose face was turned to gaze across the fields.

"Yes, the child has grown, has changed," said Madame Valmondé, slowly, as she replaced it beside its mother. "What does Armand say?"

Désirée's face became suffused with a glow that was happiness itself.

"Oh, Armand is the proudest father in the parish, I believe, chiefly because it is a boy, to bear his name; though he says not,—that he would have loved a girl as well. But I know it isn't true. I know he says that to please me. And mamma," she added, drawing Madame Valmondé's head down to her, and speaking in a whisper, "he hasn't punished one of them—not one of them—since baby is born. Even Négrillon, who pretended to have burnt his leg that he might rest from work—he only laughed, and said Négrillon was a great scamp. Oh, mamma, I'm so happy; it frightens me."

What Désirée said was true. Marriage, and later the birth of his son, had softened Armand Aubigny's imperious and exacting nature greatly. This was what made the gentle Désirée so happy, for she loved him desperately. When he frowned she trembled, but loved him. When he smiled, she asked no greater blessing of God. Armand's dark, handsome face had not often been disfigured by frowns since the day he fell in love with her.

When the baby was about three months old, Désirée awoke one day to the conviction that there was something in the air menacing her peace. It was at first too subtle to grasp. It had only been a disquieting suggestion; an air of mystery among the blacks; unexpected visits from far-off neighbors who could hardly account for their coming. Then a strange, an awful change in her husband's manner, which she dared not ask him to explain. When he spoke to her, it was with averted eyes, from which the old love-light seemed to have gone out. He absented himself from home; and when there, avoided her presence and that of her child, without excuse. And the very spirit of Satan seemed suddenly to take hold of him in his dealings with the slaves. Désirée was miserable enough to die.

She sat in her room, one hot afternoon, in her *peignoir*, listlessly drawing through her fingers the strands of her long, silky brown hair that hung about her shoulders. The baby, half naked, lay asleep upon her own great mahogany bed, that was like a sumptuous throne, with its satin lined half-canopy. One of La Blanche's little quadroon boys—half naked too—stood fanning the child slowly with a fan of peacock feathers. Désirée's eyes had been fixed absently and sadly upon the baby, while she was striving to penetrate the threatening mist that she felt closing about her. She looked from her child to the boy who stood beside him, and back again; over and over. "Ah!" It was a cry that she could not help, which she was not conscious of having uttered. The blood turned like ice in her veins, and a clammy moisture gathered upon her face.

She tried to speak to the little quadroon boy; but no sound would come, at first. When he heard his name uttered, he looked up, and his mistress was pointing to the door. He laid aside the great, soft fan, and obediently stole away, over the polished floor, on his bare tiptoes.

She stayed motionless, with gaze riveted upon her child, and her face the picture of fright.

Presently her husband entered the room, and without noticing her, went to a table and began to search among some papers which covered it.

"Armand," she called to him, in a voice which must have stabbed him, if he was human. But he did not notice. "Armand," she said again. Then she rose and tottered toward him. "Armand," she panted once more, clutching his arm, "look at our child. What does it mean? tell me."

He coldly but gently loosened her fingers from about his arm and thrust the hand away from him. "Tell me what it means!" she cried despairingly.

"It means," he answered lightly, "that the child is not white; it means that you are not white."

A quick conception of all that this accusation meant for her nerved her with unwonted courage to deny it. "It is a lie; it is not true, I am white! Look at my hair, it is brown; and my eyes are gray, Armand, you know they are gray. And my skin is fair," seizing his wrist. "Look at my hand; whiter than yours, Armand," she laughed hysterically.

"As white as La Blanche's," he returned cruelly; and went away leaving her alone with their child.

When she could hold a pen in her hand, she sent a despairing letter to Madame Valmondé.

"My mother, they tell me I am not white. Armand has told me I am not white. For God's sake tell them it is not true. You must know it is not true. I shall die. I must die. I cannot be so unhappy, and live."

The answer that came was as brief:

"My own Désirée: Come home to Valmondé; back to your mother who loves you. Come with your child."

When the letter reached Désirée she went with it to her husband's study, and laid it open upon the desk before which he sat. She was like a stone image: silent, white, motionless after she placed it there.

In silence he ran his cold eyes over the written words. He said nothing. "Shall I go, Armand?" she asked in tones sharp with agonized suspense.

"Yes, go."

"Do you want me to go?"

"Yes, I want you to go."

He thought Almighty God had dealt cruelly and unjustly with him; and felt, somehow, that he was paying Him back in kind when he stabbed thus into his wife's soul. Moreover he no longer loved her, because of the unconscious injury she had brought upon his home and his name.

She turned away like one stunned by a blow, and walked slowly towards the door, hoping he would call her back.

"Good-by, Armand," she moaned.

He did not answer her. That was his last blow at fate.

Désirée went in search of her child. Zandrine was pacing the sombre gallery with it. She took the little one from the nurse's arms with no word of explanation, and descending the steps, walked away, under the live-oak branches.

It was an October afternoon; the sun was just sinking. Out in the still fields the negroes were picking cotton.

Désirée had not changed the thin white garment nor the slippers which she wore. Her hair was uncovered and the sun's rays brought a golden gleam from its brown meshes. She did not take the broad, beaten road which led to the far-off plantation of Valmondé. She walked across a deserted field, where the stubble bruised her tender feet, so delicately shod, and tore her thin gown to shreds.

She disappeared among the reeds and willows that grew thick along the banks of the deep, sluggish bayou; and she did not come back again.

* * *

Some weeks later there was a curious scene enacted at L'Abri. In the centre of the smoothly swept backyard was a great bonfire. Armand Aubigny sat in the wide hallway that commanded a view of the spectacle; and it was he who dealt out to a half dozen negroes the material which kept this fire ablaze.

A graceful cradle of willow, with all its dainty furbishings, was laid upon the pyre, which had already been fed with the richness of a priceless *layette*. Then there were silk gowns, and velvet and satin ones added to these; laces, too, and embroideries; bonnets and gloves; for the *corbeille* had been of rare quality.

The last thing to go was a tiny bundle of letters; innocent little scribblings that Désirée had sent to him during the days of their espousal. There was the remnant of one back in the drawer from which he took them. But it was not Désirée's; it was part of an old letter from his mother to his father. He read it. She was thanking God for the blessing of her husband's love:—

"But, above all," she wrote, "night and day, I thank the good God for having so arranged our lives that our dear Armand will never know that his mother, who adores him, belongs to the race that is cursed with the brand of slavery."

For Practice

1. How does Chopin describe Armand Aubigny? Which characteristics foreshadow his reaction when he realizes the ethnicity of his child?

2. Desiree chooses to walk into the swamp with her baby rather than go home to her adopted mother where she would be loved and accepted. What motivates her choice?

3. This story was originally published in *Vogue* magazine in 1893. What judgments can you make about the magazine based on the fact that it would publish this story at that time? Do you think the magazine has changed over the nearly 100 years since this story was published?

4. Chopin's text is clearly an indictment of the caste system which is so deeply ingrained in the New Orleans society of her day. How would you characterize the argument that her text makes? Is it a call to action, or is it an example of epideictic rhetoric (the rhetoric of praise or blame)? Support your answer with good reasons.

5. Desiree's tragedy is not the result of a civil law, but of a code of conduct, unwritten laws that govern society. What kind of unwritten laws govern our own contemporary culture? Does each social group have different codes? How does "Desiree's Baby" change your perspectives on these codes of conduct?

Witness for the Prosecution

Agatha Christie

Agatha Christie (1890–1976) was born Agatha May Clarissa Miller in Torquay, England, to a conservative, well-to-do family. She was educated at home and in 1914 married Archibald Christie. She worked as a hospital dispenser (pharmacist) during WWI where she gained a knowledge of poisons that proved to be useful when she began writing detective novels. She divorced Christie in 1926, but kept his name professionally. In 1930, she married Max Mallowan, an archeologist, and accompanied him on excavations in Syria and Iraq. Her first novel, The Mysterious Affair at Styles *(1920), introduced the Belgian detective Hercule Poirot who would appear in more than 30 of her 66 detective novels and short stories and of whom she finally managed to rid herself in* Curtain *(1975), her final novel.*

Written in 1924, "Witness for the Prosecution" is one of the few Christie stories which does not feature one of her famous detectives. The short story was successfully adapted for the stage in 1953 and later made into a film version starring Charles Laughton and Marlene Dietrich. The tightly crafted, double-twist ending exemplifies the ingenuity that has attracted Christie's readers for decades. As you read this story, pay particular attention to Christie's development of character. Is the ending really a surprise?

Mr. Mayherne adjusted his pince-nez and cleared his throat with a little dry-as-dust cough that was wholly typical of him. Then he looked again at the man opposite him, the man charged with willful murder.

Mr. Mayherne was a small man, precise in manner, neatly, not to say foppishly dressed, with a pair of very shrewd and piercing gray eyes. By no means a fool. Indeed, as a solicitor, Mr. Mayherne's reputation stood very high. His voice, when he spoke to his client, was dry but not unsympathetic.

"I must impress upon you again that you are in very grave danger, and that the utmost frankness is necessary."

Leonard Vole, who had been staring in a dazed fashion at the blank wall in front of him, transferred his glance to the solicitor.

"I know," he said hopelessly. "You keep telling me so. But I can't seem to realize yet that I'm charged with murder—*murder*. And such a dastardly crime, too."

Mr. Mayherne was practical, not emotional. He coughed again, took off his pince-nez, polished them carefully, and replaced them on his nose. Then he said, "Yes, yes,

yes. Now, my dear Mr. Vole, we're going to make a determined effort to get you off—and we shall succeed—we shall succeed. But I must have all the facts. I must know just how damaging the case against you is likely to be. Then we can fix upon the best line of defense."

Still the young man looked at him in the same dazed, hopeless fashion. To Mr. Mayherne the case had seemed black enough, and the guilt of the prisoner assured. Now, for the first time, he felt a doubt.

"You think I'm guilty," said Leonard Vole, in a low voice. "But, by God, I swear I'm not! It looks pretty black against me, I know that. I'm like a man caught in a net—the meshes of it all round me, entangling me whichever way I turn. But I didn't do it, Mr. Mayherne, I didn't do it!"

In such a position a man was bound to protest his innocence. Mr. Mayherne knew that. Yet, in spite of himself, he was impressed. It might be, after all, that Leonard Vole was innocent.

"You are right, Mr. Vole," he said gravely. "The case does look very black against you. Nevertheless, I accept your assurance. Now, let us get to facts. I want you to tell me in your own words exactly how you came to make the acquaintance of Miss Emily French."

"It was one day in Oxford Street. I saw an elderly lady crossing the road. She was carrying a lot of parcels. In the middle of the street she dropped them, tried to recover them, found a bus was almost on top of her, and just managed to reach the curb safely, dazed and bewildered by people having shouted at her. I recovered her parcels, wiped the mud off them as best I could, retied the string of one, and returned them to her."

"There was no question of your having saved her life?"

"Oh, dear me, no! All I did was to perform a common act of courtesy. She was extremely grateful, thanked me warmly, and said something about my manners not being those of most of the younger generation—I can't remember the exact words. Then I lifted my hat and went on. I never expected to see her again. But life is full of coincidences. That very evening I came across her at a party at a friend's house. She recognized me at once and asked that I should be introduced to her. I then found out that she was Miss Emily French and that she lived at Cricklewood. I talked to her for some time. She was, I imagine, an old lady who took sudden and violent fancies to people. She took one to me on the strength of a perfectly simple action which anyone might have performed. On leaving, she shook me warmly by the hand and asked me to come and see her. I replied, of course, that I should be very pleased to do so, and she then urged me to name a day. I did not want particularly to go, but it would have seemed churlish to refuse, so I fixed on the following Saturday. After she had gone, I learned something about her from my friends. That she was rich, eccentric, lived alone with one maid, and owned no less than eight cats."

"I see," said Mr. Mayherne. "The question of her being well off came up as early as that?"

"If you mean that I inquired—" began Leonard Vole hotly, but Mr. Mayherne stilled him with a gesture.

"I have to look at the case as it will be presented by the other side. An ordinary observer would not have supposed Miss French to be a lady of means. She lived poorly, almost humbly. Unless you had been told the contrary, you would in all probability have considered her to be in poor circumstances—at any rate to begin with. Who was it exactly who told you that she was well off?"

"My friend, George Harvey, at whose house the party took place."

"Is he likely to remember having done so?"

"I really don't know. Of course it is some time ago now."

"Quite so, Mr. Vole. You see, the first aim of the prosecution will be to establish that you were in low water financially—that is true, is it not?"

Leonard Vole flushed.

"Yes," he said, in a low voice. "I'd been having a run of infernal bad luck just then."

"Quite so," said Mr. Mayherne again. "That being, as I say, in low water financially, you met this rich old lady and cultivated her acquaintance assiduously. Now if we are in a position to say that you had no idea she was well off, and that you visited her out of pure kindness of heart—"

"Which is the case."

"I dare say. I am not disputing the point. I am looking at it from the outside point of view. A great deal depends on the memory of Mr. Harvey. Is he likely to remember that conversation or is he not? Could he be confused by counsel into believing that it took place later?"

Leonard Vole reflected for some minutes. Then he said steadily enough, but with a rather pale face, "I do not think that that line would be successful, Mr. Mayherne. Several of those present heard his remark, and one or two of them chaffed me about my conquest of a rich old lady."

The solicitor endeavored to hide his disappointment with a wave of the hand.

"Unfortunate," he said. "But I congratulate you upon your plain speaking, Mr. Vole. It is to you I look to guide me. Your judgment is quite right. To persist in the line I spoke of would have been disastrous. We must leave that point. You made the acquaintance of Miss French, you called upon her, the acquaintanceship progressed. We want a clear reason for all this. Why did you, a young man of thirty-three, good-looking, fond of sport, popular with your friends, devote so much of your time to an elderly woman with whom you could hardly have anything in common?"

Leonard Vole flung out his hands in a nervous gesture.

"I can't tell you—I really can't tell you. After the first visit, she pressed me to come again, spoke of being lonely and unhappy. She made it difficult for me to refuse. She showed so plainly her fondness and affection for me that I was placed in an awkward position. You see, Mr. Mayherne, I've got a weak nature—I drift—I'm one of those people who can't say no. And believe me or not, as you like, after the third or fourth visit I paid her I found myself getting genuinely fond of the old thing. My mother died when I was young, an aunt brought me up, and she, too, died before I was fifteen. If I told you that I genuinely enjoyed being mothered and pampered, I dare say you'd only laugh."

Mr. Mayherne did not laugh. Instead he took off his pince-nez again and polished them, a sign with him that he was thinking deeply.

"I accept your explanation, Mr. Vole," he said at last. "I believe it to be psychologically probable. Whether a jury would take that view of it is another matter. Please continue your narrative. When was it that Miss French first asked you to look into her business affairs?"

"After my third or fourth visit to her. She understood very little of money matters, and was worried about some investments."

Mr. Mayherne looked up sharply.

"Be careful, Mr. Vole. The maid, Janet Mackenzie, declares that her mistress was a good woman of business and transacted all her own affairs, and this is borne out by the testimony of her bankers."

"I can't help that," said Vole earnestly. "That's what she said to me."

Mr. Mayherne looked at him for a moment or two in silence. Though he had no intention of saying so, his belief in Leonard Vole's innocence was at that moment strengthened. He knew something of the mentality of elderly ladies. He saw Miss French, infatuated with the good-looking young man, hunting about for pretexts that would bring him to the house. What more likely than that she should plead ignorance of business, and beg him to help her with her money affairs? She was enough of a woman of the world to realize that any man is slightly flattered by such an admission of his superiority. Leonard Vole had been flattered. Perhaps, too, she had not been averse to letting this young man know that she was wealthy. Emily French had been a strong-willed old woman, willing to pay her price, for what she wanted. All this passed rapidly through Mr. Mayherne's mind, but he gave no indication of it, and asked instead a further question.

"And did you handle her affairs for her at her request?"

"I did."

"Mr. Vole," said the solicitor, "I am going to ask you a very serious question, and one to which it is vital I should have a truthful answer. You were in low water financially. You had the handling of an old lady's affairs—an old lady who, according to her own statement, knew little or nothing of business. Did you at any time, or in any manner, convert to your own use the securities which you handled? Did you engage in any transaction for your own pecuniary advantage which will not bear the light of day?" He quelled the other's response. "Wait a minute before you answer. There are two courses open to us. Either we can make a feature of your probity and honesty in conducting her affairs while pointing out how unlikely it is that you would commit murder to obtain money which you might have obtained by such infinitely easier means. If, on the other hand, there is anything in your dealings which the prosecution will get hold of—if, to put it baldly, it can be proved that you swindled the old lady in any way, we must take the line that you had no motive for the murder, since she was already a profitable source of income to you. You perceive the distinction. Now, I beg of you, take your time before you reply."

But Leonard Vole took no time at all.

"My dealings with Miss French's affairs were all perfectly fair and above board. I acted for her interests to the very best of my ability, as anyone will find who looks into the matter."

"Thank you," said Mr. Mayherne. "You relieve my mind very much. I pay you the compliment of believing that you are far too clever to lie to me over such an important matter."

"Surely," said Vole eagerly, "the strongest point in my favor is the lack of motive. Granted that I cultivated the acquaintanceship of a rich old lady in the hopes of getting money out of her—that, I gather, is the substance of what you have been saying—surely her death frustrates all my hopes?"

The solicitor looked at him steadily. Then, very deliberately, he repeated his unconscious trick with his pince-nez. It was not until they were firmly replaced on his nose that he spoke.

"Are you not aware, Mr. Vole, that Miss French left a will under which you are the principal beneficiary?"

"What?" The prisoner sprang to his feet. His dismay was obvious and unforced. "My God! What are you saying? She left her money to me?"

Mr. Mayherne nodded slowly. Vole sank down again, his head in his hands.

"You pretend you know nothing of this will?"

"Pretend? There's no pretense about it. I knew nothing about it."

"What would you say if I told you that the maid, Janet Mackenzie, swears that you *did* know? That her mistress told her distinctly that she had consulted you in the matter, and told you of her intentions?"

"Say? That she's lying! No, I go too fast. Janet is an elderly woman. She was a faithful watchdog to her mistress, and she didn't like me. She was jealous and suspicious. I should say that Miss French confided her intentions to Janet, and that Janet either mistook something she said, or else was convinced in her own mind that I had persuaded the old lady into doing it. I dare say that she herself believes now that Miss French actually told her so."

"You don't think she dislikes you enough to lie deliberately about the matter?"

Leonard Vole looked shocked and startled.

"No, indeed! Why should she?"

"I don't know," said Mr. Mayherne thoughtfully. "But she's very bitter against you."

The wretched young man groaned again.

"I'm beginning to see," he muttered. "It's frightful. I made up to her, that's what they'll say, I got her to make a will leaving her money to me, and then I go there that night, and there's nobody in the house—they find her the next day—oh, my God, it's awful!"

"You are wrong about there being nobody in the house," said Mr. Mayherne. "Janet, as you remember, was to go out for the evening. She went, but about half past nine she returned to fetch the pattern of a blouse sleeve which she had promised to a friend. She let herself in by the back door, went upstairs and fetched it, and went out again. She heard voices in the sitting-room, though she could not distinguish what they said, but she will swear that one of them was Miss French's and one was a man's."

"At half past nine," said Leonard Vole. "At half past nine—" He sprang to his feet. "But then I'm saved—saved—"

"What do you mean, saved?" cried Mr. Mayherne, astonished.

"By half past nine I was at home again! My wife can prove that. I left Miss French about five minutes to nine. I arrived home about twenty past nine. My wife was there waiting for me. Oh, thank God—thank God! And bless Janet Mackenzie's sleeve pattern."

In his exuberance, he hardly noticed that the grave expression on the solicitor's face had not altered. But the latter's words brought him down to earth with a bump.

"Who, then, in your opinion, murdered Miss French?"

"Why, a burglar, of course, as was thought at first. The window was forced, you remember. She was killed with a heavy blow from a crowbar, and the crowbar was found lying on the floor beside the body. And several articles were missing. But for Janet's absurd suspicions and dislike of me, the police would never have swerved from the right track."

"That will hardly do, Mr. Vole," said the solicitor. "The things that were missing were mere trifles of no value, taken as a blind. And the marks on the window were not at all conclusive. Besides, think of yourself. You say you were no longer in the house by half past nine. Who, then, was the man Janet heard talking to Miss French in the sitting-room? She would hardly be having an amicable conversation with a burglar."

"No," said Vole. "No—" He looked puzzled and discouraged. "But, anyway," he added with reviving spirit, "it lets me out. I've got an alibi. You must see Romaine—my wife—at once."

"Certainly," acquiesced the lawyer. "I should already have seen Mrs. Vole but for her being absent when you were arrested. I wired to Scotland at once, and I understand that she arrives back tonight. I am going to call upon her immediately I leave here."

Vole nodded, a great expression of satisfaction settling down over his face.

"Yes, Romaine will tell you. My God! it's a lucky chance that."

"Excuse me, Mr. Vole, but you are very fond of your wife?"

"Of course."

"And she of you?"

"Romaine is devoted to me. She'd do anything in the world for me."

He spoke enthusiastically, but the solicitor's heart sank a little lower. The testimony of a devoted wife—would it gain credence?

"Was there anyone else who saw you return at nine-twenty? A maid, for instance?"

"We have no maid."

"Did you meet anyone in the street on the way back?"

"Nobody I knew. I rode part of the way in a bus. The conductor might remember."

Mr. Mayherne shook his head doubtfully.

"There is no one, then, who can confirm your wife's testimony?"

"No. But it isn't necessary, surely?"

"I dare say not. I dare say not," said Mr. Mayherne hastily. "Now here's just one thing more. Did Miss French know that you were a married man?"

"Oh, yes."

"Yet you never took your wife to see her. Why was that?"

For the first time, Leonard Vole's answer came halting and uncertain.

"Well—I don't know."

"Are you aware that Janet Mackenzie says her mistress believed you to be single, and contemplated marrying you in the future?"

Vole laughed. "Absurd! There was forty years' difference in age between us."

"It has been done," said the solicitor dryly. "The fact remains. Your wife never met Miss French?"

"No—" Again the constraint.

"You will permit me to say," said the lawyer, "that I hardly understand your attitude in the matter."

Vole flushed, hesitated, and then spoke.

"I'll make a clean breast of it. I was hard up, as you know. I hoped that Miss French might lend me some money. She was fond of me, but she wasn't at all interested in the struggles of a young couple. Early on, I found that she had taken it for granted that my wife and I didn't get on—were living apart. Mr. Mayherne—I wanted the money—for Romaine's sake. I said nothing, and allowed the old lady to think what she chose. She spoke of my being an adopted son to her. There was never any question of marriage—that must be just Janet's imagination."

"And that is all?"

"Yes—that is all."

Was there just a shade of hesitation in the words? The lawyer fancied so. He rose and held out his hand.

"Good-by, Mr. Vole." He looked in the haggard young face and spoke with an unusual impulse. "I believe in your innocence in spite of the multitude of facts arrayed against you. I hope to prove it and vindicate you completely."

Vole smiled back at him.

"You'll find the alibi is all right," he said cheerfully.

Again he hardly noticed that the other did not respond.

"The whole thing hinges a good deal on the testimony of Janet Mackenzie," said Mr. Mayherne. "She hates you. That much is clear."

"She can hardly hate me," protested the young man.

The solicitor shook his head as he went out. *Now for Mrs. Vole*, he said to himself. He was seriously disturbed by the way the thing was shaping.

The Voles lived in a small shabby house near Paddington Green. It was to this house that Mr. Mayherne went.

In answer to his ring, a big slatternly woman, obviously a char-woman, answered the door.

"Mrs. Vole? Has she returned yet?"

"Got back an hour ago. But I dunno if you can see her."

"If you will take my card to her," said Mr. Mayherne quietly, "I am quite sure that she will do so."

The woman looked at him doubtfully, wiped her hand on her apron, and took the card. Then she closed the door in his face and left him on the step outside.

In a few minutes, however, she returned with a slightly altered manner.

"Come inside, please."

She ushered him into a tiny drawing-room. Mr. Mayherne, examining a drawing on the wall, started up suddenly to face a tall, pale woman who had entered so quietly that he had not heard her.

"Mr. Mayherne? You are my husband's solicitor, are you not? You have come from him? Will you please sit down?"

Until she spoke he had not realized that she was not English. Now, observing her more closely, he noticed the high cheekbones, the dense blue-black of the hair, and an occasional very slight movement of the hands that was distinctly foreign. A strange woman, very quiet. So quiet as to make one uneasy. From the very first Mr. Mayherne was conscious that he was up against something that he did not understand.

"Now, my dear Mrs. Vole," he began, "you must not give way—"

He stopped. It was so very obvious that Romaine Vole had not the slightest intention of giving way. She was perfectly calm and composed.

"Will you please tell me about it?" she said. "I must know everything. Do not think to spare me. I want to know the worst." She hesitated, then repeated in a lower tone, with a curious emphasis which the lawyer did not understand, "I want to know the worst."

Mr. Mayherne went over his interview with Leonard Vole. She listened attentively, nodding her head now and then.

"I see," she said, when he had finished. "He wants me to say that he came in at twenty minutes past nine that night?"

"He did come in at that time?" said Mr. Mayherne sharply.

"That is not the point," she said coldly. "Will my saying so acquit him? Will they believe me?"

Mr. Mayherne was taken aback. She had gone so quickly to the core of the matter.

"That is what I want to know," she said. "Will it be enough? Is there anyone else who can support my evidence?"

There was a suppressed eagerness in her manner that made him vaguely uneasy.

"So far, there is no one else," he said reluctantly.

"I see," said Romaine Vole.

She sat for a minute or two perfectly still. A little smile played over her lips.

The lawyer's feeling of alarm grew stronger and stronger.

"Mrs. Vole—" he began. "I know what you must feel—"

"Do you?" she asked. "I wonder."

"In the circumstances—"

"In the circumstances—I intend to play a lone hand."

He looked at her in dismay.

"But, my dear Mrs. Vole—you are overwrought. Being so devoted to your husband—"

"I beg your pardon?"

The sharpness of her voice made him start. He repeated in a hesitating manner, "Being so devoted to your husband—"

Romaine Vole nodded slowly, the same strange smile on her lips.

"Did he tell you that I was devoted to him?" she asked softly. "Ah! yes, I can see he did. How stupid men are! Stupid—stupid—stupid—"

She rose suddenly to her feet. All the intense emotion that the lawyer had been conscious of in the atmosphere was now concentrated in her tone.

"I hate him, I tell you! I hate him. I hate him. I hate him! I would like to see him hanged by the neck till he is dead."

The lawyer recoiled before her and the smoldering passion in her eyes.

She advanced a step nearer and continued vehemently.

"Perhaps I shall see it. Supposing I tell you that he did not come in that night at twenty past nine, but at twenty past ten? You say that he tells you he knew nothing about the money coming to him. Supposing I tell you he knew all about it, and counted on it, and committed murder to get it? Supposing I tell you that he admitted to me that night when he came in what he had done? That there was blood on his coat? What then? Supposing that I stand up in court and say all these things?"

Her eyes seemed to challenge him. With an effort he concealed his growing dismay, and endeavored to speak in a rational tone.

"You cannot be asked to give evidence against your husband—"

"He is not my husband!"

The words came out so quickly that he fancied he had misunderstood her.

"I beg your pardon? I—"

"He is not my husband."

The silence was so intense that you could have heard a pin drop.

"I was an actress in Vienna. My husband is alive but in a madhouse. So we could not marry. I am glad now." She nodded defiantly.

"I should like you to tell me one thing," said Mr. Mayherne. He contrived to appear as cool and unemotional as ever. "Why are you so bitter against Leonard Vole?"

She shook her head, smiling a little.

"Yes, you would like to know. But I shall not tell you. I will keep my secret."

Mr. Mayherne gave his dry little cough and rose.

"There seems no point in prolonging this interview," he remarked. "You will hear from me again after I have communicated with my client."

She came closer to him, looking into his eyes with her wonderful dark ones.

"Tell me," she said, "did you believe—honestly—that he was innocent when you came here today?"

"I did," said Mr. Mayherne.

"You poor little man." She laughed.

"And I believe so still," finished the lawyer. "Good evening, madam."

He went out of the room, taking with him the memory of her startled face. *This is going to be the devil of a business*, said Mr. Mayherne to himself as he strode along the street.

Extraordinary, the whole thing. An extraordinary woman. A very dangerous woman. Women were the devil when they got their knife into you.

What was to be done? That wretched young man hadn't a leg to stand upon. Of course, possibly he did commit the crime.

No, said Mr. Mayherne to himself. *No—there's almost too much evidence against him. I don't believe this woman. She was trumping up the whole story. But she'll never bring it into court.*

He wished he felt more conviction on the point.

The police court proceedings were brief and dramatic. The principal witnesses for the prosecution were Janet Mackenzie, maid to the dead woman, and Romaine Heilger, Austrian subject, the mistress of the prisoner.

Mr. Mayherne sat in court and listened to the damning story that the latter told. It was on the lines she had indicated to him in their interview.

The prisoner reserved his defense and was committed for trial.

Mr. Mayherne was at his wits' end. The case against Leonard Vole was black beyond words. Even the famous K. C. who was engaged for the defense held out little hope.

"If we can shake that Austrian woman's testimony, we might do something," he said dubiously. "But it's a bad business."

Mr. Mayherne had concentrated his energies on one single point. Assuming Leonard Vole to be speaking the truth, and to have left the murdered woman's house at nine o'clock, who was the man Janet heard talking to Miss French at half past nine?

The only ray of light was in the shape of a scapegrace nephew who had in bygone days cajoled and threatened his aunt out of various sums of money. Janet Mackenzie, the solicitor learned, had always been attached to this young man, and had never ceased urging his claims upon her mistress. It certainly seemed possible that it was this nephew who had been with Miss French after Leonard Vole left, especially as he was not to be found in any of his old haunts.

In all other directions, the lawyer's researches had been negative in their result. No one had seen Leonard Vole entering his own house, or leaving that of Miss French. No one had seen any other man enter or leave the house in Cricklewood. All inquiries drew blank.

It was the eve of the trial when Mr. Mayherne received the letter which was to lead his thoughts in an entirely new direction.

It came by the six-o'clock post. An illiterate scrawl, written on common paper and enclosed in a dirty envelope with the stamp stuck on crooked.

Mr. Mayherne read it through once or twice before he grasped its meaning.

> Dear Mister:
>
> Youre the lawyer chap wot acts for the young feller. If you want that painted foreign hussy showd up for wot she is an her pack of lies you come to 16 Shaw's Rents Stepney to-night It ull cawst you 2 hundred quid Arsk for Missis Mogson.

The solicitor read and reread this strange epistle. It might, of course, be a hoax, but when he thought it over, he became increasingly convinced that it was genuine, and also convinced that it was the one hope for the prisoner. The evidence of Romaine Heilger damned him completely, and the line the defense meant to pursue, the line that the evidence of a woman who had admittedly lived an immoral life was not to be trusted, was at best a weak one.

Mr. Mayherne's mind was made up. It was his duty to save his client at all costs. He must go to Shaw's Rents.

He had some difficulty in finding the place, a ramshackle building in an evil-smelling slum, but at last he did so, and on inquiry for Mrs. Mogson was sent up to a room on the third floor. On this door he knocked, and getting no answer, knocked again.

At this second knock, he heard a shuffling sound inside, and presently the door was opened cautiously half an inch and a bent figure peered out.

Suddenly the woman, for it was a woman, gave a chuckle and opened the door wider.

"So it's you, dearie," she said, in a wheezy voice. "Nobody with you, is there? No playing tricks? That's right. You can come in—you can come in."

With some reluctance the lawyer stepped across the threshold into the small, dirty room, with its flickering gas jet. There was an untidy unmade bed in a corner, a plain deal table, and two rickety chairs. For the first time Mr. Mayherne had a full view of the tenant of this unsavory apartment. She was a woman of middle age, bent in figure, with a mass of untidy gray hair and a scarf wound tightly round her face. She saw him look-ing at this and laughed again, the same curious, toneless chuckle.

"Wondering why I hide my beauty, dear? He, he, he. Afraid it may tempt you, eh? But you shall see—you shall see."

She drew aside the scarf, and the lawyer recoiled involuntarily before the almost formless blur of scarlet. She replaced the scarf again.

"So you're not wanting to kiss me, dearie? He, he I don't wonder. And yet I was a pretty girl once—not so long ago as you'd think, either. Vitriol, dearie, vitriol—that's what did that. Ah! but I'll be even with 'em—"

She burst into a hideous torrent of profanity which Mr. Mayherne tried vainly to quell. She fell silent at last, her hands clenching and unclenching themselves ner-vously.

"Enough of that," said the lawyer sternly. "I've come here because I have reason to believe you can give me information which will clear my client, Leonard Vole. Is that the case?"

Her eyes leered at him cunningly.

"What about the money, dearie?" she wheezed. "Two hundred quid, you remember."

"It is your duty to give evidence, and you can be called upon to do so."

"That won't do, dearie. I'm an old woman, and I know nothing. But you give me two hundred quid, and perhaps I can give you a hint or two. See?"

"What kind of hint?"

"What should you say to a letter? A letter from *her*. Never mind how I got hold of it. That's my business. It'll do the trick. But I want my two hundred quid."

Mr. Mayherne looked at her coldly, and made up his mind.

"I'll give you ten pounds, nothing more. And only that if this letter is what you say it is."

"Ten pounds?" She screamed and raved at him.

"Twenty," said Mr. Mayherne, "and that's my last word."

He rose as if to go. Then, watching her closely, he drew out a pocketbook, and counted out twenty one-pound notes.

"You see," he said. "that is all I have with me. You can take it or leave it."

But already he knew that the sight of the money was too much for her. She cursed and raved impotently, but at last she gave in. Going over to the bed, she drew something out from beneath the tattered mattress.

"Here you are, damn you!" she snarled. "It's the top one you want."

It was a bundle of letters that she threw to him, and Mr. Mayherne untied them and scanned them in his usual cool, methodical manner. The woman, watching him eagerly, could gain no clue from his impassive face.

He read each letter through, then returned again to the top one and read it a second time. Then he tied the whole bundle up again carefully.

They were love letters, written by Romaine Heilger, and the man they were written to was not Leonard Vole. The top letter was dated the day of the latter's arrest.

"I spoke true, dearie, didn't I?" whined the woman. "It'll do for her, that letter?"

Mr. Mayherne put the letters in his pocket, then he asked a question.

"How did you get hold of this correspondence?"

"That's telling," she said with a leer. "But I know something more. I heard in court what that hussy said. Find out where she was at twenty past ten, the time she says she was at home. Ask at the Lion Road Cinema. They'll remember—a fine upstanding girl like that—curse her!"

"Who is the man?" asked Mr. Mayherne. "There's only a Christian name here."

The other's voice grew thick and hoarse, her hands clenched and unclenched. Finally she lifted one to her face.

"He's the man that did this to me. Many years ago now. She took him away from me—a chit of a girl she was then. And when I went after him—and went for him, too—he threw the cursed stuff at me! And she laughed—damn her! I've had it for her for years. Followed her, I have, spied upon her. And now I've got her! She'll suffer for this, won't she, Mr. Lawyer? She'll suffer?"

"She will probably be sentenced to a term of imprisonment for perjury," said Mr. Mayherne quietly.

"Shut away—that's what I want. You're going, are you? Where's my money? Where's that good money?"

Without a word, Mr. Mayherne put down the notes on the table. Then, drawing a deep breath, he turned and left the squalid room. Looking back, he saw the old woman crooning over the money.

He wasted no time. He found the cinema in Lion road easily enough, and, shown a photograph of Romaine Heilger, the commissionaire recognized her at once. She had arrived at the cinema with a man some time after ten o'clock on the evening in question. He had not noticed her escort particularly, but he remembered the lady who had spoken to him about the picture that was showing. They stayed until the end, about an hour later.

Mr. Mayherne was satisfied. Romaine Heilger's evidence was a tissue of lies from beginning to end. She had evolved it out of her passionate hatred. The lawyer wondered whether he would ever know what lay behind that hatred. What had Leonard Vole done to her? He had seemed dumfounded when the solicitor had reported her attitude to him. He had declared earnestly that such a thing was incredible—yet it had seemed to Mr. Mayherne that after the first astonishment his protests had lacked sincerity.

He did know. Mr. Mayherne was convinced of it. He knew, but he had no intention of revealing the fact. The secret between those two remained a secret. Mr. Mayherne wondered if some day he should come to learn what it was.

The solicitor glanced at his watch. It was late, but time was everything. He hailed a taxi and gave an address.

"Sir Charles must know of this at once," he murmured to himself as he got in.

The trial of Leonard Vole for the murder of Emily French aroused widespread interest. In the first place the prisoner was young and good-looking, then he was accused of a particularly dastardly crime, and there was the further interest of Romaine Heilger, the principal witness for the prosecution. There had been pictures of her in many papers, and several fictitious stories as to her origin and history.

The proceedings opened quietly enough. Various technical evidence came first. Then Janet Mackenzie was called. She told substantially the same story as before. In cross-examination counsel for the defense succeeded in getting her to contradict herself once or twice over her account of Vole's association with Miss French; he emphasized the fact that though she had heard a man's voice in the sitting-room that night, there was nothing to show that it was Vole who was there, and he managed to drive home a feeling that jealousy and dislike of the prisoner were at the bottom of a good deal of her evidence.

Then the next witness was called.

"Your name is Romaine Heilger?"

"Yes."

"You are an Austrian subject?"

"Yes."

"For the last three years you have lived with the prisoner and passed yourself off as his wife?"

Just for a moment Romaine Heilger's eyes met those of the man in the dock. Her expression held something curious and unfathomable.

"Yes."

The questions went on. Word by word the damning facts came out. On the night in question the prisoner had taken out a crowbar with him. He had returned at twenty minutes past ten, and had confessed to having killed the old lady. His cuffs had been stained with blood, and he had burned them in the kitchen stove. He had terrorized her into silence by means of threats.

As the story proceeded, the feeling of the court which had, to begin with, been slightly favorable to the prisoner, now set dead against him. He himself sat with downcast head and moody air, as though he knew he were doomed.

Yet it might have been noted that her own counsel sought to restrain Romaine's animosity. He would have preferred her to be more unbiased.

Formidable and ponderous, counsel for the defense arose.

He put it to her that her story was a malicious fabrication from start to finish, that she had not even been in her own house at the time in question, that she was in love with another man and was deliberately seeking to send Vole to his death for a crime he did not commit.

Romaine denied these allegations with superb insolence.

Then came the surprising denouement, the production of the letter. It was read aloud in court in the midst of a breathless stillness.

"Max, beloved, the Fates have delivered him into our hands! He has been arrested for murder—but, yes, the murder of an old lady! Leonard, who would not hurt a fly! At last I shall have my revenge. The poor chicken! I shall say that he came in that night with blood upon him—that he confessed to me. I shall hang him, Max—and when he hangs he will know and realize that it was Romaine who sent him to his death. And then—happiness, Beloved! Happiness at last!"

There were experts present ready to swear that the handwriting was that of Romaine Heilger, but they were not needed. Confronted with the letter, Romaine broke down utterly and confessed everything. Leonard Vole had returned to the house at the time he said, twenty past nine. She had invented the whole story to ruin him.

With the collapse of Romaine Heilger, the case for the Crown collapsed also. Sir Charles called his few witnesses, the prisoner himself went into the box and told his story in a manly straightforward manner, unshaken by cross-examination.

The prosecution endeavored to rally, but without great success. The judge's summing up was not wholly favorable to the prisoner, but a reaction had set in and the jury needed little time to consider their verdict.

"We find the prisoner not guilty."

Leonard Vole was free!

Little Mr. Mayherne hurried from his seat. He must congratulate his client.

He found himself polishing his pince-nez vigorously, and checked himself. His wife had told him only the night before that he was getting a habit of it. Curious things, habits. People themselves never knew they had them.

An interesting case—a very interesting case. That woman, now, Romaine Heilger.

The case was dominated for him still by the exotic figure of Romaine Heilger. She had seemed a pale, quiet woman in the house at Paddington, but in court she had flamed out against the sober background, flaunting herself like a tropical flower.

If he closed his eyes he could see her now, tall and vehement, her exquisite body bent forward a little, her right hand clenching and unclenching itself unconsciously all the time.

Curious things, habits. That gesture of hers with the hand was her habit, he supposed. Yet he had seen someone else do it quite lately. Who was it now? Quite lately—

He drew in his breath with a gasp as it came back to him. The woman in Shaw's Rents—

He stood still, his head whirling. It was impossible—impossible—Yet, Romaine Heilger was an actress.

The K. C. came up behind him and clapped him on the shoulder.

"Congratulated our man yet? He's had a narrow shave, you know. Come along and see him."

But the little lawyer shook off the other's hand.

He wanted one thing only—to see Romaine Heilger face to face.

He did not see her until some time later, and the place of their meeting is not relevant.

"So you guessed," she said, when he had told her all that was in his mind. "The face? Oh! that was easy enough, and the light of that gas jet was too bad for you to see the make-up."

"But why—why—"

"Why did I play a lone hand?" She smiled a little, remembering the last time she had used the words.

"Such an elaborate comedy!"

"My friend—I had to save him. The evidence of a woman devoted to him would not have been enough—you hinted as much yourself. But I know something of the psychology of crowds. Let my evidence be wrung from me, as an admission, damning me in the eyes of the law, and a reaction in favor of the prisoner would immediately set in."

"And the bundle of letters?"

"One alone, the vital one, might have seemed like a—what do you call it?—put-up job."

"Then the man called Max?"

"Never existed, my friend."

"I still think," said little Mr. Mayherne, in an aggrieved manner, "that we could have got him off by the—er—normal procedure."

"I dared not risk it. You see you thought he was innocent—"

"And you knew it? I see," said little Mr. Mayherne.

"My dear Mr. Mayherne," said Romaine, "you do not see at all. I knew—he was guilty!"

For Practice

1. Many scholars do not consider that a mystery story such as "Witness for the Prosecution" is an appropriate text for serious study. Nevertheless, it is a very popular story which has been adapted for both the stage and screen. Do you think that it is possible for a popular story to be considered literature? If so, is this story an example of such a story?

2. Describe Mayherne's character. What in his character makes it possible for him to be so easily deceived by Romaine Heilger and Leonard Vole? How do they exploit the situation in the text to carry off their deception?

3. What part, if any, did prejudice play in the trial of Leonard Vole?

4. It may seem that Christie herself has perpetrated a trick on her readers, similar to the one that Heilger and Vole perpetrate on the court. However, you might consider that both Christie and her characters simply use their audiences' own preconceived notions against them. How might you articulate what you have learned about human nature from this story as an argument either for, or against the jury system?

5. Does Christie's short story challenge or strengthen your own opinions on the criminal justice system?

America

Allen Ginsberg

Allen Ginsberg (1926–1997) first acquired fame as a poet of the Beat generation, an American counter-cultural literary movement of the 1950s. While Beats quickly became satirically portrayed as wearing black turtleneck sweaters and berets while reading incomprehensible poetry accompanied by bongo drums at coffee houses, the shock and energy of the original Beats' work cannot be overstated. The shock came from subject matter seldom addressed in American literature previously (including but not limited to drug use, homosexuality, and mental illness), and the energy came from inventive uses of language sometimes based upon bebop jazz music.

Due to his open homosexuality and drug use, leftist politics, and occasional employment of profanity in his poetry, Ginsberg was anathema to mainstream 1950 American culture. In fact, his best known work, Howl and Other Poems *(1956), led to an obscenity trial, which Ginsberg's publisher won. However, Ginsberg quickly became embraced by the literary mainstream, winning a Guggenheim Fellowship and other awards. He was so widely appreciated by the time of his death in 1997 that many national magazines printed full-page obituaries.*

"America," from Howl, *is an excellent example of Ginsberg's countercultural stances and poetic virtuosity. By turns earnest and satiric, "America" exposes many problems within mainstream 1950s American culture: blind acceptance of mass media, Cold War paranoia, economic inequality, racial and religious prejudice, and an aversion to the human body. The concluding line, "America I'm putting my queer shoulder to the wheel," is not only a sexual coming-out but also recapitulates a major theme in the poem—that many American citizens do not fit constrictive definitions of "American."*

America

America I've given you all and now I'm nothing.
America two dollars and twentyseven cents January 17, 1956.
I can't stand my own mind.
America when will we end the human war?

Go fuck yourself with your atom bomb.
I don't feel good don't bother me.
I won't write my poem till I'm in my right mind.
America when will you be angelic?
When will you take off your clothes?
When will you look at yourself through the grave?   10
When will you be worthy of your million Trotskyites?
America why are your libraries full of tears?
America when will you send your eggs to India?
I'm sick of your insane demands.
When can I go into the supermarket and buy what I need with my good looks?
America after all it is you and I who are perfect not the next world.
Your machinery is too much for me.
You made me want to be a saint.
There must be some other way to settle this argument.
Burroughs is in Tangiers I don't think he'll come back it's sinister.   20
Are you being sinister or is this some form of practical joke?
I'm trying to come to the point.
I refuse to give up my obsession.
America stop pushing I know what I'm doing.
America the plum blossoms are falling.
I haven't read the newspaper for months, everyday somebody goes on trial for
    murder.
America I feel sentimental about the Wobblies.
America I used to be a communist when I was a kid I'm not sorry.
I smoke marijuana every chance I get.
I sit in my house for days on end and stare at the roses in the closet.   30
When I go to Chinatown I get drunk and never get laid.
My mind is made up there's going to be trouble.
You should have seen me reading Marx.
My psychoanalyst thinks I'm perfectly right.
I won't say the Lord's Prayer.
I have mystical visions and cosmic vibrations.
America I still haven't told you what you did to Uncle Max after he came over
    from Russia.

I'm addressing you.
Are you going to let your emotional life be run by Time Magazine?   40
I'm obsessed by Time Magazine.
I read it every week.
Its cover stares at me every time I slink past the corner candystore.
I read it in the basement of the Berkeley Public Library.
It's always telling me about responsibility. Businessmen are serious. Movie
producers are serious. Everybody's serious but me.
It occurs to me that I am America.
I am talking to myself again.
Asia is rising against me.
I haven't got a chinaman's chance.
I'd better consider my national resources.

My national resources consist of two joints of marijuana millions of genitals an
    unpublishable private literature that goes 1400 miles an hour and
    twentyfive-thousand mental institutions.   50
I say nothing about my prisons nor the millions of underprivileged who live in
    my flowerpots under the light of five hundred suns.
I have abolished the whorehouses of France, Tangiers is the next to go.
My ambition is to be President despite the fact that I'm a Catholic.

America how can I write a holy litany in your silly mood?
I will continue like Henry Ford my strophes are as individual as his
    automobiles more so they're all different sexes.
America I will sell you strophes $2500 apiece $500 down on your old strophe
America free Tom Mooney
America save the Spanish Loyalists
America Sacco & Vanzetti must not die
America I am the Scottsboro boys.   60
America when I was seven momma took me to Communist Cell meetings they
    sold us garbanzos a handful per ticket a ticket costs a nickel and the
    speeches were free everybody was angelic and sentimental about the
    workers it was all so sincere you have no idea what a good thing the
    party was in 1935 Scott Nearing was a grand old man a real mensch
    Mother Bloor made me cry I once saw Israel Amter plain. Everybody
    must have been a spy.
America you don't really want to go to war.
America it's them bad Russians.
Them Russia wants to eat us alive. The Russia's power mad. She wants to take
    our cars from out our garages.
Her wants to grab Chicago. Her needs a Red Readers' Digest. Her wants our
    auto plants in Siberia. Him big bureaucracy running our fillingstations.
That no good. Ugh. Him make Indians learn read. Him need big black niggers.
    Hah. Her make us all work sixteen hours a day. Help.
America this is quite serious.
America this is the impression I get from looking in the television set.
America is this correct?
I'd better get right down to the job.   70
It's true I don't want to join the Army or turn lathes in precision parts
    factories, I'm nearsighted and psychopathic anyway.
America I'm putting my queer shoulder to the wheel.

                                         1956

For Practice

1. The structure of "America" violates formal expectations for poetry in that
every line is at least one complete sentence. Furthermore, the lines vary in
length and there is no rhyme nor meter. Instead, the poem relies on repetition of words, sentence structure, and rhetorical strategies. Why do you
think Ginsberg structures his poem this way? Does his violation of formal
expectations have anything to do with the substance of his argument?

2. "America" appears to have a highly chaotic organization. The speaker jumps from topic to topic without indicating how those topics are related. What effect does this produce? Why might Ginsberg have wanted to produce this effect?

3. The speaker of the poem addresses, questions, and reacts to America as if it were a person. Why might this be the case?

4. Though Ginsberg at one point claims "America this is quite serious" (line 68), portions of the poem are comic, ironic, sarcastic, or satiric. Ginsberg even adopts a horribly stereotyped Native American voice in one section. Why does Ginsberg frequently shift tone, if not persona, throughout the poem? Would the poem be more effective if it were written exclusively in one mood or tone?

5. One of Ginsberg's concerns in "America" is how our perceptions of the world are frequently determined by mass media. What precisely, in your own words, is Ginsberg's argument about mass media? What kinds of evidence does he offer to support his claims? Consider both the logic of the argument and the literary strategies he uses.

A Bronzeville Mother Loiters in Mississippi. Meanwhile, a Mississippi Mother Burns Bacon

Gwendolyn Brooks

Gwendolyn Brooks (b. 1917) is one of the most acclaimed African-American writers. When her poetry collection Annie Allen *won the Pulitzer Prize in 1950, she became the first African American to win a Pulitzer in any category. Since that time, the awards have never ceased and include the Frost Medal from the Poetry Society of America, two Guggenheim Fellowships, the National Endowment for the Arts Lifetime Achievement Award, the National Book Awards Medal for Distinguished Contribution to American Letters, and the National Medal of Arts. In addition, Brooks has been the recipient of over seventy honorary degrees, has been the Poet Laureat of Illinois since 1968, and was inducted into the Women's Hall of Fame in 1988. She is the author of numerous volumes of poetry.*

In her poetry, Brooks seamlessly weaves together the psychology of individual characters, conflicts within familial and romantic relationships, and broader social and political injustices and struggles. "A Bronzeville Mother Loiters in Mississippi. Meanwhile, a Mississippi Mother Burns Bacon," from the collection The Bean Eaters *(1960), is a good example of how Brooks deftly examines multiple relationships simultaneously—one's relationships with one's own conscience, with immediate family members, and with humanity. The historical event which sparked the poem was the acquittal of two men from Money, Mississippi, who were tried for the 1955 murder of Emmett Louis Till, a fourteen-year-old African-American boy from Chicago who allegedly "wolf-whistled" at one defendant's wife. Instead of merely expressing outrage in her poem, Brooks imagines the wife's attempts at self-justification, her pangs of conscience, and her eventual realization that her husband's rage is not only a threat to African-Americans but also to herself and her own children.*

From the first it had been like a
Ballad. It had the beat inevitable. It had the blood.
A wildness cut up, and tied in little bunches.
Like the four-line stanzas of the ballads she had never quite
Understood—the ballads they had set her to, in school.

Herself: the milk-white maid, the "maid mild"
Of the ballad. Pursued
By the Dark Villain. Rescued by the Fine Prince.
The Happiness-Ever-After.
That was worth anything.   10
It was good to be a "maid mild."
That made the breath go fast.

Her bacon burned. She
Hastened to hide it in the step-on can, and
Drew more strips from the meat case. The eggs and sour-milk biscuits
Did well. She set out a jar
Of her new quince preserve.

. . . But there was a something about the matter of the Dark Villain.
He should have been older, perhaps.
The hacking down of a villain was more fun to think about   20
When his menace possessed undisputed breadth, undisputed height,
And a harsh kind of vice.
And best of all, when his history was cluttered
With the bones of many eaten knights and princesses.

The fun was disturbed, then all but nullified
When the Dark Villain was a blackish child
Of fourteen, with eyes still too young to be dirty,
And a mouth too young to have lost every reminder
Of its infant softness.
That boy must have been surprised! For   30
These were grown-ups. Grown-ups were supposed to be wise.
And the Fine Prince—and that other—so tall, so broad, so
Grown! Perhaps the boy had never guessed
That the trouble with grown-ups was that under the magnificent shell of
        adulthood, just under,
Waited the baby full of tantrums.
It occurred to her that there may have been something
        ridiculous in the picture of the Fine Prince
Rushing (rich with the breadth and height and
Mature solidness whose lack, in the Dark Villain, was impressing her,
Confronting her more and more as this first day after the trial
And acquittal wore on) rushing
With his heavy companion to hack down (unhorsed)   40
That little foe.
So much had happened, she could not remember now what that foe had done
Against her, or if anything had been done.
The one thing in the world that she did know and knew

With terrifying clarity was that her composition
Had disintegrated. That, although the pattern prevailed,
The breaks were everywhere. That she could think
Of no thread capable of the necessary
Sew-work.

She made the babies sit in their places at the table.   50
Then, before calling Him, she hurried
To the mirror with her comb and lipstick. It was necessary
To be more beautiful than ever.
The beautiful wife.
For sometimes she fancied he looked at her as though
Measuring her. As if he considered, Had she been worth It?
Had *she* been worth the blood, the cramped cries, the little stuttering bravado,
The gradual dulling of those Negro eyes,
The sudden, overwhelming *little-boyness* in that barn?
Whatever she might feel or half-feel, the lipstick necessity was something
          apart. He must never conclude   60
That she had not been worth It.

He sat down, the Fine Prince, and
Began buttering a biscuit. He looked at his hands.
He twisted in his chair, he scratched his nose.
He glanced again, almost secretly, at his hands.
More papers were in from the North, he mumbled. More meddling headlines.
With their pepper-words, "bestiality," and "barbarism," and
"Shocking."
The half-sneers he had mastered for the trial worked across
His sweet and pretty face.   70

What he'd like to do, he explained, was kill them all.
The time lost. The unwanted fame.
Still, it had been fun to show those intruders
A thing or two. To show that snappy-eyed mother,
That sassy, Northern, brown-black—

Nothing could stop Mississippi.
He knew that. Big Fella
Knew that.
And, what was so good, Mississippi knew that.
Nothing and nothing could stop Mississippi.   80
They could send in their petitions, and scar
Their newspapers with bleeding headlines. Their governors
Could appeal to Washington.

"What I want," the older baby said, "is 'lasses on my jam."
Whereupon the younger baby
Picked up the molasses pitcher and threw
The molasses in his brother's face. Instantly
The Fine Prince leaned across the table and slapped
The small and smiling criminal.

She did not speak. When the Hand   90
Came down and away, and she could look at her child.
At her baby-child,
She could think only of blood.
Surely her baby's cheek
Had disappeared, and in its place, surely,
Hung a heaviness, a lengthening red, a red that had no end.
She shook her head. It was not true, of course.
It was not true at all. The
Child's face was as always, the
Color of the paste in her paste-jar.   100

She left the table, to the tune of the children's lamentations, which
        were shriller
Than ever. She
Looked out of a window. She said not a word. *That*
Was one of the new Somethings—
The fear,
Tying her as with iron.

Suddenly she felt his hands upon her. He had followed her
To the window. The children were whimpering now.
Such bits of tots. And she, their mother,
Could not protect them. She looked at her shoulders, still   110
Gripped in the claim of his hands. She tried, but could not resist the idea
That a red ooze was seeping, spreading darkly, thickly, slowly,
Over her white shoulders, her own shoulders,
And over all of Earth and Mars.

He whispered something to her, did the fine Prince, something
About love, something about love and night and intention.

She heard no hoof-beat of the horse and saw no flash of the shining steel.
He pulled her face around to meet
His, and there it was, close close,
For the first time in all those days and nights.   120
His mouth, wet and red,
So very, very, very red,
Closed over hers.

Then a sickness heaved within her. The courtroom Coca-Cola,
The courtroom beer and hate and sweat and drone,
Pushed like a wall against her. She wanted to bear it.
But his mouth would not go away and neither would the
Decapitated exclamation points in that Other Woman's eyes.

She did not scream.
She stood there.   130
But a hatred for him burst into glorious flower,
And its perfume enclasped them—big,
Bigger than all magnolias.

The last bleak news of the ballad.
The rest of the rugged music.
The last quatrain.

1960

For Practice

1. We often think of poetry as a kind of abstract literary form which deals with abstract concepts and high ideals. Brooks poem, however, is particular, personal, and political. What are your expectations about poetic genres? Did anything about this poem surprise you?

2. What do you observe about the use of color imagery in this text? How are the colors black, red, and white used? What symbolic weight do these colors carry in the poem?

3. Brooks's poem moves back and forth between internal thought patterns and exterior events. Note the various places where a character's stream of consciousness get disrupted by an action or sensory perception. Why does Brooks choose these moments to break the characters' thoughts, and how do the actions which break them interact with or comment on those thoughts? Why is it that we never hear the thoughts of Emmett Till ("the Dark Villain") or his mother (the "Bronzeville Mother" of the title)?

4. In addition to examining an instance of racial inequality, prejudice, and violence, this poem depicts family and gender dynamics. What roles do the children, the father, and the mother play in this poem? Why does the mother feel the need to have "been worth It" to her husband? How does feeling this need cause her to act? Do her feelings for her husband change during the poem?

5. Ultimately, who are the victims and villains in the poem? Are we asked to pity the Mississippi Mother and consider her a victim also, or does she indict herself? Does Brooks find a way to reach across color lines and provide reasons why both blacks and whites should fight against racial inequality, prejudice, and violence? Does she suggest that violence against others indicates potential violence against oneself and one's family?

6. In what ways, if any, has Brooks provoked you to change your thinking about race matters?

Riot Act, April 29, 1992

Ai

Ai (b. 1947) was born Florence Anthony in Tucson, Arizona, to a Japanese father and an African-American–Choctaw–Irish mother. After growing up in Las Vegas and San Francisco, she attended the University of Arizona, majoring in Japanese. While there she immersed herself in Buddhism. She has received awards from the Guggenheim Foundation, the National Endowment for the Arts, and various universities, and is a frequent reader-performer of her work.

"Riot Act, April 29, 1992" was published in 1993 in Greed, *her fifth volume of poetry. A dramatic monologue, "Riot Act" is spoken by an unnamed black rioter taken into police custody in South Central Los Angeles in the aftermath of the Rodney King trial. The speaker sees the results of the riots, looting, and fires as "the day the wealth finally trickled down/to the rest of us." This poem poignantly describes the frustration felt by many African-Americans with this country's justice system.*

I'm going out and get something.
I don't know what.
I don't care.
Whatever's out there, I'm going to get it.
Look in those shop windows at boxes
and boxes of Reeboks and Nikes
to make me fly through the air
like Michael Jordan
like Magic.
While I'm up there, I see Spike Lee.   10
Looks like he's flying too
straight through the glass
that separates me
from the virtual reality
I watch everyday on TV.
I know the difference between
what it is and what it isn't.
Just because I can't touch it
doesn't mean it isn't real.

All I have to do is smash the screen,   20
reach in and take what I want.
Break out of prison.
South Central homey's newly risen
from the night of living dead,
but this time he lives,
he gets to give the zombies
a taste of their own medicine.
Open wide and let me in,
or else I'll set your world on fire,
but you pretend that you don't hear.   30
You haven't heard the word is coming down
like the hammer of the gun
of this black son, locked out of the big house,
while massa looks out the window and sees only smoke.
Massa doesn't see anything else,
not because he can't,
but because he won't.
He'd rather hear me talking about mo' money,
mo' honeys and gold chains
and see me carrying my favorite things   40
from looted stores
than admit that underneath my Raiders' cap,
the aftermath is staring back
unblinking through the camera's lens,
courtesy of CNN,
my arms loaded with boxes of shoes
that I will sell at the swap meet
to make a few cents on the declining dollar.
And if I destroy myself
and my neighborhood   50
"ain't nobody's business, if I do,"
but the police are knocking hard
at my door
and before I can open it,
they break it down
and drag me in the yard.
They take me in to be processed and charged,
to await trial,
while Americans forget
the day the wealth finally trickled down   60
to the rest of us.

1993

For Practice

1. The glossary of this book suggests that the speakers of "dramatic monologues" often reveal more than they intend to. Is that the case with this speaker? If so, what things does this rioter unintentionally reveal? If not, why do you think this case is different from the usual dramatic monologue?

2. Explore Ai's use of television as a symbol in the poem? What does this symbol mean to the speaker of the poem? Does television carry the same symbolic importance to more affluent Americans?

3. What are some of the ironies at work in this poem? How is the irony achieved? What would you consider the ultimate irony of the poem?

4. Put yourself in the position of the lawyer assigned to defend the speaker. What argument could you make in defense of the speaker? How would you implicate television and the rest of American culture in this crime?

5. This poem represents a very painful incident in recent American history. The violence of the riots may make us unwilling to accept the reasons offered as justification for the narrator's behavior. What do you think about Ai's choice of a dramatic monologue as a form for presenting her argument? Do you think other forms might present it more effectively?

Creating Your Own Arguments

1. The texts in this unit demonstrate that social justice is a very complex concept because multiple and contradictory notions of justice can, and often do, co-exist. Compare, for example, the view of justice held by the speaker of Ai's "Riot Act" with that held by Antigone. Both Antigone and this speaker disobey civil authority. How do they justify their disobedience? How would you evaluate the strength of their arguments?

2. Both Gertrude Bonnin and the children of Blake's Chimney Sweeper poems are victims of social injustices, but Bonnin is a "real" human while the chimney sweeps, at least those in the poem, are creatures of Blake's imagination. In your opinion, which of these two literary arguments is the stronger one? Why? Be sure to give good reasons for your argument. Consider the relative merits of the rhetorical appeals of *pathos, ethos,* and *logos* and how these appeals are used in these two texts as part of your answer.

3. In several of these texts, the author's view of what constitutes social injustice is very clear. In others, it is not so clear. Choose two texts which represent these different perspectives on social justice. Explain how the author treats the issue of social injustice. Try to account for the authors' different perspectives by referring to the cultures and times in which the texts were produced. Use library resources to help you with this question.

4. Unreliable narrators always complicate the issues of a text. Choose from this unit any two texts in which there is a strong narrative voice. Evaluate the reliability of the narrator, being sure to give good reasons from the text itself. Then discuss how the narrator's reliability either strengthens or weakens the argument of the text.

5. Imagine that you are a defense attorney who has been assigned to defend some of the characters found in texts in this unit. Choose the character you would feel most comfortable defending and write a closing argument for his or her case.

6. The Los Angeles riot which forms a context for the poem "Riot Act" is a historical reality. Do some library research to find contemporary news reports about the riots. Compare the perspectives on the riots which the news media present with those of the poem's narrator. If you think they are different, try to account for the difference.

7. Not all crimes are punished. When does the failure to punish a crime constitute a social injustice? Consider at least two texts as examples for your argument. In addition to those texts in this section, you might also consider the play *Trifles* in Unit One.

UNIT
FIVE

Living, Dying, and the
Quest for Meaning

"The Meaning of Life" is a term most of us don't really take seriously. There is something strange, and perhaps even a little funny, in our preoccupation with finding out the purpose of our short lives. Nevertheless, in every culture, people have had to find ways to deal with the fact of mortality and have struggled to make sense of a world that includes both joy and suffering. Some people derive meaning from religious faith; others find religion difficult to accept. Some regard meaning as something we find; for others, meaning is something we must make. For many, life is most meaningful when shared with others; yet there are also those who find pleasure in a more solitary journey. Political activity, scientific endeavors, art, music, work, family life—all of these activities serve as a deep source of meaning for some, while remaining relatively unimportant to others. In fact, there are many people who, for a variety of reasons, would rather avoid words like "meaning" or "values" altogether. Some fear that too much concern about "the meaning of life" may cause us to impose our ideas and values on others, or to place unrealistic demands on life and miss out on the joy of day-to-day experience.

While few of us can comfortably sit down with someone else and talk directly about these beliefs, or about "the meaning of life," we discuss these issues indirectly through a wide variety of contexts. For example, most of us have probably had the experience of getting into a serious discussion with friends after we have watched a good movie together. Like film, other forms of literature provide us with one method of examining how different people cope with their common mortality. The question recurs in every era and culture. No matter how different our belief systems, no matter how different our perceptions about issues of gender, morality, religion, sexuality, or government, all human beings know that eventually their bodies will die. In the meantime, most of us want to live lives that matter in some way, at least to ourselves and usually to others as well.

The literary works in this unit all deal with questions of life, death, and meaning. As you read these selections, there are several issues you should keep in mind. How do the characters or speakers in the different texts describe death? Is it a friend, an enemy? Is there any connection between the characters' attitudes towards death and the values they recommended living by? How does the community help or hurt the individual who seeks to face death or to make meaning of the present moment? Are there things worth dying for, worth killing for? What do the characters believe in? Why? When is belief dangerous gullibility and when does it lead to a fuller and more fruitful life? For what are they searching?

Looking at these issues may not give you a greater ability to answer any nagging questions you may have about your purpose in this world.

Nor is it likely to satisfy whatever concerns you may have about mortality. Indeed, the point of this unit is not to sway anyone to or from any particular beliefs. But investigating the ideas presented by the readings in this unit may heighten your awareness of your own beliefs and values, as well as the beliefs and values of others.

Celestial Music

Louise Glück

Poet Louise Glück (b. 1943) has published several books of poetry. Her work has also appeared in periodicals as well as a variety of anthologies. Among her many honors is the National Book Critics Circle Award for Poetry, awarded in 1985 for her poetry collection The Triumph of Achilles. *Glück is a native of New York City, but she has worked as a teacher or artist-in-residence at a variety of colleges and universities around the country.*

Glück's poem "Celestial Music," from her 1990 collection, Ararat, *presents the speaker's comments on the differences between many of her own and her friend's beliefs. They each respond differently to death and suffering. Each of them holds different beliefs about what makes life meaningful and what makes suffering bearable. Yet they both value life and find ways to accept death. As you read this poem, pay particular attention to the speaker's tone. How does this tone give us clues concerning the poem's overall message?*

I have a friend who still believes in heaven.
Not a stupid person, yet with all she knows, she literally talks to god,
she thinks someone listens in heaven.
On earth, she's unusually competent.
Brave, too, able to face unpleasantness.

We found a caterpillar dying in the dirt, greedy ants crawling over it.
I'm always moved by weakness, by disaster, always eager to oppose vitality.
But timid, also, quick to shut my eyes.
Whereas my friend was able to watch, to let events play out
according to nature. For my sake, she intervened,   10
brushing a few ants off the torn thing, and set it down across the road.

My friend says I shut my eyes to god, that nothing else explains
my aversion to reality. She says I'm like the child who buries her head in
    the pillow

so as not to see, the child who tells herself
that light causes sadness—
My friend is like the mother. Patient, urging me
to wake up an adult like herself, a courageous person—

In my dreams, my friend reproaches me. We're walking
on the same road, except it's winter now;
she's telling me that when you love the world you hear celestial music;   20
look up, she says. When I look up, nothing.
Only clouds, snow, a white business in the trees
like brides leaping to a great height—
Then I'm afraid for her; I see her
caught in a net deliberately cast over the earth—

In reality, we sit by the side of the road, watching the sun set,
from time to time the silence pierced by a birdcall.
It's this moment we're both trying to explain, the fact
that we're at ease with death, with solitude.
My friend draws a circle in the dirt; inside, the caterpillar doesn't move.   30
She's always trying to make something whole, something beautiful, an image
capable of life apart from her.
We're very quiet. It's peaceful sitting here, not speaking, the composition
fixed, the road turning suddenly dark, the air
going cool, here and there the rocks shining and glittering—
it's this stillness that we both love.
The love of form is a love of endings.

For Practice

1. What is the tone of this poem? What words help create this tone? How does this tone affect the poem's overall meaning?

2. What *ethos* does the narrator present? How does she present the beliefs of her friend? What does each of the two characters believe about God and heaven? In particular, what does the speaker's friend believe causes the speaker's squeamishness about death? Does the speaker credit the friend's courage to her religious beliefs?

3. In the third stanza, the speaker says that both characters are "trying to explain" the same thing, that each of them is "at ease with death, with solitude." How does the speaker find common ground with the friend? What is this common ground?

4. Consider the final line of the poem. What does this line mean? How does it relate to the rest of the poem? How is poetry a "love of form"? How is religion a "love of form"? Why does Glück end the poem in this way?

5. What are your own attitudes toward death and dying? Do you think any differently about death as a result of reading this poem? Why or why not?

The Titanic

David R. Slavitt

An amazingly prolific novelist, poet, translator and film critic, David R. Slavitt (b.1935) has over 50 books to his credit. Born in White Plains, New York, Slavitt was forced by his father to attend Andover and the Yale University. Defying his father's wishes, Slavitt decided not to attend Harvard Law School and became a writer instead. His first job was for Reader's Digest; *he also worked for* Newsweek *for seven years. Slavitt currently lives in Philadelphia.*

"Titanic" is taken from his 1983 collection of poetry, Big Nose. *Thanks to the Academy award-winning film, the story of the "unsinkable' ocean liner's tragic collision with an iceberg on its maiden voyage in 1912 has been very much in the public eye recently. As you read this poem, think about similar rituals and outpourings of grief which follow some deaths (for example, Princess Diana or Mother Teresa).*

Who does not love the *Titanic?*
If they sold passage tomorrow for that same crossing,
who would not buy?

To go down . . . We all go down, mostly
alone. But with crowds of people, friends, servants,
well fed, with music, with lights! Ah!

And the world, shocked, mourns, as it ought to do
and almost never does. There will be the books and movies
to remind our grandchildren who we were
and how we died, and give them a good cry.   10

Not so bad, after all. The cold
water is anesthetic and very quick.
The cries on all sides must be a comfort.

We all go, only a few, first-class.

For Practice

1. What is the speaker of this poem suggesting about the way the world treats death? About the way it should treat death?

2. Why might Slavitt have chosen the *Titanic* as his central metaphor? What seems to be his speaker's attitude towards the ship and the public's continued fascination with it? How is this attitude conveyed?

3. How does Slavitt's presentation of the *Titanic* compare with the way the ship and its fate *were* presented in the 1997 mega-hit feature film? What do you think he would say about the film?

4. Consider the speaker's tone. Is he being entirely serious when he suggests that cold water is anesthetic and that the cries must be a comfort? How do you know?

5. What does the speaker mean by the last line?

6. If you are interested, you might look up the most famous poem written on the sinking of the *Titanic,* Thomas Hardy's "The Convergence of the Twain," written just a few weeks after the news of the disaster in 1912. How do the two poems compare?

7. The success of the movie *Titanic* has re-inserted this event into our national consciousness. How does Slavitt's poem alter your perspective on the sinking of the *Titanic?*

Guests of the Nation

Frank O'Connor

Born Michael Francis O'Donovan in Cork, Ireland, Frank O'Connor (1903–1966) was the poor son of an abusive and alcoholic soldier. As a teenager, he participated in the Irish revolt against British rule following the 1916 Easter Rebellion, in which a minority of Irish nationalists declared Ireland a republic. Within a week the rebellion was defeated, and the British government decided to execute fifteen of its leaders, an act that outraged the Irish people.

In the following story, first published in O'Connor's 1928 short story collection of the same name, Belcher and Hawkins are English soldiers who have been captured by Irish partisans. Bonaparte, Noble, and Donovan are members of the Irish Republican Army who are charged with holding and hiding them in the Irish countryside. The story's central conflict centers around the clash between different versions of duty—military, religious, and ethical—and addresses the legitimacy of the use of violence in the name of a cause.

I

At dusk the big Englishman, Belcher, would shift his long legs out of the ashes and say "Well, chums, what about it?" and Noble or me would say "All right, chum" (for we had picked up some of their curious expressions), and the little Englishman, Hawkins, would light the lamp and bring out the cards. Sometimes Jeremiah Donovan would come up and supervise the game and get excited over Hawkins's cards, which he always played badly, and shout at him as if he was one of our own "Ah, you divil, you, why didn't you play the tray?"

But ordinarily Jeremiah was a sober and contented poor devil like the big Englishman, Belcher, and was looked up to only because he was a fair hand at documents, though he was slow enough even with them. He wore a small cloth hat and big gaiters over his long pants, and you seldom saw him with his hands out of his pockets. He reddened when you talked to him, tilting from toe to heel and back, and looking down all the time at his big farmer's feet. Noble and me used to make fun of his broad accent, because we were from the town.

I couldn't at the time see the point of me and Noble guarding Belcher and Hawkins at all, for it was my belief that you could have planted that pair down anywhere from this to Claregalway and they'd have taken root there like a native weed. I never in my short experience seen two man to take to the country as they did.

They were handed on to us by the Second Battalion when the search for them became too hot, and Noble and myself, being young, took over with a natural feeling of responsibility, but Hawkins made us look like fools when he showed that he knew the country better than we did.

"You're the bloke they calls Bonaparte," he says to me. "Mary Brigid O'Connell told me to ask you what you done with the pair of her brother's socks you borrowed."

For it seemed, as they explained it, that the Second used to have little evenings, and some of the girls of the neighborhood turned in, and, seeing they were such decent chaps, our fellows couldn't leave the two Englishmen out of them. Hawkins learned to dance "The Walls of Limerick," "The Siege of Ennis," and "The Waves of Tory" as well as any of them, though, naturally, he couldn't return the compliment, because our lads at that time did not dance foreign dances on principle.

So whatever privileges Belcher and Hawkins had with the Second they just naturally took with us, and after the first day or two we gave up all pretense of keeping a close eye on them. Not that they could have got far, for they had accents you could cut with a knife and wore khaki tunics and overcoats with civilian pants and boots. But it's my belief that they never had any idea of escaping and were quite content to be where they were.

It was a treat to see how Belcher got off with the old woman of the house where we were staying. She was a great warrant to scold, and cranky even with us, but before ever she had a chance of giving our guests, as I may call them, a lick of her tongue, Belcher had made her his friend for life. She was breaking sticks, and Belcher, who hadn't been more than ten minutes in the house, jumped up from his seat and went over to her.

"Allow me, madam," he says, smiling his queer little smile, "please allow me"; and he takes the bloody hatchet. She was struck too paralytic to speak, and after that, Belcher would be at her heels, carrying a bucket, a basket, or a loaf of turf, as the case might be. As Noble said, he got into looking before she leapt, and hot water, or any little thing she wanted, Belcher would have it ready for her. For such a huge man (and though I am five foot ten myself I had to look up at him) he had an uncommon shortness—or should I say lack?—of speech. It took us some time to get used to him, walking in and out, like a ghost, without a word. Especially because Hawkins talked enough for a platoon, it was strange to hear big Belcher with his toes in the ashes come out with a solidary "Excuse me, chum," or "That's right, chum." His one and only passion was cards, and I will say for him that he was a good card-player. He could have fleeced myself and Noble, but whatever we lost to him Hawkins lost to us, and Hawkins played with the money Belcher gave him.

Hawkins lost to us because he had too much old gab, and we probably lost to Belcher for the same reason. Hawkins and Noble would spit at one another about religion into the early hours of the morning, and Hawkins worried the soul out of Noble, whose brother was a priest, with a string of questions that would puzzle a cardinal. To make it worse even in treating of holy subjects, Hawkins had a deplorable tongue. I never in all my career met a man who could mix such a variety of cursing and bad language into an argument. He was a terrible man, and a fright to argue. He never did a stroke of work, and when he had no one else to talk to, he got stuck in the old woman.

He met his match in her, for one day when he tried to get her to complain profanely of the drought, she gave him a great come-down by blaming it entirely on Jupiter Pluvius (a deity neither Hawkins nor I had ever heard of, though Noble said

The Gate by Hans Hofmann (1880–1966)

What is your first impression of this painting? How does learning that it is called *The Gate* change your experience of the painting? What are the functions of a gate? Consider not only the physical properties of a gate, but also the social and cultural connotations that are attached to gates. Hofmann argued that the artist's vision transforms nature so that it takes on new meaning. How do these geometric shapes and the use of color transform the traditional architectural meaning of a gate?

Hans Hofmann, *The Gate,* 1960. Oil on canvas. Copyright
© Estate of Hans Hofmann/Licensed by VAGA, New York, NY.
Photo by David Heald, courtesy of Solomon R. Guggenheim
Museum, New York. Copyright © The Solomon R. Guggenheim
Foundation, New York.

The Arnolfini Wedding Portrait by Jan van Eyck (c. 1390–1441)

Van Eyck was a Flemish painter who was interested in creating for the viewer of his paintings an almost tactile experience through the use of minute detail. This painting commemorates the wedding of a wealthy Italian merchant who lived in Flanders. Observe and describe the many details that you see in this painting. Several objects in the painting—the dog, the shoes, the chandelier, the mirror—carried special coded meanings which we can no longer readily decipher. Nevertheless, the painting can still tell us much about what the people of this era valued. For example, the woman is not pregnant, though she holds her drapery in such a way that it appears as though she were. What might this tell us about the "value" of bearing children at this time? Based on the details of this painting, what can you infer about the roles of men and women in this society? How is this wedding portrait similar or different from wedding portraits of today? What do you make of those similarities and differences? How does this painting connect to the texts in the "Everyday Use" unit?

Jan van Eyck, *The Marriage of Giovanni Arnolfini and Giovanna Cenami,* 1434. Photograph by Bridgeman. Art Resource, NY.

Street Scene. Atlanta, Georgia, 1936 by Walker Evans

Walker Evans was a documentary photographer whose work has been instrumental in forming our impression of life during the Great Depression. Evans was particularly intrigued by the disparity between life during the Depression and the images he found in commercial art of the time. Look at the images on the billboards. What do they advertise? How does the lifestyle portrayed in these posters compare to that lived in the houses behind the fence? How does the photographer use light and dark to arouse the emotion of the viewer? The rhetorical appeal in this photograph is *pathos.* Could you articulate a *logos*-based argument that is as effective as the one you see here? In what ways is this photograph's argument similar to those in Unit Three?

Walker Evans, (1903–1975), *Street Scene, Atlanta, Georgia, 1936.* Farm Security Administration— Office of War Information, Photograph Collection/Library of Congress.

Arcitas and Palamon Looking at Emilia in the Garden by Barthelemy d'Eyck

This painting is an illustration for Boccaccio's *Tessida*. The book was produced sometime between 1460 and 1470. Boccaccio's story of Palamon and Arcite is the basis of Chaucer's "The Knight's Tale." This painting depicts Emilia in the garden where Arcite and Palamon see and fall in love with her. The theme of two friends who love the same woman is a common one in literature and art. What do you think this tells us about the nature of human relationships? According to "The Knight's Tale," what are the consequences of Arcite's and Palamon's competition over Emilia? In this painting, Emilia is seated with her back to the young men, who are in prison. Why do you think the artist chose to reproduce this image instead of portraying another scene from the story? How is this illustration different from and similar to book illustrations of today?

Barthelemy d'Eyck, *Arcitas and Palamon Looking at Emilia in the Garden*, c. 1460-1470 from the manuscript of *Tessida* by Boccaccio. Courtesy of the Picture Archive of the Austrian National Library, Vienna, Austria.

Landscape with the Fall of Icarus
by Pieter Brueghel the Elder (1558)

Each of these images represents a scene from the story of the fall of Icarus, a Greek myth in which a father and son, Daedalus and Icarus, attempt to escape from an island by fashioning wings from feathers and wax. Although Daedalus warns his son not to fly close to the sun, lest his wax wings be damaged, Icarus ignores his father, flies too high, and plunges to his death in the sea when the heat of the sun melts his wings. Where is Icarus in Brueghel's painting? What is significant about his position in this scene? What argument does Brueghel seem to be making by decentering Icarus as the focus of this painting?

In contrast to Brueghel's version of this episode, Matisse's image (see next page), made by pasting pieces of paper on a sheet of colored background, foregrounds Icarus's silhouette. How does Matisse's use of solid colors affect the tone of his work? How does this tone differ from Brueghel's?

Pieter Brueghel the Elder, *Landscape with the Fall of Icarus*. Musées Royaux des Beaux-Arts, Brussels, Belgium. Copyright © Scala/Art Resource, NY.

Icarus by Henri Matisse (1947)

Henri Matisse, *Icarus*, Plate VIII from *Jazz,* by Henri Matisse. Paris, E. Tériade, 1947. The Museum of Modern Art, New York. The Louis E. Stern Collection. Photograph © 1998 The Museum of Modern Art, New York.

The Ox-Bow (The Connecticut River Near Northampton) by Thomas Cole (1836)

This image portrays the coming of a storm to a portion of the Connecticut River Valley and represents the Romantic movement in art, which we often associate with the poetry of William Wordsworth and William Blake and the novels of James Fenimore Cooper. Romanticism emphasized the power of emotions which are evoked by nature. Notice how small the single human figure in the foreground seems in the context of this vast landscape. What argument does this painting make about the relationship between humans and nature? How does it make this argument? How does our culture's view of nature compare to Cole's? What emotions does this painting continue to evoke? Do you think that this emotional response is the same as that experienced by Cole's contemporaries in an era before such vistas gave way to civilization?

Thomas Cole (1801–1848) *View from Mount Holyoke, Northampton, Massachusetts, After a Thunderstorm—The Ox-Bow*, 1836. Oil on canvas, 51-1/2 in. x 76 in. The Metropolitan Museum of Art, Gift of Mrs. Russell Sage, 1908. Photograph © 1995 The Metropolitan Museum of Art.

Severo, Buckskin Charlie, and Others
The Messenger (1894) by H. S. Poley

These two images are different versions of the same photograph made by H. S. Poley in 1894. The original version includes a suburban background and another group of Native American people on the left side. The second image was apparently altered by landscape artist Charles Craig in 1898. How do these alterations change the message of the original photograph, which was itself posed? What stereotypes of American Indians does each of these photographs present? What do you think of the practice of altering a photograph in this way? What do these images show us concerning the reliability of photography as a way of representing "reality"? How do this photograph and Cole's painting articulate the tensions between nature, human kind, and technology that the texts in Unit Six address?

H. S. Poley, *Severo, Buckskin Charlie, and Others.* Courtesy of Denver Public Library, Western History Department.

H. S. Poley, altered by Chas Craig, *The Messenger.* Copyright © 1898 by Chas Craig. Courtesy of Denver Public Library, Western History Department.

that among the pagans it was believed that he had something to do with the rain). Another day he was swearing at the capitalists for starting the German War when the old lady laid down her iron, puckered up her little crab's mouth, and said: "Mr. Hawkins, you can say what you like about the war, and think you'll deceive me because I'm only a simple poor countrywoman, but I know what started the war. It was the Italian Count that stole the heathen divinity out of the temple in Japan. Believe me, Mr. Hawkins, nothing but sorrow and want can follow the people that disturb the hidden powers."

A queer old girl, all right.

2

We had our tea one evening, and Hawkins lit the lamp and we all sat into cards. Jeremiah Donovan came in too, and sat down and watched us for a while, and it suddenly struck me that he had no great love for the two Englishmen. It came as a great surprise to me, because I hadn't noticed anything about him before.

Late in the evening a really terrible argument blew up between Hawkins and Noble, about capitalists and priests and love of your country.

"The capitalists," says Hawkins with an angry gulp, "pays the priests to tell you about the next world so as you don't notice what the bastards are up to in this."

"Nonsense, man!" says Noble, losing his temper. "Before ever a capitalist was thought of, people believed in the next world."

Hawkins stood up as though he was preaching a sermon.

"Oh, they did, did they?" he says with a sneer. "They believed all the things you believe, isn't that what you mean? And you believe that God created Adam, and Adam created Shem, and Shem created Jehoshophat. You believe all that silly old fairy tale about Eve and Eden and the apple. Well, listen to me, chum. If you're entitled to hold a silly belief like that, I'm entitled to hold my silly belief—which is that the first thing your God created was a bleeding capitalist, with morality and Rolls-Royce complete. Am I right, chum?" he says to Belcher.

"You're right, chum," says Belcher with his amused smile, and got up from the table to stretch his long legs into the fire and stroke his moustache. So, seeing that Jeremiah Donovan was going, and that there was no knowing when the argument about religion would be over, I went out with him. We strolled down to the village together, and then he stopped and started blushing and mumbling and saying I ought to be behind, keeping guard on the prisoners. I didn't like the tone he took with me, and anyway I was bored with life in the cottage, so I replied by asking him what the hell we wanted guarding them at all for. I told him I'd talked it over with Noble, and that we'd both rather be out with a fighting column.

"What use are those fellows to us?" says I.

He looked at me in surprise and said: "I thought you knew we were keeping them as hostages."

"Hostages?" I said.

"The enemy have prisoners belonging to us," he says, "and now they're talking of shooting them. If they shoot our prisoners, we'll shoot theirs."

"Shoot them?" I said.

"What else do you think we were keeping them for?" he says.

"Wasn't it very unforeseen of you not to warn Noble and myself of that in the beginning?" I said.

"How was it?" says he. "You might have known it."

"We couldn't know it, Jeremiah Donovan," says I. "How could we when they were on our hands so long?"

"The enemy have our prisoners as long and longer," says he.

"That's not the same thing at all," says I.

"What difference is there?" says he.

I couldn't tell him, because I knew he wouldn't understand. If it was only an old dog that was going to the vet's, you'd try and not get too fond of him, but Jeremiah Donovan wasn't a man that would ever be in danger of that.

"And when is this thing going to be decided?" says I.

"We might hear tonight," he says. "Or tomorrow or the next day at latest. So if it's only hanging around here that's a trouble to you, you'll be free soon enough."

It wasn't the hanging round that was a trouble to me at all by this time. I had worse things to worry about. When I got back to the cottage the argument was still on. Hawkins was holding forth in his best style, maintaining that there was no next world, and Noble was maintaining that there was; but I could see that Hawkins had had the best of it.

"Do you know what, chum?" he was saying with a saucy smile. "I think you're just as big a bleeding unbeliever as I am. You say you believe in the next world, and you know just as much about the next world as I do, which is sweet damn-all. What's heaven? You don't know. Where's heaven? You don't know. You know sweet damn-all! I ask you again, do they wear wings?"

"Very well, then," says Noble, "they do. Is that enough for you? They do wear wings."

"Where do they get them, then? Who makes them? Have they a factory for wings? Have they a sort of store where you hands in your chit and takes your bleeding wings?"

"You're an impossible man to argue with," says Noble. "Now, listen to me—" And they were off again.

It was long after midnight when we locked up and went to bed. As I blew out the candle I told Noble what Jeremiah Donovan was after telling me. Noble took it very quietly. When we'd been in bed about an hour he asked me did I think we ought to tell the Englishmen. I didn't think we should, because it was more than likely that the English wouldn't shoot our men, and even if they did, the brigade officers, who were always up and down the the Second Battalion and knew the Englishmen well, wouldn't be likely to want them plugged. "I think so too," says Noble. "It would be great cruelty to put the wind up them now."

"It was very unforeseen of Jeremiah Donovan anyhow," says I.

It was next morning that we found it so hard to face Belcher and Hawkins. We went about the house all day scarcely saying a word. Belcher didn't seem to notice; he was stretched into the ashes as usual, with his usual look of waiting in quietness for something unforeseen to happen, but Hawkins noticed and put it down to Noble's being beaten in the argument of the night before.

"Why can't you take a discussion in the proper spirit?" he says severely. "You and your Adam and Eve! I'm a Communist, that's what I am. Communist or anarchist, it all comes to much the same thing." And for hours he went round the house, muttering when the fit took him. "Adam and Eve! Adam and Eve! Nothing better to do with their time than picking bleeding apples!"

3

I don't know how we got through that day, but I was very glad when it was over, the tea things were cleared away, and Belcher said in his peaceable way: "Well, chums, what about it?" We sat round the table and Hawkins took out the cards, and just then I heard Jeremiah Donovan's footstep on the path and a dark presentiment crossed my mind. I rose from the table and caught him before he reached the door.

"What do you want?" I asked.

"I want those two soldier friends of yours," he says, getting red.

"Is that the way, Jeremiah Donovan?" I asked.

"That's the way. There were four of our lads shot this morning, one of them a boy of sixteen."

"That's bad," I said.

At that moment Noble followed me out, and the three of us walked down the path together, talking in whispers. Feeney, the local intelligence officer, was standing by the gate.

"What are you going to do about it?" I asked Jeremiah Donovan.

"I want you and Noble to get them out; tell them they're being shifted again; that'll be the quietest way."

"Leave me out of that," says Noble under his breath.

Jeremiah Donovan looks at him hard.

"All right," he says. "You and Feeney get a few tools from the shed and dig a hole by the far end of the bog. Bonaparte and myself will be after you. Don't let anyone see you with the tools. I wouldn't like it to go beyond ourselves."

We saw Feeney and Noble go round to the shed and went in ourselves. I left Jeremiah Donovan to do the explanations. He told them that he had orders to send them back to the Second Battalion. Hawkins let out a mouthful of curses, and you could see that though Belcher didn't say anything, he was a bit upset too. The old woman was for having them stay in spite of us, and she didn't stop advising them until Jeremiah Donovan lost his temper and turned on her. He had a nasty temper, I noticed. It was pitch-dark in the cottage by this time, but no one thought of lighting the lamp, and in the darkness the two Englishmen fetched their topcoats and said goodbye to the old woman.

"Just as a man makes a home of a bleeding place, some bastard at headquarters thinks you're too cushy and shunts you off," says Hawkins, shaking her hand.

"A thousand thanks, madam," says Belcher. "A thousand thanks for everything"— as though he'd made it up.

We went round to the back of the house and down towards the bog. It was only then that Jeremiah Donovan told them. He was shaking with excitement.

"There were four of our fellows shot in Cork this morning and now you're to be shot as a reprisal."

"What are you talking about?" snaps Hawkins. "It's bad enough being mucked about as we are without having to put up with your funny jokes."

"It isn't a joke," says Donovan. "I'm sorry, Hawkins, but it's true," and begins on the usual rigmarole about duty and how unpleasant it is.

I never noticed that people who talk a lot about duty find it much of a trouble to them.

"Oh, cut it out!" says Hawkins.

"Ask Bonaparte," says Donovan, seeing that Hawkins isn't taking him seriously. "Isn't it true, Bonaparte?"

"It is," I say, and Hawkins stops.

"Ah, for Christ's sake, chum!"

"I mean it, chum," I say.

"You don't sound as if you meant it."

"If he doesn't mean it, I do," says Donovan, working himself up.

"What have you against me, Jeremiah Donovan?"

"I never said I had anything against you. But why did your people take out four of our prisoners and shoot them in cold blood?"

He took Hawkins by the arm and dragged him on, but it was impossible to make him understand that we were in earnest. I had the Smith and Wesson in my pocket and I kept fingering it and wondering what I'd do if they put up a fight for it or ran, and wishing to God they'd do one or the other. I knew if they did run for it, that I'd never fire on them. Hawkins wanted to know was Noble in it, and when we said yes, he asked us why Noble wanted to plug him. Why did any of us want to plug him? What had he done to us? Weren't we all chums? Didn't we understand him and didn't he understand us? Did we imagine for an instant that he'd shoot us for all the so-and-so officers in the so-and-so British Army?

By this time we'd reached the bog, and I was so sick I couldn't even answer him. We walked along the edge of it in the darkness, and every now and then Hawkins would call a halt and begin all over again, as if he was wound up, about our being chums, and I knew that nothing but the sight of the grave would convince him that we had to do it. And all the time I was hoping that something would happen; that they'd run for it or that Noble would take over the responsibility from me. I had the feeling that it was worse on Noble than on me.

4

At last we saw the lantern in the distance and made towards it. Noble was carrying it, and Feeney was standing somewhere in the darkness behind him, and the picture of them so still and silent in the bogland brought it home to me that we were in earnest, and banished the last bit of hope I had.

Belcher, on recognizing Noble, said: "Hallo, chum," in his quiet way, but Hawkins flew at him at once, and the argument began all over again, only this time Noble had nothing to say for himself and stood with his head down, holding the lantern between his legs.

It was Jeremiah Donovan who did the answering. For the twentieth time, as though it was haunting his mind, Hawkins asked if anybody thought he'd shoot Noble.

"Yes, you would," says Jeremiah Donovan.

"No, I wouldn't, damn you!"

"You would, because you'd know you'd be shot for not doing it."

"I wouldn't, not if I was to be shot twenty times over. I wouldn't shoot a pal. And Belcher wouldn't—isn't that right, Belcher?"

"That's right, chum," Belcher said, but more by way of answering the question than of joining in the argument. Belcher sounded as though whatever unforeseen thing he'd always been waiting for had come at last.

"Anyway, who says Noble would be shot if I wasn't? What do you think I'd do if I was in his place, out in the middle of a blasted bog?"

"What would you do?" asks Donovan.

"I'd go with him wherever he was going, of course. Share my last bob with him and stick by him through thick and thin. No one can ever say of me that I let down a pal."

"We had enough of this," says Jeremiah Donovan, cocking his revolver.

"Is there any message you want to send?"

"No, there isn't."

"Do you want to say your prayers?"

Hawkins came out with a cold-blooded remark that even shocked me and turned on Noble again.

"Listen to me, Noble," he says. "You and me are chums. You can't come over to my side, so I'll come over to your side. That show you I mean what I say? Give me a rifle and I'll go along with you and the other lads."

Nobody answered him. We knew that was no way out.

"Hear what I'm saying?" he says. "I'm through with it. I'm a deserter or anything else you like. I don't believe in your stuff, but it's no worse than mine. That satisfy you?"

Noble raised his head, but Donovan began to speak and he lowered it again without replying.

"For the last time, have you any messages to send?" says Donovan in a cold, excited sort of voice.

"Shut up, Donovan! You don't understand me, but these lads do. They're not the sort to make a pal and kill a pal. They're not the tools of any capitalist."

I alone of the crowd saw Donovan raise his Webley to the back of Hawkins's neck, and as he did so I shut my eyes and tried to pray. Hawkins had begun to say something else when Donovan fired, and as I opened my eyes at the bang, I saw Hawkins stagger at the knees and lie out flat at Noble's feet, slowly and as quiet as a kid falling asleep, with the lantern light on his lean legs and bright farmer's boots. We all stood very still, watching him settle out in the last agony.

Then Belcher took out a handkerchief and began to tie it about his own eyes (in our excitement we'd forgotten to do the same for Hawkins), and, seeing it wasn't big enough, turned and asked for the loan of mine. I gave it to him and he knotted the two together and pointed with his foot at Hawkins.

"He's not quite dead," he says. "Better give him another."

Sure enough, Hawkins's left knee is beginning to rise. I bent down and put my gun to his head; then, recollecting myself, I get up again. Belcher understands what's in my mind.

"Give him his first," he says. "I don't mind. Poor bastard, we don't know what's happening to him now."

I knelt and fired. By this time I didn't seem to know what I was doing. Belcher, who was fumbling a bit awkwardly with the handkerchief, came out with a laugh as he heard the shot. It was the first time I heard him laugh and it sent a shudder down my back; it sounded so unnatural.

"Poor bugger!" he said quietly. "And last night he was so curious about it all. It's very queer, chums, I always think. Now he knows as much about it as they'll ever let him know, and last night he was all in the dark."

Donovan helped him to tie the handkerchiefs about his eyes. "Thanks, chum." he said. Donovan asked if there were any messages he wanted sent.

"No, chum," he says. "Not for me. If any of you would like to write to Hawkins's mother, you'll find a letter from her in his pocket. He and his mother were great chums. But my missus left me eight years ago. Went away with another fellow and took the kid with her. I like the feeling of a home, as you may have noticed, but I couldn't start again after that."

It was an extraordinary thing, but in those few minutes Belcher said more than in all the weeks before. It was just as if the sound of the shot had started a flood of talk in him and he could go on the whole night like that, quite happily, talking about himself. We stood round like fools now that he couldn't see us any longer. Donovan looked at Noble, and Noble shook his head. Then Donovan raised his Webley, and at that moment Belcher gives his queer laugh again. He may have thought we were talking about him, or perhaps he noticed the same thing I'd noticed and couldn't understand it.

"Excuse me, chums," he says. "I feel I'm talking the hell of a lot, and so silly, about my being so handy about a house and things like that. But this thing came on me suddenly. You'll forgive me, I'm sure."

"You don't want to say a prayer?" asks Donovan.

"No, chum," he says. "I don't think it would help. I'm ready and you boys want to get it over."

"You understand that we're only doing our duty?" says Donovan.

Belcher's head was raised like a blind man's, so that you could only see his chin and the tip of his nose in the lantern light.

"I never could make out what duty was myself," he said. "I think you're all good lads, if that's what you mean. I'm not complaining."

Noble, just as if he couldn't bear anymore of it, raised his fist at Donovan, and in a flash Donovan raised his gun and fired. The big man went over like a sack of meal, and this time there was no need of a second shot.

I don't remember much about the burying, but that it was worse than all the rest because we had to carry them to the grave. It was all mad lonely with nothing but a patch of lantern-light between ourselves and the dark, and birds hooting and screeching all round, disturbed by the guns. Noble went through Hawkins's belongings to find the letter from his mother, and then joined his hands together. He did the same with Belcher. Then, when we'd filled in the grave, we separated from Jeremiah Donovan and Feeney and took our tools back to the shed. All the way we didn't speak a word. The kitchen was dark and cold as we'd left it, and the old woman was sitting over the hearth, saying her beads. We walked past her into the room, and Noble struck a match to light the lamp. She rose quietly and came to the doorway with all her cantankerousness gone.

"What did ye do with them?" she asked in a whisper, and Noble started so that the match went out in his hand.

"What's that?" he asked without turning around.

"I heard ye," she said.

"What did you hear?" asked Noble.

"I heard ye. Do ye think I didn't hear ye, putting the spade back in the houseen?"

Noble struck another match and this time the lamp lit for him.

"Was that what ye did to them?" she asked.

Then, by God, in the very doorway, she fell on her knees and began praying, and after looking at her for a minute or two Noble did the same by the fireplace. I pushed my way out past her and left them at it. I stood at the door, watching the stars and listening to the shrieking of the birds dying out over the bogs. It is so strange what you feel at times like that you can't describe it. Noble says he saw everything ten times the size, as though there were nothing in the whole world but that little patch of bog with the two Englishmen stiffening into it, but with me it was as if the patch of bog where the Englishmen were was a million miles away, and even Noble and the old woman, mumbling behind me, and the birds and the bloody stars were all far away, and I was somehow very small and very lost and lonely like a child astray in the snow. And anything that happened to me afterwards, I never felt the same about again.

For Practice

1. What is the significance of this story's title?

2. Where does Donovan feel his primary duty lies? How does he justify his position? Why does he dislike the prisoners? Is his shooting of the prisoners justified legally? Ethically? Why or why not?

3. What does the narrator, Bonaparte, think of Donovan's sense of duty? What do the other characters say about duty? Where does O'Connor himself seem to stand on this issue? What aspects of the text suggest his view? Has he loaded the debate, or has he been fair to both sides?

4. Consider the final paragraph. How has Bonaparte been affected by his participation in the incident?

5. What values are implied by the different attitudes that Donovan and Bonaparte take towards their prisoners and towards their own duties as soldiers? Do the varying responses of the characters reveal different attitudes about life—both its purpose and its value? What are these different attitudes?

6. How does each of the characters deal with death? What does O'Connor hope his readers will learn from these differing reactions?

7. Recent constitutional changes in Northern Ireland have greatly altered the political situation in that country. What effect might "Guests of the Nation" and other stories like it have in reorienting entrenched attitudes that stand in the way of peace in Northern Ireland?

Musee des Beaux Arts[1]

W. H. Auden

The son of a physician, W. H. Auden (1907–1973) was fascinated as a child with his father's medical books. His poetry often reflects this fascination: his tone usually possesses the cool, diagnostic manner of the medical profession and his themes often revolve around disease and human suffering. He was born in Great Britain but immigrated to the United States in 1939, eventually becoming an American citizen. Shortly after this immigration, Auden met and fell in love with Chester Kallman. The relationship soon developed into a lifelong companionship.

Auden experimented extensively with poetic forms and published more than ten books of poetry, as well as plays, essays, travel books and opera libretti. "Musee des Beaux Arts" was written in 1938 and published two years later. The poem's title is French and means "Museum of Fine Arts," an appropriate title, since the work directly refers to painting. In particular, the poem's speaker mentions the painting "The Fall of Icarus" by 16th century Dutch artist Pieter Brueghel. (See the color plates section of this book.) The story of Icarus originates in Greek mythology. Icarus' father, Daedalus, gives his son a pair of wings made of feathers and wax, along with instructions that he not fly too close to the sun. When the young man ignores his father's warning, the wings melt, and Icarus plunges into the ocean. Auden's poem offers a reflection on Brueghel's depiction of this mythological incident, but it also reflects on real life experiences of suffering and death.

About suffering they were never wrong,
The Old Masters: how well they understood
Its human position; how it takes place
While someone else is eating or opening a window or just walking dully along;
How, when the aged ate reverently, passionately waiting   5
For the miraculous birth, there always must be
Children who did not specially want it to happen, skating
On a pond at the edge of the wood:
They never forgot
That even the dreadful martyrdom must run its course   10
Anyhow in a corner, some untidy spot

Where the dogs go on with their doggy life and the torturer's horse
Scratches its innocent behind on a tree.

In Brueghel's *Icarus*,[2] for instance: how everything turns away
Quite leisurely from the disaster; the plowman may   15
Have heard the splash, the forsaken cry,
But for him it was not an important failure; the sun shone
As it had to on the white legs disappearing into the green
Water; and the expensive delicate ship that must have seen
Something amazing, a boy falling out of the sky,   20
Had somewhere to get to and sailed calmly on.

1938

Notes

1. The Museum of Fine Arts, in Brussels.
2. *Landscape with the Fall of Icarus,* by Pieter Brueghel the elder (1525?–1569), located in the Brussels Museum. According to Greek myth, Daedalus and his son Icarus escaped from imprisonment by using homemade wings of wax; but Icarus flew too near the sun, the wax melted, and he fell into the sea and drowned. In the Brueghel painting the central figure is a peasant plowing, and several other figures are more immediately noticeable than Icarus, who, disappearing into the sea, is easy to miss in the lower right-hand corner. Equally ignored by the figures is a dead body in the woods. (A copy of this painting is in the art and photography section of this book.)

For Practice

1. What does this poem imply about the way people respond to death? Does the speaker seem to be criticizing these responses, or just describing?
2. Does the speaker of "Musee des Beaux Arts" take a different attitude toward death from the speaker of Slavitt's "Titanic"? What similarities or differences do you observe?
3. After you have read the poem "Musee des Beaux Arts," examine Brueghel's painting, "The Fall of Icarus." Compare the two. Do you notice details in the painting that Auden omits? What does the poem help you see in the painting? Does the painting help you better understand the poem?
4. Auden's poetry is often recognized for its understatement—its tendency to treat serious matters with wry humor and emotional matters in an unemotional tone. Is that true of this poem? Give examples to defend your answer.
5. There is a marked difference between the two stanzas of the poem. What does each stanza do? How does each stanza contribute to the overall argument of the poem?
6. The last stanza describes three reactions to Icarus' fall. Identify the three. How are the responses alike and how are they different? Can we tell what the speaker thinks about the three responses? What do you think about them?

Ulysses

Alfred, Lord Tennyson

Alfred, Lord Tennyson (1809–1892) is generally considered one of the greatest of the English poets of the Victorian period. His works were immensely popular during his lifetime, and despite unfavorable reception after his death, his reputation as a deliberate thinker and skillful crafts-man remains intact. His works are rich with echoes of the past; for exam-ple, in his famous epic, "Idylls of the King," he creates his own version of the famous King Arthur legends.

"Ulysses" was written in 1833 and published in Tennyson's Poems *in 1842. In this poem, Tennyson imagines the thoughts of an aged Ulysses (Odysseus), the famous hero of Homeric epic* The Odyssey. *The episode on which this poem is based is not, however, from Homer but Dante's* Inferno. *Readers familiar with* The Odyssey *will be acquainted with Ulysses' heroic deeds during the prime of his life, but here Tennyson uses the aged hero to explore the condition of old age: with his most heroic work complete and with death drawing nearer; what is left for the man of action to do? Tennyson presents a character on a quest for meaning, but leaves unan-swered questions about what Ulysses is trying to attain, as well as about the motivations for his quest.*

It little profits that an idle king,
By this still hearth, among these barren crags,
Matched with an aged wife, I mete and dole
Unequal laws unto a savage race,
That hoard, and sleep, and feed, and know not me.   5

    I cannot rest from travel; I will drink
Life to the lees. All times I have enjoyed
Greatly, have suffered greatly, both with those
That loved me, and alone; on shore, and when
Through scudding drifts the rainy Hyades   10
Vexed the dim sea. I am becoming a name;
For always roaming with a hungry heart
Much have I seen and known—cities of men
And manners, climates, councils, governments,
Myself not least, but honored of them all—   15

And drunk delight of battle with my peers,
Far on the ringing plains of windy Troy.
I am a part of all that I have met;
Yet all experience is an arch wherethrough
Gleams that untraveled world, whose margin fades   20
For ever and for ever when I move.
How dull it is to pause, to make an end,
To rust unburnished, not to shine in use!
As though to breathe were life. Life piled on life
Were all too little, and of one to me   25
Little remains; but every hour is saved
From that eternal silence, something more,
A bringer of new things; and vile it were
For some three suns to store and hoard myself,
And this gray spirit yearning in desire   30
To follow knowledge like a sinking star,
Beyond the utmost bound of human thought.
This is my son, mine own Telemachus,
To whom I leave the scepter and the isle—
Well-loved of me, discerning to fulfill   35
This labor by slow prudence to make mild
A rugged people, and through soft degrees
Subdue them to the useful and the good.
Most blameless is he, centered in the sphere
Of common duties, decent not to fail   40
In offices of tenderness, and pay
Meet adoration to my household gods,
When I am gone. He works his work, I mine.

    There lies the port; the vessel puffs her sail:
There gloom the dark, broad seas. My mariners.   45
Souls that have toiled, and wrought, and thought with me—
That ever with a frolic welcome took
The thunder and the sunshine, and opposed
Free hearts, free foreheads—you and I are old;
Old age hath yet his honor and his toil.   50
Death closes all; but something ere the end,
Some work of noble note, may yet be done,
Not unbecoming men that strove with Gods.
The lights begin to twinkle from the rocks;
The long day wanes; the slow moon climbs; the deep   55
Moans round with many voices. Come, my friends.
'Tis not too late to seek a newer world.
Push off, and sitting well in order smite
The sounding furrows; for my purpose holds
To sail beyond the sunset, and the baths   60
Of all the western stars, until I die.
It may be that the gulfs will wash us down;
It may be we shall touch the Happy Isles,

And see the great Achilles, whom we knew.
Though much is taken, much abides; and though   65
We are not now that strength which in old days
Moved earth and heaven, that which we are, we are:
One equal temper of heroic hearts.
Made weak by time and fate, but strong in will
To strive, to seek, to find, and not to yield.   70

1833

For Practice

1. Tennyson uses the first-person voice to narrate the poem. What effect does this have on the meaning of the poem? How might the poem have been different if Tennyson has used a third-person narrator? How does the use of first person allow the poem to raise subtle questions about Ulysses' decision-making process? What are these questions?

2. How much does "Ulysses" represent concerns that are common to all humans? What factors would Tennyson seem to suggest as possible motivations of a quest for meaning?

3. The old saying goes, "You can't teach an old dog new tricks." Ulysses points out how his son Telemachus is better suited to peacetime governing than he is (lines 33–43). Do you interpret that as a legitimate argument, or a poor excuse for dodging his responsibilities? Do our personalities become fixed after a certain age? How much do the actions of our younger days determine what we will be like in old age?

4. Tennyson wrote "Ulysses" partly to help himself recover from the loss of his close friend Arthur Hallam, to help himself in "braving the struggle of life." How does the poem reflect this purpose?

5. Does Ulysses' desire to journey seem to be a search to find meaning, or an attempt to make meaning? What is the difference between these two kinds of quests? How does the nature of his desire affect your reading of the poem?

6. This poem is based on two very old texts: Homer's *The Odyssey* which dates back to ancient Greece and Dante's *Inferno*, a Renaissance epic poem which is itself based on classical literature. What is the effect of grounding a literary argument in ancient texts like these? Why do you suppose Tennyson and, for that matter, Dante, want to remind us of these old stories? Is such a rhetorical move as effective today as it seems to have been in earlier times?

Gimpel the Fool

Isaac Bashevis Singer
translated by Saul Bellow

Isaac Bashevis Singer (1904–1991) was born in Poland to Orthodox Jewish parents. He came to America in 1935, but continued to write stories and newspaper articles in Yiddish, his native language. Though translation of literature tends to obscure its full depth and meaning, Singer has worked closely with translators (in this case, the Jewish novelist Saul Bellow) to ensure that the quality of his storytelling remains intact. Singer's stories have the ring of fable: deceptively straightforward in their telling, they provoke complex moral and intellectual thought.

In "Gimpel the Fool," Singer creates a man who believes everything and explores, among other issues, what it really means to believe. He also investigates the ways people know things, questioning the grounds upon which people build their systems of belief. Though his story retains a distinctly ethnic feel, the humor and simple appeal of this tale make it easily accessible to the non-Jewish reader. This translation of "Gimpel the Fool" first appeared in 1957.

1

I am Gimpel the fool. I don't think myself a fool. On the contrary. But that's what folks call me. They gave me the name while I was still in school. I had seven names in all: imbecile, donkey, flax-head, dope, glump, ninny, and fool. The last name stuck. What did my foolishness consist of? I was easy to take in. They said, "Gimpel, you know the rabbi's wife has been brought to childbed?" So I skipped school. Well, it turned out to be a lie. How was I supposed to know? She hadn't had a big belly. But I never looked at her belly. Was that really so foolish? The gang laughed and hee-hawed, stomped and danced and chanted a good-night prayer. And instead of the raisins they give when a woman's lying in, they stuffed my hand full of goat turds. I was no weakling. If I slapped someone he'd see all the way to Cracow. But I'm really not a slugger by nature. I think to myself: Let it pass. So they take advantage of me.

I was coming home from school and heard a dog barking. I'm not afraid of dogs, but of course I never want to start up with them. One of them may be mad, and if he bites there's not a Tartar in the world who can help you. So I made tracks. Then I looked around and saw the whole market place wild with laughter. It was no dog at all but Wolf-Leib the Thief. How was I supposed to know it was he? It sounded like a howling bitch.

When the pranksters and leg-pullers found that I was easy to fool, every one of them tried his luck with me. "Gimpel, the Czar is coming to Frampol; Gimpel, the moon fell down in Turbeen; Gimpel, little Hodel Furpiece found a treasure behind the bathhouse." And I like a golem believed everyone. In the first place, everything is possible, as it is written in the Wisdom of the Fathers. I've forgotten just how. Second, I had to believe when the whole town came down on me! If I ever dared to say, "Ah, you're kidding!" there was trouble. People got angry. "What do you mean! You want to call everyone a liar?" What was I to do? I believed them, and I hope at least that did them some good.

I was an orphan. My grandfather who brought me up was already bent toward the grave. So they turned me over to a baker, and what a time they gave me there! Every woman or girl who came to bake a batch of noodles had to fool me at least once. "Gimpel, there's a fair in heaven; Gimpel, the rabbi gave birth to a calf in the seventh month; Gimpel, a cow flew over the roof and laid brass eggs." A student from the yeshiva came once to buy a roll, and he said, "You, Gimpel, while you stand here scraping with your baker's shovel the Messiah has come. The dead have arisen." "What do you mean?" I said. "I heard no one blowing the ram's horn!" He said, "Are you deaf?" And all began to cry, "We heard it, we heard!" Then in came Rietze the Candle-dipper and called out in her hoarse voice, "Gimpel, your father and mother have stood up from the grave. They're looking for you."

To tell the truth, I knew very well that nothing of the sort had happened, but all the same, as folks were talking, I threw on my wool vest and went out. Maybe something had happened. What did I stand to lose by looking? Well, what a cat music went up! And then I took a vow to believe nothing more. But that was no go either. They confused me so that I didn't know the big end from the small.

I went to the rabbi to get some advice. He said, "It is written, better to be a fool all your days than for one hour to be evil. You are not a fool. They are the fools. For he who causes his neighbor to feel shame loses Paradise himself." Nevertheless the rabbi's daughter took me in. As I left the rabbinical court she said, "Have you kissed the wall yet?" I said, "No; what for?" She answered, "It's the law; you've got to do it after every visit." Well, there didn't seem to be any harm in it. And she burst out laughing. It was a fine trick. She put one over on me, all right.

I wanted to go off to another town, but then everyone got busy matchmaking, and they were after me so they nearly tore my coat tails off. They talked at me and talked until I got water on the ear. She was no chaste maiden, but they told me she was virgin pure. She had a limp, and they said it was deliberate, from coyness. She had a bastard, and they told me the child was her little brother. I cried, "You're wasting your time. I'll never marry that whore." But they said indignantly, "What a way to talk! Aren't you ashamed of yourself? We can take you to the rabbi and have you fined for giving her a bad name." I saw then that I wouldn't escape them so easily and I thought: They're set on making me their butt. But when you're married the husband's the master, and if that's all right with her it's agreeable to me too. Besides, you can't pass through life unscathed, nor expect to.

I went to her clay house, which was built on the sand, and the whole gang, hollering and chorusing, came after me. They acted like bear-baiters. When we came to the well they stopped all the same. They were afraid to start anything with Elka. Her mouth would open as if it were on a hinge, and she had a fierce tongue. I entered the house. Lines were strung from wall to wall and clothes were drying. Barefoot she stood by the tub, doing the wash. She was dressed in a worn hand-me-down gown of plush. She had her hair put in braids and pinned across her head. It took my breath away, almost, the reek of it all.

Evidently she knew who I was. She took a look at me and said, "Look who's here! He's come, the drip. Grab a seat."

I told her all; I denied nothing. "Tell me the truth," I said, "are you really a virgin, and is that mischievous Yechiel actually your little brother? Don't be deceitful with me, for I'm an orphan."

"I'm an orphan myself," she answered, "and whoever tries to twist you up, may the end of his nose take a twist. But don't let them think they can take advantage of me. I want a dowry of fifty guilders, and let them take up a collection besides. Otherwise they can kiss my you-know-what." She was very plainspoken. I said, "It's the bride and not the groom who gives a dowry." Then she said, "Don't bargain with me. Either a flat 'yes' or a flat 'no'—Go back where you came from."

I thought: No bread will ever be baked from *this* dough. But ours is not a poor town. They consented to everything and proceeded with the wedding. It so happened that there was a dysentery epidemic at the time. The ceremony was held at the cemetery gates, near the little corpse-washing hut. The fellows got drunk. While the marriage contract was being drawn up I heard the most pious high rabbi ask, "Is the bride a widow or a divorced woman?" And the sexton's wife answered for her, "Both a widow and divorced." It was a black moment for me. But what was I to do, run away from under the marriage canopy?

There was singing and dancing. An old granny danced opposite me, hugging a braided white *chalah*. The master of revels made a "God's mercy" in memory of the bride's parents. The schoolboys threw burrs, as on Tishe b'Av fast day. There were a lot of gifts after the sermon: a noodle board, a kneading trough, a bucket, brooms, ladles, household articles galore. Then I took a look and saw two strapping young men carrying a crib. "What do we need this for?" I asked. So they said, "Don't rack your brains about it. It's all right, it'll come in handy," I realized I was going to be rooked. Take it another way though, what did I stand to lose? I reflected: I'll see what comes of it. A whole town can't go altogether crazy.

2

At night I came where my wife lay, but she wouldn't let me in. "Say, look here, is this what they married us for?" I said. And she said, "My monthly has come." "But yesterday they took you to the ritual bath, and that's afterward, isn't it supposed to be?" "Today isn't yesterday," said she, "and yesterday's not today. You can beat it if you don't like it." In short, I waited.

Not four months later she was in childbed. The townsfolk hid their laughter with their knuckles. But what could I do? She suffered intolerable pains and clawed at the walls. "Gimpel," she cried, "I'm going. Forgive me!" The house filled with women. They were boiling pans of water. The screams rose to the welkin.

The thing to do was to go to the House of Prayer to repeat Psalms, and that was what I did.

The townsfolk like that, all right. I stood in a corner saying Psalms and prayers, and they shook their heads at me. "Pray, pray!" they told me. "Prayer never made any woman pregnant." One of the congregation put a straw to my mouth and said, "Hay for the cows." There was something to that too, by God!

She gave birth to a boy. Friday at the synagogue the sexton stood up before the Ark, pounded on the reading table, and announced, "The wealthy Reb Gimpel invites the congregation to a feast in honor of the birth of a son." The whole House of Prayer rang with laughter. My face was flaming. But there was nothing I could do. After all, I *was* the one responsible for the circumcision honors and rituals.

Half the town came running. You couldn't wedge another soul in. Women brought peppered chick-peas, and there was a keg of beer from the tavern. I ate and drank as much as anyone, and they all congratulated me. Then there was a circumcision, and I named the boy after my father, may he rest in peace. When all were gone and I was left with my wife alone, she thrust her head through the bed-curtain and called me to her.

"Gimpel," said she, "why are you silent? Has your ship gone and sunk?"

"What shall I say?" I answered. "A fine thing you've done to me! If my mother had known of it she'd have died a second time."

She said, "Are you crazy, or what?"

"How can you make such a fool," I said, "of one who should be the lord and master?"

"What's the matter with you?" she said. "What have you taken it into your head to imagine?"

I saw that I must speak bluntly and openly. "Do you think this is the way to use an orphan?" I said. "You have borne a bastard."

She answered, "Drive this foolishness out of your head. The child is yours."

"How can he be mine?" I argued. "He was born seventeen weeks after the wedding."

She told me then that he was premature. I said, "Isn't he a little too premature?" She said, she had had a grandmother who carried just a short a time and she resembled this grandmother of hers as one drop of water does another. She swore to it with such oaths that you would have believed a peasant at the fair if he had used them. To tell the plain truth, I didn't believe her; but when I talked it over next day with the schoolmaster he told me that the very same thing had happened to Adam and Eve. Two they went up to bed, and four they descended.

"There isn't a woman in the world who is not the granddaughter of Eve," he said.

That was how it was; they argued me dumb. But then, who really knows how such things are?

I began to forget my sorrow. I loved the child madly, and he loved me too. As soon as he saw me he'd wave his little hands and want me to pick him up, and when he was colicky I was the only one who could pacify him. I bought him a little bone teething ring and a little gilded cap. He was forever catching the evil eye from someone, and then I had to run to get one of those abracadabras for him that would get him out of it. I worked like an ox. You know how expenses go up when there's an infant in the house. I don't want to lie about it; I didn't dislike Elka either, for that matter. She swore at me and cursed, and I couldn't get enough of her. What strength she had! One of her looks could rob you of the power of speech. And her orations! Pitch and sulphur, that's what they were full of, and yet somehow also full of charm. I adored her every word. She gave me bloody wounds though.

In the evening I brought her a white loaf as well as a dark one, and also poppyseed rolls I baked myself. I thieved because of her and swiped everything I could lay my hands on: macaroons, raisins, almonds, cakes. I hope I may be forgiven for stealing from the Saturday pots the women left to warm in the baker's oven. I would take out scraps of meat, a chunk of pudding, a chicken leg or head, a piece of tripe, whatever I could nip quickly. She ate and became fat and handsome.

I had to sleep away from home all during the week, at the bakery. On Friday nights when I got home she always made an excuse of some sort. Either she had heartburn, or a stitch in the side, or hiccups, or headaches. You know what women's excuses are. I had a bitter time of it. It was rough. To add to it, this little brother of hers, the bastard, was growing bigger. He'd put lumps on me, and when I wanted to hit back she'd open her mouth and curse so powerfully I saw a green haze floating before my eyes. Ten times a day she threatened to divorce me. Another man in my place would have taken French leave and disappeared. But I'm the type that bears it and says nothing. What's one to do? Shoulders are from God, and burdens too.

One night there was a calamity in the bakery; the oven burst, and we almost had a fire. There was nothing to do but go home, so I went home. Let me, I thought, also taste the joy of sleeping in bed in mid-week. I didn't want to wake the sleeping mite and tiptoed into the house. Coming in, it seemed to me that I heard not the snoring of one but, as it were, a double snore, one a thin enough snore and the other like the snoring of a slaughtered ox. Oh, I didn't like that! I didn't like it at all. I went up to the bed, and things suddenly turned black. Next to Elka lay a man's form. Another in my place would have made an uproar, and enough noise to rouse the whole town, but the thought occurred to me that I might wake the child. A little thing like that—why frighten a little swallow, I thought. All right then, I went back to the bakery and stretched out on a sack of flour and till morning I never shut an eye. I shivered as if I had had malaria. "Enough of being a donkey," I said to myself. "Gimpel isn't going to be a sucker all his life. There's a limit even to the foolishness of a fool like Gimpel."

In the morning I went to the rabbi to get advice, and it made a great commotion in the town. They sent the beadle for Elka right away. She came, carrying the child. And what do you think she did? She denied it, denied everything, bone and stone! "He's out of his head," she said. "I know nothing of dreams or divinations." They yelled at her, warned her, hammered on the table, but she stuck to her guns: it was a false accusation, she said.

The butchers and the horse-traders took her part. One of the lads from the slaughterhouse came by and said to me, "We've got our eye on you, you're a marked man." Meanwhile the child started to bear down and soiled itself. In the rabbinical court there was an Ark of the Covenant, and they couldn't allow that, so they sent Elka away.

I said to the rabbi, "What shall I do?"

"You must divorce her at once," said he.

"And what if she refuses?" I asked.

He said, "You must serve the divorce. That's all you'll have to do."

I said, "Well, all right, Rabbi. Let me think about it."

"There's nothing to think about," said he. "You mustn't remain under the same roof with her."

"And if I want to see the child?" I asked.

"Let her go, the harlot," said he, "and her brood of bastards with her."

The verdict he gave was that I mustn't even cross her threshold—never again, as long as I should live.

During the day it didn't bother me so much. I thought: It was bound to happen, the abscess had to burst. But at night when I stretched out upon the sacks I felt it all very bitterly. A longing took me, for her and for the child. I wanted to be angry, but that's my misfortune exactly, I don't have it in me to be really angry. In the first place— this was how my thoughts went—there's bound to be a slip sometimes. You can't live without errors. Probably that lad who was with her led her on and gave her presents and what not, the women are often long on hair and short on sense, and so he got around her. And then since she denies it so, maybe I was only seeing things? Hallucinations do happen. You see a figure of a mannikin or something, but when you come up closer it's nothing, there's not a thing there. And if that's so, I'm doing her an injustice. And when I got so far in my thoughts I started to weep. I sobbed so that I wet the flour where I lay. In the morning I went to the rabbi and told him that I had made a mistake. The rabbi wrote on with his quill, and he said that if that were so he would have to reconsider the whole case. Until he had finished I wasn't to go near my wife, but I might send her bread and money by messenger.

3

Nine months passed before all the rabbis could come to an agreement. Letters went back and forth. I hadn't realized that there could be so much erudition about a matter like this.

Meanwhile Elka gave birth to still another child, a girl this time. On the Sabbath I went to the synagogue and invoked a blessing on her. They called me up to the Torah, and I named the child for my mother-in-law—may she rest in peace. The louts and loudmouths of the town who came into the bakery gave me a going over. All Frampol refreshed its spirits because of my trouble and grief. However, I resolved that I would always believe what I was told. What's the good of *not* believing? Today it's your wife you don't believe; tomorrow it's God Himself you won't take stock in.

By an apprentice who was her neighbor I sent her daily a corn or a wheat loaf, or a piece of pastry, rolls or bagels, or, when I got the chance, a slab of pudding, a slice of honeycake, or wedding strudel—whatever came my way. The apprentice was a good-hearted lad, and more than once he added something on his own. He had formerly annoyed me a lot, plucking my nose and digging me in the ribs, but when he started to be a visitor to my house he became kind and friendly. "Hey, you, Gimpel," he said to me, "you have a very decent little wife and two fine kids. You don't deserve them."

"But the things people say about her," I said.

"Well, they have long tongues," he said, "and nothing to do with them but babble. Ignore it as you ignore the cold of last winter."

One day the rabbi sent for me and said, "Are you certain, Gimpel, that you were wrong about your wife?"

I said, "I'm certain."

"Why, but look here! You yourself saw it."

"It must have been a shadow," I said.

"The shadow of what?"

"Just one of the beams, I think."

"You can go home then. You owe thanks to the Yanover rabbi. He found an obscure reference in Maimonides that favored you."

I seized the rabbi's hand and kissed it.

I wanted to run home immediately. It's no small thing to be separated for so long a time from wife and child. Then I reflected: I'd better go back to work now, and go home in the evening. I said nothing to anyone, although as far as my heart was concerned it was like one of the Holy Days. The women teased and twitted me as they did every day, but my thought was: Go on, with your loose talk. The truth is out, like the oil upon the water. Maimonides says it's right, and therefore it is right!

At night, when I had covered the dough to let it rise, I took my share of bread and a little sack of flour and started homeward. The moon was full and the stars were glistening, something to terrify the soul. I hurried onward, and before me darted a long shadow. It was winter, and a fresh snow had fallen. I had a mind to sing, but it was growing late and I didn't want to wake the householders. Then I felt like whistling, but I remembered that you don't whistle at night because it brings the demons out. So I was silent and walked as fast as I could.

Dogs in the Christian yards barked at me when I passed, but I thought: Bark your teeth out! What are you but mere dogs? Whereas I am a man, the husband of a fine wife, the father of promising children.

As I approached the house my heart started to pound as though it were the heart of a criminal. I felt no fear, but my heart went thump! Well, no drawing back. I quietly lifted the latch and went in. Elka was asleep. I looked at the infant's cradle. The shutter was closed, but the moon forced its way through the cracks. I saw the newborn child's face and loved it as soon as I saw it—immediately—each tiny bone.

Then I came nearer to the bed. And what did I see but the apprentice lying there beside Elka. The moon went out all at once. It was utterly black, and I trembled. My teeth chattered. The bread fell from my hands, and my wife waked and said, "Who is that, ah?"

I muttered, "It's me."

"Gimpel?" she asked. "How come you're here? I thought it was forbidden."

"The rabbi said," I answered and shook as with a fever.

"Listen to me, Gimpel," she said, "go out to the shed and see if the goat's all right. It seems she's been sick." I have forgotten to say that we had a goat. When I heard she was unwell I went into the yard. The nannygoat was a good little creature. I had a nearly human feeling for her.

With hesitant steps I went up to the shed and opened the door. The goat stood there on her four feet. I felt her everywhere, drew her by the horns, examined her udders, and found nothing wrong. She had probably eaten too much bark. "Good night, little goat," I said. "Keep well." And the little beast answered with a "Maa" as though to thank me for the good will.

I went back. The apprentice had vanished.

"Where," I asked, "is the lad?"

"What lad?" my wife answered.

"What do you mean?" I said. "The apprentice. You were sleeping with him."

"The things I have dreamed this night and the night before," she said, "may they come true and lay you low, body and soul! An evil spirit has taken root in you and dazzles your sight." She screamed out, "You hateful creature! You moon calf! You spook! You uncouth man! Get out, or I'll scream all Frampol out of bed!"

Before I could move, her brother sprang out from behind the oven and struck me a blow on the back of the head. I thought he had broken my neck. I felt that something about me was deeply wrong, and I said, "Don't make a scandal. All that's needed now is that people should accuse me of raising spooks and *dybbuks*." For that was what she had meant. "No one will touch bread of my baking."

In short, I somehow calmed her.

"Well," she said, "that's enough. Lie down, and be shattered by wheels."

Next morning I called the apprentice aside. "Listen here, brother!" I said. And so on and so forth. "What do you say?" He stared at me as though I had dropped from the roof or something.

"I swear," he said. "you'd better go to an herb doctor or some healer. I'm afraid you have a screw loose, but I'll hush it up for you." And that's how the thing stood.

To make a long story short, I lived twenty years with my wife. She bore me six children, four daughters and two sons. All kinds of things happened, but I neither saw nor heard. I believed, and that's all. The rabbi recently said to me, "Belief in itself is beneficial. It is written that a good man lives by his faith."

Suddenly my wife took sick. It began with a trifle, a little growth upon the breast. But she evidently was not destined to live long; she had no years. I spent a fortune on her. I have forgotten to say that by this time I had a bakery of my own and in Frampol was considered to be something of a rich man. Daily the healer came, and every witch doctor in the neighborhood was brought. They decided to use leeches, and after that to try cupping. They even called a doctor from Lublin, but it was too late. Before she died she called me to her bed and said, "Forgive me, Gimpel."

I said, "What is there to forgive? You have been a good and faithful wife."

"Woe, Gimpel!" she said. "It was ugly how I deceived you all these years. I want to go clean to my Maker, and so I have to tell you that the children are not yours."

If I had been clouted on the head with a piece of wood it couldn't have bewildered me more.

"Whose are they?" I asked.

"I don't know," she said. "There were a lot . . . but they're not yours." And as she spoke she tossed her head to the side, her eyes turned glassy, and it was all up with Elka. On her whitened lips there remained a smile.

I imagined that, dead as she was, she was saying, "I deceived Gimpel. That was the meaning of my brief life."

4

One night, when the period of mourning was done, as I lay dreaming on the flour sacks, there came a Spirit of Evil himself and said to me, "Gimpel, why do you sleep?"

I said, "What should I be doing? Eating *kreplach*?"

"The whole world deceives you," he said, "and you ought to deceive the world in your turn."

"How can I deceive the world?" I asked him.

He answered, "You might accumulate a bucket of urine every day and at night pour it into the dough. Let the sages of Frampol eat filth."

"What about the judgment in the world to come?" I said.

"There is no world to come," he said. "They've sold you a bill of goods and talked you into believing you carried a cat in your belly. What nonsense!"

"Well, then," I said, "and is there a God?"

He answered, "There is no God either."

"What," I said, "*is* there then?"

"A thick mire."

He stood before my eyes with a goatish beard and horn, long-toothed, and with a tail. Hearing such words, I wanted to snatch him by the tail, but I tumbled from the flour sacks and nearly broke a rib. Then it happened that I had to answer the call of nature, and, passing, I saw the risen dough, which seemed to say to me, "Do it!" In brief, I let myself be persuaded.

At dawn the apprentice came. We kneaded the bread, scattered caraway seeds on it, and set it to bake. Then the apprentice went away, and I was left sitting in the little trench by the oven, on a pile of rags. Well, Gimpel, I thought, you've revenged yourself on them for all the shame they've put on you. Outside the frost glittered, but it was warm beside the oven. The flames heated my face. I bent my head and fell into a doze.

I saw a dream, at once, Elka in her shroud. She called to me, "What have you done, Gimpel?"

I said to her, "It's all your fault," and started to cry.

"You fool!" she said. "You fool! Because I was false is everything false too? I never deceived anyone but myself. I'm paying for it all, Gimpel. They spare you nothing here."

I looked at her face. It was black; I was startled and waked, and remained sitting dumb. I sensed that everything hung in the balance. A false step now and I'd lose Eternal Life. But God gave me His help. I seized the long shovel and took out the loaves, carried them into the yard, and started to dig a hole in the frozen earth.

My apprentice came back as I was doing it. "What are you doing, boss?" he said, and grew pale as a corpse.

"I know what I'm doing," I said, and I buried it all before his very eyes.

Then I went home, took my hoard from its hiding place, and divided it among the children. "I saw your mother tonight," I said. "She's turning black, poor thing."

They were so astounded they couldn't speak a word.

"Be well," I said, "and forget that such a one as Gimpel ever existed." I put on my short coat, a pair of boots, took the bag that held my prayer shawl in one hand, my stock in the other, and kissed the *mezzuzah*. When people saw me in the street they were greatly surprised.

"Where are you going?" they said.

I answered, "Into the world." And so I departed from Frampol.

I wandered over the land, and good people did not neglect me. After many years I became old and white; I heard a great deal, many lies and falsehoods, but the longer I lived the more I understood that there were really no lies. Whatever doesn't really happen is dreamed at night. It happens to one if it doesn't happen to another, tomorrow if not today, or a century hence if not next year. What difference can it make? Often I heard tales of which I said, "Now this is a thing that cannot happen." But before a year had elapsed I heard that it actually had come to pass somewhere.

Going from place to place, eating at strange tables, it often happens that I spin yarns—improbable things that could never have happened—about devils, magicians, windmills, and the like. The children run after me, calling, "Grandfather, tell us a story." Sometimes they ask for particular stories, and I try to please them. A fat young boy once said to me, "Grandfather, it's the same story you told us before." The little rogue, he was right.

So it is with dreams too. It is many years since I left Frampol, but as soon as I shut my eyes I am there again. And whom do you think I see? Elka. She is standing by the washtub, as at our first encounter, but her face is shining and her eyes are as radiant as the eyes of a saint, and she speaks outlandish words to me, strange things. When I wake I have forgotten it all. But while the dream lasts I am comforted. She answers all my queries, and what comes out is that all is right. I weep and implore, "Let me be with you." And she consoles me and tells me to be patient. The time is nearer than it is far. Sometimes she strokes and kisses me and weeps upon my face. When I awaken I feel her lips and taste the salt of her tears.

No doubt the world is entirely an imaginary world, but it is only once removed from the true world. At the door of the hovel where I lie, there stands the plank on which the dead are taken away. The gravedigger Jew has his spade ready. The grave waits and the worms are hungry; the shrouds are prepared—I carry them in my beggar's sack. Another *shnorrer* is waiting to inherit my bed of straw. When the time comes I will go joyfully. Whatever may be there, it will be real, without complication, without ridicule, without deception. God be praised: there even Gimpel cannot be deceived.

For Practice

1. How is the title of this story significant? Is Gimpel really a fool? Using evidence from the story, explain and defend the reasons for your answers.

2. How much do you think the townspeople are responsible for Gimpel's fate? What role do they play in the story?

3. At the end of the story Gimpel looks forward to the afterlife as a time when he will finally not be deceived. Is this claim just another one of Gimpel's gullible notions? Explain your answer using evidence from the story. What do you think Singer's attitude is here?

4. One of the themes Singer investigates is how we come to know and believe the things we do. Where does Gimpel get his beliefs from? Do the sources of his beliefs affect the truth of them?

5. Is Gimpel simply a follower? Explain why or why not. What are the benefits to being someone like Gimpel? What are the drawbacks?

6. Singer brings supernatural elements into this story. What purpose do you think he is trying to achieve? Does it enhance or detract from the story?

7. What argument does this story make about the possibility of finding truth in this world? Has Singer's argument altered your thinking about this issue?

Zaabalawi

Naguib Mahfouz

Naguib Mahfouz (b. 1911) is one of Egypt's finest writers. In 1988, he was awarded the Nobel Prize for Literature, which greatly increased worldwide demand for his works. Mahfouz's novels and short stories have distinguished him within an Arab culture that traditionally reveres poetry. Despite this fame, some of Mahfouz's writings have aroused controversy: in 1994, he survived an assassination attempt by Muslim extremists. His works often deal with the lives of the common and poor of urban Egypt.

This translation of "Zaabalawi" first appeared in 1967. In this story, Mahfouz takes his readers on a strange quest for healing, a quest that is rich in symbolic value. Mahfouz explores the mysterious nature of belief, including its unlikely beginnings and unpredictable developments. As you read this story, consider this story's use of symbolism and the broader significance of this journey.

Finally I became convinced that I had to find Sheikh Zaabalawi. The first time I had heard of his name had been in a song:

"What's wrong with the world, O Zaabalawi?
They've turned it upside down and made it insipid."

It had been a popular song in my childhood and one day it had occurred to me—in the way children have of asking endless questions—to ask my father about him.

"Who is Zaabalawi, father?"

He had looked at me hesitantly as though doubting my ability to understand the answer. However, he had replied:

"May his blessing descend upon you, he's a true saint of God, a remover of worries and troubles. Were it not for him I would have died miserably—"

In the years that followed I heard him many a time sing the praises of this good saint and speak of the miracles he performed. The days passed and brought with them many illnesses from each one of which I was able, without too much trouble and at a cost I could afford, to find a cure, until I became afflicted with that illness for which no one possesses a remedy. When I had tried everything in vain and was overcome by despair, I remembered by chance what I had heard in my childhood: Why, I asked myself, should I not seek out Sheikh Zaabalawi? I recollected that my father had said that he had made his acquaintance in Khan Gaafar at the house of Sheikh Kamar, one of those sheikhs who practised law in the religious courts, and I therefore took myself off to his house. Wishing to make sure that he was still living there, I made enquiries of a vendor of beans whom I found in the lower part of the house.

"Sheikh Kamar!" he said, looking at me in amazement. "He left the quarter ages ago. They say he's now living in Garden City and has his office in Al-Azhaar Square:"

I looked up the office address in the telephone book and immediately set off to the Chamber of Commerce Building, where it was located. On asking to see him I was ushered into a room just as a beautiful woman with a most intoxicating perfume was leaving it. The man received me with a smile and motioned me towards a fine leather-upholstered chair. My feet were conscious of the costly lushness of the carpet despite the thick soles of my shoes. The man wore a lounge suit and was smoking a cigar; his manner of sitting was that of someone well satisfied both with himself and his worldly possessions. The look of warm welcome he gave me left no doubt in my mind that he thought me a prospective client, and I felt acutely embarrassed at encroaching upon his valuable time.

"Welcome!" he said, prompting me to speak.

"I am the son of your old friend Sheikh Ali al-Tatawi," I answered so as to put an end to my equivocal position.

A certain languor was apparent in the glance he cast at me; the languor was not total in that he had not as yet lost all hope in me.

"God rest his soul," he said. "He was a fine man."

The very pain that had driven me to go there now prevailed upon me to stay.

"He told me," I continued, "of a devout saint named Zaabalawi whom he met at Your Honour's. I am in need of him, sir, if he be still in the land of the living."

The languor became firmly entrenched in his eyes and it would have come as no surprise to me if he had shown the door to both me and my father's memory.

"That," he said in the tone of one who has made up his mind to terminate the conversation, "was a very long time ago and I scarcely recall him now."

Rising to my feet so as to put his mind at rest regarding my intention of going, I asked:

"Was he really a saint?"

"We used to regard him as a man of miracles."

"And where could I find him today?" I asked, making another move towards the door.

"To the best of my knowledge he was living in the Birgawi Residence in al-Azhar," and he applied himself to some papers on his desk with a resolute movement that indicated he wouldn't open his mouth again. I bowed my head in thanks, apologized several times for disturbing him and left the office, my head so buzzing with embarrassment that I was oblivious to all sounds around me.

I went to the Birgawi Residence which was situated in a thickly populated quarter. I found that time had so eaten into the building that nothing was left of it save an antiquated facade and a courtyard which, despite it being supposedly in the charge of a caretaker, was being used as a rubbish dump. A small insignificant fellow, a mere prologue to a man, was using the covered entrance as a place for the sale of old books on theology and mysticism.

On my asking him about Zaabalawi, he peered at me through narrow, inflamed eyes and said in amazement:

"Zaabalawi! Good heavens, what a time ago that was! Certainly he used to live in this house when it was livable in, and many was the time he would sit with me talking of bygone days and I would be blessed by his holy presence. Where, though, is Zaabalawi today?"

He shrugged his shoulders sorrowfully and soon left me to attend to an approaching customer. I proceeded to make enquiries of many shopkeepers in the district. While I found that a large number of them had never even heard of him, some, though recalling nostalgically the pleasant times they had spent with him, were ignorant of his present whereabouts, while others openly made fun of him, labelled him a charlatan, and advised me to put myself in the hands of a doctor—as though I had not already done so. I therefore had no alternative but to return disconsolately home.

With the passing of the days like motes in the air my pains grew so severe that I was sure I would not be able to hold out much longer. Once again I fell to wondering about Zaabalawi and clutching at the hopes his venerable name stirred within me. Then it occurred to me to seek the help of the local Sheikh of the district; in fact, I was surprised I hadn't thought of this to begin with. His office was in the nature of a small shop except that it contained a desk and a telephone, and I found him sitting at his desk wearing a jacket over his striped *galabia*. As he did not interrupt his conversation with a man sitting beside him, I stood waiting till the man had gone. He then looked up at me coldly. I told myself that I should win him over by the usual methods, and it wasn't long before I had him cheerfully inviting me to sit down.

"I'm in need of Sheikh Zaabalawi," I answered his enquiry as to the purpose of my visit.

He gazed at me with the same astonishment as that shown by those I had previously encountered.

"At least," he said, giving me a smile that revealed his gold teeth, "he is still alive. The devil of it is, though, he has no fixed abode. You might well bump into him as you go out of here, on the other hand you might spend days and months in fruitless search of him."

"Even you can't find him!"

"Even I! He's a baffling man, but I thank the Lord that he's still alive!"

He gazed at me intently, and murmured:

"It seems your condition is serious."

"Very!"

"May God come to your aid! But why don't you go about it rationally?"

He spread out a sheet of paper on the desk and drew on it with unexpected speed and skill until he had made a full plan of the district showing all the various quarters, lanes, alleyways, and squares. He looked at it admiringly and said, "These are dwelling-houses, here is the Quarter of the Perfumers, here the Quarter of the Coppersmiths, the Mouski, the Police and Five Stations. The drawing is your best guide. Look carefully in the cafés, the places where the dervishes perform their rites, the mosques and prayer-rooms, and the Green Gate, for he may well be concealed among the beggars and be indistinguishable from them. Actually, I myself haven't seen him for years, having been somewhat preoccupied with the cares of the world and was only brought back to those most exquisite times of my youth by your enquiry."

I gazed at the map in bewilderment. The telephone rang and he took up the receiver.

"Take it," he told me, generously. "We're at your service."

Folding up the map, I left and wandered off through the quarter, from square to street to alleyway, making enquiries of everyone I felt was familiar with the place. At last the owner of a small establishment for ironing clothes told me:

"Go to the calligrapher Hassanein in Umm al-Ghulam—they were friends."

I went to Umm al-Ghulam where I found old Hassenein working in a deep, narrow shop full of signboards and jars of colour. A strange smell, a mixture of glue and perfume, permeated its every corner. Old Hassanein was squatting on a sheepskin rug in front of a board propped against the wall; in the middle of it he had inscribed the word "Allah" in silver lettering. He was engrossed in embellishing the letters with prodigious care. I stood behind him, fearful to disturb him or break the inspiration that flowed to his masterly hand. When my concern at not interrupting him had lasted some time, he suddenly enquired with unaffected gentleness:

"Yes?"

Realizing that he was aware of my presence, I introduced myself.

"I've been told that Sheikh Zaabalawi is your friend and I'm looking for him," I said.

His hand came to a stop. He scrutinized me in astonishment.

"Zaabalawi! God be praised!" he said with a sigh.

"He is a friend of yours, isn't he?" I asked eagerly.

"He was, once upon a time. A real man of mystery: he'd visit you so often that people would imagine he was your nearest and dearest, then would disappear as though he'd never existed. Yet saints are not to be blamed."

The spark of hope went out with the suddenness of a lamp by a power-cut.

"He was so constantly with me said the man, "that I felt him to be a part of everything I drew. But where is he today?"

"Perhaps he is still alive?"

"He's alive, without a doubt. He had impeccable taste and it was due to him that I made my most beautiful drawings."

"God knows," I said, in a voice almost stifled by the dead ashes of hope, "that I am in the direst need of him and no one knows better than you of the ailments in respect of which he is sought."

"Yes—yes. May God restore you to health. He is, in truth, as is said of him, a man, and more—"

Smiling broadly, he added: "And his face is possessed of an unforgettable beauty. But where is he?"

Reluctantly I rose to my feet, shook hands and left. I continued on my way eastwards and westwards through the quarter, enquiring about him from everyone who, by reason of age or experience, I felt was likely to help me. Eventually I was informed by a vendor of lupine that he had met him a short while ago at the house of Sheikh Gad, the well-known composer. I went to the musician's house in Tabakshiyya where I found him in a room tastefully furnished in the old style, its walls redolent with history. He was seated on a divan, his famous lute lying beside him, concealing within itself the most beautiful melodies of our age, while from within the house came the sound of pestle and mortar and the clamour of children. I immediately greeted him and introduced myself, and was put at my ease by the unaffected way in which he received me. He did not ask, either in words or gesture, what had brought me, and I did not feel that he even harboured any such curiosity. Amazed at his understanding and kindness, which boded well, I said:

"O Sheikh Gad, I am an admirer of yours and have long been enchanted by the renderings of your songs."

"Thank you," he said with a smile.

"Please excuse my disturbing you," I continued timidly, "but I was told that Zaabalawi was your friend and I am in urgent need of him."

"Zaabalawi!" he said, frowning in concentration. "You need him? God be with you, for who knows, O, Zaabalawi, where you are?"

"Doesn't he visit you?" I asked eagerly.

"He visited me some time ago. He might well come now; on the other hand I mightn't see him till death!"

I gave an audible sigh and asked:

"What made him like that?"

He took up his lute. "Such are saints or they would not be saints," he said laughing.

"Do those who need him suffer as I do?"

"Such suffering is part of the cure!"

He took up the plectrum and began plucking soft strains from the strings. Lost in thought, I followed his movements. Then, as though addressing myself, I said:

"So my visit has been in vain!"

He smiled, laying his cheek against the side of the lute.

"God forgive you, he said, "for saying such a thing of a visit that has caused me to know you and you me!"

I was much embarrassed and said apologetically:

"Please forgive me; my feelings of defeat made me forget my manners!"

"Do not give in to defeat. This extraordinary man brings fatigue to all who seek him. It was easy enough with him in the old days when his place of abode was known. Today, though, the world has changed and after having enjoyed a position attained only by potentates, he is now pursued by the police on a charge of false pretences. It is therefore no longer an easy matter to reach him, but have patience and be sure that you will do so."

He raised his head from the lute and skillfully led into the opening bars of a melody. Then he sang:

> "I make lavish mention, even though I blame myself,
> of those I have loved,
> For the words of lovers are my wine."

With a heart that was weary and listless I followed the beauty of the melody and the singing.

"I composed the music to this poem in a single night," he told me when he had finished. "I remember that it was the night of the Lesser Bairam. He was my guest for the whole of that night and the poem was of his choosing. He would sit for a while just where you are, then would get up and play with my children as though he were one of them. Whenever I was overcome by weariness or my inspiration failed me he would punch me playfully in the chest and joke with me, and I would bubble over with melodies and thus I continued working till I finished the most beautiful piece I have ever composed."

"Does he know anything about music?"

"He was the epitome of things musical. He had an extremely beautiful speaking voice and you had only to hear him to want to burst into song. His loftiness of spirit stirred within you—"

"How was it that he cured those diseases before which men are powerless?"

"That is his secret. Maybe you will learn it when you meet him."

But when would that meeting occur? We relapsed into silence and the hub-bub of children once more filled the room.

Again, the Sheikh began to sing. He went on repeating the words "and I have a memory of her" in different and beautiful variations until the very walls danced in ecstasy. I expressed my wholehearted admiration and he gave me a smile of thanks. I then got up and asked permission to leave and he accompanied me to the outer door. As I shook him by the hand he said, "I hear that nowadays he frequents the house of Haag Wanas al-Damanhouri. Do you know him?"

I shook my head, a modicum of renewed hope creeping into my heart.

"He is a man of private means," he told me, "who from time to time visits Cairo, putting up at some hotel or other. Every evening, though, he spends at the Negma Bar in Alfi Street."

I waited for nightfall and went to the Negma Bar. I asked a waiter about Hagg Wanas and he pointed to a corner which was semi-secluded because of its position behind a large pillar with mirrors on its four sides. There I saw a man seated alone at a table with a bottle three-quarters empty and another empty one in front of him; there were no snacks or food to be seen and I was sure that I was in the presence of a hardened drinker. He was wearing a loosely flowing silk *galabia* and a carefully wound turban; his legs were stretched out towards the base of the pillar, and as he gazed into the mirror in rapt contentment the sides of his face, rounded and handsome despite the fact that he was approaching old age, were flushed with wine. I approached quietly till I stood but a few feet away from him. He did not turn towards me or give any indication that he was aware of my presence.

"Good evening, Mr. Wanas." I said with amiable friendliness.

He turned towards me abruptly as though my voice had roused him from slumber and glared at me in disapproval. I was about to explain what had brought me to him when he interrupted me in an almost imperative tone of voice which was none the less not devoid of an extraordinary gentleness:

"First, please sit down, and, second, please get drunk!"

I opened my mouth to make my excuses but, stopping up his ears with his fingers, he said:

"Not a word till you do what I say."

I realized that I was in the presence of a capricious drunkard and told myself that I should go along with him at least halfway.

"Would you permit me to ask one question?" I said with a smile, sitting down.

Without removing his hands from his ears he indicated the bottle.

"When engaged in a drinking bout like this I do not allow any conversation between myself and another unless, like me, he is drunk, otherwise the session loses all propriety and mutual comprehension is rendered impossible."

I made a sign indicating that I didn't drink.

"That's your look-out," he said offhandedly. "And that's my condition!"

He filled me a glass which I meekly took and drank. No sooner had it settled in my stomach than it seemed to ignite.

I waited patiently till I had grown used to its ferocity, and said:

"It's very strong, and I think the time has come for me to ask you about—"

Once again, however, he put his fingers in his ears.

"I shan't listen to you until you're drunk!"

He filled up my glass for the second time. I glanced at it in trepidation; then, over-coming my innate objection, I drank it down at a gulp. No sooner had it come to rest inside me than I lost all will-power. With the third glass I lost my memory and with the fourth the future vanished. The world turned round about me and I forgot why I had gone there. The man leaned towards me attentively but I saw him—saw everything—as a mere meaningless series of coloured planes. I don't know how long it was before my head sank down on to the arm of the chair and I plunged into deep sleep. During it I had a beautiful dream the like of which I had never experienced. I dreamed that I was in an immense garden surrounded on all sides by luxuriant trees and the sky was nothing but stars seen between the entwined branches, all enfolded in an atmosphere like that of sunset or a sky overcast with cloud. I was lying on a small hummock of jas-mine petals which fell upon me like rain, while the lucent spray of a fountain unceas-ingly sprinkled my head and temples. I was in a state of deep contentedness, of ecstat-ic serenity. An orchestra of warbling and cooing played in my ear. There was an extra-ordinary sense of harmony between me and my inner self, and between the two of us and the world, everything being in its rightful place without discord or distortion. In the whole world there was no single reason for speech or movement, for the universe moved in a rapture of ecstasy. This lasted but a short while. When I opened my eyes consciousness struck at me like a policeman's fist and I saw Wanas al-Damanhouri regarding me with concern. In the bar only a few drowsy people were left.

"You have slept deeply," said my companion; "you were obviously hungry for sleep."

I rested my heavy head in the palms of my hands. When I took them away in aston-ishment and looked down at them I found that they glistened with drops of water.

"My head's wet," I protested.

"Yes, my friend tried to rouse you," he answered quietly.

"Somebody saw me in this state?"

"Don't worry, he is a good man. Have you not heard of Sheikh Zaabalawi?"

"Zaabalawi!" I exclaimed, jumping to my feet.

"Yes," he answered in surprise. "What's wrong?"

"Where is he?"

"I don't know where he is now. He was here and then he left."

I was about to run off in pursuit but found I was more exhausted than I had imag-ined. Collapsed over the table, I cried out in despair:

"My sole reason for coming to you was to meet him. Help me to catch up with him or send someone after him."

The man called a vendor of prawns and asked him to seek out the Sheikh and bring him back. Then he turned to me.

"I didn't realize you were afflicted. I'm very sorry—"

"You wouldn't let me speak," I said irritably.

"What a pity! He was sitting on this chair beside you the whole time. He was play-ing with a string of jasmine petals he had round his neck, a gift from one of his admir-ers, then, taking pity on you, he began to sprinkle some water on your head to bring you round."

"Does he meet you here every night?" I asked, my eyes not leaving the doorway through which the vendor of prawns had left.

"He was with me tonight, last night and the night before that, but before that I hadn't seen him for a month."

"Perhaps he will come tomorrow," I answered with a sigh.

"Perhaps."

"I am willing to give him any money he wants."

Wanas answered sympathetically:

"The strange thing is that he is not open to such temptations, yet he will cure you if you meet him."

"Without charge?"

"Merely on sensing that you love him."

The vendor of prawns returned, having failed in his mission.

I recovered some of my energy and left the bar, albeit unsteadily. At every street corner I called out, "Zaabalawi!" in the vague hope that I would be rewarded with an answering shout. The street boys turned contemptuous eyes on me till I sought refuge in the first available taxi.

The following evening I stayed up with Wanas al-Damanhouri till dawn, but the Sheikh did not put in an appearance. Wanas informed me that he would be going away to the country and wouldn't be returning to Cairo until he'd sold the cotton crop.

I must wait, I told myself; I must train myself to be patient. Let me content myself with having made certain of the existence of Zaabalawi, and even of his affection for me, which encourages me to think that he will be prepared to cure me if a meeting between us takes place.

Sometimes, however, the long delay wearied me. I would become beset by despair and would try to persuade myself to dismiss him from my mind completely. How many weary people in this life know him not or regard him as a mere myth! Why, then, should I torture myself about him in this way?

No sooner, however, did my pains force themselves upon me than I would again begin to think about him, asking myself as to when I would be fortunate enough to meet him. The fact that I ceased to have any news of Wanas and was told he had gone to live abroad did not deflect me from my purpose; the truth of the matter was that I had become fully convinced that I had to find Zaabalawi.

Yes, I have to find Zaabalawi.

For Practice

1. The narrator has not yet met Zaabalawi face-to-face. What do you think Mahfouz is trying to say about belief by ending the story the way he does? Has the narrator been wasting his time, or has he gained something of value out of the experience?

2. Why do you think the narrator turns to Zaabalawi for help when so many other possibilities might be available? What symbolic value does Zaabalawi hold for the narrator? What message is Mahfouz trying to communicate about how people come to hold their beliefs? What is your reaction?

3. Why do you think the townspeople are so reluctant to talk about Zaabalawi? What role does the community play in shaping the narrator's (and your own) perceptions about Zaabalawi?

4. We hear about Zaabalawi only through the words of other characters, who each give different, incomplete pictures of this "saint." We never hear from Zaabalawi himself. Reconstruct what you think Zaabalawi is like, based upon the descriptions given by the various characters.

5. The narrator says near the end of the story that whenever his pains would

renew, he would renew his search for Zaabalawi. Is his search for Zaabalawi self-centered, or are there more altruistic, selfless goals he seeks? What do you think your interpretation implies about belief or meaning? How does his motivation compare to that of Tennyson's Ulysses?

6. Few of the characters the narrator meets seem to be current followers of Zaabalawi; they speak of him as a figure of the past. Why do you think they have changed? What broader significance do you attribute to their changes in attitudes?

Ode to a Nightingale

John Keats

John Keats (1795–1821) lived only twenty-five years and published only fifty-four poems in his lifetime, yet today he is considered one of the foremost poets in the English language. The eldest of four children of the manager of a prosperous stable, he attended a village academy and studied to be a surgeon. Though he had no formal literary education, Keats mastered a wide range of poetic forms including the sonnet and ode, as well as longer works in the tradition of the Spenserian romance and the epic. He saw his work as part of the new romantic style of poetry, following in the tradition begun by William Wordsworth.

"To a Nightingale" is one of five great odes which Keats wrote in 1819 and which are widely believed to be the most perfect examples of this form. In this ode, the narrator attempts to come to terms with the "weariness, fever, and the fret" of human existence. As you read, think about how his awareness and understanding of his own mortality changes as he listens to the song of the nightingale. Pay particular attention to the way that Keats uses language in this poem.

I

My heart aches, and a drowsy numbness pains
   My sense, as though of hemlock I had drunk,
Or emptied some dull opiate to the drains
   One minute past, and Lethe-wards had sunk:
'Tis not through envy of thy happy lot,   5
   But being too happy in thine happiness
      That thou, light-winged Dryad of the trees,
         In some melodious plot
Of beechen green, and shadows numberless,
      Singest of summer in full-throated ease.   10

II

O, for a draught of vintage! that hath been
   Cooled a long age in the deep-delvéd earth,

Tasting of Flora and the country green,
    Dance, and Provencal song, and sunburnt mirth!
O for a beaker full of the warm South,   15
      Full of the true, the blushful Hippocrene,
        With beaded bubbles winking at the brim,
          And purple-stained mouth;
      That I might drink, and leave the world unseen,
        And with thee fade away into the forest dim: 20

III

Fade far away, dissolve, and quite forget
    What thou among the leaves hast never known,
The weariness, the fever, and the fret
    Here, where men sit and hear each other groan;
Where palsy shakes a few, sad, last gray hairs,   25
      Where youth grows pale, and specter-thin, and dies;
        Where but to think is to be full of sorrow
          And leaden-eyed despairs,
      Where Beauty cannot keep her lustrous eyes,
        Or new Love pine at them beyond tomorrow.   30

IV

Away! away! for I will fly to thee,
    Not charioted by Bacchus and his pards,
But on the viewless wings of Poesy,
    Though the dull brain perplexes and retards:
Already with thee! tender is the night,   35
      And haply the Queen-Moon is on her throne,
        Clustered around by all her starry Fays;
          But here there is no light,
      Save what from heaven is with the breezes blown
        Through verdurous glooms and winding mossy ways.   40

V

I cannot see what flowers are at my feet,
    Nor what soft incense hangs upon the boughs,
But, in embalméd darkness, guess each sweet
    Wherewith the seasonable month endows
The grass, the thicket, and the fruit-tree wild;   45
      White hawthorn, and the pastoral eglantine;
        Fast fading violets covered up in leaves;
          And mid-May's eldest child,
      The coming musk-rose, full of dewy wine,
        The murmurous haunt of flies on summer eves.   50

VI

Darkling I listen; and, for many a time
    I have been half in love with easeful Death,
Called him soft names in many a muséd rhyme,
    To take into the air my quiet breath;
Now more than ever seems it rich to die,   55
    To cease upon the midnight with no pain,
       While thou art pouring forth thy soul abroad
        In such an ecstasy!
    Still wouldst thou sing, and I have ears in vain—
    To thy high requiem become a sod.   60

VII

Thou wast not born for death, immortal Bird!
    No hungry generations tread thee down;
The voice I hear this passing night was heard
    In ancient days by emperor and clown:
Perhaps the selfsame song that found a path   65
    Through the sad heart of Ruth, when, sick for home,
       She stood in tears amid the alien corn;
        The same that ofttimes hath
    Charmed magic casements, opening on the foam
    Of perilous seas, in faery lands forlorn.   70

VIII

Forlorn! the very word is like a bell
    To toll me back from thee to my sole self!
Adieu! the fancy cannot cheat so well
    As she is famed to do, deceiving elf.
Adieu! adieu! thy plaintive anthem fades   75
    Past the near meadows, over the still stream,
       Up the hillside; and now 'tis buried deep
        In the next valley-glades:
    Was it a vision, or a waking dream?
       Fled is that music:—Do I wake or sleep?   80

May 1819

For Practice

1. Look in the Glossary for the definition of the term "ode." How does this poem fit with that definition? How is this form appropriate to the subject of the poem? Would you consider this poem to be in an "elevated style"? Why?

2. What words seemed to stand out for you as you read the poem? Keats uses many words taken from classical myth and ancient legends: "Dryad," "Lethewards," "Hippocrene," "Fays." How do these words shape the poem's atmosphere?

3. Keats uses many images in the poem: "purple stained mouth," "the grass, the thicket, and the fruit tree wild," "dewy wine," among others. What kind of picture do these images paint? How does this picture change from stanza to stanza? How does Keats use language to make these images more vivid?

4. Stanzas 6 and 7, in which the narrator discusses his thoughts about death, seem to be pivotal to the poem. How would you characterize the difference between the first five stanzas and the last stanza? How does Keats accomplish this change in stanzas 6 and 7?

5. How does this poem try to change the reader's attitude toward life and death? Do you see these things differently because of your reading of the poem? Why or why not?

Because I Could Not Stop for Death

Emily Dickinson

Emily Dickinson (1830–1886) was the reclusive daughter of a lawyer in Amherst, Massachusetts. She spent almost all of her life in the same house. Only seven of her poems were published during her lifetime, most edited to make them more conventional. Dickinson wrote and rewrote her poems until she considered them perfect. She bundled together more than eight hundred poems into forty-three collections which she called "fascicles" and which were found by her sister in a bureau drawer after the poet's death. At least as many manuscripts for other poems, in various stages of completion, were also found. A full collection of her works was not issued until 1960 when Thomas H. Johnson of Harvard released The Complete Poems. *His numbering system and chronological ordering are accepted as the standard.*

This poem (#712) is considered by many to be the greatest of Dickinson's works. In it, she unites love and death as she represents death as a gentleman caller. As you read, try to identify the speaker's attitude toward death. Does the matter-of-fact tone of the poem belie her true emotions?

Because I could not stop for Death—
He kindly stopped for me—
The Carriage held but just Ourselves—
And Immortality.

We slowly drove—He knew no haste   5
And I had put away
My labor and my leisure too,
For His Civility—

We passed the School, where Children strove
At Recess—in the Ring—   10
We passed the Fields of Gazing Grain—
We passed the Setting Sun—

Or rather—He passed Us—
The Dews drew quivering and chill—
For only Gossamer, my Gown—   15
My Tippet—only Tulle—

We paused before a House that seemed
A Swelling of the Ground—
The Roof was scarcely visible—
The Cornice—in the Ground—   20

Since then—'tis Centuries—and yet
Feels shorter than the Day
I first surmised the Horses' Heads
Were toward Eternity—

—1863

For Practice

1. Dickinson's poems do not conform to the conventions of lyric poetry. In what ways is this poem different from other poems that you have read? You might consider punctuation, capitalization, rhyme, and meter. How does Dickinson's departure from these conventions affect your understanding of the poem?

2. How does this poem depict the passage of time? What is the speaker's attitude toward the passing of time? How is this attitude conveyed in the physical appearance of the poem? Consider, in particular, the unusual punctuation and Dickinson's use of conjunctions.

3. Is the poem's atmosphere in the second three stanzas different from that in the first three stanzas? In what ways does Dickinson's use of images bring about this change?

4. Dickinson uses the metaphor of a gentleman caller to represent death in this poem. To what extent is this metaphor an allegory? (Look in the Glossary for the definition of this term.) What is the literal meaning of the poem? What is the figurative meaning of the poem? What "moral or political lesson" might the figurative meaning contain? Is this lesson convincing to you? Why or why not?

Why I Write:
Making No Become Yes

Elie Wiesel

*Elie Wiesel (b. 1928) is a Romanian Jew who miraculously survived intern-
ment in the concentration camps Birkenau, Auschwitz, Buna, and
Buchenwald where most of the other members of his family were killed.
After his release from Buchenwald at the end of the war, he went to France
where he was educated at the Sorbonne. He emigrated to the United States
in 1956 and became a naturalized citizen in 1963. Wiesel has also been a
journalist and professor in the humanities, as well as a writer of novels
and essays. His many awards include the Nobel Prize for Literature in
1986. His first novel,* Night, *which is largely autobiographical, relates the
story of a young concentration camp survivor who experiences tremendous guilt because he has lived while so many others did not. Wiesel's
many books, both fiction and non-fiction, deal with the themes of the
Holocaust and Jewishness.*

*"Why I Write: Making No Become Yes" first appeared in April 1985 in
the* New York Times Book Review. *In this essay, Wiesel tries to explain why
he continues to write about the Holocaust forty years after the end of
World War II and the liberation of the camps. As you read through this
essay, try to determine precisely what Wiesel means by the sub-title,
"making no become yes."*

Why do I write?

Perhaps in order not to go mad. Or, on the contrary, to touch the bottom of madness. Like Samuel Beckett, the survivor expresses himself "en désespoir
de cause"—out of desperation.

Speaking of the solitude of the survivor, the great Yiddish and Hebrew poet and
thinker Aaron Zeitlin addresses those—his father, his brother, his friends—who have
died and left him: "You have abandoned me," he says to them. "You are together, without me. I am here. Alone. And I make words."

So do I, just like him. I also say words, write words, reluctantly.

There are easier occupations, far more pleasant ones. But for the survivor, writing
is not a profession, but an occupation, a duty. Camus calls it "an honor." As he puts it:
"I entered literature through worship." Other writers have said they did so through
anger, through love. Speaking for myself, I would say—through silence.

It was by seeking, by probing silence that I began to discover the perils and power of the word. I never intended to be a philosopher, or a theologian. The only role I sought was that of witness. I believed that, having survived by chance, I was duty-bound to give meaning to my survival, to justify each moment of my life. I knew the story had to be told. Not to transmit an experience is to betray it. This is what Jewish tradition teaches us. But how to do this? "When Israel is in exile, so is the word," says the Zohar. The word has deserted the meaning it was intended to convey—impossible to make them coincide. The displacement, the shift, is irrevocable.

This was never more true than right after the upheaval. We all knew that we could never, never say what had to be said, that we could never express in words, coherent, intelligible words, our experience of madness on an absolute scale. The walk through flaming night, the silence before and after the selection, the monotonous praying of the condemned, the Kaddish of the dying, the fear and hunger of the sick, the shame and suffering, the haunted eyes, the demented stares. I thought that I would never be able to speak of them. All words seemed inadequate, worn, foolish, lifeless, whereas I wanted them to be searing.

Where was I to discover a fresh vocabulary, a primeval language? The language of night was not human, it was primitive, almost animal—hoarse shouting, screams, muffled moaning, savage howling, the sound of beating. A brute strikes out wildly, a body falls. An officer raises his arm and a whole community walks toward a common grave. A soldier shrugs his shoulders, and a thousand families are torn apart, to be reunited only by death. This was the concentration camp language. It negated all other language and took its place. Rather than a link, it became a wall. Could it be surmounted? Could the reader be brought to the other side? I knew the answer was negative, and yet I knew that "no" had to become "yes." It was the last wish of the dead.

The fear of forgetting remains the main obsession of all those who have passed through the universe of the damned. The enemy counted on people's incredulity and forgetfulness. How could one foil this plot? And if memory grew hollow, empty of substance, what would happen to all we had accumulated along the way? Remember, said the father to his son, and the son to his friend. Gather the names, the faces, the tears. We had all taken an oath: "If, by some miracle, I emerge alive, I will devote my life to testifying on behalf of those whose shadow will fall on mine forever and ever."

That is why I write certain things rather than others—to remain faithful.

Of course, there are times of doubt for the survivor, times when one gives in to weakness, or longs for comfort. I hear a voice within me telling me to stop mourning the past. I too want to sing of love and of its magic. I too want to celebrate the sun, and the dawn that heralds the sun. I would like to shout, and shout loudly: "Listen, listen well! I too am capable of victory, do you hear? I too am open to laughter and joy! I want to stride, head high, my face unguarded, without having to point to the ashes over there on the horizon, without having to tamper with facts to hide their tragic ugliness. For a man born blind, God himself is blind, but look, I see, I am not blind." One feels like shouting this, but the shout changes to a murmur. One must make a choice; one must remain faithful. A big word, I know. Nevertheless I use it, it suits me. Having written the things I have written, I feel I can afford no longer to play with words. If I say that the writer in me wants to remain loyal, it is because it is true. This sentiment moves all survivors; they owe nothing to anyone, but everything to the dead.

I owe them my roots and my memory. I am duty-bound to serve as their emissary, transmitting the history of their disappearance, even if it disturbs, even if it brings pain. Not to do so would be to betray them, and thus myself. And since I am incapable of communicating their cry by shouting, I simply look at them. I see them and I write.

While writing, I question them as I question myself. I believe I have said it before, elsewhere. I write to understand as much as to be understood. Will I succeed one day? Wherever one starts, one reaches darkness. God? He remains the God of darkness. Man? The source of darkness. The killers' derision, their victims' tears, the onlookers' indifference, their complicity and complacency—the divine role in all that I do not understand. A million children massacred—I shall never understand.

Jewish children—they haunt my writings. I see them again and again. I shall always see them. Hounded, humiliated, bent like the old men who surround them as though to protect them, unable to do so. They are thirsty, the children, and there is no one to give them water. They are hungry, but there is no one to give them a crust of bread. They are afraid, and there is no one to reassure them.

They walk in the middle of the road, like vagabonds. They are on the way to the station, and they will never return. In sealed cars, without air or food, they travel toward another world. They guess where they are going, they know it, and they keep silent. Tense, thoughtful, they listen to the wind, the call of death in the distance.

All these children, these old people, I see them. I never stop seeing them. I belong to them.

But they, to whom do they belong?

People tend to think that a murderer weakens when facing a child. The child reawakens the killer's lost humanity. The killer can no longer kill the child before him, the child inside him.

But with us it happened differently. Our Jewish children had no effect upon the killers. Nor upon the world. Nor upon God.

I think of them, I think of their childhood. Their childhood is a small Jewish town, and this town is no more. They frighten me; they reflect an image of myself, one that I pursue and run from at the same time—the image of a Jewish adolescent who knew no fear, except the fear of God, whose faith was whole, comforting, and not marked by anxiety.

No, I do not understand. And if I write, it is to warn the reader that he will not understand either. "You will not understand, you will never understand," were the words heard everywhere during the reign of night. I can only echo them. You, who never lived under a sky of blood, will never know what it was like. Even if you read all the books ever written, even if you listen to all the testimonies ever given, you will remain on this side of the wall, you will view the agony and death of a people from afar, through the screen of a memory that is not your own.

An admission of impotence and guilt? I do not know. All I know is that Treblinka and Auschwitz cannot be told. And yet I have tried. God knows I have tried.

Have I attempted too much or not enough? Among some 25 volumes, only three or four penetrate the phantasmagoric realm of the dead. In my other books, through my other books, I have tried to follow other roads. For it is dangerous to linger among the dead, they hold on to you and you run the risk of speaking only to them. And so I have forced myself to turn away from them and study other periods, explore other destinies and teach other tales—the Bible and the Talmud, Hasidism and its fervor, the shtetl and its songs, Jerusalem and its echoes, the Russian Jews and their anguish, their awakening, their courage. At times, it has seemed to me that I was speaking of other things with the sole purpose of keeping the essential—the personal experience—

unspoken. At times I have wondered: And what if I was wrong? Perhaps I should not have heeded my own advice and stayed in my own world with the dead.

But then, I have not forgotten the dead. They have their rightful place even in the works about the Hasidic capitals Ruzhany and Korets, and Jerusalem. Even in my biblical and Midrashic tales, I pursue their presence, mute and motionless. The presence of the dead then beckons in such tangible ways that it affects even the most removed characters. Thus they appear on Mount Moriah, where Abraham is about to sacrifice his son, a burnt offering to their common God. They appear on Mount Nebo, where Moses enters solitude and death. They appear in Hasidic and Talmudic legends in which victims forever need defending against forces that would crush them. Technically, so to speak, they are of course elsewhere, in time and space, but on a deeper, truer plane, the dead are part of every story, of every scene.

"But what is the connection?" you will ask. Believe me, there is one. After Auschwitz everything brings us back to Auschwitz. When I speak of Abraham, Isaac and Jacob, when I invoke Rabbi Yohanan ben Zakkai and Rabbi Akiba, it is the better to understand them in the light of Auschwitz. As for the Maggid of Mezeritch and his disciples, it is in order to encounter the followers of their followers that I reconstruct their spellbound, spellbinding universe. I like to imagine them alive, exuberant, celebrating life and hope. Their happiness is as necessary to me as it was once to themselves.

And yet—how did they manage to keep their faith intact? How did they manage to sing as they went to meet the Angel of Death? I know Hasidim who never vacillated— I respect their strength. I know others who chose rebellion, protest, rage—I respect their courage. For there comes a time when only those who do not believe in God will not cry out to him in wrath and anguish.

Do not judge either group. Even the heroes perished as martyrs, even the martyrs died as heroes. Who would dare oppose knives to prayers? The faith of some matters as much as the strength of others. It is not ours to judge, it is only ours to tell the tale.

But where is one to begin? Whom is one to include? One meets a Hasid in all my novels. And a child. And an old man. And a beggar. And a madman. They are all part of my inner landscape. The reason why? Pursued and persecuted by the killers, I offer them shelter. The enemy wanted to create a society purged of their presence, and I have brought some of them back. The world denied them, repudiated them, so I let them live at least within the feverish dreams of my characters.

It is for them that I write, and yet the survivor may experience remorse. He has tried to bear witness; it was all in vain.

After the liberation, we had illusions. We were convinced that a new world would be built upon the ruins of Europe. A new civilization would see the light. No more wars, no more hate, no more intolerance, no fanaticism. And all this because the witnesses would speak. And speak they did, to no avail.

They will continue, for they cannot do otherwise. When man, in his grief, falls silent, Goethe says, then God gives him the strength to sing his sorrows. From that moment on, he may no longer choose not to sing, whether his song is heard or not. What matters is to struggle against silence with words, or through another form of silence. What matters is to gather a smile here and there, a tear here and there, a word here and there, and thus justify the faith placed in you, a long time ago, by so many victims.

Why do I write? To wrench those victims from oblivion. To help the dead vanquish death.

For Practice

1. This text is clearly an argumentative essay that is about a real event. Does that fact keep it from being "literary," or could we consider this text literature? What points would you make in arguing on one side or the other of this question?

2. How does your knowledge of Wiesel's own experience alter your understanding of this essay? Do you think you would react to it differently if it were written by someone who had not lived through the concentration camps?

3. Describe the literary techniques that Wiesel uses to appeal to the reader's emotions? In your opinion, does the pathetic appeal support his logical argument or does it detract from it?

4. The title of this essay, "Why I Write: Making No Become Yes" seems very mundane and ordinary compared to the content of the article. What do you think Wiesel might be trying to accomplish with this contrast?

5. In what way, according to Wiesel, can mere words alter the reality of the Holocaust?

6. What does Wiesel mean when he says, "making no become yes?" What does the subtitle of this essay suggest to you about Wiesel's belief about the power of language and argument?

7. Has Wiesel succeeded in making "no become yes" for you?

Writing Your Own Arguments

1. Several of the works in this unit make us consider the reasons that people hold certain beliefs. Choose at least two of these works and explore what motivates people to have belief in the first place. What causes people to be superstitious, religious, trusting? Are there innate human desires we wish to fulfill? Write an essay in which you attempt to explore these issues.

2. How do you decide what to believe and what not to believe? What assumptions are behind our decisions about belief? Even if we claim to be guided by "gut reactions," what are behind those? How consistent are we in selecting what ideas, doctrines, theories, or hopes to follow? Is it even important that we be consistent? Consider how some of the works in this unit treat this decision process, and examine how you make your own choices about what to accept or reject.

3. Since we are always changing with time, adapting ourselves to different events, contacts, and conditions, our own beliefs and our understanding of them also fluctuate. Several of the works in this unit, including "Guests of the Nation," "Zaabalawi," and "Gimpel the Fool," portray this process of belief, showing shifts in values over time. Select two or three works and compare how the authors treat this process and what attitudes they are attempting to communicate about it. You may wish to discuss your own reactions.

4. The awareness of impending death seems to make the quest for meaning more urgent for several of the characters in the works we have read. Is that something that tends to be true for most people? Explain why or why not. What do our reactions to death say about the rest of our lives? You may also want to consider which literary work you found most compelling in its approach to death.

5. Several works in this unit, particularly the pieces by Auden, Glück, and Wiesel, discuss the relationship between suffering or death and creative activity—painting, writing, and so forth. Other texts, like "Ulysses," examine the importance of active work as a source of meaning in life. Select two or three works, either from this unit or from some other unit in our textbook, that explore the relationship between creative activity, or work, and the quest for meaning. How does art or work function to create meaning in the texts you selected? Do you find any of these approaches compelling? Why or why not?

6. People do not find life meaningful all by themselves. We human beings learn to face life and death within communities that help us figure out what we think about the world and how we will live in it. Select two or three works and explore this question. How do the characters' communities assist and/or hinder them in the process of forming values and beliefs? Or, what is the role of the community in the process of dying? How do you evaluate the relationship between these characters and their communities?

7. Most of you have recently seen a movie or a television show that concerns themes similar to the ones we have been exploring in this chapter. How does the recent text deal with issues of death, or issues of meaning and value? How does it compare with the texts we have explored in this unit? Select one or two works from our text and compare them with a contemporary work from popular culture.

UNIT
SIX

*Nature, Technology, and
Romancing the Self*

As you sit down to breakfast on any given morning—eating cereal and reading the paper—you probably do not feel alienated from your environment. You are at home, a safe comfortable place which you may have furnished and organized yourself. You know how to get the things you need to maintain your way of living (how to drive a car, where the grocery store is, how to open a checking account), and some of your lifestyle decisions may be ethically driven. For example, you may not own a television because you think it is damaging to your education, or you may own a fuel-efficient automobile in order to decrease your stress on the environment. If you feel in control of your surroundings, how can you be alienated?

The idea of alienation implies a rupture or distance between people and their origins or their environment. Such a rupture might include the inability to make the food and clothing on which one depends for survival. Do you know, for example, how to produce the raw materials from which the cereals we eat everyday are made? Do you know how the chemicals used to preserve your cereal are produced? Would you be able to find a locally produced nutritional equivalent to your cereal if all cereal factories closed down or, if the bridge which crosses the river into your town collapsed? The inability of most people in contemporary America to answer "Yes" to such questions suggests that many humans are alienated from their means of survival.

Since the beginnings of modern industrial society, scholars and poets have speculated that our culture's dependence on mass production and technology would also bring about ethical alienation. Even if you do not know a lot about history, you will probably be familiar with the notion that industrialization is considered responsible for many social evils such as colonialism, materialism, and the destruction of our environment. Theoretically, the separation between humans and the materials and modes of production which sustain them also impairs their ability to live and act ethically. For example, the curtains which keep the sun off your paper as you eat breakfast may have been made by workers in a foreign factory who are paid only a few cents a day. The non-biodegradable plastic bowl you use for cereal will eventually end up in a solid waste landfill, adding to the pollution destroying the environment. Who is responsible for solving these problems? The governments which are supposed to regulate industry? The factory which abuses workers? The consumer who refuses to choose the more expensive or less convenient products made under more ethical conditions? Cultural critics suggest that our alienation from the natural world has consequences that are reflected in our aesthetics (as represented by both our elite and popular forms of art), our religions (which many people use to determine what it means to be good), and our social relations.

The readings in this section explore the stories we tell about our alienated relationship with our environment. As you read these texts, determine what type of alienation underlies the problem that is at issue in each. Does the author take only a negative view of modem culture, or are there some positive effects of industrialization? What visions of the good life are criticized or valued by each author? How has our alienation changed over time, for example, between the era of Shelley and Blake and that of Silko and Klinkenborg?

Ozymandias

Percy Bysshe Shelley

Percy Bysshe Shelley (1792–1822) was born at Field Place, Sussex, the eldest son of a member of Parliament, and he received an upper-class education at Eton and Oxford. From his early pamphlet, The Necessity of Atheism, *which led to his expulsion from Oxford, to later works such as* Prometheus Unbound, *Shelley's poetry and prose is marked by a commitment to freeing individuals from the social, economic, and religious oppression of society. For Shelley, progress and societal improvement would be brought about not through outward reform of institutions but by a gradual change of the consciousness of individuals, which could be fostered through literature.*

"Ozymandias," written in 1817 and published in 1818, is a work that addresses the concept of progress as well as the representation and glorification of progress. In this poem, Shelley demonstrates the vanity of human progress through the description of the remains of the monument of Ozymandias (the Greek name for Ramses II). This poem provides a stark contrast between the advances of humankind and the ravaging forces of nature, prompts readers to see the vanity of overcoming the environment with human progress, and challenges readers to redefine progress in light of what we learn from the natural world.

I met a traveller from an antique land
Who said: Two vast and trunkless legs of stone
Stand in the desert . . . Near them, on the sand,
Half sunk, a shattered visage lies, whose frown,
And wrinkled lip, and sneer of cold command,   5
Tell that its sculptor well those passions read
Which yet survive, stamped on these lifeless things,
The hand that mocked them, and the heart that fed:
And on the pedestal these words appear:
"My name is Ozymandias, king of kings: 10
Look on my works, ye Mighty, and despair!'
Nothing beside remains. Round the decay
Of that colossal wreck, boundless and bare
The lone and level sands stretch far away.

For Practice

1. What is the central irony of this poem and what argument does it propose in the debate concerning nature and technology? Is nature or culture presented more positively? How does this poem define progress?

2. Is Shelley's argument here against progress in general, or is he addressing the means that we use to commemorate our progress? What does this poem say about the role that art plays in how we view ourselves and our world? How is this poem relevant to current attitudes toward progress (specifically, technological progress) or representations of progress?

3. How do the lines "Two vast and trunkless legs of stone/Stand in the desert" function as an effective introduction to the traveler's story?

6. Note the word choice in the last three lines. How is Shelley's word choice especially effective for his argument? What kind of rhetorical appeal do his linguistic choices mobilize: *ethos, pathos,* or *logos*?

7. What is your reaction to Shelley's poem? In what ways does it alter your perspective on nature and technology?

Design

Robert Frost

Robert Frost (1874–1963) ranks among America's greatest poets. During his lifetime, Frost produced more than a dozen collections of poetry, beginning with A Boy's Will *in 1913. His last collection,* In the Clearing, *was published in 1962 when he was 88 years old. Frost enjoys great popular appeal and several of his poems, such as "Stopping by the Woods on a Snowy Evening" and "The Path Not Taken" have achieved the status of cultural icons. In addition to the popular approval of his work, Frost has received recognition as a literary artist. He won the Pulitzer Prize an unprecedented four times and was nominated in 1949 for the Nobel Prize for Literature. Much of the reason for this popularity among critics and the public alike can be accounted for by the fact that the poems can be read on many levels. Frost's poetry dramatizes simple, homely subjects drawn from the rural New England environment in which he lived much of his life. Their plain vocabulary and simple style make them accessible to even the most unsophisticated reader of poetry. At the same time, his sophisticated use of literary techniques complicates in extraordinary ways apparently straightforward themes.*

"Design" is perhaps the quintessential example of the artful simplicity of Robert Frost. In this brief sonnet, he addresses the big issues of life and death, innocence and evil, chance and design. As you read, pay close attention to the different literary techniques Frost uses in this poem.

I found a dimpled spider, fat and white,
On a white heal-all, holding up a moth
Like a white piece of rigid satin cloth—
Assorted characters of death and blight
Mixed ready to begin the morning right,   5
Like the ingredients of a witches' broth—
A snow-drop spider, a flower like a froth,
And dead wings carried like a paper kite.

What had that flower to do with being white,
The wayside blue and innocent heal all?   10
What brought the kindred spider to that height,
Then steered the white moth thither in the night?

What but design of darkness to appall?—
If design govern in a thing so small.

For Practice

1. Read the description of the term "sonnet" in the Glossary of this book. Why is the sonnet an appropriate form for a poem called "Design"? How does Frost play with sonnet conventions to complicate this poem?

2. Make a list of the images Frost uses in this poem. Are they consistent with one another, or do some evoke different kinds of emotional responses? How would you characterize these images?

3. In this poem, Frost brings together three white things: the spider, the moth, and the flower. However, two of these things are not usually white, the spider and the flower, which is usually blue. What does Frost make of this strange coincidence? How does it relate to the title of the poem?

4. A hallmark of Frost's poetry is ambiguity. For example, at the end of this poem, Frost's questions suggest two very different ideas about the meaning of this coincidence, but he provides no answers for these questions. He leaves the issue open for the reader to think about. How would you say this technique works as an argument? What does it say about Frost's view of the world? How is our own view of the world changed by our encounter with Frost's ambiguity?

5. Has your perspective on the question of whether the universe exists by design or by chance been altered by your experience with this text?

Long Time Ago/
In the Beginning

Leslie Marmon Silko

Since the 1977 publication of her novel Ceremony, *Leslie Silko (b. 1948) has been recognized as an important North American writer and a central figure among contemporary Indian writers. Born of mixed Indian and Anglo ancestry in Albuquerque, New Mexico and raised in the close-knit Laguna Pueblo community, Silko draws upon knowledge of traditional Laguna storytelling and Indian culture in her work. She retells old stories, re-examines the relationship between indigenous people and European colonists, reasserts the value of Indian cultures, and creates narratives of Indian survival, struggle, and change.*

The piece below is an excerpt from Storyteller *(1981), a multi-genre collection including autobiographical writings, family photographs, short fiction, verse, re-tellings of traditional Laguna stories. Other selections from* Storyteller *such as the short stories "Lullaby" and "Yellow Woman" are often anthologized in college texts. "Long time ago/in the beginning" recounts a creation myth in the form of a narrative poem, and it offers a somewhat surprising explanation for the existence of a particular kind of evil.*

Long time ago
in the beginning
there were no white people in this world
there was nothing European.
And this world might have gone on like that
except for one thing:
witchery.
This world was already complete
even without white people.
There was everything   10
including witchery.

Then it happened.
These witch people got together.
Some came from far far away

across oceans
across mountains.
Some had slanty eyes
others had black skin.
They all got together for a contest
the way people have baseball tournaments nowadays   20
except this was a contest
in dark things.

So anyway
they all got together
witch people from all directions
witches from all the Pueblos
and all the tribes.
They had Navajo witches there,
some from Hopi, and a few from Zuni.
They were having a witches' conference,   30
that's what it was
Way up in the lava rock hills
north of Cañoncito
they got together
to fool around in caves
with their animal skins.
Fox, badger, bobcat, and wolf
they circled the fire
and on the fourth time
they jumped into that animal's skin.   40

But this time it wasn't enough
and one of them
maybe a Sioux or some Eskimos
started showing off.
"That wasn't anything,
watch this."

The contest started like that.
Then some of them lifted the lids
on their big cooking pots,
calling the rest of them over   50
to take a look:
dead babies simmering in blood
circles of skull cut away
all the brains sucked out.
Witch medicine
to dry and grind into powder
for new victims.

Others untied skin bundles of disgusting objects:
dark flints, cinders from burned hogans where the
dead lay   60

Whorls of skin
cut from fingertips
sliced from the penis and clitoris tip.

Finally there was only one
who hadn't shown off charms or powers.
The witch stood in the shadows beyond the fire
and no one ever knew where this witch came from
which tribe
or if it was a woman or a man.
But the important thing was   70
this witch didn't show off any dark thunder charcoals
or red ant-hill beads.
This one just told them to listen:
"What I have is a story."

At first they all laughed
but this witch said
Okay
go ahead
laugh if you want to
but as I tell the story   80
it will begin to happen.

Set in motion now
set in motion by our witchery
to work for us.

Caves across the ocean
in caves of dark hills
white skin people
like the belly of a fish
covered with hair.

Then they grow away from the earth   90
then they grow away from the sun
then they grow away from the plants and animals.
They see no life
When they look
they see only objects.
The world is a dead thing for them
the trees and rivers are not alive
the mountains and stones are not alive.
The deer and bear are objects
They see no life.   100

They fear
They fear the world.
They destroy what they fear.
They fear themselves.

The wind will blow them across the ocean
thousands of them in giant boats
swarming like larva
out of a crushed ant hill.

They will carry objects
which can shoot death 110
faster than the eye can see.

They will kill the things they fear
all the animals
the people will starve.

They will poison the water
they will spin the water away
and there will be drought
the people will starve.

They will fear what they find
They will fear the people 120
They kill what they fear.

Entire villages will be wiped out
They will slaughters whole tribes.
Corpses for us
Blood for us
Killing killing killing killing.

And those they do not kill
will die anyway
at the destruction they see
at the loss 130
at the loss of the children
the loss will destroy the rest.

Stolen rivers and mountains
the stolen land will eat their hearts
and jerk their mouths from the Mother.
The people will starve.

They will bring terrible diseases
the people have never known.
Entire tribes will die out
covered with festering sores 140
shitting blood
vomiting blood.
Corpses for our work.

Set in motion now
set in motion by our witchery
set in motion
to work for us.

They will take this world from ocean to ocean
they will turn on each other
they will destroy each other   150
Up here
in these hills
they will find the rocks,
rocks with veins of green and yellow and black.
They will lay the final pattern with these rocks
they will lay it across the world
and explode everything.

Set in motion now
set in motion
To destroy   160
To kill
Objects to work for us
objects to act for us
Performing the witchery
for suffering
for torment
for the stillborn
the deformed
the sterile
the dead.   170

Whirling
Whirling
Whirling
set into motion now
set into motion.

So the other witches said
"Okay you win; you take the prize,
but what you said just now—
it isn't so funny
It doesn't sound so good.   180
We are doing okay without it
we can get along without that kind of thing.
Take it back.
Call that story back."

But the witch just shook its head
at the others in their stinking animal skins, fur
and feathers.
It's already turned loose.
It's already coming.
It can't be called back.   190

For Practice

1. Consider "Long time ago/in the beginning" in light of other narratives of origin with which you are familiar (Classical myths, Genesis, etc.). What characteristics do these narratives share? How do they differ? What, if anything, do these similarities and differences suggest to you about the nature of humankind and culture?

2. What kind of people has the witch's spell created? How might this poem be read as a comment on the relationship between Europeans and indigenous North Americans? What comment does the poem make about the groups' different relationships to the land?

3. The people created by the witch's spell bring death and destruction to Indians and their lands, and yet, Silko seems to indicate that the fault ultimately lies with the Indians, or at least the witches who created the destructive people in the first place. What is your reaction to this paradoxical situation? How can you read the ambiguity at the heart of this legend as an argument about human culture in general?

4. What specific phrases, words, or details contribute to an unflattering depiction of the people created by the witch's spell?

5. Why do the other witches want the spell called back? Why can't it be called back? What does the conclusion of the poem imply about the power of the spoken word? Does Silko's story suggest that spoken words are more powerful than written words? If so, what does this suggest about the power relationship between cultures with written language and those without?

Rappaccini's Daughter

Nathaniel Hawthorne
(from the writings of Aubépine)

Nathaniel Hawthorne (1804–1864) has long been considered one of America's most important writers. A descendant of Puritan immigrants, Hawthorne often used his novels and short stories to explore his era's reverent beliefs concerning Puritanism and revolutionary America. After graduating from Bowdoin College in 1825, Hawthorne set out to become a writer and published his first short novel in 1828. In 1837 he published his Twice-Told Tales, *a volume of short stories that included such famous works as "The Minister's Black Veil," "My Kinsman Major Molineux," and "Young Goodman Brown." While these stories have become standard readings in high school and college literature classes, Hawthorne's collection received little attention at the time. This lack of attention changed, however, in 1949 when Hawthorne published* The Scarlet Letter, *a novel that depicts one woman's struggle to overcome her society's strictures against female sexuality. "Rappaccini's Daughter" was first published in 1844 and tells the story of a young college student who moves to a new city and soon falls in love with the beautiful young woman next door. This woman lives in a beautiful, but deadly garden of poisonous plants created by her father. The story raises many questions concerning the ethics of science, human beings' relationships to nature, and male anxieties concerning women's sexuality.*

We do not remember to have seen any translated specimens of the productions of M. de l'Aubépine—a fact the less to be wondered at, as his very name is unknown to many of his own countrymen as well as to the student of foreign literature. As a writer, he seems to occupy an unfortunate position between the Transcendentalists (who, under one name or another, have their share in all the current literature of the world) and the great body of pen-and-ink men who address the intellect and sympathies of the multitude. If not too refined, at all events too remote, too shadowy, and unsubstantial in his modes of development to suit the taste of the latter class, and yet too popular to satisfy the spiritual or metaphysical requisitions of the former, he must necessarily find himself without an audience, except here and there an individual or possibly an isolated clique. His writings, to do them justice, are not altogether destitute of fancy and originality; they might have won him greater reputation but for an inveterate love of allegory, which is apt to invest his plots and characters with the aspect of scenery and people in the clouds, and to steal away the human warmth out of his conceptions. His fictions are sometimes historical, sometimes of the present day, and sometimes, so far as can be discovered, have little or no reference either to time or space. In any case, he generally contents himself with a very slight embroidery of outward manners,—the faintest possible counterfeit of real life,—and endeavors to create an interest by some less obvious peculiarity of the subject. Occasionally a breath of Nature, a raindrop of pathos and tenderness, or a gleam of humor, will find its way into the midst of his fantastic imagery, and make us feel as if, after all, we were yet within the limits of our native earth. We will only add to this very cursory notice that M. de l'Aubépine's productions, if the reader chance to take them in precisely the proper point of view, may amuse a leisure hour as well as those of a brighter man; if otherwise, they can hardly fail to look excessively like nonsense.

Our author is voluminous; he continues to write and publish with as much praiseworthy and indefatigable prolixity as if his efforts were crowned with the brilliant success that so justly attends those of Eugene Sue. His first appearance was by a collection of stories in a long series of volumes entitled "Contes deux fois racontées." The titles of some of his more recent works (we quote from memory) are as follows: "Le Voyage Céleste à Chemin de Fer," 3 tom., 1838; "Le nouveau Père Adam et la nouvelle Mère Eve," 2 tom., 1839; "Roderic; ou le Serpent à l'estomac," 2 tom., 1840; "Le Culte du Feu," a folio volume of ponderous research into the religion and ritual of the old Persian Ghebers, published in 1841; "La Soirée du Chateau en Espagne," 1 tom., 8vo, 1842; and "L'Artiste du Beau; on le Papillon Mécanique," 5 tom., 4to, 1843. Our somewhat wearisome perusal of this startling catalogue of volumes has left behind it a certain personal affection and sympathy, though by no means admiration, for M. de l'Aubépine; and we would fain do the little in our power towards introducing him favorably to the American public. The ensuing tale is a translation of his "Beatrice; on la Belle Empoisonneuse," recently published in "La Revue Anti-Aristocratique." This journal, edited by the Comte de Bearhaven, has for some years past led the defence of liberal principles and popular rights with a faithfulness and ability worthy of all praise.

A young man, named Giovanni Guasconti, came, very long ago, from the more southern region of Italy, to pursue his studies at the University of Padua. Giovanni who had but a scanty supply of gold ducats in his pocket, took lodgings in a high and gloomy chamber of an old edifice which looked not unworthy to have been the palace of a Paduan noble, and which, in fact, exhibited over its entrance the armorial bearings of a family long since extinct. The young stranger, who was not unstudied in the great poem of his country, recollected that one of the ancestors of this family, and perhaps an occupant of this very mansion, had been pictured by Dante as a partaker of the immortal agonies of his *Inferno*. These reminiscences and associations, together with the tendency to heartbreak natural to a young man for the first time out of his native sphere, caused Giovanni to sigh heavily as he looked around the desolate and ill-furnished apartment.

"Holy Virgin, signor!" cried old Dame Lisabetta, who, won by the youth's remarkable beauty of person, was kindly endeavoring to give the chamber a habitable air, "what a sigh was that to come out of a young man's heart! Do you find this old mansion gloomy? For the love of Heaven, then, put your head out of the window, and you will see as bright sunshine as you have left in Naples."

Guasconti mechanically did as the old woman advised, but could not quite agree with her that the Paduan sunshine was as cheerful as that of southern Italy. Such as it was, however, it fell upon a garden beneath the window and expended its fostering influences on a variety of plants, which seemed to have been cultivated with exceeding care.

"Does this garden belong to the house?" asked Giovanni.

"Heaven forbid, signor, unless it were fruitful of better pot herbs than any that grow there now," answered old Lisabetta. "No; that garden is cultivated by the own hands of Signor Giacomo Rappaccini, the famous doctor, who, I warrant him, has been heard of as far as Naples. It is said that he distils these plants into medicines that are as potent as a charm. Oftentimes you may see the signor doctor at work, and perchance the signora, his daughter, too, gathering the strange flowers that grow in the garden."

The old woman had now done what she could for the aspect of the chamber; and, commending the young man to the protection of the saints, took her departure.

Giovanni still found no better occupation than to look down into the garden beneath his window. From its appearance, he judged it to be one of those botanic gardens which were of earlier date in Padua than elsewhere in Italy or in the world. Or, not improbably, it might once have been the pleasure-place of an opulent family; for there was the ruin of a marble fountain in the centre, sculptured with rare art, but so woefully shattered that it was impossible to trace the original design from the chaos of remaining fragments. The water, however, continued to gush and sparkle into the sunbeams as cheerfully as ever. A little gurgling sound ascended to the young man's window, and made him feel as if the fountain were an immortal spirit that sung its song unceasingly and without heeding the vicissitudes around it, while one century imbodied it in marble and another scattered the perishable garniture on the soil. All about the pool into which the water subsided grew various plants, that seemed to require a plentiful supply of moisture for the nourishment of gigantic leaves, and, in some instances, flowers gorgeously magnificent. There was one shrub in particular, set in a marble vase in the midst of the pool, that bore a profusion of purple blossoms, each of which had the lustre and richness of a gem; and the whole together made a show so resplendent that it seemed enough to illuminate the garden, even had there been no sunshine. Every portion of the soil was peopled with plants and herbs, which, if less beautiful, still bore tokens of assiduous care, as if all had their individual virtues, known to the scientific mind that fostered them. Some were placed in urns, rich with old carving, and others in common garden pots; some crept serpent-like along the ground or climbed on high, using whatever means of ascent was offered them. One plant had wreathed itself round a statue of Vertumnus, which was thus quite veiled and shrouded in a drapery of hanging foliage, so happily arranged that it might have served a sculptor for a study.

While Giovanni stood at the window he heard a rustling behind a screen of leaves, and became aware that a person was at work in the garden. His figure soon emerged into view, and showed itself to be that of no common laborer, but a tall, emaciated, sallow, and sickly-looking man, dressed in a scholar's garb of black. He was beyond the middle term of life, with gray hair, a thin, gray beard, and a face singularly marked with intellect and cultivation, but which could never, even in his more youthful days, have expressed much warmth of heart.

Nothing could exceed the intentness with which this scientific gardener examined every shrub which grew in his path: it seemed as if he was looking into their inmost nature, making observations in regard to their creative essence, and discovering why one leaf grew in this shape and another in that, and wherefore such and such flowers differed among themselves in hue and perfume. Nevertheless, in spite of this deep intelligence on his part, there was no approach to intimacy between himself and these vegetable existences. On the contrary, he avoided their actual touch or the direct inhaling of their odors with a caution that impressed Giovanni most disagreeably; for the man's demeanor was that of one walking among malignant influences, such as savage beasts, or deadly snakes, or evil spirits, which, should he allow them one moment of license, would wreak upon him some terrible fatality. It was strangely frightful to the young man's imagination to see this air of insecurity in a person cultivating a garden, that most simple and innocent of human toils, and which had been alike the joy and labor of the unfallen parents of the race. Was this garden, then, the Eden of the present world? And this man, with such a perception of harm in what, his own hands caused to grow,—was he the Adam?

The distrustful gardener, while plucking away the dead leaves or pruning the too luxuriant growth of the shrubs, defended his hands with a pair of thick gloves. Nor were these his only armor. When, in his walk through the garden, he came to the magnificent plant that hung its purple gems beside the marble fountain, he placed a kind of mask over his mouth and nostrils, as if all this beauty did but conceal a deadlier malice; but, finding his task still too dangerous, he drew back, removed the mask, and called loudly, but in the infirm voice of a person affected with inward disease,—

"Beatrice! Beatrice!"

"Here am I, my father. What would you?" cried a rich and youthful voice from the window of the opposite house—a voice as rich as a tropical sunset, and which made Giovanni, though he knew not why, think of deep hues of purple or crimson and of perfumes heavily delectable. "Are you in the garden?"

"Yes, Beatrice," answered the gardener, "and I need your help."

Soon there emerged from under a sculptured portal the figure of a young girl, arrayed with as much richness of taste as the most splendid of the flowers, beautiful as the day, and with a bloom so deep and vivid that one shade more would have been too much. She looked redundant with life, health, and energy; all of which attributes were bound down and compressed, as it were, and girdled tensely, in their luxuriance, by her virgin zone. Yet Giovanni's fancy must have grown morbid while he looked down into the garden; for the impression which the fair stranger made upon him was as if here were another flower, the human sister of those vegetable ones, as beautiful as they, more beautiful than the richest of them, but still to be touched only with a glove, nor to be approached without a mask. As Beatrice came down the garden path, it was observable that she handled and inhaled the odor of several of the plants which her father had most sedulously avoided.

"Here, Beatrice," said the latter, "see how many needful offices require to be done to our chief treasure. Yet, shattered as I am, my life might pay the penalty of approaching it so closely as circumstances demand. Henceforth, I fear, this plant must be consigned to your sole charge."

"And gladly will I undertake it," cried again the rich tones of the young lady, as she bent towards the magnificent plant and opened her arms as if to embrace it. "Yes, my sister, my splendor, it shall be Beatrice's task to nurse and serve thee; and thou shalt reward her with thy kisses and perfumed breath, which to her is as the breath of life."

Then, with all the tenderness in her manner that was so strikingly expressed in her words, she busied herself with such attentions as the plant seemed to require; and Giovanni, at his lofty window, rubbed his eyes and almost doubted whether it were a girl tending her favorite flower, or one sister performing the duties of affection to another. The scene soon terminated. Whether Dr. Rappaccini had finished his labors in the garden, or that his watchful eye had caught the stranger's face, he now took his daughter's arm and retired. Night was already closing in; oppressive exhalations seemed to proceed from the plants and steal upward past the open window; and Giovanni, closing the lattice, went to his couch and dreamed of a rich flower and beautiful girl. Flower and maiden were different, and yet the same, and fraught with some strange peril in either shape.

But there is an influence in the light of morning that tends to rectify whatever errors of fancy, or even of judgment, we may have incurred during the sun's decline, or among the shadows of the night, or in the less wholesome glow of moonshine. Giovanni's first movement, on starting from sleep, was to throw open the window and gaze down into the garden which his dreams had made so fertile of mysteries. He was surprised and a little ashamed to find how real and matter-of-fact an affair it proved to be, in the first rays of the sun which gilded the dew-drops that hung upon leaf and blossom, and, while giving a brighter beauty to each rare flower, brought everything within the limits of ordinary experience. The young man rejoiced that, in the heart of the barren city, he had the privilege of overlooking this spot of lovely and luxuriant vegetation. It would serve, he said to himself, as a symbolic language to keep him in communion with Nature. Neither the sickly and thought-worn Dr. Giacomo Rappaccini, it is true, nor his brilliant daughter, were now visible; so that Giovanni could not determine how much of the singularity which he attributed to both was due to their own qualities and how much to his wonder-working fancy; but he was inclined to take a most rational view of the whole matter.

In the course of the day he paid his respects to Signor Pietro Baglioni, professor of medicine in the university, a physician of eminent repute, to whom Giovanni had brought a letter of introduction. The professor was an elderly personage, apparently of genial nature, and habits that might almost be called jovial. He kept the young man to dinner, and made himself very agreeable by the freedom and liveliness of his conversation, especially when warmed by a flask or two of Tuscan wine. Giovanni, conceiving that men of science, inhabitants of the same city, must needs be on familiar terms with one another, took an opportunity to mention the name of Dr. Rappaccini. But the professor did not respond with so much cordiality as he had anticipated.

"Ill would it become a teacher of the divine art of medicine," said Professor Pietro Baglioni, in answer to a question of Giovanni, "to withhold due and well-considered praise of a physician so eminently skilled as Rappaccini; but, on the other hand, I should answer it but scantily to my conscience were I to permit a worthy youth like yourself, Signor Giovanni, the son of an ancient friend, to imbibe erroneous ideas respecting a man who might hereafter chance to hold your life and death in his hands. The truth is, our worshipful Dr. Rappaccini has as much science as any member of the faculty—with perhaps one single exception—in Padua, or all Italy; but there are certain grave objections to his professional character."

"And what are they?" asked the young man.

"Has my friend Giovanni any disease of body or heart, that he is so inquisitive about physicians?" said the professor, with a smile. "But as for Rappaccini, it is said of him—and I, who know the man well, can answer for its truth—that he cares infinitely more for science than for mankind. His patients are interesting to him only as subjects for some new experiment. He would sacrifice human life, his own among the rest, or whatever else was dearest to him, for the sake of adding so much as a grain of mustard seed to the great heap of his accumulated knowledge."

"Methinks he is an awful man indeed," remarked Guasconti, mentally recalling the cold and purely intellectual aspect of Rappaccini. "And yet, worshipful professor, is it not a noble spirit? Are there many men capable of so spiritual a love of science?"

"God forbid," answered the professor, somewhat testily; "at least, unless they take sounder views of the healing art than those adopted by Rappaccini. It is his theory that all medicinal virtues are comprised within those substances which we term vegetable poisons. These he cultivates with his own hands, and is said even to have produced new varieties of poison, more horribly deleterious than Nature, without the assistance of this learned person, would ever have plagued the world withal. That the signor doctor does less mischief than might be expected with such dangerous substances is undeniable. Now and then, it must be owned, he has effected, or seemed to effect, a marvellous cure; but, to tell you my private mind, Signor Giovanni, he should receive little credit for such instances of success,—they being probably the work of chance,—but should be held strictly accountable for his failures, which may justly be considered his own work."

The youth might have taken Baglioni's opinions with many grains of allowance had he known that there was a professional warfare of long continuance between him and Dr. Rappaccini, in which the latter was generally thought to have gained the advantage. If the reader be inclined to judge for himself, we refer him to certain black-letter tracts on both sides, preserved in the medical department of the University of Padua.

"I know not, most learned professor," returned Giovanni, after musing on what had been said of Rappaccini's exclusive zeal for science,—"I know not how dearly this physician may love his art; but surely there is one object more dear to him. He has a daughter."

"Aha!" cried the professor, with a laugh. "So now our friend Giovanni's secret is out. You have heard of this daughter, whom all the young men in Padua are wild about, though not half a dozen have ever had the good hap to see her face. I know little of the Signora Beatrice save that Rappaccini is said to have instructed her deeply in his science, and that, young and beautiful as fame reports her, she is already qualified to fill a professor's chair. Perchance her father destines her for mine! Other absurd rumors there be, not worth talking about or listening to. So now, Signor Giovanni, drink off your glass of lachryma."

Guasconti returned to his lodgings somewhat heated with the wine he had quaffed, and which caused his brain to swim with strange fantasies in reference to Dr. Rappaccini and the beautiful Beatrice. On his way, happening to pass by a florist's, he bought a fresh bouquet of flowers.

Ascending to his chamber, he seated himself near the window, but within the shadow thrown by the depth of the wall, so that he could look down into the garden with little risk of being discovered. All beneath his eye was a solitude. The strange plants were basking in the sunshine, and now and then nodding gently to one another, as if in acknowledgment of sympathy and kindred. In the midst, by the shattered fountain, grew the magnificent shrub, with its purple gems clustering all over it; they glowed in the air, and gleamed back again out of the depths of the pool, which thus seemed to overflow with colored radiance from the rich reflection that was steeped in it. At first, as we have said, the garden was a solitude. Soon, however,—as Giovanni had half hoped, half feared, would be the case,—a figure appeared beneath the antique sculptured portal, and came down between the rows of plants, inhaling their various perfumes as if she were one of those beings of old classic fable that lived upon sweet odors. On again beholding Beatrice, the young man was even startled to perceive how much her beauty exceeded his recollection of it; so brilliant, so vivid, was its character, that she glowed amid the sunlight, and, as Giovanni whispered to himself, positively illuminated the more shadowy intervals of the garden path. Her face being now more revealed than on the former occasion, he was struck by its expression of simplicity and sweetness,—qualities that had not entered into his idea of her character, and which made him ask anew what manner of mortal she might be. Nor did he fail again to observe, or imagine, an analogy between the beautiful girl and the gorgeous shrub that hung its gemlike flowers over the fountain,—a resemblance which Beatrice seemed to have indulged a fantastic humor in heightening, both by the arrangement of her dress and the selection of its hues.

Approaching the shrub, she threw open her arms, as with a passionate ardor, and drew its branches into an intimate embrace—so intimate that her features were hidden in its leafy bosom and her glistening ringlets all intermingled with the flowers. "Give me thy breath, my sister," exclaimed Beatrice; "for I am faint with common air. And give me this flower of thine, which I separate with gentlest fingers from the stem and place it close beside my heart." With these words the beautiful daughter of Rappaccini plucked one of the richest blossoms of the shrub, and was about to fasten it in her bosom. But now, unless Giovanni's draughts of wine had bewildered his senses, a singular incident occurred. A small orange-colored reptile, of the lizard or chameleon species, chanced to be creeping along the path, just at the feet of Beatrice. It appeared to Giovanni,—but, at the distance from which he gazed, he could scarcely have seen anything so minute,—it appeared to him, however, that a drop or two of moisture from the broken stem of the flower descended upon the lizard's head. For an instant the reptile contorted itself violently, and then lay motionless in the sunshine. Beatrice observed this remarkable phenomenon, and crossed herself, sadly, but without surprise; nor did she therefore hesitate to arrange the fatal flower in her bosom. There it blushed, and almost glimmered with the dazzling effect of a precious stone, adding to her dress and aspect the one appropriate charm which nothing else in the world could have supplied. But Giovanni, out of the shadow of his window, bent forward and shrank back, and murmured and trembled.

"Am I awake? Have I my senses?" said he to himself. "What is this being? Beautiful shall I call her, or inexpressibly terrible?"

Beatrice now strayed carelessly through the garden, approaching closer beneath Giovanni's window, so that he was compelled to thrust his head quite out of its concealment in order to gratify the intense and painful curiosity which she excited. At this moment there came a beautiful insect over the garden wall; it had, perhaps, wandered through the city, and found no flowers or verdure among those antique haunts of men until the heavy perfumes of Dr. Rappaccini's shrubs had lured it from afar. Without alighting on the flowers, this winged brightness seemed to be attracted by Beatrice, and lingered in the air and fluttered about her head. Now, here it could not be but that Giovanni Guasconti's eyes deceived him. Be that as it might, he fancied that, while Beatrice was gazing at the insect with childish delight, it grew faint and fell at her feet; its bright wings shivered; it was dead—from no cause that he could discern, unless it were the atmosphere of her breath. Again Beatrice crossed herself and sighed heavily as she bent over the dead insect.

An impulsive movement of Giovanni drew her eyes to the window. There she beheld the beautiful head of the young man—rather a Grecian than an Italian head, with fair, regular features, and a glistening of gold among his ringlets—gazing down upon her like a being that hovered in mid air. Scarcely knowing what he did, Giovanni threw down the bouquet which he had hitherto held in his hand. "Signora," said he, "there are pure and healthful flowers. Wear them for the sake of Giovanni Guasconti."

"Thanks, Signor," replied Beatrice, with her rich voice, that came forth as it were like a gush of music, and with a mirthful expression half childish and half woman-like. "I accept your gift and would fain recompense it with this precious purple flower; but if I toss it into the air it will not reach you. So Signor Guasconti must even content himself with my thanks."

She lifted the bouquet from the ground, and then, as if inwardly ashamed at having stepped aside from her maidenly reserve to respond to a stranger's greeting, passed swiftly homeward through the garden. But few as the moments were, it seemed to Giovanni, when she was on the point of vanishing beneath the sculptured portal, that, his beautiful bouquet was already beginning to wither in her grasp. It was an idle thought; there could be no possibility of distinguishing a faded flower from a fresh one at so great a distance.

For many days after this incident the young man avoided the window that looked into Dr. Rappaccini's garden, as if something ugly and monstrous would have blasted his eyesight had he been betrayed into a glance. He felt conscious of having put himself, to a certain extent, within the influence of an unintelligible power by the communication which he had opened with Beatrice. The wisest course would have been, if his heart were in any real danger, to quit his lodgings and Padua itself at once; the next wiser, to have accustomed himself, as far as possible, to the familiar and daylight view of Beatrice—thus bringing her rigidly and systematically within the limits of ordinary experience. Least of all, while avoiding her sight, ought Giovanni to have remained so near this extraordinary being that the proximity and possibility even of intercourse should give a kind of substance and reality to the wild vagaries which his imagination ran riot continually in producing. Guasconti had not a deep heart—or, at all events, its depths were not sounded now; but he had a quick fancy, and an ardent southern temperament, which rose every instant to a higher fever pitch. Whether or no Beatrice possessed those terrible attributes, that fatal breath, the affinity with those so beautiful and deadly flowers which were indicated by what Giovanni had witnessed, she had at least instilled a fierce and subtle poison into his system. It was not love, although her rich beauty was a madness to him; nor horror, even while he fancied her spirit to be imbued with the same baneful essence that seemed to pervade her physical frame; but a wild offspring of both love and horror that had each parent in it, and burned like one and shivered like the other Giovanni knew not what to dread; still less did he know what to hope; yet hope and dread kept a continual warfare in his breast, alternately vanquishing one another and starting up afresh to renew the contest. Blessed are all simple emotions, be they dark or bright! It is the lurid intermixture of the two that produces the illuminating blaze of the internal regions.

Sometimes he endeavored to assuage the fever of his spirit by a rapid walk through the streets of Padua or beyond its gates: his footsteps kept time with the throbbings of his brain, so that the walk was apt to accelerate itself to a race. One day he found himself arrested; his arm was seized by a portly personage, who had turned back on recognizing the young man and expended much breath in overtaking him.

"Signor Giovanni! Stay, my young friend!" cried he. "Have you forgotten me? That might well be the case if I were as much altered as yourself."

It was Baglioni, whom Giovanni had avoided ever since their first meeting, from a doubt that the professor's sagacity would look too deeply into his secrets. Endeavoring to recover himself, he stared forth wildly from his inner world into the outer one and spoke like a man in a dream.

"Yes; I am Giovanni Guasconti. You are Professor Pietro Baglioni. Now let me pass!"

"Not yet, not yet, Signor Giovanni Guasconti," said the professor, smiling, but at the same time scrutinizing the youth with an earnest glance. "What! did I grow up side by side with your father? and shall his son pass me like a stranger in these old streets of Padua? Stand still, Signor Giovanni; for we must have a word or two before we part."

"Speedily, then, most worshipful professor, speedily," said Giovanni, with feverish impatience. "Does not your worship see that I am in haste?"

Now, while he was speaking there came a man in black along the street, stooping and moving feebly like a person in inferior health. His face was all overspread with a most sickly and sallow hue, but yet so pervaded with an expression of piercing and active intellect that an observer might easily have overlooked the merely physical attributes and have seen only this wonderful energy. As he passed, this person exchanged a cold and distant salutation with Baglioni, but fixed his eyes upon Giovanni with an intentness that seemed to bring out whatever was within him worthy of notice. Nevertheless, there was a peculiar quietness in the look, as if taking merely a speculative, not a human, interest in the young man.

"It is Dr. Rappaccini!" whispered the professor when the stranger had passed. "Has he ever seen your face before?"

"Not that I know," answered Giovanni, starting at the name.

"He *has* seen you! he must have seen you!" said Baglioni, hastily. "For some purpose or other, this man of science is making a study of you. I know that look of his! It is the same that coldly illuminates his face as he bends over a bird, a mouse, or a butterfly, which, in pursuance of some experiment, he has killed by the perfume of a flower; a look as deep as Nature itself, but without Nature's warmth of love. Signor Giovanni, I will stake my life upon it, you are the subject of one of Rappaccini's experiments!"

"Will you make a fool of me?" cried Giovanni, passionately. "*That*, signor professor, were an untoward experiment."

"Patience! patience!" replied the imperturbable professor. "I tell thee, my poor Giovanni, that Rappaccini has a scientific interest in thee. Thou hast fallen into fearful hands! And the Signora Beatrice,—what part does she act in this mystery?"

But Guasconti, finding Baglioni's pertinacity intolerable, here broke away, and was gone before the professor could again seize his arm. He looked after the young man intently and shook his head.

"This must not be," said Baglioni to himself. "The youth is the son of my old friend, and shall not come to any harm from which the arcana of medical science can preserve him. Besides, it is too insufferable an impertinence in Rappaccini, thus to snatch the lad out of my own hands, as I may say, and make use of him for his infernal experiments. This daughter of his! It shall be looked to. Perchance, most learned Rappaccini, I may foil you where you little dream of it!"

Meanwhile Giovanni had pursued a circuitous route, and at length found himself at the door of his lodgings. As he crossed the threshold he was met by old Lisabetta, who smirked and smiled, and was evidently desirous to attract his attention; vainly, however, as the ebullition of his feelings had momentarily subsided in dull vacuity. He turned his eyes full upon the withered face that was puckering itself into a smile, but seemed to behold it not. The old dame, therefore, laid her grasp upon his cloak.

"Signor! signor!" whispered she, still with a smile over the whole breadth of her visage, so that it looked not unlike a grotesque carving in wood, darkened by centuries. "Listen, signor! There is a private entrance into the garden!"

"What do you say?" exclaimed Giovanni, turning quickly about, as if an inanimate thing should start into feverish life. "A private entrance into Dr. Rappaccini's garden?"

"Hush! hush! not so loud!" whispered Lisabetta, putting her hand over his mouth. "Yes; into the worshipful doctor's garden, where you may see all his fine shrubbery. Many a young man in Padua would give gold to be admitted among those flowers."

Giovanni put a piece of gold into her hand.

"Show me the way," said he.

A surmise, probably excited by his conversation with Baglioni, crossed his mind, that this interposition of old Lisabetta might perchance be connected with the intrigue, whatever were its nature, in which the professor seemed to suppose that Dr. Rappaccini was involving him. But such a suspicion, though it disturbed Giovanni, was inadequate to restrain him. The instant that he was aware of the possibility of approaching Beatrice, it seemed an absolute necessity of his existence to do so. It mattered not whether she were angel or demon; he was irrevocably within her sphere, and must obey the law that whirled him onward, in ever-lessening circles, towards a result which he did not attempt to foreshadow; and yet, strange to say, there came across him a sudden doubt whether this intense interest on his part were not delusory; whether it were really of so deep and positive a nature as to justify him in now thrusting himself into an incalculable position; whether it were not merely the fantasy. of a young man's brain, only slightly or not at all connected with his heart.

He paused, hesitated, turned half about, but again went on. His withered guide led him along several obscure passages, and finally undid a door, through which, as it was opened, there came the sight and sound of rustling leaves, with the broken sunshine glimmering among them. Giovanni stepped forth, and, forcing himself through the entanglement of a shrub that wreathed its tendrils over the hidden entrance, stood beneath his own window in the open area of Dr. Rappaccini's garden.

How often is it the case that, when impossibilities have come to pass and dreams have condensed their misty substance into tangible realities, we find ourselves calm, and even coldly self-possessed, amid circumstances which it would have been a delirium of joy or agony to anticipate! Fate delights to thwart us thus. Passion will choose his own time to rush upon the scene, and lingers sluggishly behind when an appropriate adjustment of events would seem to summon his appearance. So was it now with Giovanni. Day after day his pulses had throbbed with feverish blood at the improbable idea of an interview with Beatrice, and of standing with her, face to face, in this very garden, basking in the Oriental sunshine of her beauty, and her full gaze the mystery which he deemed the riddle of his own exist there was a singular and untimely equanimity within his breast. He threw a glance around the garden to discover if Beatrice or her father were present, and, perceiving that he was alone, began a critical observation of the plants.

The aspect of one and all of them dissatisfied him; their gorgeousness seemed fierce, passionate, and even unnatural. There was hardly an individual shrub which a wanderer, straying by himself through a forest, would not have been startled to find growing wild, as if an unearthly face had glared at him out of the thicket. Several also would have shocked a delicate instinct by an appearance of artificialness indicating that there had been such commixture, and, as it were, adultery, of various vegetable species, that the production was no longer of God's making, but the monstrous offspring of man's depraved fancy, glowing with only an evil mockery of beauty. They were probably the result of experiment, which in one or two cases had succeeded in mingling plants individually lovely into a compound possessing the questionable and ominous character that distinguished the whole growth of the garden. In fine, Giovanni recognized but two or three plants in the collection, and those of a kind that he well knew to be poisonous. While busy with these contemplations he heard the rustling of a silken garment, and, turning, beheld Beatrice emerging from beneath the sculptured portal.

Giovanni had not considered with himself what should be his deportment; whether he should apologize for his intrusion into the garden, or assume that he was there with the privity at least, if not by the desire, of Dr. Rappaccini or his daughter; but Beatrice's manner placed him at his ease, though leaving him still in doubt by what agency he had gained admittance. She came lightly along the path and met him near the broken fountain. There was surprise in her face, but brightened by a simple and kind expression of pleasure.

"You are a connoisseur in flowers, signor," said Beatrice, with a smile, alluding to the bouquet which he had flung her from the window. "It is no marvel, therefore, if the sight of my father's rare collection has tempted you to take a nearer view. If he were here, he could tell you many strange and interesting facts as to the nature and habits of these shrubs; for he has spent a lifetime in such studies, and this garden is his world."

"And yourself, lady," observed Giovanni, "if fame says true,—you likewise are deeply skilled in the virtues indicated by these rich blossoms and these spicy perfumes. Would you deign to be my instructress, I should prove an apter scholar than if taught by Signor Rappaccini himself."

"Are there such idle rumors?" asked Beatrice, with the music of a pleasant laugh. "Do people say that I am skilled in my father's science of plants? What a jest is there! No; though I have grown up among these flowers, I know no more of them than their hues and perfume; and sometimes methinks I would fain rid myself of even that small knowledge. There are many flowers here, and those not the least brilliant, that shock and offend me when they meet my eye. But pray, signor, do not believe these stories about my science. Believe nothing of me save what you see with your eyes."

"And must I believe all that I have seen with my own eyes?" asked Giovanni, pointedly, while the recollection of former scenes made him shrink. "No, signora; you demand too little of me. Bid me believe nothing save what comes from your own lips."

It would appear that Beatrice understood him. There came a deep flush to her cheek; but she looked full into Giovanni's eyes, and responded to his gaze of uneasy suspicion with a queenlike haughtiness.

"I do so bid you, signor," she replied. "Forget whatever you may have fancied in regard to me. If true to the outward senses, still it may be false in its essence; but the words of Beatrice Rappaccini's lips are true from the depths of the heart outward. Those you may believe."

A fervor glowed in her whole aspect and beamed upon Giovanni's consciousness like the light of truth itself, but while she spoke there was a fragrance in the atmosphere around her, rich and delightful, though evanescent, yet which the young man, from an indefinable reluctance, scarcely dared to draw into his lungs. It might be the odor of the flowers. Could it be Beatrice's breath which thus embalmed her words with a strange richness, as if by steeping them in her heart? A faintness passed like a shadow over Giovanni and flitted away; he seemed to gaze through the beautiful girl's eyes into her transparent soul, and felt no more doubt or fear.

The tinge of passion that had colored Beatrice's manner vanished; she became gay, and appeared to derive a pure delight from her communion with the youth not unlike what the maiden of a lonely island might have felt conversing with a voyager from the civilized world. Evidently her experience of life had been confined within the limits of that garden. She talked now about matters as simple as the daylight or summer clouds, and now asked questions in reference to the city, or Giovanni's distant home, his friends, his mother, and his sisters—questions indicating such seclusion, and such lack of familiarity with modes and forms, that Giovanni responded as if to an infant. Her spirit gushed out before him like a fresh rill that was just catching its first glimpse of the sunlight and wondering at the reflections of earth and sky which were flung into its bosom. There came thoughts, too, from a deep source, and fantasies of a gemlike brilliancy, as if diamonds and rubies sparkled upward among the bubbles of the fountain. Ever and anon there gleamed across the young man's mind a sense of wonder that he should be walking side by side with the being who had so wrought upon his imagination, whom he had idealized in such hues of terror, in whom he had positively witnessed such manifestations of dreadful attributes,—that he should be conversing with Beatrice like a brother, and should find her so human and so maidenlike. But such reflections were only momentary; the effect of her character was too real not to make itself familiar at once.

In this free intercourse they had strayed through the garden, and now, after many turns among its avenues, were come to the shattered fountain, beside which grew the magnificent shrub, with its treasury of glowing blossoms. A fragrance was diffused from it which Giovanni recognized as identical with that which he had attributed to Beatrice's breath, but incomparably more powerful. As her eyes fell upon it, Giovanni beheld her press her hand to her bosom as if her heart were throbbing suddenly and painfully.

"For the first time in my life," murmured she, addressing the shrub, "I had forgotten thee."

"I remember, signora," said Giovanni, "that you once promised to reward me with one of these living gems for the bouquet which I had the happy boldness to fling to your feet. Permit me now to pluck it as a memorial of this interview."

He made a step towards the shrub with extended hand; but Beatrice darted forward, uttering a shriek that went through his heart like a dagger. She caught his hand and drew it back with the whole force of her slender figure. Giovanni felt her touch thrilling through his fibers.

"Touch it not!" exclaimed she, in a voice of agony. "Not for thy life! It is fatal!"

Then, hiding her face, she fled from him and vanished beneath the sculptured portal. As Giovanni followed her with his eyes, he beheld the emaciated figure and pale intelligence of Dr. Rappaccini, who had been watching the scene, he knew not how long, within the shadow of the entrance.

No sooner was Guasconti alone in his chamber than the image of Beatrice came back to his passionate musings, invested with all the witchery that had been gathering around it ever since his first glimpse of her, and now likewise imbued with a tender warmth of girlish womanhood. She was human; her nature was endowed with all gentle and feminine qualities; she was worthiest to be worshipped; she was capable, surely, on her part, of the height and heroism of love. Those tokens which he had hitherto considered as proofs of a frightful peculiarity in her physical and moral system were now either forgotten, or, by the subtle sophistry of passion transmitted into a golden crown of enchantment, rendering Beatrice the more admirable by so much as she was the more unique. Whatever had looked ugly was now beautiful; or, if incapable of such a change, it stole away and hid itself among those shapeless half ideas which throng the dim region beyond the daylight of our perfect consciousness. Thus did he spend the night, nor fell asleep until the dawn had begun to awake the slumbering flowers in Dr. Rappaccini's garden, whither Giovanni's dreams doubtless led him. Up rose the sun in his due season, and, flinging his beams upon the young man's eyelids, awoke him to a sense of pain. When thoroughly aroused, he became sensible of a burning and tingling agony in his hand—in his right hand—the very hand which Beatrice had grasped in her own when he was on the point of plucking one of the gemlike flowers. On the back of that hand there was now a purple print like that of four small fingers, and the likeness of a slender thumb upon his wrist.

Oh, how stubbornly does love,—or even that cunning semblance of love which flourishes in the imagination, but strikes no depth of root into the heart,—how stubbornly does it hold its faith until the moment comes when it is doomed to vanish into thin mist! Giovanni wrapped a handkerchief about his hand and wondered what evil thing had stung him, and soon forgot his pain in a reverie of Beatrice.

After the first interview, a second was in the inevitable course of what we call fate. A third; a fourth; and a meeting with Beatrice in the garden was no longer an incident in Giovanni's daily life, but the whole space in which he might be said to live; for the anticipation and memory of that ecstatic hour made up the remainder. Nor was it otherwise with the daughter of Rappaccini. She watched for the youth's appearance, and flew to his side with confidence as unreserved as if they had been playmates from early infancy—as if they were such playmates still. If, by any unwonted chance, he failed to come at the appointed moment, she stood beneath the window and sent up the rich sweetness of her tones to float around him in his chamber and echo and reverberate throughout his heart: "Giovanni! Giovanni! Why tarriest thou? Come down!" And down he hastened into that Eden of poisonous flowers.

But, with all this intimate familiarity, there was still a reserve in Beatrice's demeanor, so rigidly and invariably sustained that the idea of infringing it scarcely occurred to his imagination. By all appreciable signs, they loved; they had looked love with eyes that conveyed the holy secret from the depths of one soul into the depths of the other, as if it were too sacred to be whispered by the way; they had even spoken love in those gushes of passion when their spirits darted forth in articulated breath like tongues of long-hidden flame; and yet there had been no seal of lips, no clasp of hands, nor any slightest caress such as love claims and hallows. He had never touched one of the gleaming ringlets of her hair; her garment—so marked was the physical barrier between them—had never been waved against him by a breeze. On the few occasions when Giovanni had seemed tempted to overstep the limit, Beatrice grew so sad, so stern, and withal wore such a look of desolate separation, shuddering at itself, that not a spoken word was requisite to repel him. At such times he was startled at the horrible suspicions that rose, monster-like, out of the caverns of his heart and stared him in the face; his love grew thin and faint as the morning mist, his doubts alone had substance. But, when Beatrice's face brightened again after the momentary shadow, she was transformed at once from the mysterious, questionable being whom he had watched with so much awe and horror; she was now the beautiful and unsophisticated girl whom he felt that his spirit knew with a certainty beyond all other knowledge.

A considerable time had now passed since Giovanni's last meeting with Baglioni. One morning, however, he was disagreeably surprised by a visit from the professor, whom he had scarcely thought of for whole weeks, and would willingly have forgotten still longer. Given up as he had long been to a pervading excitement, he could tolerate no companions except upon condition of their perfect sympathy with his present state of feeling. Such sympathy was not to be expected from Professor Baglioni.

The visitor chatted carelessly for a few moments about the gossip of the city and the university, and then took up another topic.

"I have been reading an old classic author lately," said he, "and met with a story that strangely interested me. Possibly you may remember it. It is of an Indian prince, who sent a beautiful woman as a present to Alexander the Great. She was as lovely as the dawn and gorgeous as the sunset; but what especially distinguished her was a certain rich perfume in her breath—richer than a garden of Persian roses. Alexander, as was natural to a youthful conqueror, fell in love at first sight with this magnificent stranger; but a certain sage physician, happening to be present, discovered a terrible secret in regard to her."

"And what was that?" asked Giovanni, turning his eyes downward to avoid those of the professor.

"That this lovely woman," continued Baglioni, with emphasis, "had been nourished with poisons from her birth upward, until her whole nature was so imbued with them that she herself had become the deadliest poison in existence. Poison was her element of life. With that rich perfume of her breath she blasted the very air. Her love would have been poison—her embrace death. Is not this a marvellous tale?"

"A childish fable," answered Giovanni, nervously starting from his chair. "I marvel how your worship finds time to read such nonsense among your graver studies."

"By the by," said the professor, looking uneasily about him, "what singular fragrance is this in your apartment? Is it the perfume of your gloves? It is faint, but delicious; and yet, after all, by no means agreeable. Were I to breathe it long, methinks it would make me ill. It is like the breath of a flower; but I see no flowers in the chamber."

"Nor are there any," replied Giovanni, who had turned pale as the professor spoke; "nor, I think, is there any fragrance except in your worship's imagination. Odors, being a sort of element combined of the sensual and the spiritual, are apt to deceive us in this manner. The recollection of a perfume, the bare idea of it, may easily be mistaken for a present reality."

"Ay; but my sober imagination does not often play such tricks," said Baglioni; "and, were I to fancy any kind of odor, it would be that of some vile apothecary drug, wherewith my fingers are likely enough to be imbued. Our worshipful friend Rappaccini, as I have heard, tinctures his medicaments with odors richer than those of Araby. Doubtless, likewise, the fair and learned Signora Beatrice would minister to her patients with draughts as sweet as a maiden's breath; but woe to him that sips them!"

Giovanni's face evinced many contending emotions. The tone in which the professor alluded to the pure and lovely daughter of Rappaccini was a torture to his soul; and yet the intimation of a view of her character, opposite to his own, gave instantaneous distinctness to a thousand dim suspicions, which now grinned at him like so many demons. But he strove hard to quell them and to respond to Baglioni with a true lover's perfect faith.

"Signor professor," said he, "you were my father's friend; perchance, too, it is your purpose to act a friendly part towards his son. I would fain feel nothing towards you save respect and deference; but I pray you to observe, signor, that there is one subject on which we must not speak. You know not the Signora Beatrice. You cannot, therefore, estimate the wrong—the blasphemy, I may even say—that is offered to her character by a light or injurious word."

"Giovanni! my poor Giovanni!" answered the professor, with a calm expression of pity, "I know this wretched girl far better than yourself. You shall hear the truth in respect to the poisoner Rappaccini and his poisonous daughter; yes, poisonous as she is beautiful. Listen; for, even should you do violence to my gray hairs, it shall not silence me. That old fable of the Indian woman has become a truth by the deep and deadly science of Rappaccini and in the person of the lovely Beatrice."

Giovanni groaned and hid his face.

"Her father," continued Baglioni, "was not restrained by natural affection from offering up his child in this horrible manner as the victim of his insane zeal for science; for, let us do him justice, he is as true a man of science as ever distilled his own heart in an alembic. What, then, will be your fate? Beyond a doubt you are selected as the material of some new experiment. Perhaps the result is to be death; perhaps a more awful still. Rappaccini, with what he calls the interest of science before his eyes, will hesitate at nothing."

"It is a dream," muttered Giovanni to himself, "surely it is a dream."

"But," resumed the professor, "be of good cheer, son of my friend. It is not yet too late for the rescue. Possibly we may even succeed in bringing back this miserable child within the limits of ordinary nature, from which her father's madness has estranged her. Behold this little silver vase! It was wrought by the hands of the renowned Benvenuto Cellini, and is well worthy to be a love gift to the fairest dame in Italy. But its contents are invaluable. One little sip of this antidote would have rendered the most virulent poisons of the Borgias innocuous. Doubt not that it will be as efficacious against those of Rappaccini. Bestow the vase, and the precious liquid within it, on your Beatrice, and hopefully await the result."

Baglioni laid a small, exquisitely wrought silver vial on the table and withdrew, leaving what he had said to produce its effect upon the young man's mind.

"We will thwart Rappaccini yet, " thought he, chuckling to himself, as he descended the stairs; "but, let us confess the truth of him, he is a wonderful man—a wonderful man indeed; a vile empiric, however, in his practice, and therefore not to be tolerated by those who respect the good old rules of the medical profession."

Throughout Giovanni's whole acquaintance with Beatrice, he had occasionally, as we have said, been haunted by dark surmises as to her character; yet so thoroughly had she made herself felt by him as a simple, natural, most affectionate, and guileless creature, that the image now held up by Professor Baglioni looked as strange and incredible as if it were not in accordance with his own original conception. True, there were ugly recollections connected with his first glimpses of the beautiful girl; he could not quite forget the bouquet that withered in her grasp, and the insect that perished amid the sunny air, by no ostensible agency save the fragrance of her breath. These inci-

dents, however, dissolving in the pure light of her character, had no longer the efficacy of facts, but were acknowledged as mistaken fantasies, by whatever testimony of the
senses they might appear to be substantiated. There is something truer and more real
than what we can see with the eyes and touch with the finger. On such better evidence
had Giovanni founded his confidence in Beatrice, though rather by the necessary force
of her high attributes than by any deep and generous faith on his part. But now his
spirit was incapable of sustaining itself at the height to which the early enthusiasm of
passion had exalted it; he fell down, grovelling among earthly doubts, and defiled
therewith the pure whiteness of Beatrice's image. Not that he gave her up; he did but
distrust. He resolved to institute some decisive test that should satisfy him, once for
all, whether there were those dreadful peculiarities in her physical nature which could
not be supposed to exist without some corresponding monstrosity of soul. His eyes,
gazing down afar, might have deceived him as to the lizard, the insect, and the flowers;
but if he could witness, at the distance of a few paces, the sudden blight of one fresh
and healthful flower in Beatrice's hand, there would be room for no further question.
With this idea he hastened to the florist's and purchased a bouquet that was still
gemmed with the morning dew-drops.

It was now the customary hour of his daily interview with Beatrice. Before
descending into the garden, Giovanni failed not to look at his figure in the mirror,—a
vanity to be expected in a beautiful young man, yet, as displaying itself at that troubled
and feverish moment, the token of a certain shallowness of feeling and insincerity of
character. He did gaze, however, and said to himself that his features had never before
possessed so rich a grace, nor his eyes such vivacity, nor his cheeks so warm a hue of
super-abundant life.

"At least," thought he, "her poison has not yet insinuated itself into my system. I
am no flower to perish in her grasp."

With that thought he turned his eyes on the bouquet, which he had never once laid
aside from his hand. A thrill of indefinable horror shot through his frame on perceiving that those dewy flowers were already beginning to droop; they wore the aspect of
things that had been fresh and lovely yesterday. Giovanni grew white as marble, and
stood motionless before the mirror, staring at his own reflection there as at the likeness of something frightful. He remembered Baglioni's remark about the fragrance
that seemed to pervade the chamber. It must have been the poison in his breath! Then
he shuddered—shuddered at himself. Recovering from his stupor, he began to watch
with curious eye a spider that was busily at work hanging its web from the antique cornice of the apartment, crossing and recrossing the artful system of interwoven lines—
as vigorous and active a spider as ever dangled from an old ceiling. Giovanni bent
towards the insect, and emitted a deep, long breath. The spider suddenly ceased its toil;
the web vibrated with a tremor originating in the body of the small artisan. Again
Giovanni sent forth a breath, deeper, longer, and imbued with a venomous feeling out
of his heart: he knew not whether he were wicked, or only desperate. The spider made
a convulsive gripe with his limbs and hung dead across the window.

"Accursed! accursed!" muttered Giovanni, addressing himself "Hast thou grown so
poisonous that this deadly insect perishes by thy breath?"

At that moment a rich, sweet voice came floating up from the garden.

"Giovanni! Giovanni! it is past the hour! Why tarriest thou? Come down!"

"Yes," muttered Giovanni again. "She is the only being whom my breath may not
slay! Would that it might!"

He rushed down, and in an instant was standing before the bright and loving eyes of Beatrice. A moment ago his wrath and despair had been so fierce that he could have desired nothing so much as to wither her by a glance; but with her actual presence there came influences which had too real an existence to be at once shaken off: recollections of the delicate and benign power of her feminine nature, which had so often enveloped him in a religious calm; recollections of many a holy and passionate outgush of her heart, when the pure fountain had been unsealed from its depths and made visible in its transparency to his mental eye; recollections which, had Giovanni known how to estimate them, would have assured him that all this ugly mystery was but an earthly illusion, and that, whatever mist of evil might seem to have gathered over her, the real Beatrice was a heavenly angel. Incapable as he was of such high faith, still her presence had not utterly lost its magic. Giovanni's rage was quelled into an aspect of sullen insensibility. Beatrice, with a quick spiritual sense, immediately felt that there was a gulf of blackness between them which neither he nor she could pass. They walked on together, sad and silent, and came thus to the marble fountain and to its pool of water on the ground, in the midst of which grew the shrub that bore gem-like blossoms. Giovanni was affrighted at the eager enjoyment—the appetite, as it were— with which he found himself inhaling the fragrance of the flowers.

"Beatrice," asked he, abruptly, "whence came this shrub?"

"My father created it," answered she, with simplicity.

"Created it! created it!" repeated Giovanni. "What mean you, Beatrice?"

"He is a man fearfully acquainted with the secrets of Nature," replied Beatrice: and, at the hour when I first drew breath, this plant sprang from the soil, the offspring of his science, of his intellect, while I was but his earthly child. Approach it not!" continued she, observing with terror that Giovanni was drawing nearer to the shrub. "It has qualities that you little dream of. But I, dearest Giovanni,—I grew up and blossomed with the plant and was nourished with its breath. It was my sister, and, I loved it with a human affection; for, alas!—hast thou not suspected it?—there was an awful doom."

Here Giovanni frowned so darkly upon her that Beatrice paused and trembled. But her faith in his tenderness reassured her, and made her blush that she had doubted for an instant.

"There was an awful doom," she continued, "the effect of my father's fatal love of science, which estranged me from all society of my kind. Until Heaven sent thee dearest Giovanni, oh, how lonely was thy poor Beatrice!"

"Was it a hard doom?" asked Giovanni, fixing his eyes upon her.

"Only of late have I known how hard it was," answered she, tenderly. "Oh, yes; but my heart was torpid, and therefore quiet."

Giovanni's rage broke forth from his sullen gloom like a lightning flash out of a dark cloud.

"Accursed one!" cried he, with venomous scorn and anger. "And, finding thy solitude wearisome, thou hast severed me likewise from all the warmth of life and enticed me into thy region of unspeakable horror!"

"Giovanni!" exclaimed Beatrice, turning her large bright eyes upon his face. The force of his words had not found its way into her mind; she was merely thunderstruck.

"Yes, poisonous thing!" repeated Giovanni, beside himself with passion. "Thou hast done it! Thou hast blasted me! Thou hast filled my veins with poison! Thou hast made me as hateful, as ugly, as loathsome and deadly a creature as thyself—a world's wonder of hideous monstrosity! Now, if our breath be happily as fatal to ourselves as to all others, let us join our lips in one kiss of unutterable hatred, and so die!"

"What has befallen me?" murmured Beatrice, with a low moan out of her heart. "Holy Virgin, pity me, a poor heart-broken child!"

"Thou,—dost thou pray?" cried Giovanni, still with the same fiendish scorn. "Thy very prayers, as they come from thy lips, taint the atmosphere with death. Yes, yes: let us pray! Let us to church and dip our fingers in the holy water at the portal! They that come after us will perish as by a pestilence! Let us sign crosses in the air! It will be scattering curses abroad in the likeness of holy symbols!"

"Giovanni," said Beatrice, calmly, for her grief was beyond passion, "why dost thou join thyself with me thus in those terrible words? I, it is true, am the horrible thing thou namest me. But thou,—what hast thou to do, save with one other shudder at my hideous misery to go forth out of the garden and mingle with thy race, and forget that there ever crawled on earth such a monster as poor Beatrice?"

"Dost thou pretend ignorance?" asked Giovanni, scowling upon her. "Behold! this power have I gained from the pure daughter of Rappaccini."

There was a swarm of summer insects flitting through the air in search of the food promised by the flower odors of the fatal garden. They circled round Giovanni's head, and were evidently attracted towards him by the same influence which had drawn them for an instant within the sphere of several of the shrubs. He sent forth a breath among them, and smiled bitterly at Beatrice as at least a score of the insects fell dead upon the ground.

"I see it! I see it!" shrieked Beatrice. "It is my father's fatal science! No, no, Giovanni; it was not I! Never! never! I dreamed only to love thee and be with thee a little time, and so to let thee pass away, leaving but thine image in mine heart; for, Giovanni, believe it, though my body be nourished with poison, my spirit is God's creature, and craves love as its daily food. But my father,—he has united us in this fearful sympathy. Yes; spurn me, tread upon me, kill me! Oh, what is death after such words as thine? But it was not I. Not for a world of bliss would I have done it."

Giovanni's passion had exhausted itself in its outburst from his lips. There now came across him a sense, mournful, and not without tenderness, of the intimate and peculiar relationship between Beatrice and himself. They stood, as it were, in an utter solitude, which would be made none the less solitary by the densest throng of human life. Ought not, then, the desert of humanity around them to press this insulated pair closer together? If they should be cruel to one another, who was there to be kind to them? Besides, thought Giovanni, might there not still be a hope of his returning within the limits of ordinary nature, and leading Beatrice, the redeemed Beatrice, by the hand? O, weak, and selfish, and unworthy spirit, that could dream of an earthly union and earthly happiness as possible, after such deep love had been so bitterly wronged as was Beatrice's love by Giovanni's blighting words! No, no; there could be no such hope. She must pass heavily, with that broken heart, across the borders of Time—she must bathe her hurts in some fount of paradise, and forget her grief in the light of immortality, and *there* be well.

But Giovanni did not know it.

"Dear Beatrice," said he, approaching her, while she shrank away as always at his approach, but now with a different impulse, "dearest Beatrice, our fate is not yet so desperate. Behold! there is a medicine, potent, as a wise physician has assured me, and almost divine in its efficacy. It is composed of ingredients the most opposite to those by which thy awful father has brought this calamity upon thee and me. It is distilled of blessed herbs. Shall we not quaff it together, and thus be purified from evil?"

"Give it me!" said Beatrice, extending her hand to receive the little silver vial which Giovanni took from his bosom. She added, with a peculiar emphasis, "I will drink; but do thou await the result."

She put Baglioni's antidote to her lips; and, at the same moment, the figure of Rappaccini emerged from the portal and came slowly towards the marble fountain. As he drew near, the pale man of science seemed to gaze with a triumphant expression at the beautiful youth and maiden, as might an artist who should spend his life in achieving a picture or a group of statuary and finally be satisfied with his success. He paused; his bent form grew erect with conscious power; he spread out his hands over them in the attitude of a father imploring a blessing upon his children; but those were the same hands that had thrown poison into the stream of their lives. Giovanni trembled. Beatrice shuddered nervously, and pressed her hand upon her heart.

"My daughter," said Rappaccini, "thou art no longer lonely in the world. Pluck one of those precious gems from thy sister shrub and bid thy bridegroom wear it in his bosom. It will not harm him now. My science and the sympathy between thee and him have so wrought within his system that he now stands apart from common men, as thou dost, daughter of my pride and triumph, from ordinary women. Pass on, then, through the world, most dear to one another and dreadful to all besides!"

"My father," said Beatrice, feebly,—and still as she spoke she kept her hand upon her heart,—"wherefore didst thou inflict this miserable doom upon thy child?"

"Miserable!" exclaimed Rappaccini. "What mean you, foolish girl? Dost thou deem it misery to be endowed with marvellous gifts against which no power nor strength could avail an enemy—misery, to be able to quell the mightiest with a breath—misery, to be as terrible as thou art beautiful? Wouldst thou, then, have preferred the condition of a weak woman, exposed to all evil and capable of none?"

"I would fain have been loved, not feared," murmured Beatrice, sinking down upon the ground. "But now it matters not. I am going, father, where the evil which thou hast striven to mingle with my being will pass away like a dream—like the fragrance of these poisonous flowers, which will no longer taint my breath among the flowers of Eden. Farewell, Giovanni! Thy words of hatred are like lead within my heart; but they, too, will fall away as I ascend. Oh, was there not, from the first, more poison in thy nature than in mine?"

To Beatrice,—so radically had her earthly part been wrought upon by Rappaccini's skill,—as poison had been life, so the powerful antidote was death; and thus the poor victim of man's ingenuity and of thwarted nature, and of the fatality that attends all such efforts of perverted wisdom, perished there, at the feet of her father and Giovanni. just at that moment Professor Pietro Baglioni looked forth from the window, and called loudly, in a tone of triumph mixed with horror, to the thunderstricken man of science,—

"Rappaccini! Rappaccini! and is *this* the upshot of your experiment!"

1844

For Practice

1. "Rappaccini's Daughter" begins with a framing device. (*Aubépine* is French for "Hawthorne" and the second paragraph is a mock survey of Hawthorne's own career.) What rhetorical purpose does this frame serve? Why do you think Hawthorne used it?

2. How does Hawthorne describe Beatrice? How does this description affect your view of her motivations throughout the story? Is she a sympathetic character? Why or why not?

3. How does Hawthorne describe Giovanni? How does this description affect your view of his motivations throughout the story? Is he a sympathetic character? Why or why not?

4. "Rappaccini's Daughter" presents three separate descriptions of Rappaccini's garden: Giovanni's initial impressions, his account of the garden on the next day, and his narration of his first entrance into the garden. Reread each of these passages in the story, noting which words standout for you in each description. How do these words create a specific mood in each passage? What is the mood of each passage? Use the concept of qualitative progression (see Glossary) to analyze these passages. Does the changing mood in these passages constitute an argument? What is that argument?

5. Rappaccini seems to argue for a vision of science as a nonmoral study of nature, as an investigation that disregards human emotion and interests. Does the story as a whole agree with this view? Do Beatrice's last words affect the other characters' indictments of Rappaccini's experiments? If so, how?

London

William Blake

William Blake (1757–1827) grew up in a Soho London community of artisans and tradespeople. He was apprenticed to an engraver in 1772, and after his apprenticeship, worked to establish a reputation as an artistic engraver and visionary poet. Blake's work was strongly influenced by his reading of the Bible and other works on spirituality, and through his studies, he came to believe that the opposition of positive and negative forces is essential to human existence. This view of the necessity of what Blake called 'contraries' is central to his work. Blake also maintained a strong belief in the prophetic possibility of art, and his work is imbued with visionary sensibilities.

The poem "London" appeared in the 1794 volume Songs of Experience, *the companion to the 1789* Songs of Innocence. *In addition to writing the* Songs *and designing the illustrations for each volume, Blake produced and printed these works himself through a labor-intensive etching and coloring technique he developed specifically for the purpose of creating illuminated prints and books. In this way, Blake was able to maintain creative control of the entire book-making process without the intervention of commercial publishers. However, this approach to bookmaking limited the number of copies which were produced and thus restricted sales and profits.*

I wander through each chartered street,
Near where the chartered Thames does flow,
And mark in every face I meet
Marks of weakness, marks of woe.

In every cry of every man,   5
In every infant's cry of fear,
In every voice, in every ban,
The mind-forged manacles I hear.

How the chimney-sweeper's cry
Every black'ning church appalls   10
And the hapless soldier's sigh
Runs in blood down palace walls.

But most through midnight streets I hear
How the youthful harlot's curse
Blasts the new born infants tear   15
And blights with plagues the marriage hearse.

For Practice

1. Consider this poem in relationship to the "Chimney Sweeper" poems appearing in Unit Four in this volume. What images of urban industrial life do the poems share? How do these images compare with representations of urban life in other literary works and films with which you are familiar?

2. How might this poem be read as an expression of concern with religious or social problems? What visionary or prophetic qualities does the poem have? How does it illustrate Blake's sense of 'contraries'? (See page 346 for a further discussion of Blake's contraries.)

3. How does the poem's theme relate to the title of the volume in which it originally appeared, *Songs of Experience*?

4. Blake uses powerful images to underscore his argument in this text. What is Blake's argument and how do the phrases "mind-forged manacles," "black-'ning Church" and "marriage hearse" work as a rhetorical appeal?

Riders to the Sea

John Millington Synge

In 1898, on the advice of William Butler Yeats, one of Ireland's most respected poets, J.M. Synge (1871–1909) journeyed to the Aran Islands off the west coast of Ireland. It was here that Synge, an upper middle class, highly educated novice writer gained his appreciation for the Irish language and the Irish-influenced English dialect spoken by the impoverished Aran islanders. He wrote about his many subsequent visits to this rocky, isolated land in a memoir, The Aran Islands, *and made the lives and language of the people who lived there the subjects of several plays, including "Riders to the Sea".*

The one-act play, first performed in Dublin in 1904, focuses on a family whose existence is shaped by the harsh landscape and marginal economy of an island culture. The dialogue contains phrases and rhythms particular to the Aran Islands dialect, and the action reflects aspects of the islanders' traditional beliefs and concerns. The sea is an omnipresent and seemingly malevolent force; it is both the cause of grief and the means by which the characters make their livelihoods.

Persons in the Play

*First performed at the Molesworth Hall, Dublin,
February 25, 1904.*

MAURYA (an old woman)	HONOR LAVELLE
BARTLEY (her son)	W .G. FAY
CATHLEEN (her daughter)	SARAH ALLGOOD
NORA (a younger daughter)	EMMA VERNON
MEN AND WOMEN	

Scene: *An Island off the West of Ireland.*
(Cottage kitchen, with nets, oil-skins, spinning wheel, some new boards standing by the wall, etc. CATHLEEN, *a girl of about twenty, finishes kneading cake, and puts it down in the pot-oven by the fire, then wipes her hands, and begins to spin at the wheel. Nora, a young girl, puts her head in at the door.)*

NORA *(in a low voice):* Where is she?
CATHLEEN: She's lying down, God help her, and may be sleeping, if she's able.

[Nora comes in softly, and takes a bundle from under her shawl.]

CATHLEEN *(spinning the wheel rapidly):* What is it you have?

NORA: The young priest is after bringing them. It's a shirt and a plain stocking were got off a drowned man in Donegal.

[Cathleen stops her wheel with a sudden movement, and leans out to listen.]

NORA: We're to find out if it's Michael's they are, some time herself will be down looking by the sea.

CATHLEEN: How would they be Michael's, Nora. How would he go the length of that way to the far north?

NORA: The young priest says he's known the like of it. "If it's Michael's they are," says he, "you can tell herself he's got a clean burial by the grace of God, and if they're not his, let no one say a word about them, for she'll be getting her death," says he, "with crying and lamenting."

[The door which NORA *half closed is blown open by a gust of wind.]*

CATHLEEN *(looking out anxiously):* Did you ask him would he stop Bartley going this day with the horses to the Galway fair?

NORA: "I won't stop him," says he, "but let you not be afraid. Herself does be saying prayers half through the night, and the Almighty God won't leave her destitute," says he, "with no son living."

CATHLEEN: Is the sea bad by the white rocks, Nora?

NORA: Middling bad, God help us. There's a great roaring in the west, and it's worse it'll be getting when the tide's turned to the wind.

[She goes over to the table with the bundle.]

Shall I open it now?

CATHLEEN: Maybe she'd wake up on us, and come in before we'd done. *(Coming to the table.)* It's a long time we'll be, and the two of us crying.

NORA *(goes to the inner door and listens):* She's moving about on the bed. She'll be coming in a minute.

CATHLEEN: Give me the ladder, and I'll put them up in the turf-loft, the way she won't know of them at all, and maybe when the tide turns she'll be going down to see would he be floating from the east.

[They put the ladder against the gable of the chimney, CATHLEEN *goes up a few steps and hides the bundle in the turf-loft.* MAURYA *comes from the inner room.]*

MAURYA *(looking up at Cathleen and speaking querulously):* Isn't it turf enough you have for this day and evening?

CATHLEEN: There's a cake baking at the fire for a short space *(throwing down the turf)* and Bartley will want it when the tide turns if he goes to Connemara.

[Nora picks up the turf and puts it round the pot-oven.]

MAURYA *(sitting down on a stool at the fire):* He won't go this day with the wind rising from the south and west. He won't go this day, for the young priest will stop him surely.

NORA: He'll not stop him, mother, and I heard Eamon Simon and Stephen Pheety and Colum Shawn saying he would go.

MAURYA: Where is he itself?

NORA: He went down to see would there be another boat sailing in the week, and I'm thinking it won't be long till he's here now, for the tide's turning at the green head, and the hooker's tacking from the east.

CATHLEEN: I hear some one passing the big stones.

NORA *(looking out):* He's coming now, and he in a hurry.

BARTLEY *(Comes in and looks round the room. Speaking sadly and quietly):* Where is the bit of new rope, Cathleen, was bought in Connemara?

CATHLEEN *(coming down):* Give it to him, Nora; it's on a nail by the white boards. I hung it up this morning, for the pig with the black feet was eating it.

NORA *(giving him a rope):* Is that it, Bartley?

MAURYA: You'd do right to leave that rope, Bartley, hanging by the boards. *(Bartley takes the rope.)* It will be wanting in this place, I'm telling you, if Michael is washed up to-morrow morning, or the next morning, or any morning in the week, for it's a deep grave we'll make him by the grace of God.

BARTLEY *(beginning to work with the rope):* I've no halter the way I can ride down on the mare, and I must go now quickly. This is the one boat going for two weeks or beyond it, and the fair will be a good fair for horses I heard them saying below.

MAURYA: It's a hard thing they'll be saying below if the body is washed up and there's no man in it to make the coffin, and I after giving a big price for the finest white boards you'd find in Connemara.

[She looks round at the boards.]

BARTLEY: How would it be washed up, and we after looking each day for nine days, and a strong wind blowing a while back from the west and south?

MAURYA: If it wasn't found itself, that wind is raising the sea, and there was a star up against the moon, and it rising in the night. If it was a hundred horses, or a thousand horses you had itself, what is the price of a thousand horses against a son where there is one son only?

BARTLEY *(working at the halter, to CATHLEEN):* Let you go down each day, and see the sheep aren't jumping in on the rye, and if the jobber comes you can sell the pig with the black feet if there is a good price going.

MAURYA: How would the like of her get a good price for a pig?

BARTLEY *(to CATHLEEN):* If the west wind holds with the last bit of the moon let you and Nora get up weed enough for another cock for the kelp. It's hard set we'll be from this day with no one in it but one man to work.

MAURYA: It's hard set we'll be surely the day you're drownd'd with the rest. What way will I live and the girls with me, and I an old woman looking for the grave?

[BARTLEY lays down the halter, takes off his old coat, and puts on a newer one of the same flannel.]

BARTLEY *(to NORA):* Is she coming to the pier?

NORA *(looking out):* She's passing the green head and letting fall her sails.

BARTLEY *(getting his purse and tobacco):* I'll have half an hour to go down, and you'll see me coming again in two days, or in three days, or maybe in four days if the wind is bad.

MAURYA *(turning round to the fire, and putting her shawl over her head):* Isn't it a hard and cruel man won't hear a word from an old woman, and she holding him from the sea?

CATHLEEN: It's the life of a young man to be going on the sea, and who would listen to an old woman with one thing and she saying it over?

BARTLEY *(taking the halter):* I must go now quickly. I'll ride down on the red mare, and the gray pony'll run behind me. . . . The blessing of God on you.

[He goes out.]

MAURYA *(crying out as he is in the door):* He's gone now, God spare us, and we'll not see him again. He's gone now, and when the black night is falling I'll have no son left me in the world.

CATHLEEN: Why wouldn't you give him your blessing and he looking round in the door? Isn't it sorrow enough is on every one in this house without your sending him out with an unlucky word behind him, and a hard word in his ear?

[MAURYA takes up the tongs and begins raking the fire aimlessly without looking round.]

NORA *(turning towards her):* You're taking away the turf from the cake.

CATHLEEN *(crying out):* The Son of God forgive us, Nora, we're after forgetting his bit of bread.

[She comes over to the fire.]

NORA: And it's destroyed he'll be going till dark night, and he after eating nothing since the sun went up.

CATHLEEN *(turning the cake out of the oven):* It's destroyed he'll be, surely. There's no sense left on any person in a house where an old woman will be talking for ever.

[MAURYA sways herself on her stool.]

CATHLEEN *(cutting off some of the bread and rolling it in a cloth; to Maurya):* Let you go down now to the spring well and give him this and he passing. You'll see him then and the dark word will be broken, and you can say "God speed you," the way he'll be easy in his mind.

MAURYA *(taking the bread):* Will I be in it as soon as himself?

CATHLEEN: If you go now quickly.

MAURYA *(standing up unsteadily):* It's hard set I am to walk.

CATHLEEN *(looking at her anxiously):* Give her the stick, Nora, or maybe she'll slip on the big stones.

NORA: What stick?

CATHLEEN: The stick Michael brought from Connemara.

MAURYA *(taking a stick NORA gives her):* In the big world the old people do be leaving things after them for their sons and children, but in this place it is the young men do be leaving things behind for them that do be old.

[She goes out slowly. NORA goes over to the ladder.]

CATHLEEN: Wait, Nora, maybe she'd turn back quickly. She's that sorry, God help her, you wouldn't know the thing she'd do.

NORA: Is she gone round by the bush?

CATHLEEN *(looking out):* She's gone now. Throw it down quickly, for the Lord knows when she'll be out of it again.

NORA *(getting the bundle from the loft):* The young priest said he'd be passing to-morrow, and we might go down and speak to him below if it's Michael's they are surely.

CATHLEEN *(taking the bundle):* Did he say what way they were found?

NORA *(coming down):* "There were two men," says he, "and they rowing round with poteen before the cocks crowed, and the oar of one of them caught the body, and they passing the black cliffs of the north."

CATHLEEN *(trying to open the bundle):* Give me a knife, Nora, the string's perished with the salt water, and there's a black knot on it you wouldn't loosen in a week.

NORA *(giving her a knife):* I've heard tell it was a long way to Donegal.

CATHLEEN *(cutting the string):* It is surely. There was a man in here a while ago—the man sold us that knife—and he said if you set off walking from the rocks beyond, it would be seven days you'd be in Donegal.

NORA: And what time would a man take, and he floating?

[CATHLEEN *opens the bundle and takes out a bit of a stocking.*
They look at them eagerly.]

CATHLEEN *(in a low voice):* The Lord spare us, Nora! isn't it a queer hard thing to say if it's his they are surely?

NORA: I'll get his shirt off the hook the way we can put the one flannel on the other. *(She looks through some clothes hanging in the corner.)* It's not with them, Cathleen, and where will it be?

CATHLEEN: I'm thinking Bartley put it on him in the morning, for his own shirt was heavy with the salt in it *(pointing to the corner).* There's a bit of a sleeve was of the same stuff. Give me that and it will do.

[NORA *brings it to her and they compare the flannel.*]

CATHLEEN: It's the same stuff, Nora; but if it is itself aren't there great rolls of it in the shops of Galway, and isn't it many another man may have a shirt of it as well as Michael himself?

NORA *(who has taken up the stocking and counted the stitches, crying out):* It's Michael, Cathleen, it's Michael; God spare his soul, and what will herself say when she hears this story, and Bartley on the sea?

CATHLEEN *(taking the stocking):* It's a plain stocking.

NORA: It's the second one of the third pair I knitted, and I put up three score stitches, and I dropped four of them.

CATHLEEN *(counts the stitches):* It's that number is in it *(crying out).* Ah, Nora, isn't it a bitter thing to think of him floating that way to the far north, and no one to keen him but the black hags that do be flying on the sea?

NORA *(Swinging herself round, and throwing out her arms on the clothes):* And isn't it a pitiful thing when there is nothing left of a man who was a great rower and fisher, but a bit of an old shirt and a plain stocking?

CATHLEEN *(after an instant):* Tell me is herself coming, Nora? I hear a little sound on the path.

NORA *(looking out):* She is, Cathleen. She's coming up to the door.

CATHLEEN: Put these things away before she'll come in. Maybe it's easier she'll be after giving her blessing to Bartley, and we won't let on we've heard anything the time he's on the sea.

NORA *(helping CATHLEEN to close the bundle):* We'll put them here in the corner.

[*They put them into a hole in the chimney corner.*
CATHLEEN *goes back to the spinning-wheel.*]

NORA: Will she see it was crying I was?

CATHLEEN: Keep your back to the door the way the light'll not be on you.

[Nora sits down at the chimney corner, with her back to the door.
Maurya comes in very slowly, without looking at the girls, and goes over to her
stool at the other side of the fire. The cloth with the bread is still in her hand.
The girls look at each other, and Nora points to the bundle of bread.]

CATHLEEN *(after spinning for a moment):* You didn't give him his bit of bread?

[Maurya begins to keen softly, without turning round.]

CATHLEEN: Did you see him riding down?

[Maurya goes on keening.]

CATHLEEN *(a little impatiently):* God forgive you; isn't it a better thing to raise your
voice and tell what you seen, than to be making lamentation for a thing that's
done? Did you see Bartley, I'm saying to you.

MAURYA *(with a weak voice):* My heart's broken from this day.

CATHLEEN *(as before):* Did you see Bartley?

MAURYA: I seen the fearfulest thing.

CATHLEEN *(leaves her wheel and looks out):* God forgive you; he's riding the mare now
over the green head, and the gray pony behind him.

MAURYA *(starts, so that her shawl falls back from her head and shows her white tossed
hair. With a frightened voice):* The gray pony behind him.

CATHLEEN *(coming to the fire):* What is it ails you, at all?

MAURYA *(speaking very slowly):* I've seen the fearfulest thing any person has seen, since
the day Bride Dara seen the dead man with the child in his arms.

CATHLEEN and NORA: Uah.

[They crouch down in front of the old woman at the fire.]

NORA: Tell us what it is you seen.

MAURYA: I went down to the spring well, and I stood there saying a prayer to myself.
Then Bartley came along, and he riding on the red mare with the gray pony behind
him. *(She puts up her hands, as if to hide something from her eyes.)* The Son of
God spare us, Nora!

CATHLEEN: What is it you seen.

MAURYA: I seen Michael himself.

CATHLEEN *(speaking softly):* You did not, mother; It wasn't Michael you seen, for his
body is after being found in the far north, and he's got a clean burial by the grace
of God.

MAURYA *(a little defiantly):* I'm after seeing him this day, and he riding and galloping.
Bartley came first on the red mare; and I tried to say "God speed you," but something choked the words in my throat. He went by quickly; and "the blessing of God
on you," says he, and I could say nothing. I looked up then, and I crying, at the
gray pony, and there was Michael upon it—with fine clothes on him, and new
shoes on his feet.

CATHLEEN *(begins to keen):* It's destroyed we are from this day. It's destroyed, surely.

NORA: Didn't the young priest say the Almighty God wouldn't leave her destitute with
no son living?

MAURYA *(in a low voice, but clearly):* It's little the like of him knows of the sea. . . .
Bartley will be lost now, and let you call in Eamon and make me a good coffin out
of the white boards, for I won't live after them. I've had a husband, and a husband's
father, and six sons in this house—six fine men, though it was a hard birth I had

with every one of them and they coming to the world—and some of them were found and some of them were not found, but they're gone now the lot of them. ... There were Stephen, and Shawn, were lost in the great wind, and found after in the Bay of Gregory of the Golden Mouth, and carried up the two of them on the one plank, and in by that door.

[She pauses for a moment, the girls start as if they heard something through the door that is half open behind them.]

NORA *(in a whisper):* Did you hear that, Cathleen? Did you hear a noise in the northeast?

CATHLEEN *(in a whisper):* There's some one after crying out by the seashore.

MAURYA *(continues without hearing anything):* There was Sheamus and his father, and his own father again, were lost in a dark night, and not a stick or sign was seen of them when the sun went up. There was Patch after was drowned out of a curagh that turned over. I was sitting here with Bartley, and he a baby, lying on my two knees, and I seen two women, and three women, and four women coming in, and they crossing themselves, and not saying a word . I looked out then, and there were men coming after them, and they holding a thing in the half of a red sail, and water dripping out of it—it was a dry day, Nora—and leaving a track to the door.

[She pauses again with her hand stretched out towards the door.
It opens softly and old women begin to come in, crossing themselves on the threshold, and kneeling down in front of the stage with red petticoats over their heads.]

MAURYA *(half in a dream, to* CATHLEEN*):* Is it Patch, or Michael, or what is it at all?

CATHLEEN: Michael is after being found in the far north, and when he is found there how could he be here in this place?

MAURYA: There does be a power of young men floating round in the sea, and what way would they know if it was Michael they had, or another man like him, for when a man is nine days in the sea, and the wind blowing, it's hard set his own mother would be to say what man was it.

CATHLEEN: It's Michael, God spare him, for they're after sending us a bit of his clothes from the far north.

[She reaches out and hands MAURYA *the clothes that belonged to* MICHAEL.
MAURYA *stands up slowly and takes them in her hands. Nora looks out.]*

NORA: They're carrying a thing among them and there's water dripping out of it and leaving a track by the big stones.

CATHLEEN *(in a whisper to the women who have come in):* Is it Bartley it is?

ONE OF THE WOMEN: It is surely, God rest his soul.

[Two younger women come in and pull out the table. Then men carry in the body of BARTLEY, *laid on a plank, with a bit of a sail over it, and lay it on the table.]*

CATHLEEN *(to the women, as they are doing so):* What way was he drowned?

ONE OF THE WOMEN: The gray pony knocked him into the sea, and he was washed out where there is a great surf on the white rocks.

[MAURYA has gone over and knelt down at the head of the table. The women are keening softly and swaying themselves with a slow movement. CATHLEEN and NORA kneel at the other end of the table. The men kneel near the door.]

MAURYA *(raising her head and speaking as if she did not see the people around her):* They're all gone now, and there isn't anything more the sea can do to me. . . . I'll have no call now to be up crying and praying when the wind breaks from the south, and you can hear the surf is in the east, and the surf is in the west, making a great stir with the two noises, and they hitting one on the other. I'll have no call now to be going down and getting Holy Water in the dark nights after Samhain, and I won't care what way the sea is when the other women will be keening. *(To Nora.)* Give me the Holy Water, Nora, there's a small sup still on the dresser.

*[*Nora *gives it to her.]*

Maurya *(drops* Michael's *clothes across* Bartley's *feet, and sprinkles the Holy Water over him):* It isn't that I haven't prayed for you, Bartley, to the Almighty God. It isn't that I haven't said prayers in the dark night till you wouldn't know what I'd be saying; but it's a great rest I'll have now, and it's time surely. It's a great rest I'll have now, and great sleeping in the long nights after Samhain, if it's only a bit of wet flour we do have to eat, and maybe a fish that would be stinking.

[She kneels down again, crossing herself, and saying prayers under her breath.]

Cathleen *(to an old man):* Maybe yourself and Eamon would make a coffin when the sun rises. We have fine white boards herself bought, God help her, thinking Michael would be found, and I have a new cake you can eat while you'll be working.

The Old Man *(looking at the boards):* Are there nails with them?

Cathleen: There are not, Colum; we didn't think of the nails.

Another Man: It's a great wonder she wouldn't think of the nails, and all the coffins she's seen made already.

Cathleen: It's getting old she is, and broken.

*[*Maurya *stands up again very slowly and spreads out the pieces of* Michael's *clothes beside the body, sprinkling them with the last of the Holy Water.]*

Nora *(in a whisper to* Cathleen*):* She's quiet now and easy; but the day Michael was drowned you could hear her crying out from this to the spring well. It's fonder she was of Michael, and would any one have thought that?

Cathleen *(slowly and clearly):* An old woman will be soon tired with anything she will do, and isn't it nine days herself is after crying and keening, and making great sorrow in the house?

Maurya *(puts the empty cup mouth downwards on the table, and lays her hands together on* Bartley's *feet):* They're all together this time, and the end is come. May the Almighty God have mercy on Bartley's soul, and on Michael's soul, and on the souls of Sheamus and Patch, and Stephen and Shawn *(bending her head)*; and may He have mercy on my soul, Nora, and on the soul of every one is left living in the world.

[She pauses, and the keen rises a little more loudly from the women, then sinks away.]

Maurya *(continuing):* Michael has a clean burial in the far north, by the grace of the Almighty God. Bartley will have a fine coffin out of the white boards, and a deep grave surely. What more can we want than that? No man at all can be living for ever, and we must be satisfied.

[She kneels down again and the curtain falls slowly.]

For Practice

1. Describe the experience of reading a play written in the dialect Synge has employed in *Riders to the Sea*. How does the dialect help to create your sense of the characters in this text? Do you think that Synge's intended audience was people who spoke this dialect? If not, what do you imagine might be the effect of this dialect on an audience?

2. In the stage directions, Synge lists the following set pieces: "nets, oilskins, spinning wheel, some new boards standing by the wall." What is the significance of these details? What do they tell the audience about the characters' situation?

3. Describe Maurya's understanding of fate and loss. Do you think this understanding corresponds with that of the author? Why or why not?

4. Some scholars have observed that the three female characters may be said to represent the Fates of classical mythology, or the Wyrds of Anglo-Saxon tradition. What do these characters from ancient tradition symbolize? If the three female characters really do represent the Fates or the Wyrds, how does that affect your understanding of the argument of this play?

5. The culture of a small community on the Aran Islands at the end of the 19th century is a very different from the highly technological culture we inhabit 100 years later. What is the relationship of the island community depicted by Synge to the world beyond its shores? To our own twentieth-century culture?

Back to Love Canal: Recycled Homes, Rebuilt Dreams

Verlyn Klinkenborg

Verlyn Klinkenborg (b. 1953) is a writer and teacher of creative writing at Harvard. He is the author of two non-fiction books. Making Hay *(1986) is a collection of essays in which Klinkenborg reflects on his experiences on a Minnesota farm.* The Last Fine Time *(1991) is a history of a Buffalo, New York, neighborhood bar owned by his father. The book is a memoir, not only of the bar, but of the Polish neighborhood where it is located and the changes there between 1947 and 1970. Klinkenborg has also published essays in several respected American journals.*

This essay first appeared in Harper's *magazine in March 1991, ten years after the Love Canal neighborhood was condemned when it was discovered that the houses were built on a toxic waste dump. In this essay, Klinkenborg reflects on the history of Love Canal and speculates about its future. As you read, consider the relationships between neighborhoods and place, and between neighborhoods and the larger cultural and governmental entities to which they belong. Notice how Klinkenborg describes the physical environment surrounding the Love Canal. Compare his description of the natural world to his description of the interior of the building where he listens to the sales pitch for the Love Canal property.*

They wore walking shorts, but school had started and I could feel the Niagara Frontier tightening up for autumn, which is only a pause before winter here. I drove from Buffalo through Tonawanda and Wheatfield to the city of Niagara Falls, past the airport, past the few small farms still standing on Cayuga Drive. Around me lay suburbs and malls and, farther north, the beginnings of the fruit belt, the cherry and apple orchards that border Lake Ontario. I crossed the bridge over Bergholtz Creek and entered a quiet residential district, where children had just trailed off to school. The everyday hung over lawns and sidewalks like leaf smoke, creating a sense of protective closure, insulation against the unexpected.

A few blocks away, indiscernible, the Niagara River flowed—opaque, glacial, morbid, bound for its tumult a mile or two downstream. No one moves to Niagara Falls for the falls. It is not that kind of city and not that kind of attraction. Parts of the city sizzle and stink with industry, with refineries, power stations, chemical plants. The Power

Vista, as they call it, and the hydroelectric reservoirs—clean arcs of concrete—seem to mock the casual shambles of rock that shape the falls. The city fathers still debate how plainly to mark the route to the precipice. Confusion is profitable. The falls should come as a surprise, they seem to feel.

I followed the map to Frontier Avenue in the easternmost section of the city and found a discrepancy. The map showed 97th and 99th streets running north from Frontier Avenue to Colvin Boulevard. In reality 97th and 99th streets and the houses on both sides of them, together with the cross streets of Read Avenue and Wheatfield Avenue, as well as the 99th Street School and its playground and its parking lot, were demolished in 1982 and 1983 and lie buried under many tons of sod, clay, and high-density polyethylene in what is now called the "Canal Site Containment Area." The sod, a well-kept grass field that mounds attractively in the middle, is surrounded by an eight-foot chain-link fence and pierced by vertical fluorescent-orange pipes. Beneath the field lies the Love Canal, 3,000 feet long, 80 to 100 feet wide, and 15 to 40 feet deep, where between 1942 and 1953 the Hooker Electrochemical Company dumped nearly 22,000 tons of chemical waste, much of it toxic, including, as one of the reporters who broke the story of Love Canal wrote, as much dioxin as fell upon Vietnam in the form of Agent Orange.

"Love Canal," "Hooker Chemical," "Toxic Waste Dump"—these phrases return in a lump after so much time, so much intervening history. Many persons—perhaps most persons—now think that the drama of Love Canal lay in the negligent deposit of chemicals, the unwitting exposure to those chemicals of nearby residents, the ultimate relocation of hundreds of families. They forget that Love Canal became a national story, a byword, because it radicalized apparently ordinary people. Love Canal severed the bond between citizens and their city, their state, and their country. The battle there was fought over that bond, and it was fought in public, through protest marches and press releases, because the public, not the state, was at risk.

I came upon Love Canal too suddenly. It was like stepping out of a lodgepole forest onto the site of an old bum. I wanted a transition. One minute I was savoring the taste of the ordinary, and it lulled me, as it is meant to do. Then, abruptly, almost in the instant I looked up from my map, the streets fell empty of cars, people, sound. The grass had grown long, and the hedges were untrimmed; fallen branches lay ungathered in yards, and at the curb piles of brush moldered here and there. I turned up 100th Street. Houses lined only its east side. The electric meter had been removed from every house. Sidewalks and driveways were turning to rubble. Nearly all the windows had been boarded up, and on most of the doors a number had been chalked in black, a number that was once an address but now seemed more like an inventory mark. At 723 a yellow lawn chair sat alone on a concrete porch, facing the chain-link fence and mounded field to the west. There were houses with rock-faced fronts and metal awnings, with brick and shingle facades, simple clapboard houses redone in aluminum siding, houses as plain as one ever finds in the suburbs. They were poignant only because they were deserted.

These were not the houses that lay across the street from Love Canal in the 1970s. These were the houses that lay across the street from the backyards of the houses that once lay across the street from the houses whose backyards once lined the canal. Everything west of 100th Street for a quarter mile was buried and fenced. When the buyout of homes at Love Canal was finally settled a decade ago, the state of New York found itself the owner of nearly all the property within what came to be called the EDA, the Emergency Declaration Area: a district one mile long and a half mile wide containing 789 single houses. Now, in order to recoup some of its losses and to restore the neighborhood to life, the state is offering some of those houses for sale through the Love Canal Area Revitalization Agency. You can buy one of the houses LCARA has chosen to offer, or you can deposit one hundred dollars and LCARA will order an appraisal on a vacant house of your own choosing. But to settle at Love Canal, you'll have to forget how these houses came to be empty. You'll have to pretend that the past has little meaning.

Near Frontier Avenue, the houses are old and rural in character, barely salable. But a mile to the north, above Colvin Boulevard, near Bergholtz Creek, and a block or two away from the canal, the streets are in better condition and the houses are more likely to be modern in an early Sixties manner and built of brick. These are the houses LCARA had decided to sell. On 98th Street, which dead-ends at the canal, I stopped and inspected 1071, a small ranch, 1,026 square feet, with gray shingle siding and a pink door. The asking price was forty-eight thousand dollars. That included a long list of renovations yet to be done by LCARA: new driveway, new insulation, new external doors, new paint. I examined 1076, across the street—a gray ranch with a breezeway, two bedrooms, one bath, 1,144 square feet, corner lot, patio, barbecue pit, sixty thousand dollars. It had a clean, urbane fireplace notched into the end of a wall like a missing cornerstone. Behind it flows Black Creek, from whose bed dioxin-contaminated sediments were scraped a year ago as part of the Love Canal remediation plan.

On 98th Street, a telephone lineman was preparing to restore service. A block away, an LCARA maintenance man was working with a languor that looked official. A man who had seen me inspecting houses walked over and began to talk. He wore a blue work shirt and a trim gray beard and was taking the day off from painting his house because of the threat of rain. He was a longtime resident, one of the few persons who had not accepted the federal buyout. I said he must be happy to be getting neighbors again at last.

"Who needs neighbors?" he said. "I like it the way it is. Nice and quiet."

The lineman joined the conversation. They talked about a mysterious section of Love Canal buried under a golf course in another part of town. The reason it had never been dug up, they suggested, was best expressed by rubbing the thumb over the first two fingers in a lucrative motion. The conversation became a workshop in worldly wisdom, a lesson in lump-taking. They talked of people who had lived "inside the fence" and "outside the fence" as if the fence around Love Canal had always been there and as if having lived inside the fence conferred a special authority where suffering was concerned. The talk grew strong. Environmental activists were in it for themselves, the government was a patsy, the chemical industry had been good for the city, life was full of risks, you took your chances.

Are the houses safe? I asked.

"I never moved," said the resident.

"What's safe?" said the lineman.

To find out I drove to 9820 Colvin Boulevard, a ranch house typical of the kind LCARA is selling, perfect for a young family or a retired couple. Michael Podd, the New York State Department of Environmental Conservation's citizen-participation specialist, sat at his desk in someone's former living room. An assistant administrator sat not far away at a desk in someone's former dining room. Podd gave me a sheaf of official documents. He took me back into someone's former bedroom and showed me an elaborate three-dimensional model, complete with geological strata and transparent overlays depicting the lapse of time. He explained what happened at Love Canal in more informal language than that used in the official documents. It was a sad story, full of good intentions gone awry but with a great evil remedied in the end. "I don't tell people what's safe or not," Podd concluded. "My job is to give them enough information so that they can make up their own minds." From his desk, Podd could look directly across the street to the Canal Site Containment Area, or to what LCARA calls the "reservation," Love Canal itself, capped and fenced and monitored through groundwater wells. It was like looking at the buffer zone of a minimum-security prison.

I visited the LCARA sales office. The realtor there was a good-humored, slender man named Leonard Rinallo, seventeen years in the real estate business. He wore a mustache and white pants and drove a Mercury Cougar, which he parked in the driveway of 1010 96th Street, another small ranch house. Someone's former living room, where in 1978, 1979, or 1980 someone might have watched the news coverage of the emotional protests occurring a block away at Love Canal, was now Leonard Rinallo's office. A brightly colored "Adopted Land Use Diagram" was pinned to the wall. Outlined in yellow was "Black Creek Village," the new name for the cluster of streets north of the Canal Site Containment Area. Future parkland was outlined in green, planned residential development in orange. In the red areas east of the canal—areas the present health commissioner has deemed uninhabitable (though several families live there)—plans are afoot for commercial and light industrial development. The empty houses on 100th, 101st, and 102nd streets will eventually be destroyed.

The interior of the LCARA sales office was resonantly empty. It had the midmorning feel I have always associated with the homes of neat, childless housewives, for whom the day's work is done quickly and a vacancy fashioned by ten o'clock. But there was no television, and there were no neighbors, and a realtor's desk stood where a sofa might once have been. By chance, I visited Rinallo on the day after the state supreme court threw out a plea brought by several environmental groups for an injunction against house sales at Love Canal. He expressed measured happiness with the decision, renewed satisfaction with his job. Rinallo would have been more cheerful had a source of mortgages been found as well. "The banks can't redline," he said, "but they can sit on an application forever." Sales were not brisk. (In the coming months, sales would improve. By early November, thirteen houses were under contract though still awaiting financing. A coalition of environmental groups including the National Resources Defense Council would later sue to stop the sales.)

Rinallo treated me like a customer. He gave me a state-prepared packet of information and took me back into someone's former bedroom, where he played an LCARA sales video for me. It outlined the slow but inexorable process that led from the digging of the canal by William T. Love for a turn-of-the-century model industrial city to the moment when the first new homeowner in the revitalization plan turns the key in the lock of his newly refurbished house. The video was worth watching to see pictures of Love Canal in the Thirties, when it was just a long pond. It was worth watching to hear the cheerful music and the narrator's march-of-time voice and to sense the high pitch of official optimism. (The video is currently being revised. The state attorney general's office protested the video's description of Love Canal as a suitable dumpsite for its era, a problem that Rinallo described as "a play on words type thing." The state may merely be protecting its own litigation. Its case against Occidental Petroleum, Hooker's parent company, for its role at Love Canal has just come to trial in Buffalo after a decade of legal positioning.)

I drove back to the edge of the Canal Site Containment Area and parked. I watched the neatly groomed field that lay behind the chain-link fence. It was hard to imagine that it had once been a school and a playground and two streets full of houses. It was hard to imagine the 44 million pounds of chemical waste still lying beneath it. It was especially hard to imagine those chemicals lying on the surface of the earth, suppurating, as they had in the late Seventies, and to picture those streets filled with distraught homeowners protesting their fate and the corporate and governmental negligence that had brought it on.

Many of those homeowners—bedrock, blue-collar Americans—worked in the Niagara Falls chemical industry or had friends or relatives who did. It did not surprise all of them to learn that Hooker had dumped 22,000 tons of toxic chemicals, covered the pit, and walked away, wiping its hands. They knew that a chemical plant "is not a chocolate factory," as a Hooker official in Michigan remarked in the late Seventies. What surprised them was the discovery that an attempt had been made to shift liability for those chemicals all down the line. With a warning in the final paragraph of its 1953 deed of sale—the inadequacy of which the attorney general is testing in court, though LCARA includes the same limitation of liability in its current sales contracts— Hooker sold the canal for the sum of one dollar to the Niagara Falls Board of Education, which erected a grammar school on the site. Sensing its own legal jeopardy, the Board of Education deeded part of the property in 1960, with another annulment of liability, to the city of Niagara Falls, where, if you possessed faith in government, you would suppose liability might safely rest. But the mayor of Niagara Falls, Michael O'Laughlin—still mayor in 1990 and chairman of LCARA since 1980—told protesting homeowners, "You are hurting Niagara Falls with your publicity. There is no problem here."

Prospective buyers would visit the LCARA sales office and the Department of Environmental Conservation's Public Information Office, as I had. They would collect pamphlets and brochures. Perhaps they would read them. If they did, they might get the impression that the city, state, and federal governments had willingly initiated the chemical analyses, the health studies, the temporary removal of residents, and the final buyout of homes in the Emergency Declaration Area. They might notice that in the fact sheet on "Love Canal EDA Habitability," the New York State Department of Health said, in effect, that it was up to prospective buyers to decide whether the houses there were safe, houses offered at 15 to 20 percent less than local market prices. With a bundle of encouraging official documents under one's arm and the sight in one's eye of a fenced "reservation" and a scientific-looking leachate treatment plant, the plea of money would always prevail. A bargain is a bargain.

As I sat and stared at the vacancy that was once Love Canal, I found myself temporarily persuaded of, if not by, the state's rationality. But rationality is not always a virtue, and credulity is an old failing of mine, the residue of an upbringing in which deference meant a lot and reasonableness was more important than reason. No one ever called it tractability, that predisposition to reasonableness, but that is what it amounts to. At Love Canal, after visiting Michael Podd and Leonard Rinallo, I found myself eager again to believe what I was told because it was the least depressing choice. I wanted to feel again that the past had, been a nice place, or, conversely, that the future would be. I knew better, though not half as well as the former inhabitants of the empty houses that surrounded me.

The question naturally arises: Who would move to Love Canal? The question is imprecise. It assumes that the answer is, No one in his right mind. (It also assumes a full awareness of what happened at Love Canal.) The state of New York, through LCARA, has gone out of its way to appeal to the right-minded. Its brochures and fact sheets bear the stamp of rationality, of solid, official information. Its realtor looks like other realtors, its houses like other houses. The streets where it does its business are as quiet as the streets in brand-new developments. The right-minded may well move to Love Canal, but they will need to believe that their predecessors were wrong when they formed a homeowner's association and insisted on a government buyout of all homes in the area. Either that, or the right-minded will need to believe that the state has fixed the problem. The past was a nice place. Or the future will be.

The potential buyers of homes at Love Canal are middle-aged. They are young. They are mostly blue-collar workers, squeezed, as everyone is, by the rise in housing costs. They resemble no one so much as they do the people who used to live there. And what do they say about the area?

"You can't beat the price. If the neighborhood does catch on, in five or six or ten years, I've got a great investment."

"I'd like a place where there's some sense of values, where you can take pride in where you live."

"They must have cleaned it up pretty well. It's probably one of the safest places to live in Niagara Falls by now. There are problems no matter where you live in the world."

"There are chemicals all over this town. My attitude is, if you find a place where they've at least paid attention to cleaning it up, you should go."

"I think it was all a lot of hooey. This street should never have been condemned to begin with. If it was contaminated, I don't think you'd be seeing so many green trees."

"Or all these squirrels."

Who would move to Love Canal?

"Everyone's waiting for someone else," said Leonard Rinallo in September. "Most people are followers."

"Former residents are coming back," he added in November, "people from the Niagara Falls area. One man sold his home in California and bought the most expensive house we had. He's moving here in the spring. Another family with three children. They wouldn't be coming if they didn't think it was safe."

Is it safe? Beneath the "reservation," the toxins in the canal have been "contained," though no one will guarantee their perpetual containment. There is no problem here, the state implies, as it has all along. "I've got an hour-and-a-half commute to work," says Michael Podd, the citizen-participation specialist. "I'd buy a house here." Podd also told me a story about one longtime Love Canal resident who said to an interviewer, "I know what's in my backyard. Do you know what's in yours?" When the validity of the state's habitability studies is challenged, LCARA's executive director, William Broderick, says, "Just about every place is contaminated. If we shouldn't put people in here, then maybe the rest of the city should be evacuated."

Life at Love Canal halted a decade ago: Its streets are still; traffic, nonexistent. As I sat beside the fence around the canal, it seemed as if all the men were at work, all the wives shopping, all the children at school, all the grandparents still living in rural homes. The style of the houses dates back to the Fifties and early Sixties, when America was a different country. The threat of toxic contamination around me was invisible, intangible, but the sense of nostalgia was extraordinarily pungent. These deserted streets evoked an era when, as one potential home-buyer remarked, Love Canal was the "kind of place where you had street parties all the time, where you really knew the people next door. It was the kind of place where if a father was taking his kids for ice cream, he'd take the whole block along."

That man, a former resident, was describing a time when no one expected to be surprised by the presence of chemical waste in the backyard, a time in the minds of its people when government was generous and watchful, not obdurate and evasive, as it was when the Love Canal Homeowner's Association began to press for chemical analyses, medical testing, and, ultimately, the buyout of homes. What many prospective buyers see when they look at Love Canal, and what its first residents saw too, is a suburban innocence that harks back a generation or more, a neighborhood where the everyday creates a sense of protective closure. They are eager to believe, paradoxically, that everything has changed and that the past can be recaptured. The state would like to foster that faith. It is selling the past, and it hopes to purchase forgetfulness. In the informational packets and video that LCARA shows prospective buyers, there is no allusion to the ardor of homeowner's protests at Love Canal, no trace whatever of the emotions that erupted there a decade ago. The state will replace furnaces and windows and driveways, repaint and reroof and replaster the houses it sells, but it will never be able to restore innocence. That will return, briefly, when the moving vans come, when lights burn again in those houses at night.

For Practice

1. According to Klinkenborg, in what ways is the government acting irresponsibly? What evidence does he give to support this claim? What can you infer from his argument about what he believes the role of government ought to be?

2. Why do you think that blue-collar workers would be the most likely buyers of the Love Canal homes? What do you think about Klinkenborg's characterization of such workers? Look at the words he imagines them saying. Does he give a fair representation of the working class? Why or why not? Why is it important to his argument that these workers are characterized in this way?

3. The author uses many numbers in this text. How does he use them? What do numbers imply about the authority of the information one gives? What does Klinkenborg's use of numbers imply about authority?

4. After reading this article, would you move into the Love Canal area? How would you feel if today you found out that your house was sitting on top of a former toxic waste dump? Would you believe the local or federal government if they said that the area had been cleaned and was now safe to live in? Why or why not? What kind of proof, if any, would be sufficient to persuade you to move there?

5. What argument do you think Klinkenborg is making in this essay? Has this argument succeeded in persuading you?

"Repent Harlequin!" Said the Ticktockman

Harlan Ellison

Harlan Ellison (b. 1934) has written more than 1300 stories, essays, articles, and columns. He is the author of two dozen screenplays and teleplays, including the famous Star Trek *episode "The City on the Edge of Forever," and is a creative consultant for the television series* Babylon 5 *and the revival of* The Twilight Zone *series. Dust jacket biographies appearing on many of Ellison's books are as creative as what is between the covers. They record life experiences most writers, including Ellison, only dream of having, among them: hand-coloring the etchings accompanying his stories with a 64-box set of Crayolas, being sentenced to life in prison for the brutal murders of four literary nobodies, saving actor Brad Pitt from an assassin's bullet, and driving a big yellow bus for the Kenosha and Racine school districts. Ellison's work often features protagonists in direct conflict with authority and establishments of all kinds, and his trademarks of an irreverent writing style and a sharp wit are those of a seriously mischievous non-conformist.*

"'Repent Harlequin!' Said the Ticktockman" was first published in 1965 in Galaxy, *a science fiction magazine. Since then it has often been reprinted in literary anthologies and science fiction collections. Depicting a hero at odds with the sinister political establishment of a hyper-efficient, technology-dependent society, the story investigates the consequences of conformity and non-conformity in a world of authoritarian excess and absolutes. As a vision of dystopia, "Repent Harlequin!" is very much in the tradition of George Orwell's* 1984 *or Aldous Huxley's* Brave New World.

There are always those who ask, what is it all about? For those who need to ask, for those who need points sharply made, who need to know "where it's at," this:

> The mass of men serve the state thus, not as men mainly, but as machines, with their bodies. They are the standing army, and the militia, jailors, constables, posse comitatus, etc. In most cases there is no free exercise whatever of the judgment or of the moral sense; but they put themselves on a level with wood and earth and *stones;* and wooden men can perhaps be manufactured that will serve the

purpose as well. Such command no more respect than men of straw or a lump of dirt. They have the same sort of worth only as horses and dogs. Yet such as these even are commonly esteemed good citizens. Others—as most legislators, politicians, lawyers, ministers, and officeholders—serve the state chiefly with their heads; and, as they rarely make any moral distinctions, they are as likely to serve the Devil, without intending it, as God. A very few, as heroes, patriots, martyrs, reformers in the great sense, and men, serve the state with their consciences also, and so necessarily resist it for the most part; and they are commonly treated as enemies by it.

Henry David Thoreau
Civil Disobedience

That is the heart of it. Now begin in the middle, and later learn the beginning; the end will take care of itself.

But because it was the very world it was, the very world they had allowed it to *become*, for months his activities did not come to the alarmed attention of The Ones Who Kept The Machine Functioning Smoothly, the ones who poured the very best butter over the cams and mainsprings of the culture. Not until it had become obvious that somehow, someway, he had become a notoriety, a celebrity, perhaps even a hero for (what Officialdom inescapably tagged) "an emotionally disturbed segment of the populace," did they turn it over to the Ticktockman and his legal machinery. But by then, because it was the very world it was, and they had no way to predict he would happen—possibly a strain of disease long-defunct, now, suddenly, reborn in a system where immunity had been forgotten, had lapsed—he had been allowed to become too real. Now he had form and substance.

He had become a *personality*, something they had filtered out of the system many decades before. But there it was, and there *he* was, a very definitely imposing personality. In certain circles—middle-class circles—it was thought disgusting. Vulgar ostentation. Anarchistic. Shameful. In others, there was only sniggering: those strata where thought is subjugated to form and ritual, niceties, proprieties. But down below, ah, down below, where the people always needed their saints and sinners, their bread and circuses, their heroes and villains, he was considered a Bolivar; a Napoleon; a Robin Hood; a Dick Bong (Ace of Aces); a Jesus; a Jomo Kenyatta.

And at the top—where, like socially-attuned Shipwreck Kellys, every tremor and vibration threatening to dislodge the wealthy, powerful and titled from their flagpoles—he was considered a menace; a heretic; a rebel; a disgrace; a peril. He was known down the line, to the very heart-meat core, but the important reactions were high above and far below. At the very top, at the very bottom.

So his file was turned over, along with his time-card and his cardioplate, to the office of the Ticktockman.

The Ticktockman: very much over six feet tall, often silent, a soft purring man when things went timewise. The Ticktockman.

Even in the cubicles of the hierarchy, where fear was generated, seldom suffered, he was called the Ticktockman. But no one called him that to his mask.

You don't call a man a hated name, not when that man, behind his mask, is capable of revoking the minutes, the hours, the days and nights, the years of your life. He was called the Master Timekeeper to his mask. It was safer that way.

"That is *what* he is," said the Ticktockman with genuine softness, "but not *who* he is. This time-card I'm holding in my left hand has a name on it, but it is the name of *what* he is, not *who* he is. The cardioplate here in my right hand is also named, but not *whom* named, merely *what* named. Before I can exercise proper revocation, I have to know *who* this *what* is."

To his staff, all the ferrets, all the loggers, all the finks, all the commex, even the mineez, he said, "Who is this Harlequin?"

He was not purring smoothly. Timewise, it was jangle.

However, it *was* the longest speech they had ever heard him utter at one time, the staff, the ferrets, the loggers, the finks, the commex, but not the mineez, who usually weren't around to know, in any case. But even they scurried to find out.

Who is the Harlequin?

High above the third level of the city, he crouched on the humming aluminum-frame platform of the air-boat (foof! air-boat, indeed! swizzleskid is what it was, with a tow-rack jerry-rigged) and he stared down at the neat Mondrian arrangement of the buildings.

Somewhere nearby, he could hear the metronomic left-right-left of the 2:47 PM shift, entering the Timkin roller-bearing plant in their sneakers. A minute later, precisely, he heard the softer right-left-right of the 5:00 AM formation, going home.

An elfin grin spread across his tanned features, and his dimples appeared for a moment. Then, scratching at his thatch of auburn hair, he shrugged within his motley, as though girding himself for what came next, and threw the joystick forward, and bent into the wind as the air-boat dropped. He skimmed over a slidewalk, purposely dropping a few feet to crease the tassels of the ladies of fashion, and—inserting thumbs in large ears—he stuck out his tongue, rolled his eyes and went wugga-wugga-wugga. It was a minor diversion. One pedestrian skittered and tumbled, sending parcels every-whichway, another wet herself, a third keeled slantwise and the walk was stopped automatically by the servitors till she could be resuscitated. It was a minor diversion.

Then he swirled away on a vagrant breeze, and was gone. Hi-ho.

As he rounded the cornice of the Time-Motion Study Building, he saw the shift, just boarding the sidewalk. With practiced motion and an absolute conservation of movement, they sidestepped up onto the slow-strip and (in a chorus line reminiscent of a Busby Berkeley film of the antediluvian 1930s) advanced across the strips ostrich-walking till they were lined up on the expresstrip.

Once more, in anticipation, the elfin grin spread, and there was a tooth missing back there on the left side. He dipped, skimmed, and swooped over them; and then, scrunching about on the air-boat, he released the holding pins that fastened shut the ends of the home-made pouring troughs that kept his cargo from dumping prematurely. And as he pulled the trough-pins, the air-boat slid over the factory workers and one hundred and fifty thousand dollars' worth of jelly beans cascaded down on the expresstrip.

Jelly beans! Millions and billions of purples and yellows and green and licorice and grape and raspberry and mint and round and smooth and crunchy outside and soft-mealy inside and sugary and bouncing jouncing tumbling clattering clattering skittering fell on the heads and shoulders and hardhats and carapaces of the Timkin workers, tinkling on the slidewalk and bouncing away and rolling about underfoot and filling the sky on their way down with all the colors of joy and childhood and holidays, coming down in a steady rain, a solid wash, a torrent of color and sweetness out of the sky from above, and entering a universe of sanity and metronomic order with quite-mad coocoo newness. Jelly beans!

The shift workers howled and laughed and were pelted, and broke ranks, and the jelly beans managed to work their way into the mechanism of the slidewalks after which there was a hideous scraping as the sound of a million fingernails rasped down a quarter of a million blackboards, followed by a coughing and a sputtering, and then the slidewalks all stopped and everyone was dumped thisawayandthataway in a jack-straw tumble, still laughing and popping little jelly bean eggs of childish color into their mouths. It was a holiday, and a jollity, an absolute insanity, a giggle. But . . .

The shift was delayed seven minutes.

They did not get home for seven minutes.

The master schedule was thrown off by seven minutes.

Quotas were delayed by inoperative slidewalks for seven minutes.

He had tapped the first domino in the line, and one after another, like chik chik, chik, the others had fallen.

The System had been seven minutes' worth of disrupted. It was a tiny matter, one hardly worthy of note, but in a society where the single driving force was order and unity and equality and promptness and clocklike precision and attention to the clock, reverence of the gods of the passage of time, it was a disaster of major importance.

So he was ordered to appear before the Ticktockman. It was broadcast across every channel of the communications web. He was ordered to be *there* at 7:00 dammit on time. And they waited, and they waited, but he didn't show up till almost ten-thirty, at which time he merely sang a little song about moonlight in a place no one had ever heard of, called Vermont, and vanished again. But they had all been waiting since seven, and it wrecked *hell* with their schedules. So the question remained: Who is the Harlequin?

But the *unasked* question (more important of the two) was: how did we get *into* this position, where a laughing, irresponsible japer of jabberwocky and jive could disrupt our entire economic and cultural life with a hundred and fifty thousand dollars' worth of jelly beans ...

Jelly for God's sake *beans!* This is madness! Where did he get the money to buy a hundred and fifty thousand dollars' worth of jelly beans? (They knew it would have cost that much, because they had a team of Situation Analysts pulled off another assignment, and rushed to the slidewalk scene to sweep up and count the candies, and produce findings, which disrupted their schedules and threw their entire branch at least a day behind.) Jelly beans! Jelly . . . *beans?* Now wait a second—a second accounted for—no one has manufactured jelly beans for over a hundred years. Where did he get jelly beans?

That's another good question. More than likely it will never be answered to your complete satisfaction. But then, how many questions ever are?

The middle you know. Here is the beginning. How it starts:

A desk pad. Day for day, and turn each day. 9:00—open the mail. 9:45—appointment with planning commission board. 10:30—discuss installation progress charts with J.L. 11:45—pray for rain. 12:00—lunch. *And so it goes.*

"I'm sorry, Miss Grant, but the time for interviews was set at 2:30, and it's almost five now. I'm sorry you're late, but those are the rules. You'll have to wait till next year to submit application for this college again." *And so it goes.*

The 10:10 local stops at Cresthaven, Galesville, Tonawanda Junction, Selby and Farnhurst, but not at Indiana City, Lucasville and Colton, except on Sunday. The 10:35 express stops at Galesville, Selby and Indiana City, except on Sundays & Holidays, at which time it stops at . . . *and so it goes.*

"I couldn't wait, Fred. I had to be at Pierre Cartain's by 3:00, and you said you'd meet me under the clock in the terminal at 2:45, and you weren't there, so I had to go on. You're always late, Fred. If you'd been there, we could have sewed it up together, but as it was, well, I took the order alone ..." *And so it goes.*

Dear Mr. and Mrs. Atterley: In reference to your son Gerold's constant tardiness, I am afraid we will have to suspend him from school unless some more reliable method can be instituted guaranteeing he will arrive at his classes on time. Granted he is an exemplary student, and his marks are high, his constant flouting of the schedules of this school makes it impractical to maintain him in a system where the other children seem capable of getting where they are supposed to be on time *and so it goes.*

YOU CANNOT VOTE UNLESS YOU APPEAR AT 8:45 A.M.

"I don't care if the script is *good,* I need it Thursday!"

CHECK-OUT TIME IS 2:00 P.M.

"You got here late. The job's taken. Sorry."

YOUR SALARY HAS BEEN DOCKED FOR TWENTY MINUTES TIME LOST.

"God, what time is it, I've gotta run!"

And so it goes. And so it goes. And so it goes. And so it goes goes goes goes goes tick tock tick tock tick tock and one day we no longer let time serve us, we serve time and we are slaves of the schedule, worshippers of the sun's passing, bound into a life predicated on restrictions because the system will not function if we don't keep the schedule tight.

Until it becomes more than a minor inconvenience to be late. It becomes a sin. Then a crime. Then a crime punishable by this:

EFFECTIVE I5 JULY 2389 12:00:00 midnight, the office of the Master Timekeeper will require all citizens to submit their time-cards and cardioplates for processing. In accordance with Statute 555-7-SGH-999 governing the revocation of time per capita, all cardioplates will be keyed to the individual holder and—

What they had done, was devise a method of curtailing the amount of life a person could have. If he was ten minutes late, he lost ten minutes of his life. An hour was proportionately worth more revocation. If someone was consistently tardy, he might find himself, on a Sunday night, receiving a communiqué from the Master Timekeeper that his time had run out, and he would be "turned off" at high noon on Monday, please straighten your affairs, sir, madame or bisex.

And so, by this simple scientific expedient (utilizing a scientific process held dearly secret by the Ticktockman's office) the System was maintained. It was the only expedient thing to do. It was, after all, patriotic. The schedules had to be met. After all, there *was* a war on!

But, wasn't there always?

"Now that is really disgusting," the Harlequin said, when Pretty Alice showed him the wanted poster. "Disgusting and *highly* improbable. After all, this isn't the Day of the Desperado. A *wanted* poster!"

"You know," Pretty Alice noted, "you speak with a great deal of inflection."

"I'm sorry," said the Harlequin, humbly.

"No need to be sorry. You're always saying 'I'm sorry.' You have such massive guilt, Everett, it's really very sad."

"I'm sorry," he said again, then pursed his lips so the dimples appeared momentarily. He hadn't wanted to say that at all. "I have to go out again. I have to *do* something."

Pretty Alice slammed her coffee-bulb down on the counter. "Oh for God's sake, Everett, can't you stay home just *one* night! Must you always be out in that ghastly clown suit, running around an*noy*ing people?"

"I'm—" he stopped, and clapped the jester's hat onto his auburn thatch with a tiny tingling of bells. He rose, rinsed out his coffee-bulb at the spray, and put it into the dryer for a moment. "I have to go."

She didn't answer. The faxbox was purring, and she pulled a sheet out, read it, threw it toward him on the counter. "It's about you. Of course. You're ridiculous."

He read it quickly. It said the Ticktockman was trying to locate him. He didn't care, he was going out to be late again. At the door, dredging for an exit line, he hurled back petulantly, "Well, *you* speak with inflection, *too!*"

Pretty Alice rolled her pretty eyes heavenward. "You're ridiculous." The Harlequin stalked out, slamming the door, which sighed shut softly, and locked itself.

There was a gentle knock, and Pretty Alice got up with an exhalation of exasperated breath, and opened the door. He stood there. "I'll be back about ten-thirty, okay?"

She pulled a rueful face. "Why do you tell me that? Why? You *know* you'll be late! You *know* it! You're *always* late, so why do you tell me these dumb things?" She closed the door.

On the other side, the Harlequin nodded to himself. *She's right. She's always right. I'll be late. I'm always late. Why do I tell her these dumb things?*

He shrugged again, and went off to be late once more.

He had fired off the firecracker rockets that said: I will attend the 115th annual International Medical Association Invocation at 8:00 PM precisely. I do hope you will all be able to join me.

The words had burned in the sky, and of course the authorities were there, lying in wait for him. They assumed, naturally, that he would be late. He arrived twenty minutes early, while they were setting up the spiderwebs to trap and hold him. Blowing a large bullhorn, he frightened and unnerved them so, their own moisturized encirclement webs sucked closed, and they were hauled up, kicking and shrieking, high above the amphitheater's floor. The Harlequin laughed and laughed, and apologized profusely. The physicians, gathered in solemn conclave, roared with laughter, and accepted the Harlequin's apologies with exaggerated bowing and posturing, and a merry time was had by all, who thought the Harlequin was a regular foofaraw in fancy pants; all, that is, but the authorities, who had been sent out by the office of the Ticktockman; they hung there like so much dockside cargo, hauled up above the floor of the amphitheater in a most unseemly fashion.

(In another part of the same city where the Harlequin carried on his "activities," totally unrelated in every way to what concerns us here, save that it illustrates the Ticktockman's power and import, a man named Marshall Delahanty received his turn-off notice from the Ticktockman's office. His wife received the notification from the gray-suited minee who delivered it, with the traditional "look of sorrow" plastered hideously across his face. She knew what it was, even without unsealing it. It was a billet-doux of immediate recognition to everyone these days. She gasped, and held it as though it were a glass slide tinged with botulism, and prayed it was not for her. Let it be for Marsh, she thought, brutally, realistically, or one of the kids, but not for me, please dear God, not for me. And then she opened it, and it *was* for Marsh, and she was at one and the same time horrified and relieved. The next trooper in the line had caught the bullet. "Marshall, she screamed, "Marshall! Termination, Marshall!

OhmiGod, Marshall, whattl we do, whattl we do, Marshall omigod-marshall . . ." and in their home that night was the sound of tearing paper and fear, and the stink of madness went up the flue and there was nothing, absolutely nothing they could do about it.

(But Marshall Delahanty tried to run. And early the next day, when turn-off time came, he was deep in the Canadian forest two hundred miles away, and the office of the Ticktockman blanked his cardioplate, and Marshall Delahanty keeled over, running, and his heart stopped, and the blood dried up on its way to his brain, and he was dead that's all. One light went out on the sector map in the office of the Master Timekeeper, while notification was entered for fax reproduction, and Georgette Delahanty's name was entered on the dole roles till she could remarry. Which is the end of the footnote, and all the point that need be made, except don't laugh, because that is what would happen to the Harlequin if ever the Ticktockman found out his real name. It isn't funny.)

The shopping level of the city was thronged with the Thursday-colors of the buyers. Women in canary yellow chitons and men in pseudo-Tyrolean outfits that were jade and leather and fit very tightly, save for the balloon pants.

When the Harlequin appeared on the still-being-constructed shell of the new Efficiency Shopping Center, his bullhorn to his elfishly-laughing lips, everyone pointed and stared, and he berated them:

"Why let them order you about? Why let them tell you to hurry and scurry like ants or maggots? Take your time! Saunter a while! Enjoy the sunshine, enjoy the breeze, let life carry you at your own pace! Don't be slaves of time, it's a helluva way to die, slowly, by degrees . . . down with the Ticktockman!"

Who's the nut? most of the shoppers wanted to know. Who's the nut oh wow I'm gonna be late I gotta run. . . .

And the construction gang on the Shopping Center received an urgent order from the office of the Master Timekeeper that the dangerous criminal known as the Harlequin was atop their spire, and their aid was urgently needed in apprehending him. The work crew said no, they would lose time on their construction schedule, but the Ticktockman managed to pull the proper threads of governmental webbing, and they were told to cease work and catch that nitwit up there on the spire; up there with the bullhorn. So a dozen and more burly workers began climbing into their construction platforms, releasing the a-grav plates, and rising toward the Harlequin.

After the debacle (in which, through the Harlequin's attention to personal safety, no one was seriously injured), the workers tried to reassemble, and assault him again, but it was too late. He had vanished. It had attracted quite a crowd, however, and the shopping cycle was thrown off by hours, simply hours. The purchasing needs of the System were therefore falling behind, and so measures were taken to accelerate the cycle for the rest of the day, but it got bogged down and speeded up and they sold too many float-valves and not nearly enough wegglers which meant that the popli ratio was off, which made it necessary to rush cases and cases of spoiling Smash-O to stores that usually needed a case only every three or four hours. The shipments were bollixed, the transshipments were misrouted, and in the end, even the swizzleskid industries felt it.

"Don't come back till you have him!" the Ticktockman said, very quietly, very sincerely, extremely dangerously.

They used dogs. They used probes. They used cardioplate crossoffs. They used teepers. They used bribery. They used stiktytes. They used intimidation. They used torment. They used torture. They used finks. They used cops. They used search & seizure. They used fallaron. They used betterment incentive. They used fingerprints. They used the Bertillon system. They used cunning. They used guile. They used treachery. They used Raoul Mitgong, but he didn't help much. They used applied physics. They used techniques of criminology.

And what the hell: they caught him.

After all, his name was Everett C. Marm, and he wasn't much to begin with, except a man who had no sense of time.

"Repent, Harlequin! " said the Ticktockman.

"Get stuffed!" the Harlequin replied, sneering.

"You've been late a total of sixty-three years, five months, three weeks two days, twelve hours, forty-one minutes, fifty-nine seconds, point oh three six one one one microseconds. You've used up everything you can, and more. I'm going to turn you off."

"Scare someone else. I'd rather be dead than live in a dumb world with a bogey-man like you."

"It's my job."

"You're full of it. You're a tyrant. You have no right to order people around and kill them if they show up late."

"You can't adjust. You can't fit in."

"Unstrap me, and I'll fit my fist into your mouth."

"You're a nonconformist."

"That didn't used to be a felony."

"It is now. Live in the world around you."

"I hate it. It's a terrible world."

"Not everyone thinks so. Most people enjoy order."

"I don't, and most of the people I know don't."

"That's not true. How do you think we caught you?"

"I'm not interested'"

"A girl named Pretty Alice told us who you were."

"That's a lie."

"It's true. You unnerve her. She wants to belong; she wants to conform; I'm going to turn you off."

"Then do it already, and stop arguing with me."

"I'm not going to turn you off."

"You're an idiot!"

"Repent, Harlequin!" said the Ticktockman.

"Get stuffed."

So they sent him to Coventry. And in Coventry they worked him over. It was just like what they did to Winston Smith in NINETEEN EIGHTY-FOUR, which was a book none of them knew about, but the techniques are really quite ancient, and so they did it to Everett C. Marm; and one day, quite a long time later, the Harlequin appeared on the communications web, appearing elfin and dimpled and bright-eyed, and not at all brainwashed, and he said he had been wrong, that it was a good, a very good thing indeed, to belong, to be right on time hip-ho and away we go, and everyone stared up at him on the public screens that covered an entire city block, and they said to themselves, well, you see, he was just a nut after all, and if that's the way the system is run, then let's do it that way, because it doesn't pay to fight city hall, or in this case, the

Ticktockman. So Everett C. Marm was destroyed, which was a loss, because of what Thoreau said earlier, but you can't make an omelet without breaking a few eggs, and in every revolution a few die who shouldn't, but they have to, because that's the way it happens, and if you make only a little change, then it seems to be worthwhile. Or, to make the point lucidly:

"Uh, excuse me, sir, I, uh, don't know how to uh, to uh, tell you this, but you were three minutes late. The schedule is a little, uh, bit off."

He grinned sheepishly.

"That's ridiculous" murmured the Ticktockman behind his mask. "Check your watch." And then he went into his office, going *mrmee, mrmee, mrmee, mrmee.*

For Practice

1. Consider the structure of this story. We are told at the outset that the quote from Thoreau's *Civil Disobedience* is "the heart of it," and that we are to "begin in the middle, and later learn the beginning; the end will take care of itself." What is the significance of this set of reading instructions? Based on these instructions, what assumptions can be made about the story? How can "the heart," "the beginning," "the middle," and "the end" of a story be defined?

2. Re-read the quote from Thoreau. What is your understanding of the quote itself? What is its relationship to Ellison's story? How do Thoreau's life and philosophy create a cultural context for reading this text?

3. What is your definition of technology? How does it compare to Ellison's view of technology? Mark passages in the story where there are references to technology. Does technology play a primarily productive or destructive role in the lives of the characters?

4. What is the difference in connotation between the titles "Master Timekeeper" and "Ticktockman?"

5. Describe the tone of the narrator. How does the tone influence our perceptions of Harlequin/Everett C. Marm and the Ticktockman? What qualities can we appreciate in Harlequin? How do the character and actions of Harlequin become an argument in this text?

6. Are your attitudes toward technology altered as a result of reading this text? Why or why not?

Ozymandias

Terry Carr

Terry Carr (1937–1987), born in Grant's Pass, Oregon, attended the City College of San Francisco and the University of California at Berkeley. Though Carr produced some fiction, notably a novel Cirque *and the short story collection* The Light at the End of the Universe, *he is best known as an editor of science-fiction series and anthologies. He founded the "Ace Science Fiction Specials" series, co-edited the influential* World's Best Science Fiction *(1965–71), and edited over a dozen other science-fiction anthologies, including* Classic Science Fiction *and the* Universe *series. Carr's choice of what was the best in science fiction helped set the standard in science fiction for years, and he has been recognized for this excellence by being awarded a total of four Hugo Awards.*

"Ozymandias," published in 1972, is a story that engages some of the same themes as Shelley's poem of the same name. Instead of using a broken statue in the middle of a desert to make his point, Carr uses cryogenic burial vaults in the midst of land racked by atomic war. The question of the overall good of technological progress and the effects of tampering with nature is brought into focus not only by the plundered burial vaults but by the emergence of a person who tries to escape the natural process of death and, unlike Shelley's "Ozymandias," awakes to see the destruction of the modern achievements of his world.

They came up out of the groundstars howling and leaping, laughing and pushing, singing into the night a strange, tuneless, polyphonal chant. They proceeded past the markers and twice around them, still giggling and chanting, and spread out in a wavering line that went up the hill like a snake. It took them ten minutes to go from the markers to the boundary, a distance of no more than fifty paces for a walker—but these were not walkers, they were robbers, and they had the laws to follow.

Sooleyrah was in the lead, because he was the best dancer among them—the most graceful and quick and, even more important, the most inventive. No approach to the vaults could be made in just the same way any had been made before, and if the watcher, who was always second in line, noticed a pattern developing that he thought he might have seen before, it was his job to trip the leader, or shove him, or kick him, or whatever was necessary to shake him into a new rhythm or direction. On those raids when the leader invented enough new variations, and the watcher made sure there were no repeats from the past, then they had a successful raid. When leader and watcher failed, there were explosions, blindings, gases, and sometimes the sound-without-sound, and then there was death.

But Sooleyrah was in good form tonight, and even Kreech, who was watcher, had to admit that.

"Go good," he chanted. "Go good, good, good, go good." Then he tripped Sooleyrah, but only for the fun of it, and danced in a circle till the leader bounded up and continued.

"Watchers got easy, yeah easy," Sooleyrah sang. "Easy trip leader, no reason; damn no reason." He did a double-back step, and whirled, his flying foot narrowly missing Kreech's mouth.

"Reason next time," he sang, and laughed.

Behind him, Kreech did the whirling step, just missing the next in line, and he too laughed; then the third man followed it, and the kick and laugh traveled back down the hill, undulating in the darkness. Sooleyrah, slim and graceful and dark-bearded, did a slide, three jumps, then rolled on the ground, leading always upward, toward the vaults. They stood black and distant against the night sky at hillcrest, jagged storehouses of darkness.

"Don't matter anyway," Kreech told him. "Don't matter, Sooleyrah, don't leader matter. Go good, go bad, no difference." He rolled, following Sooleyrah up the hill, and the small bells he carried in his tattered shirt pocket tinkled dully. "You heard he said, don't matter."

"Hell damn, yeah," Sooleyrah sang. "Damn yeah, damn fat boy, damn he knows." He paused, straining on tiptoes to look back down the line. The fat boy was only a little way behind them, puffing and gasping already as he tried to follow the upward dance; he wasn't accustomed to it, as anyone could see. His gray-washed tunic was splotching dark with sweat; his hair, cut short at ear-length, fell in sweat-strings down his forehead.

Kreech paused, turned, looked back, and so did the next man, and the next, and so on until the one in front of the fat boy turned suddenly to stare at him; and the fat boy yipped, startled, then caught on to it and turned to look back himself.

Sooleyrah laughed again, and returned to his dance. "Damn fat boy no good anyway," he sang. "No good, know nothing, no good, know nothing."

"Hell damn yourself," Kreech said. "Damn fat boy almost a thinker. *Damn* almost."

Sooleyrah snorted, and did a particularly difficult series of jump-steps deliberately for the confounding of the almost-thinker back down the line. "Damn-almost as good as nowhere, nowhere," he sang. "That's thinkers now anyway, nowhere, nowhere. Nowhere."

"Except fat boy," Kreech said.

"Hell fat boy," Sooleyrah said, lapsing from song in his disgust. "Fat boy don't know, but you know, I know. Vaults still there—*there*!"—he pointed up the hill, still dancing—"so what's fat boy know? So we dance, we sing, careful, damn careful."

They were halfway up the hill now, the luminescent groundstars merging into a bright mist spread over the valley below, where only occasional widely spaced bones of buildings thrust up into the open night air. The rest of the valley, all the way to the mountains, was groundstars from here.

Above them, up the hill, blackness grew and deepened with each step, and the massive vaults loomed black against the weak, scattered light of the skystars. The vaults covered the crown of the hill, most of them broken or crumbled or even exploded by now—the result of centuries of raids by the valley robbers. Those that still stood were all empty inside, or so the thinkers had said, but Sooleyrah didn't believe them. There were always more vaults to open—always had been, always would be. Hell damn foolishness to say there weren't, or wouldn't be.

If the vaults all became empty, there would be no toys, no starboxes, no tools to replace those worn and broken or maybe thrown away dull, and no samesongs or pictures or any of the other things that had been stored there for the valley people. Which was ridiculous, and unthinkable, and Sooleyrah wouldn't think it.

So he danced on upward, darting to right and left, rolling and tumbling, laughing into the empty air, while behind him, one by one, the others pointed after him to the vaults, and danced and tumbled, and echoes of his laugh faded back down the line.

Lasten, the fat boy, was frightened. He had never been on a raid before, had never been trained for it. He knew he would make some disastrous mistake at any moment, and then the others would turn on him. Or, if they did get to the vaults without trouble, it would be a night for the Immortals.

Probably gas or the sound-without-sound, he thought. *Not so afraid of a blinding—least you can get back down the hill from that. But it be something killing for me, yeah.*

Well, he was lucky to be alive anyway: all the other thinkers had been killed the night before. Massacred by the robbers—just lined up in the hub-square and stoned to death. Oh, the screaming and panic, the ones who tried to run with their ankles hobbled, the manic singing and shouting of the robbers—Lasten shuddered, hating himself for his cowardice, hating the way he had hidden in an unused basement where groundstars were so thick they made a shimmering fog. Hiding, he had heard all of it anyway, had even seen some of the worst scenes, the most vivid ones; they'd invaded his mind in waves of terror from the thinkers or, sometimes, exultation and a kind of crazed kill-frenzy from the robbers. For Lasten, the fat boy, was a weird, one of the 10% of human mutations that managed to live in each generation.

Some were born with extra toes, or no feet at all; these were the common ones, the ones who lived as easily as anyone else, accepting tithes from the market thieves as they rocked back and forth in the dirt and listened for rumors to sell. Others were born already dead or dying, with jellied skulls or tiny hearts unable to support life. And a few, a very few, had extra things that no one else had: not just extra hands or grotesquely oversized private parts (like Kreech, like Kreech), but *talents.* Lasten's father, for instance, had had a talent for numbers; he could remember how many seasons ago a thing had happened, or how often it had happened during his lifetime, or even put numbers together in his head to make new numbers. And Sooleyrah claimed he had a place somewhere in his head where everything was always level, and that was why he was such a good dancer.

Lasten could hear people's minds. Not their thoughts, for people don't have thoughts inside; Lasten heard emotions and mind-pictures, whatever was strongest in the consciousness of those around him. Red hate, boiling and exploding; sometimes pure fear, blue-white, rigid; sex fantasies that echoed disturbingly in Lasten's own mind. They came at him unbidden; he couldn't shut them out when they were really strong, as they had been last night. Blood, blood on the ground, dark blood spurting from crushed skulls, a trail of red where one man had tried to drag his battered body away to safety. And screaming: Lasten had heard the screams of both the killers and the dying, and had found himself, when it was over, huddled in a corner and still screaming himself, his throat hoarse and ragged. He was crying, and he had emptied his stomach and his bowels simultaneously, helpless to stop either.

And it had all been unnecessary, because they wouldn't have killed him anyway. He wasn't yet a thinker.

Yeah, only thinkers got the death, only official thinkers. Dumb robbers don't know I'm a thinker too, just not entered yet. Dumb robbers don't know hell damn thing.

Lasten tripped over his feet trying to accomplish a whirling jump-step; he fell gasping to the ground, and for a second he thought he'd lie there, let the line pass him while he caught his breath. But the next in line kicked him sharply, kicked him again and again, and Lasten moaned and struggled to his feet. He ran weakly to catch up to the line ahead, sweating and whimpering. He knew he'd never get back alive from this raid. Probably none of them would.

Should try to get away, roll out into the dark where they can't see, maybe they'd go right on by. Couldn't stop to look for me, no; rest of the line has to keep up or the approach goes bad, sure it does. Damn dumb robbers.

But he didn't have the quickness to get out of sight before they'd catch him and drag him back into line, and he knew it. Yeah, damn dumb robbers were going to get themselves killed, blown up, burned—and fat boy thinker Lasten was going to get killed with them, because he couldn't get away.

"Fat boy fell down," Kreech laughed, stepping high behind Sooleyrah's lead. "Daipell kicked him, kicked him, kicked him, fat boy got up."

Sooleyrah paused, looked angrily back down the hill. The fat boy was back in line now, clumsily following the steps. Sooleyrah could hardly see him now, they had progressed so far up into the skystar darkness; but the fat boy's size stood out against the brightness of the valley groundstars below.

"Fat boy messes up my approach, I'll kill him, smash him with rocks, rocks," Sooleyrah chanted. "Yeah, like the rest, make him a thinker too. No good, any thinker." Abruptly he whirled, and did an easy dance-skip straight up the hill. Kreech immediately followed him.

"Told you leave him back, leave him back," Kreech sang. "No good dancer yeah you're right, *damn* right. No good for the rest."

"Fat boy dances right or I damn smash him with rocks," Sooleyrah said.

"We don't smash nobody if we're dead too. No good dancer, no good approach, no good at the vaults. Get ourselves dead, because of fat boy."

Sooleyrah slowed his dancing even more than he already had. He did a waddle-step, then giggled and broke into a tension-high laugh. "Go slow, go easy for fat boy. Go easy so he can follow, so we get into vaults right, no killing tonight. Waddle waddle, kind of dance fat boy does all the time anyway." He giggled again. "Make sure no killing at vaults, show damn almost-thinker vaults still there. Yeah, let him see for himself, no different from always, always . . ."

Kreech leaped forward quickly and tripped him. Their feet tangled together and they both fell, Sooleyrah's lean form sprawling loosely, Kreech's bulkier body hitting the sparse grass heavily. Sooleyrah rolled over quickly and was on his feet almost immediately. Kreech grunted and bounded up too.

"Go bad there," he sang. "Too much the same, go bad, go lousy. Got to go *good*, Sooleyrah, *go good, go good.*"

The next man in line caught up to them, and he deftly tripped Kreech and fell to the ground beside him, following the lead. Sooleyrah whooped his laughter, whirled and danced on up the hill.

"Yeah, go good tonight," he sang. "Just let fat boy thinker see, yeah, then tomorrow we smash him, *damn* yeah."

And it was all so useless, so senseless. Lasten puffed and sweated trying to follow the lead of the man ahead of him in the line, trying to duplicate each movement, each step, every twist or hop or gesture; that was the rule when the robbers went up to the vaults, and if you didn't follow it they might stop long enough to kill you. Senselessly, uselessly.

Because it didn't matter. The whole ritual of the dance-approach, the singsong chanting, the leader and the watcher . . . all unnecessary. The robbers thought they were conquering taboos by the skill of their dancing whenever they made a successful approach to the vaults, and they thought they'd failed when instead they encountered the vault-fires, the blindings, the deaths . . . but fat boy Lasten who had been trained as a thinker knew better.

Damn yeah, know better than dumb robbers.

The robbers could have walked straight up the hill to the vaults, no wandering snakelike line, no jumping and dancing, no chanting. They could have approached any of the vaults, and they would have gotten in without incident . . . or else they would have been gassed or blinded or killed. Sometimes a raid would get through the Immortals' defenses, and sometimes it would mean danger and death, but it had nothing to do with the dance or the rituals.

Yeah, dance it right and you get in, or dance it wrong and you get killed. Stupid, stupid.

Lasten's people had been thinkers, the ones who kept the old knowledge . . . or what remained of it. They knew that the vaults were guarded not by curses or demons, nor by strange magic laws that judged and recorded the dance steps of generations of ignorant vault robbers. No, these vaults had been protected by the Immortals in ways even the thinkers no longer knew . . . but it was not magic. There were hidden eyes surrounding each vault, and they defended against invasion with a variety of weapons. Gas was one, explosions were another; that was plain enough. The sound-without-sound was not so simple, nor the blinding lights, but they were all the same, only defenses left to guard the vaults.

The world that had created those vaults was gone, destroyed in bombings and explosions and gases so powerful they had killed most of the Immortals. They screamed and died, screamed and died, until only a handful were left, grubbing among the ruins, their women bearing strange children, and all of them dazzled by the groundstars that filled the low places everywhere.

Each spring now, as soon as the thaw was complete, the people of the valley held a memorial for the past and the thinkers told the story.

The man ahead of Lasten was waddling now, laughing as he glanced back to see the fat boy follow the lead. Lasten cursed in ragged gasps, but he waddled after him as the man leaped forward to trip the dancer in front of him. The two of them fell sprawling to the ground, and giggled and laughed as they rose.

"Hey, yeah, fat boy," the dancer ahead of him sang, "come get me, fat boy, your turn to trip ole Sharksey," and he danced in a circle, waiting, giggling, challenging.

Lasten sucked harsh air into his lungs, gathered what strength he had and ran forward to swing a leg and trip the man. But his aim was short; he felt himself falling, off balance, saw Sharksey's face suddenly angry, and then he was on the ground gasping weakly, and Sharksey muttered "Sisterson!" and leaped upon him.

The man's weight was not great, but the impact knocked the rest of Lasten's wind out of him. He moaned weakly, hardly feeling the elbows Sharksey was wielding freely as he rolled off him and got to his feet. "Damn lousy fat Lasten, should've been made a thinker so you'd be killed too. No good dancer, *damn* no good. Get us all killed, yeah, only maybe we kill you, kill Lasten, hey kill fat boy, yeah? Yeah? Unless you get *up*, fat boy, *up* right now, right *now!*"

And Lasten struggled to his feet while Sharksey continued to dance around him cursing and threatening. He stood up shuddering, and Sharksey sang, "Okay, dance it right, dance right . . . oh yeah, or we kill you, Lasten, and you know it, you know it, don't you?" He laughed, whirled and danced on upward to follow the others.

Lasten watched him go, seeing him through a red mist like crimson groundstars swarming around his head. In his mind he still felt the throbbing hatred, the promise of death that was more than just promise; Sharksey really *wanted* to kill him. He gasped in air, and the mist began to dissipate—and suddenly his legs were cut from beneath him as the next dancer in line leaped forward to trip him in his turn. Again he was on the ground, but this time, driven by fear of the anticipation he'd felt from Sharksey's mind, he got up quickly and danced, or lurched, or shambled, step by step up the hill after the line.

No more mistakes for Lasten, no, he told himself. *Dancing don't matter to the Immortals, but it does to the filthy robbers, murdering robbers, and they'll really kill you, won't make no difference why you die.*

But damn them, damn them forcing me here when I've told them the vaults are empty.

Sooleyrah had reached the gates now. There had once been a strong wall here, he'd heard that, but it was virtually demolished by generations of robbers who had torn it down barehanded, stone by stone, and the stones were littered all around, some scattered back down the hill where they'd rolled or been thrown. Fifteen or twenty yards to the right was a pit where once a bad dancer had caused an explosion. Of the wall only the gates remained, twin steel markers pitted and rust-flaking with age. Night moss had crept up the sides of the gates, half covering them with dark green fur. Overhead the cold skystars hung silently.

"Okay, we go in," Sooleyrah chanted. "We go in, go in—hey we go in *now!*" and he danced forward, through the gates as quickly as he could (many robbers had been killed there, though none within Sooleyrah's memory), and on the other side, the inside, he paused and did shuffle-steps, humming a high keening song while Kreech and one, two, three more followed him through.

"Now we're in," he said softly to Kreech, and they turned to survey the vaults. Behind them more of the line danced through the gates, slowed and finally stopped like Sooleyrah and Kreech, panting, staring around them at the vaults.

"Which one?" Kreech asked. "You been here three, four times in a row now, so which one we go into?"

Sooleyrah's eyes narrowed as he studied the vaults. They crowned the entire hilltop, vaults of many sizes and shapes, some tall, like obelisks, others domelike, still others jointed with odd angels and designs. Sooleyrah had always been afraid of the vaults—for their size alone, even if they hadn't been so dangerous. They towered into the sky above; and when the robbers entered those doorways the arches stretched far overhead to encompass echoing empty darkness.

"Starboxes are kept in the vaults for us, no other reason, yeah?" he said to Kreech. "And samesongs, and tools; some toys maybe too, lots of shapes, yeah? Plug 'em into the starboxes and yeah, they work, they work. Now why unless they're for us? Who else, Kreech, who else?"

"Nobody," Kreech said. "Nobody but us to take 'em."

"Yeah, yeah, nobody," Sooleyrah said, turning slowly in the night, in the poised silence of the hilltop and the looming vaults. He looked back down the hill and saw the rest of the line coming through the gates, and the gates themselves now seemed to lead out, to lead downward, back to the brightness of the groundstars. He saw Lasten come panting and shuffling through, and suddenly he grinned.

"Hey, fat boy Lasten can pick us a vault. Almost-thinker says they're all empty, hell he knows. Remember what the rest said? Rest of the thinkers Said they could remember which vaults were used up, remember how many vaults there were, and all empty now. You remember? Yeah? Damn dumb thinkers been fooling us for hey *long* time. Send us up here instead of them, make us take the chances, oh yeah, they just tell us which vaults to go to. Oh sure, oh yeah, smart old thinkers, and every one dead now, about time."

Kreech kicked over a loosely planted stone; underneath it were faintly glowing crawling things that scurried in small circles and quickly burrowed into the ground, hiding.

"Yeah, always hated the thinkers," Kreech said. "Always knew they were liars—well, didn't all of us? Hey yeah, good, get Lasten up here and make him pick out our vault tonight."

"Yeah okay, pass the word back," Sooleyrah said, then turned his back to the line and stared again at the vaults. But almost immediately he had another thought; he said to Kreech, "Lasten picks our vault, and he's first one to go in tonight. First one. Place of honor, yeah?" He laughed.

"First one in gets killed if the approach wasn't good," Kreech said. "Oh yeah, place of honor."

"Fat boy needs it," Sooleyrah said. "Bring him here."

Lasten's fear sharpened when they came for him. Why did they want him now, when they were through the gates and at the portals of the vaults themselves? Surely they wouldn't kill him now, up here on the silent hilltop. What reason, what reason? (Unless they were going back to human sacrifice in front of the vaults. *No.*)

But the flickering impressions that reached him from Sooleyrah's mind, when he was brought to the leader, had nothing of murder in them. There was hatred, yes, and the soft spongy feel of gloating. But not murder, no, nothing overt.

"Hey Lasten, you almost a thinker, yeah?" Sooleyrah said, and his voice was so quiet, almost friendly. But not his mind.

"I wasn't entered," Lasten said cautiously.

"Yeah, we know. Okay, but you know a lot of stuff, yeah? Know a lot about vaults, which ones are dangerous, which ones maybe empty, we hear. Now, not *all* of 'em empty, Lasten, not *all* of 'em. You almost a thinker, you not dumb, yeah?"

"The thinkers told you they were all empty," Lasten said, "so you killed the thinkers. Now if I still say that, you'll kill *me*."

Sooleyrah smiled widely, glancing at Kreech. "No, no, Lasten, you not dumb. Okay, now what vault do we go to tonight?"

A chill scurried up Lasten's back, touching the nape of his neck spider-softly.

"You want me to pick the vault?" he asked. "Why me? Why, Sooleyrah?"

Sooleyrah laughed, enjoying himself. "Hell damn *I* know what vault to pick. Thinkers always do that, always. So no more thinkers, but we got you, Lasten. So you pick."

So I pick—and if the vault is empty, it's my fault, not Sooleyrah's. Sooleyrah maybe not so sure about the vaults after all, eh?

"You scared to pick one yourself, Sooleyrah? Scared you can't find a vault with your pretty things? Yeah, you're scared, scared."

But he shouldn't have said that. Sooleyrah leaped forward and grasped Lasten's arm, painfully squeezing the soft flesh, twisting the arm behind him. Lasten cried out in pain, and bent over trying to escape the pressure. Sooleyrah jammed his arm up against his shoulder blades.

"Not scared, fat boy; not scared, just smart. Thinkers knew about vaults, they taught you, yeah? Sure, Lasten, sure, we know. Then thinkers said all vaults empty, no use making raids any more, yeah? Yeah? Well, maybe thinkers got something up here they don't want found, eh? Robbers not so dumb, Lasten, and Sooleyrah not dumb either. You pick vault, *you*, and it *better* not be empty!"

Or they'll stone me right here, Lasten thought, seeing that as a bright certainty in Sooleyrah's mind. *Only way Sooleyrah could make up for leading a failure raid. Yeah, and the robbers would love another stoning, especially up here where the magic is. Magic and death, oh yeah, they'll love it.*

"And *you* go into vault first, Lasten," Kreech told him with happy malice. "Sure, *you*, Lasten, place of honor for you."

Place of death, Lasten thought. *Oh you dumb damn robbers, lousy murdering superstitious—*

"Which one, Lasten?" Sooleyrah said, applying pressure to his arm. "Which one?"

And Lasten, the almost-thinker, suddenly laughed.

"Yeah, okay," he said, and giggled again, a giggle just like Sooleyrah's or Kreech's, only higher pitched, thinner. "Okay, yeah, okay, okay . . ."

Sooleyrah let go of his arm, stepping back. "You take us to an empty vault, you won't be laughing," he warned.

"Yeah, oh yeah, I know," Lasten said, managing to stop his giggling. It wasn't that funny, after all; in fact, probably it wasn't funny at all.

"That one," he said, pointing to the vault nearest to them. "We go there."

Sooleyrah and Kreech both stared. "*That* one? Fat boy, you crazy? Nothing in that vault, nothing there since before you or me born!"

"Hey, yeah," Kreech said. "First vault ever emptied was that one, that one right there, don't you know that?"

"Sure, I know, sure. But that's the one we go to tonight. And you look close, robber leader and watcher, you look close and you'll see vault's *not* empty. You want more pretty stuff stored in vaults, you just look close tonight!"

He began to walk confidently toward the nearest vault, while behind him Sooleyrah and Kreech looked angry, then uneasy, and finally they turned and motioned the rest of the party to follow them as they moved after Lasten.

Sure, damn robbers emptied this vault first thing, Lasten was thinking. *Been in this one so often you can't count, clearing it out, every piece they could find, everything the Immortals stored here. Only that just means it's a safe vault, all the defenses used up or burned out so long ago. Nothing here to blind me, burn me, kill me. Safe vault, yeah . . . but maybe not so empty as they think.*

The door to the vault gaped open, leading into blackness. Lasten called for torches, and two of the robbers came forward and lit them. "Okay, now we go in," Lasten said, and sullenly the torchbearers followed him through the wide doorway, Sooleyrah and Kreech right behind them.

Inside was a high-ceilinged room littered with dust and stones and broken pieces of once-complete artifacts; one wall of the room was dark and misshapen, its plastoid seared by some long-forgotten fire-explosion. A hole in the ceiling, so far above them it was barely discernible in the flickering torchlight, showed where once there had been lighting fixtures, long since ripped out by the robbers. The sounds of footsteps were flat and harsh in the bare room, and the faint smell of old torchsmoke seemed to come from the shadows. Sooleyrah moved closer to Lasten, saying with dangerous softness, "Don't see nothing in here, thinker."

Lasten nodded, looking carefully around the vault.

"*You* see anything in here, Kreech? Looks empty to me, just empty as damn, yeah?"

Kreech grinned. "Oh no, not empty. Can't be' fat thinker brought us here. That right, fat thinker? Something hidden in here?"

Lasten got down on hands and knees in the middle of the floor, picking through the rubble. Here and there he brushed aside dust and stones to look closely at the floor.

"Yeah hey, he got something hidden all right," Sooleyrah said. "Hey, move in with the torches there, move closer." The torchbearers edged suspiciously forward; Sooleyrah grabbed one, swung him around and placed him where he wanted him, standing right over Lasten. "You too," he told the other man, and that one too held his torch close over the fat boy.

Lasten giggled.

"You find it, hey?" Sooleyrah said. "What is it, fat boy? Better be good, and you know it, now don't you? What is it?"

Lasten knew Sooleyrah and the others were more frightened than they acted. The robbers had always been afraid of these vaults, no matter how often they'd pillaged them, and despite the lower and lower frequency of maimings or killings by the defense systems. *Robbers think this is all demon-stuff, something like that. Hell, no demons, not even lousy magic. Just stuff we forgot, even the thinkers forgot.*

But yeah, I know one more thing about vaults that Sooleyrah don't know.

Lasten rose to his feet, puffing, then looked around and picked out the south wall. In the center of it was a metal plaque with writing on it—devil marks, the robbers called it: another kind of magic to fear.

Lasten couldn't read it, but he knew what it must be. He motioned Sooleyrah over to him and pointed at the plaque. "Take that off the wall," he said.

Sooleyrah stared at him; so did Kreech, and so did the rest, the torchbearers and the ones crowded around the doorway.

"Take it off the wall!" Lasten said sharply, a little shrilly. "Pry it, use your knives— but be careful."

Sooleyrah hesitated only a moment more; then he turned and picked out one of the men in the doorway. "Takker—you. Bring your knife, do what thinker says. Rest of you, you keep door blocked so thinker can't run out."

Takker came into the vault reluctantly, drawing his knife. It was crude but strong; once it had been just a slim bar of metal, but Takker had filed it sharp. He worked the edge under the plaque and pried; the plaque began to loosen.

"Secret place in there?" Sooleyrah asked, and Lasten didn't have to feel the suppressed fear from his mind; it was apparent in his voice.

"Yeah, secret place," he said. "Surprise for you."

The plaque came off and dropped to the floor with a sharp metallic ring. Lasten stepped forward, motioned for the light and looked into the small hole opened in the wall.

There was a round dial, with markings and writing—the short writing they'd used for numbers. A time-lock, set for sometime in the future, after the wars. But the time could be changed, no reason it couldn't be changed.

Lasten twisted the dial, heard its faint scraping clearly in the suddenly silent vault. Turn, turn, and seasons flowed by, more and more time was marked off. Years, years. He kept turning the dial, waiting for the time-lock to release. (Maybe he was turning it the wrong direction? But no; it wouldn't turn at all the other way.)

All around him he tasted fear. He stood in semidarkness as the torchbearers edged away; shadows sprang up to claim more of the vault. Even Sooleyrah and Kreech had moved away, toward the door.

Then the floor of the vault began to rise.

There was a section of the flooring, twice as long as the height of a man and half as wide, that was separate from the rest; Lasten had searched for and found the edges of that section when he'd been on hands and knees earlier. Now the section was rising out of the floor, accompanied by a low subterranean hum of machinery. It was a block of heavy plastoid, and as Lasten and the others stared in wonder and terror it raised itself steadily to a height almost up to their shoulders.

It was a compartment, transparent-sided; inside it lay the body of an Immortal— or a demon, a god, a monster. He was huge, twice the size of Lasten or Sooleyrah or any of the rest of them; they could see that even while he was lying down, in the moving shadows of torchlight.

The mechanisms of the compartment were whirring to life; Lasten saw the top of the case lifting off, smelled stale air as it was released from the case, saw a needle-thin marker on the side of the compartment leap to the end of its dial, and at the same time the giant's body convulsed, back arching, muscles quivering. It settled back, but again the dial-marker leaped, and the huge body with it.

This time there came a moan, low and weak, and the monster's head rolled onto its side. Its mouth was open, slack; the eyes fluttered; the hands shook and moved.

Needles and tubes withdrew from the body, sinking back into their seats within the case. The dials settled to rest.

The Immortal's eyes opened and stared emptily at them.

Hell hell hell hell hell big monstrous inhuman devil hell hell kill us all kill us no no!

The eyes opened wider, and the creature moaned again, louder now. It was a deep growl, half-choked, and it echoed from the walls.

Hate us hate us all kill us kill me me me me no!

And the giant tried to sit up.

Its hands scratched at the sides of the case, lacking coordination, lacking strength. The creature grunted and fell back; it breathed in pain-wracked gobbets of air, making harsh gasping sounds deep in its throat.

Kreech screamed. He threw himself at the men standing frozen in the doorway and fought his way through them, still screaming. He sent others reeling backward as he burst through, and several followed him, adding their screams to his. Sooleyrah yelled after him, started to run too but hesitated.

Lasten stood rooted in fright, his whole being filled with terror, both from himself and from the flood of panic in the minds around him. Red, bursting fear, splashing white-hot into his stomach, his chest . . .

Kill me kill me kill me me me me kill—

The giant sat up, and it was monstrous. Twice the height of a man, it swayed and moaned above them in the dark vault. Its fingers scrabbled spasmodically; it slipped back onto one elbow; its eyes rolled as it stared down at them. And it spoke.

"God . . . oh God . . . what are you? What *are* you?"

A weak, thin voice. Frightened.

"Help me . . . please, help—"

Suddenly it tumbled over, falling off the side of its mount, headfirst onto the floor at Lasten's feet. It crashed heavily and noisily, sending Lasten staggering back in fright. The monster writhed there on the floor, hands clutching air, legs jerking, spittle falling from its mouth. And then it slumped, and sobbed weakly, hopelessly. "Oh God, please . . ."

Kill me kill me me me kill kill and Lasten suddenly had a large stone in his hands and he ran forward and brought it down with all his strength on the monster's face. It smashed in one eye, a side of the head, and thin red blood spurted. The giant thrashed about wildly, arms flung up and feet kicking spasmodically, and faint little sobs came from its gaping mouth. Lasten hit it again, and again, and again, and he was screaming now, screaming to drown out the cries of the monster, and he hit it again, and again, and *harder* . . .

And at last there were only his own screams in the vault. The monster, the Immortal, the inhuman giant lay silent and destroyed at his feet. Sooleyrah and the rest had fled. Lasten choked off his cries and dropped the slippery red stone. He fell against the case, hardly noticing the blood that covered his legs and hands.

I'm alive I'm alive, alive . . . I'm alive . . .

It was more than an hour later when Sooleyrah and Kreech crept back up to the vault. There had been silence for all that time, and the monster had not come out after them.

Kreech carried a torch; he thrust it before him through the doorway. He saw the demon-monster, and he recoiled; but then he realized that it lay completely still and there was blood all around its smashed head.

Sooleyrah pushed past him and entered the vault. He saw Lasten standing beside the monster's case, a dark stone in his hands. Lasten brought the stone down once, twice, and the molding broke; pieces showered to his blood-caked feet. He reached into the recesses of the case, yanked, and brought forth a handful of wires, red, yellow, blue, green.

He looked up and saw Sooleyrah, and smiled.

And giggled.

And said, "Come on, Sooleyrah. Come on, little dancer leader. No demon left to hurt you now, oh no, no demon, no monster. Devil scared you? But I killed him—*me.* Don't be scared, dancer, don't be scared; come inside. Plenty of stuff here, oh plenty. And in other vaults too."

He held up the fistful of many-colored wires.
"Pretty?"

For Practice

1. How does Carr's argument in this story extend, challenge, contradict, or otherwise modify Shelley's argument about progress in his version of "Ozymandias"?

2. What is the function of the distinction he makes among the classes of people (the thinkers, the weirds, the Immortals)? How does this distinction relate to the overall theme of the story and to notions of alienation described in the introduction to this chapter?

3. What is the role of magic in this story and how is it related to attitudes about nature and technology? What does this suggest about the nature of human knowledge?

4. Analyze the first paragraph. Carr does not provide an elaborate introduction to the setting and action of this story but immediately plunges the reader into an unfamiliar setting. What effect does the beginning of the story have upon the reader, and how does this technique enhance Carr's overall argument?

5. The setting of this short story is in the future, but the argument is directed toward readers of today. What does Carr gain by placing the argument in the future? How does this affect its credibility?

6. Do you feel any differently about the consequences of technology as a result of reading this story? In what ways?

Writing Your Own Arguments

1. Investigate current debates about the impact of industry on the environment. You may want to focus on one or two particular industries such as paper production or silicon chip production. Consider varying points of view from a number of sources. What are the concerns of environmentalists? How do industry supporters address these concerns? Is there always a clear line separating these two groups? How are the stances of the two groups presented in the popular media? What are the economic and environmental effects of industry on the surrounding communities? As a result of your investigation, create an argument that addresses the concerns of either the industry or its critics.

2. What are some of the environmental concerns in your local community? Select one of these issues and write an essay based on background research. You may have to go through archives of a local newspaper and interview community leaders and private citizens involved in the issue in order to gather information you will need to write your essay. Consider the following questions: How long has the concern been an issue? Which groups or individuals are in conflict with regard to the issue? What roles might class, race, and gender play in this conflict?

3. Over the years a number of films (i.e. *Blade Runner, The Terminator, The Fifth Element, The Truman Show, Brazil, Jurassic Park*) have focused on the relationship between individuals and their technological environments. Select and view one or two films and write an essay in which you analyze the position of the characters in relation to technology. In what ways are their lives determined by technology? To what degree do they act in conjunction with technology, and to what degree do they act in conflict with it? How do the narrative, the characters' thoughts and actions, and the overall theme and visual effect of the film reflect present-day thinking about technology. If possible, do some research on the film's production and try to learn more about the filmmakers' own visions of the role of technology. If the film is based on a novel, try to learn more about the relationship between the original written narrative and the film. You may also want to read reviews written at the time of the film's release.

4. Select and read a novel by William Gibson, Ursula K. LeGuin, Robert Heinlein, Harlan Ellison, or another science-fiction/fantasy author with whom you and your instructor are familiar. Do some background research on the author and the text and write an essay in which you analyze the position of the characters in relationship to technology. In what ways are their lives determined by technology? To what degree do they act in conjunction with technology, and to what degree do they act in conflict with it? How do the narrative, the characters' thoughts and actions, and novel's theme reflect present-day thinking about technology?

5. In this unit you have read works by both 19th- and 20th-century authors. Select a work from each century from this unit or another unit in the text, and write an essay in which you discuss the representation of alienation in these works. How are class, race, and gender constructed as part of the problem in the works you have selected? Describe what you see as the relationship between these works. Do some background research on each piece and

each author, and address the ideas of outside sources along with the presentation of your own ideas.

6. Many scholars and critics characterize science fiction as didactic literature, meaning that it is meant to teach a lesson. Part of the reason for this is that science fiction has long passages of expository prose. How do you react to this type of exposition in a novel? Does it hold your interest? Does it persuade you? Or do you find it boring and skip over it? Consider how the relative merits of expository prose and action and figurative language. Is it possible that the same argument can be made using either prose or more creative forms? Support your contentions with examples from texts in this unit.

UNIT SEVEN

A Midsummer Night's Dream

A Midsummer Night's Dream

William Shakespeare
edited by Alice Griffin[1]

William Shakespeare (1564–1616) was born in Stratford-upon-Avon, a small market town north of London. Though the date of his baptism, April 26, is known, the exact date of his birth is unknown and so it is frequently celebrated on the anniversary of his death on April 23. We can assume, given the quality of his writing, that he had the regular grammar school education available to a person of his status. We know little about his early years other than that he married Anne Hathaway in 1582 and had at least three children—Susanna, born in 1583, and twins Hamnet and Judith, born in 1585. Other than these minimal details of his family life, little more is known. We do not know, for example, how or when he became involved with the stage. The first reference to Shakespeare as a member of the theatrical profession is an attack on his plays, supposed to have been written in 1592 by Robert Greene, a rival. The Comedy of Errors, *his earliest play, was probably written in the early 1590s. His last play,* The Tempest, *was probably written around 1611; there is at least one record of its performance in 1613. Between these dates, Shakespeare was involved in many theatrical productions as actor, writer, and leader of his own troupe. There are thirty-six plays in the Shakespeare canon and still others believed to have been written by him in whole or in part. In addition to the plays, he authored a sonnet sequence (see Unit Two for more information) and several long poems. Though he was respected in his lifetime, Shakespeare's literary reputation grew after his death until it achieved the extraordinary celebrity it enjoys today. Almost four hundred years after his death, his plays continue to be studied and acted and adapted.*

A Midsummer Night's Dream *was written about 1595 or 1596, probably to celebrate a courtly marriage. Unlike many of the plays whose plots derive from other sources, the plot of* A Midsummer Night's Dream *seems*

---

[1] Professor Griffin's text for *A Midsummer Night's Dream* is the First Quarto (edition) published in 1600, with modification based on the Quarto edition of 1619 and the First Folio, published in 1623. Stage directions in those editions are printed here without brackets; added stage directions are printed within brackets. We have edited Griffin's notes for this text.

to be original with Shakespeare. The action of the play is made up of several intersecting plots: the marriage of Theseus, Prince of Athens and Hippolyta, queen of the Amazons; a quarrel between Titania and Oberon, king and queen of the fairies; the confusion between the four lovers; and the comedy provided by Bottom the Weaver and his fellow players. Major themes of the play include the nature of true love, the conflict between the sexes, the contrast between law and disorder, the tension between the city and the country, and the role of art versus nature. The mischievous interference of Puck in the affairs of both humans and fairies and the comic antics of Bottom in his attempts to produce a tragic wedding play have made A Midsummer Night's Dream *a favorite play for actors, directors, and audiences. Puck and Bottom force characters and readers alike to answer Theseus' question "How shall we find the concord of this discord?"*

THE NAMES OF THE ACTORS

THESEUS, *Duke of Athens*
EGEUS, *father of Hermia*
LYSANDER, *beloved of Hermia*
DEMETRIUS, *in love with Hermia, favoured by Egeus*
PHILOSTRATE, *Master of the Revels to Theseus*
PETER QUINCE, *a carpenter (Prologue)**
NICK BOTTOM, *a weaver (Pyramus)**
FRANCIS FLUTE, *a bellows-mender (Thisby)**
TOM SNOUT, *a tinker (Wall)**
SNUG, *a joiner (Lion)**
ROBIN STARVELING, *a tailor (Moonshine)**
HIPPOLYTA, *Queen of the Amazons, betrothed to Theseus*
HERMIA, *daughter of Egeus, in love with Lysander*
HELENA, *in love with Demetrius*
OBERON, *King of the Fairies*
TITANIA, *Queen of the Fairies*
PUCK, *or* ROBIN GOODFELLOW
PEASEBLOSSOM
COBWEB
MOTH
MUSTARDSEED
Other Fairies attending Oberon *and* TITANIA. *Attendants on* THESEUS *and* HIPPOLYTA.

ACT 1

Scene: *Athens, and a wood nearby*

[SCENE 1. Athens. The palace of THESEUS*]*

---

* Characters who play in the interlude.

Enter THESEUS, HIPPOLYTA,° [PHILOSTRATE,] *with others.*

THESEUS. Now fair Hippolyta, our nuptial hour
    Draws on apace: four happy days bring in
    Another moon: but O, methinks how slow
    This old moon wanes! she lingers° my desires,
    Like to a stepdame or a dowager,°   5
    Long withering out° a young man's revenue.
HIPPOLYTA. Four days will quickly steep themselves in night:
    Four nights will quickly dream away the time:
    And then the moon, like to a silver bow
    New-bent in heaven, shall behold the night   10
    Of our solemnities.
THESEUS.   Go Philostrate,
    Stir up the Athenian youth to merriments,
    Awake the pert° and nimble spirit of mirth,
    Turn melancholy forth to funerals:
    The pale companion° is not for our pomp.   *[Exit* PHILOSTRATE.*]* 15
    Hippolyta, I wooed thee with my sword,
    And won thy love doing thee injuries;
    But I will wed thee in another key,
    With pomp, with triumph,° and with reveling.

Enter EGEUS *and his daughter* HERMIA, LYSANDER *and* DEMETRIUS.

EGEUS. Happy be Theseus, our renownèd duke.   20
THESEUS. Thanks good Egeus:° what's the news with thee?
EGEUS. Full of vexation come I, with complaint
    Against my child, my daughter Hermia.
    Stand forth Demetrius. My noble lord,
    This man hath my consent to marry her.   25
    Stand forth Lysander. And my gracious duke,
    This man hath bewitched the bosom of my child.
    Thou, thou Lysander, thou has given her rhymes,
    And interchanged love tokens with my child:
    Thou hast by moonlight at her window sung,   30
    With feigning voice, verses of feigning° love,
    And stol'n the impression of her fantasy°
    With bracelets of thy hair, rings, gauds,° conceits,°
    Knacks,° trifles, nosegays, sweetmeats—messengers
    Of strong prevailment in unhardened youth.   35
    With cunning hast thou filched my daughter's heart,
    Turned her obedience, which is due to me,
    To stubborn harshness. And my gracious duke,

0.3 S.D.: *Theseus, Hippolyta:* In Greek legend, Theseus captured the Amazon Queen Hippolyta and brought her to Athens where they were married.   **4** *lingers:* delays the fulfillment of.   **5** *dowager:* a widow supported by her dead husband's heirs.   **6** *withering out:* (1) depleting (2) growing withered.   **13** *pert:* lively.   **15** *companion:* fellow (contemptuous).   **19** *triumph:* public festival.   **21** *Egeus:* (trisyllabic).   **31** *feigning:* (1) deceptive (2) desirous ("faining").   **32** *stol'n . . . fantasy:* stealthily imprinted your image upon her fancy.   **33** *gauds:* trinkets.   *conceits:* either (a) love poetry, or (b) love tokens.   **34** *Knacks:* knick-knacks.

Be it so° she will not here before your grace
Consent to marry with Demetrius, 40
I beg the ancient privilege of Athens:
As she is mine, I may dispose of her:
Which shall be, either to this gentleman,
Or to her death, according to our law
Immediately° provided in that case. 45
THESEUS. What say you, Hermia? Be advised, fair maid.
To you your father should be as a god:
One that composed your beauties: yea and one
To whom you are but as a form in wax
By him imprinted, and within his power 50
To leave the figure, or disfigure it:
Demetrius is a worthy gentleman.
HERMIA. So is Lysander.
THESEUS.   In himself he is:
But in this kind, wanting your father's voice,°
The other man must be held the worthier. 55
HERMIA. I would my father looked but with my eyes.
THESEUS. Rather your eyes must with his judgment look.
HERMIA. I do entreat your grace to pardon me.
I know not by what power I am made bold,
Nor how it may concern my modesty, 60
In such a presence, here to plead my thoughts:
But I beseech your grace that I may know
The worst that may befall me in this case,
If I refuse to wed Demetrius.
THESEUS. Either to die the death, or to abjure 65
For ever the society of men.
Therefore fair Hermia, question your desires,
Know of your youth,° examine well your blood,°
Whether, if you yield not to your father's choice,
You can endure the livery° of a nun, 70
For aye° to be in shady cloister mewed,°
To live a barren sister all your life,
Chanting faint hymns to the cold fruitless moon.°
Thrice blessèd they that master so their blood,
To undergo such maiden pilgrimage: 75
But earthlier happy° is the rose distilled,°
Than that which, withering on the virgin thorn,
Grows, lives, and dies, in single blessedness.
HERMIA. So will I grow, so live, so die my lord,
Ere I will yield my virgin patent° up 80

39 *Be it so:* if it be that.   45 *Immediately:* precisely.   54 *in . . . voice:* in this respect, lacking your father's approval.   68 *Know . . . youth:* ask yourself as a young person.   68 *blood:* passions.   70 *livery:* habit.   71 *aye:* ever.   *mewed:* shut up.   73 *moon:* (the moon goddess Diana represented unmarried chastity).   76 *earthlier happy:* more happy on earth.   *distilled:* i.e., into perfume (thus its essence is passed on, as to a child).   80 *patent:* privilege.

Unto his lordship, whose unwishèd yoke
My soul consents not to give sovereignty.
THESEUS. Take time to pause, and by the next moon,
  The sealing day betwixt my love and me,
  For everlasting bond of fellowship,   85
  Upon that day either prepare to die
  For disobedience to your father's will,
  Or else to wed Demetrius, as he would,
  Or on Diana's altar to protest°
  For aye, austerity and single life.   90
DEMETRIUS. Relent, sweet Hermia, and Lysander, yield
  Thy crazèd° title to my certain right.
LYSANDER. You have her father's love, Demetrius:
  Let me have Hermia's: do you marry him.
EGEUS. Scornful Lysander, true, he hath my love: 95
  And what is mine, my love shall render him.
  And she is mine, and all my right of her
  I do estate° unto Demetrius.
LYSANDER. I am, my lord, as well derived° as he,
  As well possessed:° my love is more than his: 100
  My fortunes every way as fairly ranked
  (If not with vantage) as° Demetrius':
  And, which is more than all these boasts can be,
  I am beloved of beauteous Hermia.
  Why should not I then prosecute my right?   105
  Demetrius, I'll avouch it to his head,°
  Made love to Nedar's daughter, Helena,
  And won her soul: and she, sweet lady, dotes,
  Devoutly dotes, dotes in idolatry,
  Upon this spotted° and inconstant man.   110
THESEUS. I must confess that I have heard so much,
  And with Demetrius thought to have spoke thereof:
  But being over-full of self-affairs,
  My mind did lose it. But Demetrius come,
  And come Egeus, you shall go with me: 115
  I have some private schooling for you both.
  For you fair Hermia, look you arm yourself,
  To fit your fancies to your father's will;
  Or else the law of Athens yields you up
  (Which by no means we may extenuate)   120
  To death or to a vow of single life.
  Come my Hippolyta, what cheer my love?
  Demetrius and Egeus, go along:
  I must employ you in some business
  Against° our nuptial, and confer with you   125

89 *protest:* vow.   92 *crazèd:* flawed.   98 *estate:* transfer.   99 *well derived:* well born.   100 *well possessed:* wealthy.   102 *with vantage, as:* better, than.   106 *avouch . . . head:* prove it to his faces.   110 *spotted:* stained (by betrayal of Helena).   125 *Against:* in preparation for.

Of something nearly° that concerns yourselves.

EGEUS. With duty and desire we follow you.

Exeunt.° Manent° LYSANDER *and* HERMIA.

LYSANDER. How now my love? Why is your cheek so pale?
 How chance the roses there do fade so fast?

HERMIA. Belike° for want of rain, which I could well   130
 Beteem° them from the tempest of my eyes,

LYSANDER. Ay me, for aught that I could ever read,
 Could ever hear by tale or history,
 The course of true love never did run smooth;
 But either it was different in blood—   135

HERMIA. O cross! too high° to be enthralled to low.°

LYSANDER. Or else misgraffed° in respect of years—

HERMIA. O spite! too old to be engaged to young.

LYSANDER. Or else it stood upon the choice of friends—

HERMIA. O hell! to choose love by another's eyes.   140

LYSANDER. Or if there were a sympathy in choice,
 War, death, or sickness did lay siege to it;
 Making it momentany° as a sound,
 Swift as a shadow, short as any dream,
 Brief as the lightning in the collied° night,   145
 That, in a spleen,° unfolds both heaven and earth;
 And ere a man hath power to say "Behold,"
 The jaws of darkness do devour it up:
 So quick bright things come to confusion.

HERMIA. If then true lovers have been ever crossed,°   150
 It stands as an edict in destiny:
 Then let us teach our trial patience,°
 Because it is a customary cross,
 As due to love as thoughts and dreams and sighs,
 Wishes and tears; poor Fancy's° followers.   155

LYSANDER. A good persuasion: therefore hear me, Hermia:
 I have a widow aunt, a dowager,
 Of great revenue, and she hath no child:
 From Athens is her house remote seven leagues,
 And she respects° me as her only son: 160
 There gentle Hermia, may I marry thee,
 And to that place the sharp Athenian law
 Cannot pursue us. If thou lov'st me then,
 Steal forth thy father's house tomorrow night:
 And in the wood, a league without the town,   165
 Where I did meet thee once with Helena

---

126 *nearly:* closely.   127 S.D.: *Exeunt:* they exit.   *Manent:* they remain.   130 *Belike:* likely.
131 *Beteem:* (1) pour out on (2) allow.   136 *high:* high-born.   *enthralled to low:* made a slave to
one of low birth.   137 *misgraffèd:* badly joined.   143 *momentany:* momentary.   145 *collied:*
black as coal.   146 *in a spleen:* impulsively, in a sudden outburst.   150 *ever crossed:* evermore
thwarted.   153 *teach . . . patience:* teach ourselves to be patient.   155 *Fancy:* love (sometimes
infatuation).   160 *respects:* regards.

To do observance to a morn of May,°
There will I stay° for thee.
HERMIA.   My good Lysander,
   I swear to thee, by Cupid's strongest bow,
   By his best arrow, with the golden head,°   •   170
   By the simplicity of Venus's doves,
   By that which knitteth souls and prospers loves,
   And by that fire which burned the Carthage queen,
   When the false Troyan° under sail was seen,
   By all the vows that ever men have broke,   175
   (In number more than ever women spoke)
   In that same place thou has appointed me,
   Tomorrow truly will I meet with thee.
LYSANDER. Keep promise love: look, here comes Helena.

Enter HELENA.

HERMIA. God speed fair Helena: whither away?   180
HELENA. Call you me fair? That fair again unsay.
   Demetrius loves your fair:° O happy fair!
   Your eyes are lodestars,° and your tongue's sweet air°
   More tuneable than lark to shepherd's ear,
   When wheat is green, when hawthorn buds appear.
   Sickness is catching: O were favour° so,
   Yours would I catch, fair Hermia, ere I go,
   My ear should catch your voice,° my eye your eye,°   185
   My tongue should catch your tongue's sweet melody.
   Were the world mine, Demetrius being bated,°
   The rest I'ld give to be to you translated.°
   O teach me how you look, and with what art
   You sway the motion of Demetrius' heart.
HERMIA. I frown upon him; yet he loves me still.
HELENA. O that your frowns would teach my smiles such skill.   190
HERMIA. I give him curses; yet he gives me love.
HELENA. O that my prayers could such affection move.
HERMIA. The more I hate, the more he follows me.
HELENA. The more I love, the more he hateth me.
HERMIA. His folly, Helena, is no fault of mine.
HELENA. None but your beauty; would that fault were mine.
HERMIA. Take comfort: he no more shall see my face: 195
   Lysander and myself will fly this place.
   Before the time I did Lysander see,
   Seemed Athens as a paradise to me:
   O then, what graces in my love do dwell,

---

167 *do . . . May:* celebrate May Day.   168 *stay:* wait.   170 *golden head:* (The arrow with the gold head causes love).   173–174 *Carthage Queen . . . false Troyan:* Dido, who burned herself to death on a funeral pyre when Trojan Aeneas deserted her.   182 *your fair:* i.e., beauty.   183 *lodestars:* guiding stars.   *air:* music.   186 *favour:* appearance.   188 *My ear . . . voice:* my ear should catch the tone of your voice.   *my eye your eye:* my eye should catch the way you glance.   190 *bated:* subtracted, excepted.   191 *translated:* transformed.

That he hath turned a heaven unto hell!
LYSANDER. Helen, to you our minds we will unfold:
    Tomorrow night, when Phoebe° doth behold
    Her silver visage in the wat'ry glass,°   210
    Decking with liquid pearl the bladed grass
    (A time that lovers' flights doth still° conceal)
    Through Athens gates have we devised to steal.
HERMIA. And in the wood, where often you and I
    Upon faint primrose beds were wont to lie,   215
    Emptying our bosoms of their counsel° sweet,
    There my Lysander and myself shall meet,
    And thence from Athens turn away our eyes,
    To see new friends and stranger companies.°
    Farewell, sweet playfellow: pray thou for us: 220
    And good luck grant thee thy Demetrius.
    Keep word Lysander: we must starve our sight
    From lovers' food,° till morrow deep midnight.
LYSANDER. I will my Hermia.   *Exit* HERMIA.
                Helena adieu:
As you on him, Demetrius dote on you.°   *Exit* LYSANDER. 225
HELENA. How happy some, o'er other some, can be!
    Through Athens I am thought as fair as she.
    But what of that? Demetrius thinks not so:
    He will not know what all but he do know.
    And as he errs, doting on Hermia's eyes,   230
    So I, admiring of his qualities.
    Things base and vile, holding no quantity.°
    Love can transpose to form and dignity.
    Love looks not with the eyes, but with the mind:
    And therefore is winged Cupid painted blind.   235
    Nor hath Love's mind of any judgment taste:
    Wings, and no eyes, figure° unheedy haste.
    And therefore is Love said to be a child:
    Because in choice he is so often beguiled.
    As waggish boys in game themselves forswear: 240
    So the boy Love is perjured everywhere.
        For ere Demetrius looked on Hermia's eyne,°
        He hailed down oaths that he was only mine.
        And when this hail some heat from Hermia felt,
        So he dissolved, and show'rs of oaths did melt.   245
    I will go tell him of fair Hermia's flight:
    Then to the wood will he tomorrow night
    Pursue her: and for this intelligence,°

209 *Phoebe:* Diana, the moon.   210 *wat'ry glass:* mirror of the water.   212 *still:* always.   216 *counsel:* secrets.   219 *stranger companies:* the companionship of strangers.   223 *lovers' food:* the sight of the loved one.   225 *As . . . you:* As you dote on Demetrius, so may Demetrius also dote on you.   223 *holding no quantity:* out of proportion.   237 *figure:* symbolize.   242 *eyne:* eyes. 248 *intelligence:* information.

If I have thanks, it is a dear expense:°
But herein mean I to enrich my pain,   250
To have his sight° thither and back again.   *Exit.*

[SCENE 2. QUINCE's house]

Enter QUINCE *the Carpenter; and* SNUG *the Joiner; and* BOTTOM *the Weaver; and*
FLUTE *the Bellows-mender; and* SNOUT *the Tinker; and* STARVELING *the Tailor.*°

QUINCE. Is all our company here?
BOTTOM. You were the best to call them generally,° man by man,
   according to the scrip.
QUINCE. Here is the scroll of every man's name which is thought
   fit, through all Athens, to play in our interlude° before   5
   the duke and the duchess, on his wedding-day at night.
BOTTOM. First good Peter Quince, say what the play treats on,
   then read the names of the actors: and so grow to a point.
QUINCE. Marry,° our play is "The most lamentable comedy, and
   most cruel death of Pyramus and Thisby."   10
BOTTOM. A very good piece of work I assure you, and a merry. Now
   good Peter Quince, call forth your actors by the scroll.
   Masters, spread yourselves.
QUINCE. Answer as I call you. Nick Bottom the weaver?
BOTTOM. Ready: name what part I am for, and proceed.   15
QUINCE. You, Nick Bottom, are set down for Pyramus.
BOTTOM. What is Pyramus? A lover, or a tyrant?
QUINCE. A lover that kills himself, most gallant, for love.
BOTTOM. That will ask some tears in the true performing of it. If I
   do it, let the audience look to their eyes: I will move   20
   storms: I will condole° in some measure. To the rest—
   yet my chief humour° is for a tyrant. I could play Ercles°
   rarely, or a part to tear a cat in, to make all split.°
      The raging rocks
      And shivering shocks,   25
      Shall break the locks
        Of prison gates,
      And Phibbus' car°
      Shall shine from far,
      And make and mar   30
        The foolish Fates.
   This was lofty. Now name the rest of the players. This is
   Ercles' vein, a tyrant's vein: a lover is more condoling.
QUINCE. Francis Flute, the bellows-mender?

249 *dear expense:* costly outlay (on Demetrius' part).   250–251 *But . . . sight:* but I will be rewarded just by the sight of him.   0.2 S.D.: the low characters' names describe their work: *Quince:*
quoins, wooden wedges used in building. *Snug:* fitting snugly, suiting a joiner of furniture. *Bottom:*
bobbin or core on which yarn is wound. *Flute:* mender of fluted church organs and bellows. *Snout:*
spout (of the kettles he mends). *Starveling:* (tailors being traditionally thin).   2 *generally:* Bottom
often uses the wrong word; here he means the opposite: "severally, one-by-one."   5 *interlude:* short
play.   9 *Marry:* indeed (mild oath, corruption of "by the Virgin Mary").   21 *condole:* lament.   22
humour: inclination.   *Ercles:* Hercules (typified by ranting).   23 *tear . . . split:* (terms for ranting and raging on the stage).   28 *Phibbus' car:* Phoebus Apollo's chariot.

FLUTE. Here Peter Quince.   35
QUINCE. Flute, you must take Thisby on you.
FLUTE. What is Thisby? A wand'ring knight?
QUINCE. It is the lady that Pyramus must love.
FLUTE. Nay faith, let me not play a woman: I have a beard
 coming.   40
QUINCE. That's all one:° you shall play it in a mask, and you may
 speak as small° as you will.
BOTTOM. And° I may hide my face, let me play Thisby too: I'll speak
 in a monstrous little voice; "Thisne, Thisne," "Ah
 Pyramus, my lover dear, thy Thisby dear, and lady   45
 dear."
QUINCE. No, no, you must play Pyramus: and Flute, you Thisby.
BOTTOM. Well, proceed.
QUINCE. Robin Starveling, the tailor?
STARVELING. Here Peter Quince.   50
QUINCE. Robin Starveling, yoiu must play Thisby's mother. Tom
 Snout, the tinker?
STARVELING. Here Peter Quince.
QUINCE. You, Pyramus' father; myself, Thisby's father; Snug the
 joiner, you the lion's part: and I hope here is a play   55
 fitted.°
SNUG. Have you the lion's part written? Pray you, if it be, give
 it me: for I am slow of study.
QUINCE. You may do it extempore: for it is nothing but roaring.
BOTTOM. Let me play the lion too. I will roar, that° I will do any   60
 man's heart good to hear me. I will roar, that I will make
 the duke say "Let him roar again: let him roar again."
QUINCE. And you should do it too terribly, you would fright the
 duchess and the ladies, that they would shriek: and
 that were enough to hang us all.   65
ALL. That would hang us, every mother's son.
BOTTOM. I grant you, friends, if you should fright the ladies out of
 their wits, they would have no more discretion but to
 hang us: but I will aggravate° my voice so, that I will roar
 you as gently as any sucking dove: I will roar you and   70
 'twere° any nightingale.
QUINCE. You can play no part but Pyramus: for Pyramus is a
 sweet-faced man; a proper° man as one shall see in a
 summer's day; a most lovely gentleman-like man: therefore
 you must needs play Pyramus.   75
BOTTOM. Well: I will undertake it. What beard were I best to play
 it in?
QUINCE. Why, what you will.

---

41 *That's all one:* never mind.　　42 *small:* softly.　　43 *And:* if.　　56 *fitted:* cast.　　60 *that:* so that.
69 *aggravate:* (he means "moderate").　　70–71 *and 'twere:* as if it were.　　73 *proper:* handsome.

BOTTOM. I will discharge it in either your straw-colour beard, your
    orange-tawny beard, your purple-in-grain° beard, or your   80
    French-crown-colour° beard, your perfit yellow.
QUINCE. Some of your French crowns° have no hair at all; and
    then you will play barefaced. But masters here are your
    parts, and I am to entreat you, request you, and desire
    you, to con° them by tomorrow night: and meet me in the   85
    palace wood, a mile without the town, by moonlight;
    there we will rehearse: for if we meet in the city, we
    shall be dogged with company, and our devices° known.
    In the meantime, I will draw a bill of properties,° such
    as our play wants. I pray you fail me not.   90
BOTTOM. We will meet, and there we may rehearse most obscenely°
    and courageously. Take pain, be perfit: adieu.
QUINCE. At the duke's oak we meet.
BOTTOM. Enough: hold, or cut bow-strings.°   *Exeunt.*

ACT 2

[SCENE 1. A wood near Athens]

    Enter a FAIRY *at one door, and* ROBIN GOODFELLOW *[Puck] at another.*

PUCK. How now spirit, whither wander you?
FAIRY. Over hill, over dale,
    Thorough bush, thorough brier,
    Over park, over pale,°
    Thorough flood, thorough fire: 5
    I do wander everywhere,
    Swifter than the moon's sphere:
    And I serve the Fairy Queen,
    To dew° her orbs° upon the green.
    The cowslips° tall her pensioners° be,   10
    In their gold coats, spots you see:
    Those be rubies, fairy favours:°
    In those freckles live their savours.°
    I must go seek some dewdrops here,
    And hang a pearl in every cowslip's ear.   15
    Farewell thou lob° of spirits: I'll be gone,
    Our queen and all her elves come here anon.
PUCK. The king doth keep his revels here tonight.
    Take heed the queen come not within his sight.
    For Oberon is passing fell° and wrath,   20

---

80 *purple-in-grain:* dyed permanently purple.   81 *French-crown-colour:* golden, like French
crowns (gold coins).   82 *French crowns:* bald heads believed to be caused by syphilis, the "French"
disease.   85 *con:* learn by heart.   88 *devices:* plans.   89 *bill of properties:* list of stage props.
91 *obscenely:* (he may mean "fittingly" or "obscurely").   94 *hold, or cut bow-strings:* (meaning
uncertain, but equivalent to "fish, or cut bait").   4 *pale:* enclosure.   9 *dew:* bedew.   *orbs:* fairy
rings (circles of high grass).   10 *cowslips:* primroses.   *pensioners:* royal bodyguards.
12 *favours:* gifts.   13 *savours:* perfumes.   16 *lob:* lout, lubber.   20 *passing fell:* surpassingly
fierce.

Because that she, as her attendant, hath
A lovely boy, stol'n from an Indian king:
She never had so sweet a changeling.°
And jealous Oberon would have the child
Knight of his train, to trace° the forests wild.   25
But she, perforce,° withholds the lovèd boy,
Crowns him with flowers, and makes him all her joy.
And now, they never meet in grove or green,
By fountain clear, or spangled starlight sheen,
But they do square,° that all their elves for fear   30
Creep into acorn cups, and hide them there.

FAIRY. Either I mistake your shape and making quite,
Or else you are that shrewd and knavish sprite
called Robin Goodfellow. Are you not he
That frights the maidens of the villagery,   35
Skim milk,° and sometimes labour in the quern,°
And bootless° make the breathless housewife churn,
And sometimes make the drink to bear no barm,°
Mislead night-wanderers, laughing at their harm?
Those that Hobgoblin call you, and sweet Puck,   40
You do their work, and they shall have good luck.
Are you not he?

PUCK.   Thou speakest aright;
I am that merry wanderer of the night.
I jest to Oberon, and make him smile,
When I a fat and bean-fed horse beguile,   45
Neighing in likeness of a filly foal;
And sometime lurk I in a gossip's° bowl,
In very likeness of a roasted crab,°
And when she drinks, against her lips I bob,
And on her withered dewlap° pour the ale.   50
The wisest aunt, telling the saddest tale,
Sometime for three-foot stool mistaketh me:
Then slip I from her bum, down topples she,
And "tailor"° cries, and falls into a cough;
And then the whole quire° hold their hips and laugh,   55
And waxen° in their mirth, and neeze,° and swear
A merrier hour was never wasted° there.
But room° fairy: here comes Oberon.

FAIRY. And here, my mistress. Would that he were gone.

---

23 *changeling:* creature exchanged by fairies for a stolen baby (among the fairies, the stolen child).
25 *trace:* traverse.   26 *perforce:* by force.   30 *square:* quarrel.   36 *Skim milk:* steals the cream
off the milk.   *quern:* handmill for grinding grain.   37 *bootless:* without result.   38 *barm:* foamy
head (therefore the drink was flat).   47 *gossip's:* old woman's.   48 *crab:* crabapple (often put into
ale).   50 *dewlap:* loose skin hanging about the throat.   54 *"tailor":* (variously explained: perhaps
the squatting position of the tailor, or "tailard"—one with a tail).   55 *quire:* choir, group.   56
waxen: increase.   *neeze:* sneeze.   57 *wasted:* spent.

*Enter [*OBERON*] the King of Fairies, at one door with his* TRAIN, *and the*
QUEEN *[*TITANIA*], at another, with hers.*

OBERON. Ill met by moonlight, proud Titania.   60
QUEEN. What, jealous Oberon? Fairy, skip hence.
    I have forsworn his bed and company.
OBERON. Tarry, rash wanton.° Am I not thy lord?
QUEEN. Then I must be thy lady: but I know
    When thou hast stol'n away from fairyland,   65
    And in the shape of Corin° sat all day,
    Playing on pipes of corn,° and versing love
    To amorous Phillida.° Why art thou here
    Come from the farthest steep of India?
    But that, forsooth, the bouncing Amazon,°   70
    Your buskined° mistress and your warrior love,
    To Theseus must be wedded; and you come,
    To give their bed joy and prosperity.
OBERON. How canst thou thus, for shame, Titania,
    Glance at my credit with° Hippolyta,   75
    Knowing I know thy love to Theseus?
    Didst not thou lead him through the glimmering night,
    From Perigenia, whom he ravishèd?
    And make him with fair Aegles break his faith,
    With Ariadne, and Antiopa?°   80
QUEEN. These are the forgeries of jealousy:
    And never, since the middle summer's spring,°
    Met we on hill, in dale, forest, or mead,
    By pavèd° fountain, or by rushy brook,
    Or in the beachèd margent° of the sea,   85
    To dance our ringlets to the whistling wind,
    But with thy brawls thou hast disturbed our sport.
    Therefore the winds, piping to us in vain,
    As in revenge, have sucked up from the sea
    Contagious° fogs: which falling in the land,   90
    Hath every pelting° river made so proud,
    That they have overborne their continents.°
    The ox hath therefore stretched his yoke in vain,
    The ploughman lost his sweat, and the green corn°
    Hath rotted, ere his youth attained a beard:°   95
    The fold° stands empty in the drownèd field,

---

58 *room:* make room.   63 *Tarry, rash wanton:* wait, headstrong one.   66–68 *Corin, Phillida:* (traditional names in pastoral literature for a shepherd and his loved one, respectively).   67 *corn:* wheat straws.   70 *Amazon:* Hippolyta.   71 *buskined:* wearing boots.   75 *Glance . . . credit with:* hint at my favors from.   78–80 *Perigenia . . . Antiopa:* women that Theseus supposedly loved and deserted.   82 *middle . . . spring:* beginning of midsummer.   84 *pavèd:* with a pebbly bottom.   85 *margent:* margin, shore.   88–117 *Therefore . . . original:* (the disturbance in nature reflects the discord between Oberon and Titania).   90 *Contagious:* spreading pestilence.   91 *pelting:* paltry. 92 *overborne their continents:* overflown the banks which contain them.   94 *corn:* grain.   95 *beard:* the tassels on ripened grain.   96 *fold:* enclosure for livestock.

And crows are fatted with the murrion° flock.
The nine men's morris° is filled up with mud:
And the quaint mazes° in the wanton green,°
For lack of tread, are undistinguishable.   100
The human mortals want° their winter here,
No night is now with hymn or carol blest;
Therefore the moon, the governess of floods,
Pale in her anger, washes all the air,
That rheumatic diseases do abound.   105
And thorough all this distemperature,° we see
The seasons after: hoary-headed frosts
Fall in the fresh lap of the crimson rose,
And on old Hiems'° thin and icy crown,
An odorous chaplet° of sweet summer buds   110
Is, as in mockery set. The spring, the summer,
The childing° autumn, angry winter change
Their wonted liveries:° and the mazèd° world,
By their increase, now knows not which is which:
And this same progeny of evils comes   115
From our debate, from our dissension:
We are their parents and original.°
OBERON. Do you amend it then: it lies in you.
Why should Titania cross her Oberon?
I do but beg a little changeling boy,   120
To be my henchman.°
QUEEN.   Set your heart at rest.
The fairy land buys not the child of me.
His mother was a vot'ress° of my order:
And in the spicèd Indian air, by night,   125
Full often hath she gossiped by my side.
And sat with me on Neptune's yellow sands,
Marking th' embarkèd traders° on the flood:
When we have laughed to see the sails conceive,
And grow big-bellied with the wanton° wind: 130
Which she, with pretty and with swimming gait,
Following (her womb then rich with my young squire)
Would imitate, and sail upon the land,
To fetch me trifles, and return again,
As from a voyage, rich with merchandise.   135
But she, being mortal, of that boy did die,
And for her sake, do I rear up her boy:
And for her sake, I will not part with him.

---

97 *murrion:* dead from murrain, a cattle disease.   98 *nine men's morris:* game played on squares
cut in the grass on which stones or disks are moved.   99 *quaint mazes:* intricate paths.   *wanton*
green: luxuriant grass.   101 *want:* lack.   106 *distemperature:* upset in nature.   109 *Hiems:* god
of winter.   110 *odorous chaplet:* sweet-smelling wreath.   112 *childing:* fruitful.   113 *wonted*
liveries: accustomed dress.   *mazèd:* amazed.   121 *henchman:* attendant.   123 *vot'ress:* vowed
and devoted follower   127 *traders:* merchant ships.   129 *wanton:* sportive.

OBERON. How long within this wood intend you stay?

QUEEN. Perchance till after Theseus' wedding day.

    If you will patiently dance in our round,°   140

    And see our moonlight revels, go with us:

    If not, shun me, and I will spare° your haunts.

OBERON. Give me that boy, and I will go with thee.

QUEEN. Not for thy fairy kingdom. Fairies away

    We shall chide downright, if I longer stay.   145

*Exeunt [*TITANIA *and her* TRAIN.*]*

OBERON. Well, go thy way. Thou shalt not from this grove,

    Till I torment thee for this injury.

    My gentle Puck come hither: thou rememb'rest,

    Since° once I sat upon a promontory,

    And heard a mermaid, on a dolphin's back,   150

    Uttering such dulcet and harmonious breath,

    That the rude° sea grew civil° at her song,

    And certain stars shot madly from their spheres,

    To hear the sea-maid's music.

PUCK.   I remember.

OBERON. That very time, I saw (but thou couldst not)   155

    Flying between the cold moon and the earth,

    Cupid, all armed: a certain aim he took

    At a fair Vestal,° thronèd by the west,

    And loosed his love-shaft smartly from his bow,

    As it should pierce a hundred thousand hearts: 160

    But I might see young Cupid's fiery shaft

    Quenched in the chaste beams of the wat'ry moon:

    And the imperial vot'ress° passèd on,

    In maiden meditation, fancy-free.°

    Yet marked I where the bolt° of Cupid fell.   165

    It fell upon a little western flower;

    Before, milk-white, now purple with love's wound,

    And maidens call it love-in-idleness.°

    Fetch me that flow'r: the herb I showed thee once.

    The juice of it, on sleeping eyelids laid,   170

    Will make or man or woman madly dote

    Upon the next live creature that it sees.

    Fetch me this herb, and be thou here again

    Ere the leviathan° can swim a league.

PUCK. I'll put a girdle round about the earth,   175

    In forty minutes.   *[Exit.]*

OBERON. Having once this juice,

    I'll watch Titania when she is asleep,

    And drop the liquor of it in her eyes:

140 *round:* round dance.   142 *spare:* shun.   149 *Since:* when.   152 *rude:* rough.   *civil:* calm.
158 *Vestal:* virgin, probable reference to Queen Elizabeth.   162 *imperial vot'ress:* royal devotee
(Queen Elizabeth) of Diana.   164 *fancy-free:* free from love.   165 *bolt:* arrow.   168 *love-in-idle-ness:* pansy.   174 *leviathan:* whale.

The next thing then she waking looks upon,
(Be it on lion, bear, or wolf, or bull,   180
On meddling monkey, or on busy° ape)
She shall pursue it, with the soul of love.
And ere I take this charm from off her sight
(As I can take it with another herb)
I'll make her render up her page to me.   185
But who comes here? I am invisible,
And I will overhear their conference.

Enter DEMETRIUS, HELENA *following him.*

DEMETRIUS. I love thee not: therefore pursue me not.
　　Where is Lysander and fair Hermia?
　　The one I'll slay: the other slayeth me.   190
　　Thou told'st me they were stol'n unto this wood:
　　And here am I, and wood° within this wood:
　　Because I cannot meet my Hermia.
　　Hence, get thee gone, and follow me no more.
HELENA. You draw me, you hard-hearted adamant:°   195
　　But yet you draw not iron, for my heart
　　Is true as steel. Leave you your power to draw,
　　And I shall have no more power to follow you.
DEMETRIUS. Do I entice you? Do I speak you fair?°
　　Or rather do I not in plainest truth   200
　　Tell you I do not, or I cannot love you?
HELENA. And even for that, do I love you the more:
　　I am your spaniel: and Demetrius,
　　The more you beat me, I will fawn on you.
　　Use me but as your spaniel: spurn me, strike me,   205
　　Neglect me, lose me: only give me leave,
　　Unworthy as I am, to follow you.
　　What worser place can I beg in your love
　　(And yet a place of high respect with me)
　　Than to be usèd as you use your dog.   210
DEMETRIUS. Tempt not too much the hatred of my spirit,
　　For I am sick, when I do look on thee.
HELENA. And I am sick, when I look not on you.
DEMETRIUS. You do impeach° your modesty too much,
　　To leave the city and commit yourself   215
　　Into the hands of one that loves you not,
　　To trust the opportunity of night,
　　And the ill counsel of a desert° place,
　　With the rich worth of your virginity.
HELENA. Your virtue is my privilege:° for that°   220
　　It is not night, when I do see your face,

181 *busy:* mischievous.　192 *wood:* crazy.　195 *adamant:* (1) magnet (2) impenetrably hard lode-
stone.　199 *you fair:* to you in a kindly way.　214 *impeach:* discredit.　218 *desert:* deserted.
220 *Your . . . privilege:* your attraction is my excuse (for coming).　*for that:* because.

Therefore I think I am not in the night.
Nor doth this wood lack worlds of company,
For you, in my respect,° are all the world.
Then how can it be said I am alone,   225
When all the world is here to look on me?
DEMETRIUS. I'll run from thee and hide me in the brakes,°
And leave thee to the mercy of wild beasts.
HELENA. The wildest hath not such a heart as you.
Run when you will: the story will be changed;   230
Apollo flies, and Daphne° holds the chase:
The dove pursues the griffin:° the mild hind°
Makes speed to catch the tiger. Bootless° speed,
When cowardice pursues, and valour flies.
DEMETRIUS. I will not stay° thy questions. Let me go: 235
Or if thou follow me, do not believe
But I shall do thee mischief in the wood.

                                                      [Exit DEMETRIUS.*]*

HELENA. Ay, in the temple, in the town, the field,
You do me mischief. Fie Demetrius,
Your wrongs do set a scandal on my sex: 240
We cannot fight for love, as men may do:
We should be wooed, and were not made to woo.
I'll follow thee and make a heaven of hell,
To die upon the hand I love so well.   *Exit.*
OBERON. Fare thee well nymph. Ere he do leave this grove,   245
Thou shalt fly him, and he shall seek thy love.

                                  Enter PUCK.

Hast thou the flower there? Welcome wanderer.
PUCK. Ay, there it is.
OBERON. I pray thee give it me.
I know a bank where the wild thyme blows,
Where oxlips and the nodding violet grows,   250
Quite over-canopied with luscious woodbine,
With sweet musk-roses, and with eglantine:
There sleeps Titania, sometime of the night,
Lulled in these flowers, with dances and delight:
And there the snake throws° her enamelled skin,   255
Weed° wide enough to wrap a fairy in.
And with the juice of this, I'll streak her eyes,
And make her full of hateful fantasies.
Take thou some of it, and seek through this grove:
A sweet Athenian lady is in love   260
With a disdainful youth: anoint his eyes.
But do it when the next thing he espies

---

224 *respect:* regard.   227 *brakes:* thickets.   231 *Apollo . . . Daphne:* (in Ovid, Apollo pursues
Daphne, who turns into a laurel tree).   232 *griffin:* legendary beast with the head of an eagle and
the body of a lion.   *hind:* doe.   233 *Bootless:* useless.   235 *stay:* wait for.   255 *throws:* casts
off.   256 *weed:* garment.

> May be the lady. Thou shalt know the man
> By the Athenian garments he hath on.
> Effect it with some care, that he may prove   265
> More fond° on her, than she upon her love:
> And look thou meet me ere the first cock crow.

PUCK. Fear not my lord: your servant shall do so.   *Exeunt.*

[SCENE 2. Another part of the wood]

> *Enter* Titania *Queen of Fairies with her train.*

QUEEN. Come, now a roundel° and a fairy song:
> Then, for the third part of a minute, hence—
> Some to kill cankers in the musk-rose buds,
> Some war with reremice° for their leathren wings,
> To make my small elves coats, and some keep back   5
> The clamorous owl, that nightly hoots and wonders
> At our quaint° spirits. Sing me now asleep:
> Then to your offices,° and let me rest.

> *Fairies sing.*

> You spotted snakes with double° tongue,
> Thorny hedgehogs be not seen,   10
> Newts and blind-worms° do no wrong,
> Come not near our Fairy Queen.

> Philomele,° with melody,
> Sing in our sweet lullaby,
> Lulla, lulla, lullaby, lulla, lulla, lullaby.   15
> Never harm,
> Nor spell, nor charm,
> Come our lovely lady nigh.
> So good night, with lullaby.

1. FAIRY. Weaving spiders come not here: 20
> Hence you long-legged spinners, hence:
> Beetles black approach not near:
> Worm nor snail do no offence.
> Philomele, with melody, &c.   *She sleeps.*

2. FAIRY. Hence away: now all is well: 25
> One aloof stand sentinel.   *[Exeunt fairies.]*

> *Enter* OBERON *[and applies the flower juice to* TITANIA'S *eyelids.]*

OBERON. What thou seest, when thou dost wake,
> Do it for thy true love take:
> Love and languish for his sake.
> Be it ounce,° or cat, or bear,   30
> Pard,° or boar with bristled hair,
> In thy eye that shall appear,

---

265 *fond:* doting, madly in love.   1 *roundel:* dance in a ring.   4 *reremice:* bats.   7 *quaint:* dainty.   8 *offices:* duties.   9 *double:* forked.   11 *blind-worms:* legless lizards.   13 *Philomele:* the nightingale.   30 *ounce:* lynx.   31 *Pard:* leopard.

When thou wak'st, it is thy dear:
Wake when some vile thing is near.   *[Exit.]*

Enter LYSANDER *and* HERMIA.

LYSANDER. Fair love, you faint with wand'ring in the wood: 35
　　And to speak troth° I have forgot our way.
　　We'll rest us Hermia, if you think it good,
　　And tarry for the comfort of the day.
HERMIA. Be't so Lysander: find you out a bed:
　　For I upon this bank will rest my head.   40
LYSANDER. One turf shall serve as pillow for us both,
　　One heart, one bed, two bosoms, and one troth.°
HERMIA. Nay, good Lysander: for my sake, my dear,
　　Lie further off yet; do not lie so near.
LYSANDER. O take the sense, sweet, of my innocence:°   45
　　Love takes the meaning in love's conference.°
　　I mean that my heart unto yours is knit,
　　So that but one heart we can make of it:
　　Two bosoms interchainèd with an oath,
　　So then two bosoms and a single troth.   50
　　Then by your side no bed-room me deny:
　　For lying so, Hermia, I do not lie.
HERMIA. Lysander riddles very prettily.
　　Now much beshrew° my manners and my pride,
　　If Hermia meant to say Lysander lied.   55
　　But gentle friend, for love and courtesy,
　　Lie further off, in human modesty:
　　Such separation as may well be said
　　Becomes a virtuous bachelor and a maid,
　　So far be distant, and good night sweet friend: 60
　　Thy love ne'er alter till thy sweet life end.
LYSANDER. Amen, amen, to that fair prayer say I,
　　And then end life, when I end loyalty.
　　Here is my bed: sleep give thee all his rest.
HERMIA. With half that wish, the wisher's eyes be pressed.°   65

They sleep.

Enter PUCK.

PUCK. Through the forest have I gone,
　　But Athenian found I none,
　　On whose eyes I might approve°
　　This flower's force in stirring love.
　　Night and silence. Who is here?   70
　　Weeds° of Athens he doth wear:

---

36 *troth:* truth.　42 *troth:* true love.　45 *take . . . innocence:* understand the innocence of my remark.　46 *Love . . . conference:* love enables lovers to understand each other when they converse. 54 b*eshrew:* curse.　65 *pressed:* i.e., by sleep.　68 *approve:* test.

This is he (my master said)
Despisèd the Athenian maid:
And here the maiden, sleeping sound,
On the dank and dirty ground.   75
Pretty soul, she durst not lie
Near this lack-love, this kill-courtesy.
Churl, upon thy eyes I throw
All the power this charm doth owe:°
When thou wak'st, let love forbid   80
Sleep his seat on thy eyelid.°
So awake when I am gone:
For I must now to Oberon.   *Exit.*

        Enter DEMETRIUS *and* HELENA *running.*

HELENA. Stay, thou kill me, sweet Demetrius.
DEMETRIUS. I charge thee hence, and do not haunt me thus.   85
HELENA. O, wilt thou darkling° leave me? Do not so.
DEMETRIUS. Stay on thy peril: I alone will go.   *Exit* DEMETRIUS.
HELENA. O, I am out of breath in this fond° chase:
    The more my prayer, the lesser is my grace.°
    Happy is Hermia, wheresoe'er she lies: 90
    For she hath blessèd and attractive eyes.
    How came her eyes so bright? Not with salt tears:
    If so, my eyes are oft'ner washed than hers.
    No, no: I am ugly as a bear:
    For beasts that meet me run away for fear.   95
    Therefore no marvel, though Demetrius
    Do as a monster, fly my presence thus.
    What wicked and dissembling glass° of mine,
    Made me compare with Hermia's sphery eyne!°
    But who is here? Lysander, on the ground?   100
    Dead, or asleep? I see no blood, no wound.
    Lysander, if you live, good sir awake.
LYSANDER. *[Wakes]* And run through fire, I will for thy sweet sake.
    Transparent° Helena, nature shows art,
    That through thy bosom, makes me see thy heart.   105
    Where is Demetrius? O how fit a word
    Is that vile name to perish on my sword!
HELENA. Do not say so, Lysander, say not so.
    What though he love your Hermia? Lord, what though?
    Yet Hermia still loves you: then be content.   110
LYSANDER. Content with Hermia? No: I do repent
    The tedious minutes I with her have spent.
    Not Hermia, but Helena I love.
    Who will not change a raven for a dove?

---

71 *Weeds:* garments.   79 *owe:* own.   80–81 *forbid . . . eyelid:* make you sleepless (with love).
86 *darkling:* in the dark.   88 *fond:* foolishly doting.   89 *my grace:* favor shown to me.   *glass:*
looking glass.   99 *sphery eyne:* starry eyes.

The will of man is by his reason swayed:° 115
And reason says you are the worthier maid.
Things growing are not ripe until their season:
So I, being young, till now ripe° not to reason.
And touching now the point° of human skill,°
Reason becomes the marshal to my will, 120
And leads me to your eyes; where I o'erlook
Love's stories, written in love's richest book.
HELENA. Wherefore° was I to this keen mockery born?
When at your hands did I deserve this scorn?
Is't not enough, is't not enough, young man, 125
That I did never, no, nor ever can,
Deserve a sweet look from Demetrius' eye,
But you must flout° my insufficiency?
Good troth you do me wrong, good sooth you do,
In such disdainful manner me to woo. 130
But fare you well: perforce I must confess,
I thought you lord or more true gentleness.°
O, that a lady, of one man refused,
Should of another, therefore be abused! *Exit.*
LYSANDER. She sees not Hermia. Hermia, sleep thou there, 135
And never mayst thou come Lysander near.
For, as a surfeit of the sweetest things
The deepest loathing to the stomach brings:
Or as the heresies that men do leave,
Are hated most of those they did deceive: 140
So thou, my surfeit and my heresy,
Of all be hated; but the most, of me:
And all my powers, address your love and might,
To honour Helen, and to be her knight.

Exit.

HERMIA. *[Wakes.]* Help me Lysander, help me: do thy best 145
To pluck this crawling serpent from my breast.
Ay me, for pity. What a dream was here?
Lysander, look how I do quake with fear.
Methought a serpent eat my heart away.
And you sat smiling at his cruel prey.° 150
Lysander: what, removed? Lysander, lord!
What, out of hearing, gone? No sound, no word?
Alack, where are you? Speak, and if you hear:
Speak, of° all loves. I swoon almost with fear.
No? Then I well perceive you are not nigh: 155
Either death, or you, I'll find immediately. *Exit.*

---

104 *Transparent:* radiant.   115 *swayed:* ruled.   118 *ripe:* mature.   119 *point:* peak.   *skill:*
knowledge.   123 *Wherefore:* why.   128 *flout:* mock.   132 *lord . . . gentleness:* more of a gentleman.   150 *prey:* preying.   154 *of:* for the sake of.

ACT 3

[SCENE 1. The wood]

Enter the CLOWNS *[*QUINCE, SNUG, BOTTOM, FLUTE, SNOUT, *and* STARVELING.*]*

BOTTOM. Are we all met?

QUINCE. Pat, pat: and here's a marvellous convenient place for
our rehearsal. This green plot shall be our stage, this
hawthorn brake° our tiring-house,° and we will do it in
action, as we will do it before the duke.   5

BOTTOM. Peter Quince?

QUINCE. What sayest thou, bully° Bottom?

BOTTOM. There are things in this Comedy of Pyramus and Thisby
that will never please. First, Pyramus must draw a sword
to kill himself; which the ladies cannot abide. How   10
answer you that?

SNOUT. By'r lakin,° a parlous° fear.

STARVELING. I believe we must leave the killing out, when all is done.

BOTTOM. Not a whit: I have a device to make all well. Write me
a prologue, and let the prologue seem to say, we will   15
do no harm with our swords, and that Pyramus is not
killed indeed: and for the more better assurance, tell
them that I Pyramus am not Pyramus, but Bottom the
weaver: this will put them out of fear.

QUINCE. Well, we will have such a prologue, and it shall be   20
written in eight and six.°

BOTTOM. No, make it two more: let it be written in eight and eight.

SNOUT. Will not the ladies be afeared of the lion?

STARVELING. I fear it, I promise you.

BOTTOM. Masters, you ought to consider with yourselves, to bring   25
in (God shield us) a lion among ladies, is a most dreadful
thing. For there is not a more fearful wild-fowl than
your lion living: and we ought to look to't.

SNOUT. Therefore another prologue must tell he is not a lion.

BOTTOM. Nay, you must name his name, and half his face must be   30
seen through the lion's neck, and he himself must speak
through, saying thus, or to the same defect:° "Ladies,"
or "Fair ladies—I would wish you," or "I would request
you," or "I would entreat you, not to fear,
not to tremble: my life for yours. If you think I come   35
hither as a lion, it were pity of my life. No, I am no
such thing: I am a man as other men are." And there
indeed let him name his name, and tell them plainly he
is Snug the joiner.

---

4 *brake:* thicket.   *tiring-house:* dressing room.   7 *bully:* "old pal."   12 *By'r lakin:* mild oath, "by
Our Lady."   *parlous:* awful, perilous.   21 *eight and six:* alternate lines of eight and six syllables
(the ballad meter).   33 *defect:* (he means "effect").

QUINCE. Well, it shall be so, but there is two hard things: that is,
    to bring the moonlight into a chamber: for you know,
    Pyramus and Thisby meet by moonlight.
SNOUT. Doth the moon shine that night we play our play?
BOTTOM. A calendar, a calendar: look in the almanac: find out   45
    moonshine, find out moonshine.
QUINCE. Yes, it doth shine that night.
BOTTOM. Why then may you leave a casement of the great
    chamber-window, where we play, open; and the moon may
    shine in at the casement.   50
QUINCE. Ay, or else one must come in with a bush of thorns° and
    a lantern, and say he comes to disfigure,° or to present,
    the person of Moonshine. Then, there is another thing;
    we must have a wall in the great chamber: for Pyramus
    and Thisby, says the story, did talk through the chink   55
    of a wall.
SNOUT. You can never bring in a wall. What say you, Bottom?
BOTTOM. Some man or other must present wall: and let him have
    some plaster, or some loam, or some rough-cast° about
    him, to signify wall; and let him hold his fingers thus: 60
    and through that cranny, shall Pyramus and Thisby whisper.
QUINCE. If that may be, then all is well. Come, sit down every
    mother's son, and rehearse your parts. Pyramus, you
    begin: when you have spoken your speech, enter into that
    brake, and so every one according to his cue.   65

Enter PUCK.

PUCK. What hempen homespuns° have we swagg'ring here,
    So near the cradle of the Fairy Queen?
    What, a play toward?° I'll be an auditor,
    An actor too perhaps, if I see cause.
QUINCE. Speak Pyramus. Thisby stand forth.   70
PYRAMUS. Thisby, the flowers of odious savours sweet—
QUINCE. "Odorous, odorous."
PYRAMUS. —odours savours sweet,
    So hath thy breath, my dearest Thisby dear.
    But hark, a voice: stay thou but here awhile,   75
    And by and by I will to thee appear.   *Exit* PYRAMUS.
                                          [Exit.]
PUCK. A stranger Pyramus than e'er played here.
THISBY. Must I speak now?
QUINCE. Ay marry must you. For you must understand he goes
    but to see a noise that he heard, and is to come again.   80
THISBY. Most radiant Pyramus, most lily-white of hue,
    Of colour like the red rose, on triumphant brier,
    Most brisky juvenal,° and eke most lovely Jew,°

---

51 *bush of thorns:* bundle of firewood (the man in the moon was supposed to have been placed there as a punishment for gathering wood on Sundays).   52 *disfigure:* (he means "figure," symbolize). 59 *rough-cast:* coarse plaster of lime and gravel.   66 *hempen homespuns:* wearers of clothing spun at home from hemp.   68 *toward:* in preparation.   83 *brisky juvenal:* lively youth.   *Jew:* diminutive of either "juvenal" or "jewel."

As true as truest horse, that yet would never tire,
I'll meet thee Pyramus, at Ninny's tomb.   85
QUINCE. "Ninus' tomb,"° man: why, you must not speak that yet.
That you answer to Pyramus. You speak all your part
at once, cues and all. Pyramus, enter; your cue is past:
it is "never tire."
THISBY. O—As true as truest horse, that yet would never tire.   90

Enter PYRAMUS *with the ass-head [followed by* PUCK*].*

PYRAMUS. If I were fair, Thisby, I were only thine.
QUINCE. O monstrous! O strange! We are haunted. Pray masters,
fly masters. Help!   *The clowns all exeunt.*
PUCK. I'll follow you: I'll lead you about a round,°
Through bog, through bush, through brake, through brier.   95
Sometime a horse I'll be, sometime a hound,
A hog, a headless bear, sometime a fire,
And neigh, and bark, and grunt, and roar, and burn,
Like horse, hound, hog, bear, fire, at every turn.   *Exit.*
BOTTOM. Why do they run away? This is a knavery of them to   100
make me afeared.

Enter SNOUT.

SNOUT. O Bottom, thou art changed. What do I see on thee?
BOTTOM. What do you see? You see an ass-head of your own, do
you?   *[Exit* SNOUT.*]*

Enter QUINCE.

QUINCE. Bless thee Bottom, bless thee. Thou art translated.°   *Exit.* 105
BOTTOM. I see their knavery. This is to make an ass of me, to
fright me if they could: but I will not stir from this
place, do what they can. I will walk up and down here,
and will sing that they shall hear I am not afraid.
[*Sings.*] The woosel° cock, so black of hue,   110
With orange tawny bill,
The throstle,° with his note so true,
The wren, with little quill.°
TITANIA. What angel wakes me from my flow'ry bed?
BOTTOM. [*Sings.*] The finch, the sparrow, and the lark,   115
The plain-song° cuckoo gray:
Whose note full many a man doth mark,
And dares not answer, nay.
For indeed, who would set his wit to° so foolish a bird?
Who would give a bird the lie,° though he cry "cuckoo"°   120
never so?°

86 *Ninus' tomb:* (tomb of the founder of Nineveh, and meeting place of the lovers in Ovid's version
of the Pyramus story).   94 *about a round:* in circles, like a round dance (round about).   105
translated: transformed.   110 *woosel:* ousel, blackbird.   112 *throstle:* thrush.   113 *quill:* piping
note.   116 *plain-song:* sounding a simple unvaried note.   119 *set . . . to:* match his wit against.
120 *Who . . . lie:* who could call a bird a liar. *"cuckoo":* (which sounded like "cuckold" = a deceived
husband).   121 *never so:* i.e., often.

TITANIA. I pray thee, gentle mortal, sing again.
    Mine ear is much enamoured of thy note:
    So is mine eye enthrallèd to thy shape,
    And thy fair virtue's force (perforce°) doth move me,   125
    On the first view to say, to swear, I love thee.
BOTTOM. Methinks mistress, you should have little reason for
    that. And yet, to say the truth, reason and love keep
    little company together now-a-days. The more the pity,
    That some honest neighbors will not make them friends.   130
    Nay, I can gleek° upon occasion.
TITANIA. Thou art as wise as thou art beautiful.
BOTTOM. Not so neither: but if I had wit enough to get out of
    this wood, I have enough to serve mine own turn.
TITANIA. Out of this wood do not desire to go: 135
    Thou shalt remain here, whether thou wilt or no.
    I am a spirit of no common rate:°
    The summer still doth tend upon my state,°
    And I do love thee: therefore go with me.
    I'll give thee fairies to attend on thee: 140
    And they shall fetch thee jewels from the deep,
    And sing, while thou on pressèd flowers dost sleep:
    And I will purge thy mortal grossness so,
    That thou shalt like an airy spirit go.
    Peaseblossom, Cobweb, Moth,° and Mustardseed!   145

Enter four FAIRIES.

PEASEBLOSSOM. Ready.
COBWEB. And I.
MOTH.   And I.
MUSTARDSEED.   And I.
ALL.   Where shall we go?
TITANIA. Be kind and courteous to this gentleman,
    Hop in his walks and gambol° in his eyes,
    Feed him with apricocks° and dewberries,°   150
    With purple grapes, green figs, and mulberries.
    The honey-bags steal from the humblebees,°
    And for night-tapers, crop° their waxen thighs,
    And light them at the fiery glow-worm's eyes.
    To have my love to bed and to arise: 155
    And pluck the wings from painted butterflies,
    To fan the moonbeams from his sleeping eyes.
    Nod to him elves, and do him courtesies.
PEASEBLOSSOM. Hail, mortal.
COBWEB. Hail.

---

125 *perforce:* by force.   131 *gleek:* joke satirically.   137 *rate:* rank, value.   138 *still . . . state:* always serves as an attendant in my royal train.   145 *Moth:* mote (so pronounced), tiny speck. 149 *gambol in:* caper before.   150 *apricocks:* apricots.   *dewberries:* blackberries.   152 *humblebees:* bumblebees.   153 *crop:* clip.

MOTH. Hail.

MUSTARDSEED. Hail.

BOTTOM. I cry your worships mercy,° heartily: I beseech your
    worship's name.

COBWEB. Cobweb.   165

BOTTOM. I shall desire you of more acquaintance, good Master
    Cobweb: if I cut my finger,° I shall make bold with you.
    Your name, honest gentleman?

PEASEBLOSSOM. Peaseblossom.

BOTTOM. I pray you commend me° to Mistress Squash,° your mother,   170
    and to Master Peascod,° your father. Good Master Peaseblossom,
    I shall desire you of more acquaintance, too.
    Your name I beseech you sir?

MUSTARDSEED. Mustardseed.

BOTTOM. Good Master Mustardseed, I know your patience well.   175
    That same cowardly giant-like ox beef hath devoured
    many a gentleman of your house. I promise you, your
    kindred hath made my eyes water ere now. I desire you
    of more acquaintance, good Master Mustardseed.

TITANIA. Come wait upon him: lead him to my bower.   180
    The moon methinks looks with a wat'ry eye:
    And when she weeps, weeps every little flower,
    Lamenting some enforcèd° chastity.
    Tie up my lover's tongue, bring him silently.   *Exeunt.*

[SCENE 2. Another part of the wood]

*Enter [*OBERON,*] King of Fairies, solus.*°

OBERON. I wonder if Titania be awaked;
    Then what it was that next came in her eye,
    Which she must dote on in extremity.

Enter PUCK.

    Here comes my messenger. How now, mad spirit?
    What night-rule° now about this haunted grove?   5

PUCK. My mistress with a monster is in love.
    Near to her close and consecrated bower,
    While she was in her dull° and sleeping hour,
    A crew of patches,° rude mechanicals,°
    That work for bread upon Athenian stalls,°   10
    Were met together to rehearse a play,
    Intended for great Theseus' nuptial day:
    The shallowest thickskin of that barren sort,°
    Who Pyramus presented in their sport,
    Forsook his scene and entered in a brake: 15

163 *I . . . mercy:* I respectfully beg your pardons.   167 *cut my fingers:* (cobwebs were used to stop
bleeding).   170 *commend me:* offer my respects.   *Squash:* unripe peapod.   171 *Peascod:* ripe
peapod.   180 *enforcèd:* violated.   S.D.: *solus:* alone.   5 *night-rule:* diversion ("misrule") in the
night.   8 *dull:* drowsy.   9 *patches:* fools.   *mechanicals:* workers.   10 *stalls:* shops.   13 *barren sort:* stupid crew.

When I did him at this advantage take,
An ass's nole° I fixèd on his head.
Anon° his Thisby must be answerèd,
And forth my mimic° comes. When they him spy,
As wild geese, that the creeping fowler° eye,   20
Or russet-pated choughs,° may in sort,°
Rising and cawing at the guns report,
Sever themselves and madly sweep the sky,
So at his sight away his fellows fly:
And at our stamp, here o'er and o'er one falls: 25
He murder cries, and help from Athens calls.
Their sense thus weak, lost with their fears thus strong,
Made senseless things begin to do them wrong.
For briers and thorns at their apparel snatch:
Some° sleeves, some hats; from yielders, all things catch.°   30
I led them on in this distracted° fear,
And left sweet Pyramus translated there:
When in that moment (so it came to pass)
Titania waked, and straightway loved an ass.
OBERON. This falls out better than I could devise.   35
    But has thou yet latched° the Athenian's eyes
    With the love-juice, as I did bid thee do?
PUCK. I took him sleeping (that is finished too)
    And the Athenian woman by his side;
    Then when he waked, of force° she must be eyed.   40

Enter DEMETRIUS *and* HERMIA.

OBERON. Stand close:° this is the same Athenian.
PUCK. This is the woman: but not this the man.
DEMETRIUS. O why rebuke you him that loves you so?
    Lay breath so bitter on your bitter foe.
HERMIA. Now I but chide: but I should use thee worse,   45
    For thou, I fear, hast given me cause to curse.
    If thou hast slain Lysander in his sleep,
    Being o'er shoes in blood, plunge in the deep,
    And kill me too.
    The sun was not so true unto the day,   50
    As he to me. Would he have stolen away
    From sleeping Hermia? I'll believe as soon
    This whole° earth may be bored,° and that the moon
    May through the center creep, and so displease
    Her brother's noontide with th' Antipodes.°   55

---

17 *nole:* head, noodle.   18 *Anon:* presently.   19 *mimic:* actor.   20 *fowler:* hunter of fowl.   21 *russet-pated choughs:* grey-headed jackdaws.   *sort:* a flock.   30 *Some:* i.e., snatch.   *from yielders . . . catch:* (everything joins in to harm the weak).   31 *distracted:* maddened.   36 *latched:* moistened.   40 *of force:* by necessity.   41 *close:* hidden.   53 *whole:* solid.   *be bored:* have a hole bored through it.   55 *Her brother's . . . Antipodes:* the noon of her brother sun, by appearing among the Antipodes (the people on the other side of the earth).

It cannot be but thou hast murdered him.
So should a murderer look; so dead,° so grim.
DEMETRIUS. So should the murdered look, and so should I,
    Pierced through the heart with your stern cruelty.
    Yet you, the murderer, look as bright, as clear,   60
    As yonder Venus in her glimmering sphere.°
HERMIA. What's this to my Lysander? Where is he?
    Ah good Demetrius, wilt thou give him me?
DEMETRIUS. I had rather give his carcass to my hounds.
HERMIA. Out dog, out cur! Thou driv'st me past the bounds   65
    Of maiden's patience. Hast thou slain him then?
    Henceforth be never numbered among men.
    O, once tell true: tell true, even for my sake:
    Durst thou have looked upon him, being awake?
    And hast thou killed him sleeping? O brave touch!°   70
    Could not a worm,° an adder, do so much?
    An adder did it: for with doubler tongue°
    Than thine, thou serpent, never adder stung.
DEMETRIUS. You spend your passion on a misprised mood:°
    I am not guilty of Lysander's blood: 75
    Nor is he dead, for aught that I can tell.
HERMIA. I pray thee, tell me then that he is well.
DEMETRIUS. And if I could, what should I get therefore?
HERMIA. A privilege never to see me more:
    And from thy hated presence part I so: 80
    See me no more, whether he be dead or no.   *Exit.*
DEMETRIUS. There is no following her in this fierce vein.
    Here therefore for a while I will remain.
    So sorrow's heaviness doth heavier grow
    For debt that bankrout sleep doth sorrow owe:°   85
    Which now in some slight measure it will pay,
    If for his tender° here I make some stay.°   *Lies down.*
OBERON. What hast thou done? Thou hast mistaken quite,
    And laid the love-juice on some true-love's sight.
    Of thy misprision° must perforce° ensue   90
    Some true love turned, and not a false turned true.
PUCK. Then fate o'errules, that one man holding troth,
    A million fail, confounding° oath on oath.°
OBERON. About the wood, go swifter than the wind,
    And Helena of Athens look thou find.   95
    All fancy-sick° she is, and pale of cheer,°
    With sighs of love, that costs the fresh blood dear.

---

57 *dead:* deadly.   61 *sphere:* (in the Ptolemaic system, each planet moved in its own sphere around
the earth).   70 *brave touch:* splendid stroke (ironic).   71 *worm:* snake.   72 *doubler tongue:* (1)
tongue more forked (2) more deceitful speech.   74 *on . . . mood:* in mistaken anger.   85 *For debt
. . . owe:* because sleep cannot pay the debt of repose he owes the man who is kept awake by sorrow.
87 *tender:* offer.   *stay:* pause.   *misprision:* mistake.   *perforce:* of necessity.   93 *confounding:*
destroying.   *oath on oath:* one oath after another.   96 *fancy-sick:* lovesick.   *cheer:* face.

By some illusion see thou bring her here:
I'll charm his eyes against she do appear.°
PUCK. I go, I go, look how I go.   100
   Swifter than arrow from the Tartar's bow.°   *Exit.*
OBERON. Flower of this purple dye,
   Hit with Cupid's archery,
   Sink in apple of his eye:
   When his love he doth espy,   105
   Let her shine as gloriously
   As the Venus of the sky.
   When thou wak'st, if she be by,
   Beg of her for remedy.

                   Enter PUCK.

PUCK. Captain of our fairy band,   110
   Helena is here at hand,
   And the youth, mistook by me,
   Pleading for a lover's fee.°
   Shall we their fond pageant° see?
   Lord, what fools these mortals be!   115
OBERON. Stand aside. The noise they make
   Will cause Demetrius to awake.
PUCK. Then will two at once woo one:
   That must needs be sport alone.°
   And those things to best please me   120
   That befall prepost'rously.

                Enter LYSANDER *and* HELENA.

LYSANDER. Why should you think that I should woo in scorn?
   Scorn and derision never come in tears.
   Look when I vow, I weep: and vows so born,
      In their nativity all truth appears.°   125
   How can these things in me seem scorn to you,
   Bearing the badge° of faith to prove them true?
HELENA. You do advance your cunning more and more.
   When truth kills truth,° O devilish-holy fray!
   These vows are Hermia's. Will you give her o'er?   130
   Weigh oath with oath, and you will nothing weigh.
   Your vows to her and me, put in two scales,
   Will even weigh: and both as light as tales.
LYSANDER. I had no judgment, when to her I swore.
HELENA. Nor none, in my mind, now you give her o'er.   135
LYSANDER. Demetrius loves her: and he loves not you.

---

99 *against . . . appear:* in preparation for her appearance.   101 *Tartar's bow:* (the Tartars, who used powerful Oriental bows, were famed as archers).   113 *fee:* reward.   114 *fond pageant:* foolish spectacle.   119 *alone:* unique.   124–125 *vows . . . appears:* vows born in weeping must be true ones.   127 *badge:* (1) outward signs (2) family crest.   129 *truth kills truth:* former true love is killed by vows of present true love.

DEMETRIUS. [*Awakes.*] O Helen, goddess, nymph, perfect divine,
    To what, my love, shall I compare thine eyne!
    Crystal is muddy. O, how ripe in show,
    Thy lips, those kissing cherries, tempting grow!   140
    That pure congealèd white, high Taurus'° snow,
    Fanned with the eastern wind, turns to a crow,
    When thou hold'st up thy hand. O let me kiss
    This princess of pure white,° this seal of bliss.
HELENA. O spite! O hell! I see you are all bent   145
    To set against me, for your merriment.
    If you were civil,° and knew courtesy,
    You would not do me thus much injury.
    Can you not hate me, as I know you do,
    But you must join in souls° to mock me too?   150
    If you were men, as men you are in show,
    You would not use a gentle lady so;
    To vow, and swear, superpraise my parts,°
    When I am sure you hate me with your hearts.
    You both are rivals, and love Hermia: 155
    And now both rivals, to mock Helena.
    A trim° exploit, a manly enterprise,
    To conjure tears up in a poor maid's eyes
    With your derision. None of noble sort
    Would so offend a virgin, and extort°   160
    A poor soul's patience, all to make you sport.
LYSANDER. You are unkind, Demetrius: be not so.
    For you love Hermia: this you know I know.
    And here, with all good will, with all my heart,
    In Hermia's love I yield you up my part: 165
    And yours of Helena to be bequeath,
    Whom I do love, and will do to my death.
HELENA. Never did mockers waste more idle breath.
DEMETRIUS. Lysander, keep thy Hermia: I will none.°
    If e'er I loved her, all that love is gone.   170
    My heart to her but as guest-wise sojourned:°
    And now to Helen it is home returned,
    There to remain.
LYSANDER. Helen, it is not so.
DEMETRIUS. Disparage not the faith thou dost not know,   175
    Lest to thy peril thou aby it dear.°
    Look where thy love comes: yonder is thy dear.

Enter HERMIA.

---

141 *Taurus:* mountain range in Asia Minor.   144 *princess . . . white:* sovereign example of white-ness (her hand).   147 *civil:* well behaved.   150 *join in souls:* agree in spirit.   153 *parts:* quali-ties.   157 *trim:* fine (ironic).   160 *extort:* wring.   169 *none:* have none of her.   171 *to her . . . sojourned:* visited her only as a guest.   176 *aby it dear:* buy it at a high price.

HERMIA. Dark night, that from the eye his function takes,
　　The ear more quick of apprehension makes.
　　Wherein it doth impair the seeing sense,
　　It pays the hearing double recompense.　　　　　　　　　　180
　　Thou are not by mine eye, Lysander, found:
　　Mine ear, I thank it, brought me to thy sound.
　　But why unkindly didst thou leave me so?
LYSANDER. Why should he stay, whom love doth press to go?
HERMIA. What love could press Lysander from my side?　　　185
LYSANDER. Lysander's love, that would not let him bide—
　　Fair Helena: who more engilds the night
　　Than all your fiery oes and eyes of light.°
　　Why seek'st thou me? Could not this make thee know,
　　The hate I bear thee made me leave thee so?　　　　　　190
HERMIA. You speak not as you think: it cannot be.
HELENA. Lo: She is one of this confederacy.
　　Now I perceive they have conjoined all three,
　　To fashion this false sport in spite of° me.
　　Injurious° Hermia, most ungrateful maid,　　　　　　　195
　　Have you conspired, have you with these contrived
　　To bait° me with this foul derision?
　　Is all the counsel° that we two have shared,
　　The sisters' vows, the hours that we have spent,
　　When we have chid the hasty-footed time　　　　　　　200
　　For parting us; O, is all forgot?
　　All schooldays' friendship, childhood innocence?
　　We Hermia, like two artificial° gods,
　　Have with our needles created both one flower,
　　Both on one sampler,° sitting on one cushion,　　　　　205
　　Both warbling of one song, both in one key;
　　As if our hands, our sides, voices, and minds
　　Had been incorporate.° So we grew together,
　　Like to a double cherry, seeming parted,
　　But yet an union in partition,　　　　　　　　　　　　210
　　Two lovely berries moulded on one stem:
　　So with two seeming bodies but one heart,
　　Two of the first, like coats in heraldry,
　　Due but to one, and crownèd with one crest.°
　　And will you rent° our ancient love asunder,　　　　　215
　　To join with men in scorning your poor friend?
　　It is not friendly, 'tis not maidenly.
　　Our sex, as well as I, may chide you for it;
　　Though I alone do feel the injury.

---

188 *oes . . . light:* stars.　　194 *in spite of:* to spite.　　195 *Injurious:* insulting.　　197*bait:* attack.
198 *counsel:* secrets.　　203 *artificial:* skilled in art.　　205 *sampler:* work of embroidery.　　208
incorporate: in one body.　　213–214 *Two . . . crest:* (the two bodies being) like double coats of arms
joined under one crest (with one heart).

HERMIA. I am amazèd at your passionate words: 220
    I scorn you not. It seems that you scorn me.
HELENA. Have you not set Lysander, as in scorn,
    To follow me, and praise my eyes and face?
    And made your other love, Demetrius
    (Who even but now did spurn° me with his foot)   225
    To call me goddess, nymph, divine, and rare,
    Precious, celestial? Wherefore speaks he this
    To her he hates? And wherefore doth Lysander
    Deny your love, so rich within his soul,
    And tender° me (forsooth) affection,   230
    But by your setting on, by your consent?
    What though I be not so in grace° as you,
    So hung upon with love, so fortunate,
    But miserable most, to love unloved?
    This you should pity, rather than despise.   235
HERMIA. I understand not what you mean by this.
HELENA. Ay, do. Persèver, counterfeit sad° looks:
    Make mouths upon° me when I turn my back:
    Wink at each other, hold the sweet jest up.
    This sport well carried, shall be chronicled.°   240
    If you have any pity, grace, or manners,
    You would not make me such an argument.°
    But fare ye well: 'tis partly my own fault:
    Which death or absence soon shall remedy.
LYSANDER. Stay, gentle Helena: hear my excuse,   245
    My love, my life, my soul, fair Helena.
HELENA. O excellent!
HERMIA.   Sweet, do not scorn her so.
DEMETRIUS. If she cannot entreat,° I can compel.
LYSANDER. Thou canst compel no more than she entreat.
    Thy threats have no more strength than her weak prayers.   250
    Helen, I love thee, by my life I do:
    I swear by that which I will lose for thee,
    To prove° him false that says I love thee not.
DEMETRIUS. I say I love thee more than he can do.
LYSANDER. If thou say so, withdraw, and prove° it too.   255
DEMETRIUS. Quick, Come.
HERMIA.   Lysander, whereto tends all this?
LYSANDER. Away, you Ethiope.°
DEMETRIUS.   No, no, sir,
    Seem to break loose: take on as you would follow;
    But yet come not.° You are a tame man, go.

215 *rent:* rend, tear.   225 *spurn:* kick.   230. *tender:* offer.   232 *in grace:* favored.   237 *sad:* serious.   238 *mouths upon:* faces at.   240 *chronicled:* written down in the history books.   242 *argument:* subject (of your mockery).   248 *entreat:* sway you by entreaty.   253, 255 *prove:* i.e., by a duel.   257 *Ethiope:* (because she is a brunette).   258–259 *Seem . . . not:* You only seem to break loose from Hermia and pretend to follow me to a duel, but you actually hold back.

LYSANDER. Hang off,° thou cat, thou burr: vile thing, let loose;   260
    Or I will shake thee from me like a serpent.
HERMIA. Why are you grown so rude? What change is this,
    Sweet love?
LYSANDER.   Thy love? Out, tawny Tartar, out:
    Out, loathèd med'cine: O hated potion, hence!
HERMIA. Do you not jest?
HELENA.   Yes sooth: and so do you.   265
LYSANDER. Demetrius, I will keep my word° with thee.
DEMETRIUS. I would I had your bond.° For I perceive
    A weak bond holds you. I'll not trust your word.
LYSANDER. What? Should I hurt her, strike her, kill her dead?
    All though I hate her, I'll not harm her so.   270
HERMIA. What? Can you do me greater harm than hate?
    Hate me, wherefore?° O me, what news,° my love?
    Am I not Hermia? Are you not Lysander?
    I am as fair now, as I was erstwhile.°
    Since night, you loved me; yet since night, you left me.   275
    Why then, you left me—O the gods forbid—
    In earnest, shall I say?
LYSANDER.   Ay, by my life:
    And never did desire to see thee more.
    Therefore be out of hope, of question, of doubt:
    Be certain: nothing truer: 'tis no jest   280
    That I do hate thee, and love Helena.
HERMIA. O me, you juggler,° you canker blossom,°
    You thief of love: what, have you come by night,
    And stol'n my love's heart from him?
HELENA. Fine, i' faith.
    Have you no modesty, no maiden shame,   285
    No touch of bashfulness? What, will you tear
    Impatient answers from my gentle tongue?
    Fie, fie, you counterfeit, you puppet,° you.
HERMIA. Puppet? Why so—ay, that way goes the game.
    Now I perceive that she hath made compare   290
    Between our statures, she hath urged her height,
    And with her personage, her tall personage,
    Her height (forsooth) she hath prevailed with him.
    And are you grown so high in his esteem,
    Because I am so dwarfish and so low?   295
    How low am I, thou painted maypole? Speak:
    How low am I? I am not yet so low,
    But that my nails can reach unto thine eyes.

---

260 *Hang off:* let go.   266 *keep my word:* i.e., to duel.   267 *bond:* written agreement.   272
wherefore: why.   *what news:* what's the matter.   274 *erstwhile:* a short while ago.   282 *juggler:*
deceiver.   *canker blossom:* worm that causes canker in blossoms.   288 *puppet:* (Hermia is short
and Helena tall).

HELENA. I pray you, though you mock me, gentlemen,
    Let her not hurt me. I was never curst:°   300
    I have no gift at all for shrewishness:
    I am a right maid for my cowardice:°
    Let her not strike me. You perhaps may think,
    Because she is something lower than myself,
    That I can match her.
HERMIA. Lower? Hark again.   305
HELENA. Good Hermia, do not be so bitter with me,
    I evermore did love you Hermia.
    Did ever keep your counsels, never wronged you;
    Save that in love unto Demetrius,
    I told him of your stealth unto this wood.   310
    He followed you: for love, I followed him.
    But he hath chid me hence, and threatened me
    To strike me, spurn me, nay to kill me too;
    And now, so° you will let me quiet go,
    To Athens will I bear my folly back,   315
    And follow you no further. Let me go.
    You see how simple and how fond° I am.
HERMIA. Why, get you gone. Who is't that hinders you?
HELENA. A foolish heart, that I leave here behind.
HERMIA. What, with Lysander?
HELENA.   With Demetrius.   320
LYSANDER. Be not afraid: she shall not harm thee Helena.
DEMETRIUS. No sir: she shall not, though you take her part.
HELENA. O when she's angry, she is keen and shrewd.°
    She was a vixen when she went to school:
    And though she be but little, she is fierce.   325
HERMIA. "Little" again? Nothing but "low" and "little"?
    Why will you suffer her to flout° me thus?
    Let me come to her.
LYSANDER.   Get you gone, you dwarf;
    You minimus,° of hind'ring knot-grass° made;   330
    You bead, you acorn.
DEMETRIUS.   You are too officious
    In her behalf that scorns your services.
    Let her alone: speak not of Helena,
    Take not her part. For if thou dost intend°
    Never so little show of love to her,
    Thou shalt aby it.°
LYSANDER.   Now she holds me not: 335
    Now follow, if thou dar'st, to try whose right,
    Of thine or mine, is most in Helena.°

300 *curst:* bad-tempered.   302 *right . . . cowardice:* true woman in being cowardly.   314 *so:* if.
317 *fond:* foolish.   323 *keen and shrewd:* sharp and malicious.   327 *flout:* mock.   329 *minimus:* smallest of creatures.   *knot-grass:* weed believed to stunt the growth if eaten.   333 *intend:*
extend.   335 *aby it:* buy it dearly.   336–337 *try . . . Helena:* prove by fighting which of us has mos
right to Helena.

DEMETRIUS. Follow? Nay, I'll go with thee, cheek by jowl.

           Exeunt LYSANDER *and* DEMETRIUS.

HERMIA. You, mistress, all this coil is long of° you.
    Nay, go not back.

HELENA.   I will not trust you, I,   340
    Nor longer stay in your curst company
    Your hands than mine are quicker for a fray:
    My legs are longer though to run away.   *[Exit.]*

HERMIA. I am amazed,° and know not what to say.   *Exit.*

OBERON. This is thy negligence: still thou mistak'st,   345
    Or else commit'st thy knaveries wilfully.

PUCK. Believe me, king of shadows, I mistook.
    Did you not tell me I should know the man
    By the Athenian garments he had on?
    And so far blameless proves my enterprise,   350
    That I have 'nointed an Athenian's eyes:
    And so far am I glad it so did sort,°
    As this their jangling I esteem a sport.

OBERON. Thou seest these lovers seek a place to fight;
    Hie therefore Robin, overcast the night,   355
    The starry welkin° cover thou anon
    With drooping fog as black as Acheron,°
    And lead these testy° rivals so astray,
    As° one come not within another's way.
    Like to Lysander sometime frame thy tongue: 360
    Then stir Demetrius up with bitter wrong:°
    And sometime rail thou like Demetrius:
    And from each other look thou lead them thus;
    Till o'er their brows death-counterfeiting sleep
    With leaden legs and batty wings doth creep: 365
    Then crush this herb into Lysander's eye;
    Whose liquor hath this virtuous° property,
    To take from thence all error with his might,
    And make his eyeballs roll with wonted° sight.
    When next they wake, all this derision°   370
    Shall seem a dream, and fruitless vision,
    And back to Athens shall the lovers wend,
    With league whose date° till death shall never end.
    Whiles I in this affair do thee employ,
    I'll to my queen and beg her Indian boy: 375
    And then I will her charmèd eye release
    From monster's view, and all things shall be peace.

---

339 *coil is long of:* turmoil is because of.   344 *amazed:* confused.   352 *sort:* turn out.   356
welkin: sky.   357 *Acheron:* one of the four rivers in the underworld.   358 *testy:* irritable.   359
As: so that.   361 *wrong:* insult.   367 *virtuous:* potent.   369 *wonted:* (previously) accustomed.
370 *derision:* laughable interlude.   373 *date:* term.

PUCK. My fairy lord, this must be done with haste,
    For night's swift dragons cut the clouds full fast:
    And yonder shines Aurora's harbinger,°   380
    At whose approach, ghosts wand'ring here and there,
    Troop home to churchyards: damnèd spirits all,
    That in crossways° and floods° have burial,
    Already to their wormy beds are gone:
    For fear lest day should look their shames upon,   385
    They wilfully themselves exile from light,
    And must for aye consort° with black-browed night.
OBERON. But we are spirits of another sort.
    I with the morning's love have oft made sport,°
    And, like a forester, the groves may tread   390
    Even till the eastern gate all fiery red,
    Opening on Neptune, with fair blessèd beams,
    Turns into yellow gold his salt green streams.
    But notwithstanding, haste, make no delay:
    We may effect this business yet ere day.   *[Exit.]* 395
PUCK. Up and down, up and down,
    I will lead them up and down.
    I am feared in field and town.
    Goblin, lead them up and down.
    Here comes one.   400

Enter LYSANDER.

LYSANDER. Where art thou, proud Demetrius? Speak thou now.
PUCK. Here villain, drawn° and ready. Where art thou?
LYSANDER. I will be with thee straight.
PUCK.   Follow me then
    To plainer° ground.   *[Exit* LYSANDER.*]*

Enter DEMETRIUS.

DEMETRIUS. Lysander, speak again.
    Thou runaway, thou coward, art thou fled?   405
    Speak: in some bush? Where dost thou hide thy head?
PUCK. Thou coward, art thou bragging to the stars,
    Telling the bushes that thou look'st for wars,
    And wilt not come? Come recreant,° come thou child,
    I'll whip thee with a rod. He is defiled   410
    That draws a sword on thee.
DEMETRIUS.   Yea, art thou there?
PUCK. Follow my voice: we'll try no manhood° here.   *Exeunt.*

[Enter LYSANDER.*]*

380 *Aurora's harbinger:* the morning star heralding Aurora, the dawn.   383 *crossways:* crossroads, where suicides were buried.   *floods:* those who drowned.   387 *aye consort:* ever associate.   389 *morning's . . . sport:* hunted with Cephalus (beloved of Aurora and himself devoted to his wife Procris, whom he killed by accident; "sport" also = "amorous dalliance," and "love" = Aurora's love for Oberon).   402 *drawn:* with sword drawn.   404 *plainer:* more level.   409 *recreant:* oath-breaker, coward.   412 *try no manhood:* test no valor.

LYSANDER. He goes before me and still dares me on:
    When I come where he calls, then he is gone
    The villain is much lighter-heeled than I;   415
    I followed fast: but faster did he fly,
    That fallen am I in dark uneven way,
    And here will rest me. *[Lies down.]* Come thou gentle day,
    For if but once thou show me thy grey light.
    I'll find Demetrius and revenge this spite.   *[Sleeps.]* 420

            Enter PUCK *and* DEMETRIUS.

PUCK. Ho, ho, ho! Coward, why com'st thou not?
DEMETRIUS. Abide° me, if thou dar'st, for well I wot°
    Thou run'st before me, shifting every place,
    And dar'st not stand, nor look me in the face.
    Where art thou now?
PUCK.   Come hither: I am here.   425
DEMETRIUS. Nay then thou mock'st me. Thou shalt buy this dear,°
    If ever I thy face by daylight see.
    Now go thy way. Faintness constraineth me
    To measure out my length on this cold bed.
    By day's approach look to be visited.   *[Lies down and sleeps.]* 430

               Enter HELENA.

HELENA. O weary night, O long and tedious night,
    Abate° thy hours; shine comforts° from the east,
    That I may back to Athens by daylight,
    From these that my poor company detest:
    And sleep, that sometimes shuts up sorrow's eye.   435
    Steal me awhile from mine own company.   *Sleeps.*
PUCK. Yet but three? Come one more,
    Two of both kinds makes up four.
    Here she comes, curst° and sad.
    Cupid is a knavish lad,   440
    Thus to make poor females mad.

               Enter HERMIA.

HERMIA. Never so weary, never so in woe,
        Bedabbled with the dew, and torn with briers:
    I can no further crawl, no further go:
        My legs can keep no pace with my desires.   445
    Here will I rest me till the break of day.
    Heavens shield Lysander, if they mean a fray.   *[Lies down and sleeps.]*
PUCK.   On the ground,
        Sleep sound:
        I'll apply
        To your eye,
    Gentle lover, remedy.   *[Squeezes the love-juice on* LYSANDER'S *eyelids.]*

---

422 *Abide:* wait for.   *wot:* know.   426 *buy this dear:* pay dearly for this.   432 *Abate:* shorten.
shine comforts: may comforts shine.   439 *curst:* cross.

When thou wak'st
Thou tak'st
True delight
In the sight
Of thy former lady's eye:
And the country proverb known,
That every man should take his own,
In your waking shall be shown.
    Jack shall have Jill:
    Naught shall go ill:
The man shall have his mare again, and all shall be well.
[*Exit* PUCK. *The lovers remain asleep on stage.*]

ACT 4

[SCENE 1. *The wood*]

    Enter [TITANIA] QUEEN OF FAIRIES, *and* [BOTTOM] THE CLOWN, *and* FAIRIES,
        and the KING [OBERON] *behind them [unseen].*

TITANIA. Come sit thee down upon this flow'ry bed,
    While I thy amiable° cheeks do coy,°
And stick musk-roses in thy sleek smooth head,
    And kiss thy fair large ears, my gentle joy.
BOTTOM. Where's Peaseblossom?   5
PEASEBLOSSOM. Ready.
BOTTOM. Scratch my head, Peaseblossom. Where's Mounsieur
    Cobweb?
COBWEB. Ready.
BOTTOM. Mounsieur Cobweb, good mounsieur, get you your weapons   10
    in your hand, and kill me a red-hipped humblebee on
    the top of a thistle: and good mounsieur, bring me the
    honey-bag. Do not fret yourself too much in the action,
    mounsieur: and good mounsieur have a care the honey-
    bag break not, I would be loath to have you overflowen   15
    with a honey-bag, signior. Where's Mounsieur
    Mustardseed?
MUSTARDSEED. Ready.
BOTTOM. Give me your neaf,° Mounsieur Mustardseed. Pray you
    leave your curtsy,° good mounsieur.   20
MUSTARDSEED. What's your will?
BOTTOM. Nothing, good mounsieur, but to help Cavalery° Cobweb
    to scratch. I must to the barber's mounsieur, for
    methinks I am marvellous hairy about the face. And I am
    such a tender ass, if my hair do but tickle me, I must   25
    scratch.
TITANIA. What, will thou hear some music, my sweet love?

---

2 *amiable:* lovely.   *coy:* caress.   19 *neaf:* fist.   20 *leave your curtsy:* either (a) stop bowing, or
(b) replace your hat.   22 *Cavalery:* (he means "cavalier").

BOTTOM. I have a reasonable good ear in music. Let's have the tongs°
    and the bones.°

TITANIA. Or say, sweet love, what thou desirest to eat.   30

BOTTOM. Truly, a peck of provender. I could munch your good
    dry oats. Methinks I have a great desire to a bottle° of hay.
    Good hay, sweet hay, hath no fellow.

TITANIA. I have a venturous fairy that shall seek
    The squirrel's hoard, and fetch thee new nuts.   35

BOTTOM. I had rather have a handful or two of dried pease. But
    I pray you, let none of your people stir me: I have an
    exposition° of sleep come upon me.

TITANIA. Sleep thou, and I will wind thee in my arms.
    Fairies, be gone, and be all ways° away.   *[Exeunt* FAIRIES.*]* 40
    So doth the woodbine the sweet honeysuckle
    Gently entwist: the female ivy so
    Enrings the barky fingers of the elm.
    O how I love thee! how I dote on thee!   *[They sleep.]*

        Enter ROBIN GOODFELLOW [PUCK.]

OBERON. *[Advances.]* Welcome good Robin. Seest thou this sweet sight?   45
    Her dotage now I do begin to pity.
    For meeting her of late behind the wood,
    Seeking sweet favours° for this hateful fool,
    I did upbraid her and fall out with her.
    For she his hairy temples then had rounded   50
    With coronet of fresh and fragrant flowers
    And that same dew which sometime° on the buds
    Was wont to° swell like round and orient° pearls,
    Stood now within the pretty flowerets' eyes,
    Like tears that did their own disgrace bewail.   55
    When I had at my pleasure taunted her,
    And she in mild terms begged my patience,
    I then did ask of her her changeling child:
    Which straight she gave me, and her fairy sent
    To bear him to my bower in fairy land.   60
    And now I have the boy, I will undo
    This hateful imperfection of her eyes.
    And gentle Puck, take this transformèd scalp
    From off the head of this Athenian swain;
    That he awaking when the other do,   65
    May all to Athens back again repair,°
    And think no more of this night's accidents,°
    But as the fierce vexation of a dream.

---

28 *tongs:* crude music made by striking tongs with a piece of metal.   *bones:* pieces of bone held
between the fingers and clapped together rhythmically.   32 *bottle:* bundle.   38 *exposition:* (he
means "disposition to").   40 *all ways:* in every direction.   48 *favours:* bouquets as love tokens.
52 *sometime:* formerly.   53 *Was wont to:* used to.   *orient:* (where the most beautiful pearls came
from).   66 *repair:* return.   67 *accidents:* incidents.

But first I will release the Fairy Queen.
    Be as thou wast wont to be: 70
    See, as thou was wont to see.
    Dian's bud o'er Cupid's flower°
    Hath such force and blessèd power.
    Now my Titania, wake you, my sweet queen.

TITANIA. My Oberon, what visions have I seen!   75
    Methought I was enamoured of an ass.

OBERON. There lies your love.

TITANIA.   How came these things to pass?
    O, how mine eyes do loathe his visage now!

OBERON. Silence awhile Robin, take off this head:
    Titania, music call, and strike more dead   80
    Than common sleep of all these five the sense.°

TITANIA. Music, ho music! such as charmeth sleep.

PUCK. Now, when thou wak'st, with thine own fools' eyes peep.

OBERON. Sound music: *Music still.*°
                Come my queen, take hands with me,
    And rock the ground whereon these sleepers be.   *[Dance.]* 85
    Now thou and I are new in amity,
    And will tomorrow midnight solemnly
    Dance in Duke Theseus' house triumphantly,°
    And bless it to all fair prosperity.
    There shall the pairs of faithful lovers be   90
    Wedded, with Theseus, all in jollity.

PUCK. Fairy King, attend and mark:
    I do hear the morning lark.

OBERON. Then my queen, in silence sad,°
    Trip we after the night's shade: 95
    We the globe can compass soon,
    Swifter than the wand'ring moon.

TITANIA. Come my lord, and in our flight,
    Tell me how it came this night,
    That I sleeping here was found,   100
    With these mortals on the ground.   *Exeunt.*

       Wind horns. Enter THESEUS, HIPPOLYTA, EGEUS *and all his train.*

THESEUS. Go one of you, find out the forester:
    For now our observation° is performed.
    And since we have the vaward° of the day,
    My love shall hear the music of my hounds.   105
    Uncouple° in the western valley, let them go:
    Dispatch I say, and find the forester.   *[Exit an* ATTENDANT.*]*

---

72 *Dian's bud . . . flower:* (Diana's bud counteracts the effects of love-in-idleness, the pansy).   80–81 *strike . . . sense:* Make these five (the lovers and Bottom) sleep more soundly.   84.1 S.D. *still:* continuously.   88 *triumphantly:* in celebration.   94 *sad:* serious.   101.1 S.D.: *wind:* blow, sound. 103 *observation:* observance of the May Day rites.   104 *vaward:* vanguard, earliest part.   106 *Uncouple:* unleash (the dogs).

We will, fair queen, up to the mountain's top,
And mark the musical confusion
Of hounds and echo in conjunction.   110
HIPPOLYTA. I was with Hercules and Cadmus° once,
When in a wood of Crete they bayed the bear,°
With hounds of Sparta:° never did I hear
Such gallant chiding. For besides the groves,
The skies, the fountains, every region near   115
Seemed all one mutual cry. I never heard
So musical a discord, such sweet thunder.
THESEUS. My hounds are bred out of the Spartan kind:
So flewed, so sanded:° and their heads are hung
With ears that sweep away the morning dew,   120
Crook-kneed, and dewlapped° like Thessalian bulls:
Slow in pursuit; but matched in mouth like bells,
Each under each.° A cry° more tuneable
Was never holloa'd to, nor cheered with horn,
In Crete, in Sparta, nor in Thessaly.   125
Judge when you hear. But soft.° What nymphs are these?
EGEUS. My lord, this is my daughter here asleep,
And this Lysander, this Demetrius is,
This Helena, old Nedar's Helena.
I wonder of their being here together.   130
THESEUS. No doubt they rose up early to observe
The rite of May: and hearing our intent,
Came here in grace° of our solemnity.
But speak Egeus, is not this the day
That Hermia should give answer of her choice?   135
EGEUS. It is, my lord.
THESEUS. Go bid the huntsmen wake them with their horns.

Shout within: wind horns. They all start up.

Good morrow, friends. Saint Valentine is past.
Begin these wood-birds but to couple now?°
LYSANDER. Pardon, my lord.   *[They kneel.]*
THESEUS.   I pray you all, stand up.   140
I know you two are rival enemies.
How comes this gentle concord in the world,
That hatred is so far from jealousy,°
To sleep by hate° and fear no enmity?
LYSANDER. My lord, I shall reply amazedly,   145
Half sleep, half waking. But as yet, I swear,
I cannot truly say how I came here.

---

111 *Cadmus:* mythical builder of Thebes.   112 *bayed the bear:* brought the bear to bay, to its last stand.   113 *hounds of Sparta:* (a breed famous for their swiftness and quick scent).   119 *flewed, so sanded:* with hanging cheeks, so sand-colored.   121 *dewlapped:* with skin hanging from the chin.   122–123 *matched . . . each:* with each voice matched for harmony with the next in pitch, like bells in a chime.   123 *cry:* pack of dogs.   126 *soft:* wait.   133 *grace:* honor.   138–139 *Saint . . . now:* (birds traditionally chose their mates on St. Valentine's Day).   143 *jealousy:* suspicion. 144 *hate:* one it hates.

But as I think—for truly would I speak,
And now I do bethink me, so it is—
I came with Hermia hither. Our intent   150
Was to be gone from Athens, where we might,
Without° the peril of the Athenian law—
EGEUS. Enough, enough, my lord: you have enough.
    I beg the law, the law upon his head:
    They would have stol'n away, they would, Demetrius,   155
    Thereby to have defeated you and me:
    You of your wife, and me of my consent:
    Of my consent that she should be your wife.
DEMETRIUS. My lord, fair Helen told me of their stealth,
    Of this their purpose hither, to this wood,   160
    And I in fury hither followed them;
    Fair Helena in fancy° following me.
    But my good lord, I wot not by what power
    (But by some power it is) my love to Hermia,
    Melted as the snow, seems to me now   165
    As the remembrance of an idle gaud,°
    Which in my childhood I did dote upon:
    And all the faith, the virtue of my heart,
    The object and the pleasure of mine eye,
    Is only Helena. To her, my lord,   170
    Was I betrothed ere I saw Hermia:
    But like a sickness,° did I loathe this food.
    But as in health, come° to my natural taste,
    Now I do wish it, love it, long for it.
    And will for evermore be true to it.   175
THESEUS. Fair lovers, you are fortunately met.
    Of this discourse we more will hear anon.
    Egeus, I will overbear your will:
    For in the temple, by and by,° with us,
    These couples shall eternally be knit.   180
    And for the morning now is something worn,°
    Our purposed hunting shall be set aside.
    Away with us to Athens. Three and three,
    We'll hold a feast in great solemnity.
    Come Hippolyta.   185

Exeunt DUKE [HIPPOLYTA, EGEUS] *and* LORDS.

DEMETRIUS. These things seem small and undistinguishable,
    Like far-off mountains turnèd into clouds.
HERMIA. Methinks I see these things with parted° eye,
    When everything seems double.
HELENA.   So methinks:

---

152 *Without:* beyond.   162 *in fancy:* out of doting love.   166 *idle gaud:* trifling toy.   172 *sick-ness:* sick person.   173 *come:* i.e., back.   179 *by and by:* immediately.   181 *something worn:* somewhat worn on.   188 *parted:* divided (each eye seeing a separate image).

And I have found Demetrius, like a jewel,   190
  Mine own, and not mine own.°
DEMETRIUS.   Are you sure
  That we are awake? It seems to me,
  That we yet sleep, we dream. Do not you think
  The duke was here, and bid us follow him?
HERMIA. Yea, and my father.
HELENA.   And Hippolyta.   195
LYSANDER. And he did bid us follow to the temple.
DEMETRIUS. Why then, we are awake: let's follow him,
  And by the way let us recount our dreams.   *Exeunt Lovers.*
BOTTOM. *(Wakes.)* When my cue comes, call me, and I will answer.
  My next is "Most fair Pyramus." Hey ho. Peter Quince?   200
  Flute the bellows-mender? Snout the tinker? Starveling?
  God's my life! Stol'n hence, and left me asleep? I have
  had a most rare vision. I have had a dream, past the wit
  of man to say what dream it was. Man is but an ass, if he
  go about° to expound this dream. Methought I was—   205
  there is no man can tell what. Methought I was, and
  methought I had—but man is but a patched fool,° if he
  will offer to say what methought I had. The eye of man
  hath not heard, the ear of man hath not seen, man's hand is
  not able to taste, his tongue to conceive, nor his   210
  heart to report, what my dream was. I will get Peter
  Quince to write a ballad of this dream: it shall be called
  Bottom's Dream; because it hath no bottom: and I
  will sing it in the latter end of our play, before the duke.
  Peradventure, to make it the more gracious, I shall sing   215
  it at her° death.   *Exit.*

[SCENE 2. *Athens,* QUINCE's *house]*

Enter QUINCE, FLUTE, SNOUT, *and* STARVELING.

QUINCE. Have you sent to Bottom's house? Is he come home yet?
STARVELING. He cannot be heard of. Out of doubt he is transported.°
FLUTE. If he come not, then the play is marred. It goes not forward,
  doth it?
QUINCE. It is not possible. You have not a man in all Athens able   5
  to discharge° Pyramus but he.
FLUTE. No, he hath simply the best wit of any handicraft man in Athens.
QUINCE. Yea, and the best person too, and he is a very paramour
  for a sweet voice.
FLUTE. You must say "paragon." A paramour is (God bless us)   10
  a thing of naught.°

Enter SNUG THE JOINER.

190–191 *like . . . own:* like a person who finds a jewel: the finder is the owner, but insecurely so.
205 *go about:* attempt.   207 *patched fool:* fool dressed in motley.   216 *her:* Thisby's.   2 *trans-*
ported: carried away (by spirits).   6 *discharge:* portray.   11 *of naught:* wicked, naughty.

SNUG. Masters, the duke is coming from the temple, and there
    is two or three lords and ladies more married. If our
    sport had gone forward, we had all been made men.°
FLUTE. O sweet bully Bottom. Thus hath he lost sixpence a day°   15
    during his life: he could not have 'scaped sixpence a day.
    And the duke had not given him sixpence a day for playing
    Pyramus, I'll be hanged. He would have deserved it.
    Sixpence a day in Pyramus, or nothing.

Enter BOTTOM.

BOTTOM. Where are these lads? Where are these hearts?   20
QUINCE. Bottom! O most courageous° day! O most happy hour!
BOTTOM. Masters, I am to discourse wonders: but ask me not what.
    For if I tell you, I am not true Athenian. I will tell you
    everything, right as it fell out.
QUINCE. Let us hear, sweet Bottom.   25
BOTTOM. Not a word of me. All that I will tell you is, that the
    duke hath dined. Get your apparel together, good
    strings to your beards, new ribbands to your pumps, meet
    presently° at the palace, every man look o'er his part: for
    the short and the long is, our play is preferred.° In any   30
    case, let Thisby have clean linen: and let not him that
    plays the lion pare his nails, for they shall hang out for
    the lion's claws. And most dear actors, eat no onions nor
    garlic, for we are to utter sweet breath: and I do not
    doubt but to hear them say it is a sweet comedy. No more   35
    words: away, go away.   *Exeunt.*

ACT 5

[SCENE 1. The palace of Theseus*]*

Enter THESEUS, HIPPOLYTA, *and* PHILOSTRATE, *and his* LORDS.

HIPPOLYTA. 'Tis strange, my Theseus, that these lovers speak of.
THESEUS. More strange than true. I never may believe
    These antick° fables, nor these fairy toys.°
    Lovers and madmen have such seething brains,
    Such shaping fantasies,° that apprehend   5
    More than cool reason ever comprehends.
    The lunatic, the lover, and the poet,
    Are of imagination all compact.°
    One sees more devils than vast hell can hold:
    That is the madman. The lover, all as frantic,   10
    Sees Helen's beauty in a brow of Egypt.°

---

14 *made men:* men made rich.   15 *sixpence a day:* i.e., as a pension.   21 *courageous:* (he may
mean "auspicious").   29 *presently:* immediately.   30 *preferred:* recommended (for presentation).
3 *antick:* fantastic.   *fairy toys:* trivial fairy stories.   5 *fantasies:* imaginations.   8 *of . . . compact:* totally composed of imagination.   11 *a brow of Egypt:* the swarthy face of a gypsy (believed to
come from Egypt).

The poet's eye, in a fine frenzy rolling,
Doth glance from heaven to earth, from earth to heaven.
And as imagination bodies forth
The forms of things unknown, the poet's pen   15
Turns them to shapes, and gives to airy nothing,
A local habitation and a name.
Such tricks hath strong imagination,
That if it would but apprehend some joy,
It comprehends° some bringer of that joy.   20
Or in the night, imagining some fear,
How easy is a bush supposed a bear.
HIPPOLYTA. But all the story of the night told over,
And all their minds transfigured so together,
More witnesseth than fancy's images,°   25
And grows to something of great constancy:°
But howsoever, strange and admirable.°

      Enter LOVERS: LYSANDER, DEMETRIUS, HERMIA, *and* HELENA.

THESEUS. Here come the lovers, full of joy and mirth.
Joy, gentle friends, joy and fresh days of love
Accompany your hearts.
LYSANDER.   More° than to us   30
Wait in your royal walks, your board, your bed.
THESEUS. Come now, what masques,° what dances shall we have,
To wear away this long age of three hours
Between our after-supper° and bed-time?
Where is our usual manager of mirth?   35
What revels are in hand? Is there no play,
To ease the anguish of a torturing hour?
Call Philostrate.
PHILOSTRATE.   Here, mighty Theseus.
THESEUS. Say, what abridgment° have you for this evening?
What masque,° what music? How shall we beguile   40
The lazy time, if not with some delight?
PHILOSTRATE. There is a brief° how many sports are ripe:°
Make choice of which your highness will see first.

             [Gives a paper.]

THESEUS. "The battle with the Centaurs, to be sung
By an Athenian eunuch to the harp."   45
We'll none of that. That I have told my love
In glory of my kinsman Hercules.
"The riot of the tipsy Bacchanals,
Tearing the Thracian singer in their rage."°

---

20 *comprehends:* includes.   25 *Move . . . images:* testifies that it is more than just imagination.
26 *constancy:* certainty.   27 *admirable:* to be wondered at.   30 *More:* even more (joy and love).
32, 40 *masques:* lavish courtly entertainments combining song and dance.   34 *after-supper:* late
supper.   39 *abridgment:* either (a) diversion to make the hours seem shorter or (b) short entertainment.   42 *brief:* list.   *ripe:* ready.   48–49 *riot . . . rage:* (The singer Orpheus of Thrace was
torn limb from limb by the Maenads, frenzied female priests of Bacchus).

That is an old device: and it was played   50
When I from Thebes came last a conqueror.
"The thrice three Muses mourning for the death
Of Learning, late deceased in beggary."
That is some satire keen and critical,
Not sorting with° a nuptial ceremony.   55
"A tedious brief scene of young Pyramus
And his love Thisby; very tragical mirth."
Merry and tragical? Tedious and brief?
That is hot ice and wondrous strange snow.
How shall we find the concord of this discord?   60
PHILOSTRATE. A play there is, my lord, some ten words long,
    Which is as brief as I have known a play:
    But by ten words, my lord, it is too long,
    Which makes it tedious: for in all the play
    There is not one word apt, one player fitted.°   65
    And tragical, my noble lord, it is:
    For Pyramus therein doth kill himself.
    Which when I saw rehearsed, I must confess,
    Made mine eyes water; but more merry tears
    The passion of loud laughter never shed.   70
THESEUS. What are they that do play it?
PHILOSTRATE. Hard-handed men, that work in Athens here,
    Which never laboured in their minds till now:
    And now have toiled their unbreathed° memories
    With this same play, against° your nuptial.   75
THESEUS. And we will hear it.
PHILOSTRATE.   No, my noble lord,
    It is not for you. I have heard it over,
    And it is nothing, nothing in the world;
    Unless you can find sport in their intents,
    Extremely stretched and conned° with cruel pain.   80
    To do your service.
THESEUS.   I will hear that play.
    For never anything can be amiss,
    When simpleness and duty tender° it.
    Go bring them in, and take your places, ladies.   *[Exit* PHILOSTRATE.*]*
HIPPOLYTA. I love not to see wretchedness o'ercharged,°   85
      And duty in his service perishing.
THESEUS. Why gentle sweet, you shall see no such thing.
HIPPOLYTA. He says they can do nothing in this kind.°
THESEUS. The kinder we, to give them thanks for nothing.
    Our sport shall be to take what they mistake.   90

---

55 *sorting with:* befitting.   65 *fitted:* (well) cast.   74 *unbreathed:* unpracticed, unexercised.   75 *against:* in preparation for.   80 *stretched and conned:* strained and memorized.   83 *tender:* offer.   85 *wretchedness o'ercharged:* poor fellows taxing themselves too much.   88 *in this kind:* of this sort.

And what poor duty cannot do, noble respect
Takes it in might, not merit.°
Where I have come, great clerks° have purposèd
To greet me with premeditated welcomes;
Where I have seen them shiver and look pale,   95
Make periods in the midst of sentences,
Throttle° their practised accent in their fears,
And in conclusion dumbly have broke off,
Not paying me a welcome. Trust me, sweet,
Out of this silence yet I picked a welcome: 100
And in the modesty of fearful duty°
I read as much as from the rattling tongue
Of saucy and audacious eloquence.
Love, therefore, and tongue-tied simplicity,
In° least, speak most, to my capacity.°   105

[Enter PHILOSTRATE.*]*

PHILOSTRATE. So please your grace, the Prologue is addressed.°
THESEUS. Let him approach.

Flourish trumpets. Enter the PROLOGUE [QUINCE].

PROLOGUE. If we offend, it is with our good will.
     That you should think, we come not to offend,
     But with good will. To show our simple skill,   110
     That is the true beginning of our end.
     Consider then, we come but in despite.°
     We do not come, as minding to content you,
     Our true intent is. All for your delight,
     We are not here. That you should here repent you,   115
     The actors are at hand: and by their show,
     You shall know all, that you are like to know.°
THESEUS. This fellow doth not stand upon points.°
LYSANDER. He hath rid his prologue like a rough colt: he knows
     not the stop.° A good moral my lord: it is not enough   120
     to speak; but to speak true.
HIPPOLYTA. Indeed he hath played on his prologue like a child on a
     recorder:° a sound, but not in government.°
THESEUS. His speech was like a tangled chain: nothing impaired, but
     all disordered. Who is next?   125

Enter PYRAMUS *and* THISBY, WALL, MOONSHINE, *and* LION.

91–92 *noble . . . merit:* a noble nature considers the sincerity of effort rather than the skill of execution.   93 *clerks:* scholars.   97 *Throttle:* choke on.   101 *fearful duty:* subjects whose devotions gave them stage fright.   105 *In:* i.e., saying.   *capacity:* way of thinking.   106 *addressed:* ready. 108–117 *If . . . know:* (Quince's blunders in punctuation exactly reverse the meaning).   112 *despite:* malice.   111 *stand upon points:* (1) pay attention to punctuation (2) bother about the niceties (of expression).   120 *stop:* (1) halt (2) period.   123 *recorder:* flutelike wind instrument. *in government:* well managed.

PROLOGUE. Gentles, perchance you wonder at this show,
    But wonder on, till truth make all things plain.
    This man is Pyramus, if you would know:
    This beauteous lady, Thisby is certain.
    This man, with lime and rough-cast,° doth present   130
    Wall, that vile wall which did these lovers sunder:
    And through Wall's chink, poor souls, they are content
    To whisper. At the which, let no man wonder.
    This man, with lantern, dog, and bush of thorn,
    Presenteth Moonshine. For if you will know,   135
    By moonshine did these lovers think no scorn
    To meet at Ninus' tomb, there, there to woo:
    This grisly beast (which Lion hight° by name)
    The trusty Thisby, coming first by night,
    Did scare away, or rather did affright: 140
    And as she fled, her mantle she did fall:°
    Which Lion vile with bloody mouth did stain.
    Anon comes Pyramus, sweet youth and tall,°
    And finds his trusty Thisby's mantle slain:
    Whereat, with blade, with bloody blameful blade,   145
    He bravely broached° his boiling bloody breast.
    And Thisby, tarrying in mulberry shade,
    His dagger drew, and died. For all the rest,
    Let Lion, Moonshine, Wall, and lovers twain.
    At large° discourse, while here they do remain.   150
THESEUS. I wonder if the lion be to speak.
DEMETRIUS. No wonder, my lord: one lion may, when many asses do.

        Exeunt [PROLOGUE, PYRAMUS,] LION, THISBY, MOONSHINE.

WALL. In this same interlude° it doth befall
    That I, one Snout by name, present a wall:
    And such a wall, as I would have you think,   155
    That had in it a crannied hole or chink:
    Through which the lovers, Pyramus and Thisby,
    Did whisper often, very secretly.
    This loam, this rough-cast, and this stone doth show
    That I am that same wall: the truth is so.   160
    And this the cranny is, right and sinister,°
    Through which the fearful lovers are to whisper.
THESEUS. Would you desire lime and hair to speak better?
DEMETRIUS. It is the wittiest° partition° that ever I heard discourse,
    my lord.   165

        Enter PYRAMUS.

---

130 *rough-cast:* rough plaster made of lime and gravel.   138 *hight:* is called.   141 *fall:* let fall.
143 *tall:* brave.   146 *broached:* opened (Shakespeare parodies the overuse of alliteration in the earlier bombastic Elizabethan plays).   150 *At large:* in full.   153 *interlude:* short play.   161 *right
and sinister:* from right to left (he probably uses the fingers of his right and left hands to form the
cranny).   164 *wittiest:* most intelligent.   *partition:* (1) wall (2) section of a learned book or
speech.

THESEUS. Pyramus draws near the wall: silence.
PYRAMUS. O grim-looked night, O night with hue so black,
 O night, O night, alack, alack, alack,
 I fear my Thisby's promise is forgot   170
 And thou O wall, O sweet, O lovely wall,
 That stand'st between her father's ground and mine,
 Thou wall, O wall, O sweet and lovely wall,
 Show me thy chink, to blink through with mine eyne.°

             [WALL holds up his fingers.]

 Thanks, courteous wall. Jove shield thee well for this.   175
 But what see I? No Thisby do I see.
 O wicked wall, through whom I see no bliss,
 Cursed by thy stones for thus deceiving me.
THESEUS. The wall methinks being sensible,° should curse again.°
PYRAMUS. No in truth sir, he should not. "Deceiving me" is   180
 Thisby's cue: she is to enter now, and I am to spy her
 through the wall. You shall see it will fall pat° as I told you:
 yonder she comes.

         Enter THISBY.

THISBY. O wall, full often hast thou heard my moans,
 For parting my fair Pyramus and me.   185
 My cherry lips have often kissed thy stones;
 Thy stones with lime and hair knit up in thee.
PYRAMUS. I see a voice: now will I to the chink,
 To spy and I can hear my Thisby's face.
 Thisby?   190
THISBY. My love thou art, my love I think.
PYRAMUS. Think what thou wilt, I am thy lover's grace:
 And, like Limander,° am I trusty still.
THISBY. And I like Helen,° till the Fates me kill.
PYRAMUS. Not Shafalus to Procrus,° was so true.   195
THISBY. As Shafalus to Procrus, I to you.
PYRAMUS. O kiss me through the hole of this vile wall.
THISBY. I kiss the wall's hole, not your lips at all.
PYRAMUS. Wilt thou at Ninny's° tomb meet me straightway?
THISBY. Tide° life, tide death, I come without delay.   200

       [Exeunt PYRAMUS *and* THISBY.*]*

WALL. Thus have I, Wall, my part dischargèd so;
 And being done, thus Wall away doth go.   *Exit.*
THESEUS. Now is the mural° down between the two neighbours.
DEMETRIUS. No remedy my lord, when walls are so willful to hear
 without warning.°   210

---

174 *eyne:* eyes.   179 *sensible:* capable of feelings and perception.   *again:* back.   182 *pat:* exactly.   193 *Limander:* (he means "Leander").   194 *Helen:* (he means "Hero").   195 *Shafalus to Procrus:* (he means "Cephalus" and "Procris" [see Act III, scene 2, 389 n.]).   199 *Ninny:* fool (he means "Ninus").   200 *Tide:* come, betide.   203 *mural:* wall.   205 *without warning:* either (a) without warning the parents or (b) unexpectedly.

HIPPOLYTA. This is the silliest stuff that ever I heard.

THESEUS. The best in this kind are but shadows:° and the worst are
    no worse, if imagination amend them.

HIPPOLYTA. It must be your imagination then, and not theirs.

THESEUS. If we imagine no worse of them than they of themselves,   215
    they may pass for excellent men. Here come two noble
    beasts in, a man and a lion.

Enter LION and MOONSHINE.

LION. You ladies, you, whose gentle hearts do fear
    The smallest monstrous mouse that creeps on floor,
    May now perchance both quake and tremble here.   220
    When lion rough in wildest rage doth roar.
    Then know that I, as Snug the joiner am
    A lion fell,° nor else no lion's dam:°
    For if I should as lion come in strife   225
    Into this place, 'twere pity on my life.

THESEUS. A very gentle beast, and of a good conscience.

DEMETRIUS. The very best at a beast,° my lord, that e'er I saw.

LYSANDER. This lion is a very fox for his valour.

THESEUS. True, and a goose for his discretion.   230

DEMETRIUS. Not so my lord: for his valour cannot carry his discretion,
    and the fox carries the goose.

THESEUS. His discretion, I am sure, cannot carry his valour: for the
    goose carries not the fox. It is well: leave it to his discretion,
    and let us listen to the moon.   235

MOONSHINE. This lanthorn° doth the hornèd moon present—

DEMETRIUS. He should have worn the horns upon his head.°

THESEUS. He is no crescent, and his horns are invisible within the
    circumference.

MOONSHINE. This lanthorn doth the hornèd moon present,   240
    Myself, the man i' th' moon do seem to be.

THESEUS. This is the greatest error of all the rest; the man should
    be put into the lanthorn. How is it else the man i' th'
    moon?

DEMETRIUS. He dares not come there for the candle; for you see, it   245
    is already in snuff.°

HIPPOLYTA. I am aweary of this moon. Would he would change.

THESEUS. It appears, by his small light of discretion, that he is in
    the wane: but yet in courtesy, in all reason, we must stay°
    the time.   250

LYSANDER. Proceed, Moon.

MOONSHINE. All that I have to say, is to tell you that the lanthorn is

---

207 *in . . . shadows:* of this sort are only plays (or only actors).   218 *fell:* fierce.   *nor . . . dam:* and
not a lioness.   222 *best beast:* (pronounced similarly).   230 *lanthorn:* lantern (once made of
horn).   230–231 *hornèd . . . head:* (referring to the cuckold or deceived husband, who supposedly
grew horns).   240 *in snuff:* (1) in need of snuffing (having a long, burnt-out wick or snuff) (2) in a
temper.   243 *stay:* await.

the moon, I the man i' th' moon, this thornbush my
thornbush, and this dog my dog.

DEMETRIUS. Why, all these should be in the lanthorn: for all these are
in the moon. But silence: here comes Thisby.   255

Enter THISBY.

THISBY. Tis old Ninny's tomb. Where is my love?
LION. Oh!   *The* LION *roars.* THISBY *runs off.*
DEMETRIUS. Well roared, Lion.
THESEUS. Well run, Thisby.
HIPPOLYTA. Well shone, Moon. Truly, the moon shines with a good   260
grace.

[The LION *shakes* THISBY'S *mantle.]*

THESEUS. Well moused,° Lion.
DEMETRIUS. And then came Pyramus.

Enter PYRAMUS. *[Exit* LION.]

LYSANDER. And so the lion vanished.
PYRAMUS. Sweet moon, I thank thee for thy sunny beams,   265
        I thank thee, moon, for shining now so bright.
    For by thy gracious, golden, glittering gleams,
        I trust to take of truest Thisby sight.
            But stay: O spite!
            But mark, poor knight,   270
        What dreadful dole° is here?
            Eyes, do you see!
            How can it be!
        O dainty duck, O dear!
            Thy mantle good,   275
            What, stained with blood?
        Approach, ye Furies° fell:
            O Fates!° come, come:
            Cut thread and thrum.°
            Quail,° crush, conclude, and quell.°   280
THESEUS. This passion, and the death of a dear friend, would go
near to make a man look sad.
HIPPOLYTA. Beshrew° my heart, but I pity the man.
PYRAMUS. O wherefore Nature, didst thou lions frame?   285
        Since lion vile hath here deflowered my dear.
    Which is—no, no—which was the fairest dame
        That lived, that loved, that liked, that looked with cheer.
        Come tears, confound:
            Out sword, and wound

---

257 *moused:* shaken, as a cat shakes a mouse.   266 *dole:* grief.   272 *Furies:* classical spirits of the
underworld who avenged murder.   273 *Fates:* three sisters who spun the thread of human destiny,
which at will was cut with a shears.   274 *thrum:* fringelike end of the warp in weaving.   275
Quail: subdue.   *quell:* kill.   278 *Beshrew:* curse (meant lightly).

The pap° of Pyramus: 290
   Ay, that left pap,
   Where heart doth hop.   *[Stabs himself.]*
Thus die, I, thus, thus, thus.
   Now am I dead,
   Now am I fled,   295
My soul is in the sky.
   Tongue lose thy light,
   Moon° take thy flight,   *[Exit MOONSHINE.]*
Now die, die, die, die, die.   *[Dies.]*

DEMETRIUS. No die,° but an ace° for him. For he is but one.   300
LYSANDER. Less than an ace, man. For he is dead, he is nothing.
THESEUS. With the help of a surgeon, he might yet recover, and
   prove an ass.
HIPPOLYTA. How chance Moonshine is gone before Thisby comes   303
   back and finds her lover?

Enter THISBY.

THESEUS. She will find him by starlight. Here she comes, and her
   passion ends the play.
HIPPOLYTA. Methinks she should not use a long one for such a
   Pyramus: I hope she will be brief.   310
DEMETRIUS. A mote will turn the balance, which Pyramus, which
   Thisby, is the better: he for a man, God warr'nt° us;
   she for a woman, God bless us.
LYSANDER. She hath spied him already with those sweet eyes.
DEMETRIUS. And thus she means,° videlicet—°   315
THISBY. Asleep my love?
   What, dead, my dove?
O Pyramus, arise,
   Speak, speak. Quite dumb?
   Dead, dead? A tomb   320
Must cover thy sweet eyes.
   These lily lips,
   This cherry nose,
These yellow cowslip° cheeks,
   Are gone, are gone: 325
   Lovers, make moan:
His eyes were green as leeks.
   O Sisters Three,°
   Come, come to me,
With hands as pale as milk,   330
   Lay them in gore,
   Since you have shore
With shears his thread of silk.

---

285 *pap:* breast.   292–293 *Tongue . . . Moon:* (he reverses the two subjects).   295 *die:* (singular of
"dice").   *ace:* a throw of one at dice.   306 *warr'nt:* warrant, protect.   309 *means:* laments.
videlicet: namely.   318 *cowslip:* yellow primrose.   322 *Sisters Three:* the Fates.

       Tongue, not a word:
       Come trusty sword,
   Come blade, my breast imbrue°   *[Stabs herself.]* 335
       And farewell friends:
       Thus Thisby ends:
   Adieu, adieu, adieu.   *[Dies.]*

THESEUS. Moonshine and Lion are left to bury the dead.
DEMETRIUS. Ay, and Wall too.   340
BOTTOM. *[Starts up]* No, I assure you, the wall is down that parted
   their fathers. Will it please you to see the Epilogue, or
   to hear a Bergomask° dance between two of our company?
THESEUS. No epilogue, I pray you; for your play needs no excuse.   345
   Never excuse: for when the players are all dead, there
   need none to be blamed. Marry, if he that writ it had
   played Pyramus and hanged himself in Thisby's garter,
   it would have been a fine tragedy: and so it is truly, and
   very notably discharged. But come, your Bergomask: 350
   let your Epilogue alone.   *[A dance.]*
   The iron tongue° of midnight hath told° twelve.
   Lovers, to bed, 'tis almost fairy time.°
   I fear we shall outsleep the coming morn,
   As much as we this night have overwatched.   355
   This palpable gross° play hath well beguiled
   The heavy gait of night. Sweet friends, to bed.
   A fortnight hold we this solemnity,
   In nightly revels, and new jollity.   *Exeunt.*

              Enter PUCK *[with a broom].*

PUCK. Now the hungry lion roars,   360
     And the wolf behowls the moon;
   Whilst the heavy° ploughman snores,
     All with weary task fordone.°
   Now the wasted brands° do glow,
   Whilst the screech-owl, screeching loud,   365
     Puts the wretch that lies in woe°
   In remembrance of a shroud.
     Now it is the time of night,
   That the graves, all gaping wide,
     Every one lets forth his sprite,°   370
   In the church-way paths to glide.
     And we fairies, that do run
   By the triple Hecate's° team,°
     From the presence of the sun,

330 *imbrue:* stain with gore.   338 *Bergomask:* exaggerated country dance.   346 *iron tongue:* i.e.,
of the bell.   *told:* counted, tolled.   347 *fairy time:* (from midnight to daybreak).   350 *palpable
gross:* obvious and crude.   356 *heavy:* sleepy.   357 *fordone:* worn out, "done in."   358 *wasted
brands:* burnt logs.   360 *wretch . . . woe:* sick person.   364 *sprite:* spirit, ghost.   367 *triple
Hecate:* the moon goddess, identified as Cynthia in heaven, Diana on earth, and Hecate in hell.
team: dragons that pull the chariot of the night moon.

Following darkness like a dream,
    Now are frolic:° not a mouse   375
Shall disturb this hallowed house.
I am sent with broom before,
To sweep the dust° behind° the door.

            Enter KING *and* QUEEN OF FAIRIES, *with all their train.*

OBERON. Through the house give glimmering light,
    By the dead and drowsy fire,   380
Every elf and fairy sprite,
    Hop as light as bird from brier,
And this ditty after me,
    Sing, and dance it trippingly.
TITANIA. First rehearse your song by rote,   385
To each word a warbling note.
Hand in hand, with fairy grace,
Will we sing and bless this place.   *[Song and dance.]*
OBERON. Now, until the break of day,
Through this house each fairy stray.   390
To the best bride-bed will we,
Which by us shall blessèd be:
And the issue° there create,°
Ever shall be fortunate:
So shall all the couples three   395
Ever true in loving be:
And the blots of Nature's hand°
Shall not in their issue° stand.
Never mole, harelip, nor scar,
Nor mark prodigious,° such as are   400
Despisèd in nativity,
Shall upon their children be.
With this field-dew consecrate.
Every fairy take his gait,°
And each several° chamber bless,   405
Through this palace, with sweet peace;
And the owner of its blest,
Ever shall in safety rest.
Trip away: make no stay: *Exeunt [all but* PUCK*].*
Meet me all by break of day.   410
PUCK. If we shadows have offended,
Think but this, and all is mended,
That you have but slumbered here,
While these visions did appear.
And this weak and idle° theme,   415

---

370 *frolic:* frolicsome.   373 *To sweep the dust:* (Puck often helped with household chores).
behind: from behind.   388, 393 *issue:* children.   388 *create:* created.   392 *blots . . . hand:* birth
defects.   395 *mark prodigious:* unnatural birthmark.   399 *take his gait:* proceed.   400 *several:*
separate.   410 *idle:* foolish.

No more yielding but° a dream,
Gentles, do not reprehend.
If you pardon, we will mend.°
And as I am an honest Puck,
If we have unearnèd luck,
Now to scape the serpent's tongue,°   420
We will make amends, ere long:
Else the Puck a liar call.
So good night unto you all.
Give me your hands,° if we be friends;   425
And Robin shall restore amends.°   *[Exit.]*

411 *No . . . but:* yielding nothing more than.   413 *mend:* improve.   416 *serpent's tongue:* hissing
of the audience.   420 *hands:* applause.   421 *restore amends:* do better in the future.

For Practice

1. *A Midsummer Night's Dream* was likely written to celebrate a courtly marriage. Consider all the marriages and impending marriages in the play. Do you think that Shakespeare intended his play, not simply for enjoyment, but as a story with a moral? What argument might he be making about marriage in this play? Support your claims with good reasons from the text.

2. What is the function of dreaming in the play? How does dreaming link to or comment upon some of the major themes of this play? (See the introduction for the play for some ideas about these themes.) Consider how the rules of the real world do not apply in a dream world.

3. Many of the women in this play do not submit easily to male power, but behave as unruly subjects. At the time this play was written, Queen Elizabeth I was in the final third of a long and relatively prosperous and stable reign. How do you think the unruliness of the women in the play represents a change in attitudes toward women? You might consider the degrees of freedom the various female characters have in Athens and in the forest as a way of examining these values.

4. In *A Midsummer Night's Dream*, Shakespeare presents us with two courts: the Athenian court headed by Theseus, and the fairy court ruled by Oberon. How does the court of the fairies mirror or comment on the mortal court of Theseus? How might either or both of these constitute a commentary on the English court?

5. In Act II, Scene i, Helena says to Demetrius:

   > Your wrongs do set a scandal on my sex.
   > We cannot fight for love, as men may do;
   > We should be wooed, and were not made to woo.

   What is the issue she raises with him here? Do you agree with her perspective as it applies to her and Demetrius? How do you personally feel about this issue?

6. In Act 3, Scene ii, Lines 203–219, Helena describes the relationship she has with Hermia. What kinds of images does she use to describe this relationship? What words are repeated throughout this passage? Reflect upon how Helena's stylistic use of language reinforces the meaning of her speech here. You might consider such features as the addition or deletion of connecting words, the use of a single verb to describe the action of several objects (a figure of speech known as *zeugma*), repetition of words, or parallelism of phrases.

7. Theseus' statements concerning the activities of poets in Act V, Scene iv, lines 4–22, have been read by many critics as Shakespeare's comment about both *A Midsummer Night's Dream* in particular and about drama in general. What do you think of Theseus' explanation of the contrasts between lunatics, lovers, and poets? What perspectives do all three share? What are the boundaries between them? How are these boundaries defined and held in place? How might the definition of a lunatic, a lover, or a poet change over time or in different societies? Consider how each of the characters in the play might belong to at least two of these categories over the course of the play.

UNIT
EIGHT

*Casebook on
Judith Ortiz Cofer*

Judith Ortiz Cofer

*J*udith Ortiz Cofer was born February 24, 1952 in Hormigueros, Puerto Rico. Two years later, her family moved to Paterson, New Jersey, near where her father was stationed at Brooklyn Navy Yard. The family returned to Puerto Rico several times for extended periods, such as during Cofer's first and second grade years. Even when living in the United States, Cofer was exposed to a combination of Puerto Rican and Anglo influences. Spanish was her first language of acquisition.

As she notes in "The Paterson Public Library," Cofer was always an avid reader and, through her exposure to books, developed a "sense of inner freedom, a feeling of power and the ability to fly that is the main reward of the writer" (132). In 1986, she published a book of poetry called Peregrina *and in 1987 published two more,* Reaching for the Mainland *and* Terms of Survival. *Her 1989 novel,* The Line of the Sun, *was nominated for a Pulitzer Prize in 1990, and her collection of essays,* Silent Dancing: A Partial Remembrance of a Puerto Rican Childhood *appeared in the same year. In 1993, she published* The Latin Deli: Telling the Lives of Barrio Women, *which is a collection of essays, short stories and poetry, and a collection of short stories entitled* An Island Like You: Stories of the Barrio, *appeared in 1996. She now resides in Atlanta, Georgia, where she teaches and continues to write.*

As a native of Puerto Rico, Cofer has experienced, in her own words, a sort of "cultural schizophrenia" growing up in the United States. Cofer reflects in her work the sense of "countrylessness" described by Ana Castillo in her book Massacre of the Dreamers, *a work that explores the cultural, economic, political and spiritual effects of living as a non-white in the U.S. Castillo argues that many Americans are "countryless," in that they cannot claim either the legacy of White America or that of their ancestors' native land.[1] In "The Myth of the Latin American Woman," Cofer describes what it is like to walk through the streets of a White Western world as a Latina, in the body a brown woman from "Rita Moreno's gene pool" (594).*

Important themes in Cofer's work include the inter-relationship between literature and everyday life; the power and importance of nar- rative and art (particularly various forms of literature) in shaping one's identity, both as an individual and as a member of larger com- munities; the impact of the past on the future, specifically as it is communicated through women's stories to their daughters and grand- daughters in a multigenerational setting; and concerns of ethnicity, race, gender, marginalization, and border-crossing. Language is a key factor for Cofer in confronting these issues. In her interview with

Marilyn Kallet, she admits that when translating to English stories told in Spanish, "[s]omething is lost" (588), yet she insists that she does not want the Spanish in her stories to "alienate." On the contrary, she explains: "I use it to try to bridge, so that when I write a poem I don't send my reader to the dictionary. Rather I'm saying 'Read closely, it will become clear to you. "What we speak and how we say things shapes the way we see the world" (586).

Although Cofer says she does not intend to send her reader to the dictionary, we have included at the end of this section a glossary of Spanish terms employed in the following selections of Cofer's work. We have done so in order that the reader might engage more fully in each piece. We have selected from Cofer's poetry, essays, and stories works that we hope offer a sampling of her writing techniques and of the subjects that she often explores. In addition, we have included Marilyn Kallet's 1993 interview with Cofer, which sheds light not only on Cofer as a person, but also on her concerns and choices as a writer. Finally, in order to provide some background on the issues of cultural assimilation/destruction and memory/narrative as an important weapon against such assimilation, we have added to this section excerpts from Terry DeHay's essay, "Narrating Memory," from the collection Narrative and Identity: New Essays in Ethnic American Literature.

Note

[1]Ana Castillo, *Massacre of the Dreamer* (Albuquerque: University of New Mexico Press, 1994) 21.

The Art of Not Forgetting: An Interview with Judith Ortiz Cofer

Marilyn Kallet

Marilyn Kallet, director of the Creative Writing program at the University of Tennessee, first recorded "The Art of Not Forgetting: An Interview with Judith Ortiz Cofer" on November 9, 1993; she completed the interview the following May. During that time, Cofer gave several readings in Knoxville and taught classes at Oak Ridge High School as a Distinguished Writer-in-Residence, funded by an NEA Audience Development Grant which had been awarded to UT. The interview was first published in Prairie Schooner *(1994) and then in* Worlds in Our Words: Contemporary American Women Writers *(1997). The interview presents a number of the themes which are important common aspects in the primary works included in this casebook. This conversation between two women writers and university teachers stresses how what we read, write, experience, and say shapes our perception and understanding of the world, as well as how and where we belong in that world.*

MK: The concept of not forgetting plays a central part in your work and aesthetics. Why is not forgetting so important to you as a writer?

JOC: It's a complex concept for me. Many people of my parents' generation felt that if we assimilated, if we learned to live within the culture, it would be easier for us. I can see that as an economic survival technique, but as an artist I discovered that assimilation is exactly what destroys the artistic—to blend so well that you forget what makes you unique. When I started to write I really thought—like most English majors and graduate students—that I had to abstract all my ideas to be able to communicate the large concepts. I found out that what I really needed to communicate were the basics in our culture. Language and memory became important, because I realized that memory was the treasure in my backyard. My education had allowed me to become perceptive enough to be able to use memory plus imagination, to transform remembering into art. Not forgetting is a spiritual matter with me. It connects me to the reality of my life. As long as I understand that I will continue to produce art. One falls into the error of forgetting basic concepts like language and its power to affect reality. The language one speaks at home shapes the original reality, and then one learns other versions of that to survive in the world. As a poet I have to be able to tell the difference, to transmit that. In a poem like "The Latin Deli" I don't just put in Spanish words as decoration. They are used to transmit a special kind of reality, to communicate to my English-speaking reader, to say, "Yes, this is a different reality, but you can understand it by paying close attention."

MK: So you are inviting the reader in?

JOC: Right. I don't use language to alienate. I use it to try to bridge, so that when I write a poem I don't send my reader to the dictionary. Rather I'm saying, "Read closely, it will become clear to you." What we speak and how we say things shapes the way we see the world.

MK: When you were little, was Spanish spoken at home?

JOC: Absolutely, especially since my mother was the one who was with us in the house all the time. She spoke nothing but Spanish. Our apartments were a microcosm of her casa. This is where she listened to her Spanish-language records, where the Spanish-language newspaper came in, and her books. She encouraged us to succeed in the outside world, but that was not her reality.

MK: How old were you when you first moved to Paterson?

JOC: The first time I was two, but then my father left on an extended tour with the navy, and we went back to Puerto Rico. Then directly after that he was transferred to the Roosevelt Roads Navy Base in Puerto Rico. We spent a couple of years in Paterson and then I attended first and second grade in Puerto Rico. The first time that I came back to Paterson to enter the world of school I was already in the third grade. By that time Spanish had become my first language again and there was the culture shock of going into the classroom. So you can understand how I trace my obsession with language back to that early time when I had to determine what language would serve me best.

MK: You were trying to figure out where you belonged, and where to find a sense of belonging.

JOC: Yes. I have an essay about that in *Silent Dancing*, about the teacher not understanding my needs. I decided at an early age that language was my best defense.

MK: And books?

JOC: They were not only a refuge but a guide. What people could not tell me or would not tell me I would find in books.

MK: Was your father bilingual?

JOC: Fully. He spoke textbook English. He was a perfectionist and he insisted on the correct pronunciation. I remember clearly one time when he had come to pick me up at catechism. One of my friends, a Puerto Rican, said tousand instead of thousand. He was too kind to correct her but later he said, "I want you to know that the word is thousand." He made me repeat it and I thought that he was just being pushy. I finally understood that he felt that he would be treated better if he spoke well and he transmitted that to us.

MK: Language was a passport to . . . ?

JOC: The usual immigrant idea that if you speak intelligently people will treat you with respect. He was of that mind. Even though he was very authoritarian and the military shaped him, he understood that I needed books, and he encouraged me in that area and bought me books. In fact, he was the one who told my mother not to push me to cook if I didn't want to, that that was something I wasn't going to need. That was the most liberated decision he ever made in the sense that he thought my intelligence could take me farther than he had gone. He was the one who emphasized the importance of education. He insisted that my brother and I keep up with our studies no matter how unstable our lives were. He facilitated my move into the literary life by encouraging me to read voraciously, to think of education as empowering.

MK: Do you remember which books you were looking at, which ones influenced you at the beginning?

JOC: In fact I do. I have an essay called "The Paterson Public Library" coming out in my new book, *The Latin Deli*. In it, I talk about how nothing prevented me from going to the library. I was allowed a certain amount of time to go on Saturday mornings. There was a girl who hated me because the teacher used to humiliate her by making me tutor her in spelling. She lived on the way to the library and she had promised to beat me up. I remember fearing this girl—she was twice as big as I was. I guess I wanted books more than to save my life because she did carry through with her threat. That hour or so that I was given to go and get books was my best time. The library was impressive to a little girl. I don't know what it would look like now and I have resisted going back because at that time I felt like I was in one of those paintings of philosophers and their disciples sitting on the steps of a great temple. I would approach this magnificent library which was incongruously placed in the worst neighborhood you can imagine where this Greek temple arose from chaos with its lions and its columns.

I had a pink card which meant for a long time I could only check out children's books. So I started reading the world's fairy tales and folk tales at one end of the children's room and worked my way to the other. I experienced a sense of discovery when I found out that the Cinderella story appears in Africa and China, and that heroines didn't have to have pink skin and gold hair, that sometimes they had braided kinky hair and sometimes they had Asian features. That reassured me in my reality that the world was populated by people as different-looking as I thought I was.

MK: Did you identify with Cinderella?

JOC: Not so much with Cinderella as with the woman rising out of her condition and situation in life. I had decided at an early age that I wouldn't get married, mainly because my model for marriage was the passive wife and the domineering husband—not so much in my grandmother's time but in the next generation. The fifties generation of my mother was a lot more traditional than the old women I knew as I child. . . . I wasn't looking for the prince, I was looking for how in the world was I going to be more than just a housewife, how could I leave Paterson and do other things. The fairy tales allowed me to see that sometimes by the use of wit and intelligence a girl could leave her allotted place in the ashes and come out into the sunlight! We didn't live in dire poverty, we were better off than most of the people in my neighborhood because my father had a military career. But I did not want a typical life for myself, I wanted to be a teacher. I wanted to get out into the wider world.

MK: It seems like writing has been a way into adventure. You have written eloquently about the atmosphere of women's lives as you were growing up. You mentioned earlier that you wanted to write more about your father.

JOC: I do, mainly because he was absent during my childhood. He was a man who came home every six months or so and spent some time with us. Because of the navy, most frequently he was home during the weekends and the rest of the time he was away. So I didn't really get to know him except that he usually made the final decisions. He was a quiet man, and year by year became more quiet and more depressed. I understood that this was not the life he had chosen. He had accepted his life. He would have really been a completely different kind of man had he been able to explore his potential. He was very intelligent and military life stifled him. And yet he looked around him and saw his friends who were factory workers and others imprisoned by the economy and their own lack of skills, so he stayed in the navy and became more and more withdrawn. I can only imagine his loneliness on a ship full of people who did not speak his native language far away from his family. So I never got to know my real father. I knew only what he became. And then he died. And so I need to explore that and yet have resisted doing so. First of all I have to explore my life as a woman and I know how to do that. I have the language, the avenues, the models. At some point I will begin to write about my father with some maturity and more hindsight.

MK: In terms of your gift for storytelling, does some of that come from your father as well as your mother and grandmother?

JOC: He wasn't a talker. He was a silent man and he directed our lives through silence. My mother's people owned land and were farmers, and they have a basic joy for life that seems to go with lives connected to the seasons and the earth. I didn't learn storytelling from my father so much as discipline. He knew exactly what he needed to do and he did it. I'm not the stoic that he was, however.

MK: Then the storytelling ability comes from your mother?

JOC: Yes, from my mother's mother. In my baby years I stayed close to my father's mother, but after that it was Mamá, my mother's mother, who was really the grandmother in my life. And she is a joyful storyteller. Hardships to her have been hurdles. She overcomes one and goes to the next, she doesn't dwell on them. I come from a tradition where the women tell stories. I trace the storyteller's impulse to the months I spent at my Mamá's house, listening to the women communicate and teach through their powerful narratives.

MK: What were you learning from them?

JOC: In "Casa," from *Silent Dancing*, I describe a scene where in the late afternoon the women gathered to tell stories and gossip and commiserate with each other while the men were at work and the boys were playing baseball. The girls learned by listening to the women. The women did not censor their speech. We listened to birthing stories, to marital problems. In some cases I assumed that the women were talking for our benefit, so that we would understand that a woman's life was hard. I started listening to them with the natural curiosity of a young girl to learn about the facts of life, and there was a simple pleasure in hearing them talk. Later when I started delving into my memories to find material for my work, these stories the women told became the triggers for early poems and later for the novels and the essays in *Silent Dancing*. The deeper I probed with the hindsight of an adult woman, the more I understood the subtext, which was lessons in life for a woman. In my work I try to shed light on what were at one time simply amusing little stories which I have now chosen to interpret as the handing-down of knowledge.

MK: In "Casa" language becomes a place; I can see you sitting there in the late afternoon.

JOC: Wasn't it Milosz who said that "language is the only homeland"? I believe that. The women spoke in Spanish of course, and I have to translate that into English. Something is lost. What people say to one another under intimate circumstances can never fully survive translation. There's a lot of nonverbal communication going on, many shared intimacies. The only way I can regain the power of the original storytelling is not to be a slave to the factual story, but rather to present it as drama, with me as the witness or audience. I try to give back to the women's voices the original power that they had for me as a child by using the techniques of the poet and fiction writer.

MK: Who are the writers who have most influenced your writing?

JOC: That's always a hard one for me to answer because I have done such eclectic reading. I am an English teacher and my background is in American literature. If any writers excited me during my early years in college it was Faulkner and Eudora Welty and Flannery O'Connor and the southern writers who used language with such delight. It's not that their themes were delightful, but that they really took language and went with it. They ignited something in my own storytelling impulse. I was definitely not influenced by the minimalists, for example, and the restrained language-users. It was interesting to me later when I did read Gabriel Garcia Márquez, Manuel Puig, Mario Vargas Llosa, Isabel Allende, and other Latin American storytellers that they had a lot in common with the southern writers. They use language with what Márquez calls "plenitude." Language to them is a feast. Later I found out that there was a direct link between Faulkner and Márquez, that Márquez considers Faulkner his primary influence. So it comes full circle.

I have to admit also that as a child I read everything I could find, from Harlequin-style Spanish romances to the encyclopedia. I think my writing finally became a blend between my formal education and my eclectic reading in both English and Spanish.

MK: Which poets have influenced you most?

JOC: I've been an avid reader of poetry for many years. While I was in graduate school I read the "standard" poets. The first poet who gave me that "jolt,' that shock of recognition, who made me feel that she was speaking directly to me, was Denise Levertov. After I looked up her poetry I seriously began to think of writing poetry myself.

MK: What was it about her work that impressed you?

JOC: It was both the control and the flexibility. She was speaking with emotion about certain subjects that were close to her, but she kept a certain control. The lines were naturally flowing and yet they seemed to have a reason for being. Later I read some of her essays about the lines. She was very conscious of what she was doing without being self-conscious. By studying Levertov's poetry I realized the art and craft involved in writing poetry, as well as the emotional release and self-discovery involved.

MK: Do you remember the first time you consciously thought of yourself as a writer?

JOC: I didn't consciously think of myself as a writer when I was writing my thesis, that's for sure! [Laughter.] As you know, I wasn't really able to give my own creative writing any time until after I finished graduate school. I did get married at nineteen and I did have a child at twenty-one and continued to go to school. All of my waking hours were involved in trying to keep my world from becoming chaos.

When I finished school I went to work for a wonderful woman named Betty Owen, who was the head of the English Department at Broward Community College in Hollywood, Florida. She was the first person to whom I showed my poetry, and she told me, "Send it out!" She became my reader and mentor. In 1978 when Betty Owen was saying "you can write," and occasionally a poem would get accepted, I began to think of myself as a writer. Then writing became so much a part of my life that I can hardly remember a time when I didn't write.

MK: Do you think of yourself as a poet at heart?

JOC: I do. I like that term better than any other. I remember when my novel came out I had a couple of poetry friends say, half-kiddingly, "I see you've sold out!" I felt horrible. It was like being accused of abandoning a child. But I have never stopped writing poetry. When I get up in the morning and I have two hours to write, I still give the first hour to poetry. I'm always working on a new poem. . . . I consider myself primarily a poet.

MK: How do you decide which genre to pursue, or does the work itself make that decision for you?

JOC: The work itself sometimes makes a double decision. Right now I'm working on a short story based on the character in "The Latin Deli" [a poem]. The direction is based on the strength of my obsession. If I write a poem and the subject continues to intrigue me, and I need to explore it in a more ample way, it might become an essay, a short story, or even a novel. I now have twenty pages of a story called "Corazon's Cafe." In this story, the woman from my poem has a husband who has just died and she is considering closing their grocery store. This woman intrigued me and I wanted to explore her character in more depth.

I recently wrote an essay called "The Story of My Body" for an anthology. . . . It's about how walking around in this body has affected my life. About how not being tall, being a "shrimp," and unathletic has influenced my individual reality. When I started writing it I knew that it couldn't be a poem, it couldn't be anything but a very structured essay which I divided into skin color, size, and physical appearance and the relativity of these to my sense of self. To my mother I'm tall, because she's 4'11". To everyone else, I'm short.

MK: Physical appearance does affect our reality but it's not something we talk about.

JOC: I resisted writing about it. . . . And then I started thinking about how having been the last chosen for sports at school inspired my best secret stories. . . . I fantasized about being Wonder Woman and scooping up all of the P.E. teachers and putting them on a barren asteroid where they would perish because they had no inner resources. I didn't realize how much I disliked them until I wrote that! I needed to say this in an essay. An essay is an attempt to explore ideas. A poem is an attempt to concentrate ideas into their essential core.

Basically, the decision about genre is made when I sit down and decide the parameters of what I'm writing. Some fit very nicely into the poem because I see them as images. Others require language to be ample and generous.

MK: Storytelling unifies various genres you work with.

JOC: And obsessions! I have obsessions that are explored in different ways and genres.

MK: What are they?

JOC: Language as identity and as the mechanism for defining our world is something that I think about a lot. How saying one thing in a particular way is completely different than saying the same thing in another way. The relationships that women create, the intricate patterns that we weave out of affection and family loyalties, and how those have changed and shifted in a cosmic way from my grandmother's time to my own. And absences, absences leave a very real space people must fill. . . . These are some ideas that pop up in any work that I do, and I predict that whatever I do these ideas will always concern me.

MK: What are you working on now?

JOC: I am trying to finish *The Latin Deli.* I'm working on the title story based on the poem "The Latin Deli."

MK: Is there anything else you would like to say?

JOC: At universities, students are very concerned with becoming writers. They should also understand that writing is a vocation—more so than a profession, that when you commit yourself to it it is like a religious calling. It's not just about a public life or the publishing market. The power of the artist comes from being disciplined and comes through the creation of the work. Many new writers want to know, "*If* I write this, who will publish it?" I say to them, "Just write it!" The work is the important thing. Creation is the main reward. It's great to have the work published, but the process itself is what I need in my life.

For Practice

1. What does Cofer mean by the concept of "not forgetting"? How and why is this concept essential to her writing?

2. In this interview, Cofer notes that she does not "use language to alienate. I use it to try to bridge" (586). To achieve this goal, Cofer constructs her works so that a reader will not necessarily need to race to a dictionary. She hopes that readers will rely instead on close reading of her works. For each of the works by Cofer included in this casebook, select a word, phrase, or passage which illustrates this goal of her writing and explain how that item functions within that text as a bridge.

3. What does Cofer believe was her father's most enlightened decision as a parent? How and why did that decision affect her in terms of gender, ethnicity, identity, marginalization, and "border crossing" issues and concerns?

4. Cofer points out that "what people say to one another under intimate circumstances can never fully survive translation" (588). Using an example from your own experience, explain how and why her argument here is either valid or unjustified. Then write a brief creative narrative in which you include the untranslatable shared communication from your own experience and try to give back to the voice(s) of the speaker(s) the original power which she/he/they had.

5. How was the Cinderella story an important learning experience for Cofer? Does her argument in that segment of this interview reflect or challenge the arguments presented in the DeHay essay? How so? What is an example from one of the works by Cofer included in this casebook in which she illustrates what she claims here to have gleaned from learning the Cinderella story? How so?

6. Cofer explains that reading the poetry of Denise Levertov impressed upon her two key aspects about writing. What are these two aspects? Identify an excerpt from one of the works by Cofer included in the casebook which demonstrates both of these key aspects of writing. Explain how that excerpt illustrates these aspects. Then locate a poem by Levertov and identify and explain how an excerpt from that poem illustrates these two aspects of writing. Finally, select a passage from one of your own papers written this semester and show how it either illustrates both these key aspects of writing or how it does not include one or both of them.

Latin Deli: An Ars Poetica

This poem is the title work from Cofer's 1993 collection The Latin Deli. *The
"Latin" of the title refers to Latin America, including Puerto Rico, Cuba,
and Mexico (all of which are mentioned in the poem). The poem deals with
the cultural "exile" of various Latin Americans in the United States and
with the attempt to preserve their cultural identities. The term* ars poetica
*in the subtitle is Latin for "the art of poetry." (It is also the title of a poem
by Horace which describes how to be a successful poet.) As you read this
poem, consider the ways that it is about both exile and the art of writing
poetry.*

Presiding over a formica counter,
plastic Mother and Child magnetized
to the top of an ancient register,
the heady mix of smells from the open bins
of dried codfish, the green plantains   5
hanging in stalks like votive offerings,
she is the Patroness of Exiles,
a woman of no-age who was never pretty,
who spends her days selling canned memories
while listening to the Puerto Ricans complain   10
that it would be cheaper to fly to San Juan
than to buy a pound of Bustelo coffee here,
and to Cubans perfecting their speech
of a "glorious return" to Havana—where no one
has been allowed to die and nothing to change until then;   15
to Mexicans who pass through, talking lyrically
of *dólares* to be made in El Norte—

                                  all wanting the comfort
of spoken Spanish, to gaze upon the family portrait
of her plain wide face, her ample bosom   20
resting on her plump arms, her look of maternal interest
as they speak to her and each other
of their dreams and disillusions—
how she smiles understanding,
when they walk down the narrow aisles of her store   25
reading the labels of packages aloud, as if
they were the names of lost lovers: *Suspiros*,
Merengues, the stale candy of everyone's childhood.

> She spends her days
> slicing *jamón y queso* and wrapping it in wax paper   30
> tied with string: plain ham and cheese
> that would cost less at the A&P, but it would not satisfy
> the hunger of the fragile old man lost in the folds
> of his winter coat, who brings her lists of items
> that he reads to her like poetry, or the others,   35
> whose needs she must divine, conjuring up products
> from places that now exist only in their hearts—
> closed ports she must trade with.

For Practice

1. Why do people come to the Latin Deli when they could get many of the same things more cheaply elsewhere?

2. The poet describes the store's proprietor as the "Patroness [or Patron Saint] of Exiles." How is this description appropriate?

3. In the interview included in this section, Cofer says that she includes Spanish words in her works in order to "transmit a special kind of reality" and to build a bridge between cultures. Do you think her use of Spanish words in this poem serves those purposes? Why or why not?

4. The poem is rich in metaphors and similes. Identify some and discuss how they contribute to the theme.

5. Judging from what the poem says (its content) and how it says it (its form), what does the poem say about the art of writing poetry? Explain how both its content and form contribute to this argument.

The Myth of the Latin Woman: I Just Met a Girl Named María

This essay, originally published in The Latin Deli *in 1993, is also included in the anthology* Against the Current. *In this essay, Cofer exposes people's tendencies to classify others based on stereotypes. She also explores the effects of being a "María." Cofer explains that as a Latina, she is often assumed to be both inferior—socially, economically, and intellectually— and "hotblooded"—exotic and passionate as only a "dark" woman can be. As you read this essay, think about the ways in which this stereotype compares to others our culture makes concerning Latinos.*

On a bus trip to London from Oxford University where I was earning some graduate credits one summer, a young man, obviously fresh from a pub, spotted me and as if struck by inspiration went down on his knees in the aisle. With both hands over his heart he broke into an Irish tenor's rendition of "María" from *West Side Story*. My politely amused fellow passengers gave his lovely voice the round of gentle applause it deserved. Though I was not quite as amused, I managed my version of an English smile: no show of teeth, no extreme contortions of the facial muscles— I was at this time of my life practicing reserve and cool. Oh, that British control, how I coveted it. But María had followed me to London, reminding me of a prime fact of my life: you can leave the Island, master the English language, and travel as far as you can, but if you are a Latina, especially one like me who so obviously belongs to Rita Moreno's gene pool, the Island travels with you.

This is sometimes a very good thing—it may win you that extra minute of someone's attention. But with some people, the same things can make *you* an island—not so much a tropical paradise as an Alcatraz, a place nobody wants to visit. As a Puerto Rican girl growing up in the United States and wanting like most children to "belong," I resented the stereotype that my Hispanic appearance called forth from many people I met.

Our family lived in a large urban center in New Jersey during the sixties, where life was designed as a microcosm of my parents' casas on the island. We spoke in Spanish, we ate Puerto Rican food bought at the bodega, and we practiced strict Catholicism complete with Saturday confession and Sunday mass at a church where our parents were accommodated into a one-hour Spanish mass slot, performed by a Chinese priest trained as a missionary for Latin America.

As a girl I was kept under strict surveillance, since virtue and modesty were, by cultural equation, the same as family honor. As a teenager I was instructed on how to behave as a proper señorita. But it was a conflicting message girls got, since the Puerto Rican mothers also encouraged their daughters to look and act like women and to dress in clothes our Anglo friends and their mothers found too "mature" for our age. It was, and is, cultural, yet I often felt humiliated when I appeared at an American friend's party wearing a dress more suitable to a semiformal than to a playroom birthday celebration. At Puerto Rican festivities, neither the music nor the colors we wore could be too loud. I still experience a vague sense of letdown when I'm invited to a "party" and it turns out to be a marathon conversation in hushed tones rather than a fiesta with salsa, laughter, and dancing—the kind of celebration I remember from my childhood.

I remember Career Day in our high school, when teachers told us to come dressed as if for a job interview. It quickly became obvious that to the barrio girls, "dressing up" sometimes meant wearing ornate jewelry and clothing that would be more appropriate (by mainstream standards) for the company Christmas party than as daily office attire. That morning I had agonized in front of my closet, trying to figure out what a "career girl" would wear because, essentially, except for Marlo Thomas on TV, I had no models on which to base my decision. I knew how to dress for school: at the Catholic school I attended we all wore uniforms; I knew how to dress for Sunday mass, and I knew what dresses to wear for parties at my relatives' homes. Though I do not recall the precise details of my Career Day outfit, it must have been a composite of the above choices. But I remember a comment my friend (an Italian-American) made in later years that coalesced my impressions of that day. She said that at the business school she was attending the Puerto Rican girls always stood out for wearing "everything at once." She meant, of course, too much jewelry, too many accessories. On that day at school, we were simply made the negative models by the nuns who were themselves not credible fashion experts to any of us. But it was painfully obvious to me that to the others, in their tailored skirts and silk blouses, we must have seemed "hopeless" and "vulgar." Though I now know that most adolescents feel out of step much of the time, I also know that for the Puerto Rican girls of my generation that sense was intensified. The way our teachers and classmates looked at us that day in school was just a taste of the culture clash that awaited us in the real world, where prospective employers and men on the street would often misinterpret our tight skirts and jingling bracelets as a come-on.

Mixed cultural signals have perpetuated certain stereotypes—for example, that of the Hispanic woman as the "Hot Tamale" or sexual firebrand. It is a one-dimensional view that the media have found easy to promote. In their special vocabulary, advertisers have designated "sizzling" and "smoldering" as the adjectives of choice for describing not only the foods but also the women of Latin America. From conversations in my house I recall hearing about the harassment that Puerto Rican women endured in factories where the "boss men" talked to them as if sexual innuendo was all they understood and, worse, often gave them the choice of submitting to advances or being fired.

It is custom, however, not chromosomes, that leads us to choose scarlet over pale pink. As young girls, we were influenced in our decisions about clothes and colors by the women—older sisters and mothers who had grown up on a tropical island where the natural environment was a riot of primary colors, where showing your skin was one way to keep cool as well as to look sexy. Most important of all, on the island, women perhaps felt freer to dress and move more provocatively, since, in most cases, they were protected by the traditions, mores, and laws of a Spanish/Catholic system of morality and machismo whose main rule was: *You may look at my sister, but if you touch her I will kill you.* The extended family and church structure could provide a young woman with a circle of safety in her small pueblo on the island; if a man "wronged" a girl, everyone would close in to save her family honor.

This is what I have gleaned from my discussions as an adult with older Puerto Rican women. They have told me about dressing in their best party clothes on Saturday nights and going to the town's plaza to promenade with their girlfriends in front of the boys they liked. The males were thus given an opportunity to admire the women and to express their admiration in the form of *piropos*: erotically charged street poems they composed on the spot. I have been subjected to a few piropos while visiting the Island, and they can be outrageous, although custom dictates that they must never cross into obscenity. This ritual, as I understand it, also entails a show of studied indifference on the woman's part; if she is "decent," she must not acknowledge the man's impassioned words. So I do understand how things can be lost in translation. When a Puerto Rican girl dressed in her idea of what is attractive meets a man from the mainstream culture who has been trained to react to certain types of clothing as a sexual signal, a clash is likely to take place. The line I first heard based on this aspect of the myth happened when the boy who took me to my first formal dance leaned over to plant a sloppy overeager kiss painfully on my mouth, and when I didn't respond with sufficient passion said in a resentful tone: "I thought you Latin girls were supposed to mature early"—my first instance of being thought of as a fruit or vegetable—I was supposed to *ripen*, not just grow into womanhood like other girls.

It is surprising to some of my professional friends that some people, including those who should know better, still put others "in their place." Though rarer, these incidents are still commonplace in my life. It happened to me most recently during a stay at a very classy metropolitan hotel favored by young professional couples for their weddings. Late one evening after the theater, as I walked toward my room with my new colleague (a woman with whom I was coordinating an arts program), a middle-aged man in a tuxedo, a young girl in satin and lace on his arm, stepped directly into our path. With his champagne glass extended toward me, he exclaimed, "Evita!"

Our way blocked, my companion and I listened as the man half-recited, half-bellowed "Don't Cry for Me, Argentina." When he finished, the young girl said: "How about a round of applause for my daddy?" We complied, hoping this would bring the silly spectacle to a close. I was becoming aware that our little group was attracting the attention of the other guests. "Daddy" must have perceived this too, and he once more barred the way as we tried to walk past him. He began to shout-sing a ditty to the tune of "La Bamba"—except the lyrics were about a girl named María whose exploits all rhymed with her name and gonorrhea. The girl kept saying "Oh, Daddy" and looking at me with pleading eyes. She wanted me to laugh along with the others. My companion and I stood silently waiting for the man to end his offensive song. When he finished, I looked not at him but at his daughter. I advised her calmly never to ask her father what he had done in the army. Then I walked between them and to my room. My friend complimented me on my cool handling of the situation. I confessed to her that I really had wanted to push the jerk into the swimming pool. I knew that this same man—probably a corporate executive, well educated, even worldly by most standards—would not have been likely to regale a white woman with a dirty song in public. He would perhaps have checked his impulse by assuming that she could be somebody's wife or mother, or at least *somebody* who might take offense. But to him, I was just an Evita or a María: merely a character in his cartoon-populated universe.

Because of my education and my proficiency with the English language, I have acquired many mechanisms for dealing with the anger I experience. This was not true for my parents, nor is it true for the many Latin women working at menial jobs who must put up with stereotypes about our ethnic group such as: "They make good domestics." This is another facet of the myth of the Latin woman in the United States. Its origin is simple to deduce. Work as domestics, waitressing, and factory jobs are all that's available to women with little English and few skills. The myth of the Hispanic menial has been sustained by the same media phenomenon that made "Mammy" from *Gone with the Wind* America's idea of the black woman for generations; María, the housemaid or counter girl, is now indelibly etched into the national psyche. The big and the little screens have presented us with the picture of the funny Hispanic maid, mispronouncing words and cooking up a spicy storm in a shiny California kitchen.

This media-engendered image of the Latina in the United States has been documented by feminist Hispanic scholars, who claim that such portrayals are partially responsible for the denial of opportunities for upward mobility among Latinas in the professions. I have a Chicana friend working on a Ph.D. in philosophy at a major university. She says her doctor still shakes his head in puzzled amazement at all the "big words" she uses. Since I do not wear my diplomas around my neck for all to see, I too have on occasion been sent to that "kitchen," where some think I obviously belong.

One such incident that has stayed with me, though I recognize it as a minor offense, happened on the day of my first public poetry reading. It took place in Miami in a boat-restaurant where we were having lunch before the event. I was nervous and excited as I walked in with my notebook in my hand. An older woman motioned me to her table. Thinking (foolish me) that she wanted me to autograph a copy of my brand new slender volume of verse, I went over. She ordered a cup of coffee from me, assuming that I was the waitress. Easy enough to mistake my poems for menus, I suppose. I know that it wasn't an intentional act of cruelty, yet of all the good things that happened that day, I remember that scene most clearly, because it reminded me of what I had to overcome before anyone would take me seriously. In retrospect I understand that my anger gave my reading fire, that I have almost always taken doubts in my abilities as a challenge—and that the result is, most times, a feeling of satisfaction at having won a convert when I see the cold, appraising eyes warm to my words, the body language change, the smile that indicates that I have opened some avenue for communication. That day I read to that woman and her lowered eyes told me that she was embarrassed at her little faux pas, and when I willed her to look up at me, it was my victory, and she graciously allowed me to punish her with my full attention. We shook hands at the end of the reading, and never saw her again. She has probably forgotten the whole thing but maybe not.

Yet I am one of the lucky ones. My parents made it possible for me to acquire a stronger footing in the mainstream culture by giving me the chance at an education. And books and art have saved me from the harsher forms of ethnic and racial prejudice that many of my Hispanic *compañeras* have had to endure. I travel a lot around the United States, reading from my books of poetry and my novel, and the reception I most often receive is one of positive interest by people who want to know more about my culture. There are, however, thousands of Latinas without the privilege of an education or the entrée into society that I have. For them life is a struggle against the misconceptions perpetuated by the myth of the Latina as whore, domestic or criminal. We cannot change this by legislating the way people look at us. The transformation, as I see it, has to occur at a much more individual level. My personal goal in my public life is to try to replace the old pervasive stereotypes and myths about Latinas with a much more interesting set of realities. Every time I give a reading, I hope the stories I tell, the dreams and fears I examine in my work, can achieve some universal truth which will get my audience past the particulars of my skin color, my accent, or my clothes.

I once wrote a poem in which I called us Latinas "God's brown daughters." This poem is really a prayer of sorts, offered upward, but also, through the human-to-human channel of art, outward. It is a prayer for communication, and for respect. In it, Latin women pray "in Spanish to an Anglo God/with a Jewish heritage," and they are "fervently hoping/that if not omnipotent, at least He be bilingual."

For Practice

1. Can you identify with Cofer in her response to having been judged based on a stereotype as inferior and/or sexually exotic? If so, how? If not, what is the significance of this difference between you and Cofer?

2. While the Latina stereotype at times brings Cofer attention that might be interpreted positively, why is this kind of attention disturbing to her? How does the issue of sexuality become a dangerous one for Latinas living in Western cultures?

3. Think about the paradoxes, described here by Cofer, of the Latina's role as "woman" (pure/sexy, modest/assertive, childish/womanly). Do these same paradoxes exist in Anglo-American culture as well? How are they different from those described by Cofer? How are they similar?

4. How does Cofer's position as a Catholic affect her experience?

5. How does memory function for Cofer in this essay?

By Love Betrayed

This fictional story is from The Latin Deli *(1993). It deals with several themes that recur in Cofer's works: relationships between women and men and between parents and children, the Puerto Rican "exile" in America, and the role of religion (specifically, Catholicism) in the lives of Puerto Ricans. Also important are issues of perspective. The story is told in first person by an adult narrator who is remembering events that happened when she was in third grade. As you read this selection, think about the gaps between what the narrator understood as a young girl and what she understands as an adult.*

As a little girl I imagined my father was a genie that came out of a magic bottle at night. It was a green bottle of cologne that he splashed on his face before leaving the house. I thought it was the strong smell that made my mother cry.

I loved him more than anyone. He was beautiful to me with his dark, shiny black hair combed back like one of the handsome men on the *telenovelas* my mother watched while she waited for him to come home at night. I was allowed to stay up for the early one: *Traicionado por el amor:* By Love Betrayed.

My *papi* had a mustache like a thin brush that tickled me when he kissed me. If they had not been shouting at each other, he would sometimes come into my room and say good-night before he left for his job at the nightclub. Then his perfume would get on my blanket and I would hold it to my face until I fell asleep. I dreamed of him and me walking on a beach. I had never been to the ocean, but he told me stories about growing up in a house on the beach in Puerto Rico. It had been blown away by a hurricane.

When my mother got angry at my father, she made me think of a hurricane. Blowing him away from us with her screams and her tears. Once, she scratched his cheek. He covered it with her makeup before he left for work. Another time I heard a sound like a slap, but I did not know who hit whom, because my mother always cried, and he always left.

Sometimes I would hear her saying the rosary aloud, the dozens of Hail Marys and Our Fathers was a song that would put me to sleep better than any lullaby. She had come back to the church after leaving it when she had run away with Papi. My mother said that Tito had taken her away from God but that now she was back to stay. She had the priest come to our apartment and sprinkle it with holy water, which doesn't smell like anything.

My mother made our apartment look like a church too: she put a cross with Christ on it over their bed and mine—Papi liked to say that one day it would fall on their heads and kill them, and my mother would answer, "Well, Tito, I'm ready to go to my

Dios any time, are you?" He would just laugh. She hung a picture of the Holy Mother and Baby Jesus on the wall facing my bed, and one of Christ knocking at a door in the hallway. On her dresser she had a painted statue of the Virgin Mary crushing a black snake. When you saw it on the mirror it looked as if she was a real little person who was about to trip over a snake because she wasn't looking where she was going. I used to play pretend and try to take the snake out. But it was glued on under her little foot. My mother did not like me to play with the saint dolls, though, and I had to sneak into their room when she was busy in the kitchen or watching TV.

My parents argued a lot. Our apartment was small, and I heard them saying the same things over and over in as many different hurting words as possible. I learned my fighting words in Spanish then: the words to hurt and also the words of the church that my mother taught me so that I would not turn out a sinner like my father.

"Who made you?"

"God made me."

"Why did He make you?"

"To glorify His Name and to obey His commands and those of His Church."

We said this lesson over and over in our catechism class with Sister Teresa who was preparing us for First Communion.

When I got older, I tried to ask my mother questions about my father. Her answers were always the same:

"Where does Papi go at night?"

"To his job."

"But he has a job during the day. He's the super of our building, right?"

"He has two jobs. Finish your cereal. It's getting late for school."

When she made up her mind not to talk about my father, I could not make her say a word. For many years I could not talk to him, since the only time he was at home, in between his jobs, she was also there, watching me. Finally I got my chance to see my papi alone after she started volunteer work at the church several mornings a week when I was in third grade.

One day she had to leave early to help plan a women's religious retreat. She put a bowl of cereal in front of me and told me to walk carefully to school. I was big enough to walk the four blocks alone, especially since there were crossing guards at every corner. I kissed her good-bye and asked for my blessing: "Dios te bendiga, Hija," she said and crossed herself.

"Amén," I said and crossed myself.

I ran to the living room window from where I could see her come out on the street and walk toward the church. After she disappeared around the corner, I took the house key and left our apartment to look for my father. I was not sure what I would do when I found him. I felt scared and excited, though, knowing that I was doing something that would make my mother angry if she found out. I knew that Papi would not tell.

It was a big building with long dark hallways that wound around each other for seven floors. I had never been above our third floor. When I reached the fifth floor, I smelled his cologne. I followed it to the door of 5-A. I knew for sure that he was somewhere near because his toolbox was in the corner of the landing. I stood in front of the door with my knees shaking, afraid to knock and afraid to turn back. The building was quiet at that hour. All the children were in school and most people at work. I put my head to the door and listened.

First I heard a woman's voice saying my father's name in a strange way: "Tito, Tito . . . " She said it as if they were playing a game. Then I heard his voice, but I could not understand the words. Then they both laughed. I decided to knock.

The woman who opened the door was wearing a red robe and her hair was a mess. Her lipstick was purple. I remember thinking that she looked like a vampire. I felt like running away, especially since she looked a little wild with her blonde-streaked hair all over her face. She had dark skin and blonde-streaked hair. I remember that.

"What do you want?" she said in an angry voice.

"I . . . I'm looking for my father."

"Your *father?*" She looked behind her. He had come out of her bedroom. I knew it was her bedroom because her apartment was just like ours, except for the furniture. Her sofa was black, and she had no curtains on her windows. My father was combing his hair with the black comb he always carried in his shirt pocket. He looked really surprised to see me at the door.

"Eva, what are you doing here?" Before I could answer, though, he closed the door behind him—right on the woman's face. I was really nervous. I couldn't tell him what I was doing there because I didn't know myself. He bent down and looked at me. He looked nervous too. I could tell because his left eye twitched when he was upset; I've seen it do that after he and my mother had a fight. "Are you sick, Evita? Why aren't you at school? Where is your mother?" He looked around as if he thought she was behind me somewhere.

"I stayed home, Papi. I had a headache. She's gone to church." He had been squeezing my shoulder with his hand, but he let go of me then. He smiled in a way my mother called his "devil smile." She said that meant he thought he knew it all. That nobody could fool him. He claimed that he always knew when somebody had a secret around the house. And that's how he found the money she had been saving behind her underwear drawer.

"Are you really sick or just taking the day off, *mi amor?*"

I just smiled, trying for a "devil smile" myself.

"I thought so. Well, maybe I'll do the same. The señora's clogged sink can wait another day. How about a hamburger at the White Castle for lunch?"

"It's only 9:30, Papi. Not time for lunch."

"Says who? Today *we* decide everything by ourselves. Deal?" He gave me his hand and I took it.

For Practice

1. How is the title important? How are the characters in the story betrayed by various kinds of "love?" Do you see this theme in other works by Cofer included in this section? Which ones? Does her treatment of this theme remain the same in each work or change according to the situation? How would you explain the similarities or differences?

2. How much do you think the narrator as a young girl understood about the events in the story? What portions of the story indicate her understanding or lack of it?

3. What role does religion play in the story? How do the characters in the story differ in their attitudes towards religion?

4. The narrator describes in detail one of her mother's religious icons: the Virgin Mary crushing a black snake. Why do you think she devotes so much space to this image? What symbolic significance lies in this description?

5. The girl in the story is named Eva (the Spanish equivalent of Eve). How does this story parallel the Biblical story of Eve's temptation and fall? What is the significance of this allusion?

Casa

"Casa" is a personal non-fiction essay by Judith Ortiz Cofer that first appeared in Prairie Schooner *(1989) and then as the opening piece in* Silent Dancing: A Partial Remembrance of A Puerto Rican Childhood *(1990), a collection of essays and poems by Cofer. In the preface to* Silent Dancing, *Cofer points out that often "my writing begins as a meditation on past events" (12).*

As she explains in the Kallet interview, "Casa" describes a frequent experience from her past, when several generations of women in her family gathered to gossip and tell "amusing little stories" (76) which served to provide life lessons for the young girls. "Casa" details one such afternoon of story-telling by Cofer's maternal grandmother to members of both the next two generations. Cofer interweaves this version of the cuentos *about Maria la Loca with observations on many of the themes reflected throughout the works included in this casebook, much as her Mama worked at braiding her grand-daughter's tangled mane of hair that typical afternoon. Thus, as in her other non-fiction prose, Cofer strives here to generate "not just family history, but also creative explorations of known territory" (12).*

At three or four o'clock in the afternoon, the hour of *café con leche*, the women of my family gathered in Mamá's living room to speak of important things and to tell stories for the hundredth time, as if to each other, meant to be overheard by us young girls, their daughters. In Mamá's house (everyone called my grandmother Mamá) was a large parlor built by my grandfather to his wife's exact specifications so that it was always cool, facing away from the sun. The doorway was on the side of the house so no one could walk directly into her living room. First they had to take a little stroll through and around her beautiful garden where prize-winning orchids grew in the trunk of an ancient tree she had hollowed out for that purpose. This room was furnished with several mahogany rocking chairs, acquired at the births of her children, and one intricately carved rocker that had passed down to Mamá at the death of her own mother. It was on these rockers that my mother, her sisters and my grandmother sat on these afternoons of my childhood to tell their stories, teaching each other and my cousin and me what it was like to be a woman, more specifically, a Puerto Rican woman. They talked about life on the island, and life in *Los Nueva Yores*, their way of referring to the U.S., from New York City to California: the other place, not home, all the same. They told real-life stories, though as I later learned, always embellishing them with a little or a lot of dramatic detail, and they told *cuentos*, the morality and cautionary tales told by the women in our family for generations: stories that became a part of my subconscious as I grew up in two worlds, the tropical island and the cold city, and which would later surface in my dreams and in my poetry.

One of these tales was about the woman who was left at the altar. Mamá liked to tell that one with histrionic intensity. I remember the rise and fall of her voice, the sighs, and her constantly gesturing hands, like two birds swooping through her words. This particular story would usually come up in a conversation as a result of someone mentioning a forthcoming engagement or wedding. The first time I remember hearing it, I was sitting on the floor at Mamá's feet, pretending to read a comic book. I may have been eleven or twelve years old: at that difficult age when a girl is no longer a child who can be ordered to leave the room if the women wanted freedom to take their talk into forbidden zones, or really old enough to be considered a part of their conclave. I could only sit quietly, pretending to be in another world, while absorbing it all in a sort of unspoken agreement of my status as silent auditor. On this day, Mamá had taken my long, tangled mane of hair into her ever busy hands. Without looking down at me or interrupting her flow of words, she began braiding my hair, working at it with the quickness and determination which characterized all her actions. My mother was watching us impassively from her rocker across the room. On her lips played a little ironic smile. I would never sit still for *her* ministrations, but even then, I instinctively knew that she did not possess Mamá's matriarchal power to command and keep everyone's attention. This was particularly evident in the spell she cast when telling a story.

"It is not like it used to be when I was a girl." Mamá announced, "Then, a man could leave a girl standing at the church altar with a bouquet of fresh flowers in her hands and disappear off the face of the earth. No way to track him down if he was from another town. He could be a married man, with maybe even two or three families all over the island. There was no way to know. And there were men who did this. Hombres with the devil in their flesh who would come to a pueblo, like this one, take a job at one of the haciendas, never meaning to stay, only to have a good time and to seduce the women."

The whole time she was speaking, Mamá was weaving my hair into a flat plait which required pulling apart the two sections of hair with little jerks that made my eyes water; but knowing how grandmother detested whining and *boba* (sissy) tears, as she called them, I just sat up as straight and stiff as I did at La Escuela San José, where the nuns enforced good posture with a flexible plastic ruler they bounced off slumped shoulders and heads. As Mamá's story progressed, I noticed how my young aunt Laura had lowered her eyes, refusing to meet Mamá's meaningful gaze. Laura was seventeen, in her last year of high school, and already engaged to a boy from another town who had staked his claim with a tiny diamond ring, then left for Los Nueva Yores to make his fortune. They were planning to get married in a year; but Mamá had expressed serious doubts that the wedding would ever take place. In Mamá's eyes, a man set free without a legal contract was a man lost. She believed that marriage was not something men desired, but simply the price they had to pay for the privilege of children, and of course, for what no decent (synonymous with "smart") woman would give away for free. "María la Loca was only seventeen when *it* happened to her." I listened closely at the mention of this name. María was a town "character," a fat middle-aged woman who lived with her old mother on the outskirts of town. She was to be seen around the pueblo delivering the meat pies the two women made for a living. The most peculiar thing about María, in my eyes, was that she walked and moved like a little girl, though she had the thick body and wrinkled face of an old woman. She would swing her hips in an exaggerated, clownish way, and sometimes even hop and skip up to someone's house. She spoke to no one. Even if you asked her a question, she would just look at you and smile, showing her yellow teeth. But I had heard that if you got close enough, you could hear her humming a tune without words. The kids yelled out nasty things at her, calling her *la Loca*, and the men who hung out at the bodega playing dominoes sometimes whistled mockingly as she passed by with her funny, outlandish walk. But María seemed impervious to it all, carrying her basket of *pasteles* like a grotesque Little Red Riding Hood through the forest.

María la Loca interested me, as did all the eccentrics and "crazies" of our pueblo. Their weirdness was a measuring stick I used in my serious quest for a definition of "normal." As a Navy brat, shuttling between New Jersey and the pueblo, I was constantly made to feel like an oddball by my peers, who made fun of my two-way accent: a Spanish accent when I spoke English; and, when I spoke Spanish, I was told that I sounded like a "Gringa." Being the outsiders had already turned my brother and me into cultural chameleons, developing early the ability to blend into a crowd, to sit and read quietly in a fifth story apartment building for days and days when it was too bitterly cold to play outside; or, set free, to run wild in Mamá's realm, where she took charge of our lives, releasing mother for a while from the intense fear for our safety that our father's absences instilled in her. In order to keep us from harm when father was away, mother kept us under strict surveillance. She even walked us to and from Public School No. 11, which we attended during the months we lived in Paterson, New Jersey, our home base in the States. Mamá freed the three of us like pigeons from a cage. I saw her as my liberator and my model. Her stories were parables from which to glean the *Truth*.

"Maria la Loca was once a beautiful girl. Everyone thought she would marry the Méndez boy." As everyone knew, Rogelio Méndez was no other than the richest man in town. "But," Mamá continued, knitting my hair with the same intensity she was putting into her story, "this *macho* made a fool out of her and ruined her life." She paused for the effect of her use of the word "*macho*," which at that time had not yet become a popular epithet for an unliberated man. This word had for us the crude and comical connotation of "male of the species," stud; a *macho* was what you put in a pen to increase your stock.

I peeked over my comic book at my mother. She too was under Mamá's spell, smiling conspiratorially at this little swipe at men. She was safe from Mamá's contempt in this area. Married at an early age, an unspotted lamb, she had been accepted by a good family of strict Spaniards whose name was old and respected, though their fortune had been lost long before my birth. In a rocker Papá had painted sky blue sat Mamá's oldest child, Aunt Nena. Mother of three children, stepmother of two more, she was a quiet woman who liked books but had married an ignorant and abusive widower whose main interest in life was accumulating wealth. He too was in the mainland working on his dream of returning home rich and triumphant to buy the *finca* of his dreams. She was waiting for him to send for her. She would leave her children with Mamá for several years while the two of them slaved away in factories. He would one day be a rich man, and she a sadder woman. Even now her life-light was dimming. She spoke little, an aberration in Mamá's house, and she read avidly, as if storing up spiritual food for the long winters that awaited her in Los Nueva Yores without her family. But even Aunt Nena came alive to Mamá's words, rocking gently, her hands over a thick book in her lap. Her daughter, my cousin Sara, played jacks by herself on the tile porch outside the room where we sat. She was a year older than I. We shared a bed and all our family's secrets. Collaborators in search of answers, Sara and I discussed everything we heard the women say, trying to fit it all together like a puzzle that once assembled would reveal life's mysteries to us. Though she and I still enjoyed taking part in boy's games—chase, volleyball and even *vaqueros*, the island version of cowboys and Indians involving cap-gun battles and violent shootouts under the mango tree in Mamá's backyard—we loved best the quiet hours in the afternoon when the men were still at work and the boys had gone to play serious baseball at the park. Then Mamá's house belonged only to us women. The aroma of coffee perking in the kitchen, the mesmerizing creaks and groans of the rockers, and the women telling their lives in *cuentos* are forever woven into the fabric of my imagination, braided like my hair that day I felt my grandmother's hands teaching me about strength, her voice convincing me of the power of story-telling.

That day Mamá told of how the beautiful María had fallen prey to a man whose name was never the same in subsequent versions of the story; it was Juan one time, José, Rafael, Diego, another. We understood that the name, and really any of the facts, were not important, only that a woman had allowed love to defeat her. Mamá put each of us in María's place by describing her wedding dress in loving detail: how she looked like a princess in her lace as she waited at the altar. Then, as Mamá approached the tragic denouement of her story, I was distracted by the sound of my Aunt Laura's violent rocking. She seemed on the verge of tears. She knew the fable was intended for her. That week she was going to have her wedding gown fitted, though no firm date had been set for the marriage. Mamá ignored Laura's obvious discomfort, digging out a ribbon from the sewing basket she kept by her rocker while describing María's long illness, "a fever that would not break for days." She spoke of a mother's despair: "that woman climbed the church steps on her knees every morning, wore only black as a *promesa* to the Holy Virgin in exchange for her daughter's health." By the time María returned from her honeymoon with death, she was ravished, no longer young or sane. "As you can see she is almost as old as her mother already," Mamá lamented while tying the ribbon to the ends of my hair, pulling it back with such force that I just knew that I would never be able to close my eyes completely again.

"That María is getting crazier every day." Mamá's voice would take a lighter tone now, expressing satisfaction, either for the perfection of my braid, or for a story well-told; it was hard to tell. "You know that tune she is always humming?" Carried away by her enthusiasm, I tried to nod, but Mamá would still have me pinned between her knees.

"Well, that's the wedding march." Surprising us all, Mamá sang out, "Da, da, dará . . . da, da, dará." Then lifting me off the floor by my skinny shoulders, she lead me around the room in an impromptu waltz—another session ending with the laughter of women, all of us caught up in the infectious joke of our lives.

For Practice

1. How does Cofer use details about setting (time and place) in this essay to create *ethos* and *pathos*? How do these details also help to introduce the essay's examination of gender, ethnicity, identity, marginalization, and "border crossing" issues and concerns?

2. How do the passages in the essay about Mamá's braiding of young Judith's hair parallel and comment on the central focus of the essay, her grandmother's story-telling? Does this parallel reflect and affirm or refute the thesis of the Dehay essay included in this casebook? Explain your answer.

3. In the Kallet interview, Cofer notes that an essential aspect of her writing is the ability "to use memory plus imagination, to transform remembering into art" (see page 585). How does "Casa" exemplify this core concern of Cofer's work?

4. How are Mamá, young Judith, Cofer's mother, Aunt Nena, Laura, María la Loca, and Rogelio Méndez each described in this essay? Why does Cofer choose to include each in this essay?

5. What "known territory" (especially gender, ethnic, identity, marginalization, and "border crossing") issues and concerns does Cofer examine through the "family history" narrative of "Casa"? How does she examine these issues?

6. What is an example of a story that you recall from your own childhood or adolescence which served the same purpose as *cuentos*? Explain the societal message encoded in that story. What cultural values was the story designed to convey?

Dear Joaquín

"Dear Joaquín" is written in epistolary form, a kind of fiction written as if it were a letter from one person to another. Cofer's use of this form emphasizes the issue of the narrator's distance from her lover, her family, and her country. Cofer has commented that "absences leave a very real space people must fill" (see page 590). This story/letter traces the narrator's experience of falling into discord with her family and culture over issues of her morality and honor. It also reveals her subsequent attempt to deal with her alienation from the man and the place she loves. In light of what Cofer says in "The Myth of the Latin Woman" about Puerto Rican girls' being expected to be both virtuous and "womanly" at the same time, Olga's alienation from her family in this story takes on particular significance.

This may never reach your hands. It is unlikely that it will. With your mamá watching her nest like a jealous hen and Rosaura keeping you drugged with sex and her witch's brews. You are lucky if you still know your name, much less remember me, the woman who truly loves you. Joaquín, I wait for you in America. My love, I come home from the factory every day to an empty, cold room. I am drinking a glass of our favorite wine—you once said my skin tasted like this—and writing to you, sealing all my hopes in this envelope. This is unbearable, *mi amor*. How could you abandon me when I needed you the most? Do you know that after my mother caught us on the beach that night she locked me in my room and called the priest in to confess me? I felt like a murderer on death row. I told him I was almost eighteen, a woman now, older than my mother when she had me. He refused me absolution and walked out of our house. Mamá came in yelling, *mala, perdida*, and said I was no longer her daughter. On my birthday that Sunday, Joaquín, I got two gifts from my family: a suitcase and a one–way ticket to New York City. But you must have heard all this. At first I thought you would come to me, but ten months have passed and not a word. My sister finally wrote me that you were hiding in your mother's house, from my mother's fury and the priest's tongue, and about Rosaura. You, hiding like a frightened child. You, my brave Joaquín of the night, my valiant Joaquín of the moon, the sand, skin, and wine. Hiding behind your mamá's big bottom, under Rosaura's mambo skirts. I will write to you every day of this long winter. My letters will gather like a storm cloud over your clear blue island sky until they burst in a downpour. The passion that you awakened in me will shadow you, Joaquín, until I come home to claim you. You are my man. In the meantime, forget about Rosaura. That *bruja* has put you under a spell. Don't eat anything from her *cocina*. And keep my image in your mind, Joaquín.

If this page should find its way to you, write to me and tell me how it is on the *playa* now. Tell me how it is to feel the sun on your skin in November.

Amor y besos
Olga

For Practice

1. Consider the impact—on Olga, on her lover, and on her family—of her having transgressed her culture's definitions of what a woman should be. What are the effects of her actions? What are the ideological implications of such definitions of womanhood; in other words, what do these definitions say about how Olga's culture values women?

2. Considering some of Cofer's comments about language in the Kallet interview, examine her choice to write this story mostly in English. What are the effects of this choice? Why does she include a few Spanish words? What are their effects?

3. Why has Cofer chosen the epistolary form for this story? What are the effects of her having done so? How might the story be different if she had used a different narrative technique (i.e., a third–person narrator)?

"Who Will Not Be Vanquished?"

"Who Will Not Be Vanquished?" was published in The Latin Deli: Telling the Lives of Barrio Women *(1993), a collection of short stories, poems, and non-fiction essays by Cofer. In this poem, Cofer once again mines her own experiences for the raw material of a creative work of art. Two particular memories, both relating to her own daughter, provide Cofer the opportunity to explore a number of the common themes of this casebook. For example, the inter-text of Cofer's recollections of Pasternak's* Doctor Zhivago *with her naming and the birth of her daughter, Tanya, creates a locus for examination of gender, ethnicity, marginalization, "border crossing," and identity issues and concerns. Then the near-tragic adolescent experience of Tanya's fifteen-year-old friend provides a chance to re-investigate these same issues and concerns, as well as the interrelationship between literature and everyday life, and the importance and power of language and narrative in shaping one's individual and communal identity.*

—For Tanya

1.
I named you for a snow-princess
in a Russian novel,
a woman of noble bearing
who would not be vanquished
by war nor passion: not Lara,   5
the other one—the quiet aristocrat
who inspired no poems from the man
but for whom he walked the frozen miles.

2.
Gold earrings flashing
through your black hair, you pirouette   10
so that your wide skirt blooms
around the long stems of your legs
for me to admire your wild beauty.
You are transformed
into one of the gypsy ancestors   15
we have never discussed.

3.
On the fall day of your birth,
in a city not far enough north
of the equator for my fantasy,
I held onto *Doctor Zhivago*   20
so hard, that when the first pain came,
I broke the spine. While the hot wires
announcing your arrival shot through me,
I imagined a sleigh pulled
by strong white horses, gliding   25
over a landscape of powdery snow.
In the distance: an ice palace.

4.
Today you want to go somewhere exotic:
an island in the Caribbean
inhabited only by beautiful young people;   30
a place where a girl might pick
from anyone's garden, a red hibiscus
for her hair, and wear a dress so light
that any breeze might make it dance;
where a dark-haired man   35
wearing a flowered shirt
leans against the bright blue wall
of a café, holding a guitar,
waiting for inspiration.

5.
Mourning suits us Spanish women.   40
Tragedy turns us into Antigone—maybe
we are bred for the part.

6.
Your best friend, also fifteen,
leaped from her father's speeding car
during an argument. After the call,   45
I saw how your eyes darkened
as you listened to my careful words;
I saw the women of our family in black,
gathering in a circle around you.

7.
On the ride to the hospital,   50
you sit up straight, averting your gaze.
I place my hand on your trembling shoulder,
and assure you that it's OK to cry.
But, gently, you disengage yourself
from my intrusive touch.   55

Without looking back, you walk away from me,
and into the antiseptic castle where she waits
like a captive maiden in her costume of gauze.

8.
She waits there, regal in her pain, eager
to recount her wingless flight, to show you   60
her wounds, and to tell you
about the betrayals of parents.

For Practice

1. As described in this poem, how are Tanya and Lara (the characters in *Doctor Zhivago*) different from one another?

2. According to stanzas 2 and 4, what is Cofer's daughter like? How does Cofer develop this description?

3. What is the function of stanza 5 in the poem? How does this stanza relate to the story of Maria la Loca which is narrated in "Casa"?

4. What metaphors and similes does Cofer use in the last six lines of the poem? What does the use of these figures of speech say about the position, roles, and constraints upon women and adolescents n this society? How do the metaphors and similes convey these messages?

5. In an interview with Rafael Ocasio, Cofer noted that through her writing she has discovered "that memory is subject to revision according to gender, age, circumstances, and many other criteria" (50). Explain how this poem either reflects or refutes that viewpoint.

6. In "Narrating Memory," Dehay explains that a "fragmented narrative creates the possibility that the other, the past that has been repressed or unknown, is emerging into the story in spite of the power inherent in the typical narrative voice" (see page 617). How does Cofer fragment the narrative of this poem? Who/what represents the typical (dominant) narrative voice? How so? Who/what represents the other (emergent) narrative voice? How so? In terms of the relationship between and validity of each of these kinds of voices, what does the poem conclude? Explain your answer.

Excerpt from "Narrating Memory"

Terry DeHay

The following selection is excerpted from a longer study in the essay col-lection Memory, Narrative, and Identity *(eds. Amritjit Singh, Joseph T. Skerrett, Jr., and Robert E. Hogan. Boston: Northeastern UP, 1994). Dehay's essay focuses on novels by minority women writers, and his ideas are relevant to the stories, poems, and essays by Cofer in this casebook. Dehay argues that women minority writers attempt to preserve "alterna-tive histories" to the dominant (or majority) one. These writers want to protect their cultures from being forgotten or distorted by the majority culture. Dehay also argues that these writers "deconstruct" the typical structure of a realist narrative, with its unified point of view. Instead, their narratives often contain several different points of view, each of which is "true" in some sense.*

As you read, compare Dehay's ideas with what Cofer says in her inter-view with Marilyn Kallet about her own writings. Also, consider how Dehay's ideas apply to the selections by Cofer in this section, as well as to works by other minority women writers elsewhere in the textbook.

Third World writers in the United States are increasingly confronting the need to construct alternative histories to those of the dominant culture in order to combat the appropriation and oppression of marginalized cultures. They are creating narratives that actively confront the dominant culture's attempt to destroy and/or neutralize these marginalized cultures through the destruction or appropria-tion of their collective history. As Barbara Harlow writes in her book *Resistance Literature*, "an important consequence of the First World's military, economic, and political intervention in the Third World . . . has been the catastrophic disruption of Third World people's cultural and literary traditions . . ." (33), which would generally be essential in the preservation of authentic history. This assault on history under-scored its power, especially in terms of a dialectic of individual and collective remem-bering, to give a people a common understanding of beginnings and processes in the act of becoming or resisting. Often a dominant culture will negate the importance of a minority group's shared and different past in favor of a more universal reading— We're all Americans—implying that the difference that the minority group *senses* is not real, but rather imagined. This is the myth of assimilation, "the melting pot"; the mainstream history then incorporates, assimilates, these differences. Even more difficult and more destructive, the dominant culture inevitably writes this "official" version of history and presents it as "fact" and unquestionable. Until recently, history has presented itself as an objective science, against which the intuitive challenge of marginalized memory remained virtually powerless.

Harlow convincingly outlines the importance of *not* reading Third World literature with the "European writer's mania for man without history—solitary and free—with unexplainable despair and anguish and death as the ultimate movements "not be confined by the First World imagination to what Gayatri Spivak, in her seminar "Third World under Erasure" at the Summer Institute for Culture and Society, Pittsburgh, in 1986, criticized as mere representative allegories of "correct political practice" (29, cited by Harlow). Many Third World writers are emphatically attempting to affect and even rewrite the historical record through their work and therefore directly address historical and factual incidences. Their work must not be neutralized by removing specifics to the plane of the symbolic or allegorical, but rather should be recognized in its full historical and political context. At the same time, Harlow points out that the personal accounts related in much literature of the resistance point to convergences within the larger context of the struggle against oppression.

Although Harlow's book focuses on resistance to colonial and neocolonial repression in Third World countries, many of her concepts can also be applied to the literature of Third World writers living in the United States, especially women of color. As Fredric Jameson points out in "Modernism and Imperialism": "in the United States itself, we have come to think and to speak of the emergence of an *internal* Third World and of internal Third World voices, as in Black women's literature or Chicano literature, for example" (51). Women of color in the United States live on the margin in at least two important ways: as members of marginalized "minority" groups and as women in a dominant white male culture. As Alice Walker points out in her essay "In Search of Our Mothers' Gardens," black women, as women from a marginalized culture, were effectively excluded from the institutions of the dominant ideology through the inaccessibility of education. Their creativity was limited to those materials that were appropriate to their marginalized space—scraps of cloth, flower seeds—or to modes of expression that cannot easily be denied—singing, dancing, story-telling. At times, the dominant culture has appropriated or reinterpreted even these cultural expressions to reenforce its values rather than reading them as historical records of struggle as Walker does in her essay. The example she gives of the quilt hanging in the Smithsonian Institution in Washington, D. C., is a poignant example of this process of appropriation: ". . . there hangs a quilt unlike any other in the world. . . . Though it follows no known pattern of quilt making, though it is made of bits and pieces of worthless rags, it is obviously the work of a powerful imagination and deep spiritual feeling. Below the quilt I saw a note that said it was made by 'an anonymous black woman in Alabama, a hundred years ago'" (239). A product both of a creative force of the woman who patched it together from "worthless rags" and the oppressive forces of the dominant culture, the quilt, isolated and objectified, hanging in a museum, loses much of the meaning of the circumstances of its creation. This creator is anonymous in large part because of her position in this culture. As Walker states, "If we could locate this 'anonymous black woman from Alabama,' she would turn out to be one of our grandmothers" (239). Today, through new acts of creation, Third World women are looking back, locating these lost ancestors, freeing them from the confines of museums, and reclaiming their histories.

Novels by minority women writers challenge the domination of hegemonic history and memory in the very structure of the narrative, as they directly confront the importance of memory to personal and cultural identity. Works have common strategies of interrupting the surface of the traditional linear narrative to allow for the entry of a multiplicity of voices and perspectives. This deconstruction is a response to what Colin MacCabe calls the "classical [nineteenth century] realist novel," in which the narrative creates "a hierarchy amongst the discourses that compose the text": "In the classical realist novel the narrative prose functions as a metalanguage that can state all the truths in the object language—those words held in inverted commas—and can also explain the relation of this object language to the real" (35). In other words, the narrative "metalanguage" mediates between the "text" and the reader, providing a "window of words" to frame the reader's relationship to the "real." The narrative, according to MacCabe, "simply allows reality to appear and denies its own status as articulation" (35). However, although this metalanguage is "transparent," like all language, it is ideological, and therefore the reality, or "truth" to which it points, is also ideologically informed. In the case of the realist novel, the dominant ideology is that of the patriarchal culture of western Europe and later the United States.

Multiethnic American women's literature, like other marginalized literatures, often uses this deconstruction of the traditional realist narrative metalanguage to produce alternative narrative patterns to those of the dominant culture and to destabilize the "hierarchy amongst discourses" within the text. By providing openings for other narratives, other versions of history, these texts lead to a revisioning or "re-membering" (to borrow Mary DeShazer's term) of minority women's identities. Theirs is not a quest for a new metalanguage, but rather the celebration of what MacCabe calls the "multifarious nature of the real" (34). Barbara Christian, in *Black Women Novelists: The Development of a Tradition, 1892-1976*, identifies this tendency toward perspectives in her analysis of Paule Marshall's novels, *Browngirl, Brownstones* and *The Chosen Place, The Timeless People*:

> . . . her emphasis moves from the way the world affects an individual psyche to how our many psyches create a world . . . toward a unity of rather than a specialization of, experience. That type of movement is one of the reasons why persistent creative artists are so important to a culture. In graphically depicting their own growth, in analyzing abstract concepts through the concrete experiences of particular human beings, they fuse the personal and social areas that our fragmented world thrusts one against the other. Only when we see the oneness between politics and the individual psyche, oppression and the nature of human history, culture and the individual, their voices sing, will our species move beyond biting its tail to create its mouth. The wholeness of the creative process continually reminds us that we purposely sleep through much of our lives. (135)

By taking apart the traditional narrative, minority women writers are able to identify the artificial nature of accepted patterns and to reveal authentic unities.

Raymond Williams, in *Marxism and Literature*, defines three distinct aspects of culture that create "internal dynamic relations" within any system. The most easily identifiable is the *hegemonic* or *dominant*. But along with the dominant, the *residual* and the *emergent* function as part of the dynamic process that is, in Williams's terms, culture. The 'residual,' according to Williams "has been effectively formed in the past, but it is still active in the cultural process, not only and often not at all as an element of the past, but as an effective element of the present. Thus certain experiences, meanings, and values which cannot be expressed or substantially verified in terms of the dominant culture, are nevertheless lived and practiced on the basis of the residue—cultural as well as social—of some previous social and cultural institution or formation" (122). He also distinguishes between the residual that has been incorporated into the hegemony and that which presents an alternative or opposition to the dominant aspects of culture. The emergent aspects of culture are "new meanings and values, new practices, new relationships and kinds of relationships" that are continually being created (123).

These categories of the dominant, recessive, and emergent help clarify the importance of the past to the reconstruction of repressed cultural identity. To return to the past is not sufficient, nor is it possible in the dynamic process of cultural formation. However, the past does supply powerful and important connections that are essential to the revisioning of minority women's identities. Steven Knapp, in his article "Collective Memory and the Actual Past," states that, regardless of whether or not remembered events actually happened, "the narratives preserved sometimes play a *normative* role—that is, they may in various ways provide criteria, implicit or explicit, by which contemporary models of action can be shaped or corrected, or even by which practical ethical or political proposals can be authorized or criticized" (123). He refers to this function as "collective *authority*," by which a culture defines itself. Clearly, understanding one's relationship to this "collective authority" is essential to resisting hegemonic control. If marginalized cultures accept the dominant culture's narratives as normative, they will be powerless to resist domination. If, instead, they denaturalize these narratives, at the same time recuperating their own collective (recessive) memories, they can provide alternative "collective authorities," with alternative (emergent) "models of action" to resist domination.

Adrienne Rich, in her essay "When We Dead Awaken," defines this dialectical process as *re-vision*: "the act of looking back, of seeing with fresh eyes, of entering an old text from a new critical direction," asserting that re-visioning is an "act of survival": "Until we can understand the assumptions in which we are drenched, we cannot know ourselves" (35). For minority women, this means a positive recuperation of residual cultural alternatives, as well as the recognition of the distortion of their history by the dominant culture. The act of re-visioning creates fresh connections with the past, which can supply an alternative culture or cultures to stand in opposition to the dominant culture, which has historically both absorbed and repressed them. The emergent provides a synthesis: "new meanings and values, new practices, new relationships and kinds of relationships," which are continually created (Williams 123).

This process of synthesis is often recreated in minority women's novels through the relationships between mothers, as repositories of the recessive culture, and daughters, in their attempts to live in the modern white world. The cultures represented by the mothers provide a means of finding power as women of color in a male-dominated white culture. DeShazer, in *Inspiring women: Reimagining the Muse*, states that women writers "name their muses not by casting off or consuming or appropriating, but by taking on, connecting, inheriting" (6). She extends her reading of the

Demeter/Kore, mother/daughter relationship, so prevalent in women's writing, to women writers of color, in terms of a *familial muse*, the muse that comes not from a distant mythology or tradition, but from their own lives. She cites Maya Angelou: "Image making is very important for every human being. It is especially important for black American women in that we are, by being black, a minority in the United States, and by being female the less powerful of the genders. . . . We need to see our mothers, aunts, our sisters, and grandmothers. We need to see Frances Harper, Sojourner Truth, Fannie Lou Hamer, women of our heritage. We need to have these women preserved" (40 [from *Black Women Writers at Work*, ed. Claudia Tate, 1–2]). The minority woman must look to her history, both to preserve it and to find out who she is. She needs to have a clear vision of her past, in order to re-vision her present. This is the process of re-membering. The female muse, then, in these texts, inspires the writer with a sense of the history of her culture, a connection to a past that the dominant culture may be repressing or reinterpreting away from the authentic history.

Their mothers' histories as they run counter to that of the dominant or official history are primarily oral and generally passed through stories and other acts of creation. These stories may, in fact, conflict directly with the mother's advice on how to survive in the closed world of the dominant culture. But the mothers' stories, memories, and works of art provide other models and choices, the possibility of alternative and oppositional identities. . . .

The deconstructive act that these minority women's narratives perform demonstrates the importance of recognizing the type of control that the traditional narrative form exercises over the material it contains. The traditional narrative voice, regardless of its position, implies unity of vision, linear progression, a comfortable beginning, middle, and end. Perspective is always centered in the individual with whom the narrative originates. John Berger's analysis of perspective in the visual arts points to the importance of drawing attention to the subjective nature of perspective in narration: "Perspective makes the single eye the centre of the visible world. . . . The visible world is arranged for the spectator as the universe was once thought to be arranged for God" (10). By choosing to open up the narrative form, dispersing the points of origin and denying artificial cohesion, these minority women writers are challenging the very nature of patriarchal authority. Unseating the singular eye or I, they are acknowledging, and often celebrating, differences between cultures and even within themselves.

Perhaps even more importantly, however, these writers are providing models for marginalized groups for recovering and revising their own history, based on a respect for memory and a recognition of the subjectivity of all narrative. Their works disorder and decenter the narrative without losing track of the primary task of telling the stories. The fragmented narrative creates the possibility that the other, the past that has been repressed or unknown, is emerging into the story in spite of the power inherent in the typical narrative voice. This produces the impression that multiple voices can disrupt or interrupt the narrative flow, inserting their own voices and stories. Although this is clearly only, in a sense, an impression, and the writer is still selecting and ordering these disruptions, the narrative acts as a mimetic representation of the way in which other voices have inserted themselves into the writer's consciousness and contribute to an understanding of the structure of society.

Some counter in their work what Fredric Jameson in *The Political Unconscious* calls master narratives: "ideological paradigms which contain within their plots a determined ending." Minority women writers, like other marginalized writers, reverse this process, producing works that openly examine the economic, political situations in which they are writing. Writing against established narrative patterns becomes a way of questioning the way in which these master narratives shape our ways of seeing. Remembering is the process of reclaiming and protecting a past often suppressed by the dominant culture, and in this sense, as re-visioning, it is essential in the process of gaining control over one's life. As Rich states, it is an act of survival.

Works Cited

Anzaldúa, Gloria, ed. *Making Face, Making Soul = Haciendo Caras: Creative and Critical Perspectives by Women of Color*. San Francisco: Aunt Lute Foundation Books, 1990.

Berger, John. *Ways of Seeing*. New York: Penguin, 1972.

Christian, Barbara. *Black Women Novelists: The Development of a Tradition, 1892-1976*. Westport, CT: Greenwood, 1980.

Cisneros, Sandra. *The House on Mango Street*. Houston: Arte Público, 1988.

DeShazer, Mary K. *Inspiring Women: Reimagining the Muse*. New York: Pergamon, 1986.

Erdrich, Louise. *Tracks*. New York: Holt, 1988.

Harlow, Barbara. *Resistance Literature*. New York: Methuen, 1987.

Horno-Delgado, Asuncion, Eliana Ortega, Nina M. Scott, and Nancy Saporta Sternback, eds. *Breaking Boundaries: Latina Writings and Critical Readings*. Amherst: U of Massachusetts P, 1989.

Jameson, Fredric. "Modernism and Imperialism." *Nationalism, Colonialism and Literature*. Minneapolis: U of Minnesota P, 1990.

_____. *The Political Unconscious: Narrative as a Socially Symbolic Act*. Ithaca: Cornell UP, 1981.

Knapp, Steven. "Collective Memory and the Actual Past." *Representations* 26 (Spring 1989): 123–49.

MacCabe, Colin. "Realism and the Cinema: Notes on Some Brechtian Theses." *A Critical and Cultural Theory Reader*. Ed. Anthony Easthope and Kate McGowan. Toronto: Toronto UP, 1992. 35–39.

Rich, Adrienne. "When We Dead Awaken: Writing as Revision." *On Lies, Secrets and Silence, Selected Prose, 1966–1978*. New York: Norton, 1979. 33–49.

Tan, Amy. *The Joy Luck Club*. New York: Putnam's, 1989.

Walker, Alice. *In Search of Our Mother's Gardens: Womanist Prose*. New York: Harcourt, 1983.

_____. *The Temple of My Familiar*. New York: Harcourt, 1989.

Williams, Raymond. *Marxism and Literature*. New York: Oxford UP, 1977.

For Practice

1. DeHay argues that minority women writers oppose what he calls the "myth . . . of the melting pot" (see page 614). Why does he call it a myth? How does Cofer seem to resist that myth in her works?

2. DeHay says that minority women writers need a "recognition of the distortion of their history by the dominant culture" (see page 616). How does this

idea of cultural distortion relate to Cofer's essay "I Just Met a Girl Named Maria"?

3. In his essay, DeHay stresses how minority women writers resist the dominant culture in their writings. But, in her interview, Cofer also talks about building a "bridge" to the dominant culture through her works. Do some works by Cofer seem to emphasize resistance, while others emphasize building cultural bridges? Which ones fit into these categories? How do these works differ?

4. DeHay quotes Steven Knapp's idea that stories remembered and retold can serve as "collective authority" for a culture. What does he mean by the term "collective authority"? (See page 616.) How can stories fulfill such a role? Relate Knapp's idea to what Cofer says about story-telling in her interview and to the role story-telling plays in "Casa."

5. Relate DeHay's idea about minority women writers' "deconstructing" the typical narrative to Cofer's narratives. Which of Cofer's narratives seem more "deconstructed" than others? Why?

Writing Your Own Arguments

1. What role does language play in shaping our experience? How is the influence of language complicated when one's native language is not that of the mainstream? How does language contribute to or determine definitions of what is American? How do Judith Ortiz Cofer's works reflect these issues?

2. How are relationships shaped by cultural values, habits, and customs? How do relationships benefit from those influences? How are relationships negatively affected by those same factors? How do Cofer's works reflect these positive and negative influences?

3. What part does the past play in making us who we are? Are there ways in which we act unconsciously on the past? Explain. How does Cofer answer these questions? Do you agree with her answers? Why or why not?

4. Several of the works in this section deal with relationships between parents and children or between men and women. Discuss how one of these types of relationships is portrayed in Cofer's works. Do you share her attitudes toward this kind of relationship? Why or why not?

5. Many of Cofer's works refer to Catholicism. Discuss the role that Catholicism plays in the lives of the characters in Cofer's stories. What do you think is Cofer's own attitude toward Catholicism? How is this attitude reflected in her stories?

6. All of Cofer's works deal in some way with people caught between cultures. Analyze the different ways characters in Cofer's works deal with cross-cultural tensions.

7. Cofer herself exists between two cultures, American and Puerto Rican. She sees her role as a bridge between these cultures. Do her writings successfully build such a bridge? Why or why not?

8. Compare one of Cofer's poems to Pat Mora's "Sonrisas." Do these women share the same attitudes about living between two cultures? How do their poems differ? How are they similar? Which poem do you think is more effective in conveying these attitudes? Why?

GLOSSARY

from
**Literary Conversation, *by*
Patsy Callaghan
and Ann Dobyns**

abstract language: See concrete language.

allegory: A story with two parallel and consistent levels of meaning, one literal and one figurative, in which the figurative level offers a moral or political lesson. One reader of "Where Are You Going, Where Have You Been?" says that Arnold Friend is the devil, and offers evidence that his two roles, as Friend and devil, are parallel and consistent. People who read Arnold Friend as an allegorical figure will then attempt to define the moral lesson Connie learned, or the one we learn as we read the story.

alliteration: Repetition of sound. When a sound or set of sounds is repeated in close proximity, the repetition calls attention to itself. The repetition may be used for emphasis or to link related words, or the purpose of repeating the sound may have something to do with the sound itself.

antagonist: A person or persons in conflict with or opposing the **protagonist**, though a force or a circumstance can also function as antagonist. Our most obvious example of an antagonist is Arnold Friend, who terrorizes Connie in "Where Are You Going, Where Have You Been?"

archaic language: Words that were, but are no longer, in common use. Inexperienced readers may find that archaic terms distance them from a literary work, but experienced readers take into account that in the context of works written in earlier times archaic language offers us a glimpse of that historical moment. In contemporary works, archaic words may be used to connote past ideas, attitudes, or circumstances.

archetype: Generally, archetypes are what we perceive to be original patterns, models of being and behaving we recognize from the collective unconscious we all share; for example, we recognize the stories, personalities, emotions, and situations of the Olympian gods and goddesses as familiar models in literature. We also refer to a perfect example of a type or group as an archetype. Referring to a character, an archetype is a figure so seemingly familiar that it registers imaginatively as universal—for example, the hero who sacrifices his own life for the betterment of humanity (e.g., Prometheus), or the scapegoat, or the sorceress.

atmosphere, mood, or ambiance: These terms refer to the emotional or psychological climate of a work. Although subjective, the way works register with readers is important and predictable enough to be a part of most literary discussions. One reader of "Where Are You Going, Where Have You Been?" said it was "scary"; *Trifles* might be seen as anxious or conspiratorial. In either case, the atmosphere generates reader expectations about the progression of events in the work. Sustained or changing, it is usually communicated through details of setting. Reading for atmosphere, particularly with other readers, helps foster an ability to recognize and name complex emotional responses to experience and to become aware of the way a prevailing mood can influence events and behaviors.

ballad: A story poem that usually comes out of an oral or song tradition and is arranged in four-line stanzas rhyming "abab." Usually a refrain, or repeating part, contains a line that advances the story. The formula and repetition enhance the emotional effect and help the singer remember the words.

canon: A term that has come to denote "works worth reading," as determined by a broad consensus of scholars with diverse critical viewpoints and over the passage of time. Words like "masterpieces" and "classics" and "great books" also refer to canonical works. The ongoing critical conversation about what is worth reading is called "canon formation," and as the group involved in that process evolves from its rather homogeneous composition to include women and ethnic minorities, it has become obvious that the criteria used to judge literary merit are contextual and negotiable. For example, knowing about a writer's culture or the culture represented in the text can help you see how the language choices are effective within that cultural context and may allow you to make an evaluation that is relevant to the cultural origins of the work.

character: The representation of a person in an imaginative work whom we come to know from the words on the page. When characters are one dimensional, stereotypical, predictable, or simple we refer to them as *flat*. Flat characters usually act as foils or backdrops, offering motivation for or an interpretive clue about the main characters. When characters seem real, are fully developed, are unpredictable and difficult to pin down, we refer to them as *round*. Round characters usually are aligned with the central conflicts or questions at issue in the work; it is their dilemmas which concern us and their interests with which we identify. In "Where Are You Going, Where Have You Been?" we know almost nothing about the strange, silent Ellie, yet his presence lends palpable density to the threatening atmosphere.

When characters grow and change in the course of the action, they are said to be *dynamic*; remaining unchanged, they are *static*. Sometimes the change occurs not in the protagonist but in someone watching, as the reader or another character becomes aware that the protagonist is more complicated than was first realized. These classifications of characters are important when we are reflecting on the way the work progresses, what happens or what changes, which usually requires us to align our understanding of plot or circumstance with our understanding of character.

characterization: How would you describe an old friend to a new one? You might use physical description—green teeth, Brillo pad hair—which is called *exposition*. But you also would show what he or she is like through characterization—with stories and anecdotes about what the person does or has done, with indirect presentation through objects or details or the reactions of others, with the words of others about your friend. This is precisely how writers control characterization in literature. Observing the various kinds of information the writer has given you about a character, you form generalizations the same way you might in your everyday interactions. This is one of the most valuable kinds of practice literary interpretation offers: how to take stock of others, taking into account everything you can and in the process recognizing human complexity, rather than making hasty judgments based on little information or preconceived notions and biases.

Plot and character are interdependent; one evokes the other. For example, in *Trifles*, the character Mrs. Peters changes over the course of the play; in the beginning, she is "married to the law," and in the end, she subverts it. But we had to believe she would do it, or we wouldn't find the plot credible. This is one of our requirements for good characterization: characters must register as believable; their actions must seem probable. They also must be consistent, or we must be able to infer reasons for changes. When we perceive changes, we must understand possible motives for those changes. Although the characters may stretch our credulity, and although their motivations may not be obvious, a writer's artful choices will give us some basis for speculation and generalization.

chorus: In classical Greek drama, a group of actors stood together alongside the action, commenting on it, offering opinions, and often advising the hero. We have come to think of them as the voice of public response, formally representing a dialogic relationship between the work and the audience. The importance of this idea goes beyond the study of ancient theater, however, because often characters in literary works still fill this role, not as participants in the action but as commentators, a reflective voice. Some readers have seen the men in *Trifles* acting as a chorus, voicing the accepted perspective of the status quo, the traditional way of seeing attributed to the institutions of law.

concrete language: Because literature communicates imaginatively and emotionally as well as intellectually, it is particularly dependent on concrete language. Concrete words are specific, vivid, graphic, and appeal to the senses. Abstract language on the other hand is general or without material references and appeals primarily to the intellect. Grief, love, fatherhood, and evil are abstract; teeth, oil can, a hand on my wrist, and Arnold Friend are concrete.

Concrete language appears in literature as imagery, which is often called "mental pictures" experienced by readers through the senses. Imagery engages the reader's imagination, thereby aiding identification with the experience, through words that appeal to our senses of sight, hearing, smell, touch, and taste directly through description or metaphorically through comparisons.

connotation: The associations, feelings, and attitudes that a word suggests or implies, as opposed to the denotation, which is a word's primary meaning. While the word "home" denotes one's place of residence, it connotes familiarity, privacy, and intimacy. Sharing connotations brings richness to poetic language; relating the various connotations promotes a fuller understanding.

conventional form; As you discovered in the descriptions of designs, specific combinations of design elements can become traditional or conventional through their application and recognition. With conventional forms, you come to desire and expect certain kinds of progressions, such as the way a sonnet often raises a question in the first eight lines and addresses it in the last six. These anticipations are raised by the design itself, and thus conventional expectations connect design to development. Because the design is familiar, or conventional, it leads you to expect a related sequence, or development.

When you reflect on the progression in terms of its conventions, ask yourself whether the story seemed similar to other works you have read: a mystery, a tale of growing up, a journey of discovery, an adventure tale. Then ask yourself if, in the middle of reading, you had expectations of how the work would end. Are these two observations related? Did the kind of work you perceived it to be influence your expectations of the progression or the outcome? "Where Are You Going,

Where Have You Been?" is an example of a short story that uses categorical expectations to move the story forward (see **short story** and **plot**).

critical approaches: When your reading group discusses literature, you are engaging in literary criticism. As this text shows in every chapter, conversation about literature naturally elicits critical questions. When critics formulate general principles that characterize a particular method of inquiry, a particular way of investigating a work, we call it a critical approach, or a critical school. Although the six brief descriptions that follow do not cover the spectrum of critical approaches, they represent ways of reading that will be a part of most programs of literary study. We list them separately, but critics often combine the approaches to explain and develop their readings.

Formalist criticism: The formalist critic regards the literary work as a unified artistic object. To a formalist, the key interpretive information is in a work's intrinsic features, or the elements found in the work itself: the form, diction, syntax, sound, or genre. Formalists are not concerned with social, biographical, or historical information; they ask instead, how do all of the parts of the work fit together to create a particular effect. The "close reading" strategy employed by the formalist critic is a careful, step-by-step analysis involving observation, generalization, and interpretation.

Historical criticism: Historical critics place a literary work in the historical context from which it emerged. Some reconstruct the world that existed at the time the text was written in order to understand it the way it might have been understood by the people of the time, or to investigate how the conditions of its creation may have affected its meaning. Others gather historical data that can lend significance to elements of the text for which modern readers have no specific context. Still others examine the ways particular works have been interpreted over the passing of time to understand something about the interpreters' view of the world.

Feminist criticism: Feminist critics ask how works represent and relate issues of sexuality and power. They are concerned with how works were created and how they are interpreted and valued. Feminist critics are concerned with the ways in which male-oriented assumptions have permeated literary culture and given privilege to the ideas and works that matched those assumptions. Others look at how a writer's gender influences his or her writing, or how sexual orientation influences literary creation and interpretation.

Biographical criticism: Critics interested in biography focus on the fact that literary works emerge from the experiences of real people, and believe that information about writers can help us understand the meanings of their writings. As our experiences shape our readings of literary works, so the experiences of writers shape their creations. Knowing specific facts about an author's life often deepens our appreciation of or engagement with a work. Biographical critics explain literary works in terms of their knowledge of an author's life.

Psychoanalytic criticism: Psychoanalytic critics ask how particular theories of psychology can explain the human behavior and motivation of writers and/or their characters. Typically, they look at what a work suggests about what is operating at unconscious levels, treating the literary work as a psychoanalyst might regard a dream. The systems for finding significance in scenes, events, feelings, and behaviors vary according to the psychological or psychoanalytic theory being applied. However, in specific works of psychoanalytic criticism, these theories are usually summarized in the body of the work, to help the reader make the same assumptions as the critic.

Cultural criticism: Cultural critics regard literary works as artifacts of a culture, or a set of beliefs, assumptions, and practices that connect a group of people. They prefer to describe rather than to evaluate. Literature, to cultural critics, is political and ideological, and should be read as a product of and as a means of revealing those agendas. They attempt to discover the criteria on the basis of which cultural phenomena are considered "high" or "low," and seek to dismantle the political hierarchies that are the basis of those judgments. They also consider the ways in which specific literary products perpetuate systems of cultural privilege among and between class, ethnic, and gender groups. Thus their reading strategy involves connecting works to a whole setting of other ideas, contexts, or issues within which the works make sense.

culture: In modern literary studies, culture has come to mean the whole milieu of ideas, morals, art, historical circumstances, customs, popular forms and figures, laws, and habits of a group of people. Lest you begin to believe that such a concept is too broad to be useful, remember that the readers of "Where Are You Going, Where Have You Been?" referred to the culture, or various cultures, of youth that could provide a context for comprehending and even judging Connie's behavior. The limits and extensions of a culture are evident in its prohibitions, its reward and punishment systems, the way adherence is promoted, and the consequences of violating the rules or norms of the culture.

When we read about a cultural moment, we can recover some of the conditions of existence that may have influenced the creation of, or the actions, events, and behaviors presented within, a work. Reading literature with an eye for what is praised, blamed, valued, or devalued by narrators and characters can help us imagine ourselves standing outside our own biases and assumptions and within a set of cultural boundaries unlike our own. Those boundaries may be ethnic, ideological, economic, or gender-marked, or they may exist between one neighborhood and another.

diction: The vocabulary and phrasing in a literary work. Diction can be analyzed in a number of ways, but the best way to read for significance in diction is *substitution*: think of an alternative for a word or phrase and note meaningful differences between your choice and the writer's. Overall, we can read for whether the words are simple or complex, abstract or concrete, contemporary or archaic, familiar or formal. We can look at patterns in the way the writer uses particular parts of speech. We can look at denotations, or literal meanings, and connotations, or associations words have beyond their dictionary definitions. Finally, we can look at relationships between and among word choices within the text, observing patterns of meaning created by the writer's combinations and sequences.

dramatic irony: Irony is dramatic when it involves an incongruity between what the audience knows and what the character or characters have not yet realized. At the conclusion of *Trifles*, the county attorney, baffled by the circumstances of the crime, says facetiously to Mrs. Hale, "Well, at least we found out that she was not going to quilt it. She was going to—what is it you call it, ladies?" When Mrs. Hale replies, the audience, not the attorney, understands the relationship of her answer to the strangling: "We call it—knot it, Mr. Henderson."

elegy: A poem commemorating a death or loss, the style and form of which suggest a mournful reflection.

epic: Epic poems celebrate the exploits of heroes. The stories are long, the subjects are the values and destinies of cultures, and the style is elevated. They usually begin by asking audiences and muses to listen (some variation of "hear ye, hear ye"), then open in the middle of the action (*in medias res*). Along the way, supernatural helpers often assist the hero.

essay: A form of prose, mainly in the form of persuasion, which makes an appeal to the reader's way of thinking about a subject. As Montaigne employed the form, it became a kind of intellectual, emotional, and imaginative exploration of a subject. Modern examples range from the formal essay, which is relatively impersonal, authoritative, and orderly, to the informal essay, which assumes a tone of familiarity, focuses on everyday experiences, and is self-revealing, relaxed, and often humorous.

figurative language: When language is used to mean something other than the usual or standard meaning, it is being used "figuratively," that is, in order to achieve some special meaning or effect. These figures once were studied primarily as stylistic devices, but we know that they go beyond their classifications as elements of literary language to describing indispensable characteristics of all language. Imagine having to describe something unfamiliar to someone else without using comparisons like metaphors or similes to make your description comprehensible. Imagine having to express outrage without resorting to exaggeration or hyperbole. Imagine trying to raise children without telling stories that mean something to them now, but also include allegorical lessons for later reflection. Reading figuratively is an essential ability for literary interpretation, which requires that you see in multiple ways, perceiving possibilities that can reveal patterns of significance.

foreshadowing: Often events, characters, or details that at first seem insignificant acquire importance as a work progresses. Seeing these elements in a new way not only causes you to reflect back on the sequence, connecting and relating what came before to see the progression of the work, but also gives you a sense of recognition and familiarity that propels you further into the reading experience. You become a part of the work by becoming aware of connections between seemingly unrelated things.

frame story: One story frames the events and discoveries of another story. Usually a narrator in the present tells a tale from the past that in some way explains the present. There are many contemporary examples, but the most familiar frame stories come to us from Boccaccio's *Decameron*, and from Chaucer, who developed the journey and the interactions among his storytellers so fully that the frame of the *Canterbury Tales* itself includes elements of plot.

free verse/open form: Poetry that has no observable or strong pattern of rhyme or meter. Although it seems like a paradox, a "formless form" really is still a form; as the artist Ben Shahn tells us, form is "the shape of content." Look to free verse for explorations of open questions, surprises, questions unresolved but worth asking, experiences unpredictable but worth the risk, or challenges to assumptions. You have an example here in Leslie Marmon Silko's poem "Long Time Ago/In The Beginning."

genre: Genres are classes of library works. There are many genres, and the criteria used to distinguish these classes are varied. In fact, one group of literary critics has focused on "genre theory," or the study of the classification of literary works—what makes them one thing rather than another. When you figure out what a group of works has in common, you are defining a genre. Understanding that genres carry with them traditional elements can help you see how writers are choosing to use, or to manipulate, those elements to support their vision.

hyperbole: Intentional overstatement.

identification and empathy: Identifying with a person or situation in a literary work involves feeling the experience being evoked by the language. When we identify, we find the common ground in ourselves, sometimes involuntarily, that we share with the character, the situation, or even the inanimate objects we are reading about. We are asked by Joyce Carol Oates to find a way to connect with Connie in "Where Are You Going, Where Have You Been?," and although some of the readers in the conversation about the story found that identification difficult, they all recognized that the text was inviting them to try. During the course of discoveries in the play *Trifles*, the women discovered that their identification with the accused was strong enough to supplant their prior identification with the "law."

imagery: A term often used to refer to the ways writers compose mental images in writing, typically evoking visual pictures, but sometimes appealing to the other senses such as hearing, touch, smell, taste, or even movement.

incongruity: A quality of a literary work produced when the reader perceives inconsistency or discord among elements of the work. While some inexperienced readers find literary incongruities intimidating, experienced readers understand that they raise questions worth asking about form, language, participants, and situations, and invite answers that complicate the work in interesting ways. Dramatic irony is a kind of incongruity between the audience and the protagonist: we know something the character has not yet realized, and we read for the moment of discovery: A *paradox* is another kind of incongruity; an apparent contradiction which, on reflection, makes a new kind of sense.

influence: Informed readers talk about influence when their focus is the conversations between and among past and present literary texts and/or authors. The more you read, the more you will become accustomed to seeing connections between texts. Sometimes these are called *allusions*, which are direct or indirect references in one text to another. A newer term, *intertextuality*, refers to the way that the evolution of many works can be traced through historical antecedents, the concept being that all literature is in some way a reworking or revision of earlier writings. Tracing influences is scholarly work, involving immersion in the writings of various times and authors in order to establish not just reflections but conscious or unconscious connections. Such scholarship can be rewarding in our effort to perceive the work in a historical or cultural network that includes not just events and circumstances but authors and ideas.

lines, line breaks: In verse, many lines don't stop where sentences do. Thus line breaks become another meaningful division of syntactical parts that sometimes reinforce but more often skew or manipulate grammar for effect. To analyze line breaks, ask "why here, why not there?" and note differences that change the meaning or add significance. When line breaks coincide with ends of sentences, they are called *end-stopped lines*. When sentences continue beyond the end of a line, the strategy is called *enjambment*.

lyric: Any poem that, rather than telling a story, presents a speaker's state of mind or thought or feeling. It may include observation, reflection, recollection, thought, and feeling, and may be a short, simple expression of a moment, or a longer exploration of a mood or mindset, as in an elegy or an ode.

metaphor: An implied comparison between one thing and something distinctly different.

meter: The background rhythm to which the vowel, consonant, and rhyming sounds are played out. We can all hear a rhythm to spoken language, a rhythm that emphasizes certain words or sentences, that makes use of repetition and phrasing to help listeners make sense of the words. Writers of poetry consciously employ meter to reinforce their vision. When we read for meter by analyzing the rhythm, we are practicing *scansion*, or are said to be scanning the work.

The meter of a line of verse is first determined by the *pattern of stresses*, or the way stressed (or accented) and unstressed (or unaccented) syllables are arranged, and second by the number of *feet* in the line. One stressed syllable plus one or more unstressed syllables makes up what is called a foot, or a rhythmic unit that is characteristically repeated. The words used to indicate the number of feet per line from one to eight are monometer, dimeter, trimeter, tetrameter, pentameter, hexameter, heptameter, and octameter.

There are four standard feet in English:

iamb: two syllables, one unstressed followed by one stressed.

That TIME/of YEAR/thou MAYST/in ME I beHOLD (Shakespeare)

anapest: three syllables, two unstressed followed by one stressed.

Like a CHILD/from the WOMB

Like a GHOST/from the TOMB

I aRISE/and unBUILD/it aGAIN (Percy Bysshe Shelley)

trochee: two syllables, one stressed followed by one unstressed.

TROchee/TRIPS from/LONG to/SHORT (Coleridge)

dactyl: three syllables, one stressed followed by two unstressed.

PICture your/SELF on a/BOAT in a/RIVer with . . . (John Lennon and Paul McCartney)

To name the meter of a piece, we identify the type of foot used most often in the work then modify it with the typical number of feet in a line. In the examples above, Shakespeare's line is iambic pentameter; Shelley's first is anapestic dimeter; Coleridge's line is trochaic tetrameter; and the Beatles' line is dactylic tetrameter.

metonymy: One term is used for another to which it is closely related, as in referring to a ruler as "the crown."

monologue: One character talks to one or more listeners without interruption. In *dramatic monologues* such as "My Last Duchess," speakers usually reveal much more about themselves than they appear to intend. In *internal monologues* a character reflects privately on an issue or idea, usually a central concern of the work.

novel: Fictional prose works longer than short stories, novels can contain more characters and offer more complications, relationships, and changes than shorter fictional works. Traditional expectations include plot, chapter divisions, characterization, descriptions of setting and states of mind, and a frame of reference to facilitate our engagement with the world of the novel.

Although the novel form has experienced a long, complicated, and well-documented historical evolution, it has become in modern times a class distinguished primarily by its length and popularity. For every historical precedent to the current novel form, there are modern examples. The picaresque novel, which emerged in Spain in the sixteenth century and follows a character (a "rogue") through a series of adventures, has its modern counterparts in novels such as Jack Kerouac's *On the Road*. The epistolary novel, made up entirely of letters, is an eighteenth-century form made contemporary in novels such as *The Color Purple* by Alice Walker. There are, as well, novels that examine the social, economic, and political conditions of times and characters; historical novels, which borrow details and circumstances, as well as characters and events, from recorded history; nonfiction novels, which use fictional techniques to invite imaginative involvement with actual events; and "new novels," which forego the standard expectations in favor of a series of disparate impressions out of which we are to construct, or infer, a narrative coherence.

Some literature scholars have focused their research attention on the evolution and permutations of the novel form, believing that our formal expectations for order, relationship, and closure (how books should end) affect our comprehension and evaluation of the works.

ode: A long lyric poem on a serious subject. Traditionally, the ode's stanzas were presented in groups of three: the strophe, the antistrophe, and the epode (point, counterpoint, and thrust). Each kind of stanza had its own form. In the seventeenth century, "irregular" odes began to appear; these retained a serious purpose and elevated style but allowed for variation in line lengths, numbers of lines, and rhyme scheme. If you need examples, find a poem with "ode" in the title (there are many), or find a copy of one of our modern favorites: Wallace Stevens's "The Idea of Order at Key West."

onomatopoeia: The use of a word that sounds like what it means, as "hiss" or "buzz" or "twitter."

persona, speaker, or narrator: The person telling the story. The voices of the persona or narrators may be in *first person*, recounting their experiences, or they may be in *third person*, describing what happened to others. The persona may be inside or outside the work, a *participant* or an *observer*.

When a writer uses a particular speaking voice in a work, a voice to which we can attribute particular attitudes, values, and biases, it is helpful to understand that voice as a character or a role "put on" for the purposes of the telling. (The word *persona* first referred to a mask worn by actors in plays in ancient Greece.) To mistake that voice for the author often leads us to assume that the writer is advocating, rather than examining, the statements or actions of the work.

Whether the persona is seemingly close to or distant from the writer's own experience or world view, it is much more interesting to think of the persona as "constructed," because even in autobiography, what we learn about a person is what that person chooses for us to know in an order artificially arranged for best effect. Our questions, then, about persona include who tells the story? How can we describe the role the persona is assuming?

personification: Attributing human qualities to things that are not human.

plot: The structure of events in a story, what is included and in what order, is designed to arouse expectations in readers about what will happen and how characters will respond. Uncertainty, plus a concern on the part of the reader, results in suspense. If we are led to expect one thing but another happens, we experience surprise or anxiety, and we are led to reflect on the turns of plot to see if, in fact, the ending was evident, if not obvious, in the story's development.

Gustav Freytag first characterized typical plot development with what is called "Freytag's pyramid," which depicts, with a triangular shape, the rising action, climax, and falling action of many plot structures. After an *exposition*, or opening section that sets the stage for later events, the *rising action* continues by introducing various complications and conflicts that reach their emotional apex in the *climax* (where they are resolved, for better or worse), and the *catastrophe* (where the protagonist faces the outcome of the climax). Following the emotional high point of the story is the *denouement* (French for "unknotting"), during which the story reaches a new resolution or "status quo" as a result of the plot events.

This structure is more evident in some stories than in others but is a valuable tool for studying nearly all narratives, in that it makes us conscious of the changes in the emotional climate of the work. Often in modern tales the moment of climax is not as evident in an event as in a change of mood or atmosphere—nothing much seems to happen, but the characters, or our reactions to the events, have reached an emotional climax anyway.

Freytag's pyramid can help us track double or multiple plots and their relationships to each other and it can help us make more obvious the progression of an *anti-plot*, a structure grounded not in external events but in the psychological development of a character.

point of view: The perspective from which the story is told. We answer this when we ask about the persona or narrator. Narrators can know everything, not just events and details but also the thoughts and feelings of the characters, in which case they are called *omniscient*. Or they can have *limited* understanding, observing and recounting but not necessarily comprehending fully or clearly the events and details around them. When narrators seem to be all-knowing, we need to ask about their world view: what beliefs do they seem to hold? Can they be trusted? Do they project an attitude toward characters or events, and if so, is it based on assumptions we can identify? When the narrators have limited perspective, we must ask: What are those limitations? How do they influence the action, or our perceptions of characters or events?

protagonist: The main character in a story, novel, or drama around whom the action centers. Connie in "Where Are You Going, Where Have You Been?" is a protagonist.

qualitative progression: In this kind of form, feelings rather than events motivate the development. Another of Kenneth Burke's terms, qualitative progression focuses our attention on the ways in which the presence of one quality or state of mind prepares us for another that can then appropriately follow. If you are aware of the qualitative progression, you may be better able to reflect on how the work's sequence affects you as a reader. This awareness may help you understand the development of plots that are difficult to explain by an analysis of conventionally expected stages marked by events.

repetition: The repetition of an image, feeling, or detail can propel the reader through a work by setting up a point of reference from which to view the progression. Repetition can move a reader forward through a sequence even when the logical or structural progression is ambiguous.

To read for repetition as a developmental principle, watch for words, images, or ideas that are repeated, even if they don't seem obviously related. Watch, too, for words or images that seem significant, that seem to crystallize the meaning in some way, and ask whether they help to focus or explain the writer's vision.

rhyme: The most frequent types of rhymes are *close rhymes*, in which the last stressed vowel and all the sounds that follow it are alike, and end rhymes, which come at the ends of lines. *Internal rhymes* occur within a line. *Masculine or single rhymes* pair one syllable, as in "hill" and "still"; *feminine or double rhymes* pair two syllables, as in "started" and "parted."

Modern poetry may not rely on rhyme to convey or support meaning but frequently incorporates *irregular rhymes*, which occur when words don't quite rhyme but their similarity gets our attention. Irregular rhymes are also called *slant, near,* or *off* rhymes. Although different authorities define these in slightly different ways, irregular rhymes work to complicate an established order or link words that the writer wants the reader to connect.

rhyme scheme: Reading for rhyme is one way of reading for relationships. To inquire about rhyme scheme is to analyze one of the ways in which the writer may have chosen to reinforce meaning with sound. Rhyme schemes indicate the patterns of end rhymes alphabetically. Thus in the first stanza of an Italian sonnet, the pattern *abbaabba* indicates that the first, fourth, fifth, and eighth lines rhyme, as do the second, third, sixth, and seventh.

setting: The settings of literary works are the specific times, places, and circumstances against which the actions and events take place. Any reference to the place, whether it be a description of the chair in which a character sits or the landscape that surrounds her community can be considered purposeful, as can any reference to time—day, year, historical period, or era. References to circumstances, too, create a part of the environment within which characters choose, act, and respond. Their economic situation, job status, political leanings within a particular political moment, or social affiliations or disaffiliations can all influence the possibilities for characters and events in the perpetual balance of individual action and external forces. Setting contributes to meaning in a variety of ways: it can aid characterization, advance plot, create expectations, externally represent an internal mood or conflict, or suggest an attitude toward or ironic contrast with actions, behaviors, or events. Developing your skill at observing setting will help you meet a literary work on its own terms, a habit of mind that serves you well when you explore works that challenge the limitations of your own cultural experience.

short story: When Edgar Allan Poe set out to describe the "prose tale," which he so diligently and artfully composed, he included the following characteristics: it could be read at one sitting of from half an hour to two hours and it is limited to a "certain unique or single effect" to which every detail contributes. His description still seems applicable to many works of short fiction; perhaps because of the formal constraints, writers have tended to economize, making the most of every event, detail, and spoken word. Because of this concentration, the stylistic choices, the artistry of the writing, is often more evident in the short story than in the novel. You have several examples in this text, all of which can be read for the kind of "unity of effect" that Poe saw as the short story's distinguishing characteristic.

simile: A direct comparison of two unlike things using the words "like" or "as."

situational irony: A discrepancy or incongruity created when the circumstances of setting lead us to expect one thing and we get another, or when a setting seems to contrast with rather than to mirror an event or action.

sonnet: A lyric poem in fourteen lines linked by an intricate rhyme scheme. Usually composed of an octave and a sestet, or three quatrains and a couplet (see "stanza"). The Italian or Petrarchan sonnet is divided into an octave (eight lines) rhyming *abbaabba* and a sestet (six lines) rhyming *cdecde*. The octave usually presents a problem or problematic situation; the sestet usually presents the solution or resolution.

The English or Shakespearean sonnet is divided into three quatrains (four lines each) rhyming *abab cdcd efef* and a couplet (two lines) rhyming *gg*. The English sonnet also used the eight-line problem, six-line solution format, but it frequently appears with the three quatrains presenting variations of the same situation or idea, followed by a concluding or answering couplet.

The importance of the sonnet form for the reader of poetry is the same as its significance for writers: it's just long enough to present a complex idea with some resonance, and its formal requirements challenge the writer's artistry.

stanza: Italian for "stopping place," a stanza is a group of lines separated from other groups. Although the number of lines per stanza is unlimited and can vary within a poem, some stanza forms are used so frequently that they have names which help us discuss the design of the works we read. A two-line rhymed stanza is a *couplet*. A *tercet*, or *triplet*, has three lines. *Quatrains*, with four lines, are the most commonly used and are found with various rhyme schemes.

Particular combinations of stanzaic forms and rhyme schemes have become familiar by their association with classic works: *Rime royal* is a seven-line, iambic pentameter stanza rhyming *ababbcc*, and forms the structure of Chaucer's *Troilus and Criseyde*. *Ottava rima*, an Italian form, has eight lines rhyming *abababcc*. It was the perfect stanza form for Byron, who used it to write his masterwork *Don Juan*, partly because the two rhyming lines at the end often produces a comic effect.

Knowing about variation in stanza form can help us read for combinations of design elements in order to observe their effects. For example, Dylan Thomas's complicated reflection on death, "Do not go gentle into that good night," is a *villanelle*, which consists of five tercets and a quatrain. The extra line in the last stanza gives urgency and power to his vision.

style: The summation of an author's characteristic and unmistakable choices of words, syntactic structures, diction, imagery, tone, and ideas. If you imagine that the field of rhetorical choices about shape, language, participants, situations, and ideas a writer can make is just that, a "field," then a writer's style is the place in that field where he or she likes to stand. Inexperienced readers often say someone has or doesn't have style; experienced readers know to ask whether the writer's stylistic choices are or are not effective in creating and sustaining a vision. A sense of style, or the ability to distinguish the characteristic styles of various authors, comes with reading experience. Sometimes it helps to consider the style of groups rather than authors: an *idiom* is the characteristic language style of a group of people, whether that group consists of people from a particular region, occupation, ethnic group, neighborhood, or other affiliation.

syllogistic progression: A syllogism, the basic structure of an argument, is composed of a major premise, a minor premise, and a conclusion. Syllogistic progression in literature is similar; it tracks the logical progression of the argument implicit in the work. The writer is persuading us to accept a possibility, to change an assumption, to set aside a preconceived notion, or to trade a simple vision for a more complicated one. Given one thing, something must logically follow. Aristotle's contention that literary works must have beginnings, middles, and ends describes syllogistic progression, as does Freytag's definition of the five stages in dramatic plots (see **plot**).

symbol: When words acquire complex or culturally significant meanings beyond themselves, they become symbols of those meanings. The term is broad enough to be difficult to distinguish from connotation except in the degree and significance of its network of meanings. The notion of symbol includes such conventionally accepted equivalencies as flag and country, such universally recognized patterns as the journey to the underworld, and such specific symbolic connections as that of darkness to death and despair. In addition to being conventional, symbolic significance is related to culture (red is the color lighting prostitutes' windows in Amsterdam and the color of bridal gowns in traditional Hawaii), and context (red can symbolize love, and it can symbolize blood). It is more helpful, in some ways, to think about symbolic *uses* of language or ways to read *symbolically* than it is to classify specific features under the heading of symbol.

syntax: Analyzing syntax means examining the choices the writer makes in organizing the sentences that constitute the work. Literature follows predictable grammatical patterns but also varies, subverts, and manipulates them for effect. Thus when we analyze syntax, we're not always looking at complete sentences or regular grammar patterns. Instead, we are observing how words and phrases are organized into sentences in ways that support the artist's vision. We can look at whether the sentences are more often simple or complex. We can observe whether the writer tends to use or avoid certain kinds of modifiers or how those modifiers are characteristically placed within sentences. We can watch for patterns of placement of certain sentence types. Whatever we notice, we use our observations to form generalizations in support of interpretive statements about the ideas.

tone: When you speak, you express attitudes as well as explicit meaning. Using various gestures and inflections, you convey a range of attitudes. For example, you can ask the person next to you to "move over" and also communicate irritation, affection, or bored indifference. Through their stylistic choices, writers attempt to convey implicit attitudes toward the subject, the circumstances, or the audience of a work. Although tone is a subjective quality and difficult to characterize, we use and respond to it all the time. When we are offended by a message, it is most often the tone rather than the words that offends us.

Although tone in literature, as in life, can be misunderstood, writers give us a system of signals and signs to help us determine the attitude that will help us interpret the characters and events in meaningful ways. We can't know whether our reading of a work corresponds to what an author intended, nor does it really matter. When we read tone we are looking at how the signs and signals work to establish particular attitudes, assumptions, and values, and then reflecting on the way the tone influences our response and interpretation.

value: Although this may seem an odd term to include in a list of literary language, it is relevant to a consideration of situations in which we place literary works as we inquire about them. Values are assigned based on criteria. Characters seem interesting or uninteresting, significant or insignificant, engaging or distancing, depending on what criteria we bring to bear. Issues of value tend to come up in most literary discussions. They begin with comments about liking or disliking something and evolve into discussions of what should, or shouldn't be valued.

Some of the most heated debates in current literary study, in fact, concern what is worth reading. Such disagreements do not just affect what works we read in particular courses and programs; they can also influence what works are published. Gwendolyn Brook's novel *Maud Martha*, was published in 1953, the same year that James Baldwin published *Go Tell It On The Mountain*. Both books follow African-American characters from youth to adulthood. Baldwin's novel became a classic; Brooks's quickly went out of print and was unavailable for years. Why? Possibly readers did not know how to value Brooks's novel. It was poetic; it was quiet; its concern was not racial conflict or stereotypical presentations of oppression but the rich texture of ordinary life. When we judge the value of literature, our judgments are influenced by expectations that function as implicit criteria.

Criteria are contexts on the basis of which judgments of value are made. It is important for readers of literature to attempt to identify their criteria for making judgments in order to get beyond discussions at personal preference. It is also important to know that such criteria are negotiable, and that as responsible readers, you are a part of the evolving conversations going on in institutions and cultures that assign value to works over time. In this text we have included works that are generally believed to have enduring value; we also have included works less representative of traditional criteria. Which are which? All can inspire meaningful transactions between reader and work; all employ strategies of language that stretch our imaginations and challenge or clarify our way of seeing. As readers of literature, considering questions of value can help us identify our own criteria for judgment, become aware of those criteria being used by others, and argue for criteria that seem relevant to an appreciation of a work's significance.

verbal irony: When words are chosen that deliberately say something other than what they mean, the result is verbal irony, which can take the form of sarcasm, understatement, or hyperbole.

INDEX